The Routledge Who's Who series

Accessible, authoritative and enlightening, these are the definitive biographical guides to a diverse range of subjects drawn from literature and the arts, history and politics, religion and mythology.

Who's Who in Classical Mythology

MICHAEL GRANT
and JOHN HAZEL

Routledge
Taylor & Francis Group

LONDON AND NEW YORK

First published 1973 by Weidenfeld & Nicolson
First published in paperback 1993 by J. M. Dent Ltd

Reprinted 1994, 1996, 1999 by
by Routledge
2 Park Square, Milton Park, Abingdon, Oxon, OX14 4RN

This edition first published 2002
Reprinted 2004 (twice), 2005 (twice), 2006 (twice)

Simultaneously published in the USA and Canada
by Routledge
270 Madison Avenue, New York, NY 10016

Routledge is an imprint of the Taylor & Francis Group

Printed and bound in Great Britain by
TJ International Ltd, Padstow, Cornwall

British Library Cataloguing in Publication Data
A catalogue record for this book is available from the
British Library

Library of Congress Cataloging in Publication Data
A catalogue record for this title has been requested

ISBN 0–415–39112–1 (hbk)
0 415 26041-8 (pbk)

Contents

Introduction

The Greek and Roman myths are an indelible, indispensable, inescapable part of our cultural background and heritage. They originated not according to some single, all-explaining pattern – as is often sweepingly argued – but in a wide variety of different ways and in response to a great many different social and pyschological needs. They were invented to explain natural phenomena in a pre-scientific world, to elucidate sites and rituals and names of which the original meaning had been lost, to justify customs and institutions, to endow the gods with dramatic personalities and careers, to glorify nations and tribes and families and hierarchies and priesthoods, to fill out early history by inventive additions, to indulge wishful thinking by tales of adventure and heroism and, sometimes, merely to amuse and entertain: to beguile the long hours of darkness, or the tedium of a dusty journey, or a perilous tossing on the sea.

In every sort of myth, it is the story, the course of mythical 'events', which matters. The names of Achilles, Helen, Oedipus, Romulus or Horatius on the Bridge still evoke an echo today, but these echoes are dim and pointless unless the sequence of what was believed to have happened to them and what they were believed to have done are seen and pursued through their often devious courses and ramifications. That is the purpose of this book. It will endeavour to identify and describe the principal and best known and most influential incidents built into each mythological narrative over the ancient centuries, noting, from time to time, when these assumed alternative and contradictory forms.

What will then emerge, it is hoped, is a picture of the different pieces which add up to one of the greatest imaginative achievements in the history of civilisation. These are marvellous tales, which have rightly been thought worth retelling on countless thousands of occasions. As many a psychologist and anthropologist will readily confirm, they are full of profound revelations about the universal human condition and predicament. What they tell us, of course, is not historical truth. It is truth of another kind, which can perhaps be described as para-history: and in its effects upon what the Greeks and Romans, who so keenly studied these myths, did and thought, it seemed almost as significant and stimulating and uplifting as their actual past histories in which they took so much pride. And the same effects of this mythical para-history of ancient times can easily be traced onwards from then to now. It can be traced in the conscious and unconscious reliance of every intervening generation – of whatever epoch – upon the ways of thinking and ideas manifested by these mythologies. It can also be traced, very specifically, in the great and diverse fields of European art, and of European and American literature, which owe a major part of their meaning to this same mythical corpus. And as a readily apparent proof of its durability, the writers of this twentieth century have shown themselves every bit as conscious of their mythical inheritance as any of their predecessors.

Some of the Greek myths (in so far as they were not borrowed from the East) welled up from the humbler, anonymous sections of the population. Others were handed down and imposed on the people by the leaders and the ruling classes that supported them. It seems to some students more respectable and attractive to think in terms of the former process. But the latter often occurred as well, and its manifestations have been inadequately studied: they offer a wide field of research for the future. As for Roman myths, that is to say, the truly Roman myths, as opposed to those Rome adopted from the Greeks – they came up from below far less often than they were invented at the top and deliberately diffused downwards for patriotic or religious or political edification. But this does not make them any less interesting or significant, especially in our present age to which such a phenomenon is far from unfamiliar.

Everyone who compares the Greek and Roman mythologies with those of other cultures throughout the various countries of the world, and throughout the successive periods of history, will be amazed, indeed staggered, by the frequency with which the same stories recur, in closely similar or identical form, in a vast number of different lands, times and contexts. To take a single example out of many, more than nine hundred versions of the story of Cupid and Psyche are known; and they are scattered over tens of thousands of miles, and over widely separated epochs. There are two main theories about why this sort of thing has happened. One suggests that different cultures unavoidably go through the same stages of development, and that when a certain stage has been reached they tend, even without contact with each other, to produce similar myths, because their 'collective unconscious', to use the term familiarised by Karl Gustav Jung, gets to work in the same sort of fashion and in satisfaction of the same sort of inner needs. The alternative, 'diffusionist' theory maintains that, however widely the different cultures manifesting a similar myth may be separated in geographical terms, the stories were, in fact, *transmitted* from one culture to another – and, according to this view, it is only our lack of the requisite knowledge which prevents us from recognising the routes and channels and intermediaries and methods through which this transmission took place.

Both these two theories may, up to a point, be right. But sometimes the resemblances between different mythologies are too close to be explained by any 'collective unconscious'. In such cases, actual transmissions must have occurred – however difficult it may be for us today to trace the various successive links in the chain. Moreover, this conclusion tends to be confirmed by the advances of modern research: for example, it now seems that the resemblance between Greek and Far Eastern myths may be attributable to the mediating role of an Indo-Greek civilisation in northern India. As time goes on, it can be foreseen that other such channels of transmission may emerge out of the general obscurity, and become clear to us. And who knows, we may even one day be able to identify some single epoch and region in which the germs of the world's leading mythologies had their origins and began to be disseminated.

But that day lies far ahead; and meanwhile there is much else to ponder upon. For in the tales of the ancient classical world, mainly Greek but including a valuable and individual Roman corpus as well, we have before our eyes the greatest and most varied and influential of those mythological collections. What we are hoping to do here is to make it readily accessible, and to illustrate it by a representative choice from the visual art to which it so abundantly gave rise. As for terminology, no endeavour has been made to draw firm lines of delimitation between myth, legend, saga, folk-tale and märchen. For such lines are hard to draw, to say the least, and are drawn by different scholars in radically differing ways. Perhaps the most helpful distinction, at least potentially, is between myth, meaning purely fictitious material, and legend, consisting of stories which contain at least a germ or nucleus of historical truth. But even this differentiation will deliberately not be attempted here, since it is, in fact, impossible in most cases to determine whether such a nucleus is present or not. To take an obvious example, Troy was certainly destroyed by violent means – we can tell this by looking at the remains of the place for ourselves – but the question is, were its destroyers Greeks? If they were, then (according to this definition) the *Iliad*, which attributes the destruction of the city to invaders, is legend: if not, it is myth. The trouble is that we do not know the answer; and this being so, it seems more important, at least for our present purpose, to apprehend and admire the great stories that have come down to us, in all their variety, than to concentrate on attempting to classify them under different headings. Another problem of presentation, incidental, but not unimportant, is the spelling of ancient names. Here, while keeping consistency in mind as an overall aim, we have not hesitated to sacrifice it when convenience seems to exercise a prior claim, and have tried to derive the spellings adopted from the most familiar current usage.

We wish to express our acknowledgments towards many modern writers on Greek and Roman myths. In particular, we would appreciatively record our debt to H. J. Rose's *Handbook of Greek Mythology* and other works, and *Crowell's Handbook of Classical Mythology* by Edward Tripp, published in England as *The Handbook of Classical Mythology* (Arthur Barker, 1970). We are also grateful to Messrs. Weidenfeld and Nicolson Ltd for a great deal of helpful assistance, and especially to Martha Bates for seeing the book through the press.

London and Gattaiola, 1973

Note to the 2002 edition

It is nearly thirty years since the first publication of this book in a glossy illustrated coffee-table format by Weidenfeld & Nicolson. It has spent most of its career since then in paperback format, and has passed through the hands of several publishers before coming to land with Taylor & Francis. It has proved a vigorous creature and fully justified the faith we had in it at its first launch. The stories it contains are told in a straightforward, intelligible manner, and are certainly capable of being enjoyed by people of any age. We believe it will also provide useful to serious students of literature and other disciplines when they wish to refer to the characters and plots of the ancient myths. The text is the same as that originally published with but a few minor corrections. We consider that it covers its subject in a sufficiently comprehensive manner and trust that it will continue to find a useful place on the shelves of those engaged in classical studies.

Michael Grant and John Hazel

London and Gattaiola
2002

A

Abas *1.* Son of Lynceus and Hypermnestra. He succeeded his father as king of Argos, and married Aglaia, daughter of Mantineus. They had twin sons, Acrisius and Proetus, and a daughter, Idomene.

2. Son of Melampus; father of Coeranus and Lysimache.

Abderus Son of Hermes, originating from Opuntian Locris in central Greece. Heracles loved him and made him his armour-bearer, posting him to guard the man-eating horses of Diomedes, king of the Bistones; but they devoured him. Heracles founded the city of Abdera in Thrace in his memory.

Absyrtus see APSYRTUS.

Acacallis Daughter of Minos and Pasiphae. She bore Apollo a son, Amphithemis, and perhaps Miletus also.

Acamas *1.* Theseus and Phaedra had two sons, Acamas and Demophon. When Menestheus expelled their father from Athens, the two boys were lodged with Elephenor, king of the Abantes in Euboea. He took them to fight in the Trojan War. There, on an embassy to Troy to demand the return of Helen, Acamas fell in love with Priam's daughter Laodice, who bore him a son, Munychus; Theseus' mother Aethra took charge of the child. The brothers were in the Wooden Horse, and later rescued Aethra from Troy. On his way home Acamas married a Thracian princess, Phyllis. However, although offered her father's kingdom as a dowry, he left

her, promising to return later. She gave him a box containing a sacred object, telling him to open it only if he changed his mind about coming back. Settling in Cyprus, he subsequently opened the box, and was so frightened by its contents that he galloped away on his horse. It threw him, and he fell off on to his sword and died. A similar story is told of Demophon *1.*

2. Son of Antenor and Theano, and one of the leaders of Troy's Dardanian allies in the Trojan War.

Acarnan see ALCMAEON.

Acastus King of Iolcus and son of Pelias and Anaxibia. He sailed with the Argonauts against his father's wishes. On their return from Colchis, his father was deceitfully killed by Medea, and Acastus expelled Jason and her from his kingdom. In honour of his father he held funeral games to which many of the Argonauts came. He then took part in the Calydonian boar-hunt. Acastus married Astydamia, or else Hippolyta, daughter of Cretheus. They had three daughters, Laodamia, Sterope and Sthenele, as well as a number of sons.

Peleus, a fellow-Argonaut, came to Acastus after killing Eurytion, and Acastus purified him of the guilt of homicide. But Astydamia made advances to Peleus and, when he rejected them, accused him of having taken the initiative. Acastus, to punish him, took him hunting on Mount Pelion, where he treacherously stole Peleus' sword and abandoned him while he was asleep. Acastus hoped the wild Centaurs would kill Peleus, but

Chiron rescued him. Peleus later conquered Iolcus with the help of Jason and the Dioscuri; he killed Acastus' wife and, according to some, Acastus himself. Acastus' sons subsequently drove him out of Phthia.

Acca Larentia Wife of Faustulus, the shepherd who found the abandoned twins Romulus and Remus and brought them up. Since the babies had been suckled by a she-wolf, Acca was named *lupa*, which has a double meaning in Latin: 'whore' as well as 'she-wolf'. Acca was also sometimes called Faula or Fabula, another designation of harlots in Latin.

Acestes or **Aegestes** A Sicilian of Trojan descent on his mother's side. His father was the god of the river Crinisus. Acestes joined Priam's side in the Trojan War and returned to Sicily with his friend Elymus. Acestes was king of Drepanum in the west of the island, near the shrine of Venus on Mount Eryx, and twice entertained Venus' son Aeneas in his wanderings. On the second occasion Aeneas celebrated his father Anchises' funeral games. The city of Egesta was originally named Acesta after him by its founders, the Trojan followers of Aeneas who remained in Sicily.

Achaeus Son of Xuthus and the brother of Ion. He recovered his father's kingdom of Thessaly with the help of Athens and of the country of Aegialus (Achaea) in the Peloponnese, which Ion ruled. Achaeus gave his name to the Achaeans, the people of southern Thessaly. The name was also used in a broader sense by Homer and the early Greeks to designate all the Greek-speaking peoples who fought against Troy.

Achates Aeneas' armour-bearer and closest friend and companion.

Achelous The god of a river in northwestern Greece. He was a son of Ocea-

nus and Tethys. Achelous wrestled with Heracles for the hand of Deianira, but in spite of his power to change shape was defeated. He turned into a bull, but Heracles broke off one of his horns. To recover this, Achelous gave Heracles a horn from the goat Amalthea, which had suckled Zeus.

Achelous was the father of several nymphs: Callirrhoe, who married Alcmaeon; Castalia, of the famous spring at Delphi; and the Sirens.

Achilles The chief of the Greek heroes in the *Iliad*, in which his anger with Agamemnon and his duel with Hector are dominant themes.

He was the only son of the mortal Peleus, king of Phthia in Thessaly, and of the sea-nymph Thetis, daughter of Nereus. Both Zeus and Poseidon wished to have a child by the beautiful Thetis, but Themis or Prometheus warned them that her son would be greater than his father. Not wishing to run the risk of begetting a power superior to themselves, the gods arranged the marriage of Thetis with a mortal king, Peleus, and in order to recompense her they celebrated the wedding with spectacular pomp. The seeds of the conflict leading up to the Trojan War were sown at the wedding. Eris (Strife), who had deliberately not been invited so as to avoid the chance of conflict between the couple, nevertheless arrived at the proceedings and cast down before the assembly the golden apple, inscribed 'for the fairest', which was to set Hera, Athena, and Aphrodite at loggerheads.

Thetis was exceedingly attached to her son, and in the *Iliad* she seems to be the only woman for whom he feels a really close tie. In his earliest childhood she attempted to endow him with immortality by anointing him with ambrosia by day and burying him in the embers of the fire at night. Peleus, however, discovered her putting the baby in the fire and was terrified. Thetis was so angry at his interference and mistrust that she abandoned both her husband and her child and returned to the sea.

Homer does not seem to be acquainted with the well-known story of Achilles' invulnerability. According to this tale, Thetis dipped her newborn baby in the river of Hades, the Styx, but since she had to hold him by the heel, this one spot was left unprotected. It was because of this that Paris was able to kill Achilles with an arrow.

After his mother deserted him, Achilles was placed in the care of the wise Centaur Chiron, who had educated the Argonauts. Chiron taught him to practise running, and he became the swiftest of living men; Homer's favourite epithet for him is *podarkes* – 'the swift of foot'. Chiron also taught him the skills of warfare and fed him on the entrails of wild beasts to give him the quality of fierce courage. He also instructed him in music and medicine. Later on Achilles returned to Phthia and became the intimate friend of Patroclus, a rather older youth, who had taken refuge at Peleus' court. Patroclus became Achilles' squire and lover. At the same time, Achilles received training in government and diplomacy from another refugee at Phthia, Phoenix, whom Peleus made king of the Dolopes.

It was also said that Achilles was sent by Thetis to the court of Lycomedes on the island of Scyros since she knew of his tragic destiny. The doom which Thetis foretold was that Achilles would either die in inglorious old age or else – and much more probably – would join the expedition to Troy, from which he could never return. Lycomedes disguised Achilles as a girl, called him Pyrrha, and hid him in the women's quarters in his palace, because Calchas had prophesied that Troy could never be taken unless Achilles joined the expedition. While this duplicity was being maintained, Achilles took advantage of his female company by seducing the king's daugh-

ter Deidamia, who bore him Neoptolemus (sometimes called Pyrrhus).

After a while the Greeks, who needed Achilles' presence to make a success of the expedition, sent Odysseus to Scyros to find him. This clever schemer was able to penetrate Achilles' disguise by a trick. He placed weapons among some jewellery in the porch of Lycomedes' house. While the women of the royal household were admiring the jewellery, a trumpet was sounded as if to signal danger. Achilles immediately seized the weapons and gave himself away. Then, perhaps through shame at having been a party to this deception, he ignored his mother and quite freely sailed to Troy with the expedition. He owed Agamemnon no loyalty, and had not, like others, taken an oath to defend Helen's husband Menelaus, but went as if to face a personal challenge to his valour. At Aulis, where the fleet was weather-bound, Agamemnon had to sacrifice his daughter Iphigenia in order to placate Artemis, and used Achilles as a lure to attract her to the spot, offering her the bait of marriage with the young prince. According to Euripides' *Iphigenia in Aulis*, Achilles did not know what was afoot, and tried to rescue the girl; but when she realised the purpose of her sacrifice, she reconciled herself to death. Thus the Greeks were enabled to sail.

They missed their way, however, and landed by mistake in Mysia, far to the south of Troy, where the king of Teuthrania, Telephus, a son of Heracles, drove them back to their ships, with the exception of Achilles, who turned the tables and inflicted a grave wound in Telephus' thigh with his spear. The Greeks left Mysia, realising that they were far from Troy, and returned to Argos. Here, dressed in rags, came Telephus, who had learnt from an oracle that only the inflicter of his wound could cure him. Odysseus reminded Achilles that his spear was responsible for the wound, and Achilles cured it by applying rust from the spear. Telephus repaid this favour by guiding the Greeks to Troy.

On arriving off Troy, the Greeks first landed on Tenedos, where Achilles disobeyed a warning of Thetis, perhaps unintentionally, by slaying Tenes, king of the island and a son of Apollo. Achilles had been told that the archer-god Apollo would take vengeance on him for the murder, and in fact he was subsequently brought low by an arrow from Paris' bow, guided by Apollo. Thetis also warned him not to be the first to land in Troy; this time he obeyed.

Achilles' first adversary was Cycnus, a son of Poseidon, who was said to be invulnerable to weapons. Achilles strangled him with Cycnus' own helmet-strap. He also ambushed and killed Troilus.

As Troy proved impossible to take by siege or assault, Achilles led the Greek forces against many of the neighbouring towns, and sacked twelve of these on the coast and eleven inland. The most important of the latter were Lyrnessus and Thebe-under-Placus. Eetion, father of Andromache, was king of Thebe; Achilles killed him and his seven sons and ransomed the queen. At Lyrnessus he met Aeneas for the first time, and put him to flight; he also killed Mynes and Epistrophus, sons of King Evenus. It was here, too, that he captured the beautiful Briseis, whom he made his concubine and claimed to love more than any other woman. It was largely on account of her that the events described in the *Iliad* were said to have taken place.

Agamemnon had taken for his concubine Chryseis, the daughter of Apollo's prophet Chryses. He was furious at being compelled to give her back to her father to avoid Apollo's wrathful punishment, and peevishly removed Briseis from Achilles, who had urged him to restore the girl, to compensate himself for his loss. Achilles then withdrew from the war and entreated his mother to punish Agamemnon by using her influence with Zeus to persuade him to swing the tide of war against the Greeks. The plan worked beautifully for Achilles; but he later put himself in the wrong by refusing compensation consisting of an apology from Agamemnon, marriage with any of Agamemnon's three daughters, and the restoration of his concubine. From this moment Achilles' plan went astray, for his close friend and squire Patroclus, pitying the Greeks who were fighting for their lives to defend their beached ships, persuaded Achilles to lend him his armour and let him lead the Myrmidons (the people of Phthia, Peleus' country) into battle. Achilles warned Patroclus to do no more than defend the ships, but he went too far, and after great successes was killed by Hector, who stripped Achilles' armour from his body.

On learning the news Achilles was overwhelmed by anger and remorse. Thetis and the Nereids came to mourn with him and Achilles told her that he longed for death. He swore to kill Hector, and Thetis realised that he had indeed not long to live as he was doomed to die very soon after Hector. He stood by the wall and thrice shouted the war-cry, at which the Trojans retreated in confusion. Then he reconciled himself with Agamemnon and attacked the Trojans furiously, clad in new armour made for him at Thetis' request by the god of fire, Hephaestus. He killed countless Trojans and embroiled himself with the god of the River Scamander, who, being a protector of the place and naturally hostile to the invader, was enraged at the number of Trojan dead that Achilles had flung into his stream. Hephaestus saved Achilles by drying up the river.

When the Trojans were finally penned within their walls, Hector alone remained to confront him. Achilles pursued him three times round the city;

then Hector turned and faced him, with a plea that if he was killed, his body might be spared and returned to his father King Priam. Achilles refused to give him any such undertaking and slew him. He then defiled Hector's body and dragged it round Patroclus' tomb on twelve consecutive days, leaving it there as a consolation for his friend's ghost and refusing to return it to Priam. At last Thetis persuaded Achilles to relent, and after the funeral games of Patroclus, at which Achilles performed human sacrifice, Priam retrieved the corpse.

After the events described in the *Iliad*, Penthesilea, queen of the Amazons, came to reinforce the Trojans. Achilles killed her but fell in love with her dead body. When Thersites mocked him for so doing, Achilles killed him too. For this sin, Achilles was obliged to make sacrifice to Leto and her children, Apollo and Artemis, and then had to be purified by Odysseus. A second ally of Troy whom Achilles slew was the Ethiopian Memnon. Immediately after this an arrow from Paris' bow, guided by Apollo, gave Achilles a mortal wound. His body was rescued by Aias (Ajax) son of Telemon, and he was mourned for seventeen days. When Thetis and the Nereids came and sang a dirge, the whole army fled to the ships in terror. The Muses also joined the lamentation. On the eighteenth day he was cremated, his ashes laid in a golden urn made by Hephaestus, and a tomb near the sea covered his bones, mingled with those of Patroclus. According to a later tradition, the shades of Achilles and Patroclus went to live in Leuce (White Island), a place of felicity for the greatest heroes.

There was a contest as to who should be awarded Achilles' armour: Aias claimed it, but when it was granted to Odysseus by the other Greeks, Aias killed himself. This is the subject of Sophocles' tragedy *Aias*. Odysseus gave the armour to Neoptolemus to induce him to join the war, as Helenus, a

Trojan prophet, predicted that his presence was necessary for a Greek victory.

The ghost of Achilles rose from the tomb and demanded the slaughter of Priam's daughter Polyxena before the Greeks would be allowed to depart home. This is a theme of Euripides' play *Hecuba*.

Achilles' character in mythology is powerful, arrogant and cruel. He is resentful of his fate and given to violent outbursts of temper. He is a symbol of youth and strength, doomed to an early but glorious death. He was the hero whom Alexander the Great most admired.

Acis According to Ovid, Acis was a son of the god Faunus and the nymph Simaethis, and fell passionately in love with the Nereid Galatea. When the Cyclops Polyphemus saw Galatea, he too became infatuated with her, but Galatea laughed at him. Polyphemus threw a huge rock at Acis which crushed him to death. A fountain sprang up from the rock at the command of Galatea, and Acis became a river-god.

Acmon One of the Idaean Dactyls.

Acoetes When Dionysus was attacked and captured by the crew of a Tyrrhenian (Etruscan) pirate ship on which he had taken passage, Acoetes, the helmsman, was his only defender. The other sailors were turned to dolphins or fishes, but Acoetes became an ardent follower of the god.

Acontius A youth from the island of Ceos who fell in love with an Athenian girl, Cydippe, in the precincts of Artemis' temple at Delos during a festival. As he was a poor man he could not hope to marry her, but tricked her into accepting him by dropping in front of her a quince, inscribed with the words: 'I swear by Artemis to marry none but Acontius.' She picked up the apple and read the oath aloud. Whenever her parents tried to marry her to anybody else, she fell ill. Finally the Delphic Oracle declared that she was bound by the oath, and her parents allowed the match.

Acrisius *1.* King of Argos, son of Abas and father of Danae. He quarrelled with his twin brother Proetus, even fighting him inside their mother's womb. Later the two fought over their father's kingdom and Acrisius drove Proetus out. Subsequently the two divided the Argolid between themselves. They were also said to have invented the shield.

Acrisius married Eurydice *2* (or Aganippe), and had a daughter Danae. An oracle, when asked by him what he should do to have sons, foretold that Danae's son would kill him. Thereupon Acrisius, in fear, built a bronze tower, or else a stone tower with bronze doors, where he incarcerated the girl. Zeus saw her and made her pregnant by a shower of golden rain; but when she gave birth to Perseus, Acrisius launched the unhappy pair on the sea in a wooden chest. The oracle was eventually fulfilled when Perseus accidentally killed Acrisius with a discus.

2. A king of Cephallenia; the father of Laertes.

Actaeon Son of Aristaeus and Autonoe. He was trained as a hunter, by his father or by Chiron. He offended Artemis, either by claiming to have superior skill at hunting, or because he wanted to marry Semele his aunt, or (and this is the reason most frequently given) because he saw Artemis bathing naked on Mount Cithaeron. To prevent his boasting of this exploit, the goddess turned him into a stag which his own hounds then devoured; or she threw a deerskin over him, with the same result. The hounds were saddened by the disappearance of their master, but the Centaur Chiron made a statue of Actaeon so lifelike that they were appeased.

Actor Several mythical characters of this name are recorded and there is a certain confusion between them. Chief among them are:
1. A king of Phthia, who welcomed Peleus there and left him the kingdom, not having any son of his own. According to another version he had a son called Eurytion *3*, whom Peleus killed. According to a further version Actor's son Irus was the father of Eurytion.
2. Son of Deion, king of Phocis, and father of Irus, Menoetius, Patroclus' father, and of Echecles.
3. A man of Elis, the brother of Augeas and father of the Moliones by Molione.

Admetus King of Pherae in Thessaly and son of Pheres. He was an Argonaut and took part in the Calydonian boarhunt. When Admetus was still a young man, his father abdicated in his favour.

Admetus won so great a reputation for justice and hospitality that when Apollo was condemned by Zeus to act as slave to a mortal man for a year, it was to Admetus that he came, in the guise of a stranger. Admetus gave him such a kind welcome that Apollo, serving as a cow-hand, caused all his cows to have twins. He also helped Admetus to win Alcestis, whose father Pelias had decreed an impossible task for her husband-to-be – yoking a lion and a boar to a chariot.

Because Admetus forgot to pay Artemis her due ritual at his marriage, he found his wedding-bed full of snakes. Apollo explained his mistake – which was speedily remedied – and soothed the anger of his sister. He also granted Admetus the favour of being able to substitute another mortal for himself when the time came for him to die; indeed, the god even tricked the Fates so as to win this unusual privilege for his protégé. Admetus fell ill while still relatively young but, when Death came to seize him, he at first could find no one to take his place. Not even his aged parents were prepared to become his substitutes. Alcestis, however, volunteered to die instead of him, and when she duly fell ill, Death came to lead her off to the Underworld. Admetus was willing to accept her self-sacrifice, and it was only because Heracles, who happened to be a guest at his palace at the time, wrestled with Death and drove him off, that she was saved. This story is the subject of Euripides' *Alcestis*. Another version of the myth states that Persephone refused to accept the substitute.

Adonis A god of Asiatic origin who was inserted into the Greek mythology: his name is a Semitic word, *Adon*, meaning 'the Lord', and he was worshipped in many places, always in conjunction with Aphrodite or her equivalent.

He was usually said to be the son of Myrrha (or Smyrna) and of her own father, either Cinyras, king of Paphos in Cyprus, or Belus of Egypt, or Theias of Assyria. For Aphrodite, because of Myrrha's neglect of her rites, had made her fall violently in love with her father. She then tricked him by the aid of her nurse into passing a night with her, and conceived Adonis. When her father discovered what had happened he tried to kill her, but the gods turned her into a myrrh tree. This was subsequently split open by the charge of a wild boar, and Adonis fell out of the cleft – or, according to another version, Ilithyia, the goddess of childbirth, released the baby from the wood when his time had come. Aphrodite, impressed by the child's beauty, placed him in a box and gave him to Persephone to look after. Persephone also admired the child and refused to give him back to Aphrodite until Zeus had arbitrated between the two goddesses. There are two versions of the judgment. The first tells that, when Zeus decreed that Adonis should spend a third of every year with each goddess and have the remaining third to himself, he spent his own third with Aphrodite. The other version makes the Muse Calliope the umpire (Zeus being unwilling to judge) and indicates that she assigned half the year to each goddess. These stories are a reminder of Adonis' function as a god of vegetation and nature. According to the second tradition, Aphrodite punished Calliope by bringing about the death of her son Orpheus.

While spending his time with Aphrodite, Adonis lost his life as he had entered it, through the charge of a wild boar. For while hunting in the forest he was attacked. Some said that the attacker was the jealous Ares in disguise, or Aphrodite's husband Hephaestus. Aphrodite had constantly warned him to avoid hunting dangerous wild beasts: the poet Ovid says she told him the story of Atalanta as a warning. Because the goddess was so sorrowful at his loss, she made the blood-red anemone spring up from the blood he shed at his death. One variant of the myth suggests that she prevailed on Persephone to restore him to earth for four months every year, starting in the springtime.

Adranus A fire-daemon whom Hephaestus drove out of Mount Etna in Sicily.

Adrastea A Cretan nymph who nursed the baby Zeus and fed him on the milk of the goat Amalthea.

Adrastus *1.* Son of Talaus, king of Argos, and Lysimache. After a quarrel with other branches of the royal family – descended from Melampus and Proetus – he fled from Argos. Talaus was killed by Amphiaraus, a descendant of Melampus, and his son took refuge with Polybus *2*, king of Sicyon. Talaus had married Polybus' daughter, and now Polybus, who had no sons, made him his heir. After becoming king of Sicyon, Adrastus was reconciled to Amphiaraus and gave him his sister Eriphyle in marriage.

Adrastus was now restored to the throne of Argos and, in spite of warnings from Amphiaraus (a prophet), agreed to help Polynices and Tydeus to recover their thrones, of Thebes and Calydon respectively. Adrastus noticed that the two young men were wearing animal skins – Polynices a lionskin and Tydeus a boarskin – and, obeying the dictates of an oracle that bade him marry his daughters to a lion and a boar, gave the girls Argia and Deiphyle to the two young men in marriage. Adrastus, who had married his own niece Amphithea, had one other daughter, Aegialia, and two sons, Aegialeus and Cyanippus.

Adrastus led the seven armies of his allies against Thebes in the famous expedition described by Homer in the *Iliad*, by Aeschylus in his play *Seven against Thebes*, and by Euripides in *Suppliant Women* and *Phoenician Women*. This attack was a failure, Adrastus himself, alone of its leaders, escaping on his magic horse Arion. A portent of the defeat was the death of the child Archemorus, killed by a snake while his nurse Hypsipyle showed the army to a watering place. Adrastus founded the Nemean Games in his honour.

Ten years after his first attack on Thebes Adrastus accompanied the children of the first Seven, called the Epigoni, against the same city. This time there was victory, but at the cost of the life of Adrastus' son Aegialeus. Adrastus was so grief-stricken that he died on the way home. His grandson, Diomedes, became ruler of Argos.

2. Father of Eurydice, wife of Ilus.

Aeacus Son of Zeus and of the river-nymph Aegina, daughter of the river Asopus. Zeus, in the form of an eagle, carried her off from her home in Sicyon to an island off the coast of Argolis which later took her name. After she had borne Aeacus she left him on the deserted island, and he prayed to Zeus

that it should be peopled. Zeus made men from the ants (*myrmekes*), and Aeacus called them the Myrmidons.

After arbitrating between Sciron and Nisus over their claim to the throne of Megara and deciding in favour of Nisus, Aeacus married Sciron's daughter Endeis. They had two sons, Peleus, father of Achilles, and Telamon, father of Aias and Teucer.

Aeacus was renowned for his uprightness: when a drought fell on Greece, the Delphic Oracle declared that only his prayers could alleviate the trouble.

According to Pindar, Apollo and Poseidon were helped by Aeacus to build the walls of Troy. Three snakes then attacked the walls, but only one was able to penetrate them, through the section that Aeacus had built. As a result Apollo foretold that Aeacus' descendants would eventually destroy the city.

Aeacus later had another son, Phocus, by a sea-nymph, Psamathe; he was a great athlete and roused his brothers' jealousy. They killed him and were expelled from Aegina by their father, who remained upon the island as its lonely king. After his death Zeus made him a judge of the dead together with Minos and Rhadamanthys.

Aedon (Greek: 'nightingale') Daughter of Pandareos; she was married to Zethus, king of Thebes. She had two children, Itylus and Neis, and envied her sister-in-law Niobe for her twelve. She tried during the night to kill Niobe's eldest son, but mistook the bed and instead killed Itylus, who was sharing the boy's room. After this outrage, she prayed to the gods to change her from human form, and Zeus turned her into a nightingale.

Aeetes Son of Helios the Sun and the Oceanid Perse, brother of Circe and Pasiphae, and father of Medea. Aeetes was king of Colchis, at the south-eastern end of the Black Sea. His nation typifies barbarism in Greek myth, and he is depicted as a cruel, ruthless man.

He married Asterodea, a nymph of the Caucasus, by whom he had a daughter, Chalciope, who became the wife of Phrixus. Aeetes also married Idyia (in Greek 'the knowing'), an Oceanid, who bore him a daughter, Medea, and a son, Apsyrtus.

When Phrixus, in flight from Athamas, came to Aeetes on the back of the golden ram, Aeetes, at the command of Zeus, welcomed him kindly and, nailing up the ram's fleece in the grove of Ares, gave him his daughter Chalciope in marriage. Some said that Aeetes afterwards killed Phrixus because an oracle told him that one of the Greek race would kill him. Later, when Jason came to fetch the Golden Fleece (see ARGONAUTS), Aeetes feared him for the same reason.

When Jason had performed the labours imposed on him by the king as a condition for obtaining the fleece, Aeetes broke his promise to hand it over, either through fear of an oracle that he would die if the fleece left his possession, or because of his hostility to strangers in general or Jason in particular. Jason, however, aided by Medea, took the fleece and fled. Aeetes pursued him, and Apsyrtus perished in the flight. Either he died fighting as commander of his father's fleet, or he was treacherously chopped in pieces by Medea to delay her father's pursuit.

Aeetes was subsequently deposed by his brother Perses, king of the Tauri, but Medea, on her eventual return from Greece, restored him to his throne. He was succeeded by Medea's son Medus.

Aegaeon see BRIAREOS.

Aegestes see ACESTES.

Aegeus Eldest (or adopted) son of Pandion 2 and Pylia. Pandion had been king of Athens and married the daughter of the king of Megara, Pylas, whom he succeeded. Pandion had three other sons, Nisus, Pallas, and Lycus. There was a rumour, however, that he had adopted a son of Scyrius, king of the island of Scyros, and passed him off as his own. When Pandion died Nisus was made king of Megara; the other three sons invaded Attica and drove out the sons of Metion who were now ruling there. After their victory Aegeus claimed and won sole rule over Athens, although he had promised to share the territory equally with his two brothers.

Aegeus married twice but had no children. He therefore consulted the Delphic Oracle, which gave him an ambiguous answer: he was not to unfasten his wine-skin until he reached Athens. Aegeus determined to ask his friend Pittheus, king of Troezen, to interpret the oracle for him. On his way from Delphi to Troezen, Aegeus went by Corinth, where Medea appealed to him for sanctuary in Athens. She undertook to use her magic arts to give him the children he desired.

Pittheus, learning that the oracle had also foretold the birth of a great hero, made Aegeus drunk and put him to bed with his daughter Aethra. When Aegeus was aware that Aethra had conceived, he placed a sword and a pair of sandals under a large boulder. He told Aethra that when her son could raise the rock he should come to Athens with these tokens of recognition – namely, the sword and sandals – and Aegeus would accept him as his son. The boy who was then born was named Theseus (his father was also often believed to be Poseidon).

When Aegeus returned to Athens he married Medea who bore him a son, Medus. It was for this reason that Medea later showed Theseus such hatred. When Theseus came to Athens after winning a reputation for his exploits in the Isthmus, Medea recognised him, but he did not show the tokens to his father. Medea persuaded Aegeus to send the youth off to fight the wild bull of Marathon, which had killed Minos' son Androgeos. When Theseus captured the bull alive, Medea determined to kill him. Declaring to Aegeus that Theseus was going to join Pallas' fifty sons in a revolt against Aegeus' rule, she offered him, in his father's presence, a cup of poisoned wine. Aegeus, however, happened to notice that his son was wearing the sword he had left in Troezen, or saw the sword as Theseus used it to carve meat, and dashed the cup to the ground. He then granted Theseus recognition, and Medea fled with Medus back to Colchis. Theseus helped Aegeus to drive out the family of Pallas and Lycus, who were trying to seize the throne.

As a result of Theseus' journey to Crete to kill the Minotaur, Aegeus died (see THESEUS). The tribute of seven boys and seven girls to be sent to feed this beast every year (or, according to another version, every nine years) had been imposed on Athens by Minos, the powerful king of Crete, in anger at the death of his son Androgeos, killed either by the Marathonian bull or while he was going to Thebes to attend Laius' funeral games. Minos attacked Megara and Athens; Megara fell, and Athens was stricken with a plague. Aegeus obeyed the advice of Delphi and accepted Minos' terms. When Theseus came back he forgot to change the black sails of mourning for a white sail, as he had promised to do if he survived; and so Aegeus flung himself down, either from a cliff into the Aegean Sea (which is named after him), or from the Athenian Acropolis. At the latter spot, a hero's shrine was erected where he was supposed to have fallen.

Aegialeus *1*. Eldest son of Adrastus and the only one of the Epigoni to be killed in their attack on Thebes.
2. Son of Inachus, the first king of Argos.

Aegialia *see* DIOMEDES.

Aegimius In Dorian myth the king of Doris who called for the help of Heracles to drive out the Lapiths from his territory. When Heracles had done this, he refused to accept an immediate reward, but asked that his descendants might claim asylum in the land. Later the Heraclids, from whom the Dorian kings subsequently claimed descent, were believed to have settled in Doris. Aegimius' sons Dymas and Pamphylus, together with Heracles' son Hyllus, gave their names to the three Dorian tribes.

Aegina Mother of Aeacus and daughter of the River Asopus and Metope. Zeus carried her off to the island that was later called after her, and there she conceived Aeacus. Her father pursued Zeus until he was driven off by thunderbolts.

Aegipan If not the same personage as the god Pan, he was the son of Zeus and a nymph called Aex (in Greek 'she-goat'). Aegipan helped Hermes to recover Zeus' sinews when Typhon cut them out and hid them. To escape Typhon, Aegipan changed his shape into a mixture of goat and fish; in this form Zeus made him into the constellation of Capricorn.

Aegisthus Son of Thyestes and of his daughter Pelopia. Thyestes had received an oracle that he would be revenged on his brother Atreus, who had murdered his children, only if he had a son by his own daughter. He therefore raped her while she was sacrificing to Athena (or else he raped her without knowing who she was). Pelopia took his sword and hid it under a statue of Athena.

Pelopia was living in Thesprotia at the time of the rape. She was seen there by Atreus, who was searching for Thyestes. He asked for her in marriage, and Thesprotus, her guardian, gave her to him without mentioning her pregnancy or saying who she was. When

Aegisthus was born at Atreus' court in Mycenae, he was exposed by his mother and suckled by a goat. Atreus found him soon afterwards and, knowing him to be Pelopia's child, believed him to be his own and reared him.

Thyestes had his revenge in the following way. Agamemnon and Menelaus, sent to find Thyestes by their father Atreus, caught him at Delphi where they had all gone to consult the oracle. They took him back to Mycenae, where Atreus imprisoned him. He then sent Aegisthus into the prison to kill him, carrying, as it happened, the sword which Pelopia had taken from him after she had been raped. Thyestes recognised the sword and revealed himself to Aegisthus as his father. Thyestes asked to see Pelopia, who came to the prison and, realising that she had committed incest, slew herself with the sword. Aegisthus did not kill Thyestes but showed Atreus the sword stained with his mother's blood. Atreus, believing Thyestes to be dead, went to the sea and offered a thank-offering to the gods; there Aegisthus slew him.

Thyestes and Aegisthus then ruled Mycenae, but Agamemnon and Menelaus drove them out. When Agamemnon left to fight the Trojan War, Aegisthus, in spite of a warning from Hermes, came back to Mycenae and seduced Clytemnestra, Agamemnon's wife. She accepted his advances either because of her anger at the death of Iphigenia by Agamemnon's agency or because she knew that he was intending to return with a concubine, Cassandra.

The deaths of Agamemnon and Cassandra were planned by Aegisthus and Clytemnestra. Aegisthus ruled his kingdom for seven years after the murder, and was then killed in his turn by the returning son of Agamemnon, Orestes. These are the themes of Aeschylus' trilogy the *Oresteia* and of plays by Sophocles and Euripides.

Aegle There are several minor charac-

ters of this name. *See* HELIADES; THESEUS.

Aegyptus Son of Belus and twin brother of Danaus. Belus had a vast empire in Africa; he sent Aegyptus and Danaus to rule Arabia and Libya respectively. The former conquered the Melampodes ('black feet') and named his new kingdom Egypt after himself. Danaus, afraid of his brother's growing power, fled to Argos, from which his ancestress Io had come.

Aegyptus, in order to win the right to rule all the lands of Belus, asked Danaus to give his fifty daughters in marriage to his fifty sons. Danaus was finally persuaded, but, suspecting treachery, he gave each of his daughters a dagger and told them to kill their husbands on the wedding night. And so all the sons of Aegyptus were murdered, with the single exception of Lynceus.

Aello *see* HARPIES.

Aeneas Son of Venus (Greek: *Aphrodite*) and Anchises, a descendant of Tros and hence a member of the royal house of Troy, though of the junior branch. Aeneas is an important warrior on the Trojan side in the *Iliad*, second only to Hector; but his chief importance lies in the events which took place after the fall of Troy, when he led the remnant of his people to Italy. This story was in existence well before Virgil's time, but it was he who made Aeneas' coming to Italy and his subsequent settlement there the theme of his masterpiece, the *Aeneid*. In the *Iliad* Aeneas had been the only Trojan to be given any hopes for the future: for Poseidon prophesied that he would reign over Troy in years to come and save the house of Dardanus from extinction. It was ironical that Aeneas, who complained that Priam never gave him due recognition and preferred his own sons, was to be Priam's successor; though the Troy over which he was to reign was not the original one. Another link between the *Iliad* and the hero of the *Aeneid* is that Homer, like Virgil, depicts Aeneas as being the most god-fearing and pious of his race.

Aeneas was born on Mount Ida, near Troy, and given by his mother to the nymphs to look after. At the age of five he was brought to his father Anchises. When the Trojan War began Aeneas led the Dardanian troops (Dardania was a town on the slopes of Mount Ida), but Hector was supreme commander. Aeneas resented Hector's superior power, Priam's disdain, and the domination of Troy (Ilium) over his own town. Achilles drove Aeneas from Dardania and he took refuge in Lyrnessus, which was then sacked. The peoples of the Trojan region had to take refuge in Troy, the best-defended fortress, and Aeneas was there during the events described in the *Iliad*. He was married to one of Priam's daughters, Creusa *3*, and they had a son, Ascanius.

There are several versions of what happened to Aeneas after the fall of Troy. According to one account Aphrodite warned Anchises to take refuge on Mount Ida even before Troy fell, and Aeneas also left the city in time, terrified by the omen of Laocoon's death. The *Little Iliad* makes him a prisoner and slave of Neoptolemus. Again, there was a story that after the fall of the rest of Troy, Aeneas tried to defend its citadel (Pergamon) and eventually left by agreement with the Greeks, who respected his piety. The tradition that he departed from the burning city carrying Anchises on his back is much older than Virgil, as is the story of his voyages and connections with both Sicily and Carthage. The belief that Aeneas came to Central Italy goes back at least as far as the fifth century BC.

According to Roman tradition elaborated by Virgil, Aeneas and a few followers, in the final battle on the streets of the burning Troy, fought desperately and unsuccessfully. Aeneas witnessed

the death of Priam and the triumph of Neoptolemus in the royal palace. He returned to his house and, guided by his divine mother and by a message received from the shade of Hector in a dream the previous night, resolved to flee from the city with whatever he could salvage. His father at first refused to go but certain omens – a gentle flame which shone from Ascanius' head and a massive thunderbolt – persuaded him to change his mind; and so they all left home, to seek safety on Mount Ida. Aeneas carried his lame and aged father (who himself carried the Penates or household gods in his arms) and led Ascanius by the hand. Creusa followed behind, but on their way through the dark and smouldering city she became parted from them and was lost. Aeneas returned in anguish to look for her but saw only her apparition, which warned him to abandon the search. The Trojan remnant – for many others took refuge with Aeneas on Ida – remained for many months building ships, which Aeneas then launched, still ignorant of the land he was destined to settle but hoping to found a city in Thrace. There, however, the ghost of Polydorus, Priam's youngest son, warned Aeneas to leave. He sailed on to Delos, where the oracle of Apollo bade him seek the 'ancient mother' of his race. This Anchises supposed to be the isle of Crete, from which had come his ancestor Teucer, whose grandson Ilus had founded Troy. When they reached Crete, they were visited with famine. In a dream Aeneas heard the Penates tell him that the oracle of Apollo had meant the homeland not of Teucer but of his son-in-law (Ilus' father) Dardanus who had originated from Hesperia or Italy. Aeneas again set sail but was blown by a storm to the Strophades islands, where the Harpies plundered the Trojans. One of them, Celaeno, warned them that, when they became so hungry that they were compelled to eat their tables, they would be in their new country.

The Trojans sailed on to Buthrotum in Epirus where they found a fellow-Trojan, the prophet Helenus, ruling there with Hector's widow Andromache as his queen. Helenus directed Aeneas to go on to Drepanum in Sicily, and told him that he was destined to found a great nation. The Trojans avoided Scylla and Charybdis and reached Drepanum near Eryx, where Aeneas' mother Venus had her shrine. Here Anchises died and was buried.

The Trojans sailed on northwards towards Italy, but Juno (Greek: *Hera*), to foil their plan of founding a new Troy, sent a great storm to wreck the fleet, persuading Aeolus to loosen the bag of the winds. Neptune, however, stilled the sea and the Trojans came safely to Africa, near the site of Carthage which Queen Dido was newly building. Venus, anxious for her son's welfare, sent Cupid (Greek: *Eros*) in the guise of Ascanius to make Dido fall in love with Aeneas. Juno, hoping that his plans to settle in Italy would thus founder, brought about the union of the two in a cave. But Aeneas, for all Dido's protestations, did not marry her. For Jupiter sent Mercury to warn Aeneas to sail away and not to forget his destiny. From his ship he saw flames. They rose from the pyre on which the body of Dido was being consumed: for she had killed herself.

Aeneas returned to Sicily, where he was welcomed by Acestes, king of Eryx, who was the son of a Trojan mother. Funeral games were held for Anchises. But Juno caused some of the Trojan women to rebel against the prospect of further wanderings, and they set fire to the ships. A few were burnt but Jupiter sent rain to save the rest. Aeneas allowed the oldest and weakest to stay with Acestes in Eryx, and they founded the Sicilian town of Egesta.

Proceeding with his younger and abler followers, Aeneas came to Italy, losing Palinurus, his helmsman, and Misenus,

one of Hector's former companions, on the voyage; a cape in Italy was named after each of them. At Cumae Aeneas consulted the Sibyl, an aged prophetess, and following her instructions found the Golden Bough in a wood by the lake of Avernus. With this talisman he and the Sibyl went down to the Underworld. There Aeneas saw many of the shades of the dead, including Dido, who spoke no word to him and turned away. His father's shade gave him a survey of the destiny of his race and the future of Rome. Reassured by this vision, Aeneas with the Sibyl returned from the Underworld and he rejoined his men.

They then sailed to the Tiber, landed on its banks, and ate a meal there. Such was their hunger that they also ate the flat wheaten loaves they were using as tables, and Ascanius pointed out that they had fulfilled the prophecy of Celaeno. The territory in which they found themselves was Latium, named after its ruler King Latinus. He and his wife Amata had promised their only child Lavinia in marriage to Turnus, king of the neighbouring Rutulians. But even before Aeneas' arrival an unfavourable oracle had warned that Lavinia must marry a man from abroad. Latinus recognised Aeneas as a suitable candidate for her hand and welcomed him, but Juno again intervened, sending the Fury Alecto from Hades to turn Amata against the new match. Alecto also instigated Turnus to declare war on the strangers, and he summoned his allies who comprised most of the local rulers, including the Volscian Camilla and the exiled Etruscan Mezentius. Aeneas, in his turn, received the friendship of the Etruscans, who hated Mezentius for his cruelty, and of the Arcadian Evander, who was connected by blood with the Trojans and had recently founded his colony at Pallanteum (on the site of Rome's Palatine Hill). Before leaving for Pallanteum, Aeneas had a dream in which the god of the Tiber told him that on his way there he would find a huge white sow with thirty piglets, and that on that spot Ascanius would found a city thirty years later and call it Alba Longa ('Long White') after the sow. Aeneas duly sacrificed the animal to Juno in hope of softening her anger.

New armour was made for Aeneas by Vulcan (Greek: Hephaestus) at Venus' request. While he was away, Turnus attacked his camp, and tried to burn his ships, but they turned into nymphs and swam away. Nisus and Euryalus, two Trojans, tried to pass through Turnus' lines to inform Aeneas of the attack, but they were struck down. When Aeneas returned, the battle went against him. Pallas, the young son of Evander, and many others of his men were killed, but Aeneas' slaying of Mezentius and his son Lausus turned the tide. A truce was arranged and Turnus agreed to settle the issue by single combat. But Juno caused the Latini to break the agreement, and in the subsequent fighting Aeneas was wounded. Venus cured him and he attacked Laurentum, Latinus' city, with such violence that Amata, thinking Turnus was dead, killed herself. Again Turnus made a truce and arranged a single combat. But his sister Juturna, a water-nymph, who had helped him and kept him clear of Aeneas, now deserted his cause. Aeneas brought him down. Turnus' prayer for mercy was about to move the victor when he noticed Pallas' sword-belt which Turnus was wearing as a trophy. Aeneas then slew him on the spot.

Aeneas married Lavinia and ruled over a union of the Latins and Trojans. As a concession, however, to Juno's anger, the Trojans, by Jupiter's decree, forgot their language and customs and adapted themselves to Italian ways. Aeneas founded a new city, naming it Lavinium after his wife: at this place, in historic times, the cult of Venus, Vesta, and the Trojan Penates remained strong. His son Ascanius founded Alba Longa,

which became the capital of the new Trojan–Latin race, until centuries later Romulus founded Rome on the site of the Pallanteum where Aeneas had visited Evander. The family of Julius Caesar claimed descent from Aeneas through Ascanius, who was also called Iulus.

Other traditions about the later years of Aeneas recount that he met Dido's sister Anna on the banks of the River Numicius, that he was purified in the river, and that after his death he was received into the company of the gods.

Aenus A king of the Doliones of Mysia; the father of Cyzicus.

Aeolus *1.* Son of Hippotas and king of the floating island of Aeolia (perhaps the Aeolian Isles north of Sicily), a mortal to whom Zeus, as a result of his love for him, gave control of the winds. He kept the winds inside a cave on his island and could release them as he wished, or as the gods requested. Aeolus lived a carefree life with his wife Cyane, daughter of Liparus, the first king of the island, and their six sons and six daughters, who had married each other. Receiving Odysseus hospitably, he tied up the winds except for the gentle West in a leather bag for him, so that he could reach home safely. But the sailors, jealous of Odysseus' supposed treasure, untied the bag and were driven back to Aeolia, from which, however, Aeolus drove them away. Before receiving the favours of Zeus, Aeolus, an expert sailor, had invented sails and had learnt to read the signs of the weather.

2. Son of Hellen and Orseis. The three brothers Aeolus, Xuthus, and Dorus were given the three great divisions of Greece by their father, the eponym of the Hellenes. Aeolus received Thessaly and gave his name to the Aeolic race. He married Enarete and had a large and influential family: Sisyphus, Cretheus, Athamas, Salmoneus, Deion, Magnes, Perieres, and Macareus; his daughters were Canace, Alcyone, Pisidice, Calyce, Cleobule and Perimede. He killed Canace for her incestuous relationship with Macareus. Many of Aeolus' sons became kings of Greek cities. He is often confused with Aeolus *1* – for example, in Ovid's version of the story of Alcyone.

3. Son of Poseidon and Melanippe, daughter of Aeolus *2* and Hippe. He had a brother, Boeotus.

Aepytus *1.* Son of Cresphontes and king of Messenia. His mother Merope saved him when Polyphontes slew his father and usurped the throne. He was brought up in Arcadia and later returned to take vengeance on the usurper. On arriving unrecognised he pretended that he had killed Aepytus, whom Polyphontes had long sought to do away with. His mother Merope, believing his story to be true, nearly slew him in his bed, but an old man recognised him and saved him. Aepytus then killed Polyphontes at the sacrifice he was offering in thanks for Aepytus' own supposed death, and assumed his father's throne.

2. see EVADNE *2.*

Aerope Daughter of Catreus, king of Crete. Her father got rid of her either by selling her into slavery – because he believed a child of his was destined to kill him – or else by throwing her into the sea for having sexual relations with a slave. She was bought and married by Atreus, but committed adultery with his brother Thyestes. Her son was said to be Pleisthenes, though it is alternatively reported that she bore Agamemnon and Menelaus.

Aesa Fate, or one of the Fates.

Aesacus Son of King Priam and the nymph Alexirrhoe, daughter of the River Granicus. Brought up in the country near Mount Ida, Aesacus fell in love with the nymph Hesperia. Seeing her

one day drying her hair by the River Cebren, of which river her father was the god, Aesacus pursued her. Fleeing, she was bitten on the foot by a snake and died. Mortified by guilt, Aesacus leapt into the sea to drown himself. But Tethys had pity on him and turned him into a diver bird, which dashes itself constantly into the waves from a great height.

Aesculapius *see* ASCLEPIUS.

Aeson Son of Cretheus, king of Iolcus, and Tyro; father of Jason. He should have inherited the throne of Iolcus, but it was usurped by Pelias, son of Poseidon and Tyro. Aeson married Alcimede, daughter of Phylacus. When their son was born, they declared that he was dead but secretly gave him to Chiron to bring up.

While Jason was away on his quest for the Golden Fleece, Aeson died. According to one version he was forced by Pelias to drink a poison, usually described as bull's blood. Medea, on her arrival in Iolcus, brought Aeson back to life by her magic arts.

Aethalia A nymph, daughter of Hephaestus, mother of the Palici by Zeus.

Aethlius Father of Endymion by Calyce, daughter of Aeolus *2.*

Aethra Daughter of Pittheus, king of Troezen, and mother of Theseus. She was first betrothed to Bellerophon, but when he was exiled from Corinth for murder Pittheus called off the wedding. When Aegeus came to Troezen, Pittheus sent her to the island of Sphaeria, where Aegeus spent a night with her. (Later, the story was put about that she had been visited by Poseidon, perhaps to prevent scandal, and Theseus, to whom she subsequently gave birth, was often called Poseidon's son.) Before leaving Troezen, Aegeus placed the tokens proving his association with her (a sword and sandals) under a boulder. Later, after Theseus became king at Athens, Aethra went to live with him. But while he was in the Underworld with Pirithous, Castor and Polydeuces carried Aethra off to be Helen's slave, as a reprisal for Theseus' theft of Helen. At the same time they rescued Helen from Aphidnae in Attica, where Aethra had been in charge of her. Helen took Aethra with her to Troy, and after its fall Agamemnon allowed Demophon and Acamas, Aethra's grandsons, to take her back to Attica.

Aethusa Daughter of Poseidon and the Pleiad Alcyone; mother by Apollo of Hyrieus and Hyperenor.

Aetolus His father was Endymion, king of Elis, who made his three sons run a race for the right to inherit the throne. Epeius won and became king, and then his brother Aetolus succeeded him. However he was banished because, at the funeral games of Azan, he accidentally ran down Apis with his chariot and killed him. Aetolus went to the land of the Curetes on the river Achelous and conquered the country, calling it Aetolia after himself. His wife was Pronoe and they had two sons, Pleuron and Calydon, after whom two Aetolian cities were named.

Agamedes *see* TROPHONIUS.

Agamemnon Son of Atreus (or, according to one authority, of Atreus' son Pleisthenes) and Anaxibia. When Thyestes and Aegisthus had killed Atreus, Agamemnon and his brother Menelaus – who were known as the Atridae – sought help from Tyndareos, king of Sparta, and expelled the two killers. Agamemnon took the throne of Mycenae. (There is an alternative tradition that the Atridae were still small children at the time of Atreus' murder

and were rescued by a nurse and taken to Sicyon.)

Tyndareos had two daughters, Clytemnestra and Helen, who married Agamemnon and Menelaus respectively. Clytemnestra was already married to a son of Thyestes, Tantalus, whom Agamemnon slew, tearing his baby from the mother's breast to murder it. He then married her himself. The children of this union were three daughters, Iphigenia (also called Iphianassa), Electra (or Laodice), and Chrysothemis; and one son, Orestes.

In the *Iliad* Agamemnon is treated by the other Greek rulers as a high king to whom they owe allegiance and a feudal duty of military service. He took a hundred ships to Troy, the largest single contingent. He carried an ivory sceptre made by Hephaestus for Zeus, who gave it to Hermes, who in turn gave it to Agamemnon's grandfather Pelops.

When Helen was being courted by all the eligible kings of Greece, Agamemnon persuaded her father Tyndareos to give her in marriage to his brother Menelaus. The other suitors had sworn an oath to defend the rights of whoever should succeed in winning her, so that when Paris of Troy abducted Helen, they were doubly bound to go to the aid of Menelaus' brother Agamemnon in his efforts to recover his sister-in-law. This matter of honour transcended everything else for Agamemnon; he even sacrificed his eldest child Iphigenia in order to gain a favourable wind to sail from Aulis to Troy. For the reasons lying behind this act, *see* IPHIGENIA. When Agamemnon sent for her, he deceived his wife into allowing her to leave by declaring that she was to be married to Achilles. In the *Iliad* Homer seems to know nothing of the sacrifice, for Agamemnon later offers all three of his daughters to Achilles to induce him to return to active service. Euripides, in the *Iphigenia in Tauris*, follows a tradition indicating that Iphigenia did not die after all, since Artemis substituted a hind for her. But Aeschylus indicates that she was actually sacrificed, and that when Clytemnestra learnt the truth she never forgave her husband and helped Aegisthus to batter him to death after his return from the war.

After a long campaign, in the course of which the Greek army finally penned the Trojans within their city, Agamemnon had a disastrous quarrel with Achilles. When Agamemnon's slave girl Chryseis had to be returned to Chryses, Apollo's priest, to avert the wrath of that god, Agamemnon took Achilles' concubine Briseis away from him. Achilles' consequent refusal to fight led to disaster upon disaster for the Greeks, and their ships would have been burnt had not Patroclus' intervention and death brought Achilles back into the struggle.

On the fall of Troy Agamemnon took as his concubine Cassandra, the prophetess who was never believed. When he returned to Mycenae, after an absence of ten years, Aegisthus and Clytemnestra slew them both. This is the version related by Aeschylus in his Agamemnon; Homer, however, tells how Aegisthus invited Agamemnon to a feast and attacked him with a retinue of armed men.

Agapenor King of Tegea in Arcadia at the time of the Trojan War. The sons of Phegeus sold him their sister Arsinoe as a slave; but the sons of her husband Alcmaeon, finding them at Agapenor's house, killed them. Agapenor was commander of the Arcadian contingent in the Trojan War; Agamemnon lent him sixty ships. After the war his fleet was wrecked off Cyprus, where he remained and founded Paphos. In historical times the Cyprian and Arcadian dialects closely resembled one another.

Agasthenes *1.* Son of Augeas and king of Elis. His son Polyxenus led the Elean

contingent at Troy. *2.* A suitor of Helen who took part in the Trojan War.

Agathyrsus *see* HERACLES.

Agave A daughter of Cadmus and Harmonia; wife of Echion and mother of Pentheus. Her sister Semele was the mother of Dionysus by a miraculous birth in which she perished. But Agave and her sisters, Ino and Autonoe, refused to recognise Dionysus and mocked Semele's claims. For this, when Dionysus and his Maenads visited Thebes, they were punished with madness: and Agave tore her own son Pentheus to pieces when he spied on their revels. This is the theme of Euripides' *Bacchants*.

Agdistis A Phrygian name of Cybele.

Agenor *1.* Son of Poseidon and Libya and brother of Belus. Agenor became king of Phoenicia, Belus of Africa and Arabia. He married Telephassa who bore Europa, Cadmus, Phoenix, and Cilix; and according to some, Thasus and Phineus. Zeus in the form of a bull abducted Europa, and Agenor sent his sons to find her or die in the attempt. None returned; nor did his wife, who had gone with them. Phoenix settled in Libya, Cilix gave his name to Cilicia, and Cadmus founded Thebes in Greece. *2.* Son of Antenor who fought in the Trojan War. When Achilles was about to storm the Scaean Gates, Agenor saved the Trojans by challenging the Greek champion. Apollo kept him safe, and later assumed the shape of Agenor to divert the attention of Achilles. *3.* A king of Pleuron in Aetolia. He was the father of Thestius by Epicaste.

Aglaia *1. see* GRACES.
2. The wife of Abas and mother of Acrisius and Proetus.

Aglaophone One of the Sirens.

Aglaurus or **Agraulust** Two Athenian women, mother and daughter. *1.* Daughter of Actaeus, first king of Athens; she married Cecrops *1,* who inherited her father's kingdom.

2. The daughter of Cecrops 1 and Aglaurus 1. She was the mother of Alcippe by the god Ares. She and her sisters Herse and Pandrosus were entrusted by Athena with the baby Erichthonius and, though Pandrosus obeyed Athena's command not to look at him in his casket, Aglaurus and Herse disobeyed. They saw a snake coiled round the baby and, according to one tradition, threw themselves off the Acropolis. Ovid, on the other hand, makes them survive. Hermes saw Herse in the Panathenaic procession and fell in love with her. Aglaurus accepted a bribe from the god to persuade Herse to view his attentions with favour, but Athena, remembering Aglaurus' disobedience, made her jealous of her sister, so that she barred Hermes' way to her bed. In consequence Hermes turned Aglaurus to stone.

Agorius An Elean with whom Oxylus shared the government of Elis.

Agrius *1. see* GIANTS.

2. Son of Porthaon and Euryte and brother of Oeneus, king of Calydon, whose throne he usurped after the death of Oeneus' son Meleager. Subsequently Diomedes, son of Tydeus and grandson of Oeneus, took vengeance by driving out Agrius and killing his sons. Agrius thereupon killed himself.

3. Son of Odysseus and Circe.

Aias or **Ajax** *1.* Son of Telamon of Salamis and Periboea and half-brother of Teucer. The name was said to be derived from the eagle *(aietos)* seen by his father Telamon when, before his birth, Heracles prayed to Zeus to give his friend a brave son.

In the *Iliad* Aias is second only to Achilles among the Greek warriors in his prowess as a powerful fighting man; with his huge shield, he looked like a tower as he went into battle. He spoke little and slowly, but he had a good heart and tremendous courage. He often fought alongside his half-brother Teucer, the archer who shot from the shelter of the shield, and also the other Aias. He was a bulwark of the Greeks and often protected their rear in dangerous situations.

He was one of the suitors for Helen's hand, who bound themselves by oath to defend whichever of them became her husband. Aias brought twelve ships from Salamis as his contribution to the force; his personal prowess was out of proportion to the strength of his contingent. He fought a duel with Hector and nearly killed him with a great rock, but night came down to part the combatants. They then exchanged gifts, Hector giving a sword and Aias a purple sword-belt. When the Greeks sent an embassy to Achilles to urge him to return to the fight, Aias, as a close friend of his, was a member of the party but left the talking to Odysseus. The following day, when Odysseus got into difficulties and was wounded, Aias rescued him. When the Trojans reached the wall defending the beached Greek ships, Aias and his namesake performed stout service, saving Menestheus and holding back the Trojan assault. But when the Trojans attacked the fleet, though he strode the decks of the ships wielding a huge grappling-pole, thus giving the lead to the Greek resistance and becoming a target for many missiles, he could not prevent the enemy from burning a ship. It was only the timely intervention of Patroclus and the Myrmidons that saved the situation.

When Patroclus was killed and Hector had stripped off his armour, Aias covered the corpse with his shield. At Patroclus' funeral games Aias competed in several events; he drew with Odysseus at wrestling and was beaten by

Diomedes at spear-thrusting. Later, when Achilles was killed by Paris, Aias carried his body back into the Greek camp and rescued his armour, while Odysseus kept the enemy at bay.

There are several versions of his death. The most important tradition is hinted at in the *Odyssey* and developed in Sophocles' *Aias (Ajax)*. According to this story, after the death of Achilles there was a dispute as to who should receive his armour; it was claimed both by Aias and Odysseus. Either the other Greek leaders put it to the vote or, according to another version, they entrusted the decision to Helenus, the captive Trojan seer. At all events, the armour went to Odysseus. Thereupon Aias planned a night-attack on his own allies; but Athena drove him mad so that he killed a flock of sheep instead. When he came to himself, shame and remorse drove him to slay himself with his sword, the gift of Hector. Where his blood fell on the ground (or else in his homeland of Salamis) the hyacinth sprang up, with its petals marked in the shape of AI, the first two letters of his name and also, in Greek, a word meaning 'alas!'. It was also maintained that when Odysseus' ship was wrecked in his wanderings, Achilles' armour was washed ashore at the tomb of Aias in the Troad, and thus, by divine justice, Aias received the object of contention in the end. After his death Agamemnon and Menelaus refused to allow his body to be buried at first, because of the acts he had committed in his madness, but Odysseus prevailed on them to relent.

According to another story, however, he was killed by Paris with an arrow, like Achilles. It was also said that he was buried alive by the Trojans, who threw clay on him because Heracles had made him invulnerable by wrapping him while a baby in his lion-skin. Another tradition recounted that he was murdered by Odysseus.

Aias had a son, Eurysaces ('broad-shield'), by his concubine Tecmessa, whom he had taken in war against the Phrygians. This son succeeded Telamon as king of Salamis.

2. Son of Oileus of Opuntian Locris. A suitor for Helen, he was an important character in the *Iliad*, but although he often fought side by side with Aias the son of Telamon – presumably because of their common name – he presented a marked contrast to his namesake. Aias the son of Oileus was small and fleet of foot and a great spear-thrower. He wore a linen corselet, and led a large contingent of forty ships to Troy.

In character too he was markedly different from Aias the son of Telamon, being arrogant and conceited and hateful to the gods, especially Athena. At Patroclus' funeral games he gratuitously insulted Idomeneus over the chariot-race. In the foot-race, which he should have won, Athena took the victory from him and gave it to Odysseus, while Aias the son of Oileus slipped in cow-dung and cursed Athena for his failure.

After the sacking of Troy Aias brought disaster upon himself and the Greeks, for he dragged Cassandra away from Athena's statue to rape her; and in so doing he pulled down the statue itself. The image lay on the ground with its eyes averted to the sky so as to avoid the sight of the outrage. The other Greeks wanted to kill Aias for his sin, but he clung to the very image he had overturned, and the Greeks were afraid to touch him.

Athena resolved to punish Aias for his crime, and the other Greeks, too, for their failure to punish him. As the Greek fleet was sailing home, she asked Zeus to send a great storm and the ships were wrecked off Cape Caphereus in southern Euboea. Athena herself threw a thunderbolt at Aias' ship and sank it, but he swam ashore boasting that he had defied the anger of the gods and escaped with his life. He hauled himself up on a rock called Gyrae, whereupon Poseidon blasted it with a thunderbolt and drowned him.

After his death, according to one tradition, Aias was buried by Thetis on the island of Myconos, but Athena, still remorseless against him, plagued his homeland Locris until the Locrians, in obedience to the Delphic Oracle, agreed to send two virgins every year to serve in the temple of Athena at Troy: the girls had to arrive without being spied by the inhabitants, who would kill them if they saw them. The Locrians of historic times maintained that this practice continued for a thousand years.

Ajax *see* AIAS.

Alalcomeneus A hero of Plataea in Boeotia, who founded there the Great Daedala, a festival commemorating a tiff between Zeus and Hera, and its amusing conclusion (he is also called Cithaeron). *See also* ATHENA; HERA.

Alastor ('avenger') Son of Neleus of Pylos and brother of Nestor. He married Harpalyce and was killed by Heracles in raids on Pylos.

Albunea An Italian nymph with the power of prophecy who lived at Tibur (Tivoli) in central Italy, in the stream Albula which joins the Anio. She was a prophetess or Sibyl, and composed oracular verses which were deposited in the Capitol at Rome with the Sibylline books.

Alcaeus *1.* Son of Perseus and Andromeda; he married Astydamia; their children were Amphitryon and Anaxo. Heracles, his grandson, was called Alcides after him.
2. Son of Androgeos and grandson of Minos. With his brother Sthenelus he accompanied Heracles as a hostage to fetch the belt of Hippolyta, queen of the Amazons. When Heracles conquered Thasos on his return to Greece, the two young men were made its rulers.

Alcathous *1.* Son of Pelops and Hippodamia. After being exiled for murdering his brother Chrysippus, he won the kingdom of Megara and the hand of Evaechme, daughter of its king Megareus, by killing a lion which roamed Mount Cithaeron and had killed Megareus' son Evippus. Alcathous kept the animal's tongue to refute false claimants. He rebuilt the city walls which Minos of Crete had destroyed when he attacked King Nisus. Apollo rested his lyre on one of the stones in the new wall, which thereafter resounded like a lyre. The sons of Alcathous were Ischepolis and Callipolis and he had three daughters of whom one, Eriboe or Periboea, was the mother of Aias the son of Telamon, and another, Automedusa, married Iphicles and bore Iolaus.

When Ischepolis was killed in the Calydonian boar-hunt, Callipolis brought Alcathous the bad news. His father happened to be sacrificing to Apollo at the time of his arrival, and so Callipolis pulled the logs off the fire thinking the sacrifice inauspicious at such a moment. But Alcathous, misunderstanding his son's intention as impious, struck him with a log and killed him. Alcathous was purified by the prohet Polyidus. Having lost both his sons, he left his kingdom to his grandson Aias.
2. Son of Portheus. *See* TYDEUS.

Alcestis Daughter of Pelias, king of Iolcus, and Anaxibia; wife of Admetus. Her heroic self-sacrifice is the subject of Euripides' play which bears her name.

When she was of marriageable age, her father made it the condition of her betrothal that her husband should first have to yoke a lion and a boar to a chariot. Admetus, the king of Pherae, succeeded in this task thanks to the help of Apollo, to whom he had given aid and shelter when the god had to spend a year in servitude to a mortal. The chariot in which Admetus drove Alcestis away from her father's house was harnessed to this lion and boar. At the wedding Admetus forgot to sacrifice to Artemis and found a coil of snakes in his bed (or found the bedroom full of serpents) – an omen of impending death. Apollo again gave his help and placated his angry sister. He also made the Fates drunk and extracted from them an opportunity for Admetus to escape death, when it was his turn to die, if he could persuade somebody else to take his place. He could persuade nobody but his wife Alcestis, who offered to die for him. There are two versions of what ensued. Either Persephone gave Alcestis back to him, presumably because of her admiration of Alcestis' devotion to her excellent husband; or else, as Euripides tells the tale, Heracles, who was a guest at Admetus' palace at the time of the death, went after Death, wrestled with him for Alcestis, and won her back.

Alcestis had two sons, Eumelus, who fought in the Trojan War, and Hippasus. She and her husband were later exiled from Pherae.

Alcides *see* HERACLES.

Alcimede Mother of Jason and wife of Aeson. She was a daughter of Phylacus, king of Phylace. When Pelias had forced Aeson to kill himself and had killed their younger son Promachus, Alcimede committed suicide, cursing the tyrannical usurper.

Alcinous Son of Nausithous and king of the mythical Phaeacians. After the wreck of his raft, when he had been floating in the sea for two days, Odysseus landed in his country of Scheria. It was to him that Odysseus told the tale of his wanderings, caused by the wrath of Poseidon. Alcinous had married Arete, his niece (daughter of his brother Rhexenor), and they had five sons and a daughter Nausicaa, who was the first person Odysseus saw after landing.

In his splendid palace, surrounded by gardens which flourished at every season of the year, Alcinous entertained Odysseus and then helped him on his way, in spite of the enmity of Poseidon towards the voyager and a warning Alcinous had received that his constant assistance of strangers would one day bring Poseidon's wrath on his people. When the ship which took Odysseus back to Ithaca was on its return journey, Poseidon turned it into a rock and blocked the Phaeacians' harbour with a mountain.

A generation earlier Alcinous had sheltered the Argonauts on their flight from Colchis, and when the Colchian ship arrived he had decreed that if Medea was still a virgin she must be returned to her father. On the prompting of Arete, Jason and Medea made haste to consummate their marriage.

Alcippe Daughter of Ares and Aglaurus 2. She was raped at Athens by Halirrhothius, a son of Poseidon and the nymph Euryte, and Ares stuck him down for the crime. For this Ares himself had to stand trial, accused by Poseidon at the place of the rape, which was subsequently called Ares' Hill (*Areopagos*) and became the seat of the most august council and court of Athens. At this first of all murder trials, Ares was acquitted by a jury consisting of the other great Olympian gods.

Alcithoe One of the daughters of Minyas, who were turned into bats.

Alcmaeon Son of Amphiaraus and Eriphyle and brother of Amphilochus. When Polynices planned his expedition to obtain the throne of Thebes, he tried to persuade Amphiaraus to join it, but Amphiaraus, knowing through his prophetic powers that the result would be failure and death, refused. Polynices then bribed Eriphyle with the necklace of Harmonia, and she made her husband go, for there was an agreement between Adrastus and Amphiaraus that Eriphyle should arbitrate between them. Amphiaraus knew that he was doomed to die at Thebes, so before departing he made his sons swear to take vengeance for him on their mother. For ten years they did not obey him, but then the Epigoni, under Alcmaeon's lead, made war a second time against Thebes, in order to avenge their fathers. On this occasion Eriphyle was again bribed, this time by Polynices' son Thersander, who gave her Harmonia's wedding gown, and she urged her sons to join the expedition. Either before or after the expedition, Alcmaeon went to consult the Oracle of Delphi, which told him both to avenge his father and punish his mother; he also became leader of the assault. When he and his allies were victorious, Alcmaeon and his brother slew Eriphyle. The Furies, accompanied, according to one version, by the ghost of Eriphyle, drove Alcmaeon mad and pursued him. Leaving Argos, he went first to Arcadia and then to Delphi, where Manto, Tiresias' daughter, whom he had captured at Thebes and offered to Apollo from the spoils, bore him two children, Amphilochus and Tisiphone. Alcmaeon gave these children to Creon, king of Corinth, to bring up, but the queen sold Tisiphone into slavery. Alcmaeon later bought her and recovered Amphilochus.

Alcmaeon proceeded to Psophis, where the king, Phegeus, purified him and gave him his daughter Arsinoe in marriage. Alcmaeon passed on to his new wife the gifts that his mother had received as bribes, the necklace and wedding-dress of Harmonia. But since he was not cured of his madness and since a famine afflicted all Phegeus' lands, Alcmaeon consulted the Delphic Oracle. Here he was told that he must find a new, unpolluted country which the sun had not seen at the time of Eriphyle's death, and settle there. He moved to the alluvial deposits at the mouth of the river Achelous, and there the river-god gave him his daughter Cal-

lirrhoe ('fair flowing') and purified him. They had two sons, Acarnan and Amphoterus.

Callirrhoe coveted the gifts which her husband had given to Arsinoe, and sent him to obtain them by a trick. He went to Psophis and told Phegeus he would never be cured of his madness unless he dedicated the gifts at Delphi. Phegeus handed them over, but one of Alcmaeon's servants disclosed the truth. Phegeus' sons waylaid him and killed him, burying him in a grove of cypress trees.

Arsinoe, who had not been privy to the murder, complained. Thereupon her brothers shut her up in a chest and sold her as a slave to Agapenor, declaring that she had killed Alcmaeon; but they were killed at Agapenor's house by Alcmaeon's sons. Callirrhoe had asked Zeus, who had been her lover, that her children might grow up at once so as to avenge their father. The two boys then killed Phegeus and his wife and took the necklace and robe to Delphi to be dedicated to Apollo.

Alcmena Daughter of Electryon and Anaxo; the wife of her uncle Amphitryon, king of Tiryns, and the mother of Heracles. Alcmena's brothers had been killed by the men of the Taphian islands in a cattle raid, and when Amphitryon wanted to sleep with her she commanded him to avenge them first. He recovered the cattle but killed Electryon by accident as he gave them back to him. For this he was sent into exile by Sthenelus, Electryon's brother. Alcmena accompanied him to Thebes but still would not allow him to become her lover until he had punished the Taphians. He raised an army and went to war.

Zeus had arranged these difficulties because he was determined to beget a valiant mortal who would save the gods in the great forthcoming battle against the Giants. He had chosen Alcmena, the wisest and most beautiful of women, to bear this hero, and she was to be his last mortal concubine. On the night of Amphitryon's return from the campaign, Zeus came to her in her husband's form. Later, when Amphitryon himself arrived, he quickly realised that something unaccountable had happened, for Alcmena claimed to have slept with him already that night. The prophet Tiresias gave the true explanation, and Amphitryon consummated his marriage.

Alcmena was pregnant with twins, Heracles and Iphicles; but only the latter was Amphitryon's son. When the time for her delivery came, Zeus boasted to the gods that a mortal ruler, descended from him, was shortly to be born. His wife Hera realised what was afoot and saw that Zeus intended Alcmena's son to be the monarch of her native land; so she sent Ilithyia, the goddess of childbirth, to sit outside Alcmena's room and do all she could to frustrate the birth. Ilithyia set about this task by crossing her fingers, arms, legs, and toes as a magic charm to prevent the delivery. Alcmena was on the point of expiring when one of her servant-women cried out that she had given birth. Ilithyia was so astonished that she came to look, thus uncrossing herself and allowing the twins to be delivered. According to Ovid, the servant-maid, whose name was Galanthis, was turned into a weasel.

After the death of Amphitryon, who had once tried to burn his wife to death for infidelity, but was prevented when Zeus sent a rainstorm, Alcmena married the Cretan Rhadamanthys and lived in Boeotia; or else, after the death of Heracles, Eurystheus – who was the king of Mycenae and Tiryns and had persecuted him – pursued her and her grandchildren to Attica, where they took refuge at Marathon. Eurystheus attacked Attica but was defeated and captured, and Alcmena insisted on his death. When she herself died, a great stone was put in the coffin in the place of her body; and she

was carried off by Hermes to the Islands of the Blessed, where she married Rhadamanthys, now one of the judges of the dead.

Alcon A Cretan archer who, when his sleeping child was seized by a snake, shot the snake without harming the child.

Alcyone *1.* Daughter of Aeolus, king of Thessaly; wife of Ceyx, king of Trachis. They were so happy that they compared themselves to the gods, calling themselves 'Zeus' and 'Hera', for which, according to one story, they were punished by being turned into birds, Alcyone into a kingfisher and Ceyx into a gannet. The more usual version, however, is that Ceyx was drowned at sea while going to Clarus (Colophon) in search of an oracle. His wife prayed for him daily until Hera, the goddess of marriage, sent her a dream in which Morpheus told her of her husband's death. Overwhelmed with sorrow, Alcyone went to the seashore where she found the body of Ceyx washed up. The gods took pity on her grief and turned them both into kingfishers. These birds nest every winter, and for this purpose Aeolus, lord of the winds, sends calm weather; such days sailors call 'halcyon' after Alcyone. *2.* A Pleiad; the mother, by Poseidon, of Aethusa.

Alcyoneus *see* GIANTS.

Alecto or **Allecto** *see* FURIES.

Alector A king of Argos, the son of Anaxagoras and father of Iphis *2*.

Aletes ('wanderer') *1.* Son of Hippotas. He went to Dodona to enquire how he might gain the throne of Corinth and was given the answer that he would do so when someone gave him a clod of earth at a festival. So he went to a festival at Corinth disguised as a beggar and, asking for bread, was given a lump of earth. He later became king.

2. Son of Aegisthus and Clytemnestra. According to one account, he became king of Mycenae after the death of Aegisthus but Orestes later killed him.

Aleus A king of Arcadia. He lived at Tegea, and married his brother Pereus' daughter Neaera. Their children were Lycurgus, Amphidamas, Cepheus, and Auge, who was seduced by Heracles.

Alexander see PARIS.

Alexiares Son of Heracles and Hebe.

Aloadae see OTUS.

Aloeus Son of Uranus and Gaia. He married Iphimedia, but she preferred Poseidon to her husband and used to sit at the edge of the sea letting the water wash over her womb until Poseidon came to her and begot Otus and Ephialtes (the Aloadae).

Alope Daughter of Cercyon, king of Eleusis; she was loved by Poseidon, and secretly bore him a son, whom she exposed. Wild mares suckled the baby, and two shepherds found him. When they saw his fine clothes, they wanted to keep him and quarrelled as to which of them should bring him up. They asked Cercyon to arbitrate; but he, when he saw his daughter's clothes on the baby, killed her and once more exposed the child, whom wild mares once more suckled. The shepherds found him again and, realising that the child was under the protection of a god, they cared for him, calling him Hippothous, 'horse-swift', a name recalling both the mares and Poseidon's role as the patron of horses.

When Theseus killed Cercyon he gave Hippothous the rule over Eleusis, because both men claimed Poseidon as their father. Alope was buried by the road from Eleusis to Megara, and Poseidon made a spring flow from her grave.

Alpheius A river in Elis which flows past Olympia. Its god was a son of Oceanus and Tethys. The nymph Arethusa bathed in the river and Alpheius fell in love with her. He took the form of a hunter and pursued her. She fled, right across the sea as far as Sicily, where she took refuge on the island of Ortygia near Syracuse. There Artemis turned her into a spring. But Alpheius was undaunted: his waters flowed under the sea as far as Sicily, where they emerged at Ortygia and mingled with Arethusa's. Another story of Alpheius is that he fell in love with Artemis and pursued her. She and her nymphs covered their faces in mud so that Alpheius could not tell them apart and had to abandon the chase while they mocked him. His waters were diverted by Heracles to cleanse the stables of Augeas at Elis.

Alphesiboea One of the names (the other is Arsinoe) given to the daughter of King Phegeus of Psophis who married Alcmaeon.

Althaea Daughter of Thestius, king of Aetolia, and mother of Meleager, Gorge, and Deianira. She married her uncle Oeneus, king of Calydon; during the Calydonian boar-hunt her son Meleager killed her brothers Toxeus and Plexippus, and as a result she cursed him. There was a tradition that at his birth the Fates had told Althaea that when a log, burning at that moment in the fire, was consumed, her son would die. She had snatched it out and kept it in a chest, but now, in her anger at his deed, she put it on the fire and burnt it, thus causing his death. Shortly afterwards she was overcome by remorse and hanged herself.

Althaemenes Son of Catreus, king of

Crete. An oracle had declared that one of Catreus' children would kill him; hearing of it, Althaemenes emigrated to Rhodes. When his sister Apemosyne declared that Hermes had raped her and that in consequence she was pregnant, Althaemenes kicked her to death. Later his father Catreus came to fetch him home, wishing to bequeath on him his kingdom, but Althaemenes took his crew for pirates and killed his father, thus fulfilling the oracle.

Amalthea Either a nymph or a she-goat owned by the nymph. As a baby, Zeus was suckled by the goat on Mount Dicte or Ida in Crete. The goat's horns flowed with nectar and ambrosia. According to Ovid, one of them broke off and the nymphs filled it with fruit for the child – Zeus – hence the expression '*cornu copiae*' or 'horn of plenty'. The goat was turned into the star Capella (the she-goat) or the constellation Capricorn (the goat's horn). The horn came into the possession of the Naiaids and had the power of producing whatever its owner might wish for.

Amarynceus Son of Pyttius. *See* AUGEAS.

Amata Wife of Latinus, king of Latium, when Aeneas arrived in Italy. She favoured the claim of Turnus rather than Aeneas to become the husband of her daughter Lavinia. When Aeneas' son Ascanius killed a pet stag, Amata had her excuse, and war broke out. In the fighting that ensued she fervently furthered Turnus' cause. When he decided to accept a challenge from Aeneas to settle the issue by single combat, Amata tried to dissuade him, and when she learnt (falsely) that he had been killed, she hanged herself. Shortly afterwards Aeneas killed Turnus and married Lavinia.

Amazons A mythical nation of warrior-women. The name was thought by the Greeks to mean 'breastless' and to signify that the Amazons cut off and cauterised the right breasts of their daughters so that they might draw the bow. Another explanation is that they did not make bread (*maza*, 'barley'), since they lived by hunting. Originating either from the Caucasus or from Colchis, they lived in Scythia (i.e. southern Russia) or in Themiscyra in northern Asia Minor. They were thought to be descended from Ares, and worshipped him as god of war and Artemis as a goddess of virginity and female strength. They had children by occasional contact with men of neighbouring tribes, but killed or enslaved their male offspring.

In the Trojan War they took the side of the Trojans. According to one version Penthesilea, their queen, brought them reinforcements after the burial of Hector. Achilles killed her and fell in love with her corpse.

Ameinias A young admirer of Narcissus; Narcissus' sin is sometimes said to have been to cause his death.

Amor One of the gods of love, sometimes identified with Eros or Cupid. For his mythology, *see* PSYCHE.

Ampelus A beautiful youth whom Dionysus loved; a wild bull gored him, and Dionysus turned him into a vine (*ampelos*).

Amphiaraus Son of Oicles and Hypermnestra 2. He was a seer and received his prophetic powers by inheritance from his great-grandfather Melampus.

He took part in the Calydonian boar-hunt and drove Adrastus, ruler of Argos, from his throne. When Adrastus came back from Sicyon (of which he had meanwhile become king), the two were reconciled; Amphiaraus restored him his kingdom, but received Adrastus' sister Eriphyle as his wife. A further agreement was made between them, that in any further quarrels between the two Eriphyle should arbitrate and her decision should be final. He had two sons, Alcmaeon and Amphilochus, and two daughters.

Amphiaraus knew through his clairvoyance that the expedition of the Seven against Thebes was bound to fail, and so he refused to join it. But Eriphyle, bribed by Polynices with the necklace and wedding dress of Harmonia, ruled that he must go all the same. When he left he made his sons swear to avenge him on the Thebans and on their mother.

On his way to Thebes with the Seven, he reproved them bitterly for their rashness and arrogance, blaming Tydeus especially. On the battlefield, when Melanippus had fought a fatal battle with Tydeus Amphiaraus placed the severed head of Melanippus into the dying Tydeus' hands, thus cheating Athena who was just bringing ambrosia to make Tydeus immortal: for he ate the brains from Melanippus' skull, and she turned away in horror.

Amphiaraus did not die: just as the Theban Periclymenus was about to spear him in the back, Zeus, who loved him dearly, split open the rocky ground with a thunderbolt, and he was swallowed up with his horses and chariot. A spring of water issued from the place where he had disappeared.

Amphilochus *1.* Younger son of Amphiaraus and Eriphyle. He inherited his father's gift of prophecy and was one of the Epigoni who made war on Thebes ten years after the attack of the Seven. He is confused with *2*, his nephew, in the matter of the foundation of Amphilochian Argos. He seems to have been killed by Apollo at Soli in Cilicia.

2. Nephew of the above, son of Alcmaeon and Tiresias' daughter Manto. He was brought up by Creon of Thebes and later joined his father in Epirus. He

fought in the Trojan War and, with a half-brother Mopsus 2, founded cities in Pamphylia, including Mallus, where they established a dream-oracle. Later Mopsus refused to allow Amphilochus to return to Mallus, and they killed one another in single combat.

Amphimachus Son of Cteatus of Elis, a suitor of Helen, and a leader of the Eleans at Troy. He was killed by Hector.

Amphimarus A musician, sometimes said to be father of Linus by Urania.

Amphinomus One of the suitors of Penelope in the *Odyssey*. He was the least offensive of them and sought to dissuade the rest from murdering Telemachus on his return from Sparta. Nevertheless, after Odysseus came back from his wanderings, he was among those slain by Telemachus in the great hall.

Amphion and **Zethus** Twin sons of Zeus and Antiope and for a time joint rulers of Thebes. For the story of their mother's flight before their birth, *see* ANTIOPE. After they were born, their mother was thrown in prison and the twins were exposed by their uncle Lycus *1*, regent for Labdacus in his minority. The twins were reared by shepherds on the mountains, Amphion becoming adept at music and Zethus at war and stock-breeding. Amphion set up an altar in the shepherd community to Hermes, who presented him with a lyre. He learnt the Lydian mode of music from the Lydians, having married Niobe, daughter of their king Tantalus; and he added three new strings to the four which the lyre had previously possessed.

When the twins were fully grown, Antiope escaped from her long captivity and made herself known to her sons, who determined to avenge her and raised an army to attack Thebes. They killed (or expelled) Lycus, who was now acting as regent for Laius after the death of Labdacus. They also tied his wife Dirce to the horns of a bull – the fate which she had intended for Antiope. Amphion and Zethus now made themselves kings of Thebes and built its walls; Amphion played the lyre with such magical beauty that the stones followed him and fitted themselves into place. Zethus had mocked Amphion's playing but was now forced to admit that it was a more successful aid to building than his own great strength. Because the lyre had seven strings, Amphion gave Thebes seven gates. The brothers renamed the city, previously Cadmeia, after Zethus' wife, Thebe.

Amphion came to a tragic end. His wife Niobe boasted that whereas she had twelve children, Leto had only two, Apollo and Artemis. For this insult Apollo killed her sons and Artemis killed her daughters, and Niobe returned to Lydia, where the gods turned her into a pillar of stone. Amphion either killed himself then and there, or else, while trying to take vengeance upon Apollo, was killed by him during an attack on his temple. Zethus also died as a result of grief for his only son, who died in childhood; according to one account Thebe accidentally killed him. After the deaths of Amphion and Zethus, Laius returned to his throne.

In the *Odyssey* there appears a different tradition: Amphion was the son of Iasus and ruled Orchomenus in Boeotia. One of his daughters survived the arrows of Artemis and married Neleus of Pylos. Furthermore Zethus married a daughter of Pandareos, Aedon, who was transformed into a nightingale after accidentally killing their son Itylus.

Amphissus Son of Apollo and Dryope. *See* DRYOPE.

Amphithemis or **Garamas** Son of Apollo and Acacallis. Born in Libya, he had two sons by Tritonis, Nausamon and Caphaurus.

Amphitrite Daughter of Nereus and Doris (who was herself a daughter of Oceanus) and therefore a sea-goddess. Poseidon saw her dancing on the island of Naxos and fell in love with her, but she fled to the Titan Atlas for protection. Poseidon sent out the sea-creatures, his servants, to look for her, and at last the dolphin found her and pleaded for Poseidon so persuasively that she married him. And so Poseidon placed the constellation of the Dolphin in the sky. Their many children included Triton, Rhode and Benthesicyme.

Amphitryon Son of Alcaeus and grandson of Perseus. His mother was a daughter of Pelops, Astydamia or Lysidice. Electryon, his uncle, became king of the Argolid after the death of Perseus. Amphitryon wanted to marry Electryon's daughter Alcmena, but Electryon decreed that the marriage was not to be consummated until he, Electryon, had taken vengeance on the people of the Taphian islands for stealing his cattle and killing his sons in a raid. But before setting out on this expedition Electryon sent Amphitryon to Elis to recover the cattle, for the Taphians had deposited them there. When he returned with the cattle, Amphitryon, while throwing a club at one of the beasts, accidentally killed his father-in-law. Sthenelus, Electryon's brother, banished Amphitryon on a charge of murder, seizing the throne of Mycenae for himself. Amphitryon had to flee with Alcmena to Thebes, where Creon purified him.

The slaying of Alcmena's brothers had still not been avenged, a duty which now devolved on Amphitryon. Alcmena refused him his marital rights until he discharged it. He appealed to Creon for help, which Creon agreed to give, provided that Amphitryon would first rid Thebes of a pest, a vixen sent by Hera or Dionysus to ravage the territory of Teumessus and eat a young man every month. Since Cephalus of Athens had a hound, Laelaps, which was able to catch anything it was set upon, Amphitryon prevailed on him to help, offering him a share of the spoils to be taken from the Taphians. Zeus, however, turned both animals to stone, and Creon gave his help against the Taphians. His other allies were Cephalus, Amphitryon's uncle Heleius, Panopeus, and some Locrians.

This army sailed to the Taphian islands where King Pterelaus ruled the Teleboeans. This king had a golden hair on his head which had to be removed before he could die; and while he was alive his city was inviolable. But his daughter Comaetho fell in love with Amphitryon and cut the hair, at which her father fell dead. Amphitryon, far from accepting the girl's love, killed her for her treachery and gave the islands to his allies: Cephallenia to Cephalus and the rest to Heleius.

When Amphitryon returned to Thebes, he was amazed to discover that Alcmena was not surprised to see him and was under the impression that he had returned home the previous day (or night). Furthermore, according to her account, they had at last consummated their marriage. Amphitryon consulted Tiresias who lived at Thebes, and the old prophet told him that Zeus had passed the night with Alcmena, disguised as Amphitryon; moreover he had lengthened the night to thrice its normal duration in order to beget a great hero. Amphitryon accepted this explanation. Alcmena later gave birth to twins. One of them was Heracles, the son of Zeus, and the other was Amphitryon's son Iphicles, who was far weaker than his twin brother.

Amphitryon continued to live in Thebes, and had a daughter, Perimede. When Lycus usurped the throne from Creon, he threatened to kill the whole family of Heracles, but Heracles himself returned and rescued them. Then Heracles went mad and killed his children and according to some his wife Megara.

He was about to kill Amphitryon, too, when Athena prevented him by hitting him with a stone. It was for these crimes that Heracles had to perform his Labours.

Amphitryon died in battle fighting against King Erginus of Orchomenus and the Minyans. The Latin comic dramatist Plautus wrote a play about the marriage of Amphitryon and Alcmena.

Amphoterus *see* ALCMAEON.

Ampycus or **Ampyx** A Thessalian prophet, the father of Mopsus *1* by Chloris.

Amulius Son of Proca; a descendant of Aeneas and the younger brother of Numitor, from whom he violently usurped the throne of Alba Longa in Latium. He forced Numitor's daughter Rhea Silvia (or Ilia) to become a Vestal Virgin in order to prevent Numitor from having an heir. When she was raped by Mars and bore twin sons, her uncle imprisoned her and ordered his servants to drown the babies in the Tiber. The children, Romulus and Remus, were saved because the servants were content to leave the basket at the edge of the flooded river. They were subsequently found by Faustulus and brought up as shepherds.

When these twins grew to manhood, they stole goods from the local brigands to give to the shepherds, but the brigands laid a trap and caught Remus, whom they brought to Amulius. Since, however, the brigands declared that Remus had been raiding Numitor's lands, he was handed over to his grandfather, who subsequently discovered who he was. Romulus was also fetched, and the twins learnt their history and punished their great-uncle by killing him. The poet Naevius, however, followed a tradition that Amulius was a good old man who welcomed the discovery of Romulus and Remus.

Amyclas Son of Lacedaemon and Sparte; the eponym of Amyclae near Sparta.

Amycus Son of Poseidon and king of the Bebryces in Bithynia. A barbarous man, he used to challenge newcomers to his country to box with him; he always won and killed them. When the Argonauts came to his land, he once more uttered his challenge, which was accepted by the expert boxer Polydeuces. The latter beat him easily and killed him with a blow on the head. Other versions of the story recount that he was bound by the terms of the challenge to suffer whatever Polydeuces cared to inflict on him; and again that Castor and Polydeuces, meeting him at a spring, were challenged to box by him before he would let them drink, whereupon Polydeuces beat him and made him take an oath to give up his belligerent habits.

Amymone One of Danaus' fifty daughters. She was sent out by her father to find water in the Argolid, to which he had newly come in flight from Aegyptus. But Poseidon, angered because Inachus and the other Argive rivers had preferred to give the land to Hera rather than himself, had dried up the land. Amymone began to chase a deer and hit a sleeping satyr with her spear. This creature then attempted to rape her, but Poseidon appeared, drove off the satyr, and courted her himself. She lay with him; to reward her, the god struck a rock with his trident (for she had been sent out to find water), and created the spring of Lerna. Amymone bore Poseidon a son, the great sailor Nauplius 1.

Amyntor Son of Ormenus and king of Ormenium near Mount Pelion in Thessaly, or of Eleum in Boeotia. He married Cleobule, and they had a son, Phoenix, and a daughter, Astydamia or Deidamia. Phoenix quarrelled with his father Amyntor, who was keeping a mistress: his neglected wife Cleobule persuaded Phoenix to try to turn the heart of this mistress against Amyntor, and Phoenix consequently spent a night with the woman. Amyntor learnt of it and cursed Phoenix, praying to the Furies to prevent him from ever having children; and his prayer was fulfilled. Phoenix wanted to kill his father but decided to leave the country instead. Another tradition states that the concubine falsely accused Phoenix of having dealings with her though he was innocent; Amyntor believed her and blinded his son, who was cured of his blindness by Chiron.

When Heracles came to Amyntor's kingdom, he asked Amyntor to let him marry his daughter. Amyntor refused because Heracles was already married to Deianira; and then Heracles, in a rage, killed him. Another version recounts that he did this merely because Amyntor would not let him pass through his territory. Heracles had his way with Amyntor's daughter, who bore him a son, Ctesippus.

Amythaon Son of Cretheus and Tyro. He took his wife Idomene and his sons Melampus and Bias to Messenia. He supported Jason's claim to the throne of Iolcus and went to Thessaly to meet his nephew.

Anaxarete A Cypriot princess who was loved by a humble man named Iphis *1*. Ovid tells how she mocked Iphis and was unconcerned when he hanged himself; whereupon Aphrodite punished her for her callousness by turning her into a block of stone.

Anaxibia *1.* Daughter of Bias and Iphianassa and niece of Melampus; she married Pelias, to whom she bore Acastus and several daughters.
2. Sister of the Atridae, Agamemnon and Menelaus. She married Strophius, king of Phocis, and was the mother of Pylades.

Anaxo Sister of Amphitryon (who

married her daughter Alcmena). Anaxo married her uncle Electryon, the brother of her father Alcaeus. Her sons were killed by the people of the Taphian islands.

Ancaeus It is uncertain whether this is one mythical personage or two. If two, both were Argonauts and both were killed by boars.

1. Ancaeus, son of Lycurgus *3*, king of Arcadia, was sent on Jason's expedition of the *Argo* by his father, together with his uncles Amphidamas and Cepheus. He was the strongest Argonaut next to Heracles, and was paired with him on the rowing-bench. After the return of *Argo*, he was killed by the boar in the Calydonian boar-hunt, because of his foolhardy courage, or because he had claimed to be as good a hunter as Artemis. His son was Agapenor.

2. Son of Poseidon and Astydamia, daughter of Phoenix; he was king of the Leleges in Samos. On the voyage of the *Argo* he took over the helm when Tiphys died. Before he sailed with the *Argo* he planted a vineyard, of which it was prophesied by one of his servants that he would not live to taste its wine. On his return he pressed some of the grapes and was about to taste the juice when his servant said, 'there's many a slip 'twixt cup and lip'. At that moment Ancaeus heard a noise in the vineyard and, rushing out, came upon a wild boar, which gored him to death.

Anchiale A nymph who threw dust in the cave in Crete where Zeus was reared; the dust became the Idaean Dactyls.

Anchinoe A river-nymph; the wife of Belus.

Anchises Son of Capys, grandson of Assaracus, great-grandson of Tros. He was king of Dardania and father of Aeneas. He stole some of his uncle Laomedon's famous horses (the offspring of the mares which Zeus had given to Tros in payment for Ganymede) as stud for his mares.

One day Aphrodite came to Anchises while he was looking after sheep on Mount Ida. Zeus, angry with her for laughing at the other gods and goddesses when they succumbed to her snares, made her fall in love with this handsome mortal. She appeared before him as a mortal girl and from their union on the mountains Aeneas was born. When Aphrodite revealed to Anchises who she was, he was terrified because of the punishment which had been inflicted previously on mortals who had become the lovers of goddesses. But she told him that he would not suffer for what had happened, so long as he disclosed it to no one.

When Aeneas was five, Aphrodite took him away from the mountain nymphs who had reared him till then, and gave him to his father. Later Anchises boasted in his cups that Aphrodite was his mistress; for this indiscretion Zeus struck him and lamed him with a thunderbolt and Aphrodite deserted him. By the time of the Trojan War, Anchises was too old and lame to play an active part. In the war his son Aeneas led the Dardanians. When the city fell and Aeneas decided to flee with his family to Mount Ida, Anchises refused to leave until two omens, a gentle flame on the head of his grandson Ascanius and the fall of a meteor, had persuaded him that it was ordained by heaven. Aeneas carried him out of the burning town on his back. He accompanied his son on the voyage to discover a site for a new Troy and, according to Virgil, died of old age in Sicily at Drepanum. Another tradition claimed he died in Arcadia and was buried near Mount Anchisia. When Aeneas reached Cumae in Italy, the Sibyl accompanied him down to the Underworld where, in the Elysian Fields, he met the shade of his father and was given an account of the future destiny of his nation, and shown the souls of the greatest Romans to be born in years to come.

Ancus Marcius *see* MARCIUS.

Andraemon King of Calydon in Aetolia in sucession to his father-in-law Oeneus; father of Thoas *3*.

Andreus Son of the River Peneius in Thessaly; he was king of Orchomenus, and married Evippe, who bore him Eteocles.

Androgeos Son of Minos and Pasiphae. His father made him king of Paros in the Cyclades. Heracles besieged his city and took his sons Alcaeus and Sthenelus prisoner. Androgeos was believed to have come to Athens in the time of King Aegeus, and to have competed in the Panathenaic games, in which he won all the contests. There are two accounts of his death. According to the first, the young men of Athens, jealous of his victories, ambushed and killed him on his way to Thebes. The other version recounted that Aegeus sent him to rid the country of the bull of Marathon, but the bull gored him to death; it was subsequently killed by Theseus.

Andromache Daughter of Eetion, king of Thebe-under-Placus in the southern Troad. She married Hector and bore him his only child Astyanax. Her father and seven brothers were put to the sword by Achilles when he sacked Thebe, and her mother was ransomed for a large sum. In the *Iliad* she is shown with her husband and their baby son, at a moment when Hector has come from the midst of the fighting to ask the women to sacrifice to Athena, and to tear Paris away from Helen. Andromache had a firm presentiment of her husband's impending death.

When he was dead and Troy had fallen, Andromache's baby was thrown off the walls of Troy, and she was taken off into captivity by Neoptolemus, Achilles' son. He had three sons by her, Molossus, Pielus, and Pergamus; but later he married Hermione – daughter of Menelaus and Helen – who, being childless, begrudged Andromache her fruitful womb. Whether this occurred, as Euripides says, in Phthia (where Peleus defended Andromache and her children from Hermione's anger while Neoptolemus was away at Delphi) or in Epirus, Neoptolemus was shortly afterwards killed at Delphi. Then Andromache became the wife of Helenus, the Trojan seer to whom Neoptolemus had given part of Epirus to rule over. According to Virgil's *Aeneid*, however, he had already given her to Helenus when he himself married Hermione.

Helenus and Andromache lived in a new city which they called Pergamum, after Troy. They had a son called Cestrinus. Subsequently, when Helenus died, Andromache was taken by her son Pergamus to Mysia in north-western Asia Minor, where he conquered Teuthrania and founded the city of Pergamum.

Aeneas saw Andromache at the house of Helenus in Epirus; and the story of her troubles at the hands of Hermione is told in Euripides' tragedy *Andromache*.

Andromeda Daughter of Cepheus, king of Joppa in Palestine (called 'Ethiopia' in most sources), and of his wife Cassiope or Cassiopea (*Kassiepeia*), herself a daughter of Hermes' son Arabus. Cassiopea boasted that her daughter was fairer than the Nereids. They, however, complained to Poseidon, who sent a sea-serpent to ravage the country. The oracle of Zeus Ammon in Libya declared that Andromeda herself must be offered up to the serpent. She was chained to a rock at the foot of a cliff, and as the monster approached to devour her, Perseus flew by with the head of the Gorgon Medusa in his bag. He saw what was about to happen and went to Cepheus, asking for Andromeda's hand in marriage if he could dispose of the monster. Cepheus agreed and, as the serpent was already approaching, Perseus displayed the Gorgon's head to its view and turned it to stone (or slew it with his sword).

Cepheus gave a wedding feast for Perseus and Andromeda, but did not tell Perseus that Andromeda was already promised to Phineus *1*, his brother. Phineus broke into the festival with an armed band and tried to seize Andromeda but, though he was greatly outnumbered, Perseus got rid of the intruders by using the Gorgon's head to turn them to stone.

After their marriage Perseus and Andromeda lived in Palestine with Cepheus for a time. But when their first son Perses was born, Perseus resigned to him his right to inherit the throne and returned with Andromeda to the island of Seriphos. Later Perseus became king of the Argolid. There they had a number of children: Alcaeus, Sthenelus, Heleius, Mestor, Electryon, and a daughter, Gorgophone. They remained together till their death. Then Andromeda, together with her husband, parents, and the sea-serpent, were placed by Athena in the heavens as constellations; Cassiopea, however, for her sin, was laid on her back with her feet up in the air. From Andromeda's son Perses, according to Herodotus, were descended the kings of Persia.

Andromedes A fisherman who ferried Britomartis to Aegina when she was fleeing from Minos of Crete.

Anius Son of Apollo and Rhoeo. When his mother was found to be pregnant, her father Staphylus (his name means 'bunch of grapes') put her in a chest and launched her in the sea. She came to land in Delos where she bore a son, whom she placed on the altar of Apollo, bidding him to look after the infant if he acknowledged him as his son. Apollo complied, giving the child the gift of prophecy. Eventually Anius became king of the island of Delos, married Dorippa, and had a son who later became king of another island, Andros. He also had three daughters, Oeno, Spermo, and Elais, who were blessed by Dionysus and promoted the growth of wine, grain, and oil, after which they had been respectively named. On their way to Troy, the Greeks captured these three to ensure their supplies, but the girls escaped to Andros. Their brother handed them back to Agamemnon, but just as he was going to tie them up, Dionysus turned the ropes into vines and the girls into doves.

Anius entertained Aeneas and Anchises on their voyage from Troy to Italy.

Anna Sister of Queen Dido of Carthage, whom she persuaded to yield to her passion for Aeneas, thus unwittingly bringing about Dido's death. When the queen had resolved to kill herself, she made Anna help her to build a funeral pyre, without letting her know the purpose for which she intended it. After Dido's death Anna fled to Malta and then to Laurentum, where Aeneas, married to Lavinia, had succeeded Latinus as king. Lavinia was jealous of Aeneas' friendship with Anna, who in consequence threw herself into the river Numicius (or Numicus). She later reappeared and declared that she was now the nymph Anna Perenna. This story is Ovid's; but another explanation he gives of the name of Anna Perenna is that she was an old woman who gave food to the Roman plebeians when they abandoned the city of Rome and went to live on the Sacred Mountain in protest against the abuses of the patricians.

Antaeus A giant, the son of Poseidon and Gaia (the Earth), who lived in Libya and challenged all comers to wrestle with him. He was practically invincible, because contact with the earth gave him renewed strength. After he had killed his opponents, he used their skulls to roof his father's temple. When Heracles came to his country, on his way to fetch the golden apples of the Hesperides, Antaeus issued his usual challenge. But Heracles eventually got the better of him by raising him off the ground and squeezing him to death.

Antenor Son of Aesyetes and Cleomestra, a Dardanian; in the *Iliad* one of the elders who sat with Priam at the Scaean Gate when Helen explained the Greek forces to them. When Heracles had carried off Hesione after the first sack of Troy, Antenor had been sent to Greece by Priam to recover her, but he did not succeed. When Paris brought Helen to Troy, having stolen her from her husband Menelaus, Antenor was for returning her, but Priam listened to Paris instead. Similarly when Odysseus and Menelaus came as envoys with the request that she be returned, Antenor and his wife Theano entertained them in their house and protected them when Priam's sons would have killed them. After the war had begun, he did not cease to maintain this conciliatory policy and, according to some authorities, he continued to give advice to the Greeks, telling them to steal the Palladium and build the Wooden Horse. When Troy was sacked, he and his wife were saved by Odysseus and Menelaus, who put a leopard skin over Antenor's door to show his immunity. There are various accounts of what happened to him after the fall of Troy: it was said that he refounded Troy; that he went to Africa with Menelaus and settled at Cyrene; and that he led the Eneti or Veneti of Paphlagonia (who had lost their king, Pylaemenes, in the war) from Asia Minor to the head of the Adriatic Sea, where they settled in the land bearing their name, Venetia, in which Antenor founded the city of Patavium (modern Padua).

Antenor and his wife Theano, a priestess of Athena, had several sons, including Archelochus and Acamas who, together with Aeneas, led the Dardanian troops in the Trojan War.

Anteros The god of requited love. *See* EROS.

Antheas *see* EUMELUS *1.*

Antia The name Homer uses for Stheneboea, wife of Proetus. *See also* BELLEROPHON.

Anticlea *1.* Daughter of Autolycus; the mother of Odysseus and wife of Laertes. She was seduced by Sisyphus in revenge for her father's theft of some cattle. Homer regards Laertes as Odysseus' father, but later writers including Sophocles substitute Sisyphus for Laertes. Anticlea died while Odysseus was at Troy, out of sorrow for his absence; when he visited the Underworld, he met her shade.
2. Wife of Machaon.

Antigone *1.* Daughter of Oedipus, king of Thebes, and his wife and mother Jocasta (or Epicaste). Her story is best known from Sophocles' plays *Oedipus at Colonus* and *Antigone*, but there were other versions including a lost tragedy by Euripides. When Oedipus had blinded himself after the discovery of his incest with Jocasta, and Jocasta had hanged herself, he vowed to leave his polluted family and country, but was prevailed on by his brother-in-law Creon to stay for a time, while Creon acted as regent. Subsequently Oedipus' sons Eteocles and Polynices seized the throne and drove their father out, and Antigone went with him to act as his guide in his wanderings. Creon had already betrothed her to his youngest son Haemon. When Oedipus at last came to the sacred precinct of Poseidon at Colonus, where he was destined to die, Antigone's sister

Ismene came to them with the news that their brothers had quarrelled, and that Creon, supporting Eteocles, desired Oedipus to return to Thebes, because according to an oracle his presence would bring success to whichever party sheltered him. Oedipus took refuge in the sanctuary, but Creon arrived with soldiers and tried to seize Ismene and Antigone in an attempt to force Oedipus to comply. But Oedipus persuaded the inhabitants of Colonus to fetch Theseus, king of Athens, who promptly arrived and rescued the sisters. Polynices then came, and Oedipus at Antigone's entreaty listened to what he had to say; but he rejected with a curse Polynices' proposed attempt to recover Thebes from Eteocles. When Oedipus had finally disappeared from the earth, Antigone and Ismene returned voluntarily to Thebes, where Polynices attacked the city with the Seven, and he and Eteocles slew each other in single combat. Creon buried the body of Eteocles with royal pomp, but because he regarded Polynices as a rebel and a traitor he threw his body out to rot and forbade anybody to touch it. Antigone refused to tolerate this impiety and gave the body token burial, sprinkling over it three handfuls of dust. She was caught by Creon's soldiers and for her disobedience was condemned by him to death. But so that the king should avoid formal guilt for her death she was to be walled up in a cave with food and water. However Haemon, who was Creon's son and Antigone's betrothed, now spoke up for her and vainly protested to his father. Antigone rejected the plea of her sister Ismene (who had refused to help her perform her dutiful act) to be allowed to share her guilt and her doom, and was led off to her fate.

Shortly afterwards the blind old Theban prophet Tiresias appeared. He warned Creon that he had received unmistakable signs of grave pollution, and ordered him to bury the dead and

unbury the living. Creon duly buried his nephew Polynices and came to the cave where Antigone was immured and unsealed it: within he found Antigone's corpse, for she had hanged herself. Haemon cursed him, tried to kill him, and then stabbed himself. On learning of this, Creon's wife Eurydice also committed suicide.

So runs Sophocles' version. Euripides' plot, only known to us indirectly and imprecisely, probably differed in the following ways. Since the law enjoined that a married or betrothed woman should be punished by her husband, Creon ordered Haemon to execute the sentence on Antigone. Haemon pretended to have done so, but really hid her in the country, where a son was born to them. Much later the boy came to Thebes to take part in the games. When he had stripped to run a race, Creon saw on his body the spear-head birthmark borne by all the descendants of the 'Sown Men' of Thebes; whereupon he declared him a bastard, and condemned Haemon and Antigone to immediate death. Dionysus (or else Heracles) pleaded for their lives, and they were pardoned and formally married (though according to one version Heracles pleaded for them in vain). We do not know their son's name or fate.

Another variant indicates that Antigone was aided in the burial of Polynices by Argia, his wife, and that they pulled the body by moonlight on to the still burning pyre of Eteocles, where it was consumed. The guards arrested the two women, who were brought before Creon and sentenced to death, only to be saved by the arrival of an Athenian army under Theseus.

A slightly earlier tradition makes Antigone and Ismene victims of a son of Eteocles, Laodamas, who burnt them in the temple of Hera. The story of Antigone was unknown to Homer.

2. The first wife of Peleus and a daughter of Eurytion, king of Phthia. When Peleus

and Telamon had killed Phocus and were exiled from Aegina by Aeacus, Peleus came to Phthia where Eurytion purified him of his guilt and gave him Antigone in marriage, together with a third of his kingdom.

Later, after a long absence on the voyage of the *Argo*, Peleus accidentally killed Eurytion at the Calydonian boarhunt and took refuge in Iolcus, where King Acastus' wife fell in love with him. She sent word to Antigone that Peleus was about to marry her husband's daughter Sterope, and Antigone hanged herself.

3. Daughter of Laomedon, king of Troy. She compared herself with Hera in beauty and was punished by having her hair turned into snakes. The gods later took pity on her and changed her into a stork; and thenceforth that bird preyed upon snakes.

Antilochus The eldest son of Nestor, king of Pylos. He was a suitor for the hand of Helen, and went to the Trojan War with his father and brother Thrasymedes. He took a prominent part in the war and was a close friend of Achilles to whom he bore the news of the death of Patroclus. Like Achilles, Antilochus was a swift runner. He took part in Patroclus' funeral games; following his father Nestor's advice, he cheated in the chariot race and, passing Menelaus, came in second. When Menelaus was about to remonstrate, Antilochus apologised and ceded the second prize. He was also one of the three contestants in the foot-race.

While Antilochus was nobly defending his aged father, one of whose horses had been shot and killed by Paris, he was killed by Memnon. He was buried in Achilles' grave, and his shade was believed to have gone to the White Island with those of Achilles and Patroclus.

Antimachus One of the Trojan elders

who, in opposition to Antenor, advised against returning Helen to the Greeks. In hope of a bribe from Paris, he even recommended that Odysseus and Menelaus, when they came as envoys, should be killed. For this reason Agamemnon and Menelaus slew his sons.

Antinous A young Ithacan, the leader of Penelope's suitors, and the most cruel and insolent amongst them; he was the first to be killed by Odysseus.

Antiope *1.* Daughter of Nycteus, who was regent of Thebes in the infancy of Labdacus. She was a beautiful girl, and Zeus lay with her in the form of a satyr. When her pregnancy was becoming obvious, she fled to Sicyon, where she married the king, Epopeus. (According to another story, Epopeus kidnapped and ravished her, and thus made her pregnant.) Nycteus pursued her to Sicyon, fought with Epopeus, and died of his wounds, or committed suicide from shame. As he died, Nycteus enjoined his brother Lycus to take vengeance on Epopeus and punish Antiope. Lycus, therefore, invaded Sicyon with the Theban army, killed Epopeus, and took Antiope captive. When they were on their way back to Thebes, Antiope gave birth to twins at the town of Eleutherae on Mount Cithaeron. Lycus abandoned them on the mountain.

On their return to Thebes, Lycus gave Antiope as a slave to his wife Dirce, who was very cruel to her and kept her in a dungeon for many years. At last, however, Antiope escaped to Mount Cithaeron, where she was sheltered by the very shepherd who had rescued Amphion and Zethus, her twin sons. There are two versions of what ensued. Either the twins discovered that Antiope was their mother and killed Dirce and Lycus at once; or else, as Euripides told the story in his lost play *Antiope*, Zethus treated his mother as a mere runaway slave and refused to shelter her. She was then recaptured by Dirce, who was celebrating the orgies of Dionysus on Mount Cithaeron. Dirce, in her frenzy, decided to fasten Antiope to the horns of a mad bull. But at that moment Amphion and Zethus, who on the return of their shepherd foster-father had been apprised of the runaway's true identity, came up and rescued her. They then tied Dirce to the same bull she had intended for their mother. But because of Dirce's devotion to Dionysus, the god punished Antiope, driving her mad and setting her wandering through Greece. Eventually Phocus, son of Ornytion, cured her and made her his wife; and he was eventually buried beside her in Phocis.

2. Either the sister of Hippolyta, queen of the Amazons, or another name for Hippolyta herself. When Antiope was abducted by Theseus, she led her female warriors against Athens but was defeated. Antiope (or Hippolyta) bore Theseus a son, Hippolytus.

Antiphus *1.* A legitimate son of Priam; herding the sheep with his bastard half-brother Isus he was captured on Mount Ida by Achilles and ransomed by his father. Later Agamemnon caught the pair in a chariot, killed them, and stripped the bodies of their armour.

2. A friend of Odysseus, who was eaten by Polyphemus.

Apemosyne *see* ALTHAEMENES.

Aphareus King of Messenia and son of Perieres and Perseus' daughter Gorgophone. He shared his rule with his brother Leucippus. He married his half-sister Arene and named his new capital city after her. When Pelias drove the Thessalian Neleus out of Iolcus, Aphareus welcomed him to his kingdom and gave him land along the sea coast around Pylos. Aphareus' sons Ides and Lynceus died before him, so he left his kingdom to Neleus' son Nestor.

Aphrodite The Greek goddess of love, later identified with the Roman Venus to whom the mythology of Aphrodite was also attributed. One of the twelve great Olympians, she was the giver of beauty and sexual attraction, and was depicted as smiling sweetly, often in mockery. Her cult was of foreign origin, coming from the Near East by way of Cyprus and Cythera.

There are two stories of her birth. To Homer she was the daughter of Zeus and Dione, and the wife of Hephaestus. Hesiod tells a quite different tale, based on the supposed derivation of her name from *aphros* 'foam', by which she emerged fully-grown from the sea at Paphos in Cyprus or on Cythera. For when Cronos had cut off the genitals of his father Uranus, he flung them into the sea; the foam gathered round them and they were transformed into a woman. When Aphrodite landed, flowers grew in her path and she was attended by Eros (Cupid) and perhaps other divinities. She was known as *Anadyomene* ('she who emerges') and *Cypris*, 'the Cyprian'.

Aphrodite was not a faithful wife to Hephaestus; representing sexual passion rather than the bond of marriage (which was protected by Hera), she was seen as utterly irresponsible by the earlier Greek mythology. Homer tells how Helios, the sun-god, warned Hephaestus of her adultery with Ares, and her husband trapped them naked on his marriage-bed, enveloping them in an invisible net. He then invited the other gods to mock the pair, until Poseidon suggested a reconciliation. She had several children by Ares: Deimos and Phobos, whose names mean 'fear' and 'panic'; Harmonia, who married Cadmus of Thebes; and perhaps Eros, who, though he combined the attributes of Aphrodite and Ares, was nevertheless often declared to have been self-generated at a time before the coming of the Olympians.

Because of her mockery of the immortals, Aphrodite was forced by Zeus to fall in love with a mortal, Anchises. She had several affairs with other gods, and produced the phallic deity Priapus out of a union with Dionysus, and perhaps Eryx by Poseidon. She did not want to accept the advances of Hermes, but Zeus helped him by sending his eagle, which stole her sandal and gave it to Hermes. Aphrodite had to submit to him in order to recover it; she bore him Hermaphroditus who was both male and female. Aphrodite had power to make all the gods fall in love or be overcome with desire, with the exception of Athena, Artemis, and Hestia. When Hera wished to make Zeus succumb to her charms and forget the Trojan War, she borrowed from Aphrodite a girdle which made its wearer irresistible.

Aphrodite had a passion for Adonis, over whom she quarrelled with Persephone. When Adonis was killed by the boar, Aphrodite made the red anemone grow from his blood.

Aphrodite loved mortal men, such as Anchises, to whom she bore Aeneas, and she helped men who were in love with mortal women. The most important of her myths relates to the Judgment of Paris, which was the cause of the Trojan War. The golden apple, dropped at the wedding feast of Peleus and Thetis by the uninvited guest Eris (Strife), was inscribed 'for the fairest'. Hera, Athena, and Aphrodite claimed this prize of beauty, and Zeus appointed Paris, the most handsome of men, to judge between them. Each tried to bribe him, but he preferred Aphrodite's offer of the love of the most beautiful of women, and gave her the prize.

Among other mortals whom Aphrodite helped were Milanion (or Hippomenes) who wished to win Atalanta; Jason, who needed the love of Medea; Paris, whom she assisted in his abduction of Helen and constantly throughout the subsequent years in which he refused to give her up; and her own son Aeneas, with whom she made Dido fall in love.

On the other hand she punished both gods and mortals who caused her offence or boasted of being superior to her. Among these was the mother of Myrrha and her three daughters (see CINYRAS); Glaucus 2 whose mares ate him alive when he would not let them breed; Pasiphae, wife of King Minos of Crete, whom she caused to love a bull and bear the Minotaur; the women of Lemnos, whose neglect for her cult caused her to make them stink so that their husbands deserted them and were struck down by their abandoned wives – finally, however, the Argonauts came and, to please Hephaestus, Aphrodite cured the women of their smell. She was particularly cruel to Theseus' son Hippolytus, who thought himself above the call of love; for Aphrodite made his stepmother Phaedra fall in love with him, and when he would have nothing to do with her, Phaedra accused him to her husband of having raped her and hanged herself. Theseus sent his son into exile and cursed him, and Hippolytus too suffered a violent death. Aphrodite also punished the Muse Clio, who laughed at her for her passion for the mortal Adonis: for she made Clio likewise fall in love with a mortal, Pierus. The Muse Calliope, who had adjudicated between the rival claims to Adonis of Persephone and herself, was punished by the death of her son Orpheus. Aphrodite also penalised the goddess of dawn, Eos, who had lain with Aphrodite's lover Ares, by making her fall in love with two mortals, Cephalus and Tithonus. Another to experience her retribution was Helios, who had told Hephaestus of her affair with Ares; he was made to love the mortal Leucothoe. On one occasion, however, the tables were turned on Aphrodite by a mortal, for she was forced to flee from the battlefield at Troy, wounded by Diomedes.

Whereas Aphrodite often appeared as either a cruel or a ridiculous figure in early Greek literature, she was seen by the Romans as a much more serious and benevolent character: indeed Lucretius, in the exordium of his poem *On the Nature of the Universe*, saluted her as the supreme generative force.

Apis Son of Phoroneus founder of Argos, and of the nymph Teledice. Being killed by Aetolus, he left his kingdom to Argus, son of his sister Niobe.

Apollo One of the greatest gods of both the Greeks and the Romans: the principal god of prophecy and divination, and of the arts and especially music (for the Muses were directly subordinate to him), and of archery. He was a bringer of plagues, which he could also dispel; for he was a patron of medicine. He also protected herdsmen, although also associated with their principal enemy, the wolf. His origin was probably not Greek; he came to Greece from the north or east. He was also a sun god (Phoebus, 'bright'), though this identification may not have been made until the fifth century BC and only became common much later. (Alternatively his name Phoebus was attributed to his receipt of the Delphic Oracle from the Titaness Phoebe.)

Apollo was the son of Zeus and Leto, and Artemis was his twin sister. Leto, a Titaness, being pregnant by Zeus, wandered over the face of the earth seeking a place in which to give birth to her children in peace, but all places refused to take her in for fear of the wrath of Hera or because they shunned the honour of being the birthplace of two such great gods. Only Delos would receive her because it was not truly land at all but a floating island. Apollo grew up very quickly, being fed on nectar and ambrosia by the goddess Themis. After a few days he was fully grown and left Delos to find a suitable site for the oracular shrine he meant to found. He travelled through central Greece and came to a cleft in the ground which was

guarded by Python, a huge female serpent with oracular powers, on behalf of her mistress Gaia, the Earth, or the Titaness Phoebe. (The name Python was also attributed to a serpent which had been sent by Hera to prevent the pregnant Leto from giving birth.) Apollo killed Python and named his priestess Pythia after her.

Before reaching Delphi, Apollo had met the nymph Telphusa at Haliartus, and asked her if he might found his oracle at her oracular spring. But she had excused herself, pointing out how much greater the oracle at Delphi was: in fact she had sent him directly into Python's lair. For this reason Apollo returned to her spring and hid it under enormous rocks so that in future it was a much less prominent oracle than his own.

After killing Python, Apollo had to do penance for his act, for she had been a daughter of Gaia and a great prophetess. He was exiled to the Vale of Tempe for a long period of time, and the Delphians sent him envoys every eighth year. The word *delphys* means 'womb', and the sacred college insisted that Delphi was the womb or centre of the earth. It was the most important oracle of the Greek world, and was consulted by many foreigners. Games were instituted there, called Pythian in honour of Python and of Apollo. They consisted of musical contests, to which athletic competitions were added later. The priests of Apollo claimed descent from a ship-load of Cretans whom Apollo, in the form of a dolphin, had seized and diverted to Delphi.

Apollo and Artemis slew the giant Tityus for trying to rape Leto before they were born, and sent him to Tartarus where he suffered everlasting punishment. They also avenged their mother on Niobe, who had boasted that she was more fertile than Leto, by killing all or most of her children. They were both archers, and were also the deities who presided over death from natural causes or disease: thus Homer writes that Apollo slays men, and Artemis slays women, with the 'gentle arrows' of death.

Apollo twice served mortal men as a slave. His first master was Admetus, king of Pherae in Thessaly, whom he helped by giving all his cows twins and by guaranteeing him against death. This slavery was a punishment inflicted by Zeus because his sons the Cyclopes, who had made his thunderbolts in their caverns on Mount Aetna, had been slain by Apollo since Apollo's son Asclepius had been blasted by Zeus' thunderbolt for bringing Hippolytus back to life. At first Zeus, in his rage, had nearly thrown Apollo into Tartarus, but he finally relented and only imposed a year's servitude upon him. Apollo's second act of service to a mortal took place when Poseidon and he agreed to build the walls of Troy for Laomedon for a fee (in another version, Apollo pastured cattle and Poseidon built the walls alone); but Laomedon broke the agreement and the gods punished him, Apollo sending a plague on his city.

His role as patron of healing (in which he was sometimes confused with another god of healing, Paeon) was inherited by his son Asclepius. As god of music, Apollo invented the lute or cithara, and received the lyre from his half-brother Hermes; for Hermes, shortly after his birth on Mount Cyllene in Arcadia, had stolen fifty of Apollo's cattle, dragging them backwards part of the way and hiding them in a cave. Apollo, with Zeus' help, discovered the theft and made a bargain with Hermes to relinquish the cattle in exchange for the lyre. It became Apollo's favourite instrument; but one day the satyr Marsyas had the effrontery to challenge the god to a music competition. Because Apollo could play his instrument upside down as well as in the normal position, he adjudged himself the winner. The agree-

ment had been that the victor should do what he liked with the loser, so Apollo flayed Marsyas alive. He refused to allow Marsyas' instrument, the flute, to be played in his presence, but at last a musician called Sacadas dedicated a flute to Apollo and he let it be played in the Pythian dance at Delphi.

Apollo's eastern origin is shown by his support for Priam during the Trojan War, when he was Troy's most persistent and important champion. Two of the children of Priam, Helenus and Cassandra, had received prophetic gifts from Apollo. Cassandra was courted by him and given the gift of prophecy as a bribe. When, notwithstanding, she refused him her favours, Apollo cursed her by ordaining that, though she should always know the future correctly, nobody else would believe her.

Apollo had the misfortune to be rejected by other women as well. Daphne preferred to turn into a laurel rather than accept him as a lover. The Sibyl of Cumae, to whom he offered as many years of life as she had grains of sand in her hands, still refused him after receiving this proposal; and so he condemned her to live for a thousand years, but get older and older. Marpessa, when Zeus gave her the choice between Apollo and the mortal Idas, preferred Idas. Equally unsuccessful was his courtship of the nymph Sinope, who asked a favour of him before she would accept his overtures. He granted her wish and then learnt that she asked to remain a virgin until her death. His loves of young men were not much happier. He accidentally killed the Spartan youth Hyacinthus with a discus (the hyacinth flower grew from the dead youth's blood). His beloved Cyparissus killed a tame stag, and could not be consoled; so, to give him peace, Apollo turned him into the cypress tree.

At the beginning of the *Iliad*, Homer shows us Apollo in terrifying guise, punishing the Greeks with plague for the theft of Chryseis, daughter of his priest Chryses. It was Apollo, too, who slew Achilles with an arrow shot from the bow of Paris.

Apollo was the god who instructed Orestes to punish his mother Clytemnestra and her lover Aegisthus for the murder of his father Agamemnon; and when Orestes, having done this, was driven mad by the Furies, it was again Apollo who instructed him to seek trial before the Court of the Areopagus at Athens. When Orestes came before that court, Apollo defended him against the charges brought by the Furies and by Clytemnestra's ghost.

Apollo once had a quarrel with Heracles. When Heracles had killed Iphitus, he went to Delphi to enquire how he could be purified and cured of the madness that had fallen upon him. At first the Pythian priestess would have nothing to do with him, so terrible was the crime of slaying a friend. Then Heracles seized the sacred tripod, and he and Apollo began to struggle; but Zeus threw a thunderbolt and parted his two sons. Next Apollo advised Heracles that he could be cured by being sold into slavery for three years, and Heracles in thanks spread the worship of Apollo, who had likewise served as a slave.

In addition to Asclepius, Apollo's sons included Aristaeus by the sea-nymph Cyrene. Apollo is also sometimes called the father of Orpheus and Linus.

He was an important god among the Etruscans and Romans, becoming known to the latter through the oracular grotto of Cumae, whose Sibyl in Roman legend accompanied Aeneas to the Underworld. Augustus adopted him as his patron and the symbol of his civilising mission, dedicating his resplendent new temple on the Palatine Hill in 28 BC.

Appius Claudius The *decemvir: see* VERGINIA.

Apsyrtus The son of Aeetes, king of Colchis, and brother of Medea. After the departure of the Argonauts from Colchis with the Golden Fleece, there are two traditions of the pursuit of them. According to the version of Apollonius Rhodius, he was already a man, and was placed in charge of the fleet by his father; in the delta of the Ister (Danube), or on an island in the Adriatic, Medea treacherously bargained with him and lured him to a meeting, and there Jason killed him from an ambush. Ovid has the better-known variant, by which Apsyrtus was still a child; Medea took him with her in the flight as a hostage and, when Aeetes' fleet was in sight, she killed him and cut up his body, either strewing the pieces on the sea or leaving them displayed in prominent positions on the coast, so as to delay the pursuit while Aeetes collected the severed members.

Arachne A Lydian girl, the daughter of Idmon of Colophon. An expert weaver, she ventured to challenge Athena herself, the patron goddess of weaving, to do better. Athena came to her disguised as an old woman and warned her not to be presumptuous. But Arachne refused the warning, and Athena, resuming her own shape, took up the challenge. Athena wove a tapestry depicting the fates of presumptuous mortals; Arachne for her part wove the scandalous doings of the gods. Since Arachne's work equalled her own, Athena in her anger tore it to shreds and beat Arachne with a shuttle. Arachne hanged herself, and the goddess changed her into a spider, which her name denotes: the animal kept all Arachne's skill as a weaver.

Arcas Son of Zeus and Callisto. When Callisto was pregnant by him, Zeus turned her into a bear, perhaps to avoid the prying eyes of Hera, or to ward off the vengeance of Artemis, who had been her mistress and was angry because Callisto had broken a vow of chastity. Her son Arcas was rescued by Hermes (either torn from her corpse or born from her body as she changed into the bear) and given to Hermes' mother Maia to rear on Mount Cyllene. Another version of the story reported that the Arcadian king Lycaon, Callisto's father, reared the child, but cut him up and served him to Zeus in a stew; Zeus restored him to life and turned Lycaon into a wolf.

Arcas became king of Arcadia and gave his name to that country. He showed the people how to weave, grow corn, and make bread – arts he learnt from Triptolemus. One day Arcas saw a bear lumbering into the temple of Zeus Lycaeus – or else he saw it while hunting – and shot at it. The animal was his mother. Whether he killed her is not clear from the tradition; at any rate Zeus turned her into the constellation of the Great Bear, and him into the Little Bear.

Arcas had married a dryad (tree-nymph), Erato, and after his transformation his sons divided his kingdom between them.

Archemorus *see* HYPSIPYLE.

Areithous An Arcadian king, nick-named 'maceman' for his habit of fighting with an iron mace. He was killed in battle by another Arcadian king, Lycurgus.

Areius Son of Bias, an Argonaut.

Ares The Greek god of war, later equated with the important Roman god Mars.

He was the only son of Zeus and his regular consort Hera, and although the *Iliad* ridicules him as a violent braggart soldier, he ranks as one of the twelve great Olympian gods. Ares had no wife, though he engaged in frequent liaisons, especially with Aphrodite, the wife of Hephaestus, who bore him Harmonia

and the twins Phobos ('panic') and Deimos ('fear') who accompanied their father on the battlefield. The love-affair between Ares and Aphrodite came to an abrupt end when, as Homer tells through the mouth of the bard Demodocus in the *Odyssey*, Helios the sun-god spied on the pair and told Hephaestus what was going on behind his back. Thereupon Hephaestus contrived a huge net which he fixed secretly above his bed, and then pretended to leave Olympus on a visit to his worshippers on Lemnos. When Ares and Aphrodite next lay together on the bed, the net fell on them and pinned them down; Hephaestus appeared and abused them, and called the other gods to witness their shame. The goddesses out of delicacy kept away, but the gods came, laughing, to watch. Poseidon eventually persuaded Hephaestus to release them on the understanding that Ares would pay a fine.

Ares had a daughter, Alcippe, by a mortal girl, Aglaurus, daughter of Cecrops; Poseidon's son Halirrhothius raped her near the Acropolis in Athens, and Ares struck him dead on the spot. Poseidon then summoned him for murder before the council of the gods, and he was tried at the same place, which was thenceforth called Areopagus or 'Ares' hill' in memory of the event. The gods found him not guilty of murder.

Only battle and bloodshed gave Ares any pleasure: he charged around the battlefield with his twin sons and Enyo, the war goddess, rousing the martial spirit of the warriors. Athena, the goddess of strategy and true courage in battle, could easily outwit him. Moreover, on one occasion he was bound and put in a bronze jar by the giants Otus and Ephialtes, the Aloadae, and would have perished, had Hermes not learnt of his plight from the giants' stepmother Eriboea.

In the Trojan War Ares supported the Trojans, but his role is depicted as ignominious. With the help of Athena, Diomedes gave him a serious wound, which he complained about to Zeus. Subsequently he tried to join the battle after Zeus had forbidden it, and was restrained by Athena with insults. When the gods turned against each other he attacked Athena and hurled his spear at her magic breastplate (aegis): it did her no harm, but she knocked Ares down with a stone. As Aphrodite tried to help him off the field, Athena struck her, too, with her fist.

When Heracles, on his way to Delphi, was challenged by Ares' son Cycnus, Ares himself fought against him as well. Heracles, aided by Athena, killed the brigand Cycnus and wounded Ares in the thigh. Besides Cycnus, Ares had a number of other warlike sons, the most important being Diomedes, king of the Thracian Bistones, born of the nymph Cyrene; Ascalaphus; Phlegyas; and perhaps Meleager.

Arete Daughter of the Phaeacian Rhexenor and wife of Alcinous, his brother. She was of a kindly disposition and made Odysseus welcome when he came as a suppliant to her: she persuaded Alcinous to receive him as a guest. She also aided Jason and Medea and made Alcinous swear to protect them from Medea's father Aeetes if their marriage had been consummated; to achieve this end, she secretly arranged for them to lie together in a cave. Her daughter was Nausicaa, who welcomed the shipwrecked Odysseus.

Arethusa A wood-nymph who bathed in the river Alpheius; the god of the river fell in love with her. She was transformed into the spring Arethusa on the island of Ortygia at Syracuse. *See* ALPHEIUS.

Arge *see* HYPERBOREANS.

Arges One of the three Cyclopes.

Argia *1.* Daughter of Adrastus, king of Argos, and wife of Polynices. When her husband was killed by his brother Eteocles and Creon refused him burial, she helped Antigone to lift the body on to the funeral pyre of Eteocles, whom Polynices had killed. *See* ANTIGONE.
2. see AUTESION.

Argiope *1.* Daughter of Teuthras; she married Telephus, king of Teuthrania.
2. A nymph who bore Thamyris to Philammon.

Argonauts The band of heroes who took part in Jason's quest for the Golden Fleece in the ship *Argo*. The expedition, of which there were many variant accounts, is best known to us from the Hellenistic poet Apollonius Rhodius, but the story had also been familiar to Homer and Pindar.

Jason's father Aeson was the rightful king of Iolcus in Thessaly, but his throne was usurped by his half-brother Pelias. He continued to live there, but secretly sent his son, after a mock funeral, to Chiron the Centaur to rear, as he feared that Pelias would put him to death. Pelias was warned that he himself would be killed by a descendant of Aeolus who would come to him wearing only one sandal. When Jason reached manhood, he determined to go to Iolcus and lay claim to the throne. He arrived at a time when Pelias was sacrificing to his father Poseidon. Now Hera had a grudge against Pelias, and so, as Jason made his way to Iolcus, she tested him, appearing in the guise of an old woman who asked him to carry her across a swift-flowing stream that lay in their way. In spite of his haste to reach Iolcus in time for the sacrifice, Jason complied, losing his sandal in the stream. After setting her down on the other side, Jason never saw the old woman again and never knew that it had been Hera.

When he arrived at Iolcus, he came into the market-place and asked where he might find Pelias. Word was brought to the king about the young man, with one foot bare, who was asking for him. Pelias drove to the market-place to see him, and realised that the oracle was fulfilled – indeed, Jason told him quite frankly who he was and why he had come. Unwilling to desecrate the festival with his nephew's blood, Pelias invited Jason to his palace, and told him he could have the throne if he would first promise to perform one task. Jason accepted the condition, and Pelias bade him fetch home the Golden Fleece, believing that this was quite impossible and that Jason would perish in the attempt. This fleece was the wool of the ram on which Phrixus, to escape the murderous wiles of his stepmother Ino, had flown from Orchomenus in Boeotia to Colchis.

After Phrixus had arrived in Colchis, a land at the further end of the Black Sea, the fleece had been hung in the grove of Ares, where it was guarded by a monstrous serpent that never slept. There was a tradition that Aeetes, the cruel king of Colchis, had received an oracle that he would cease to reign if the fleece was removed, or that he would meet his end at the hands of a foreigner; and so, although he had given Phrixus his daughter in marriage, he had subsequently killed him.

Jason, however, consulted the Delphic Oracle about his chances of success and received a favourable reply. Hera continued to help him throughout his quest, and now inspired a fine band of young men to join him. Originally the heroes must have been Thessalians (Apollonius calls them 'Minyans', a name associated with Orchomenus in northern Boeotia), but later tradition has added Heracles and other strangers. Various lists mirror the efforts of different Greek cities to enhance their own heroes by including them in the muster of the Argonauts. Names which are universally included are the minstrel Orpheus, Zetes and

Calais (the winged sons of Boreas), Peleus, Telamon, Castor and Polydeuces (the Dioscuri), Idas, Lynceus who had superhuman eyesight, Tiphys the helmsman, Argus who built the ship, Admetus of Pherae, Augeas, and Periclymenus. Many of the heroes had some particular virtue or quality: Jason had a way with women, and the attraction Medea felt for him was the decisive factor; Mopsus *I*'s second sight helped to propitiate the goddess Cybele; Heracles, with his great strength, saved them from the giants of Arctonnesus (Bear Island); Polydeuces, by his boxing, beat Amycus; and Calais and Zetes drove off the Harpies.

The *Argo* was said to have been constructed by Argus with the help of Athena, and its figurehead was a bough from Zeus' speaking oak at Dodona: a prophetic spar which was a special gift from Athena. The ship sailed out with its complement of fifty-six men, of whom fifty-four rowed in pairs, while Orpheus sat in the bows, singing a song to still the sea and give the time to the oarsmen, and Tiphys steered in the stern. Apollo and Athena protected the vessel, and on their departure the crew sacrificed to Apollo. Pelias' son Acastus joined the company at the last moment.

The first landing place of the Argonauts was Lemnos. Aphrodite had caused the women of this island to emit a horrible smell so that their husbands had deserted them. The abandoned wives had then murdered the men who had left them, and had also killed all other males on the island. Their queen Hypsipyle welcomed Jason, Aphrodite removed the stench from the women at the intercession of Hephaestus, and Lemnos was subsequently repeopled from the offspring of the Argonauts. Some said the Argonauts stayed there a whole year.

After putting in at Samothrace, the company sailed through the Hellespont (named after Phrixus' sister Helle, who had fallen off the Golden Ram) and into the Propontis or Sea of Marmora. Here they put in at Arctonnesus, or Bear Island, which was connected with the mainland by an isthmus. The king of the Doliones, Cyzicus, received them warmly, but earth-giants called Gegeneis ('earth-born'), each with six arms, attacked the ship while the crew were away. However Heracles remained on guard, and he killed the giants and left them in a pile on the beach.

Then the Argonauts, having received instructions from Cyzicus about the remainder of their voyage, put to sea. Later in the day the wind blew them back. They beached the ship and encamped; but during the night they had to beat off an attack of the local inhabitants. In the morning they found that it was the Doliones who had attacked them, and that Cyzicus was among the slain. His funeral was honourably celebrated, but his wife Clite hanged herself from grief. Storms prevented the *Argo* from sailing on, and Mopsus, who had prophetic powers, told them that Cybele, the Phrygian goddess who lived on Mount Dindymus, must be propitiated. The Argonauts went to her open-air shrine on the mountain and danced round her image, clashing their weapons like the Corybantes who were her attendants.

When the *Argo* reached Bithynia, Heracles broke his oar, and he and his fellow-Argonauts landed. The people received them well. While Heracles was cutting wood for a new oar, the youth Hylas, whom he loved, went to draw water at a well; but the nymphs of the well were so entranced by his beauty that they pulled him into the water. Heracles was distraught at his loss and roamed the woods calling for Hylas; and the *Argo* sailed on without them both.

When the company discovered that they had left Heracles behind, the sea-god Glaucus rose from the waters to tell them that the hero had to return to

Greece to complete his labours. Polyphemus was also left behind, for he had heard Hylas' cries and had run to give him help. He later founded the city of Cius at the spot. When Heracles left, he ordered the local people to continue the search for Hylas after his departure.

The *Argo* next came to land among the Bebryces, whose king Amycus challenged all visitors to a boxing match and killed them. The Argonauts were outraged by this conduct and Polydeuces, the boxer, crushed Amycus' skull with a blow behind the ear. The Bebryces, seeing their king dead, attacked the Argonauts but were easily driven off.

Next the Argonauts put in at Salmydessus, capital of Thynia in Thrace, where the king, Phineus 2, who possessed prophetic powers, was plagued by the Harpies for having betrayed Zeus' secret plans for the human race. He had been blinded, and the Harpies constantly seized his food from his table and covered him with their droppings. He received the Argonauts well, forecast their future course, and appealed to them for help, knowing that two of them, his winged brothers-in-law Calais and Zetes, could drive away the Harpies. A feast was prepared, and when the Harpies came, Calais and Zetes pursued them as far as Acarnania, where Iris brought a message from Zeus: the Harpies were to be spared, for they were his servants; but they would never trouble Phineus again. (For another explanation of his sin, see PHINEUS 2.)

The Argonauts sailed on towards the Bosporus, knowing that they would complete their journey safely if they succeeded in passing through the Symplegades ('Clashing Rocks' – floating rocky islands at either side of the mouth of the straits, which came violently together from time to time when the wind blew). Phineus had instructed them how to cope with this danger; Euphemus, a son of Poseidon, who could run across the sea without wetting his feet, released a dove which flew between the two rocks. The rocks clashed together as it passed, but only the tip of its tail was caught. The oarsmen of the *Argo* pressed ahead so as to get through while the rocks were drawing apart again. But a great wave held them back at the point where the rocks would meet. However Athena did not desert the ship she had built; she gave it a heave through the water, and the rocks caught only the tip of the stern-oar. From that time on the straits remained open, and sailors were never troubled by the Symplegades again.

On their way thence to Colchis, which was an easy voyage, the Argonauts sacrificed to Apollo on a desert island off the shore of Thynia. They were welcomed by King Lycus of the Mariandyni, but in his country their seer Idmon was killed by a boar (as he had himself foreseen) and Tiphys the helmsman died of a sickness. Ancaeus took the helm and Dascylus, son of Lycus, became a member of the crew. At Sinope they were joined by three Thessalians who had helped Heracles in his attack on the Amazons; the Argonauts, however, as they sailed past Themiscyra, managed to avoid the Amazons. Eventually they came to the mythical Isle of Ares where they met with a flock of birds which shot out their feathers, tipped with steel so as to resemble arrows, at strangers. The Argonauts covered their heads with their shields and made a tremendous din to scare the birds away. Here they were also joined by the four sons of Phrixus who had been marooned on the island when they were fleeing from Aeetes, king of Colchis (who had killed their father). The eldest, Argus, told Jason of the difficulties in store for him in Colchis.

The Argonauts sailed up the River Phasis and anchored at the capital city, Aea. Here Jason disembarked and went to Aeetes' palace, accompanied by Telamon and Augeas. Hera threw a mist over them to conceal them, and Medea, Aeetes' second daughter and an accomplished witch, was the first person to see them. Through the wiles of Aphrodite, who was now enlisted by Hera to help her scheme, Medea immediately fell in love with Jason. Aeetes, however, was implacably hostile to the Greeks, who he believed had come to destroy him and seize his throne. But he kept his hatred secret for the time being.

Jason assured the king that the sole object of his voyage was the Golden Fleece. Aeetes pretended to consent and laid down conditions for its acquisition. These constituted a trial of strength and skill which he felt sure would bring Jason's life to a speedy end, for he was required to yoke a team of fire-breathing bulls with bronze hooves to a plough, till a field, sow it with a dragon's teeth, and then kill a host of armed men who would at once spring from the ground.

Argus went to his mother Chalciope, who was a daughter of Aeetes, to ask for help, and she suggested to Medea, who needed little persuasion, that she should use her magic art. Early next day he took Jason to a secret meeting with Medea at the temple of Hecate, goddess of witches, outside the walls of Aea. Jason promised to take her back to Greece and give her an honourable position there, and in return she gave him a magic drug and told him how to conjure up the aid of Hecate. Later in the morning Jason went to fetch the dragon's teeth from Aeetes and to receive precise instructions. That night, following Medea's commands, he sacrificed to Hecate, who came and accepted his offerings. At dawn he rubbed Medea's drug into his skin. Then, after she had sung incantations to strengthen him, he successfully performed the three tasks imposed by Aeetes. Protected by the magic drug from the flames the bulls breathed out, he succeeded in yoking them and ploughing the field, sowing the teeth behind him as he went. The armed men grew quickly and were fully grown by the afternoon. As they began to advance on him, Jason flung a boulder into their midst. Then they began fighting against each other and hacked themselves to pieces. He finished off the last survivors, and the battle was ended by sunset.

Aeetes, however, did not fulfil his promise to surrender the Golden Fleece. Instead he started to plot the destruction of the Greeks, of whom he was now greatly afraid. Medea, who suspected that her father knew she had helped Jason, left home in the middle of the night and went to the *Argo* where she found the Argonauts celebrating Jason's victory. She explained her fears, and he called on Hera to witness his pledge to marry her. She then led him to the grove of Ares where the fleece was guarded by the unsleeping serpent. By her witchcraft she succeeded in putting the beast to sleep, and Jason climbed over its coils and removed the fleece. They fled to the *Argo*, and with all haste ordered the ship to get under way and row at full speed out of the River Phasis. As the next day broke, Aeetes' fleet was already in pursuit of them.

Of the return journey of the Argonauts from Colchis there are several conflicting reports. The oldest surviving account, given by the poet Pindar, says that the ship sailed to the outer 'Ocean', presumably by going up the Phasis rather than down. It then followed the Ocean round Asia and Africa to enter the Mediterranean Sea either through the Straits of Gibraltar or up the Red Sea. Another traditional route lies across Europe: the ship was said to have sailed up the Don, down another river into the Baltic, and round western Europe into the Mediterranean through the Straits of Gibraltar. Ovid prefers a tradition that the Argonauts returned by the way they had come, having seized the king's small son Apsyrtus on their way out of Aea. Then, on the way across the Black Sea, when Aeetes' pursuing ships hove

into sight, Medea stabbed her brother Apsyrtus and cut up his body, leaving the pieces floating in the water or else exhibiting them at prominent places on the shore. So she delayed her father while he collected the body and arranged the funeral, the *Argo* meanwhile making good its escape.

According to Apollonius, however, Aeetes entrusted the pursuit of the Argonauts to his son Apsyrtus, already an adult. Apsyrtus sealed off all the exits from the Black Sea, including the Bosporus and all the mouths of the Ister (Danube), except the northern-most. The Argonauts escaped through this mouth and followed the Ister throughout its length; then, proceeding down another river, they came out into the Adriatic. Apsyrtus, however, had forestalled them, for he had blocked the exit from this river into the Adriatic and was awaiting them there. The Argonauts landed on an island sacred to Artemis, and Jason parleyed with Apsyrtus. He agreed to let Jason keep the Golden Fleece and go on his way, but insisted on the return of Medea. When she heard of this agreement, she was furious with Jason, but he pretended that his discussion with Apsyrtus had been a trick. Medea was quite prepared to see her brother die, and so she aided Jason to ambush him at a second meeting. She lured Apsyrtus there on the pretence that she wanted to be rescued from Jason who had abducted her, and Jason appeared and cut him down. After this impious act the Argonauts could not make headway down the Adriatic, and were blown back; for, as their talking bowsprit told them, Zeus had decreed that Jason and Medea must be purified by Medea's aunt Circe, who lived on an island off the western shore of Italy. The ship therefore had to sail up the river Eridanus (Po) and down the Rhone into the Tyrrhenian Sea. Hera saved them from wrong turnings.

When the *Argo* reached Aeaea, Circe's

island, Jason and Medea landed alone and were purified by her with the blood of a pig and propitiatory offerings to Zeus and the Furies. Then Circe asked them who they were and what they had done. She was so horrified by their story that although Medea was her niece she sent them away without offering hospitality. However, the purification demanded by Zeus had been secured. Helped by Hera, Thetis, and the Nereids, the *Argo* sped on southwards, past Scylla and Charybdis, the Sirens, and the Wandering Rocks. When the company reached Scheria, the island of the Phaeacians, they found that a fleet of Colchians was already there awaiting them with a demand for Medea's return. Arete, wife of the Phaeacian king Alcinous, persuaded her husband to give up Medea to the Colchians only if her marriage to Jason had not been consummated. Otherwise, she was to stay with her husband. In fact the two had not yet consummated their union, and so Arete, who favoured them, hastily arranged for its consummation that night in a cave. So the Colchians had to leave emptyhanded. They settled in Corcyra rather than return to face Aeetes' wrath.

After they had gone on and had nearly reached Greece, the Argonauts were blown off course across the sea to Libya. There they were carried inland by a huge wave and dumped in the desert. When they were dying there of thirst, three nymphs dressed in goatskins appeared to Jason, and told him that when Amphitrite unyoked the chariot of her husband Poseidon, they would repay their mother for her labour at the time when they were in her womb. Peleus interpreted the oracle, and a great white horse, which was now seen, was identified as one of Poseidon's horses; their mother was evidently the *Argo* herself, which they proceeded to carry bodily for nine days until they came to a lake, Tritonis. This lake lay near to the garden of the Hesperides, and their ar-

rival occurred just after Heracles had visited the place, killed its snake, and taken the apples. He had also caused a spring of water to gush out of a rock, and here the Argonauts were able to quench their thirst.

They launched their vessel on Lake Tritonis, but were unable to find an exit into the sea. On the suggestion of Orpheus, they offered a sacred tripod from Delphi to the gods of the place. Their prayers were answered by Triton, disguised as a certain Eurypylus; after giving Euphemus a clod of earth as a token of friendship, he pushed the *Argo* down a river as far as the sea. They sailed along the coast of Libya until they came to Crete, where the bronze man Talos, appointed by Minos to guard the island and run round it three times a day, hurled rocks at them. However, Medea put a spell on him, so that the nail which held the blood in his single vein came out of his ankle and he died. The clod of earth given by Triton fell into the sea to the north of Crete and became the island of Thera, where Euphemus' descendants, in fulfilment of a dream, subsequently settled.

Next the *Argo* was wrapped in deep darkness, and it became impossible to steer. Jason prayed to Apollo who shot a blazing arrow to a point near the ship. By its light the company saw an island nearby, which they called *Anaphe*, 'Revelation'. They landed and offered what they could to Apollo. Daylight eventually returned, and the ship completed her voyage to Iolcus, where Jason delivered the fleece to Pelias. But he never became king of Iolcus and deserted Medea who had so effectively helped him.

The *Argo* ended its days at Corinth; ironically, Jason was killed when sitting under the rotting hulk, for the prow fell on top of him. His companion, Pelias' son Acastus, became king of Iolcus. The gods raised the ship to the sky and made it into a constellation.

Argus 1. An enormous and powerful monster with many eyes (sometimes represented with eyes behind him, sometimes with a hundred eyes all over his body) for which he was nicknamed *Panoptes*, 'all-seeing'. He slew a bull which was ravaging Arcadia, and a satyr who was stealing cattle.

He himself was killed by Hermes, who was known for that reason as 'Slayer of Argus' [*Argeiphontes*]. When Io was changed into a heifer, Argus was set over her as guardian. Zeus, however, commanded Hermes to slay him. Hera set the eyes of Argus in her favourite bird, the peacock, (or else turned him into that bird). His son was Iasus 1.

2. Son of Zeus and Niobe, daughter of Phoroneus. Inheriting the latter's kingdom, he renamed it Argos.

3. The eldest son of Phrixus and Chalciope, born in Colchis. When the king of that country, Aeetes, turned against him and his brother, they fled and were shipwrecked on the Isle of Ares, where the Argonauts found them and took them back to Aea. Argus spoke up for Jason to King Aeetes. Later, when Jason had performed the tasks set him by Aeetes, Argus asked the help of his mother, the king's daughter, to save the Argonauts from the king's wrath. He and his brothers fled with Jason and Medea, and sailed to Greece in the *Argo*.

4. The builder of the *Argo*. He was helped by Athena, as no such vessel had ever existed before. He later joined the crew.

Ariadne Daughter of Minos, king of Crete, and Pasiphae. When Theseus came to Crete to kill the Minotaur, Ariadne fell in love with him and gave him a sword and a clue of thread to guide him back from the Labyrinth. Theseus had promised to take her home and marry her. After his exploit they fled together to his ship and sailed away towards Athens. On the way Theseus

put in at the island of Dia, later called Naxos. When he sailed off again he left her behind, and she was rescued by the god Dionysus, who married her. According to other versions, however, Dionysus carried her off before Theseus left; or Artemis killed her on the island because Dionysus accused her of some sin. A tradition on Naxos declared that Theseus abandoned her pregnant, and that she died in childbirth. After her death, Dionysus placed her wedding garland in the sky as a constellation, the Corona Borealis.

Arion A man of Methymna on the island of Lesbos; son of Cycleus. He was, to some extent, a historical figure – a great musician and a friend and protégé of Periander, tyrant of Corinth (625 to 585 BC). He went to Italy and Sicily where he was honoured and won rich prizes; but the traditions about him are partly mythical. It was said that he took ship at Taras (Tarentum) for Corinth, to return to Periander's court, and that when the ship was at sea he was bound by the sailors, who intended to rob him. As a final favour they allowed him to stand on the afterdeck of the ship, dressed in his poet's robes, and to play his lyre for the last time. Having sung a hymn to Apollo, he threw himself into the sea whereupon a dolphin, enchanted with his playing, carried him on its back as far as Taenarum in the Peloponnese. From there he travelled overland and reached Corinth before the ship. When it arrived, Periander, disbelieving Arion's story, questioned the captain, who declared that Arion had stayed behind in Italy. But then he appeared, to the consternation of sailors, who were crucified by Periander.

Aristaeus Son of Apollo and the nymph Cyrene. Apollo saw Cyrene wrestling with a lion on Mount Pelion in Thessaly and carried her off to Libya, where she bore him Aristaeus. Either Apollo or

Hermes gave the baby to Gaia (Earth) to rear, and the Hours helped in his upbringing. The Muses taught him the arts which his father patronised, namely healing, archery, and prophecy, and instructed him also in much country-lore, especially beekeeping, olive-growing, and cheese-making, They also gave him Cadmus' daughter Autonoe as his wife. Their son was Actaeon.

Aristaeus lived in the vale of Tempe and promoted the rustic arts among its people, who honoured him as a god. One day he saw a beautiful woman and pursued her. It was Eurydice, the wife of Orpheus. As she ran away, she stepped on a snake, which gave her a fatal bite. As a result of this accident – although he did not at first know this was the reason – Aristaeus' bees began to sicken and die. Greatly distressed, he went to his mother Cyrene, who lived in her father's house beneath the waters of the river Peneius, and called her. She told him to capture Proteus, the Old Man of the Sea, who had powers of prophecy and would explain to him what was wrong and what he must do. Proteus was hard to capture since he had the power of changing shape. But Aristaeus caught him asleep, and eventually learnt from him why his bees had died. He was told to return to Tempe, sacrifice four bulls and four bullocks to the dryads (tree-nymphs) and a black sheep to Orpheus, and return to the place nine days later. Aristaeus obeyed these instructions and, when he returned, found bees swarming in the carcasses.

After the death of his son Actaeon, Aristaeus was so distraught that he went away and lived on the island of Ceos (*see* ICARIUS 2). Later he travelled to Sicily, Sardinia, and Arcadia, teaching the people the arts of agriculture. He entered into a competition with Dionysus to see whether wine or mead was the better drink; both the gods and men preferred wine. He accompanied Diony-

sus on his triumphal progress. Some say that he had nursed the god when he was a baby on Mount Nysa, others that his daughter Macris did so. He lived with Dionysus for a time in Thrace, and then disappeared in the Haemus Mountains. The story of Aristaeus and his bees is told in Virgil's Fourth *Georgic*.

Aristodemus Son of Aristomachus. *See* TEMENUS.

Aristomachus Grandson of Hyllus and father of Temenus, Cresphontes, and Aristodemus.

Arne *1.* The nurse of Poseidon in Arcadia.
2. A Thracian woman who betrayed the island of Siphnos to Minos for gold. For her greed she was turned into a jackdaw.

Arruns An Etruscan name, found in some of the earliest Roman myths.
1. An ally of Aeneas in Italy who, in the war between the Trojans and the Rutulians under Turnus, killed the Volscian warrior-maid Camilla. For this he was slain by Diana, to whose service Camilla had been dedicated.
2. Arruns of Clusium. In about 400 BC, according to a story which is likely to be mythical, he deliberately enticed the Gauls to Clusium with a gift of wine so as to gain help in his revenge on his ward Lucumo, who had seduced his wife. Lucumo, a person of royal rank, was too powerful for Arruns to punish without external help, and the Gauls were intended to bring about his fall. After attacking Clusium, they marched on Rome and sacked it (an historical event).

Arsinoe Also called Alphesiboea. Wife of Alcmaeon, and daughter of Phegeus, king of Psophis. After Alcmaeon had gone mad, he deserted her and was later killed by Arsinoe's brothers. When she protested at this act, her brothers shut her up in a chest and sold her into slavery to Agapenor, king of Tegea. Her end is uncertain.

Arsippe One of the daughters of Minyas, who were turned into bats.

Artemis One of the twelve great Olympian deities, a goddess of hunting and archery and, paradoxically, a defender of all wild animals, children, and weak things. She was believed to roam the mountains with a band of attendant nymphs and to resent the intrusion of any who would interfere with her or her protégées. In Classical Greek literature she was characterised by a deliberately chosen and forcibly maintained virginity; she punished those who would violate this state, insisted that all her attendants should also be virgins, and defended virginity among mortal men and women. But Artemis was probably not originally a virgin goddess; she seems to derive from an earth-mother, whence her association with the many-breasted Goddess of Ephesus. In consequence she was a bringer of fertility and protector of the newly born. Artemis was the daughter of Leto and twin sister of Apollo, born either with him on Delos or just before him on Ortygia (sometimes, but not always, represented as a separate island); hence her epithets Delia and Cynthia (the latter from Mount Cynthus on Delos). Naturally Hera was jealous of her, as of all Zeus' progeny by others than herself: and in the *Iliad*, therefore, she insults her, spills her arrows, and boxes her ears, whereupon Artemis rushes to her father's knee and sits on it, weeping. With Apollo, however, she avenged the giant Tityus' attempt to rape her mother Leto; they slew him, and he was consigned to eternal punishment in Tartarus. Artemis and Apollo also killed most of Niobe's children because the latter had insulted Leto by favourably comparing her own numerous offspring with themselves.

As Apollo was considered to be responsible for the sudden but natural death of men, so Artemis was held to bring death to women. In this connection, she became closely associated or confused with the witch-goddess Hecate, sometimes called Artemis of the crossroads, who was likewise an earth-goddess and shared features with Artemis but was also much concerned with the dead.

The story of the nymph Callisto may have originally applied to Artemis herself: her titles included the epithet 'most fair' (*kalliste*). Callisto, favourite follower of Artemis, was raped by Zeus and bore Arcas. According to one variant of the story, Artemis herself changed Callisto into a bear and drove her away with her arrows, because she had ceased to be a virgin and had therefore broken her vow. On the other hand, Artemis took pity on Procris, who wished to escape her husband and live as a chaste huntress; the goddess gave her the dog Laelaps and an unerring spear (which later caused her death).

Artemis is concerned in the story of the giant hunter Orion, which appears in several versions. One of these recounts that Orion tried to rape Artemis, and was killed by her arrows. A contrary tradition suggested that she fell in love with him and that Apollo became jealous. He and Artemis were hunting in Crete when Apollo saw Orion swimming far out in the sea. Apollo, well knowing what the distant object was, challenged Artemis to try to hit it with an arrow, and thus caused her to kill her beloved. According to another story, Orion boasted that he would kill all the wild animals on earth; whereupon Artemis (or perhaps Gaia) sent a scorpion to put him to death. Alternatively, she killed him either because he loved Eos and made her his mistress or because he raped one of the nymphs, called Opis. Orion and his hounds, the scorpion, and Callisto were all placed in the heavens as constellations.

When the giants Otus and Ephialtes tried to rape Artemis and Hera, Apollo intervened in the nick of time by sending a deer between them; both cast spears at it, and killed each other instead. In the battle between the gods and giants, Artemis slew Gration with her arrows. Upon Coronis, who while pregnant with Apollo's son Asclepius lay with a mortal man, Artemis took vengeance on her brother's behalf, shooting her to death.

Artemis punished many mortals who offended her or failed to observe her rites. Among these was Actaeon who saw her bathing. Because she feared he would boast of having seen her naked body, Artemis turned him into a stag, and he was immediately devoured by his own hounds. Oeneus, who forgot to perform the rites of Artemis in his harvest festival, was punished by the visitation of a great boar, which ravaged his country and led to the disastrous Calydonian boar-hunt. Admetus was punished for a similar neglect at his wedding, for Artemis filled his bed (or bedroom) with snakes. Agamemnon, before sailing to Troy from Aulis, had to propitiate the goddess with the sacrifice of his daughter Iphigenia – either because he had boasted he was the equal of Artemis in hunting, or because he had failed to fulfil a promise he had made to her some years before, or because Artemis, as protector of wild things, was displeased by an omen of two eagles (identified with Agamemnon and Menelaus) ripping up a pregnant hare. She therefore refused to allow the wind to blow for Agamemnon's fleet.

Other deities identified with Artemis included the Cretan goddesses Britomartis and Dictynna; Selene, the moon-goddess (so that Artemis, in later times, was known as Phoebe); perhaps Iphigenia (who had originally been a local divinity); and, among the Italians, Diana.

Artemis appears prominently in Euripides' plays – *Hippolytus, Iphigenia in Aulis*, and *Iphigenia in Tauris*. The metamorphoses of Callisto and Actaeon are told by Ovid.

Ascalabus The goddess Demeter, in her long search for Persephone, one day came to his mother's house in Attica and asked for a drink to refresh her in her weariness. The woman, Misme, gave her a cup of *kykeion*, barley meal mixed with water and pennyroyal. Demeter drank it so greedily that Ascalabus laughed at her; in her anger the goddess threw the dregs in his face, turning him into the spotted lizard, which is what his name means.

Ascalaphus *1.* Son of Ares and brother of Ialmenus. The two brothers jointly ruled Orchomenus in Boeotia. They led a contingent of troops in the Trojan War, taking thirty ships. Deiphobus, aiming his spear at Idomeneus, killed Ascalaphus.
2. A son of the river Acheron and the nymph Orphne or Gorgyra. After Zeus had promised Persephone's mother Demeter that she could return to the upper world if she had eaten nothing during her sojourn in the Underworld, Ascalaphus told Hades that Persephone had eaten some pomegranate seeds; and she transformed him into an owl. Another version indicates that it was Demeter who punished him for this betrayal by putting him under a very heavy stone in Hades. Heracles, during his visit there, rolled it off him, whereupon Demeter turned Ascalaphus into an owl.

Ascanius The son of Aeneas and his first wife Creusa. He was born in Troy, and as young man sailed with Aeneas on his long voyage to find a new home for the Trojan remnant in Italy. He fought in the war against Turnus and, thirty years after Aeneas had founded Lavinium, established the city of Alba Longa.

After the fall of Troy (Ilium), according to Virgil, Ascanius' second name, which had previously been Ilus, was changed to Iulus. Livy, however, gives a different version, which makes Iulus and Ascanius two different people and states that Ascanius was the son of Aeneas and Lavinia. A refinement of the second version gives Aeneas a second son, Silvius, born to Lavinia after Aeneas' death. According to the Virgilian version, however, Silvius is the son of Ascanius.

Virgil's story emphasises the claim of the Roman family of the Julii Caesares to be descended from Iulus, and thus from Aeneas and the goddess Venus.

Asclepius (Latin: *Aesculapius*) The god of healing. He was the son of Apollo and Coronis. The baby was torn from the dead body of his mother (whom Artemis had killed) by Hermes or by his father Apollo, and given to Chiron, who brought him up and taught him the arts of medicine. There are several other versions of his birth. The people of Epidaurus, where his principal temple and cult were situated, preferred to believe that Coronis bore the baby while visiting their city with her father. Then, according to this tradition, she abandoned him on Mount Myrtium, where he was suckled by a flock of goats and found and reared by their herdsman, although he was terrified to see lightning flashes coming from the infant's body. In Messenia it was claimed that Asclepius' mother was Arsinoe, daughter of Leucippus.

Asclepius married Epione and had two sons, Machaon and Podalirius, both of whom fought at Troy and tended the wounded. In spite of his divinity, Asclepius was believed to have died. His death was brought about by Zeus, who struck him down with a thunderbolt for daring to bring the dead back to life. Asclepius' father Apollo avenged this act by killing Zeus' sons, the Cyclopes (who made their father's thunderbolts); in consequence of which Zeus imposed

upon Apollo the punishment of a year's slavery at the court of King Admetus. Snakes were sacred to Asclepius, and he was thought to be incarnate in their shape; when his worship was brought to Rome in 293 BC he was imported there from Epidaurus in the form of a snake, which was said to have swum ashore and chosen its own abode. Asclepius was put in the sky by Apollo in the form of the Serpent-holder (Ophiuchus).

Asius Two Trojan warriors. *1.* The younger brother of Hecabe and son of Dymas, a Phrygian king.
2. Son of Hyrtacus and king of Percote.

Asopus The gods of two rivers of that name, who are often confused. One of the streams runs through Sicyon's territory into the Gulf of Corinth, the other through Boeotia into the Aegean Sea. Their gods were sons of Oceanus and Tethys. One of them married the nymph Metope, a daughter of the River Ladon. They had two sons, Ismenus and Pelagon, and twenty daughters, including Aegina. The river-god searched for her and was told by Sisyphus, king of Corinth, that Zeus had abducted her to the isle of Oenone (later called Aegina after her). When he pursued Zeus, he was driven back with thunderbolts. As a result live coals were found in his bed for many years after. Other daughters of Asopus gave their names to islands, cities, and rivers: Salamis, Corcyra, Thebe, Ismene.

Assaracus A Trojan prince, the son of Tros.

Astacus A Theban, the father of Ismarus, Leades, Amphidocus, and Melanippus; his sons helped in the defence of Thebes against the Seven.

Asteria A Titaness, daughter of Coeus and Phoebe; she married Perses and bore the goddess Hecate. When Zeus pursued her, she jumped into the sea in the form of a quail. An island, Delos, later appeared at that place and was at first called Asteria or Ortygia, after *ortyx*, a quail (sometimes described as a separate island). When Leto, Asteria's sister, was pregnant, she came to this island, where she bore Apollo and Artemis.

Asterion *see* INACHUS.

Asterius or **Asterion** *1.* A king of Crete; son of Tectamus, who had colonised the island with Aeolians and Pelasgians. When Europa came to Crete, Asterius married her and adopted the three sons she had borne to Zeus, Minos, Rhadamanthys, and Sarpedon. Since he had no sons of his own, he was succeeded by Minos. Asterius and Europa had one daughter named Crete. The name Asterius was sometimes also given to the Minotaur. *2.* Son of Minos, killed by Theseus.

Asterodea Wife of Aeetes.

Asterope One of the Pleiades; often called Sterope. She was sometimes said to be the mother of Oenomaus of Elis.

Astraeus ('starry') The name of a Titan who married Eos, the Dawn.

Astyanax The little son of Hector and Andromache. In the *Iliad* he is pictured as being frightened by the horse-hair plume of Hector's helmet; Hector prays for his success in battle. His real name was Scamandrius but everybody called him Astyanax ('lord of the city') because his father was Troy's one defence. When the city fell, either Menelaus or Neoptolemus flung him from the walls, because Odysseus had warned that no male descendant of Priam should be spared. His father's shield was used as his coffin. His death is described in Euripides' tragedy *The Trojan Women*. Another, weaker, tradition states that

Astyanax was taken by the Greeks into captivity and later returned to rule a rebuilt city of Troy.

Astydamia Her parentage is obscure: the daughter either of Cretheus or Pelops or Amyntor; wife of Acastus, king of Iolcus. She fell in love with Peleus, who would have nothing to do with her; so she told her husband that he had tried to rape her. To punish Peleus, Acastus took him hunting on Mount Pelion and deserted him, asleep and defenceless. Rescued by Chiron, Peleus subsequently returned to Iolcus with his followers and some of the Argonauts. He killed Astydamia, and marched with his army between the two halves of her body.

Astyoche *1.* Daughter of the River Simois; the wife of Erichthonius 2 and mother of Tros. *2.* Daughter of Priam; she married Telephus. *3.* Daughter of Phylas, king of Thesprotia. She bore Tlepolemus by Heracles.

Astypalaea Daughter of Agenor or of his son Phoenix. She was said to have borne to Poseidon the Argonauts Ancaeus and Eurypylus. One of the Cyclades Islands was called after her.

Atalanta A famous huntress. Her story occurs in two versions, Boeotian and Arcadian. Like Artemis, she was both a huntress and a determined virgin. In the Arcadian version her father was Iasus, son of Lycurgus; in the Boeotian story he was Schoeneus, son of Athamas. In both accounts her mother was Clymene, daughter of Minyas.

When Atalanta was a baby, her father exposed her because he did not want a daughter. A she-bear found her and suckled her, and she was discovered and brought up by some hunters. She thus developed an inclination for hunting and manly pursuits, and took no interest in marriage or the arts of women. When two Centaurs, Rhoecus and Hylaeus, tried to rape her, she killed them both with her arrows. She even tried to enlist with the Argonauts, but Jason refused her application on the grounds that the presence of a single woman might cause jealousies. When the Argonauts had returned to Greece and Pelias was dead, Atalanta took part in his funeral games and beat Peleus in the wrestling match.

She is chiefly famous, however, for two myths: the Calydonian boar-hunt and the race in which the man who defeated her would gain her hand in marriage. At Calydon Atalanta joined the party which set out to kill the boar. Ancaeus and Cepheus (who appear to have been her uncles) and a few others refused to join the hunt with a woman, but Meleager, who loved Atalanta, compelled them to remain. Atalanta scored the first hit with an arrow, but Meleager finally killed the beast. He gave the hide to Atalanta, because she had drawn first blood, but his mother's brothers tried to take it from her. For this reason Meleager slew them and was in consequence slain by his mother Althaea; so he never married Atalanta.

After this episode Atalanta's fame reached the ears of her father, and he discovered she was his child. He insisted that she should marry, but she, even more unwilling than before, laid down the condition that her husband must first beat her in a race. Any man who lost, however, would be immediately killed. In spite of this condition her beauty inspired many young men to contend, but although she ran fully clothed or even armed, whereas they were naked, every one of them lost and died. At last, with the aid of Aphrodite, she was beaten. A young man – Milanion in the Arcadian version, Hippomenes in the Boeotian – was helped by Aphrodite with the gift of three golden apples which she happened to be bringing back from her orchard at Tamasus in Cyprus.

By rolling these apples off the course, the young man thrice prevented Atalanta from outstripping him: for whether from curiosity, or from greed, or because she wanted him to win, she stopped to pick them up and was overtaken. However the young man forgot to fulfil his vows to Aphrodite. Moreover, as they returned home, he consummated his union with Atalanta in the precincts of a temple, whereupon Aphrodite, for this sacrilege, turned them into lions: and lions, it was believed, do not mate with each other, but only with leopards. According to Propertius, Milanion won Atalanta by sharing her hardships in the hunt rather than by competing with her in a race. Another story makes Atalanta mother of Parthenopaeus ('son of a virgin'), whom she exposed in his infancy; and like herself, he was brought up by country-folk.

Ate The eldest daughter of Zeus; her mother was Eris (Strife). She was a personification of blind folly, rendering her victims incapable of rational choice and blinding them to distinctions of morality or expedience. In the *Iliad* Agamemnon, excusing his conduct towards Achilles, tells the story of Ate's deception of Zeus at the time of Heracles' birth. It was through her influence that Zeus once swore that a child of his own blood, then to be born, would rule Argos and the neighbouring lands. He meant Heracles, but Hera had his birth delayed by Ilithyia, and arranged for the birth of Eurystheus to take place prematurely. Thus Heracles had to serve Eurystheus, a man greatly inferior to himself, and Zeus' oath was fulfilled against his intention. Zeus, in his fury, flung Ate from Olympus with the command that she should not return; henceforward she had to live among mankind. Later Zeus sent his daughters the Prayers (*Litai*) to follow Ate through the world and give men a chance to put her mischief right.

Athamas Son of Aeolus, king of Thessaly. He became king of Orchomenus in Boeotia and married the nymph Nephele ('cloud'), who bore him Phrixus and Helle. Later he divorced Nephele, or was deserted by her, and married Ino, daughter of Cadmus and Harmonia of Thebes. This marriage produced two sons, Learchus and Melicertes. Ino, however, resented the existence of Nephele's children and decided to destroy them by the following method. She persuaded some women of Orchomenus to roast the seed-corn, rendering it useless. When the crop consequently failed and her husband consulted the Delphic Oracle, she bribed the messengers to bring back word that Phrixus (and perhaps Helle) was to be sacrificed to Laphystian Zeus in order to avert the famine. Just as Athamas was about to cut the boy's throat there appeared a magic ram sent by the god Hermes at Nephele's request (or else by Zeus, who abhorred human sacrifice). This ram could talk, and possessed a golden fleece. Phrixus and Helle, at the ram's command, immediately jumped on its back and it flew away; they were never seen again in Greece.

As a child, Dionysus was for a time cared for by Ino, the sister of his mother Semele, and by Athamas. Hera was jealous of this new son of Zeus and persecuted his foster-parents by driving them mad. Athamas shot his son Learchus with an arrow and killed him. Ino ran off with her younger son Melicertes in her arms, and flung herself into the sea from the Molurian Rock between Megara and Corinth (or, according to another version of the story, she boiled him in a cauldron). The body of Melicertes was carried ashore by a dolphin and found by his uncle King Sisyphus of Corinth, who founded the Isthmian Games in his honour. Dionysus later turned Ino and Melicertes into the sea-deities Leucothea and Palaemon, who helped sailors in distress.

Athamas, who had now lost his whole family, was banished from his kingdom and went to Delphi to consult the oracle. There he was told that a place where wild animals invited him to share their food might become his abode. As he wandered through Thessaly, he came upon wolves devouring a lamb; they ran off at his approach, leaving the remainder of their meal. Athamas settled there, calling the place Athamantia. When he was an old man, an oracle declared that Athamas was a scapegoat for the people of Thessalian Achaea. In consequence he narrowly escaped being sacrificed to Zeus, but his grandson Cytissorus, son of Phrixus, who had come from Colchis with the Argonauts, appeared and saved him. However the people of Halus in Achaea made a law that the eldest member of the clan descended from Phrixus might not enter the town hall on pain of being similarly sacrificed.

It is likely that Euripides' lost play *Ino* contained a quite different version of the story, involving a third wife of Athamas named Themisto. In his old age Athamas was given the territory round Mount Laphystius by the new ruler of Orchomenus, Andreus. Having no heirs, he adopted two of the grandsons of his brother Sisyphus. When Phrixus' children came home, however, they became Athamas' heirs instead.

Athena Daughter of Zeus; one of the twelve great Olympian gods. Athena was the patron deity of war and of many crafts and skills. She was a city-goddess and had temples in many of the leading Greek cities. She was a virgin, but unlike Artemis she did not shun men, but loved manly deeds and joined warriors on the battlefield. Athena's symbol is the owl, which is associated with wisdom, and the Romans identified her with Minerva, a goddess of the household and of craftsmen.

In art and literature Athena appears clad in full armour, with helmet, round shield, and spear; over her breast she wears the *aegis*, a goatskin breastplate with tassels. Her shield is painted with the Gorgon's head, and her owl is often seen sitting on her shoulder.

When Hephaestus clove open the head of Zeus with an axe, Athena sprang forth adult and fully armed, ready for battle. There were various explanations of this 'birth'. It was usually said that Zeus had persuaded the wise Titaness Metis, whose name means 'thought', to marry him. It was she who had caused Zeus' father Cronos to vomit his other offspring, thus releasing Poseidon and Hades. When she became pregnant, Gaia and Uranus, or Prometheus, warned Zeus that if she had a second child it would be mightier than its father and rule heaven and earth. In fear of this, Zeus swallowed Metis, pregnant as she was. In another version of the story, Zeus, who wished to have the benefit of Metis' wisdom without the disadvantage of her bearing a son to supplant him, pursued her amorously, knowing that, since she wished to remain a virgin, she would change her shape to avoid him. When she finally became a fly, Zeus swallowed her. At all events Metis was delivered inside Zeus' head, and Athena eventually emerged.

The epithet *Tritogeneia*, a word of unknown meaning, led to a belief that Athena was born beside a lake or stream called Trito or Tritonis, such as existed in Boeotia, Arcadia, and Libya. Another explanation was that she was reared by the sea-god Triton. The people of Alalcomenae in Boeotia, because their town was near a stream called Tritonis, claimed that Athena was reared by their founder Alalcomeneus.

Athena gave aid to many clever adventurers, notably Perseus, Bellerophon, Heracles, Jason, Diomedes, and Odysseus. She was also the most active champion of the Greeks at Troy. Athena helped Perseus because she wanted the destruction of the beautiful Gorgon Medusa, who had offended her; in consequence the goddess had made her so dreadful in appearance that all who looked at her were turned to stone. When Perseus offered to fetch the Gorgon's head for King Polydectes, Athena presented him with the winged sandals, wallet, and cap of invisibility that he needed in order to overcome her. When Perseus had performed the task he gave Athena the severed head, which she wore ever after upon her shield.

Athena's greatest sanctuary was the Parthenon at Athens. She did not gain Athens without a struggle, for Poseidon also claimed the place. There was a contest and Poseidon caused a spring of salt water to flow on the Acropolis. In answer Athena made an olive tree grow. Since this seemed the more useful gift, the Athenians chose the goddess rather than the god. Poseidon in his anger flooded Attica, but since Athens accorded him honours second only to Athena's, he relented and gave the city his favour. At Troy, until the war, there had supposedly been a special wooden image of Athena called the Palladium, which had fallen from heaven. It was thought that the citadel was invincible as long as it remained there. Hence the Greeks, on the advice of Helenus, a Trojan seer whom they had captured, resolved to steal the statue, and Diomedes and Odysseus crept by night into Troy and, with the help of Helen, seized and removed it. Its eventual destination, after the fall of the city, was variously identified. It was at another Trojan shrine of Athena that Aias, the son of Oileus, raped Cassandra, who clung to the statue of the goddess. Aias' violence caused the statue to fall, and at the same time it turned its eyes away from his outrageous act. After that Athena withdrew her favour from the Greeks, except Odysseus, whom she deeply loved and helped to reach his home — ten years later, it is true, but that was because Poseidon was hostile to him.

Athena's name Pallas is hard to explain. It may be that Athena took it from the giant Pallas whom she killed in the war of the gods and giants. There is also a tale that as a girl she accidentally killed a playmate called Pallas and took her friend's name in remorse. But the name is also sometimes explained as the original appellation of the warrior-goddess who was Athena's predecessor in Mycenaean times.

Further connections between Athena and Athens are provided by the stories of Erichthonius and the trial of Orestes. The former, a rather crude tale, tells of the time when Hephaestus pursued Athena and tried to rape her. The warrior-maid resisted successfully, and the god's seed fertilised the ground, out of which was subsequently born Erichthonius ('born of the earth'). The goddess gave him to King Cecrops' daughters to guard, placing him in a chest and forbidding them to look inside. Two of the girls, however, unable to resist their curiosity, peeped into the chest and saw a snake (or a child with a snake's tail, or with a snake coiled about it), whereupon they leapt down from the Acropolis. The goddess retrieved the creature and reared him in her shrine, and he later became king of Athens.

Orestes, driven by the Furies over the face of the earth after he had killed his mother Clytemnestra, finally came to Athens. Here Athena protected him, incidentally establishing the Athenian traditions of trial by jury and hospitality to foreigners. She arranged for him to be tried before the court of the Areopagus, and when the votes were equal cast her own vote in his favour. As a result the Furies were thenceforth worshipped at Athens under the name of the Eumenides, or Favourable Ones. When Orestes and Iphigenia seemed doomed to die in the Tauric peninsula (Crimea), she saved them once again.

Athena and Ares are both martial deities, but present a contrast. The Greeks, and especially Homer, preferred the former. She represents intelligence and strategy as against the wild, mindless fury of Ares. Indeed she pitted herself against him constantly in the *Iliad*, and on one occasion fought a battle against him in aid of Diomedes, guiding his spear into Ares' belly and sending the god flying from the battlefield in pain. Zeus loved Athena as warmly as he hated Ares. *See also* PALLAS.

Atlas A Titan, the son of Iapetus and the Oceanid Clymene. His name probably means 'he who carries' or 'he who endures'. He married the Oceanid Pleione.

Whereas he was originally thought of as the guardian of the pillars of heaven, he was later believed to hold the sky up himself. Atlas had been warned that a son of Zeus would one day come and steal the golden apples, guarded by the serpent Ladon, from the garden of the Hesperides, whose orchard lay nearby. Therefore, when Perseus passed that way, Atlas refused him hospitality, and for that reason Perseus showed him the head of the Gorgon Medusa, which turned him to stone; hence the Atlas Mountains of Morocco. But the far-flung local connections of his daughters, the seven Pleiades and the five Hyades, suggest that the special association of Atlas with these mountains was a secondary development.

Heracles, two generations younger than Perseus, was said to have had an encounter with Atlas. According to this story, Heracles, on his eleventh labour, came to fetch the apples of the Hesperides, and Atlas good-naturedly offered to fetch them. When he returned he told Heracles that he himself would deliver the apples to Eurystheus; for he intended to leave Heracles supporting the sky for ever. But Heracles, by pretending he needed to adjust the weight on his shoulder, tricked him into resuming his task. Thus Atlas lost both his apples and the chance to be relieved of his burden.

Atreidae *see* ATRIDAE.

Atreus Son of Pelops and Hippodamia. He became king of Mycenae, and is best known for his implacable feud with his brother Thyestes and for being the father of Agamemnon and Menelaus (or possibly the grandfather, his son Pleisthenes being sometimes regarded as their father).

Just as Pelops' father Tantalus by his wickedness had brought down a curse on himself and his descendants, and Pelops was cursed by Hermes for the death of Myrtilus, so Pelops cursed his own children for the killing of their half-brother Chrysippus, which they had carried out to satisfy their mother. Pelops, who had become king of Pisa in Elis by winning the hand of Hippodamia, banished Atreus and Thyestes from his kingdom for their crime. They went to the king of Mycenae, Sthenelus, the husband of their sister Nicippe; and Sthenelus gave them the city of Midea to govern.

Aerope, the daughter of Catreus, king of Crete, was bought as a slave by Atreus, who made her his wife; she bore him Agamemnon and Menelaus (or else, according to the alternative genealogy, their father Pleisthenes). But Aerope fell in love with Thyestes, her brother-in-law, and betrayed her husband in the following way. Atreus had vowed to sacrifice to Artemis the finest lamb born in his flocks that year. To test him, the goddess sent him a lamb with a golden fleece, which Atreus in his greed killed, keeping the fleece in a treasure-chest; this Aerope secretly gave to Thyestes. Now Sthenelus and his heir Eurystheus had both died, and their subjects consulted the Delphic Oracle, which told them to choose a king from the rulers of Midea. As they could not

agree which of the brothers should rule them, Thyestes suggested that they should take the one who could produce a golden fleece. Atreus naturally concurred, thinking he had one in his own possession. But to his astonishment it was Thyestes who produced it; and therefore it was he who became king.

But he was soon deprived of his kingdom. For, on the instructions of Zeus, who disapproved of his adultery with Aerope, Hermes visited Atreus and told him to agree that Thyestes should retain the throne unless Atreus could now produce an even greater wonder: namely, to make the sun reverse its course and the Pleiades travel backwards in the heavens. Thyestes, thinking his brother had gone mad, accepted the bargain; but the incredible happened and he had to cede the throne. Atreus sent him forthwith into exile, but shortly afterwards, when he discovered that Thyestes had cheated him in the matter of the fleece, he came to regret his leniency. Pretending good will towards his brother, he invited him to a banquet (or alternatively Thyestes came uninvited, as a suppliant). Thyestes had three sons, who had sought sanctuary at the altar of Zeus; but Atreus murdered them and served them up to his brother at the banquet. When Thyestes had finished eating, Atreus showed him the hands and feet of his dead children and told him what he had eaten. Thyestes once more went into exile and, cursing his brother, asked the Delphic Oracle how he could be avenged upon him. He was told to have a child by his own daughter Pelopia. He raped her without her knowing who he was (according to another version he did not know who she was either). But she took his sword and hid it under a statue of Athena.

As a result of Thyestes' curse and Atreus' wickedness, a famine came over the land of Argos. Atreus consulted an oracle to discover how he might atone, and was told to bring Thyestes back home. He sought for his brother, and in his wanderings came across Pelopia at the court of King Thesprotus of Thesprotia in Epirus. He fell in love with her and asked Thesprotus for her hand; whereon Thesprotus, not wishing to reveal her true parentage, passed her off as his own daughter and gave her to Atreus, pregnant as she was. When her baby, Aegisthus, was born, she abandoned it. Atreus, however, heard of the child, who had been found by a goatherd, and brought him up at the court. Meanwhile he sent his sons (or grandsons) Agamemnon and Menelaus to enquire at Delphi where his brother Thyestes might be found. Thyestes, still wishing to punish his brother, happened to visit the oracle at the same time and was seized by Agamemnon and Menelaus and hauled off to Mycenae. There Atreus locked him up and sent Aegisthus, now a grown man, into the cell to kill him, giving him by chance the very sword that Pelopia had taken from Thyestes and brought with her from Thesprotia. When Thyestes saw the sword, he asked Aegisthus where he had obtained it, and the youth told him that it belonged to his mother. Thyestes asked as a last favour that he might see her, and he told her the truth: he himself was both her father and the father of her son Aegisthus. In shame at the incest, Pelopia killed herself with the sword, and Aegisthus, refusing to slay his father, took the blood-stained weapon to Atreus, claiming that he had killed Thyestes with it. Atreus prepared a thanksgiving sacrifice to the gods because his hated brother was dead, and as he stood by the altar on the seashore Aegisthus stabbed him and so avenged his father.

The curse of Thyestes was further worked out when Aegisthus seduced Clytemnestra and the two of them murdered Agamemnon on his return from Troy. This deed, in its turn, was avenged by the murdered man's son Orestes, who killed Aegisthus.

This story forms the background of Aeschylus' trilogy the *Oresteia* and was the subject of Seneca's tragedy *Thyestes*.

Atridae A Greek patronymic meaning 'sons of Atreus', and referring to Agamemnon and Menelaus.

Atropus *see* FATES.

Atthis Daughter of Cranaus, king of Attica; The eponym of Attica.

Attis The youth loved by the Phrygian goddess Cybele, the Great Mother. There are many versions of the story of her love for him. According to the original Phrygian account, the other gods castrated the hermaphrodite deity Agdistis, whose genitals fell on the ground and grew into an almond tree. The fruit of this tree fell into the lap of Nana, a river-nymph, who bore a son. This child was abandoned, reared by a goat, and later became a shepherd. Agdistis, now female and named Cybele, saw him and loved him so jealously that she could not bear the idea of his marrying (alternatively, he had promised to be faithful to her, yet later proposed to marry a nymph, Sagaritis); she therefore made him go out of his mind and castrate himself. Attis died of his wound; Cybele was overcome with grief and turned him into a pine tree. She also caused him to be mourned every year, and ordained that, in his memory, only eunuchs could act as priests in her temple. Other traditions recounted that Cybele bore a child by Attis and that her father Meion, king of Phrygia, killed both Attis and the baby. Cybele went wild with remorse and rushed through the countryside lamenting for Attis to the accompaniment of a drum. When a famine ensued, the Phrygians were instructed by an oracle to bury Attis and revere Cybele as a goddess. Cybele then revived her dead lover and the pair were worshipped together throughout Phrygia. In a Lydian version of the myth, Attis is not killed by his castration but by a wild boar, like Adonis. *See* CYBELE.

The story of Attis and his self-castration was the background to Catullus' poem No. 63, in which a young man in ecstatic frenzy castrates himself in honour of Cybele and then bitterly repents of his deed.

Auge Daughter of Aleus, king of Arcadia, and his niece Neaera. Her father made Auge a priestess in the temple of Athena at Tegea, a post requiring her perpetual virginity. When Heracles visited Aleus he seduced her; she subsequently gave birth to a son, Telephus, and hid him in the temple. As a result of this pollution, the land became barren, and when Aleus had enquired at Delphi and learnt the cause, he had the child exposed on Mount Parthenium. He also handed his daughter to King Nauplius 2 asking him to drown her or sell her into slavery. Nauplius set her adrift on the sea in a chest, and she went aground in Mysia. There she became the property of King Teuthras, who made her his wife. When Telephus (who had been suckled by a doe and reared by shepherds) enquired at Delphi who his parents were, he was told to go to Mysia; there King Teuthras adopted him and made him his heir. According to another version of the story, Telephus was nearly married to Auge (who had not married Teuthras, but had been adopted by him as his daughter). Telephus was awarded her as his bride for defeating Idas, Teuthras' enemy, in war; but Auge wanted nothing to do with him. She took a sword to bed with her and tried to stab Telephus, but a large snake came between them. Auge told Telephus what she had meant to do and, as he prepared to punish her with death, she called on Heracles for aid. In this way Telephus discovered his mother and took her back to Arcadia. *See* TELEPHUS.

Augeas The king of Elis whose stables Heracles cleaned out. His brother was Actor, father of Eurytus and Cteatus (the Moliones). His father was either Helios or Poseidon or Phorbas. He was a Argonaut, and later attacked Pylos. He had vast numbers of cattle, whose dung caused an ever more serious blockage of his yards and stables. Eurystheus learnt of this and ordered Heracles, as the fifth of his labours, to cleanse them of dung in a day. Heracles cheated, since he demanded payment from Augeas (one tenth of the cattle), to which as a bondslave he was not entitled. Then taking Phyleus, Augeas' son, as a witness to the bargain, Heracles broke through the walls of the stables and diverted the river Alpheius through them. The river did its work well, carrying the dung out and depositing it in the sea. By evening Heracles had returned the river to its course and had rebuilt the end walls of the stables. He asked Augeas for his wages, but the latter, having grasped how Heracles had deceived him, declared the contract null and void and indeed even denied having made it at all, thereby outraging his own son Phyleus. Both Heracles and Phyleus left Elis, the former planning revenge and the latter taking refuge in Dulichium.

It was many years before Heracles returned, bringing with him a force of Arcadians. But Augeas had been expecting him and possessed an army led by Amarynceus and the Moliones. These commanders had been induced to support him by promises of a share in his kingdom. They defeated Heracles' Arcadians and drove them off. Once again Heracles left Elis. But later he ambushed the Moliones in Cleonae and again invaded the country. This time he defeated Augeas and killed him, or else deposed him. He recalled Phyleus from Dulichium and made him king of Elis. But there was also a tradition that Augeas on his deathbed gave his kingdom to a younger son, Agasthenes, and to the sons of the Moliones, and that Phyleus returned to Dulichium. Augeas had a daughter, Agamede, who was skilled in magic.

Aurora *see* EOS.

Autesion Son of Tisamenus and great-grandson of Polynices; a king of Thebes. Being persecuted by the spirits of Laius and Oedipus, he left Thebes on the advice of an oracle, and joined the Dorian invaders of the Peloponnese. He married his daughter Argia to Aristodemus. His son Theras became guardian of Argia's twins Procles and Eurysthenes, the first Heraclid kings of Sparta.

Autolycus *1.* Son of Hermes, god of thieves, and of Chione *1*: a famous thief and liar. He lived near Mount Parnassus with his wife Amphithea and his sons. His daughter Anticlea married Laertes, and was the mother of Odysseus. Autolycus was devoted to Hermes, who furthered his crafty schemes and even, it was said, gave him power to transform the goods he filched so that their owners would not recognise them. He stole the mares of Eurytus, the cattle of Sisyphus, and a leather helmet from the armoury of Amyntor. In the case of the mares he was lucky, because Eurytus suspected Heracles of the theft. But for the loss of his herds Sisyphus got his own back. As his animals gradually diminished he began to notch their hooves, and was soon able to prove Autolycus' guilt by pointing to the unusual tracks the stolen cattle had made. He recovered all the beasts he had lost, and punished Autolycus by seducing his daughter Anticlea; it was afterwards suspected that Odysseus was the offspring of this union. At all events, Autolycus when visiting Ithaca was asked to give Odysseus his name – it meant 'the victim of hatred', because so many people hated Autolycus. (*Odyssomai* means 'I hate' or 'I am angry'; according to an alternative inter-

pretation Odysseus was thus named because Autolycus was angry with so many men.)
2. A Thessalian, the son of Deimachus of Tricca. He and his brothers Phlogius and Deileon aided Heracles in his expedition against the Amazons. They then settled at Sinope, on the northern coast of Asia Minor. When the *Argo* passed on its way to Colchis, the three brothers joined the Argonauts.

Automedon Son of Diores, from the island of Scyros. He followed Achilles to the Trojan War and sometimes acted as his chariot-driver. Patroclus chose him to drive Achilles' team of horses; and when Hector killed Patroclus, the horses, in their grief, would not move until Zeus breathed fresh vigour into them to enable Automedon to escape and gain a sort of vengeance by slaying the Trojan Aretus. After Achilles was killed, Automedon became a follower of his son Neoptolemus.

Autonoe Wife of Aristaeus and mother of Actaeon and Macris. She was one of the daughters of Cadmus of Thebes and of Harmonia. She and her sisters refused to accept Zeus' choice of their sister Semele as the mother of his child, and Dionysus punished them by driving them to murder Pentheus, son of Agave, in a bacchic frenzy. After the death of Actaeon at the hands of Artemis, Autonoe and Aristaeus parted, and she went to live near Megara at a village called Ereneia.

Aventinus One of Turnus' allies against Aeneas. He was born on the Aventine Hill, later part of Rome. His father was Hercules (Heracles) and his mother a priestess, Rhea. He showed his parentage by displaying the Hydra on his shield and wearing a lion skin.

Axion *1.* Son of Phegeus, king of Psophis. *2.* Son of Priam; he was killed by Eurypylus *3*.

B

Bacchants, Bacchantes, Bacchanals *see* MAENADS.

Bacchus *see* DIONYSUS.

Balius *see* XANTHUS.

Batia *1.* Daughter of the elder Teucer, the first king of the land of Troy. When Dardanus emigrated from Samothrace to her father's kingdom, she married him and bore Erichthonius, father of Tros; she was thus the mythical ancestress of the Trojan race.
2. A Naiad who bore Icarius to King Oebalus of Sparta.

Battus *1.* The founder of the Theran colony of Cyrene in Libya. He was seventeenth in descent from the Argonaut Euphemus, whose descendants had colonised Thera in a joint venture with the Spartans.

The story of Battus' birth as preserved in Cyrenaic tradition makes him son of Phronime, daughter of a Cretan king, Etearchus. Phronime's stepmother was cruel to her and turned Etearchus against his daughter with a tale of her immorality. With lavish gifts he persuaded a Theran merchant, Themison, to grant him any favour he might desire; when Themison agreed, Etearchus asked him to throw Phronime into the sea from his ship. Themison was outraged, but had to fulfil his promise. However, he fastened a rope to the girl, and after throwing her overboard pulled her in again. Thereafter he had nothing more to do with Etearchus. Themison took Phronime to Thera where she became the concubine of a noble Theran, Polymnestus. She gave birth to Aristoteles, who acquired the nickname Battus from his stammer.

When Battus grew to manhood, he accompanied Grinnus, king of Thera, on an expedition to Delphi; the oracle told Grinnus to found a colony in the land of Libya. But he claimed to be too old for such a journey, and asked the oracle to transfer the duty to Battus. For seven years nothing was done to carry out the command, and during this time not a drop of rain fell on Thera. Realising that the drought was a punishment for their inactivity, the Therans sent a delegation to the neighbouring island of Crete to discover if anyone knew where Libya was. They found a dye-merchant called Corobius, whose ship had been blown off course to Plataea, an island off the Libyan coast. The Therans bought his service, and he guided a party to Plataea, but Battus did not join the expedition.

The colony at Plataea did not prosper, however, and when Battus went to Delphi to ask how he might cure his stammer, the oracle told him to build a city in Libya if he wished for perfect speech. The Therans then dispatched Battus with a company of colonists who, after sighting the coast of Africa, returned to Thera. The Therans drove them off again with arrows and sent them to Plataea, where they joined the first party of settlers.

Plataea, however, still did not flourish, and when the colonists enquired the reason from the Delphic Oracle, they were told that they had not even been to

Libya yet. Battus took the hint and removed his followers from the island to a nearby spot on the mainland, at Aziris. For six years they lived in this beautiful place without great success, and were then persuaded by the natives to re-establish their colony farther west at Apollo's fountain. Here the prophecy was fulfilled and the colony prospered, with hundreds of settlers flocking from the whole of Greece to join it. Battus, who was made ruler of the new city, lost his stammer when he met a lion in the country outside Cyrene. He shouted at the lion, which fled; thereafter, he found he could speak easily.

The story is told by Herodotus. Pindar refers to it in two Pythian Odes dedicated to Battus' descendant Arcesilas.

2. An old man who, near Maenalus in Arcadia, saw Hermes on the first day of the god's life driving off the cattle of Apollo which he had stolen. Hermes noticed him and offered him a cow to keep silent; Battus replied that a stone would not tell more than he. Later on Hermes returned in disguise, pretending to be the owner seeking his lost cattle. When he asked Battus if he had seen them, offering a bull and its mate as reward, the old man had no scruple in betraying him. So Hermes turned him, appropriately enough, into a stone.

Baucis and **Philemon** When Zeus and Hermes decided, before the flood descended on the world, to test mankind to see if any were worthy of preservation, they wandered over the earth disguised as travellers, seeking hospitality. All doors were closed to them, so wicked had the people become, but finally in Phrygia, one evening, they came at last to a little thatched cottage on the side of a mountain, where the elderly Philemon and his wife Baucis had lived as simple peasants ever since the time when they were married. The old couple did their very best to give the strangers a wel-

come; the meal was frugal, but it was prepared and served with devotion. A miracle then occurred, for the wine flagon kept filling itself up of its own accord. Then Baucis and Philemon prepared to kill their only goose in honour of their guests, but the gods forbade them, at the same time revealing their own identity and the doom for which the land all round them was destined. They led the aged pair up the mountain, and when they reached the summit showed them the whole country-side already drowned in water. Only their own cottage remained. This the gods transformed into a majestic temple, and Zeus asked Philemon what gift he would like. He responded by asking that he and his wife should be allowed to serve Zeus' temple as priest and priestess for the rest of their lives and to die at the same instant, lest either one should have to grieve for the other. Zeus granted their wish and at the moment of their death turned them simultaneously into trees, the oak and the lime, which often grow together. Passing strangers hung wreaths on them in memory of their piety to their divine visitors.

Begoe *see* VEGOIA.

Bellerophon Son of Glaucus, king of Corinth, or else of Poseidon. His mother was Eurynome (or Eurymede). Bellerophon was one of the greater heroes; but like Heracles, Jason, and Theseus, he often performed feats imposed by a superior. As a young man at Corinth, or rather Ephyra as its name then was, Bellerophon aspired to break in the immortal winged horse Pegasus, sprung from the blood which had fallen from Medusa's severed neck when Perseus had killed her. As she was pregnant by Poseidon, it was said that the steed owed its paternity to that god. Its name was sometimes connected with the Greek word *pege*, 'a spring of water', and the origins of at least two springs in Greece were attributed to a stamp of the horse's hoof, namely Hippocrene ('the horse-spring') on Mount Helicon, and a spring of the same name at Troezen. At first the young horse wandered over land and through the air, refusing to allow any man to approach it. Bellerophon tamed it eventually by enlisting the aid of the seer Polyidus. Polyidus told him to lie for a night upon the altar of Athena. There the young man dreamed that the goddess gave him a golden bridle and ordered him to sacrifice a bull to Poseidon the Tamer. When he awoke, he found the bridle on the ground beside him; Polyidus commanded him to obey his orders at once, and Bellerophon duly performed the sacrifice. Then he found Pegasus calmly waiting at the spring of Pirene in Corinth; it seemed to welcome his approach, and he placed the bridle on its head.

Bellerophon accidentally killed his brother Deliades, or else a tyrant at Ephyra (Corinth) called Bellerus (according to this version of the story, *Bellerophon* was a nickname meaning 'killer of Bellerus' – his original name had been Hipponous). As a result he was exiled from Ephyra and went to Argos, where King Proetus purified him of the homicide. But the king's wife Stheneboea (called Antia by Homer in the *Iliad*) fell in love with him. He rejected her advances, and she falsely accused him of trying to rape her. Proetus was unwilling to put a guest to death, but sent Bellerophon off to Lycia to the court of his father-in-law King Iobates with a sealed letter. On his arrival he was entertained warmly by Stheneboea's father; only on the tenth day did the Lycian king open the letter, which contained a request that the bearer should be killed. But by now Bellerophon was a guest of Iobates, who consequently felt the same scruple as Proetus. However Iobates ordered the youth to kill the monstrous Chimaera which was ravaging Lycia. Bellerophon,

the king was sure, would die in the attempt, but instead with the aid of Pegasus he swooped on the monster from above and successfully peppered her with arrows.

Iobates, astounded at Bellerophon's success, remained relentless, and sent him to fight single-handed against the neighbouring Solymi, the enemies of Lycia. Again Pegasus was instrumental in their destruction. A third time Iobates sent him out, this time against the Amazons. On his return, once again victorious, Bellerophon was ambushed by a picked band of Lycian soldiers sent by Iobates who was now at his wits' end. But Bellerophon slew them all. Finally accepting defeat, Iobates confided in him, showed him the secret letter, and made him his ally, giving him one of his daughters, Philonoe, in marriage and half his kingdom to rule. Bellerophon had three children, Hippolochus, Isander, and Laodamia.

According to Euripides in his lost tragedy the *Stheneboea*, Bellerophon returned to Argos and revenged himself on the queen. Pretending that he loved her, he suggested that she should ride off with him on Pegasus. But when she agreed, he pushed her off the winged horse from a great height. Her body was discovered in the sea and taken back to Argos by the fishermen who had found her.

The end of his life was miserable. Two of his children died, Isander fighting against the Solymi, Laodamia of natural causes. Bellerophon himself, according to the play by Euripides (no longer extant) that bears his name, vied with the gods and attempted to ride Pegasus up to heaven itself. Zeus in anger caused a gadfly to sting the horse, which threw Bellerophon. He survived the fall but was lamed for life. Thereafter he wandered over the face of the earth and his death was unrecorded.

Bellona A Roman goddess of war, similar to Enyo of the Greeks. Though an important cult-figure among the Romans, she had little or no mythology. She was identified in early times with Mars' wife Nerio.

Belus A Hellenised form of the Semitic *Baal*, 'lord', the name was given in Greek myth to a king of Egypt, who was the son of Poseidon and Libya and twin brother of Agenor. Belus married Anchinoe, daughter of the River Nile, and had two sons, Danaus and Aegyptus. Through Danaus and Aegyptus, Belus was the ancestor of many royal houses in Greece, Persia, and Africa. Several other mythical royal personages also bear the name of Belus, including a king of Assyria and the father of Dido, queen of Carthage.

Beroe *see* SEMELE.

Bia and **Cratos** Sons of the Titan Pallas and the River Styx. Since Zeus had been helped by Styx in his battle with the Titans, he honoured her by appointing her children as his special servants. The names of Bia and Cratos mean 'force' and 'might', and they generally appear in association. They were allotted the task of chaining Prometheus and nailing him down to the rock of Caucasus as a punishment for giving fire to mankind. In this function they appear as characters in Aeschylus' play *Prometheus Bound*. Their brother was Zelus (Zeal), and their sister Nike (Victory).

Bias Brother of the seer Melampus. *See* MELAMPUS.

Bisaltes a Thracian king. *See* THE-OPHANE.

Biton *see* CLEOBIS.

Boeotus Son of Poseidon and Mela-nippe; the brother of Aeolus *3*.

Bona Dea 'the Good Goddess'. An ob-scure Roman deity, exclusively worshipped by women, and identified with Fauna. Her mythology is slight and represents an attempt to explain her cult. In one story her father Faunus wished to commit incest with her and, to achieve his purpose, made her drunk. When she still refused him he beat her with myrtle-rods, and finally changed into a serpent to have his will with her. That is why, it was said, wine and myrtle were banned from her ceremonies, at any rate under their true names. In another story Heracles asked some women whom he found celebrating the mysteries of the Good Goddess for a drink of wine. When it was refused he forbade women to attend his own ritual at the Great Altar he founded in Rome.

Boreas God of the North Wind and son of the sky deities Astraeus and Eos (the Stars and the Dawn). His native land was said to be Thrace. He is often contrasted with Zephyrus, who represented the gentleness of the West Wind as opposed to the violence of Boreas. In mythology he courted Orithyia, a daughter of Erechtheus, an Athenian king. She resisted his advances, but when the god found her dancing in the meadows by the river Ilissus, he wrapped her in a cloud and carried her off to Thrace. She bore him two winged sons, Calais and Zetes, and two daughters, Chione and Cleopatra. Thereafter the Athenians considered Boreas to be one of their patrons; in the Persian Wars they offered him sacrifice.

Boreas was closely associated with horses and is often represented in this guise: he fathered twelve foals on a mare belonging to Danaus.

Branchus *see* SMICRUS.

Briareos A monstrous creature with a hundred arms, the offspring of Gaia (Earth) and Uranus (Sky). Poseidon is occasionally mentioned as his father.

When the other gods rebelled against Zeus, Thetis summoned Briareos to save him. He helped to put the rising down, and was rewarded by Zeus with a bride, Cymopole. He was also appointed to settle a dispute over the ownership of Corinth. He awarded the Acrocorinth (a high hill on which the citadel was built) to Helios; the rest of the place he gave to Poseidon. His normal duty, in association with his brothers Gyes and Cottus, was to guard the Titans confined in Tartarus. Homer indicates that he was also called Aegaeon.

Briseis Daughter of Briseus of Lyrnessus, a town near Troy. Achilles captured her when he sacked her native town during the years before the siege of Troy; he killed all her family and her husband Mynes, king of Lyrnessus, and made her his concubine. But when Agamemnon, at the wish of Apollo, had to return Chryseis to her father, he peevishly seized Briseis from Achilles. For this reason Achilles kept out of the war until Patroclus' death roused him to return. Briseis was then returned to Achilles, and played her part in the mourning for Patroclus.

Briseus Father of Briseis.

Britomartis A Cretan goddess similar to Artemis; the daughter of Zeus and Carme, a Cretan woman. Her name means 'the sweet maid'. She was a mistress of wild animals and lived in wild places. In Greek mythology she was brought into the cult of Artemis and made one of her attendant nymphs. Like Artemis, she was known as Dictynna in Crete. The supposed meaning of this name ('the lady of nets', though it is also possible that Dictynna may mean 'the lady of Dicte' – a mountain in Crete) is explained by the story of her nine-month flight from Minos who wanted to make her his mistress. When he was finally about to seize her, she

flung herself off the cliffs into the sea to escape him, and was caught in the fishermen's nets. Then, with the help of Artemis, she fled in Andromedes' fishing-smack to Aegina where Minos again sought her. But she had disappeared in a sacred grove of Artemis, and the people of Aegina founded a temple in her honour, where they worshipped her as *Aphaia* ('the invisible').

Bromius *see* DIONYSUS.

Broteas Son of Tantalus, king of Phrygia, and a devotee of Cybele, the Phrygian Mother-goddess, whose statue he carved in rock on Mount Sipylus. But Broteas refused to acknowledge the majesty of Artemis, and for this he was driven mad. He threw himself into a fire under the delusion that he would not be injured, and perished in the flames.

Brutus, Lucius Junius Legendary founder of the Roman Republic; it is disputed whether he ever existed. He was the nephew of Tarquinius Superbus, the last king of Rome, being the son of his sister Tarquinia. When a snake had ominously crept out of a pillar in the palace, he was said to have accompanied two of Tarquinius' sons, Titus and Arruns, on an expedition to Delphi to consult the oracle about the portent. Being suspicious of Tarquinius' policy towards the aristocracy, many of whom the king had murdered, Brutus deliberately pretended to be stupid (the meaning of his name in Latin), and was allowed to go to Greece so that he could provide amusement for his cousins. After putting the official question to the oracle, the king's sons next asked which of them would become king of Rome on their father's death. The response was that the first to kiss his mother would be supreme ruler of Rome. The princes drew lots for the right to kiss their mother on their return, and swore to keep the response secret from their youngest brother Sextus Tarquinius. But Brutus deliberately tripped up and kissed the ground – mother earth.

A little while after the return of the expedition to Delphi, King Tarquinius Superbus made war on Ardea, a rich Rutulian city, and during its siege Sextus raped Lucretia at Collatia, in the house of her husband Lucius Tarquinius Collatinus, who was his cousin. After Sextus' departure, Lucretia summoned her husband and her father, and the former brought Brutus, with whom he had been riding when the message arrived. Lucretia disclosed what had happened to her, extracted an oath from the men to avenge her honour, and stabbed herself to death. On this, Brutus led them in swearing a second oath, to expel the Tarquins and establish a republic at Rome. The others were astonished at the transformation of the presumed idiot, but willingly accepted him as leader. He led an armed rising in Rome, and the populace voted for the abolition of royal power and the exile of the royal family. Brutus then led the armed citizens to Ardea, where he won over the troops besieging the town. Meanwhile King Tarquinius Superbus, having heard of the revolt, had marched back to Rome at the head of his most faithful followers, with the intention of restoring order. He found the gates barred and his wife fled.

After the liberation, according to one account, the citizens elected Brutus consul, together with Lucius Tarquinius Collatinus. But in a short time the people repented of having elected another bearer of the hated royal name, and Brutus urged his fellow-consul to leave Rome and remove all grounds for fear. This Callatinus did, and Publius Valerius Poplicola was elected consul in his place.

Before the deposed King Tarquinius Superbus delivered his expected attack on Rome, a conspiracy of royalist sympathisers was detected among the sons of certain of the aristocratic houses. Two sons of Brutus himself, Titus and Tiberius, were implicated, and letters that were found addressed to the Tarquins proved their guilt. The consuls arrested and imprisoned the traitors, and directed the seizure of all the property of the former royal house in Rome, consecrating their estate to Mars (the Campus Martius) and destroying their standing crops. At the trial of Brutus' sons, their father displayed that fortitude and gravity which the Romans liked to consider their special hallmark. He himself, in his official capacity, pronounced his sons' guilt and witnessed their execution. The lictors bound the young men to stakes, flogged them, and beheaded them. All eyes were on Brutus who, for all his anguish, never flinched. He rewarded the informer (a slave) with citizen rights and money.

When Tarquinius Superbus invaded Roman territory, the consuls advanced to meet him. Assailing Brutus, who was leading the cavalry, with taunts, the king's son Arruns charged him on horseback. Such was the violence of their clash that each transfixed the other and both fell dead on the spot. The general battle which ensued proved inconclusive. That night, however, a voice issued from the nearby Arsian wood proclaiming a Roman victory, because they had lost one man less than Tarquinius Superbus and his Etruscan allies. The Etruscans withdrew, and Brutus was given a magnificent funeral in Rome, where all the women, in recognition of his championship of Lucretia, mourned him as if he were their father.

Busiris A king of Egypt, the son of Poseidon and of Lysianassa, daughter of Epaphus. When a drought afflicted his country, Busiris followed the advice of Phrasius, a seer from Cyprus, and introduced the practice of sacrificing all strangers who arrived in his kingdom to Zeus. This was in the hope that after a year of such 'piety' his land would receive rain. Phrasius himself was his first victim. Soon afterwards Heracles arrived and was bound so that he too could be sacrificed. But he burst his bonds and killed Busiris and his son, and all his attendants.

Butes *1*. Son of Boreas, who conspired against his half-brother Lycurgus, king of Thrace. His conspiracy was detected and he went into exile, seizing the island of Naxos, where he turned pirate. In a raid on Drius in Phthiotis he raped Coronis, a follower of Dionysus: whereupon the god punished him by driving him mad, and he drowned himself in a well.

2. An Argonaut of Athenian extraction, son of Zeuxippe (daughter of the River Eridanus) and of Poseidon or Teleon. The only member of the *Argo*'s crew unable to resist the singing of the Sirens, he jumped overboard and swam towards their island. But Aphrodite took pity on him and carried him to the western part of Sicily. There she became the mother of his son, Eryx, after whom the site of her famous shrine was named.

Byblis Daughter of Miletus and Cyanea, who fell in love with Caunus, her twin brother. Caunus, when he heard of her passion for him, left his native city of Miletus in horror and moved southwards into Caria, where he founded the city named after him. Byblis, beside herself with longing for her brother, sought him throughout the coastland of Asia Minor. But she could not find him, and the Carian nymphs turned her into a spring of water, which was named after her.

C

Cabiri (Greek: *Kabeiroi*) Early fertility gods of the northern Aegean Sea and Phrygia. They also possessed an early cult at Thebes.

There were many versions of their origins. They were sometimes called children of Hephaestus, to account for their cult on the island of Lemnos, where they were revered as smiths; sometimes their father was identified as Uranus, to account for their assistance at the birth of Zeus; and they were also said to be descendants of Proteus, the Old Man of the Sea, and providers of aid to sailors – in which capacity they were identified with the Dioscuri. On Samothrace, however, they were considered to be the sons of Zeus and Calliope. Orpheus knew of their worship, and counselled the Argonauts to put in at Samothrace in order to be initiated in their mysteries. It was said that the herms, statues of Hermes with erect phallus, came to Athens in connection with the Mysteries of the Cabiri.

Caca *see* CACUS.

Cacus Son of Vulcan; a fire-breathing monster who lived in a cave on the Palatine hill near the River Tiber, on the site of the future city of Rome. He lived on human flesh, and his cave was littered with the skulls and bones of his victims. When Hercules (Heracles) was driving the cattle he had stolen from Geryon back to Greece by way of this place, he fell asleep on the banks of the river. Cacus spotted Hercules' beautiful herd, but since he feared detection if he drove them off openly, he dragged four

prize bulls and four heifers backwards by their tails into his cave. When Hercules awoke, he searched in vain for the missing animals. However, just as he was leaving in despair, one of the heifers inside the cave answered his own cattle's lowing. Cacus rushed in terror back to the cavern and closed the entrance with a mighty boulder. Hercules could see no way to enter the hole, but finally succeeded in pushing the top off the mountain so that the interior of the cave was revealed from above. He rained arrows on Cacus, who responded with clouds of smoke and fire. Finally, in his fury, Hercules leapt on Cacus and strangled him, thus ridding the district of the scourge and recovering the cattle he had lost. In another version of the story, the monster's sister Caca fell in love with Hercules and betrayed Cacus' lair to him.

According to other versions, current in Etruria, Cacus was not an ogre but a handsome minstrel who possessed Apollo's gift of prophecy and was killed by Hercules for some reason unknown. A further Etruscan story makes him a Lydian whom Tarchon tried to imprison, and whom Hercules killed because he invaded Campania. Alternatively, he was represented as welcoming and entertaining Hercules at the site of Rome.

Cadmus Son of Agenor king of Tyre and brother of Europa; the founder of Thebes.

When Zeus, disguised as a bull, carried Europa away, Agenor sent his sons in search of her, with orders never to return unless they brought her back with them. Cadmus, accompanied by his mother Telephassa, reached Thrace, where his mother died. Then he proceeded to Delphi to ask for instructions, and was told to forget about Europa and instead to find a cow marked on her flank with a moon-shaped sign. He should follow the cow and build a city at the first place where she should choose to lie down and rest. He found the cow in the herds of King Pelagon of Phocis and drove her onwards until she eventually collapsed near the River Asopus on the site of Thebes. In preparation for the building of his citadel, Cadmus resolved to sacrifice the cow to Athena. Needing water, he sent some of his men to fetch it from the nearby spring. But a dragon sprung from Ares, which guarded the spot, killed the men and began to eat them. When Cadmus discovered their fate, he attacked the monster and slew it. Athena appeared and advised Cadmus to remove its teeth and sow half of them in the ground (she kept the other half for Aeetes, king of Colchis, to give to Jason). When Cadmus obeyed, armed men sprang up. He threw stones among them and they, suspecting each other, began a mutual slaughter until only five were left. These five Cadmus enrolled as citizens of Cadmeia, as he called his new city; they were the Spartoi, or 'Sown Men', who were ancestors of the Theban nobility.

Because he had offended Ares by killing his son the dragon, Cadmus was compelled to serve the god for the space of eight years. When his servitude was over, Athena made him king of Cadmeia, and Zeus gave him Harmonia, the daughter of Ares and Aphrodite, as his bride. Since he was marrying the daughter of one of their number, the gods, bringing splendid gifts, attended the wedding in person (the only mortal ever to receive such an honour thereafter was Peleus). However two of the gifts, a necklace made by Hephaestus and the wedding-robe, were destined to bring sorrow on subsequent owners (see ALCMAEON). Hermes gave Cadmus a lyre, and Demeter presented him with grain.

Cadmus and Harmonia ruled Thebes (as Cadmeia was later named) well, reputedly teaching the Boeotians the art of writing with Phoenician letters – from which the Greek alphabet is derived. But the children of these monarchs did not prosper, with the single exception of Polydorus. Semele became the mother of Dionysus, but perished because she asked to see her lover, Zeus, in all his glory. Autonoe, who married Aristaeus, lost her son Actaeon through the wrath of Artemis. Agave married the dragon-man Echion. Her son Pentheus, because he had spied on the Bacchic revels, was torn to pieces in the mountains by the Maenads, among whom was Agave herself: she and his aunts in their frenzy mistook him for a young lion. Another of Cadmus' daughters, Ino, and her husband Athamas fell foul of the goddess Hera for nursing the infant Dionysus. They were driven mad, Athamas killing two of his three sons, and Ino leaping into the sea with the third.

Cadmus had already abdicated in favour of Pentheus, and after the latter's death he wished to retire again. Dionysus now told him that he could assuage his grief only by emigrating from the city he had founded. So Cadmus and Harmonia travelled north to Illyria where they joined an obscure tribe called the Encheleis (eels). (Some said that they lived much nearer home, on the shores of Lake Copais in Boeotia.) Riding in an ox-cart, he led them to war against their enemies and was victorious over the whole nation of the Illyrians. Finally the Encheleis committed sacrilege by plundering a shrine of Apollo. However Ares had mercy on his daughter Harmonia and his son-in-law Cadmus, and transformed them into large, harmless snakes (which were regarded by the Greeks as containing the spirits of the dead heroes). There was a tale that Cadmus founded a dynasty in Illyria, begetting a son called Illyrius in his old age.

Cadmus was also honoured in Laconia, for the people of Brasiae in Spartan territory told a different version of the myth of Semele. According to their story, her child was born normally, and Cadmus then threw mother and son into the sea in a chest which came to land at Brasiae.

Caecilia see TANAQUIL.

Caeculus The hero or founder of the Italian city of Praeneste. Caeculus' mother, who lived with her brothers the Delpidii upon the site of the future Praeneste, conceived him when a spark flew out of the fire into her lap. His paternity was therefore attributed to Vulcan, god of fire. She abandoned and exposed her baby, who was found by some girls lying near the fire which was kept burning in a shrine of Jupiter. They called him Caeculus, it was said, because he appeared to be blinded (*caecus*) by the light of the fire. He was brought up by the country folk, and later collected them together to be the inhabitants of the new city of Praeneste. He held games to which he invited all the people of the neighbourhood. When they arrived, he urged them to join his community, telling them that his father was Vulcan. When they scoffed at his claim, he called upon Vulcan to vindicate him; and seeing the place surrounded with a wall of fire, the people flocked to become members of the city. In the war between Aeneas and Turnus for the hand of Lavinia, Caeculus led his followers in support of Turnus.

Caeles see VIBENNA.

Caeneus Originally Caenis, daughter of Elatus, a Thessalian king. In spite of her great beauty, Caenis refused to marry; but as she walked along the seashore

Poseidon saw her and raped her. As a reward, he offered her whatever she wished, and she asked him to make her a man, so that she might never again have to undergo the indignity he had inflicted on her. Poseidon granted her wish, and in addition made her invulnerable to death from the sword. Now called Caeneus, he became one of the chiefs of the Lapiths of Thessaly. At the wedding of Pirithous, when the drunken Centaurs attacked the Lapiths and tried to steal their women, Caeneus killed six Centaurs, including the mighty Latreus. Then the rest of them attacked him and, being unable to wound him with weapons, showered him with rocks and trees, until he was driven by their sheer weight under the ground and into Tartarus. There he became Caenis again. But Ovid offers another version of his end, declaring that the seer Mopsus saw Caeneus' spirit in the form of a bird ascending into the sky from the pile of rocks and trees. His son was Coronus.

Caenis see CAENEUS.

Calais and **Zetes** The twin sons of Boreas, the North Wind, and Orithyia. When these twins, known as the Boreades, were born, they were of human appearance in all respects; but after their adolescence feathers sprouted from their shoulders and formed into great golden wings. They are also sometimes depicted with winged feet. Their hair was dark, like their father's storm clouds.

It was decreed that if ever the Boreades failed to catch a fugitive they should die. They enlisted with Jason on the *Argo* in the expedition to find the Golden Fleece, and rescued Phineus, the old blind king of Salmydessus and their sister Cleopatra's husband, who was being persecuted by the Harpies. These monstrosities, in the form of female birds, would snatch up all meals set before Phineus and foul his table. The

Boreades chased them off, one as far as the River Tigres (in the Peloponnese), which was thenceforth called Harpys; the other as far as some islands in the Ionian Sea. Here Iris told them to abandon the pursuit, since the Harpies would no longer persecute Phineus; and so the islands were given the name Strophades, meaning 'Isles of Turning'. The twins returned to the *Argo* and completed the voyage. At the funeral games of King Pelias, the Boreades won the race for speed. But on their way home they were killed on the island of Tenos by Heracles because, after he lost Hylas, they had persuaded the Argonauts to sail on without him. (According to another account, however, the Boreades died at the Strophades because of their failure to catch the Harpies). Over their grave Heracles put two columns, one of which moved whenever their father the North Wind blew. *See also* ERGINUS *1*.

Calchas The seer of the Greek army in the Trojan War. He was the son of Thestor, a man of either Megara or Mycenae. Agamemnon came to Calchas in person to persuade him to accompany the expedition to Troy; and when he built a temple in honour of Artemis it was said to be to gratify the seer, who was thought to have been her priest.

Calchas, who told the future by observing birds, made many important predictions about the events of the Trojan War. When Achilles was only nine years old, Calchas declared that without his help and that of Philoctetes Troy could not be taken. At Aulis he saw a snake come out from beneath the altar, climb a plane-tree, and devour a sparrow and her eight fledgelings; it was then turned to stone. From this Calchas foretold that the war would end only after nine years. As the fleet was becalmed, he declared that Iphigenia, daughter of the commander-in-chief Agamemnon, must be fetched from Mycenae and sacrificed to appease the wrath of Artemis. When

the tenth year came, Calchas saw that the anger of Apollo could be appeased only by the return of Chryseis to her father, who was a priest of Apollo. Either he or Helenus, the Trojan seer, told the Greeks to build the Wooden Horse to deceive the Trojans.

Not long after the fall of Troy, a prophecy about Calchas' own death, which he had known from his youth, came true. It had been foretold that he would die when he met a better seer than himself. This was to be Tiresias' grandson Mopsus *2*, whom Calchas encountered at Clarus, near Colophon in Asia Minor, having refused to return to Greece with the fleet which he knew to be doomed. The two prophets held a contest. Calchas first asked Mopsus for the number of figs on a certain wild fig-tree which was especially prolific. Mopsus gave the right answer. Then Mopsus in his turn asked Calchas for the number of young in the womb of a certain pregnant sow. Calchas said eight, but Mopsus correctly forecast that there were nine piglets, which would be born the next day at the sixth hour. Calchas was mortified and died soon after. According to another version of the story, a prophet, perhaps Mopsus, watched Calchas planting vines and declared he would not live long enough to taste the wine. When the first wine of these grapes was ready, Calchas invited him to the first tasting, at which the other prophet repeated his prophecy. Calchas is said to have burst out laughing, and laughed so much that he died. His companions buried him at Notium, near Colophon.

Callidice A queen of Thesprotia in Epirus. Odysseus after his return to Ithaca went on a journey inland to appease the wrath of Poseidon. While he was travelling he came to Thesprotia, and there he married Callidice who bore him a son, Polypoetes. Odysseus led the Thesprotians against the neighbouring

Bryges, but lost the battle. On the death of Callidice Odysseus returned to Penelope, leaving Thesprotia to his son Polypoetes.

Calliope see MUSES.

Callipolis see ALCATHOUS.

Callirrhoe *1.* see ALCMAEON.
2. An Oceanid. *See* CHRYSAOR.
3. see CORESUS.

Callisto Daughter of Lycaon, king of Arcadia, or else a nymph. Her name, derived from *kalliste*, means 'most beautiful'. She followed Artemis as one of her maidens, having taken a vow to remain a virgin. But Zeus saw her and fell in love with her. He disguised himself, taking the form of Apollo or Artemis, and lured the girl into his embrace. Either Zeus or Hera or Artemis then turned Callisto into a bear. If it was Zeus, he did so to shield her from his wife's anger; if Hera, it was a penalty for invading her marriage rights; if Artemis, her action was designed to punish Callisto for breaking her vow. In the version which ascribed the transformation to Zeus, Hera avenged herself by persuading Artemis to shoot the bear, whereupon Zeus sent Hermes to rescue the baby, Arcas, from Callisto's womb. In a further variant of the story Callisto bore her son naturally, and was herself shot by Arcas when he was grown up and was hunting in the mountains of Arcadia. Yet another story tells how Callisto, in the form of a bear, was caught by some shepherds and given as a present to her father Lycaon: one day the bear happened to wander into the forbidden precinct of Zeus Lycaeus, and was shot down for this impiety by her son Arcas. According to Ovid, however, Zeus stayed Arcas' hand and turned the pair, mother and son, into stars, the constellations of the Great Bear and Arctophylax (Little Bear).

Hera was so offended by this honour to Callisto that she persuaded the Ocean to refuse to allow the Bear into his stream, so that Callisto has no rest, endlessly revolving round the Pole Star without ever setting.

Calyce Daughter of Aeolus and Enarete. *See* ENDYMION.

Calydonian Boar-Hunt see MELEAGER; ATALANTA.

Calypso A goddess or nymph, the daughter of the Titan Atlas. She lived on the mythical island of Ogygia on which Odysseus was washed up during his journey home from Troy. She loved him and kept him with her for seven years, offering to give him immortality if he would consent to stay with her. But as he pined for his home and wife, Zeus took pity on him at last and sent Hermes to persuade Calypso to help him on his way home. She gave him carpenter's tools and dry timber, and provisioned him for his voyage. She was said to have borne Odysseus a son, whose name was variously reported.

Camilla The daughter of Metabus, king of the Italian tribe the Volsci, and of Casmila. Because of his cruelty Metabus was driven out of his city of Privernum, and he took his baby daughter with him. In his flight he came to the River Amasenus, which he had no means of crossing. He bound Camilla to his spear and, with a prayer to Diana, hurled it to the other bank. When he had swum across the river, he found his daughter safe and dedicated her to Diana's service. He brought her up in the mountains, giving her mare's milk and later teaching her how to hunt and fight. Loved and protected by Diana, she was able to run through the grain without trampling it, and the sea without wetting her feet. She joined Turnus in his war against Aeneas, riding like an Amazon with one breast exposed at the head of the Volscian cavalry, with a company of picked warrior-maidens. Camilla killed many of her enemies, but finally, with the aid of Apollo, the Etruscan Arruns was able to transfix her with his spear under the naked breast. Diana empowered her nymph Opis to take swift vengeance on Arruns, whom she ambushed and shot with an arrow.

Camillus Marcus Furius Camillus, probably dictator of Rome in 396 and 389 BC (though three additional dictatorships were recorded). Although he seems to have been a historical character, a considerable body of legend grew up around his name. The Romans, according to tradition, besieged the Etruscan city of Veii for ten years without success (the same duration as the siege of Troy). A soothsayer of Veii finally let him know that the city could not fall until the Alban Lake – which had risen abnormally high – was drained. This was done, and Camillus, already thrice consul, was made dictator. Then he dug a tunnel under the town, and his men overheard the king of Veii in the temple of Juno above them declaring that whichever side offered the sacrifice he was about to make would win the war. Camillus' men burst out of the tunnel into the temple, finished the sacrifice themselves, and took possession of the city. Camillus transported the image of Juno from the temple to Rome. Shortly afterwards he was accused of misappropriating loot from Veii and of celebrating his triumph with excessive magnificence. However, it was believed that he subsequently conquered the neighbouring town of Falerii. Previously, it was said, the local schoolmaster had betrayed his charges, the sons of the leading citizens, into Camillus' hands, but Camillus had refused to accept his offer and sent the boys back home unharmed.

Some time later, after Camillus had been brought into court for mishandling the proceeds of the spoils of Veii, he went into exile – just at the time when an invading army of Gauls (Senones) was approaching Rome. The Romans were crushed by the Gauls at the River Allia (a historical event, of c. 390 BC) and Rome itself was taken and sacked, only the Capitol (according to one tradition) remaining untouched: the Gauls slaughtered the priests and elders who remained in the city. Camillus was appointed commander-in-chief and organised Roman resistance from Ardea. To gain the approval of the Senate for his appointment, a messenger was sent from there to the Capitol. But the marks he had made as he climbed up to the citadel were detected by the Gauls, and their king Brennus determined that his men should follow his example and scale the cliff. However the sacred geese of Juno roused the defenders, who drove off the assailants with great losses. But they soon ran short of supplies and tried to buy the Gauls off with gold. When the agreed thousand pounds weight of gold was being weighed, the Gauls tried to defraud the Romans; and when a Roman commander complained, Brennus threw his sword into the scales, exclaiming *vae victis* – 'woe to the losers'. At this point Camillus rode up at the head of a powerful body of troops; he repudiated the terms of capitulation and ordered the Romans to fight instead – the sword, not gold, should decide the issue. He thoroughly defeated the Gauls and was escorted home by his troops to a triumph. Many people, especially the poorer members of the community, wished to transfer the city to Veii, which they considered to have a stronger site. Camillus, however, persuaded the people that the victory was useless if they abandoned Rome, and he did not relinquish office until he had seen its buildings restored. In later years, according to the tradition, he defeated the Volscians, undertook military reforms, supported the admission of the plebeians to the principal offices of state, and in 367 vowed a Roman temple to Concord.

Camirus Grandson of Helios. He gave his name to a Rhodian city.

Camise Wife of Janus.

Canace Daughter of Aeolus. She had incestuous relations with her brother Macareus and either committed suicide or was put to death by her father. Macareus killed himself.

Canens An Italian nymph, daughter of Janus and Venilia. She was betrothed to a son of Saturn named Picus, who wandered off one day and left her singing (this is what her name means) in the woods. He was seen by the nymph Circe, who conceived a violent passion for him and fashioned a phantom boar for him to pursue. When he dismounted to chase it, she appeared before him and made advances, but he refused her. She therefore transformed him into a woodpecker. When he did not return, Canens, after wandering for a week in search of her betrothed, pined for him so grievously that she wasted away and disappeared. Only her voice remained, in the likeness of an echo.

Capaneus Son of Hipponous and Astynome; his wife was Evadne, daughter of Iphis, who bore him Sthenelus 3. He was one of the seven champions who fought for Polynices against Thebes and became known as the Seven against Thebes. He swore that even if Zeus himself forbade it he would take the city by storm, and bore on his shield the device of a man scaling a wall, accompanied by the words 'I shall burn this city'. However, as he proceeded to climb the walls, Zeus struck him down with a thunderbolt. Evadne leapt on his funeral pyre and died. After his death it was said that Asclepius resurrected him.

Caphaurus Son of Garamas (Amphithemis) of Libya; he was rich in sheep and killed two Argonauts, Canthus and Eribotes, who had attacked his flock. Their companions, however, avenged them by killing Caphaurus in his turn and driving his sheep off.

Capys *1*. The son of Assaracus; he was Anchises' father and Aeneas' grandfather. *2*. A Trojan who suspected that the Wooden Horse was a trick; he urged that it should be thrown in the sea or burnt. After the fall of Troy he followed Aeneas to Italy and was said to have founded the city of Capua in Campania.

Car Son of Phoroneus, king of Argos, and his wife Cerdo. He became king of Megara.

Cardea A Roman goddess of the Artemis type, a virgin huntress who tricked any who wished to make love to her by sending them into a shady cave to which she promised to come; she would then make off. Janus, the god of two faces, however, was not to be deceived, and took her before she could escape. In return for her favours, he gave her power over doorways (her name means 'she of the hinge') and over the whitehorn, which was sacred to Janus and thought to protect the house from evil spirits. Ovid calls her Carna, confusing her with a nymph of that name.

Carme A Cretan woman who was loved by Zeus and bore him the goddess Britomartis. Carme was later carried off as a slave to Megara, where King Nisus made her the nurse of his daughter Scylla.

Carmenta or **Carmentis** An Arcadian nymph who bore Evander to Hermes. She commanded her son to find a new home in Italy – he settled on the Palatine Hill in what was later Rome – and gave him the letters of the Roman alphabet, duly adapted from the Greek to fit the Latin tongue. Identified with the Greek goddess Themis, Carmenta was considered to have powers of prophecy. The Romans associated her name with *carmen* ('song'), a term often associated with oracles. They had a tale that she gave the goddess Leucothea (Ino) toasted cakes in memory of Phrixus. She was also a goddess of childbirth.

Carna *see* CARDEA.

Carnabon A Thracian king who killed one of the serpents which drew the chariots of Demeter's son or servant, Triptolemus, in jealousy of the powers the young man had displayed in granting benefits to his people. Demeter brought another serpent, and Triptolemus flew away; but Carnabon, as a warning to mankind, was placed by the goddess in the sky as the constellation Ophiuchus, the Serpent-Holder.

Cassandra (Also called Alexandra) Daughter of Priam, king of Troy, and of his wife Hecabe. Homer calls her their most beautiful daughter and says that Othryoneus of Cabesus became Priam's ally in the Trojan War on the understanding that he would marry Cassandra when the hostilities were over. Coroebus, son of the Phrygian king Mygdon, was another who came to Troy in the hope of marrying her. But both these suitors were killed in the war. Later traditions endowed her with great prophetic gifts. When she was young, it was said, Apollo fell in love with her and courted her, teaching her the arts of prophecy in return for the favours he hoped for. But when Cassandra refused his attentions, he condemned her to the fate of always telling truthful prophecies and never being believed. According to an alternative story, however, when she and her brother Helenus were children and were playing in the temple of Thymbraean Apollo on the feast day of that

god, they were licked on the ears and mouths by the sacred serpents and acquired their prophetic powers in this way.

Before uttering her prophecies, Cassandra went into an ecstatic trance; her family believed her to be mad. When Paris first came to Troy she realised his identity, although he had been exposed on Mount Ida as an infant and was unknown to his parents. She foretold the harm that Paris would do by going to Sparta (from which he abducted Helen), and she knew the danger of the Wooden Horse. But her warnings went entirely unheeded by the Trojans. When Troy was captured and burning, Aias, son of Oileus, caught Cassandra as she sought refuge in the temple of Athena and was clinging to the sacred image of the goddess. He dragged her away, overturning the statue, and raped her on the spot, while Athena's image turned its eyes away in horror. For this sacrilege, and because the Greeks did not take vengeance on Aias, Athena punished them by killing many of their number on their homeward journeys. She also imposed a tribute on Aias' people, the Locrians, which they had to pay for a thousand years.

Cassandra was awarded to Agamemnon as his concubine, and bore him two sons, Teledamus and Pelops. He eventually took her back to his home in Mycenae. There she fell to the sword of Agamemnon's wife Clytemnestra; but not before she had foreseen and foretold the doom that awaited him, herself, and their children, speaking in full awareness of the deeds of horror that had polluted Agamemnon's family (the house of Atreus) in past times – a scene portrayed by Aeschylus in his tragedy the *Agamemnon*.

Cassiopea *see* ANDROMEDA.

Castor and **Polydeuces** (Latin: *Castor* and *Pollux*) The 'heavenly twins', sons of Tyndareos, king of Sparta, and of Leda, and brothers of Helen and Clytemnestra. Homer regards these four as ordinary mortal children – but after his time many different stories were told about their origin. Sometimes divine parentage is ascribed to Polydeuces, sometimes both to him and Helen. According to another version, Castor and Polydeuces were both sons of Zeus; and this is the meaning of their name 'Dioscuri'. The pair were immortalised and regarded as the special patrons of sailors, to whom they appeared as Saint Elmo's Fire. They were also important gods at Sparta and at Rome. The Dioscuri in their youth took part in the expedition of the Argonauts, and although Castor, whose special skill was horsemanship, had little chance to display his ability, Polydeuces, a great boxer, was able to defeat Amycus, the bullying king of the Bebryces. After their return from the voyage, the pair helped Jason and Peleus to destroy the city of Iolcus in punishment of treachery of its king Acastus to Peleus. According to Ovid, the Dioscuri took part in the Calydonian boarhunt. When Theseus and Pirithous carried Helen off to Attica so that Theseus might marry her, the town of Aphidnae, where Theseus had left her, fell to the Dioscuri in his absence. They rescued Helen and carried off Theseus' mother Aethra to Sparta, setting a rival, Menestheus, on the throne of Athens.

Castor and Polydeuces aspired to marry Phoebe and Hilaira, the daughters of their uncle Leucippus, who lived in Messenia. The girls were already betrothed to Idas and Lynceus, who were the sons of Aphareus, king of Messenia; but the Dioscuri carried them both off to Sparta, where Hilaira bore Anogon to Castor and Phoebe bore Mnesileos to Polydeuces. This provoked the two pairs of young men (who were cousins) to begin a feud, which led to three of them dying. Their deaths occurred in this way. When the four cousins had con-

ducted a cattle-raid in Arcadia and were feasting on the proceeds, Idas suddenly announced that the man who finished eating his portion of meat first should have half the cattle, and the second to finish should take all the rest. He had divided up the meat himself and he and his brother had already eaten most of their portions. The Dioscuri were so enraged by this unfair treatment that they immediately set out for Messenia, recovered the cattle, and drove them back to Sparta. As they went, Idas and Lynceus pursued them, and Lynceus, who was endowed with marvellous vision, saw the twins from Mount Taygetus hiding far off in a hollow oak. Idas came up stealthily and struck Castor with his spear. Polydeuces then chased both his cousins back to Messenia as far as their father's tomb. Idas flung the polished stone monument at him but failed to hurt him. Thereupon Polydeuces struck Lynceus in the breast with his spear, while Zeus killed Idas with a thunderbolt. Then Polydeuces returned to Castor, who was on the point of death; but Zeus granted Polydeuces' prayer that he might share his immortality with his brother, so that each should spend a day in the house of Hades and a day in Olympus, turn and turn about. According to late Greek writers, Zeus placed the twins in the sky as the constellation Gemini.

The Romans adopted the cult of the Dioscuri very enthusiastically, especially after the epiphany of the two heroes at the battle of Lake Regillus, fought between the young Republic under Aulus Postumius and the forces of Tarquinius Superbus and his Latin allies. (In a similar way they were said to have helped the armies of Epizephyrian Locris, in southern Italy, against the neighbouring city of Croton.) At Regillus the Dioscuri charged the enemy at the head of the Roman cavalry; a short time later they also appeared in the Roman Forum, many miles away, in exactly the same garb.

There they watered their horses at the spring by Vesta's temple and told the crowds of the Roman victory. The temple of Castor and Pollux in the Forum was erected in memory of this event, and they became the patrons of the Roman order of knights (*equites*).

Catreus Son of Minos, king of Crete, and of Pasiphae. He had four children, a son, Althaemenes, and three daughters, Aerope, Clymene, and Ape mosyne. Since an oracle told him that one of his children would cause his death, he contrived to get rid of them. Althaemenes, and Apemosyne emigrated to Rhodes; the other two were to be sold into slavery by Nauplius. But Nauplius gave Aerope to Atreus as his wife, and himself married Clymene. When he grew old, Catreus decided to seek his son and name him as his heir. When he reached Rhodes, however, the people thought he and his crew were pirates and Althaemenes killed his father. Menelaus of Sparta, who was the son of Aerope and grandson of Catreus, came to his grandfather's funeral, leaving his wife Helen at home in the hands of his treacherous guest Paris, who abducted her.

Caunus *see* BYBLIS.

Cebriones Bastard son of Priam of Troy; he often acted as Hector's charioteer and accompanied him in battle. Patroclus slew him and the Greeks stripped his body.

Cecrops *1.* A snake-man sprung from the soil, the second mythical king of Attica. He married Aglaurus, daughter of Actaeus, and inherited his father-in-law's kingdom of Acte, as Attica was then called, giving it the name of Cecropia instead. He was believed to have had the body of a man and the tail of a snake. Aglaurus bore him a son, Erysichthon, who did not survive Cecrops, and three daughters, Pandrosus, Aglaurus, and Herse. When Athena and Poseidon

strove for the possession of Attica, Cecrops awarded the land to Athena, because she made an olive tree grow on the Acropolis, whereas all Poseidon could produce was a spring of brackish water. Cecrops was believed to have founded the court of the Areopagus at Athens for a trial of Ares, who was accused of the homicide of Halirrhothius and acquitted. Cecrops put an end to human sacrifice in his kingdom, and was the first to recognise the supremacy of Zeus among the gods, offering him cakes (*pelanoi*) instead of human or animal flesh. He was succeeded by Cranaus.
2. The eighth king of Athens, son of Erechtheus and Praxithea. He was the eldest son, but was chosen king not by his father but after his father's death by his Thessalian ally Xuthus. Cecrops married Metiadusa and had a son, Pandion, who succeeded him.

Cedalion A servant of Hephaestus. *See* ORION.

Celaeno *see* PLEIADES.

Celer A follower of Romulus. *See* REMUS.

Celeus A king of Eleusis in Attica. *See* METANIRA.

Centaurs A race of creatures with the body and legs of a horse and the torso, head, and arms of a man. They were the children of Centaurus, a son of Apollo and Stilbe, or else of Ixion and a cloud which Zeus made into the shape of Hera to deceive him. They lived on Mount Pelion in Thessaly, fed on meat, and were creatures of brutal and lascivious habits, except Chiron, who was gentle and wise and acted as tutor to many of the Greek heroes.

The principal myths associated with the Centaurs concern their war with the Lapiths, a neighbouring Thessalian nation, descended (like themselves, according to one version) from Ixion, but as civilised as the Centaurs were wild and unbridled. The fighting broke out at the wedding of the Lapiths' king Pirithous to Hippodamia (or Deidamia). The Centaurs had claimed Pirithous' kingdom on the ground that they were Ixion's true heirs. But Pirithous thought that the dispute had already been peacefully settled, and invited them to his wedding. The Centaurs arrived but inflamed by the wine, to which they were unaccustomed, they tried to seize the women of the Lapiths, and one of their number, Eurytion, even tried to carry off the bride. A fight ensued and many Centaurs were slain. This scene is depicted in the Parthenon metopes.

The Centaurs were driven out of Thessaly to the Peloponnese, and took refuge in Arcadia or on Cape Malea. When Heracles was entertained by the Centaur Pholus during his pursuit of the Erymanthian Boar, he was given roast meat but no wine, although there was an unopened jar in the cave. Heracles protested about his host's apparent meanness, but Pholus declared that Dionysus, when he passed through their country, had given the jar to the whole tribe of Centaurs as their common property. According to one version of the story, the god had forbidden the Centaurs to open the jar until Heracles should come, but even so Pholus hesitated. Heracles, however, insisted, indicating to Pholus that Dionysus' condition was now fulfilled. When the jar was opened, the other Centaurs, less civilised than Pholus, were attracted by its agreeable smell and gathered around. A fight broke out, and Heracles had to drive them off with his arrows poisoned with the Hydra's venom. As a result of this fight, both Pholus and Chiron accidentally met their deaths. Pholus died when he was inspecting an arrow after the fight, amazed that such a small thing could kill such large creatures as the Centaurs. He dropped the arrow on his foot and was killed by the poison. Chiron was likewise scratched by one of the arrows, which had pierced the Centaur Elatus: he had taken refuge with Chiron, and had sought a cure from him in vain. His kinsmen escaped to Eleusis in Attica, where Poseidon hid them inside a mountain. Eurytion was eventually killed by Heracles as he tried to abduct and rape a daughter of Dexamenus, king of Olenus, who at the time was Heracles' host.

But one of their number, Nessus, took a terrible vengeance on Heracles for the harm the hero had done his race. After Heracles married Deianira, they were obliged to cross the flooded river Evenus in Aetolia on their way home, and Nessus offered to carry Deianira over the stream on his back. Heracles caught him trying to rape his wife, and shot him with a poisoned arrow. As he died, Nessus, ostensibly to redeem himself, told Deianira to take some of the blood from his wound and keep it. Then, if ever Heracles lost his love for her, she could win it back by smearing a tunic with the blood and giving it to Heracles to wear. But the blood was poisoned, and when, years later, Deianira resented her husband's faithlessness and acted as Nessus had proposed, Heracles met a horrible death wrapped in the burning garment.

Centaurus *see* CENTAURS.

Cephalus Son of Deion, king of Phocis, and of Diomedes; or of Hermes and Herse, daughter of Erechtheus, king of Athens. The principal version of the romantic tale of the love of Cephalus and Procris, as told by Ovid in the *Metamorphoses*, may be a composite version of two earlier tales about mythical figures named Cephalus, one Athenian and the other Phocian.

When Cephalus married Procris, they took a vow of everlasting faithfulness. However Cephalus, who was very fond of hunting, used to leave her bed early in the morning to pursue the deer on Mount Hymettus. His good looks drew the attention of Eos, the Dawn Goddess, who fell in love with him and abducted him – much against his will, for he was passionately in love with his wife. According to some authors, Cephalus gave Eos a son, Phaethon, and remained with her for eight years; though Ovid seems to shorten this time-scale. In his story, Cephalus returned to Attica, his jealousy roused against Procris by a declaration of Eos that he would rue the day he married her. He decided to disguise himself as a stranger and test his wife by offering her a vast sum to become his mistress; and Eos helped by changing his appearance. Thus disguised, Cephalus pressed Procris until she agreed to his proposal, though with great reluctance. He then revealed his true identity and reproached her with her treachery. She was so horrified by the trick that she immediately fled, shunning the company of men and living in the mountains where she spent her time hunting, a devotee of Artemis. After a time Cephalus found her and with abject entreaties begged her to return to him. Now Procris took her vengeance: Ovid does not specify its nature, but other writers tell how, after curing King Minos of Crete of a disease which killed any woman who slept with him, she herself took him as her lover. But Pasiphae, Minos' wife, was jealous, so Procris returned to Cephalus in Athens. There is also a story that she did for another what the disguised Cephalus had tried to bribe her to do: she accepted a gold crown from a certain Pteleon and became his mistress. When she returned to Cephalus, she brought a magic spear and hunting hound. According to Ovid, who insists on her chastity, these were gifts from Artemis, but in the earlier version of the story they were rewards from Minos for curing him. Procris gave the spear and the hound, whose name was Laelaps, to her husband, who was as fond of hunting as ever.

Meanwhile at Thebes, in revenge for the death of the Sphinx, the goddess Themis (or Hera) had sent a pest in the shape of the Teumessian Fox, a vixen so terrible that the country people were afraid for themselves and their cattle. This animal was so fast that no hound could catch it. Amphitryon, who had the task of getting rid of the beast in return for a favour he hoped to receive from Creon, king of Thebes, asked Cephalus for the use of Laelaps. But when the hound chased the fox, an insoluble dilemma arose, for the hound from which Artemis had pronounced that there was no escape was pursuing a vixen which on equally good authority was uncatchable. Zeus solved the problem by turning both animals to marble. As a reward, Amphitryon gave Cephalus an island to the west of Greece, which was renamed Cephallenia after him.

After these events (or, according to some versions of the story, before them) Procris, who still resented her husband's preoccupation with hunting, was alarmed when a busybody reported to her that her husband had been heard, after a morning's strenuous exercise, calling with endearments upon a certain 'Aura' to come and soothe his weariness. It was concluded that this must be a nymph with whom Cephalus was in love, but in reality the word meant no more than 'breeze': Cephalus was simply calling for a wind to cool his heated body. At the guidance of the informer, Procris hid herself in the bushes one morning near the place where Cephalus usually rested, and when she heard him she started to move towards him. But he, thinking a wild beast was rustling the undergrowth, flung his unerring spear at his wife. As she lay dying in his arms, she begged him not to marry Aura in her place: whereupon he understood everything and told her the whole truth.

For this manslaughter of his wife Cephalus was put on trial before the

Athenian court of the Areopagus and exiled for the rest of his life. He went to Cephallenia which he ruled as its king, marrying Clymene, a daughter of Minyas. Their son was Iphiclus *3*.

Cepheus *1*. The father of Andromeda and king of a distant land, either Palestine or Ethiopia. *See* ANDR-MEDA.

2. A king of Tegea in Arcadia. He was a son of King Aleus and his wife Neaera *2*. He took part in the voyage of the *Argo* and the Calydonian boar-hunt. Heracles requested his help for an attack on Sparta, but Cepheus, in fear of an invasion from Argos while his back was turned, refused. Then Heracles gave Cepheus' daughter Sterope a lock of the hair of the Gorgon Medusa, promising that by simply holding it up three times she could repel any enemy from Tegea. Tegea was indeed preserved, but Cepheus, who joined Heracles' expedition, was killed together with all his sons except Echemus. Cepheus was succeeded by his elder brother Lycurgus *3*; and he in his turn was succeeded by Echemus, who ruled all Arcadia. According to another story it was Athena who gave the Tegeans the lock of Medusa's hair; for that reason they built the temple of Athena Polias.

Cephissus *see* INACHUS; NARCISSUS.

Cerberus The watchdog of the Underworld, offspring of Typhon and Echidna, and brother of the Hydra and the Chimaera. He is usually described as having three heads, though Hesiod ascribes to him fifty. He possessed a snake's tail, and a row of serpent heads sprouted from his back. His main function was to devour any of the inmates of the realm of Hades who tried to escape. He fawned on newly arrived shades as they entered the Underworld. He did not, however, approve of living mortals entering the realm he guarded. Orpheus had to charm him with music,

and the Sibyl of Cumae threw him a sop (cake soaked in drugged wine) to get past him: hence the expression 'a sop for Cerberus'. Heracles also had a tussle with him: his twelfth Labour was to fetch Cerberus from the Underworld. Hades permitted him to make the attempt, on the condition that he used no weapons. By sheer strength Heracles succeeded in carrying the brute to Mycenae, terrifying Eurystheus with the sight; then he returned his captive to the Underworld.

Cerberus was so hideous that a man who chanced to see him was turned to stone, and the spittle from the animal's mouth, falling on the ground, gave birth to the deadly poison of aconite.

Cercopes A pair of dwarfs of knavish habits. They lived either near Ephesus or in Thessaly and preyed on travellers. Their parents were said to be Oceanus and Theia. Their mother warned them to beware of a certain *Melampyges* (meaning a man with black buttocks). While acting as Omphale's slave, Heracles once caught the pair trying to steal his armour and hung them upside down from a pole, which he held across his shoulders like a yoke. They thus found themselves staring straight at his buttocks, which were covered with thick black hair. Amused by their ribald comments, he released them. Zeus, however, was eventually so offended by their knavery that he turned them into the monkeys they already resembled, or into stone. Ovid claims that the Pithecusae (Monkey) Island off Naples (now Ischia) was called after them.

Cercyon A king of Eleusis of Arcadian extraction, who forced all passers-by to wrestle with him. He used to kill every one of them, either during the contest or afterwards. Theseus had to undergo his challenge on his way from the Isthmus to Athens, but turned the tables on him and put him to death, thus acquiring his kingdom.

Ceres *see* DEMETER.

Cerynes Son of Temenus. He was killed by Deiphontes.

Cestrinus Son of Helenus and Andromache.

Ceto Daughter of Pontus ('Sea') and Gaia ('Land' or 'Earth'); the name means 'whale' or 'sea-monster'. She married her brother Phorcys and bore the three Graiae (Pemphredo, Enyo, and Deino, whose hair was grey from birth) and the three Gorgons (Stheno, Euryale, and Medusa). Hesiod calls her the mother of Echidna and Ladon also.

Ceyx Son of Eosphorus, the morning star, and husband of Alcyone. Ceyx was a hospitable man. He entertained Heracles when the latter was in flight from Eurystheus, and Heracles helped him in his turn by expelling the Dryopes from his kingdom. After Heracles' death, Ceyx was entrusted with the tutelage of his children, but, since he was not strong enough to stand up to Eurystheus' hostility, he felt obliged to place them under the care of Theseus. Ceyx also entertained Peleus, exiled from Aegina for the murder of Phocus.

The best-known myth about Ceyx is concerned with his death and transformation into a bird. The simpler variant merely states that he and his wife Alcyone were punished in this way for calling each other Zeus and Hera because of their blissful happiness. The story Ovid tells in the *Metamorphoses* relates how Ceyx, alarmed at certain portents – his brother Daedalion's transformation into a falcon, and the ravages of a wolf which had killed his oxen (in punishment for his hospitality to the murderer Peleus) – decided to consult the oracle at Clarus, Delphi being under blockade by the Phlegyans. He did so against the advice of Alcyone, who had a premonition of disaster. Indeed she begged him either to forego his voyage or else to take her with him. However he sailed off without her, promising to return within two months.

A great storm arose, and Ceyx was drowned. As he died he thought of Alcyone and murmured her name. She for her part was constantly sacrificing to Hera in hope of her husband's return. Hera, however, unable to bear the sight of the loving wife praying for the return of her dead husband, sent Iris to visit Sleep, who in turn dispatched his son Morpheus (whose name means changer of form), to impersonate Ceyx in a dream which would appear to Alcyone. He leaned over her bed dripping wet, tears streaming down his cheeks, and told her of the death of Ceyx in the storm. Unconsolable, Alcyone rushed down to the shore and called upon her husband's name. As she cried, the waves rolled his corpse to her feet. She was at once transformed into a kingfisher, and fluttered about her husband's corpse until the gods, taking pity on her, brought him back to life – as a kingfisher like his wife. And so they lived together once again, and mated every year in winter during the Halcyon Days, when Alcyone's father Aeolus calmed the sea for them for seven days. According to an alternative version, Ceyx became not a kingfisher but a gull.

Chalciope Daughter of Aeetes, king of Colchis, and of the Oceanid Idyia. She was married by her father to Phrixus, and bore him four children. She prevailed on her sister Medea to help Jason, so that her own children might be able to escape her father's anger. *See* ARGONAUTS.

Chalcodon Son of Abas and king of the Abantes in Euboea. While leading his people in an attack on Thebes, he was killed by Amphitryon. His son was Elephenor.

Chaos Scarcely personified in myth at

all: the gaping void out of which sprang Earth (Gaia), Tartarus, Darkness (Erebus), and Night (Nyx). Some say that Love (Eros) also came forth from Chaos, although he was usually considered to be a son of Aphrodite.

Chariclo *1.* A Boeotian nymph, the mother of Tiresias.
2. A Naiad, the wife of Chiron.

Charites *see* GRACES.

Charon Son of Erebus (Darkness) and Nyx (Night); ferryman of the dead across the river Styx to their final abode in Hades' realm. He was portrayed as a squalid, mean old man with a bad temper, but very sprightly. He demanded the fee of an obol from his passengers, and it was the custom of the Greeks to bury the dead with this coin in their mouths. When Heracles forced him to ferry him into the Underworld, Hades punished Charon by binding him in chains for a year.

Charybdis A mythical whirlpool placed at the northern end of the Straits of Messina in Sicily. It was seen as a female monster – a daughter of Poseidon and Gaia – who sucked the seawater in and cast it out three times a day, in such a way as to wreck any ship that passed nearby. Scylla was opposite on the other shore; when Odysseus had to choose between the two, he preferred to approach Scylla, as Charybdis meant certain destruction. Later on, after his men had been destroyed by Zeus for slaying the cattle of Helios, Odysseus' ship was sucked into Charybdis' whirlpool, and he survived only by clinging to a fig-tree that overhung the pool. When the ship was belched up again, hours later, he caught hold of a spar and was saved.

Chimaera A fire-breathing monster made up of the forequarters of a lion, the middle parts of a she-goat, and the

tail of a snake. It was the offspring of Typhon and Echidna. *See* BELLERO-PHON.

Chione *1.* Daughter of Daedalion. She was very beautiful (her name means 'Snow-white') and had countless suitors, among them the gods Apollo and Hermes.

Before making advances to her Apollo preferred to wait until nightfall (and then he approached in the guise of an old woman), but Hermes put her to sleep and raped her then and there. She bore twins, Autolycus to Hermes, and Philammon to Apollo. Hermes passed on his expertise in thieving to his son and Philammon too inherited his father's gift, becoming an accomplished musician. Chione, however, was induced by her beauty and success to compare herself with Artemis, to the latter's disadvantage; whereupon the goddess shot and killed her with an arrow. Daedalion was so grieved by his daughter's death that he flung himself down from a peak of Mount Parnassus and was transformed by Apollo into a hawk.
2. see BOREAS.

Chiron Unlike other Centaurs, who were descended from Ixion or his son Centaurus, Chiron was the son of Cronos and Philyra. The reason for his shape was that Cronos, wishing to conceal his passion for Philyra from his wife Rhea, had made love to the nymph in the form of a horse. In consequence, Chiron's nature was entirely different from that of his fellow Centaurs: for he was wise and kind, and well versed in medicine and all the arts, especially music. He was a friend of Apollo, who granted him the gift of archery. Chiron became the tutor of many of the great heroes of mythology, Jason, Asclepius, Asclepius' sons Machaon and Podalirius, Actaeon, and Achilles.

He lived in a cave on Mount Pelion in Thessaly and married Chariclo, who bore him a daughter, Endeis: her son Peleus, when he was abandoned weaponless on Mount Pelion by Acastus, received help from his grandfather Chiron, who found the sword which Acastus had hidden. He also taught his grandson how to woo the sea-goddess Thetis. As a son of Cronos, Chiron had the gift of immortality. But he surrendered it voluntarily, for after Heracles had attacked the other Centaurs with his poisoned arrows, one, Elatus, took refuge in Chiron's cave, and Chiron, in trying to heal him, was scratched by the arrow and overcome by unceasing agony. He was sometimes said to have transferred his immortality to the Titan Prometheus. According to another version of the tale, Chiron scratched himself while inspecting the arrows of Heracles, who was visiting him on Mount Pelion. He did not wholly lose his immortality, however, for Zeus set him in the heavens as the constellation Centaurus.

Chloris One of the surviving children of Niobe. See NELEUS.

Chromius Son of Neleus.

Chrysaor Son, perhaps of monstrous shape, created from the union of Poseidon and the Gorgon Medusa. His brother was the winged horse Pegasus. The two of them sprang from the blood shed from the severed head of their mother after her decapitation by Perseus. Chrysaor, whose name means 'golden sword', married the Oceanid Callirrhoe, who bore him the triple-headed giant Geryon and the monster Echidna.

Chryseis Daughter of Chryses, a priest of Apollo at his shrine on the isle of Chryse, near Troy. When the Greek army sacked the island, Agamemnon took the beautiful Chryseis as his concubine, declaring that he preferred her to his wife Clytemnestra. Chryses came to him and offered a rich ransom if he

would return his daughter, but Agamemnon refused. The priest then offered up special prayers and sacrifices to Apollo, asking the god to assail the Greeks with a plague until they should relent and give his daughter back. After nine days of pestilence, Agamemnon reluctantly agreed to return Chryseis to her father – but only on the condition that Achilles should compensate him by handing over his own prize, Briseis. Hence arose the anger of Achilles which is one of the main themes of Homer's *Iliad*.

There is a further story that Chryseis conceived a son by Agamemnon, calling him Chryses after his grandfather and passing him off as the child of Apollo. Later, when Orestes, Pylades, and Iphigenia (who according to this version had survived) were returning to Greece with an image of Artemis they had seized from King Thoas of the Taurians, this younger Chryses was about to betray them to Thoas, when Chryses the elder revealed that the youth was the half-brother of Orestes and Iphigenia. His grandson then changed his mind and helped Orestes to slay Thoas and return to Greece.

Chryses *1.* A priest of Apollo and the father of Chryseis.

2. Son of Agamemnon and Chryseis.

Chrysippus A beautiful young man, the son of Pelops and a nymph. Laius, king of Thebes, was so taken with the boy's looks that he kidnapped him from Pelops' court at Pisa in Elis and took him to Thebes. Rescued from Laius by his father Pelops, Chrysippus was said either to have killed himself at Thebes or else to have been murdered by his half-brothers Atreus and Thyestes, since they were jealous of Chrysippus' beauty and feared that Pelops might make him his heir.

Chrysothemis Daughter of Agamemnon and Clytemnestra, and sister of Orestes,

Iphigenia, and Electra. In Sophocles' tragedy *Electra*, she is sympathetic to her sister's desire to see Agamemnon's murder avenged but nevertheless advises Electra against defying Clytemnestra and Aegisthus.

Chthonia *see* ERECHTHEUS.

Chthonius *see* SOWN MEN.

Cicones A tribe living in south-western Thrace. Odysseus, after leaving Troy on his way home, ravaged their city of Ismarus. When the Cicones summoned help from inland, his men refused to escape and lost six of their comrades in the ensuing battle. Odysseus spared the life of Maron, son of Euanthes, priest of Apollo, and received from him the wine with which he was to fuddle the Cyclops Polyphemus. It was the Ciconian women who, in their Bacchic frenzy, tore Orpheus to pieces, after he had failed to rescue Eurydice from Hades.

Cilix Son of Agenor; the eponym of Cilicia in south-eastern Asia Minor.

Cincinnatus Lucius Quinctius Cincinnatus was a hero of the early Roman Republic; it is probable that he existed, but also likely that many of the stories related about him are mythical. According to tradition, the tribe of Aequi was besieging a Roman army on Mount Algidus in 458 BC and Rome was in danger of losing the flower of her army. In this crisis the Senate elected Cincinnatus, a humble farmer from beyond the Tiber, as dictator. A deputation dispatched to summon him to take over the command of the army found him working in the fields, clad only in a tunic. His wife Racilia ran to their cottage and fetched his toga, so that he might listen to the Senate's instructions. Wiping the dirt from his hands and face he put on the toga, and was then saluted as dictator. The plebeians, however, distrusted

Cincinnatus and feared that he would abuse his power. He conscripted all men of military age, marched to Mount Algidus, and routed the Aequians, whom he compelled to go under the 'yoke'. Thus Cincinnatus, his task completed, was able to resign his six-month dictatorship after only fifteen days and to return to work in his fields. Years later, it was said, when he was over eighty, he was again invited to be dictator in a political crisis, when Spurius Maelius was suspected of wishing to set himself up as king. Maelius was killed trying to avoid arrest; his house was razed to the ground. The tribunes of the people (officials representing plebeian interests), because they regarded this as an attack on the common people, tried to punish Cincinnatus and his followers by having military tribunes elected to the supreme office of state in the following year, instead of consuls. But tradition maintained that they could find only three eligible men – one of them being Cincinnatus' son Lucius – and were obliged to desist.

Cinyras A rich king in Cyprus who sent Agamemnon a beautiful breastplate as a present for use in the Trojan War. Cinyras, according to one account, was the son of Pygmalion's daughter Paphos, after whom the Cypriot city of that name was called. He married Cenchreis (or Metharme), who bore him a daughter, Myrrha. When Myrrha grew up, she conceived a violent infatuation for her father: this was a punishment from Aphrodite, either because the girl had neglected her rites, or because her father had boasted that she was more beautiful than the goddess. Myrrha confessed her incestuous love to an old nurse who, during a festival when the married women of Cyprus had to abstain from their husbands' beds, induced Cinyras to sleep with his daughter under the pretence that she was a girl of Myrrha's age who had fallen in love with him.

After several nights of this intercourse, Cinyras brought a lamp into his room and saw the girl's face. When he recognised his daughter, he tried to kill her. But she fled, coming eventually to the land of the Sabaeans in South Arabia where the gods turned her into a myrrh tree. She was pregnant and the goddess of childbirth released her baby, Adonis, from the treetrunk, or else a wild boar charged the tree and the baby was born through the cleft its tusks had made.

Another version of Cinyras' ancestry makes him the son of the Syrian Sandoces, a descendant of Tithonus and Eos. He was also sometimes called a Cilician who migrated to Cyprus. It was believed that when Agamemnon sent Menelaus, Odysseus, and Talthybius to the city of Paphos to enlist Cinyras' support in the Trojan War, he offered a fleet of fifty ships but then cheated by making forty-nine of the boats little clay models manned by clay sailors. One ship commanded by his son Mygdalion set sail, but the clay models which were launched after it naturally sank.

There are two traditions about Cinyras' death. Either he killed himself after his incest with Myrrha, or he lived to a great age, favoured by Apollo and devoted to the worship of Cyprian Aphrodite, whose priest he was.

Circe ('hawk') Daughter of Helios the Sun-god and Perse, an Oceanid; sister of Aeetes, king of Colchis. A powerful witch, she lived on the island of Aeaea, identified by Classical writers with Cape Circeium on the western coast of Italy. She transformed her enemies, or those who offended her, into animals. Picus she turned into a woodpecker for refusing her love; and when the sea-god Glaucus asked her for a potion to make Scylla love him, she fell in love with Glaucus herself and made Scylla into the monster which lurked in a cave opposite Charybdis in the Straits of Messina. Nevertheless Glaucus mourned for Scylla and rejected Circe's advances.

Homer calls Circe a goddess, and describes her home on Aeaea as a stone house standing in the middle of a clearing in a dense wood. Round the house prowled lions and wolves, the drugged victims of Circe's sorcery; they were not dangerous, but fawned on all comers. Circe worked at a huge divinely-artificed loom.

When Jason and Medea were fleeing from Aeetes, they came at Zeus' command to Aeaea to be purified by Circe for the murder of Apsyrtus. She conducted the purification, but when she discovered the nature of the crime from which they had required to be cleansed, she drove them away in horror at their deed, even though Medea was her niece. When Odysseus came to Aeaea, the members of the advance party he sent to explore the island were all turned by Circe into swine, except Eurylochus, who had suspected treachery. Odysseus himself, setting out to rescue his men, was intercepted by Hermes who taught him how to counter Circe's magic. He gave Odysseus the herb *moly* and warned him, before he slept with her, to make her swear a solemn oath not to harm him. He spent a year in Circe's company, and when he felt he had to leave, she gave him instructions for his homeward journey, directing him to go to the realm of Hades to consult the spirits of the dead.

The Italians had certain other traditions about Circe, believing that she bore Odysseus three sons, Telegonus, Agrius, and Latinus. She sent Telegonus to find Odysseus, who had long since returned to Ithaca, but on his arrival Telegonus accidentally killed his father. He brought the body back to Aeaea, and took Odysseus' widow Penelope and his son Telemachus with him. Circe made them immortal and married Telemachus; while Telegonus made Penelope his wife. *See also* CANENS.

Cithaeron *see* ALALCOMENEUS.

Claudia Quinta *see* CYBELE.

Cleobis and **Biton** Two young Argive brothers. Their mother, a priestess of Hera at Argos, had to go to the temple for a festival. As the oxen were late, her sons pulled her to the temple in the ox-cart, a distance of about five miles. On her arrival, the priestess thanked Hera for her dutiful sons, praying that they might have whatever was best for mortal men. They slept that night in the temple, expecting to take their mother home the next day; but they never awoke again. The Athenian statesman Solon described them as the happiest of mortals, and statues dedicated to them by the Argives have been discovered at Delphi.

Cleobule *see* PHOENIX 2.

Cleodaeus Son of Hyllus and Iole.

Cleopatra *1*. The wife of Meleager; daughter of Idas and Marpessa. She persuaded her husband to save Calydon from the Curetes when, through anger at his mother, he refused to fight.
2. A daughter of Boreas, the North Wind, and Orithyia. Cleopatra married Phineus, king of Salmydessus in Thrace. Phineus subsequently took a second wife, Idaea, and at her instigation blinded – or, according to another version, merely imprisoned and whipped – his sons by Cleopatra, Pandion and Plexippus. The Argonauts blinded or killed Pheneus, and gave his kingdom to the young men, who in turn handed it over to Cleopatra so that they could join the Argonauts' expedition.

Cleothera Daughter of Pandareos. Brought up by goddesses, she became a slave of the Furies.

Clio *see* MUSES.

Clite Daughter of Merops, king of Percote, and wife of Cyzicus, king of the

Doliones in Mysia. Cyzicus was killed accidentally by the Argonauts. Clite was so grief-stricken that she took her own life; the wood nymphs wept for her, their tears forming a pool that was called after her.

Clitus Son of Mantius. Because of his beauty, he was carried off by the goddess of the Dawn, Eos, to live with the gods.

Cloelia When the Etruscan Lars Porsenna finally gave up his attempt to restore Tarquinius Superbus to the throne of Rome from which he had been expelled, he made a treaty with the Romans according to which they handed over hostages in exchange for the Janiculum Hill across the Tiber, which was to be returned by the Etruscans. One of the hostages was a girl called Cloelia who, while in the Etruscans' camp, obtained permission to bathe in the Tiber. After sending her guards away while she undressed, she swam across the river to Rome, accompanied by other girl hostages. The Etruscans shot at the swimming figures, but Cloelia was able to restore the whole band safe and sound to their families. Although Porsenna complained of the breach of the treaty and demanded Cloelia's return, he was so impressed by her bravery that he guaranteed her safety and soon restored her to Rome, together with a number of other hostages of her own choosing. So Cloelia's act opened up friendly relations between Porsenna and the new Republic; and the Romans erected an equestrian statue of her on the Sacred Way.

Clotho *see* FATES.

Clymene *1*. Daughter of Catreus. Nauplius married her and she bore him Palamedes, Oeax, and Nausimedon.
2. A nymph who bore Phaethon to Helios.

3. Daughter of Minyas; the second wife of Cephalus.

Clymenus *1*. A king of Argos, the father of Harpalyce, whom he raped. When her child was born, Harpalyce cut it up and served it to her father at a feast (or, according to an alternative version, she thus killed her brother). Clymenus, when he discovered what she had done, killed both himself and his daughter.
2. Grandson of Phrixus and a king of Orchomenus in Boeotia. He was struck by a stone thrown by Perieres, charioteer to the Theban Menoeceus. Before he died, Clymenus made his son Erginus swear to take vengeance on the Thebans.

Clytemnestra (Greek: *Klytaimestra*) Daughter of Tyndareos, king of Sparta, and Leda; sister of Helen, Castor, and Polydeuces. She was first married to Tantalus (son of Thyestes), to whom she bore a child. Tantalus' cousin Agamemnon, king of Mycenae, killed them both and took Clytemnestra as his wife. She bore him four children: Iphigenia, Electra, Chrysothemis, and Orestres. Clytemnestra was turned against her husband by his sacrifice of his eldest daughter Iphigenia to Artemis, in order to obtain a favourable wind to sail to Troy. She therefore plotted with Tantalus' brother Aegisthus, her lover, to overthrow her husband on his return from Troy. Aegisthus killed Agamemnon, and Clytemnestra killed the Trojan princess Cassandra whom Agamemnon had brought back from Troy as his concubine. Orestes escaped to Phocis on his father's murder. But he later returned to Mycenae and, with the help of Electra, killed his mother and Aegisthus. For this crime the Furies visited Orestes with madness.

Clytia or **Clytie** *see* HELIOS.

Clytius *1*. An Argonaut, the son of Eury-

tus, king of Oechalia. He was killed by Aeetes in Colchis.
2. A Trojan elder, the son of Laomedon and a brother of Priam.
3. A giant, killed with torches by Hecate in the war between the gods and the giants.

Clytoneus A king of Nauplia in the Argolid; the father of Nauplius *2*.

Cocalus The king of Camicus in Sicily. *See* DAEDALUS.

Cocles *see* HORATIUS.

Codrus A king of Athens; son of Melanthus, a descendant of Neleus and a member of the Messenian royal family. When the Dorians captured Messenia, Codrus came to Athens, slew the Boeotian king Xuthus in single combat in a frontier war, and became the ruler of Athens in place of the house of Theseus, marrying an Athenian woman to improve his title to the throne. The Dorians made an attack on Attica, which was a haven for all the Ionian peoples whom they had displaced. The Delphic Oracle pronounced that they might beat the Athenians if Codrus' life were spared; and a friendly Delphian communicated this news to the Athenians. Thereupon Codrus went to battle against the Dorians dressed as a woodcutter and deliberately courted death so that Attica should be saved. Codrus was succeeded by his son Medon. His family were said to have retained the throne until the eighth century, when the monarch (according to a tradition which may be accurate) was replaced by the three archons of early historical times.

Coeus A Titan, the son of Uranus and Gaia. He fathered Leto and Asteria on the Titaness Phoebe, his sister.

Comaetho *1*. A legendary priestess of Artemis at Patrae. In spite of this goddess's hatred of sexual relations, Comaetho was taken by her lover Melanippus in Artemis' temple. As a result, a famine affected Patrae, and the pair were sacrificed to appease Artemis' anger. Human sacrifice continued in this way for many years, until Eurypylus the Thessalian arrived, bringing an image of Dionysus he had found at Troy. The arrival of a strange king with a strange god was the signal for the abandonment of the ritual.

2. *see* PTERELAUS.

Cometes Son of Sthenelus *3*. He seduced Diomedes' wife Aegialia.

Copreus ('dung-layer') Son of Pelops and herald of his nephew King Eurystheus of Mycenae, employed to deliver his master's commands to Heracles. He was a fugitive from Elis, where he had killed a man called Iphitus; but Eurystheus purified him of the murder.

Copreus' son Periphetes was killed at Troy by Hector.

Corcyra A nymph after whom the island of Corcyra (Corfu) was named. She was a daughter of the river-god Asopus. Poseidon carried her off to the island that bears her name. Alternatively it was said that Black Corcyra (Korčula) was her island.

Coresus According to Pausanias, Coresus, a priest of Dionysus at Calydon, fell in love with a girl called Callirrhoe, who rejected his suit. Dionysus, in answer to his prayers, sent madness upon the people of Calydon. They were told by an oracle that to cure their affliction they must sacrifice Callirrhoe to Dionysus unless she could find a substitute for herself. It was Coresus' task to carry out the sacrifice, and at the moment of its execution he decided to offer himself as a substitute for Callirrhoe, plunging the knife into his own breast. Then Callirrhoe, who until this

moment had been indifferent and even hostile to Coresus, was filled with remorse and stabbed herself as well.

Coriolanus The legendary Gnaeus Marcius (his historical existence is in doubt) was considered to have won the surname Coriolanus for the conquest of the Volscian city of Corioli. According to Livy, the date of this achievement was 493 BC. Tradition maintained, however, that he was not only an excellent commander but politically an archconservative. When the Senate proposed to distribute free bread to the lower classes, who were starving as a result of their recent secession from Rome to the adjacent Sacred Mountain, Coriolanus was said to have objected to the distribution, unless the plebeians were willing to restore to the patricians their full ancient privileges. He so greatly offended the plebeians by this speech that it was believed he would have been lynched had not the tribunes of the people (the representatives of the plebeians) summoned him to court. Since, however, he rejected their authority, he failed to appear and was condemned to exile. Ironically enough, it was to Rome's Volscian enemies at Antium that he went for refuge. There he quickly became general and led a successful Volscian army to the very gates of his own native city. No pleas of the Roman government or embassies of priests and senators could prevail on him to relent.

Finally, when the situation seemed desperate, his aged mother Volumnia (called Veturia by Livy), his wife Vergilia (whom Livy calls Volumnia), and his two small sons went forth from the city to plead with him. When Coriolanus tried to kiss his mother, she first asked him whether it was as his mother or as a prisoner of war that he received her. And so Coriolanus' resolution was broken by the entreaties of his womenfolk – much to the anger of the Volscians who, according to one version of the story, put him to death for his weakness. Livy, on the other hand, believed that he lived to a bitter old age in exile.

Corobius see BATTUS 1.

Coroebus Son of Mygdon. See CASSANDRA.

Coronides Daughters of the giant Orion, named Metioche and Menippe. After their father's death, they were brought up by their mother Side. When a famine and drought came upon their city of Orchomenus and Apollo's oracle declared that two virgins must be sacrificed to the Furies, the Coronides killed themselves with the shuttles of their loom. The famine ceased, and Hades placed the girls in the sky as comets. Ovid claims that they lived in Thebes and that two young men, the Coroni, sprang from their ashes.

Coronis 1. Daughter of Phlegyas, king of Orchomenus, and mother of Asclepius, the god of healing. She was loved by Apollo; but when she was carrying Asclepius in her womb, she was unfaithful to the god, and married Ischys, son of Elatus, an Arcadian. When Apollo heard the news from a crow, he was so angry that he turned the bird from white, which had been its colour until then, to black. He then asked Artemis to slay Coronis, but snatched his unborn son from her funeral pyre (or else Hermes did this for him). Asclepius was reared by Chiron.
2. see BUTES.

Coronus A Lapith Argonaut, the son of Caeneus. He was later killed by Heracles in a frontier-war with the Dorians. His son Leonteus fought at Troy. His daughter Anaxirrhoe married Epeius.

Corybantes The male followers of Cybele, who celebrated her rites by dancing with weapons in their hands, clashing them together and sounding drums and cymbals.

Corynetes see PERIPHETES.

Corythus 1. Son of Zeus and king of Lydia; the father of Dardanus and Iasion by the Pleiad Electra.
2. Son of Paris and the nymph Oenone. According to Hellanicus, Corythus came to Troy when fully grown to offer his services for the war against the Greeks. Helen then fell in love with him and Paris in his jealousy slew his son.

Cottus see GIANTS.

Cranae see CRANAUS.

Cranaus The third mythical king of Athens; like his predecessor Cecrops, he sprang from the soil. His wife Pedias was from Sparta and bore him two daughters, Atthis and Cranae. When Atthis died, Cranaus renamed his kingdom Attica after her. According to Athenian tradition, it was during his reign that the great flood took place and the Greek Noah, Deucalion, fled to Attica. Deucalion's son Amphictyon married Cranae and subsequently expelled Cranaus from his throne.

Cratais A sea-nymph; the mother by Phorcys of Scylla.

Cratos see BIA.

Creisus Son of Temenus. He murdered his father and supplanted him as king of Argos.

Creon (The name is a common one and simply means 'ruler'.) 1. Son of Menoeceus (a descendant of Cadmus and the 'Sown Men'). He married Eurydice or Enioche and had several sons. When Jocasta's husband King Laius of Thebes went to Delphi, Creon, who was Jocasta's brother, stayed behind. After Laius had been killed at a crossroads on Mount Cithaeron by his son Oedipus (who had been abandoned at birth on the same mountain because of an oracle, and was unaware who his parents were), Creon became regent. The Sphinx now began to ravage Theban territory, killing, according to one version, Creon's eldest son Haemon. Creon offered the kingdom and the hand of Jocasta to any man who could solve the riddle of the Sphinx and thus rid the country of the monster. Oedipus, who had been rescued in infancy and brought up in the neighbouring land of Corinth, now returned to his native land, overcame the Sphinx, and claimed his kingdom and his bride, not knowing that she was also his mother. Years later another plague, a great barrenness, fell on the land. The Delphic Oracle declared that a pollution must be driven out, and Oedipus' sins of parricide and incest were revealed. Jocasta hanged herself, Oedipus put out his own eyes, and again Creon became the ruler of Thebes. He either drove Oedipus out at once or, in another version of the story, allowed the blind ex-king to remain in Thebes, to be expelled later by his sons Eteocles and Polynices, who for a time shared rule over the city.

After a short time Eteocles and Polynices quarrelled, and Eteocles, supported by Creon, banished his brother. Creon attempted to force Oedipus, who was now in sanctuary at Colonus, near Athens, to return to Thebes, as an oracle had predicted that the place he lived and died in would be especially fortunate; Oedipus, however, refused to come, and Theseus, king of Athens, drove Creon away. Then Polynices led an Argive army with the Seven Champions against Thebes. In the fighting he lost his life in single combat against Eteocles, who also met his death. One of Creon's sons, Megareus, died in the siege, and another, Menoeceus, in obedience to an oracle, killed himself to ensure victory for the Thebans, leaping from the walls into a serpent's lair. Creon buried Eteocles' body with honour; but Polynices he ordered to be cast out in the dust of the plain, with a ban on his burial and a guard of soldiers to ensure that it was not attempted. When Antigone, Oedipus' daughter, who was betrothed to Creon's youngest son Haemon, defied the ban, she was caught by the soldiers and brought to Creon, who punished her by entombing her alive. Tiresias warned Creon to bury the dead and disinter the living, and Creon complied, but when, after burying Polynices' body, he came to the sepulchre of Antigone, he found that she had already hanged herself in the tomb. Haemon, after vainly protesting at his father's act, ran on his own sword; and then Eurydice, Creon's wife, on hearing of the death of her last surviving son, stabbed herself. Creon lived on, acting as regent for Eteocles' small son Laodamas.

Earlier in his life Creon had purified Amphitryon of the guilt of slaying his father-in-law Electryon, and helped him in his war against the Taphians. Amphitryon had then lived in Thebes, where his wife Alcmena bore Heracles. Creon eventually married his daughter Megara to Heracles, but in the hero's absence Lycus invaded Thebes, killed Creon, and seized the throne for himself. Heracles, who was in the Underworld at the time, returned and killed the usurper, but in a fit of madness wiped out Megara's children as well. According to another story, Creon was killed by Theseus, who had attacked Thebes to compel Creon to bury the corpses of the Argive dead, which he had forbidden.

There are many variants in Creon's story; see, besides Sophocles' three Theban plays (*Oedipus the King, Oedipus at Colonus, and Antigone*), Aeschylus' *Seven against Thebes* and Euripides' *Phoenician Women* and *Heracles*.

2. A king of Corinth, the son of Lycaethus. Alcmaeon entrusted Amphilochus and Tisiphone, his children by Manto, to Creon to bring up. But as Tisiphone proved to be very beautiful, Creon's

jealous wife sold her into slavery and she was bought by her father Alcmaeon. Later, when he learnt who she was, he was able to recover Amphilochus as well.

Jason and Medea came to Corinth after their return from Colchis to Iolcus. Creon welcomed them and allowed them to live in peace for ten years; they had two or three children there. Then, according to Euripides, the Corinthians began to be afraid of Medea, who was both a foreigner and a sorceress. Jason, too, started to tire of her, since she was a foreigner and could not give Jason a legitimate child as his lawful heir. Creon offered him his daughter Glauce as his wife, and ordered Medea to go into exile. Medea, before departing, gave Glauce a wedding dress, which burnt her to death when she put it on; and Creon, coming to her aid, was also burnt. In another version of the story, Medea poisoned Creon and burnt down his palace, abandoning her children in Hera's temple; whereupon Creon's kinsfolk took vengeance on her by putting the children to death, pretending that Medea had done it herself.

Cresphontes A descendant of Heracles; king of Messenia. His father was Aristomachus. With his brother Temenus and his nephews, Aristodemus' sons, he conquered the Peloponnese; they all drew lots for the kingdoms they had conquered, by throwing clay tablets into a pitcher of water. Cresphontes, however, (according to one of several versions) deliberately threw in unbaked clay, which dissolved in the water, so that the other tablets were taken out first. In consequence, as he wished, he was awarded Messenia, which it had been agreed would fall to the drawer of the last lot, after Argos and Sparta. He married Merope, daughter of Cypselus, king of Arcadia, but was killed together with two of his sons by the rich Messenians who considered him too favourable

to the commons. His third son, Aepytus 1, was brought up by Cypselus, king of Arcadia, whose daughter Merope he had married. After his father's death Aepytus avenged him by slaying Polyphontes, the leader of his murderers, who had married the dead man's widow Merope against her will.

Cretheus Son of Aeolus 2 and Enarete; the founder of Iolcus in Thessaly (from which Jason set sail on the *Argo*) and its first king. He married Tyro, his niece, the beautiful daughter of his brother Salmoneus. One of his sons was Aeson, the father of Jason.

Creusa (Greek: 'queen', 'princess') *1.* The youngest daughter of Erechtheus, king of Athens, wife of Xuthus, and mother of Ion, Achaeus, and Dorus, the eponyms of the three great branches of the Greek nation, the Ionians, Achaeans, and Dorians. *See* ION.
2. Another name for Glauce, daughter of Creon 2, king of Corinth.
3. Daughter of Priam and Hecabe (Hecuba), and wife of Aeneas; in some accounts she was the mother of Aeneas' son Ascanius, who accompanied his father to Italy. Virgil tells how, in the confusion of the sack of Troy and the flight of Aeneas' family from the burning city, Creusa, who was walking a little way behind her husband, became separated from the party and vanished. Aeneas discovered her loss when he reached the shrine of Ceres (Demeter) where they had agreed to assemble. As he dashed back into the city in search of her, he suddenly saw her apparition rise before him. The ghostly figure told him that Creusa was now in the care of Cybele, the Great Mother, and predicted his new home in Italy.
4. A Naiad (water-nymph), the mother, by Peneius, of Hypseus, Cyrene, Daphne, and Stilbe.

Crius A Titan, the son of Uranus and

Gaia. He fathered Astraeus, Pallas and Perses on his sister Eurybia.

Cronos Son of Uranus (the Sky) and Gaia (the Earth). The cleverest of their children were the Titans and Titanesses. Cronos became their king. He married his sister Rhea.

According to the best-known version of his story, his mother Gaia complained to him that Uranus was distressing her by pushing the Hundred-Armed giants (Hecatoncheires) and the Cyclopes back into her body when she was ready to bring them forth (or else he imprisoned them). She therefore gave Cronos a flint sickle with which he attacked Uranus, when next the came to lie with Gaia, and castrated him. Cronos flung the severed genitals behind him and the drops of blood became Furies, giants, and nymphs. So Cronos ruled in Uranus' place; but he quickly became as brutal as his father. He imprisoned the giants and Cyclopes once more in the earth and, being warned that one of his own children would depose him in the same way as he himself had deposed his father, swallowed them one by one as they were born. His wife Rhea, who was a Titaness and his sister, brought forth successively Hestia, Demeter, Hera, Hades, Poseidon, and Zeus. Cronos succeeded in eating all except Zeus, whom Rhea confided to her mother Gaia, substituting for him a great stone wrapped in swaddling clothes, which his father duly swallowed instead.

Zeus was reared in secret by the nymphs of Mount Dicte (or Ida) in Crete with the milk of the goat Amalthea, while the Curetes clashed their spears on their shields to prevent Cronos from hearing the baby's cries. Zeus subsequently married the Oceanid Metis, whom he persuaded to give Cronos an emetic, to make him spew up the other five children. There followed a war in which Cronos was deposed in favour of

Zeus by his children with the help of the giants and the Cyclopes, whom Zeus had released. Together with Iapetus and other Titans, Cronos was flung into the abyss of Tartarus where the Hecatoncheires were appointed to guard him. Before vomiting his children, he had vomited the stone which had been substituted for Zeus, and this was planted in Delphi to mark the navel of the earth.

According to a different tradition, Cronos had not been a grim tyrant but a benign ruler who presided over a blessed golden age; after his deposition he left to become ruler of the Isles of the Blessed in the Western Ocean. This aspect of Cronos links him with Saturn, the Roman god with whom he was identified. Some Greeks associated Cronos' name, wrongly, with the word *chronos* ('time'), and consequently depicted him as an old man with a scythe, Father Time. The oldest account of the story of Cronos is given by Hesiod in the *Theogony*.

Croton The eponym of Croton in southern Italy. While Heracles was visiting him, he was accidentally killed when Lacinius tried to steal Heracles' cattle.

Crotopus *see* LINUS.

Cteatus One of the Moliones.

Cupid or **Cupido** *see* EROS; PSYCHE.

Curetes *1.* Minor Cretan gods, associated with the nymphs of Mount Dicte or Ida who looked after the infant god Zeus. While the nymphs nursed the baby in the cave, the Curetes danced about the entrance, clashing spears on their shields to hide the infant's cries from his father Cronos. The name Curetes is derived from the Greek *kouros*, 'young man'; they were so called either because they were said to have attended Zeus in his youth, or because the Curetes were themselves thought of as taking the form of young men, resembling bands of Cretan youths who performed ritual dances.

Hesiod says that a certain Hecaterus fathered five daughters who were the mothers of the Curetes, as well as of the mountain-nymphs and the satyrs. According to another story, when Minos, king of Crete, lost his little son Glaucus, the Curetes informed him that the child could be found and restored to life by any man who could devise the aptest simile for a recently born calf that was continually changing colour. Polyidus compared it to the fruit of the dog-rose.

Zeus finally destroyed the Curetes for taking Hera's side against him and stealing Epaphus, his son by Io.

2. A nation who lived in Aetolia near Calydon. Homer tells how they tried to sack Calydon and were driven off by Meleager. See MELEAGER.

Curiatii see HORATII

Curtius The existence of the *Lacus Curtius*, a well-known site in the Roman Forum, where in primitive times there had been a marsh or pond, led to various alternative attempts to invent a mythical personage who would provide an explanation of the name.

1. Mettius Curtius A Sabine champion in the mythical war between Romulus and Titus Tatius the Sabine. According to one tradition, he engaged in single combat with the Roman Hostus Hostilius, killed him, and drove the Roman troops down from the Capitoline Hill. He taunted the Romans with being better at catching girls than fighting against men: this was a reference to their Rape of the Sabines which had allegedly taken place a short time before this event. But then Romulus delivered such a sharp attack that Mettius fled, his horse bolted, and horse and rider plunged into the pool, which was named after him. Mettius escaped only by a supreme effort, and his men went on to

lose the battle in the valley which was to become Rome's Forum.

2. Marcus Curtius When a great chasm opened up in the Forum at the site of the Lacus Curtius the young Marcus Curtius was said to have ridden his horse in full armour into the hole. He did this because the diviners had said that the god of the Underworld, to whom the Romans had neglected to offer a vow, required the immolation of the bravest Roman citizen. The chasm was a way straight down to the Underworld, and when Curtius had jumped in, it immediately closed up and was seen no more. According to this version, the exploit took place in 362 BC.

3. Gaius Curtius Chilo Legendary consul of 445 BC. He consecrated the site of the Lacus Curtius when it was struck by lightning.

Cyane *1.* A Sicilian nymph who gave her name to a famous fountain and pool (her name means 'blue' from the colour of her waters). In the *Metamorphoses* Ovid tells of her transformation. When Hades saw Persephone plucking flowers at Henna, in Sicily, and carried her off to his gloomy kingdom to be his wife, Cyane witnessed the abduction. Rising from her pool, Cyane tried to prevent him from continuing his journey; but Hades angrily flung his sceptre into the pool and opened up a road down to his realm, through which he then drove, leaving Cyane lamenting for Persephone. She grieved so much that she wasted away, melting into the waters of her pool, so that when Demeter came looking for her daughter she was unable to tell the goddess what she had seen. Persephone's girdle, however, floated on the pool and gave Demeter a clue.

2. Wife of Aeolus *1*, king of the winds.

Cyanippus *1.* The younger son of Adrastus, king of Argos.

2. Son of Aegialeus and briefly king of Argos. He died without issue.

Cybele or **Cybebe** Originally a Phrygian goddess, Cybele was fitted somewhat awkwardly into Hellenic mythology, in which the accounts of her contain many conflicting features. She was usually identified with Rhea, the mother of Zeus and the greatest Greek gods, and, like Rhea, she personified Mother Earth.

The Phrygian myth of Cybele, however, is as follows. When Zeus was lying on the ground asleep on Mount Dindymus in Phrygia, his seed fell on the earth. A strange being grew from the spot, with both male and female organs: the gods were alarmed at the potentialities of such a divinity and castrated the creature. It grew into the goddess Cybele. The severed male genitals, however, had fallen on the ground and grown into an almond tree, from which an almond one day fell into the lap of Nana, daughter of the river-god Sangarius. The fruit entered her womb and she conceived a son, Attis, whom she exposed on the mountain. A he-goat miraculously suckled the baby, which grew into a beautiful youth with whom Cybele fell in love. But Attis was neglectful or unaware of Cybele's passion for him, and instead made preparations to marry a daughter of the king of Pessinus. Cybele, wildly jealous, drove both Attis and his father-in-law mad, so that in their frenzy they castrated themselves. Attis' injury was so bad that he died. Cybele then repented of her cruelty, and obtained of Zeus a promise that Attis' body should never decay. He was buried at Pessinus in Galatia (where Cybele was known as Agdistis), but his little finger continued to move and his hair to grow. Another tradition asserts that he was changed into a pine; and this tree was made sacred to him.

A different story of Cybele makes her the daughter of Meion, king of Phrygia, and his wife Dindyme. She was abandoned on a mountain named after her, and was suckled by lions and leopards.

She instituted games and dancing on the mountain, bestowing upon her followers the Corybantes the cymbals and the drum to accompany the rites. She possessed the power of healing and was a protectress of children and wild creatures. One day she saw Attis and fell in love with him, making him her priest and demanding his absolute fidelity. However Attis had an intrigue with a river-nymph, Sagaritis, and thus broke the conditions which Cybele had imposed on him. She drove him mad, whereupon he castrated himself and died of the wound.

Another version of this myth reports that Attis and Cybele had a child, and that when her father Meion discovered this, he killed both the baby and Attis. Cybele, in despair, rushed around the country beating a drum and lamenting for her dead lover. A plague descended upon the country, and the Phrygians were instructed by an oracle to revere Cybele as a goddess and to grant Attis honourable burial. He was buried at Cybele's temple near Pessinus, but the goddess brought him back to life.

Yet another variant of the tale asserts that Attis received sexual approaches from a king and, being reluctant to comply, was castrated by him. As he lay dying under a pine-tree, Cybele's servants saw him and carried him into her temple, where he expired. Cybele instituted his cult, ordaining that only eunuchs might be his priests; and he was mourned every year by her worshippers.

Cybele had close associations with Rome, where she was a very popular divinity, identified with the Bona Dea; a myth concerning her was invented as late as 205 BC. This was during the Second Punic War, when her cult was introduced into the city because the Sibylline books had told the Romans that, if they wanted victory, they must bring the Great Mother to Rome. The Delphic Oracle directed them to Pessinus, from which the Romans obtained a venerable stone said to represent the goddess. When, however, they transported the stone to Rome, the ship stuck in the mouth of the Tiber. Then a girl called Claudia Quinta, who had been unjustly accused of unchastity, prayed to Cybele and lightly pulled the rope attached to the ship. The ship moved easily forward, thus vindicating Claudia's assertion of her innocence.

Ovid introduces Cybele into the tale of the wanderings of Aeneas. The ships in which he sailed from Troy to Italy were made from pine-trees growing on Mount Ida which were sacred to the goddess. When Turnus attacked Aeneas' ships and tried to burn them, Cybele appeared in her chariot drawn by lions (this was how she was regularly depicted by artists) with a clash of cymbals and the sound of drums and pipes. She commanded Turnus to desist, at the same time sending thunder and rain, which quenched his firebrands. A wind came, breaking the ropes which moored the Trojan ships in the Tiber; and the ships, turning into nymphs, swam out into the sea.

Cyclopes The Cyclopes (the name means 'round-eye') were giants traditionally, though not invariably, held to have but a single eye in their heads. There are conflicting traditions about them. Hesiod in the *Theogony* says that Uranus (Sky) and Gaia (Earth) brought forth three Cyclopes, Arges (the Shiner), Brontes (the Thunderer), and Steropes (the Maker of Lightning). Uranus imprisoned these three in Tartarus, together with others of his offspring whom he feared; or else he pushed them back down into Gaia's womb when she was ready to deliver them. Cronos, having castrated his father Uranus, released the Cyclopes for a time, but then imprisoned them again in Tartarus. Finally Rhea triumphed over Cronos by concealing her son Zeus from him, and when Zeus was fully grown he overthrew Cronos

and released the Cyclopes, who became his servants and, being accomplished smiths, constructed his thunderbolts. (They also made Poseidon's trident and Hades' cap of invisibility.) Apollo killed them in revenge for the death of his son Asclepius, because they had forged the thunderbolt which Zeus had used to put Asclepius to death.

Homer's Cyclopes are depicted as one-eyed pastoral giants, living in caves on an island, which was later identified with Sicily. They were savage and inhospitable, and when Odysseus reached their land, the Cyclops Polyphemus, son of the sea-god Poseidon by the nymph Thoosa, ate six members of his crew whom he caught in his cave. To Odysseus himself he promised a favour; but this merely turned out to be an offer to eat him last after all the rest. However Odysseus made him drunk, blinded him with the heated point of a stake, stole his sheep, and left him helpless.

A group of Cyclopes in the service of King Proetus built the walls of the city of Tiryns, where Heracles was born; these walls are described as 'Cyclopean'. They also built the walls of Mycenae and the Lion Gate and had a shrine on the Isthmus of Corinth. These Cyclopes are called *encheirogasteres* ('belly-hands') because they worked for their living. Virgil places the forge of Vulcan (Hephaestus), the god of fire, in Mount Etna, and represents the Cyclopes as the smiths of the god, occupied in making armour for such heroes as Aeneas, as well as thunderbolts for Jupiter (Zeus).

Cycnus *1.* Son of Ares. Using the skulls of those whom he waylaid on the road, as they were taking offerings to Delphi, Cycnus tried to build a temple to Ares. He challenged Heracles, who was on his way to fetch the apples of the Hesperides, to single combat, but was killed by him. Ares would have punished Heracles for the deed, but Zeus separated them by throwing a thunderbolt. His duel with Heracles was located either at Itonus in Phthia or on the River Echedorus in Macedonia. Heracles was aided in the battle by Athena, and some said that Ares himself suffered a wound in the thigh.

2. Son of Poseidon and Calyce; he was king of Colonae, near Troy, and an ally of Priam in his war against the Greeks. Poseidon had made Cycnus invulnerable to human weapons, but when he tried to oppose the Greek landing Achilles succeeded in strangling him to death. Poseidon transformed his body into a swan (the meaning of *kyknos* in Greek) and placed it in heaven as a constellation.

Cycnus married twice. His second wife Philonome falsely accused Tenes, son of his first wife Proclea, of trying to rape her, and Cycnus locked Tenes and his sister Hemithea in a chest and cast it on the sea. When he discovered the truth, Cycnus slew Philonome, but failed to win Tenes' forgiveness. Tenes became the founder of Tenedos.

3. A king of the Ligurians in Italy. He was related to the sun-charioteer Phaethon, who also became his lover. When Phaethon was killed, Cycnus was so grieved at his loss that Apollo in pity turned him into a swan, but because Zeus had caused the death of Phaethon, the bird shunned the sky. Since Cycnus had mourned for Phaethon in song, swans were henceforward allowed to sing a last 'swan-song' in lamentation for themselves just before they died.

4. Son of Apollo and Hyrie. According to Ovid, he was indignant because his lover Phyllius did not give him a wild bull which Heracles had helped him to capture. Accustomed to ask Phyllius for gifts in return for his favours, Cycnus had been presented on previous occasions with wild birds and a savage lion; but now Phyllius scorned him and refused the bull he had been ordered to obtain. So Cycnus flung himself off a cliff – and was transformed into a swan.

It lived on Lake Hyrie at Tempe, so called because his mother Hyrie drowned herself there in grief for her son.

Cydippe *see* ACONTIUS.

Cylarabes Son of Sthenelus *3*. He succeeded Aegialeus' son Cyanippus *2* as king of Argos.

Cyparissus The son of Telephus; a beautiful boy from the island of Ceos, whom Apollo loved dearly. There was a sacred stag, tamed by the nymphs of Carthaea, to which Cyparissus was particularly attached; he used to lead it to its grazing pastures. One day, when the stag was resting from the heat of noon, Cyparissus cast his hunting-spear and accidentally killed it. The boy was so grieved that, in spite of Apollo's protests, he wished to die. Then he asked to be allowed to go on mourning for ever, and because of his endless weeping his body dried up, and Apollo turned him into the cypress tree (Greek: *kyparissos*), a common token of mourning.

According to a variant version, he was a Cretan youth who was turned into a cypress tree while fleeing from the attentions of Apollo.

Cypris *see* APHRODITE.

Cypselus A king of Arcadia and the father of Merope, whom he gave in marriage to Cresphontes, the Heraclid king of Messenia, so as to win his alliance and preserve the autonomy of Arcadia from the Messenians; whereupon Cypselus took charge of Merope's son Aepytus, the heir to the throne of Messenia. But then Polyphontes, a kinsman of Cresphontes, killed him, and seized the throne, and forced Merope to marry him. Later Cypselus helped his grandson Aepytus to regain Messenia.

Cyrene A nymph and virgin huntress, the daughter of Hypseus, king of the

Lapiths and son of the River Peneius, and of the Naiad Creusa. When he saw her on Mount Pelion wrestling with a lion, Apollo was so attracted by her beauty and prowess that he carried her off to Africa in his chariot; the city of Cyrene was named after her. She bore Apollo two sons, Aristaeus, god of cattle and fruit trees, and the prophet Idmon.

Another version of her story tells how the land of Libya was infested by a savage lion. Eurypylus, the king of Libya, offered his kingdom to anyone who could rid the land of the beast. This Cyrene did, and founded the city named after her.

Cytorissus *see* ARGONAUTS; ATHA-MAS; PHRIXUS.

Cyzicus Son of Aeneus and Aenete; king of the Doliones. He entertained the Argonauts hospitably. But later, when driven back to his country during the night by an adverse current, they were mistaken for pirates and attacked by the Doliones, and Cyzicus accidentally met his death in the battle. His wife Clite, on learning he was dead, killed herself in her grief. The Argonauts mourned him for several days and performed his funeral games. But even then they could not start again, because, as the seer Mopsus told them, Cybele desired to be propitiated for his death; and so the Argonauts offered sacrifices to her, and danced in the manner of the Corybantes, her attendant worshippers. The city of Cyzicus on the coast of the Sea of Marmora was named after him.

D

Dactyls The Dactyls were connected with Mount Ida in Crete and Mount Ida in Phrygia near Troy, and were consequently described as Idaean. Traditions concerning them are obscure and varied. They were said to have been born on the Cretan Ida to the Titaness Rhea, or to the nymph Anchiale who, in the cave where Zeus had been born, threw up some dust which turned into the Dactyls. When they were associated with the Phrygian Ida, Cybele was sometimes named as their mother.

The Dactyls themselves were smiths. The fact that they were at times believed to have been ten in number may be due to the meaning of their name, 'fingers'. At other times they were said to comprise six gigantic males with five sisters. The males taught the Cretans the use of copper and iron, the females the mysteries of the Great Mother. Pausanias identified the male Dactyls with the Curetes: the eldest, called Heracles, was said to have founded the Olympic Games. In other sources the Dactyls were said to have numbered a hundred; or else there were thirty-two who worked magic spells and a further twenty who undid them.

Daedalion Son of Eosphorus. Apollo turned him into a falcon. His daughter was Chione *1*.

Daedalus A mythical Athenian craftsman; the name means 'the ingenious' and he was famous for many crafts and inventions. His father, who was allegedly descended from King Erechtheus, was Eupalamus, 'clever-handed', or Metion, 'knowledgeable'. Socrates pretended to claim descent from Daedalus.

Daedalus grew up to be the best painter and sculptor in Athens; his works were so lifelike that they appeared real. His sister gave him her son Perdix (also called Talus or Calus) as his apprentice. But the boy proved an even better craftsman than Daedalus himself, for he invented the saw (by copying the bone of a snake's jaw, or the backbone of a fish), the geometrician's compass, and the potter's wheel. In consequence Daedalus killed his nephew in a fit of jealousy, pushing him off the Acropolis or over a cliff into the sea. Athena, who had loved him for his skill, saw him fall and turned him into the partridge which was called after him. For this crime Daedalus was put on trial before the court of the Areopagus. He went into exile in Crete, either because he was condemned to do so, or else voluntarily.

There King Minos received him, and Daedalus performed many feats of engineering at his request. But the strangest invention he made was the artificial cow in which the queen, Pasiphae, hid herself in order to gratify her passion for a bull. The bull was deceived by the contrivance, and Pasiphae conceived the Minotaur, which was half man, half bull.

Minos, in shame at the existence of this monstrosity, determined to conceal it and commissioned Daedalus to construct the Labyrinth, an underground maze of tunnels and corridors with one entrance, so devised that any who entered it was unable to find his way out again. The Minotaur was placed in the middle. It was fed on human flesh, for the Athenians, whom Minos had beaten in war (*see* ANDROGEOS), were compelled – either annually or every nine years – to send tribute of seven youths and seven girls, who were sent one by one into the Labyrinth to provide its food. When Theseus came to Crete some years later, Daedalus was the maker of the thread which Ariadne gave him so that when he had killed the Minotaur he could make his escape from the Labyrinth.

When Minos discovered Daedalus' treachery, he shut him into the maze together with his little son Icarus (his child by one of Minos' slave girls), and kept them imprisoned. Realising that all normal methods of escape were useless, Daedalus resolved to fly out of the place on wings like those of birds. Using wax and feathers he constructed a pair of wings for Icarus and himself and after instructing the boy to fly neither too high nor too low for fear that the sun's heat might melt the wax or the sea-spray weigh down the feathers, he launched himself into the air, with Icarus following closely behind. They flew in a north-easterly direction past Paros, Delos, and Samos; but when they were in the stretch of sea that separates the Sporades Islands from the Ionian coast of Asia Minor, Icarus' exhilaration ran away with him and he flew too high. As he approached the Sun, the wax of his wings melted and he fell headlong into the sea that bears his name. Daedalus landed on the island that is now called Icaria, retrieved the body from the sea, and gave it burial. A partridge (his former nephew Perdix) beheld his sorrow with glee.

According to another story, Pasiphae released Daedalus from the Labyrinth. Then, after building a ship and inventing the first sail with which to propel it, he boarded the vessel with Icarus and escaped from the island.

He took refuge in Sicily at the court of Cocalus, the Sicanian king of Camicus. But Minos, who was determined to take his revenge, eventually traced his whereabouts. This he did by approaching all the rulers of the West and presenting them with the same problem: how to thread a spiral seashell. Only when Cocalus returned the shell threaded could Minos be sure that he had Daedalus in his grasp, for he assumed that nobody else could perform the feat. Daedalus is said to have bored a hole in the top of the shell and harnessed the thread to an ant, which proceeded to weave its way through the shell, coming out through the hole at the end.

Minos now demanded the surrender of Daedalus, but Cocalus refused, since the craftsman had built him an impregnable city. Minos then besieged the place, and Cocalus with a show of conciliation invited him to a feast, offering to give up the wanted man. First Minos was offered a bath, in which the king's three daughters were to bathe him in the traditional way. However Daedalus, having mastered the art of plumbing, had equipped the bath with pipes. Through these he now passed a torrent of boiling water which ended Minos' life in agony. According to an alternative version, Cocalus was killed fighting Minos' troops.

Many other important constructions and devices were attributed to Daedalus' ingenuity. He was said to have built Apollo's temple at Cumae and to have adorned it with pictures telling his own life-story. In Sicily he was reputed to be the builder of a reservoir on the River Alabon, a steam-bath at Selinus, a fortress at Acragas (Agrigentum), and the terrace of Aphrodite's temple at Eryx. Here he also left a model honeycomb made of gold. He was believed to have invented masts and sails and to have given mankind glue and most of the tools used in carpentry – the axe, the saw (if not the invention of Perdix), the plumbline, and the auger. Moreover, a folding chair on view in the temple of

Athena Polias, in Athens, was believed to be Daedalus' work. He was also regarded as the carver of many wooden images, some of which had moving eyes and arms and could walk; these were to be found at various places in Greece and Italy. In Sardinia certain towers called Daedalea were attributed to him. Furthermore, there were Greek traditions which attributed the Pyramids and great temples of Egypt (for example, the Shrine of Ptah at Memphis) to Daedalus' design.

Damasistratus A king of Plataea; he buried Laius when Oedipus had killed him.

Dameon Son of Phlius. An ally of Heracles against Augeas, he was killed by the Moliones.

Danae Daughter of Acrisius, king of Argos, and of Eurydice 2. As it had been prophesied that Danae's son would cause the death of Acrisius, the king imprisoned his daughter in a bronze tower (or a tower with bronze doors). Here Zeus descended on her in the form of a shower of golden rain; and the son she bore him was Perseus. Acrisius tried to dispose of this menace to his life by casting mother and baby adrift in a chest, but they landed on the isle of Seriphos. There the local king's brother, a fisherman named Dictys, saved the pair and gave them food and shelter. Perseus grew into a young man; meanwhile the king of the island, Polydectes, was plotting how he might make Danae his wife in spite of her persistent refusal. He had to rid himself of Perseus, who stood between him and Danae. Therefore, since the nobles of the island had to pay him tax, he sent Perseus off to fetch the head of the Gorgon Medusa as his contribution. While he was gone, Polydectes walled Danae up in a shrine and refused her food unless she would accept his offer

of marriage. Perseus, returning after a year with his bride Andromeda, rescued Danae in the nick of time by turning the king and his court to stone by means of the Gorgon's head. Perseus made Dictys the new king, and took his wife and mother to Argos where he accidentally killed Acrisius. According to Virgil, Danae later went to Italy, where she was driven on to the shore of Latium by a storm and founded the city of Ardea for Argive settlers. One of her grandchildren was Turnus, Aeneas' rival for the hand of Lavinia.

Danaids *see* DANAUS.

Danaus Danaus and Aegyptus were twin sons of Belus, a king whose empire included Assyria, Arabia, Egypt, and Libya. Belus gave Libya to Danaus and Arabia to Aegyptus, but the latter conquered Egypt and threatened Danaus' safety. Aegyptus had fifty sons, and Danaus had as many daughters, known as the Danaids. Aegyptus proposed that the two sets of cousins should marry, but Danaus, because he suspected that his brother's proposal was part of an attempt to overthrow him and take his kingdom, built a large boat with the help of Athena and sailed away with his fifty daughters to Argos, the city from which his ancestress Io had come. On his way there he put in at Lindus in Rhodes where he dedicated a temple to Athena in gratitude. At Argos he claimed the kingship on account of his descent from Io, but the established ruler, Gelanor, disputed the title. A debate was held in the Argive assembly, but the matter was settled by the discovery of an omen that had occurred on the eve of the meeting: a wolf fell on the Argive herds of cattle and killed the leading bull. This omen was interpreted as declaring that the outsider was to prevail, and so the kingdom passed to Danaus. He founded a temple for Apollo Lykeios (meaning 'wolf-god', according to one interpretation of the word). He also gave the people of Argos water, which their land had hitherto lacked because of Poseidon's anger: for the god had contended with Hera for the patronage of the country, and the river-gods of the country round Argos (the Argolid) had preferred the goddess. So Poseidon had dried up all their springs. Now, however, on falling in love with the Danaid Amymone, he produced a spring at Lerna. Another tradition stated that Danaus was made king for showing the people how to dig wells.

The fifty sons of Aegyptus came to Argos in search of their promised brides. Aeschylus in his play *The Suppliant Women* suggests that this happened shortly after Danaus' arrival at Argos. According to this account Pelasgus, king of the Argives, helped Danaus to defend himself from the young men, who had been ordered not to return to their father while Danaus was still alive. However Danaus was compelled to accede to their wishes, and the young men took their brides. But the girls had secretly received daggers from their father, with instructions to kill their bridegrooms in their beds. All save his eldest daughter obeyed. She, Hypermnestra, was in love with Lynceus, her husband – who respected her virginity – and told him of the plot, bidding him make his escape. He fled to Lyrcea and from there sent his wife a fire-signal announcing his safe arrival. She was imprisoned and put on trial by her father, but the Argive court, perhaps through the intervention of Aphrodite, acquitted her. In time Danaus accepted Lynceus as his son-in-law and was reconciled to the couple.

The other forty-nine Danaids brought their husbands' heads to their father to prove their loyalty. They were purified of their sin by Hermes and Athena on Zeus' orders. Then Danaus decided to marry them to youths of Argos, requiring no bridal gifts in exchange, but himself offering handsome presents along with the girls because of the natural reluctance of the local men to marry such bloodstained brides. Eventually Danaus was constrained to hold a footrace and allow the winner to take his pick, and so on until all the girls were taken. Their children were called 'Danaoi', a general name of the Greek nation in Homer. There is a tradition that Lynceus, in revenge for his brothers, eventually killed and succeeded Danaus, and also killed all his daughters except Hypermnestra. After their deaths, the Danaids were punished for their crime in Tartarus by being made to fill a leaky jar with water. Horace devoted an ode to their story, with special reference to Hypermnestra.

Daphne A nymph, the daughter of the River Peneius in Thessaly (or, in an Arcadian version, of the River Ladon); she was a virgin huntress like Artemis. Two stories are told of her. In the first Leucippus, son of King Oenomaus of Pisa in Elis, fell in love with her, but, realising her hard-heartedness, disguised himself as a girl in order to be with her; he was in any case growing his hair long in honour of the River Alpheius. So now he called himself Oeno and asked to be allowed to hunt with Daphne. She agreed, but Apollo, who was jealous, put it into the minds of her companions to bathe, and when Leucippus, disguised as Oeno, refused to participate, induced them to strip him naked. When they discovered his sex, they killed him for his deceit.

According to the second and more famous story relating to Daphne, Apollo himself also failed to win her. In was through his mockery of Eros, the god of love, that Apollo fell in love with Daphne. For after he had unfavourably compared Eros' flimsy weapons and slight stature with his own prowess at archery, Eros, to punish him, loosed two shafts from his bow from the top of Parnassus. One pierced Apollo's heart with its gold tip and made him desperate for Daphne; the other, a blunt arrow with a leaden tip, struck Daphne and made her impervious to any lover. Apollo pursued Daphne through the woodlands until, on the banks of her father's river, the Peneius, he very nearly caught her. Here she prayed fervently to the river-god to save her, and was at once rooted to the spot and changed to a laurel tree, to which she gave her name. Apollo had to abandon his courtship but, as god of music and the bow, decreed that henceforward a laurel garland should'decorate his lyre, his quiver, and the heads of minstrels.

Daphnis A Sicilian cowherd, the son of a nymph. Hermes was sometimes said to be his father and sometimes his lover or friend. Daphnis' name (derived from *daphne*, 'laurel') was given him either because he was born in a grove of laurels or because his mother exposed him in such a grove at his birth. He was brought up among the woodland nymphs, of whom he was a favourite, and among the shepherd people of Mount Etna and of Himera. He was said to be the inventor of pastoral poetry –whose ' principal exponents, notably Theocritus and Virgil, pay him special honour – and to enjoy the protection of Apollo, Artemis, and Pan, who gave him his pipes.

As a youth Daphnis boasted that he would resist the temptations of love. This was a defiance of Eros and Aphrodite; but the love-gods soon took vengeance on him. He fell violently in love with a river-nymph, Nais or Echenais. At first he would not tell her of his passion; but eventually it brought about his downfall, for when his desperate love, which was causing him to waste away, became known to the nymph, she agreed to be his on condition that he swore eternal faithfulness and forswore all other loves. But Xenia, a mortal woman (sometimes described as a prin-

cess), formed a passion for Daphnis and tricked him into making love to her by making him drunk. For this infidelity Nais struck him blind. He tried to console himself by singing of his misfortunes to the people of the countryside, setting his music to the syrinx (pipes of Pan). Finally, however, he fell into the River Anapus; and because he had broken his vow to Nais, the nymphs of the river allowed him to drown.

There are variants of this story. According to one version, Daphnis wasted away with unrequited love for Xenia. Sometimes his death was attributed to a fall from a cliff; and a spring, named after him, was said to have been placed on the spot by Hermes, who took him to heaven. An entirely different story, with a Phrygian setting, related that Daphnis loved a girl, or nymph, called Pimplea or Thalia, who was carried off by the pirates. He searched for her far and wide and eventually found her at the court of King Lityerses of Phrygia, where she was now a slave. This king compelled strangers to enter a competition with him to see which could harvest the most grain in a day; he invariably won and put the newcomer to death. Heracles, who was in Phrygia at the time, agreed to take Daphnis' place in the contest. He beat and killed Lityerses, and made Daphnis king in his stead, with Pimplea as his queen.

Dardanus *1.* Son of Zeus and Atlas' daughter Electra or of Corythus and Electra; an ancestor of the Trojans. He was generally said to have been born in Samothrace, though Arcadia, Crete, and the Troad have also been given as his birthplace. Either because of Deucalion's flood, or because of Zeus' punishment of his brother Iasion for seducing the goddess Demeter, he left Samothrace for Phrygia, where King Teucer welcomed him and gave him a part of his territory and his daughter Batia as his wife. Dardanus built a city on the slope of

Mount Ida and named it Dardania. Later he inherited the whole of Teucer's kingdom and called its inhabitants Dardanians. Dardanus' son Erechthonius was the father of Tros. Tros' children included Assaracus, who ruled Dardania, and Ilus, who founded the city of Troy, calling it Ilium. (The grandson of Assaracus was Anchises, the father of Aeneas; and the grandson of Ilus was Priam, king of Troy.)

The Roman version of the story, told by Virgil in the *Aeneid*, gives Italy as Dardanus' birthplace and Corythus as the name of his real father. According to this story, he founded Cortona in Etruria and then, separating from Iasion, departed for the Troad. This story accounted for Aeneas' final settlement in Italy; for he had received divine orders to return to the homeland of Dardanus.
2. A Scythian king, the father of Idaea, whom he slew for her cruelty to her step-children.

Dares A wealthy Trojan, the priest of Hephaestus. His sons fought Diomedes in the Trojan War; but Phegeus was killed and Idaeus put to flight.

Dascylus A king of the Mariandyni; the father of Lycus *3*.

Daunus *1*. King of the Rutulians of Ardea in Latium. His father was Pilumnus, a rustic deity, and his mother Danae, daughter of Acrisius of Argos. His wife's name was Venilia. Vulcan gave him an unbreakable sword, dipped in the waters of the Styx, which Daunus passed on to his son Turnus. His daughter was the water-nymph Juturna.
2. An Illyrian, son of Lycaon. He and his brothers, Iapyx and Peucetius, were believed to have conquered southern Italy and divided it between them. Daunus became king of Apulia, and gave his daughter to Diomedes, who took refuge with him.

Dawn *see* Eos.

Decius Mus (Publius) The name of three successive generations of Romans (the legendary dates of their consulships being 340, 312, and 279 BC respectively); only one of them, perhaps the middle one, is likely to have been a historical figure. All of them, according to tradition, 'devoted' themselves while commanding an army in the field. Devotion was the act whereby a Roman commander, clad in official dress, deliberately courted death on the field of battle, solemnly praying Mars for victory and committing himself and the enemy army to Earth and the Shades, thus bargaining with his own life for victory for his people. The death of Codrus of Athens represents a comparable idea of sacrifice.

Degmenus *see* OXYLUS.

Deianira Daughter of Oeneus, king of Calydon, and of Althaea; Heracles' second wife. Heracles had heard of Deianira's beauty in the Underworld from the ghost of her brother Meleager, who had begged him to marry her. But he had a rival, for the River Achelous also claimed her hand. The two held a wrestling match to decide the issue. Achelous changed himself into a bull, but Heracles broke off one of the horns and was the victor. So Heracles wed Deianira and helped her father Oeneus by subduing the Thesprotians. After this, however, he accidentally killed Oeneus' cupbearer and had to leave the kingdom. He took Deianira with him on the road to Trachis; but the swollen River Evenus blocked their way. The Centaur Nessus offered to carry Deianira across the river while Heracles waded. In spite of their old enmity, Heracles agreed, but when he realised that Nessus was seizing the opportunity to try to rape her, he shot the Centaur with one of the arrows poisoned with the Hydra's blood. As he died, Nessus, in pretended remorse, told Deianira that if ever Heracles' love for her should seem to wane, she should dip a garment in his blood and give it to her husband to wear, since it would bring back his affection.

Deianira took some of Nessus' blood from the wound and kept it safe in a flask. Later when she had borne Heracles several children, including Hyllus and Macaria, Deianira learnt that he had made Iole his mistress. She therefore determined to use the fatal 'love philtre' of Nessus, and sent Heracles a tunic smeared with the Centaur's blood. When he put it on, it burned him to death. Deianira, in her sorrow, killed herself. This story is the subject of Sophocles' *Women of Trachis*.

Deidamia Daughter of King Lycomedes of the island of Scyros. Achilles, when a boy, was entrusted to her father by Thetis in order that he might thus escape his destiny of fighting and dying at Troy. Lycomedes dressed the boy in female clothing, called him Pyrrha, and placed him in the women's quarters. Achilles took advantage of the situation to sleep with Deidamia, who bore him Neoptolemus. However he did not long remain undetected, and Odysseus took him to Troy, from which he never returned.

Deileon *see* AUTOLYCUS 2.

Deimos and **Phobos** Sons of Ares and Aphrodite The names mean 'Fear' and 'Panic'. These personifications of Terror accompanied their father Ares on the battlefield when he whipped up the storm of fury that made men mad for war and slaughter.

Deino *see* GRAIAE.

Deion A king of Phocis; father of Cephalus and Phylacus.

Deioneus *see* EURYTUS.

Deiphobe *see* SIBYLLA.

Deiphobus Son of Priam, king of Troy, and of Hecabe. He took a prominent part in the fighting at Troy, avenging Asius whom Idomeneus had killed. His brother Hector was very close to him. When Paris was dead, Deiphobus and Helenus competed for Helen's hand, which Deiphobus won. On the night of Troy's fall, he took Helen to examine the Wooden Horse where she tried to entice the Greek captains hiding within to give themselves away, imitating the voices of their wives. Then, wishing to ingratiate herself with Menelaus, she removed all the weapons from Deiphobus' house, so that when Menelaus and Odysseus came they killed him easily. His body disappeared, but Aeneas erected a cenotaph for him on Cape Rhoeteum; then later, according to Virgil, he heard the story of his death from Deiphobus' ghost in Hades.

Deiphontes Son of Antimachus and a descendant of Heracles. He became the protégé of King Temenus of Argos, who preferred him to his own sons, giving him his daughter Hyrnetho to wife. His brothers-in-law slew their father, and Deiphontes fled to Epidaurus where King Pityreus received him. The sons of Temenus tried to persuade Hyrnetho to leave Deiphontes, but since she loved him and had given him four children, she refused. In consequence they kidnapped her, pregnant with her fifth child as she was. Deiphontes pursued them and killed Cerynes, but Phalces dragged Hyrnetho off so roughly that both she and her baby died. Deiphontes buried her in an olive grove, and she became the object of a cult. The Argives made him their king in preference to Temenus' sons.

Deipyle Daughter of Adrastus; the wife of Tydeus.

Deipylus *see* ILIONE.

Delia *see* ARTEMIS.

Delphyne A monstrous woman with the body and tail of a serpent, who guarded Zeus' sinews for Typhon when he cut them out in his assault on the gods. She lived in the Corycian cave in Cilicia. She lost the sinews when Hermes and Aegipan retrieved them by stealth.

Demeter The great Earth-goddess, patroness of fertility and goddess of the Eleusinian Mysteries; one of the twelve major Olympian gods and one of the six children of Cronos and Rhea. By Zeus (her brother) she was mother of Persephone (Proserpina), with whom she possessed a close association in Greek cult. Her name means 'Mother Earth'. The Romans identified her with the Italian grain-goddess Ceres; she was also identified in ancient times with the Egyptian Isis, and with the Phrygian Cybele, and with her own mother Rhea. Demeter was considered to spend little time on Olympus, preferring instead to live on earth, especially at Eleusis in Attica where the Mysteries she founded commemorated her success in winning the return of her daughter Persephone (see below). They were celebrated annually in autumn, when the drama of the loss and rediscovery of Persephone was reenacted by the initiates with music and dancing.

Most of the myths about Demeter relate to the loss of her daughter Persephone. When the girl was still very young, her father Zeus, without consulting Demeter, who would have objected, agreed to Hades' request that Persephone should be his bride (the marriage of uncle and niece being common in Greece, in order to keep the estate in the family). Persephone was plucking flowers in the woods near Henna, in the fertile island of Sicily, one of Demeter's favourite lands. She was accompanied by the girls of the place, her playmates, or else by the daughters of Oceanus. Zeus made a beautiful narcissus grow in a shady, flowery dell. Persephone, at a moment when she was separated from her companions, saw the narcissus and plucked it. Immediately the earth opened up and Hades rode forth in his chariot drawn by dark-blue steeds. He snatched the girl up and at once returned with her to his realm below. Persephone shrieked for her mother but nobody came to help her; and when she reached Hades' realm she still continued to pine and would touch no food.

Demeter, when she learnt her daughter had vanished, started an immediate search. According to one account, she heard Persephone's departing cry. Carrying lighted torches, she roamed the earth for nine days and nights, refusing to eat or drink. She then met Hecate, who lived near the fields of Henna in a cave and knew of the abduction. Hecate led Demeter to Helios, the all-seeing sun-god, and asked him to tell her what he had witnessed. He unfolded the whole story, but added that Hades, as brother of Zeus, was a worthy husband for the girl and possessed a fine, ample kingdom. (According to Ovid, the river-nymph Arethusa had seen Persephone in Hades' kingdom, as she travelled underground from Greece to Sicily.)

Demeter was so distraught at the news of the abduction that she immediately cast a blight of drought and famine over the earth and especially over her beloved land of Sicily, which had betrayed its trust by not keeping Persephone safe. Descending from Olympus, she wandered throughout the earth. When she passed through Arcadia, her brother Poseidon saw her and wanted to rape her. Demeter tried to escape him by taking the form of a mare; but Poseidon's animal was the horse, and so, assuming this shape, he had his will. She bore the horse Arion and the goddess Despoina, whose name, meaning 'the lady', was not divulged except in the Arcadian Mysteries, in which Demeter was worshipped with a mare's head. Then she went into hiding in a cave, where Pan eventually found her, and reported his discovery to Zeus. Zeus sent the Fates to reason with her, and she at last recognised that her daughter's marriage with Hades must be accepted.

But a much better known version of this story is told in our oldest surviving account, the *Homeric Hymn to Demeter*. According to this poem, Demeter wandered across the earth in human form, granting the benefits of agriculture to those who received her kindly, but punishing the inhospitable. When she appeared at the house of Misme in Attica, she was given a drink of *kykeon* (penny-royal, barley-meal, and water). But Misme's son Ascalabus laughed because she drank so quickly: at which she threw the dregs in his face, and he turned into a spotted lizard. When she arrived at Eleusis, Demeter, in the guise of an old woman weighed down with sorrow, rested near a well. The daughters of King Celeus happened to come to draw water; one of them, taking pity on the stranger, invited her to return home with them for shelter and refreshment. There Metanira, the queen, welcomed her kindly, believing her to be a Cretan woman named Doso. At first Demeter refused to sit down, but then she was won over by the jokes of the slave-girl Iambe, and consented to drink a cup of *kykeon*, refusing wine because she was in mourning. Demeter was so impressed by the royal hospitality that she offered to serve in the household, and Metanira confided to her the care of her baby son Demophon. The child grew rapidly, for Demeter tried to make him immortal by anointing him with ambrosia by day and placing him in the fire by night, in order to burn the mortal part out of him. However Praxithea, one of the servants, discovered what she was doing and told her mistress. When she herself saw it, Metanira was aghast and uttered a scream; whereupon Demeter, angered at the interference, threw the child on to the floor. Then the goddess, transforming herself into her true shape, commanded Celeus to erect a temple to her at Eleusis, and taught him how to perform new and secret rites in her honour – the Eleusinian Mysteries.

Demeter spent a whole year in the new temple, refusing the company of the gods. Meanwhile the earth was becoming barren, and Zeus realised that if nothing were done to appease his sister, the race of men would soon die out and gods would cease to receive their sacrifices. In an attempt, therefore, to conciliate Demeter, he sent Iris to Eleusis to beg her to rejoin the Olympian gathering. But she refused to listen, unless Persephone were restored to her. So Zeus consented, but with a single condition: Persephone must eat nothing during her stay in the Underworld, for whoever eats and drinks in Hades' kingdom is his forever. Zeus then sent Hermes to fetch the girl, and Hades agreed to part with her. But as she left he gave her a pomegranate (according to Ovid's account Persephone had picked the pomegranate while wandering in his gardens). When Persephone reached Eleusis, Demeter asked her if she had eaten anything in the Underworld. At first Persephone denied eating anything, but Ascalaphus declared that he had seen the girl eating pomegranate seeds and she had to admit it: she had eaten a number of the seeds, variously estimated between four and seven. So Zeus decreed that she must spend a third (or half) of each year in Hades' kingdom as his wife. While the grain is in the ground, growing and ripening (that is, from the sowing in autumn to the harvest in early summer), Persephone stays with her mother and the earth is glad. But while the seed-corn is stored away in jars, in the hot summer months, the goddess goes to dwell with her gloomy husband and the earth is parched and barren. (This is contrary to some modern versions of the myth, which describe Persephone as a summer goddess who departs for Hades during the winter months and returns in spring.)

Now Zeus sent Rhea to ask Demeter to relent from her persecution of mankind, and she agreed to restore her blessings to the world. She committed the priesthood of Eleusis to Eumolpus, and instructed Triptolemus (sometimes identified with the son of Celeus, Demophon, whom Demeter had tried to make immortal) to convey the arts of agriculture to all men who would receive them. Both the Athenians and Sicilians claimed to have been the first to receive the gift of grain. Demeter lent Triptolemus her chariot, drawn by winged serpents, for his journey. She also gave Attica the figtree, for a man of that country named Phytalus, who had shown her hospitality in her wanderings, received it as his reward. When Triptolemus returned to Eleusis after his travels, Celeus wanted to kill him for impiety, but Demeter prevented him and made him yield his kingdom to Triptolemus instead.

At the feast given by Tantalus to the gods, Demeter was the only immortal to taste the stew composed of the body of Tantalus' son Pelops. When Pelops was restored to life, she gave him an ivory shoulder to replace what she had eaten.

Demeter attended the wedding of Cadmus and Harmonia, and there met Iasion, a mortal with whom she made love lying in a thrice-ploughed fallow field in Crete. For this act of presumption Zeus struck Iasion with a thunderbolt, either killing or, according to another version, crippling him. Demeter was said to have borne Iasion two sons, Plutus ('wealth') and Philomelus ('fond of song'). The latter was content to be a poor farmer, and invented the waggon; his reward from Demeter was to be made into a constellation, Bootes, the Ploughman. She was also fond of a nymph, Macris, who lived on Corcyra in a cave; and for her sake she taught the Titans how to sow and reap grain on the island, which was consequently called Drepane, the Sickle.

In Thessaly Demeter had a sacred grove, which a certain Erysichthon decided to fell in order to build himself a new dining-hall. The goddess herself, appearing in the likeness of her priestess, warned him to abandon the plan; and when he persisted, she told him to carry on with his project, as he would certainly need the hall to dine in. She then struck him with an insatiable hunger, so that however much he ate he wasted away until he was reduced to beggary (see ERYSICHTHON). He eventually devoured his own flesh and died.

Demeter's travels made it possible for her to be associated with numerous places, and she was worshipped throughout the Greek world. She was also particularly venerated by women, for example in the Thesmophoria at Athens, a ceremony named after her title *Thesmophoros* ('bringer of law') and confined to women, who prayed for fertility for themselves and the city: Aristophanes made it the subject of his comedy the *Thesmophoriazusae*.

Demodocus The minstrel of the court of King Alcinous of the Phaeacians on Scheria, the mythical island visited by Odysseus in his wanderings. Demodocus was blind (as Homer himself was believed to be). At a banquet before the games he sang of the quarrel of Odysseus and Achilles, which made Odysseus cover his head with his mantle to hide his tears. He was led out to the games by Alcinous' equerry. At the games he sang of the love of Ares and Aphrodite, and at supper Odysseus sent him a special portion of meat, with a request that he should sing the tale of the fall of Troy. His subsequent song told the story of the Wooden Horse, which caused Odysseus to weep again. Seeing this, Alcinous put an end to the song, and Odysseus, to explain his behaviour, revealed his identity and his part in the events described by the bard.

Demonice Either the mother of Thestius

by Ares or else his sister, and a daughter of Agenor and Epicaste.

Demophon or **Demophoon** *1.* Son of Theseus and Phaedra and brother of Acamas. After serving in the Trojan War with his brother, Demophon returned to Athens and became king, Menestheus the usurper having been killed at Troy. As king of Athens, Demophon protected Heracles' children against Eurystheus of Sparta. The Athenians claimed that Demophon brought the Palladium from Troy and placed it in Athena's temple at Athens.

It was also said that Demophon married the Thracian princess Phyllis; in this version (disagreeing with the story that her bridegroom was Acamas) she hanged herself in despair when Demophon did not return, and was turned into an almond tree. She did not, however, put forth leaves until the day her husband finally came back, when, in his grief, he put his arms round the tree and kissed it.

2. Son of Celeus of Eleusis. *See* DEM-ETER.

3. see MASTUSIUS.

Despoina ('Lady') Daughter of a union between Poseidon and Demeter in Arcadia, when Demeter was hiding in sorrow and anger at the loss of Persephone. She had changed herself into a mare – to avoid Poseidon's advances – and was grazing with King Oncius' horses. But Poseidon, the god of horses, saw her there and, taking the form of a stallion, mounted her.

Despoina was worshipped in Arcadia in ceremonies as mysterious as those of Eleusis. She may have been a local by-form of Persephone; the pomegranate, unhappily associated with the latter's myth, was the only fruit not offered to her. At Phigalia in Arcadia, Demeter and Despoina were worshipped in the form of women with the heads of mares.

Deucalion *1.* Son of Prometheus and Pronoia. He married Pyrrha, daughter of Epimetheus and Pandora. When Zeus determined to destroy mankind by the flood because of the wickedness of the Bronze Generation of men, or because of the evil done by the Arcadian king Lycaon and his people, Deucalion's father, the Titan Prometheus, instructed him to build an ark and stock it with food. After floating for nine days and nights, the craft came to rest on the summit of Mount Parnassus (or else near Dodona in north-western Greece). When Deucalion and Pyrrha disembarked, they sacrificed to Zeus a thank-offering for their preservation, but then realised that they were the only mortals left alive. They went to consult an oracle at the shrine of Themis either at the Boeotian river Cephisus, or on the site of the Delphic Oracle; or else Hermes came from Zeus and offered them whatever they desired, and they asked for a new race of men. The oracle or the god advised Deucalion and Pyrrha to cast the bones of their mother over their shoulders, veiling their heads and loosening their girdles. At first the pair refused, for it would have been impiety to disturb the bones of the dead. But then Deucalion realised that the mother indicated by the oracle must be their Great Mother, the Earth: so, picking up stones, they both threw them over their shoulders, as they had been told to do. Deucalion's stones became men, Pyrrha's women; and the new race was described as the Lelegians. Subsequently Deucalion and Pyrrha settled in Opuntian Locris and had children. The Athenians, however, claimed it was in their city that the pair had settled; and they showed Deucalion's grave. Their children were Hellen, Amphictyon, Protogenia, Pandora, and Thyia.

The story of the flood and the rebirth of mankind is told by Ovid in the first book of the *Metamorphoses*.

2. Son of Minos and his heir as king of

Crete. He had two sons, Idomeneus and Molus, the latter a bastard.

Dexamenus A king of Olenus who entertained Heracles. Heracles rescued his daughter Mnesimache from a forced marriage with the Centaur Eurytion. His name means 'the Hospitable'.

Dia Daughter of Eioneus of Magnesia in Thessaly. She married Ixion, to whom she bore Pirithous. More commonly, Zeus is named as Pirithous' father, having seduced Dia after Ixion, for his part, had tried unsuccessfully to rape Hera.

Diana An ancient Italian woodland goddess, a patroness of wild things and of women. She was identified with the Greek Artemis.

Dictynna An epithet of the Cretan goddess Britomartis, later identified with Artemis. It is probable that the real origin of the title is not *dictys*, 'net', as was sometimes supposed – she was thought of as the 'lady of nets' – but Mount Dicte in Crete, which was associated with her cult.

Dictys *see* DANAE.

Dido Legendary queen of Carthage; daughter of Mutto, king of Tyre in Phoenicia, and sister of Pygmalion; famous for her love of Aeneas in Virgil's *Aeneid*. She was said by Virgil to be the daughter of Belus. When Pygmalion succeeded his father as king of Tyre (in spite of a will which left the sovereignty equally to Dido and himself), he murdered Dido's husband Sychaeus or Sicharbas, his father's brother, who was priest of Tyrian Heracles (Melqart). While Dido lived in Tyre she had been called Elissa, which was the name of a goddess.

After her husband's death, Dido and his sister Anna were said to have escaped from Tyre at the head of a band of followers, landing in the region of North Africa which is now Tunisia. There, on the coast, the local king, whom Virgil calls Iarbas, sold her as much land as a bull's hide might contain: Dido cut up a hide into strips, and so secured enough land to build a citadel. This was why, it was believed, the Carthaginian citadel was named Byrsa ('hide'). According to the Greek historian Timaeus, Iarbas, with the support of the Carthaginian elders, pressed Dido to marry him. In order to avoid doing so (since she had sworn never to remarry), she cast herself into the flames of a pyre.

Virgil took the part of this tale as the basis of the earlier books of his *Aeneid*, in which he recounts the wanderings of Aeneas before his arrival on the site of Rome. He describes how Aeneas landed in Africa and saw the city of Carthage being built; later, Dido entertained him, learnt his story, and fell passionately in love with him. This respite gave him time to rebuild his fleet and refresh his men. But when he considered staying at Carthage and marrying Dido, Mercury was sent by Jupiter to warn him to be on his way to Italy, as his destiny lay there and not in Africa. By this time Dido, who had formed a sexual union with Aeneas in a cave, was convinced that he was now her husband or had irrevocably committed himself to marriage. Horrified by his intention to leave, she bitterly reproached him, but he insisted and in spite of all her pleas launched his ships. Dido ordered a pyre to be raised, ostensibly in order to destroy everything that reminded her of him. But when it was fired, she herself leapt into its flames, after running herself upon a sword he had given her.

This story is perhaps in many respects Virgil's invention, but its roots seem to be traceable to the earlier Latin epic poets, Ennius and Naevius; it probably originated in the Punic Wars. Varro, the great scholar of the first century BC, adopted the tradition, but in his version it was Anna, Dido's sister, who perished in the flames for love of Aeneas. In Virgil's story Dido's sin lay in breaking her oath not to remarry. Even after death she did not forgive Aeneas, for when he was escorted to the Underworld by the Sibyl of Cumae, he met her shade, but she refused to speak to him or answer his questions.

Diomedes 1. Son of Tydeus and Deipyle; king of Argos. In the *Iliad* he is a great warrior on the Greek side in the Trojan War, and the friend and companion of Odysseus.

In addition to the adventures mentioned in Homer's poem, he was credited with a great number of others. His father Tydeus had been killed at Thebes, trying to storm it as one of Polynices' Seven Champions; his mother was the daughter of Adrastus, the king of Argos who had led the Seven against Thebes. Diomedes was one of the sons of the Seven (known as *Epigoni* or 'the second generation') who, when they were grown up, marched on Thebes to avenge their fathers. As successful as the Seven had been ill-starred, they lost only one man, Adrastus' son Aegialeus. Adrastus himself was grief-stricken and died at Megara on his way home. Diomedes, as his daughter's son, became regent, if not king, of Argos, and guardian (with Euryalus) of Aegialeus' baby son Cyanippus; and he married his cousin Aegialia, the grand-daughter of Adrastus.

After the fall of Thebes, Diomedes went with Alcmaeon to Calydon to punish the sons of Agrius, who had wrongfully usurped the throne of Oeneus (the father of Diomedes' father Tydeus) in his old age. Diomedes drove out Agrius and his sons, many of whom were slain, and restored Oeneus to his throne. When Oeneus became too infirm to rule, Diomedes appointed Andraemon, the old man's son-in-law, to succeed him, and brought his grandfather to Argos, where he eventually

died. He was buried at Oenoe, a town named after him.

Diomedes had been one of Helen's suitors and helped Menelaus to recover her in the Trojan War. He commanded eighty ships from Argos, Tiryns, Troezen, Epidaurus, and Aegina. His subordinate officers were Sthenelus and Euryalus. According to some versions he helped Odysseus to lure Iphigenia to Aulis and to bring about Palamedes' downfall and death. Like Odysseus, Diomedes enjoyed the special protection of Athena. With her aid, in one single day he killed the Trojan prince Pandarus, wounded Aeneas, and fought with the gods, driving Ares from the field and striking Aphrodite with a spear which tore her flesh. When he found himself face to face with the Lycian captain Glaucus, instead of fighting a duel, the two discovered that they had an old family tie of friendship and exchanged armour. Diomedes had the better of the deal, for whereas his own armour was made of bronze, that of Glaucus was gold. He rescued Nestor when the old man's horse were killed, and then went with him in pursuit of Hector. In the company of Odysseus he made a night raid on the Trojan camp in the plain, killing Dolon and slaughtering the Thracian king Rhesus with twelve of his men. Again with Odysseus he went to fetch Philoctetes from Lemnos to Troy, after the seer Helenus, captured by Odysseus, had prophesied that only the presence of Philoctetes could guarantee Greek success. Diomedes was also said to have accompanied Odysseus to steal the Palladium, Athena's sacred image, from the citadel of Troy, since Helenus had declared that whichever side possessed it would win.

Helped by Athena, Diomedes was one of the few Greeks to have a safe and speedy voyage home after the war. But in the meantime Aphrodite, in revenge for the wound she had received from Diomedes' spear, had caused his wife

Aegialia to become the mistress of Sthenelus' son Cometes. This, according to one version, was the work of Nauplius 2, who persuaded Aegialia into this infidelity in order to avenge himself on Diomedes for the death of his son Palamedes. Moreover, Diomedes' claim to the throne of Argos was contested by the family of Sthenelus, which was the Argive royal house, whereas Diomedes himself only belonged to it by marriage. He was forced to take refuge at the altar of Hera and later departed from Argos, leaving his shield in her shrine. Sthenelus' son Cylarabes became king of Argos.

Accompanied by his personal followers, Diomedes sailed to Italy, where he married Evippe, the daughter of Daunus, king of Apulia. According to the Roman poets, his companions Acmon, Lycus, Idas, Nycteus, Rhexenor and Abas were turned into birds by Venus (Aphrodite) for defying her powers to do them yet greater harm. They lived on islands off Apulia called the Isles of Diomedes and showed friendship only to Greeks. When Venulus was sent by the Rutulian prince Turnus to ask his aid against Aeneas in Latium, Diomedes refused to send help, having caused Venus, Aeneas' mother, sufficient offence already. In Apulia, Daunus was said to have given him land on which he then founded a great city, which he called Argyripa, later Arpi. He was also the reputed founder of Beneventum, Sipontum, Canusium, Aequum Tuticum, and Venusia – named after Venus as a peace-offering. As a result of Athena's favour, Diomedes, after his death or disappearance from the earth, received divine honours. He was said to have been buried on the islands where his companions, now birds, sprinkled his tomb with water every day.

2. Son of Ares and the nymph Cyrene; a king of the Bistones in Thrace. He owned four mares which were so savage that they were kept fastened to bronze troughs by iron chains and halters. He fed them on human flesh. The eighth of Heracles' Labours, ordered by King Eurystheus of Mycenae, was the capture of these mares. *See* HERACLES (eighth Labour).

Dione 1. An earth-goddess who was a consort of Zeus. The name is merely the feminine of Zeus. Her cult – perhaps originally undifferentiated from that of Hera – was confined to Dodona in Aetolia, a very ancient sanctuary of Zeus, where he was worshipped in the form of an oak tree. Homer recognises Dione as the mother of the sea-goddess Amphitrite and of Aphrodite, but to Hesiod she is merely a daughter of Oceanus.
2. Daughter of Atlas. She married Tantalus *1*.

Dionysus or **Bacchus** The god of wine and of ecstatic liberation: the greatest deity of the later Greek (Hellenistic) world, to which his cult, accompanied by rich ceremonial, promised salvation. The youngest of the great Greek gods – he is only a minor deity in Homer – he appears to be an intruder from Thrace or Phrygia. He was usually accompanied by the Sileni and Satyrs who protected fertility. Originally he may, like Demeter, have been a deity of grain and agriculture in general. His followers (generally women, the Maenads or 'frenzied ones') abandoned themselves to wild dances on the hillsides: they clad themselves in fawnskins and carried torches and *thyrsoi* (staves, wrapped in grapevines or ivy stems, and crowned with pine-cones). The Greeks of early historical times were aware of the foreignness of Dionysus' spirit, and in many states the aristocratic government rejected his non-Greek orgiastic rites. Many of the myths relating to Dionysus arise from his punishment of such rejection; they may reflect a historic process whereby a foreign, ecstatic faith imposed itself on the traditional Olympian religion of the Greek ruling class. Dionysus was known as Bromius, Lenaeus 'of the wine-vat',

Lyaeus 'the releaser', and Dendrites 'of trees'; and he is often identified with Iacchus, a god associated with Demeter and the Eleusinian Mysteries. He was the patron of the two great Athenian dramatic festivals, the Lenaea and the City Dionysia, mainly associated with comic and tragic drama respectively.

The commonest story of Dionysus' birth associates him with Thebes. It was told how Zeus, in the guise of a man, seduced Semele, a daughter of Cadmus, the founder of Thebes. When Hera learnt that Semele was pregnant, she disguised herself as Semele's old nurse Beroe. In this form she extracted from Semele the name of her lover, but hearing that it was Zeus, she scoffed and refused to believe it unless Semele could persuade him to prove it by appearing to her in his true shape. So Semele enticed Zeus to grant her a favour, and when he offered whatever she might desire, she asked him to show himself in all his glory. He had to comply, and Semele, blasted by his brightness, shrivelled to nothing. Before she finally expired, Zeus rescued his divine child from her womb. He cut a gash in his own thigh, placed the child inside, and stitched the cavity up. After a couple of months, he opened himself up again and brought forth Dionysus, whom Hermes took to Semele's sister Ino, or to the nymph Macris, Aristaeus' daughter, in Euboea.

In the Theban version of the childhood of Dionysus, the god experienced great difficulty with unbelievers. First Ino, Agave, and Autonoe, Semele's sisters, refused to believe in his divine paternity, although Ino, when Hermes brought the child from Zeus, agreed to bring him up disguised as a girl. Hera, ever jealous of Zeus' amours, was angry with Ino and her husband Athamas for sheltering him, and punished them by driving them mad (see ATHAMAS). Dionysus, however, remained grateful to Ino and tried to protect her from Hera.

Later when he returned to Thebes, Ino and her sisters joined his revels. When Hera caused Ino to leap into the sea with her son Melicertes, Poseidon turned her into the sea-goddess Leucothea, in the form of a seagull.

At some time in his childhood, when danger from Hera was especially pressing, Zeus transformed Dionysus into a kid and handed him to the nymphs of Mount Nysa (variously located) to rear; these may have been the Hyades or rain-nymphs. Silenus aided them in their task. Dionysus later placed the nymphs in the sky as a a cluster of stars.

There was also an older myth of Dionysus' birth and origin, which was later added on to the Theban story so that he appeared to be 'twice born' (one of his epithets). In this version Demeter – with whom, as a god of vegetation, he had much in common – was seen as his mother by Zeus: the earth and the sky giving birth to the crops. In the tradition of the Orphic mystery religion, however, Persephone takes her mother's place. According to this account, Zeus came to her in the form of a snake, and their child was known as Zagreus. Hera, jealous, persuaded the Titans to destroy the child. In spite of his disguise as a kid, they caught him, tore him limb from limb, and devoured him, all but his heart, which Athena rescued. Zeus gave the heart to Semele to eat, and thus Dionysus was conceived afresh. (Alternatively, Demeter or Apollo gathered the remains and brought them back to life.)

When Dionysus attained manhood, he fetched his mother Semele from the Underworld so that she might receive due honour on Olympus. Diving into Lake Lerna or the bay of Troezen, he reached Hades' kingdom and carried her off, renaming her Thyone among the immortal gods.

Dionysus was often persecuted by those who refused to accept his divinity. Finally, however, after many struggles he won over the whole of Greece to his worship. While he was still in the care of the nymphs of Nysa, Lycurgus, son of Dryas, king of the Edonians, chased his nurses and tried to kill them with an ox-goad. Dionysus fled in terror and took sanctuary in the sea with Thetis, who cherished him until the gods struck Lycurgus blind, later causing him a dreadful death. At Thebes, his native city, Dionysus had to deal with his cousin Pentheus, son of Agave, who had inherited Cadmus' throne but refused to accept Dionysus' divinity. This struggle is the theme of Euripides' play *The Bacchants*. Dionysus came to Thebes in the form of a handsome young man, at the head of a band of Lydian Maenads. Through his powers he infected the women of the city and made them take to the slopes of Mount Cithaeron in Bacchic frenzy. Pentheus imprisoned the young man in a dungeon, but his chains miraculously fell off and the doors of the jail flew open. Then the stranger began to arouse the king's interest by whispering to him of the excesses he might see performed on the mountain if he disguised himself as a woman. The god dressed him in this guise and drove him with undetected mockery through the streets. Pentheus spied on the Theban Bacchants from a tree. They saw him, believed in their madness that he was a mountain lion, and, led by his mother Agave and his aunts, pulled him down and tore him limb from limb. Later Agave came to herself and sorrowfully buried him. Dionysus sent Agave and her parents Cadmus and Harmonia into exile to the land of the Encheleis. The exile of Cadmus may reflect another version of the myth of Dionysus' birth, for the people of Brasiae in Laconia declared that Semele bore her son normally, but that because she claimed he was Zeus' son, Cadmus in disbelief locked Semele and Dionysus in a chest, which he threw into the sea. The chest came ashore at Brasiae; Semele was dead, but Dionysus was rescued and

reared in a nearby cave by his aunt Ino, who had arrived there in her mad wanderings.

Another story connecting Dionysus with the sea had been told in the *Homeric Hymn to Dionysus*. Certain Tyrrhenian pirates found Dionysus, in the guise of a handsome boy drowsy with wine, on a headland on the isle of Chios or Icaria. Deciding to kidnap him and hold him for ransom, or sell him as a slave, they lured him on to their ship and offered to take him to Naxos, which he said was his home. The only member of the crew who objected to their scheme was the helmsman Acoetes, and he protested in vain: for when he steered for Naxos, the sailors bade him proceed in another direction. But then a miracle began. The wind fell, strands of grapevine covered the ship, the oars became serpents, the mast and sails were heavy with grapes, of which clusters were seen on the youth's head, and wild beasts appeared and played around his feet. Driven to madness, the sailors jumped overboard and turned into dolphins or fishes. Acoetes was terrified, but Dionysus reassured him and directed him to sail to Naxos. He became a faithful follower and priest of the god. (According to one version it was he, and not the god himself, whom Pentheus imprisoned.)

It was on Naxos that Dionysus rescued Ariadne – abandoned by Theseus – and made her his bride. Their wedding crown was set in heaven as the constellation of Corona.

A number of Greek states, it was said, were as reluctant as Thebes to accept Dionysus as a god. In Orchomenus, another Boeotian city, the daughters of King Minyas refused to join the revels and stayed at home. But the god made them insane, so that they tore one of their children apart; he then turned them into bats. At Argos too King Proetus' daughters refused to join the Maenads. They too were driven mad, and roamed the mountains imagining themselves to be cows and eating their own babies. Melampus cured them of their frenzy, though not before all the other Argive women had caught the disease as well, during the king's unwillingness to give Melampus the enormous reward he demanded – a third of the kingdom. Another Argive tradition relates that Perseus fought against Dionysus, killing many of his followers, the Haliae or 'sea-women'. But they were later reconciled, and the Argives sheltered Dionysus' wife Ariadne, who was buried in their city.

At Athens in the reign of Pandion, Dionysus was believed to have taught the cultivation of the vine to a humble man, Icarius, and his daughter Erigone. When Icarius gave his neighbours wine, they got drunk and, believing they were poisoned, put him to death. Erigone, who did not know what had happened to her father, looked for him high and low with her faithful dog Maira; when she found his body, she hanged herself. Dionysus punished the Athenians with madness, and their women hanged themselves in great numbers. Eventually the men discovered the cause of this misfortune from Apollo's oracle, and instituted a festival at which images were hung from trees in honour of Icarius and Erigone. She and her dog were commemorated in the constellations of Virgo and Procyon.

In Aetolia Dionysus was so well received that King Oeneus offered him his own wife Althaea, who subsequently bore him a daughter, Deianira, the future wife of Heracles. Dionysus rewarded Oeneus with his favour and the art of cultivating the vine.

Dionysus, as befitted a god of foreign origin, was believed to have travelled widely outside Greece. Hera drove him mad, it was said, so that he wandered through the eastern lands, Syria and Egypt, until in Phrygia Cybele or Rhea purified him and cured him of his frenzy.

He adopted Phrygian dress and was accompanied by Lydian Maenads, Satyrs, and Sileni. His female followers wore deerskins, carried the thyrsus, suckled fawns, tore to pieces and ate wild beasts, and allegedly indulged in sexual promiscuity. When his follower Silenus got lost, King Midas of Phrygia entertained him so royally that Dionysus offered him any favour he desired. He chose that whatever he touched should turn to gold – a boon that proved to be a curse as gold could be neither eaten or drunk.

In Egypt Dionysus founded the oracle of Ammon. One day he was wandering in the waterless desert with his followers when they saw a solitary ram. As they followed the animal it disappeared, but a spring of water was found where it had been. There the god placed the oracle, and set the ram in heaven as the constellation Aries. When he came to the River Euphrates, Dionysus built a bridge of ivy and vine strands, plaited together. Eventually he reached the River Ganges in India; after imposing his worship there, he returned to Greece in a chariot drawn by leopards.

In the battle between the gods and giants, Dionysus killed Eurytus with his thyrsus; and the asses ridden by his Satyrs caused terror to the giants with their braying. When the gods fled to Egypt from the monstrous Typhon, Dionysus changed himself into a goat. He was eventually reconciled to Hera and even helped her escape from a trap devised by Hephaestus – a locking chair – by making the divine smith drunk. According to one version, he had a child by a goddess, for Aphrodite was said to have borne him Priapus, who like Dionysus was a god of fertility and vegetation.

In Aristophanes' *Frogs* Dionysus was treated as a comic character. The Romans identified him with Father Liber, an ancient Italian rustic god.

Diores A leader of the contingent from Elis which went to the Trojan War; his father was Amarynceus. He was killed by Pierus, a Thracian from Aenus.

Dioscuri ('Zeus' boys') *see* CASTOR AND POLYDEUCES.

Dirce Wife of Lycus, regent of Thebes in Labdacus' infancy. After his brother Nycteus had been killed trying to recover his daughter Antiope from Epopeus, king of Sicyon, Lycus took the girl back to Thebes and handed her to Dirce, who treated her as a slave, abused her, and finally planned to fasten her to the horns of a mad bull. But Antiope's sons Amphion and Zethus rescued their mother, punishing Dirce with the very death she had tried to inflict on Antiope. However, as Dirce had been a devotee of Dionysus, the god avenged her death by driving Antiope mad; he also caused a spring of water to well up in the place where the bull had gored Dirce to death.

Dis The Roman name of the god of the Underworld, a contraction of *dives*, literally 'the Rich'. See HADES.

Dius A king of Elis. Oxylus conquered his kingdom after a battle of champions.

Dolius An old servant of Odysseus who remained faithful to his master during the latter's twenty-year absence. Six of his sons supported Odysseus, but his son Melanthius and a daughter Melantho instead favoured Penelope's suitors, who wanted to supplant her husband Odysseus; they were eventually killed on his return. Dolius and his six sons helped Odysseus overpower the Ithacans under Eupithes in the final battle.

Dolon The only son of Eumedes, a Trojan herald. In the Trojan War, at the time when Hector, in Achilles' absence, had succeeded in penning the Greeks in a fortification built to protect their beached ships, Dolon offered to go by night from the Trojan army, now encamped on the plain, and spy on the Greek dispositions, if Hector would swear to reward him with Achilles' horses. An ugly man, Dolon wore a ferret-skin cap and carried a bow which he covered in a wolfskin. As he approached the Greek lines he was seen in the darkness by Odysseus and Diomedes, who were engaged on a similar expedition. They let Dolon pass them, then chased him, captured him, and forced him to tell them all he knew about the Trojan camp, and the newly arrived force of Rhesus, king of the Thracians. Then in spite of Dolon's offer of a vast ransom, Diomedes killed him and hid his equipment, picking it up on the way back from the expedition. Ironically Hector, who had offered Dolon Achilles' team of horses, was himself destined to go behind them after his death, when Achilles dragged his body in the dust. Euripides, in his *Rhesus*, presented Dolon in a better light than Homer had.

Doris Daughter of Oceanus and Tethys; a sea-goddess who married Nereus. The fifty sea-nymphs called Nereids ('daughters of Nereus') were her children.

Dorus Deucalion's son Hellen was the mythical ancestor of the Hellenic race; for the nymph Orseis was said to have borne him three sons who in their turn begot the three main branches of the Greek people: Aeolus, the founder of the Aeolians, Xuthus, ancestor of the Achaeans and Ionians, and Dorus, from whom sprang the Dorians (in his play the *Ion*, however, Euripides makes Dorus the son of Xuthus and Creusa daughter of Erechtheus, a genealogy that enhances the status of the Ionians, and so of the Athenians, who came of their stock). The traditional home of the Dorians, in Doris, to the north of Mount Parnassus, probably reflects the historical fact of their occupation of northern Greece before they invaded the Pelopon-

nese and Crete in the twelfth and succeeding centuries before Christ. They
claimed alliance with the Heraclids, the
descendants of Heracles, who supposedly had helped the early Dorian king
Aegimius to take the land of the Lapiths,
Thessaly.

Dreams (Greek: *Oneiroi*, Latin:
Somnia) Dreams are frequently personified in Greek and Latin literature, and
especially in epic poetry. In the *Iliad*, for
instance. Zeus sends Agamemnon a false
dream ordering him to prepare to fight
the Trojans, with the news that he can
now take Troy; whereas it was really
Zeus' intention that the Trojans should
thrust the Achaeans right back to their
ships. In obedience to Zeus' command,
the dream goes to Agamemnon's bedside,
assuming the appearance of his aged
counsellor Nestor. Dreams were considered to be the children of Nyx (Night),
and Hypnos (Sleep). Ovid in his *Metamorphoses* envisaged them as living in a cave
under Hypnos' rule. They were a thousand in number, the cleverest being Morpheus who could imitate men. Another,
Icelus, assumed the form of monsters.
Virgil, after describing Aeneas' descent
to the Underworld, asserted that dreams
were sent by the spirits of the dead: those
which were true issued easily through a
gate made of horn, whereas false dreams
came out through a gate of ivory.

Dryads Dryads and hamadryads were
the nymphs of trees, originally oak trees
(*drys*). They were long-lived but not
immortal; for example, Eurydice, Orpheus' wife – killed by a snake-bite
while fleeing from Aristaeus – was a
dryad. In later times it was believed that
a dryad's existence was independent of
the tree, whereas the hamadryad lived
in a particular tree and died with it.

Dryas *see* LYCURGUS.

Dryope Daughter of Dryops or of Eury-

tus (and hence half-sister to Iole). There
are two stories of her metamorphosis
into a black poplar. According to the
first, Apollo seduced her by a trick.
Dryope had been accustomed to play
with the nymphs in the woods. Apollo
chased her, and in order to win her
favours, turned himself into a tortoise,
of which the girls made a pet. When
Dryope had the tortoise in her lap, he
turned into a snake and raped her. The
nymphs then abandoned the girl and
she gave birth to her son, Amphissus.
However she married Andraemon. Amphissus eventually built a temple for his
father Apollo in the city he founded,
Amphissa. Here the nymphs came to
converse with Dryope, and finally carried her off with them, leaving a poplar
and a spring where she had been.

In Ovid's version of the story, Dryope
was wandering by a lake, suckling her
baby Amphissus, when she saw the
bright red flowers of the lotus tree, formerly the nymph Lotis who, when fleeing from Priapus, had been changed into
the tree. Dryope wanted to give the blos-
soms to her baby to play with, but they
started to tremble and bleed and she
tried to run away. However she found
herself rooted to the spot and began to
change into a black poplar. She had
sufficient time to warn her husband Andraemon to take care of their child and
see that he did not pick flowers.

Dryops Son of Apollo or of the River
Spercheius, and ancestor of the Dryopes,
a tribe of Pelasgian (i.e. pre-Greek) peoples, who were alleged to have been
driven from their home in Doris and the
Spercheius valley by Heracles and Aegimius, an early Dorian king. The nation
then scattered to Euboea and Messenia.
Dryops' daughter (sometimes called
Penelope) was the mother of Pan.

Dymas *1.* A Phrygian king, father of
Hecabe and Asius.
2. Son of Aegimius, king of Doris.

E

Echecles Son of Actor, husband of Polymele. *See* EUDORUS.

Echemus Son of Cepheus and king of Tegea; later king of all Arcadia in succession to Cepheus' elder brother Lycurgus. In a single combat intended to determine the fate of the Peloponnese, he killed Heracles' son Hyllus; as a result of his victory, the Heraclids, descendants of Heracles, agreed to depart from the land and refrain from attacking it for a hundred years. Echemus married Tyndareos' daughter Timandra, who bore him Laodocus, but later deserted him for Phyleus, king of Dulichium.

Echenais *see* DAPHNIS.

Echetus King Echetus of Epirus is mentioned in the *Odyssey* as a man of proverbial cruelty. He blinded his daughter and made her grind bronze grain in a dungeon.

Echidna A monster (literally 'snake'), the child of the mysterious Chrysaor and of Oceanus' daughter Callirrhoe; or else of Tartarus and Gaia, or Ceto and Phorcys. The Echidna was part beautiful woman, part voracious serpent. To Typhon she bore a hideous brood, the Chimaera, the Hydra of Lerna, and Cerberus. Subsequently the Echidna mated with Orthus to produce the Sphinx, the Nemean Lion, and the Crommyonian Sow. Other creatures are sometimes called her children: Orthus, Geryon's dog, with which the Echidna mated, the serpent Ladon which guarded the garden of the Hesperides, and the

eagle that tormented Prometheus. Eventually Argus with his hundred eyes caught the Echidna asleep one day and killed it, ridding Arcadia of a grievous plague.

Echion *1*. One of the Theban 'Sown Men' (*see* CADMUS). His name means 'son of a snake'. He married Cadmus' daughter Agave and was the father of Cadmus' successor Pentheus.
2. An Argonaut, son of Hermes and Antianira, daughter of Menetes. With his twin brother Erytus he came from Alope or Pangaeum. In some versions of the story, he acted as a spy for the Argonauts.

Echo A nymph of Mount Helicon. When Hera wished to spy on Zeus in his amours, Echo infuriated the goddess by her continual chatter which seemed to be intended as deliberate assistance to Zeus. In consequence, Hera silenced her by ordaining that the nymph should be unable to speak unless first spoken to, and that her utterances should be restricted to a repetition of the final syllables of speech uttered by others. Later Echo fell in love with Narcissus, who spurned her, especially as she could only repeat his own words. In her distress she hid herself away and wasted to a shadow. Only her echoing voice remained.

Another story makes Echo a nymph whom Pan loved in vain, so that he struck her dumb, save for the power of repetition. The shepherd people were so infuriated by this habit of hers that they tore her to pieces. Gaia (Earth) hid the pieces in herself, and they still retained their repetitive powers.

Eetion Father of Andromache, Hector's wife. He was king of the Cilices, his city being Thebe-under-Placus in the Southern Troad, and an ally of Troy in the Trojan War. Achilles when he sacked Thebe killed him and all his seven sons in one day, but gave him an honourable burial.

Egeria An Italian water-nymph worshipped in association with Diana at Aricia in Latium, and with the Camenae in a grove outside the Porta Capena of Rome. The mythical second king of Rome, Numa Pompilius the Sabine, reputed for his wisdom and learning, married Egeria or made her his mistress, and relied on her counsels. They used to meet by night at the Porta Capena, where she instructed him in matters of statecraft and religion. Ovid declared that her migration to Aricia was occasioned by her grief at Numa's death. There Diana, to calm her lamentations, changed her into a spring.

Eidothea *see* IDOTHEA.

Eidyia *see* IDYIA.

Eileithyia *see* ILITHYIA.

Eioneus A king of Magnesia. *See* IXION.

Elais *see* ANIUS.

Elatus ('driver') *1.* Son of Aras; a king of Arcadia who married Cinyras' daughter Laodice; their sons included Stymphalus. Elatus emigrated to Phocis and founded Elatea.
2. A Centaur, whom Heracles killed in his battle against that race. Chiron was said to have met his death accidentally while trying to cure Elatus of the arrow-wound.

3. A Lapith; the father of Caenis, Ischys (unless this was Elatus *1*), and Polyphemus *2* the Argonaut.
4. A Trojan ally from Pedasus, killed by Agamemnon.
5. One of the suitors of Penelope, the wife of Odysseus.

Electra ('amber', perhaps originally 'fire', 'spark').
1. Daughter of Oceanus and Tethys: she married the Titan Thaumas and bore the goddess Iris and the Harpies.
2. Daughter of Atlas and Pleione; *see* PLEIADES.
3. Daughter of Agamemnon and Clytemnestra. Though not mentioned by Homer, in classical tragedy she becomes a very important character, giving her name to two extant tragedies, one by Sophocles and the other by Euripides. She is prominent also in Aeschylus' *Libation-Bearers* [*Choephoroi*] and in Euripides' *Orestes*. In these plays she performs a central role in her brother Orestes' vengeance on their mother Clytemnestra and on Clytemnestra's lover Aegisthus, because this pair had killed their father. According to Sophocles, Electra rescued Orestes, still a boy, from the murderers who wanted to slay him too. She arranged for him to go to the court of King Strophius of Phocis. When he returned as a grown man with his cousin Pylades, Strophius' son, Electra, still hostile to Clytemnestra and Aegisthus, encountered them, recognised her brother, joined him and Pylades in a ceremony at the tomb of Agamemnon, and gave them advice and encouragement. According to Euripides, however, Electra was married to a poor but honourable peasant, who out of compunction for her royal blood and the injustice of her position, respected her virginity. On the return of Orestes, she recognised him by certain tokens and joined him in the slaying of their father's murderers. But then she was overtaken by remorse, while Orestes was tor-

mented by Furies who, according to Euripides, are simply the spectres of his own guilt-ridden mind. In his play *Orestes*, the same playwright took the story further by making Menelaus appear just as the people of Mycenae were about to stone Orestes and Electra to death for matricide. Since, however, Menelaus would not persuade the people to accept Orestes as their king, Orestes and Electra, having captured his wife Helen, tried to put her to death as an act of vengeance for all the suffering her adultery with Paris had caused their house. Helen, however, as a daughter of Zeus, was immortal and escaped their vengeance; whereupon Orestes and Electra seized her daughter Hermione and held her to ransom until Apollo, who had originally insisted that Orestes should kill Clytemnestra, offered to deliver him from the madness the Furies had inflicted on him, if he would release Hermione. Electra, by Apollo's command, married her cousin Pylades, to whom she bore two sons, Strophius and Medon.

Electryon Son of Perseus, whom he succeeded as king of Mycenae, and of Andromeda. His wife Anaxo bore him Alcmena (whobecamethemotherofHeracles) and six sons; a Phrygian woman, Midea, gave him another son, Licymnius. The six sons of Pterelaus, descended from Electryon's brother Mestor and inhabiting the Taphian islands, came to Mycenae claiming a share of the kingdom. When Electryon spurned their request, they drove off his cattle. In the ensuing battle all were killed. Evenus, one of Pterelaus' sons, who had been guarding their ships, sold the cattle to Polyxenus of Elis. Then Amphitryon, to whom Alcmena was promised in marriage, bought them back and returned them to Electryon, but accidentally killed him as he threw his club at one of the cows. Sthenelus, Electryon's brother, seized the throne of Mycenae after his death, charged Amphitryon with murder, and sent him into exile.

Elephenor Son of Chalcodon; king of the Abantes of Euboea. He received the sons of Theseus of Athens, Acamas and Demophon, when they fled from the usurper Menestheus. He was the leader of the Euboean force of forty ships which joined the Greek expedition to Troy, but on the day when Pandarus broke the truce, was killed by Agenor while trying to drag off the body of Echepolus. On their way home, Elephenor's men were driven off course and shipwrecked on the coast of Epirus, where they founded the city of Apollonia.

Elissa *see* DIDO.

Elpenor The youngest member of Odysseus' crew. While Odysseus was receiving Circe's hospitality on the island of Aeaea and was due to depart the next day, Elpenor got drunk during the night and fell off the roof of the palace, where he had gone to sleep. Odysseus forgot to bury the man before sailing away; but when he visited the house of Hades he saw the shade of Elpenor which begged him to provide due funeral rites. In response to this plea, Odysseus buried the body on his return to Aeaea.

Elymus *see* ACESTES.

Emathion Son of Tithonus and Eos (Dawn); brother of Memnon. He tried to prevent Heracles from stealing the golden apples of the Hesperides and, according to one version of the story, was killed in the attempt. He was also said to have been king of Arabia.

Empusa A bogey-woman; one of Hecate's retinue. One of her feet was a donkey's; the other was made of brass. She had the power to change her shape, and liked to make love to her victims, afterwards eating them up. The way to get rid of her was to abuse her loudly, at which she would flee squeaking.

Enceladus *see* GIANTS.

Encheleis ('eels') A race of people living in Illyria or on Lake Copais in Boeotia. *See* CADMUS.

Endeis Wife of Aeacus and mother of Peleus and Telamon. Her father was Sciron or Chiron. She hated her stepson Phocus (Aeacus' son by the Nereid Psamathe): one of her sons killed him, and they both hid his body. For this Aeacus exiled them.

Endymion Son of Aethlius, son of Zeus, and Calyce, daughter of Aeolus *2*. Endymion had three sons, Aetolus, Paeon, and Epeius. He was usually described as king of Elis, and was said to have added Olympia to his domain, driving out its Cretan king Clymenus. He decided the succession to his throne by making his sons run a race, which Epeius won. The Moon, Selene, fell in love with Endymion and bore him fifty daughters. Then, because she could not bear the idea of his death, she put him to sleep for ever; and thenceforward he lay youthful and beautiful in a cave on Mount Latmus in Caria (which according to one account was his homeland). Another tale declared that Zeus gave him a wish, and that he chose to sleep forever in the cave without growing old. The people of Carian Heraclea, near Latmus, built a shrine for him there. In Elis, however, the story of his eternal sleep was unknown, for his grave was displayed at Olympia.

Enipeus The god of a river in Thessaly, who loved Tyro, daughter of Salmoneus. One day, as she wandered along the bank of her beloved's stream, Poseidon saw her and desired her. Assuming the form of the river-god, he rose out of the stream and took her, making a wave curve over them to conceal their lovemaking. She became the mother of Pelias and Neleus, and Poseidon revealed to her his true identity.

Enyo *1*. A goddess of battle, the companion of Ares. The Romans called her Bellona. She has no mythology and little personality, being no more than a personification of war.

2. The name of one of the Graiae.

Eos Goddess of Dawn, known to the Romans as Aurora; she was the daughter of the Titan Hyperion and Titaness Theia, and sister of Helios (the Sun) and Selene (the Moon). Her first husband was the Titan Astraeus ('starry'), to whom she bore the winds, the stars, and Eosphorus, the Morning Star. She drove a chariot and pair through the sky in company with her brother Helios, her horses being Phaethon ('shining') and Lampos ('bright'). Homer calls her 'early-rising', 'rosy-fingered', and 'saffron-robed'.

She fell in love with a number of handsome young mortals, usually with unhappy results (because Aphrodite bore her a grudge for taking an amorous interest in Ares). She married one of these mortals, Tithonus, and begged Zeus to give him immortality. But she forgot to ask, on his behalf, for eternal youth, so that Tithonus remained with her, endlessly ageing until he was as desiccated as a cicada and chirped like that insect. Finally Eos locked him up in his bedroom, confining him there and rising earlier and earlier to escape his bed. Their children were Memnon and Emathion, kings respectively of Ethiopia and Arabia.

Eos saw Cephalus hunting in Attica in the early morning and abducted him, thereby causing him much grief, for he longed for his wife Procris. Eos bore a son, Phaethon, to Cephalus, and inspired in him and Procris the pangs of mutual jealousy, which set them at loggerheads and resulted in Procris' eventual death at her husband's hands. Another of Eos' lovers was the gigantic hunter Orion. She took him to Delos, thus offending the virgin Artemis, to whom Delos was sacred and who consequently put Orion to death.

Eosphorus The morning star and its god. His son was Ceyx.

Epaphus Son of Zeus and Io, whom Zeus turned into a cow to avoid detection by his wife Hera. Io went from Argos to Egypt, where she recovered her natural shape and took the name Isis. In Egypt she bore Epaphus, equated by Herodotus with the Egyptian bull-god, Apis. He was stolen from her by Hera's machinations but was subsequently restored to her and became king of Egypt. He founded a city on the spot where he had been born, naming it after his wife Memphis, a daughter of the Nile. Memphis bore him Libya and Lysianassa; Libya became the mother of Agenor and Belus.

Epeiusi *1.* A son of Endymion, king of Elis. He became his father's successor by winning a footrace against his brothers Aetolus and Paeon. On ascending the throne, he named his people the Epeians after himself. He married Anaxirrhoe, Coronus' daughter, who bore him a daughter but no sons. His brother Aetolus succeeded him.
2. Son of Panopeus. After performing badly at quoits, he beat Euryalus in the boxing match at Patroclus' funeral games. He was also the builder of the Trojan Horse, with Athena's help; and Virgil lists him among the Greek warriors who hid in it. A later tradition, perhaps based on the lyric poet Stesichorus who in the *Sack of Troy* made Epeius water-carrier to the Atridae, regarded him as a coward.

Ephialtes *1. see* GIANTS. *2. see* OTUS.

Epicaste *see* JOCASTA.

Epigoni The word means 'successors' or 'second generation', and refers to the sons of the Seven Champions. Under the leadership of Adrastus, the Seven had attacked Thebes on behalf of Polynices, and all of them fell in battle except Adrastus himself. Ten years after this disaster the sons of the Seven renewed the attack on the advice of the Delphic Oracle, in order to avenge their fathers and vindicate Polynices' claim to the throne. Their leader was Alcmaeon son of Amphiaraus, and the other Epigoni were Diomedes son of Tydeus, Sthenelus son of Capaneus, Euryalus son of Mecisteus, Promachus son of Parthenopaeus, together with Thersander son of Polynices, Amphilochus brother of Alcmaeon, and Aegialeus son of Adrastus – who was the only one of them to perish. The Thebans were routed at a place called Glisas, and on Tiresias' advice abandoned their city, fleeing to the land of the Encheleis, where Cadmus and Harmonia had taken refuge after the arrival of Dionysus; Tiresias died during the flight. The Epigoni established Polynices' son Thersander on the throne of Thebes, and he invited the refugees to return. The Epigoni offered part of the booty, including Tiresias' daughter Manto, to Apollo at Delphi. Then they went home to Argos. But Adrastus, who had accompanied them, died of grief for Aegialeus, leaving Cyanippus, Aegialeus' baby son, as his heir. Diomedes became regent – he is sometimes called king – of Argos, but after the Trojan War Sthenelus or Cylarabes took the throne, since Cyanippus was now dead.

It was said that Thebes was left almost desolate by the Epigoni; the walls were razed and Thersander inherited a poor kingdom. This tradition seems to have reflected a historical situation, for in the *Iliad* only 'lower Thebes' and not the ancient citadel is mentioned in the catalogue of Greek forces.

Epimetheus Son of the Titan Iapetus and brother of Prometheus. Prometheus means 'forethought', Epimetheus 'after-thought'. Although Prometheus, who was by far the wiser, saw the danger of accepting presents from the gods, and warned his brother, Epimetheus took Pandora from Hermes and married her. The first mortal woman ever to exist, she possessed many excellent skills (her name means 'all gifts'). But Hermes had given her a treacherous nature, and placed a box full of troubles in her hand. In her feminine curiosity Pandora opened the box and released all mankind's troubles, which then for the first time burst upon the world. Hope – the only benefit the box contained – alone was left; she shut it in after the plagues had all escaped. After this disaster, Epimetheus and Pandora brought Pyrrha who later married Deucalion (the Greek Noah) into the world.

Epione Wife of Asclepius.

Epistrophius Son of Iphitus and a leader of the Phocians in the Trojan War.

Epopeus *1. see* ANTIOPE.
2. see NYCTIMENE.

Erato *see* MUSES.

Erebus ('darkness') Son of Chaos ('the primeval void') and father of Aether ('the atmosphere'), Hemera ('day'), and Charon, their mother being being Erebus' own sister Nyx ('night'). Except for Charon, the ferryman of the dead, these personifications play little part in mythology; Erebus generally refers to a place, the darkest depths of the Underworld, rather than to an immortal being.

Erechtheus A legendary king of Athens, often confused in Classical literature with his grandfather Erichthonius (they may originally have been the same). He is usually described as a son of Pandion, king of Athens, and of Zeuxippe, but

Homer indicates that he sprang directly from the soil without human parentage: Athena reared him and set him in her shrine, where he became a demigod and received sacrifices.

The commoner, later tradition makes him a mortal ruler rather than a divine being. He married Praxithea, usually described as a Naiad (water-nymph), who bore him sons, Cecrops, Pandorus, Metion, and perhaps also Thespius, Sicyon, Eupalamus, and Orneus. Their daughters were Procris (who married Cephalus), Orithyia (who married Boreas), Chthonia, and Creusa. During Erechtheus' reign at Athens, a war broke out with neighbouring Eleusis, whose people appealed to the Thracian king Eumolpus (according to an alternative version, Eumolpus was Orithyia's grandson, in which case he could not have fulfilled this role). The Athenians were hard pressed. Erechtheus enquired of Delphi how he might meet the threat, and was told that he could do so only by the sacrifice of one of his daughters. Chthonia was chosen by her parents as the victim and died, perhaps by her own consent (there was a story that her sisters killed themselves in sympathy with her, but this conflicted with other traditions). Erechtheus now proceeded to win the war, and Eleusis became Athenian territory, but kept the right to celebrate the mysteries of Demeter. During the hostilities either Eumolpus or his son was killed by Erechtheus, but Poseidon, Eumolpus' father, took vengeance on him by stabbing him with his trident. Xuthus, an ally of Erechtheus from Thessaly, may have ruled Athens for a while (and was said to have married Creusa). When, however, he was asked to nominate the new king of Athens from among Erechtheus' sons, he selected Cecrops, and was driven out of Athens by the other members of the family.

Ereuthalion An Arcadian champion who was killed by Nestor in a battle on the River Celadon.

Erginus *1*. Son of Clymenus and king of the Minyans of Orchomenus in Boeotia. As Clymenus lay dying, killed by the Thebans, he made Erginus promise to avenge him. In consequence, Erginus led his army against Thebes, which was ruled by Creon at the time. Erginus won a victory, disarmed the Thebans and removed all their armour, and forced them to pay an annual tribute of a hundred head of cattle for twenty years. After Heracles, at the age of eighteen, had killed the lion on Mount Cithaeron, he came across Erginus' heralds who were going to Thebes to collect the tribute. He cut off their ears and noses, hanging them around their necks, and sent the heralds back in this condition to their master. He then proceeded to Thebes, which Erginus attacked. Armed by Athena and supported by the Thebans, Heracles defeated Erginus and laid his territory waste; Amphitryon, Heracles' stepfather, was killed in the battle. Heracles then imposed a tribute of two hundred cattle a year on Orchomenus. Erginus' fortunes were so reduced that he reached old age without marrying. He consulted the Delphic Oracle, which advised him to fit a new tip to his ploughshare. In consequence he married a young wife, and she bore him two sons, Trophonius and Agamedes.

Pindar wrote that the son of Clymenus challenged Calais and Zetes to a race to be run in armour, and beat them; this victory silenced the mockery of the women of Lemnos. He may, however, be referring to Erginus *2*.

2. An Argonaut, usually said to be a son of Poseidon. After the death of Tiphys, he took the helm of the *Argo*.

Eriboea *1*. Second wife of Aloeus. She told Hermes of the imprisonment of Ares by the Aloadae.

2. Another name for Periboea, daughter of Alcathous.

Erichthonius *1*. An early Attic hero and king of Athens; he is described as begotten by Hephaestus. For when Athena asked him to make her some armour, Hephaestus embraced Athena and wanted to possess her, but the warrior-maiden pushed him away, and his seed fell on the ground. A child was born from it and handed by Gaia (Earth) to Athena to look after – perhaps because it was the nearest Athena ever came to having a son of her own. Athena entrusted the infant, in a covered box, to the three daughters of Cecrops to guard, with orders not to look inside. Two of the girls, Pandrosus and Herse, disobeyed, and what they saw so terrified them that they leapt from the Acropolis and killed themselves. It was said that what they saw was a snake, or a creature half-child and half-serpent, or serpents coiled round a baby. This was Erichthonius, whom Athena took back and brought up in her temple on the Acropolis. Another tradition makes him the son of Hephaestus and Atthis, daughter of Cranaus.

When he reached manhood, Erichthonius drove out Amphictyon, who had usurped the throne of Athens from Cranaus. As king of Athens, he promoted the cult of Athena, setting her olive-wood image on the Acropolis and instituting the Great Panathenaea, her principal festival. Another story relates that since he had no feet – his lower portions were the back end of a snake – he invented the chariot to make him mobile; he was, therefore, translated to the sky after his death as the constellation Auriga, the Charioteer.

Like Erechtheus, with whom he is often confused, he was stated to have been married to Praxithea. He was worshipped after his death at Athens in the form of a serpent, and was represented by the sculptor Phidias in the Parthenon, behind the shield Athena bore on her famous statue, in this way. His son Pandion succeeded him as king of Athens.

2. Son of Dardanus and Batia, the daughter of Teucer. He succeeded his father as king of Dardania. He married Astyoche, a daughter of the River Simois, who bore him Tros.

Erigone *1.* Daughter of Icarius, a humble Athenian peasant. Ovid tells how Arachne included in her tapestry the scene of her seduction by Dionysus, who disguised himself as a bunch of grapes. Dionysus had shown Icarius how to cultivate the vine, and when he offered wine to his neighbours, they killed him, thinking he had given them poison. After searching for her father high and low, Erigone found his body and hanged herself. Many Athenian girls followed her example, until finally her ghost was appeased by offerings.

2. Daughter of Aegisthus and Clytemnestra. When Orestes killed her parents he tried to slay her as well, but Artemis rescued her, and he only caught her brother Aletes. Artemis made her a priestess of her cult in Attica. There were two accounts of what followed. One stated that Erigone brought Orestes to court for matricide (this was presumably his trial before the Areopagus, at which Athena acquitted him). The other recorded that she bore him an illegitimate son, Penthilus.

Erinyes *see* FURIES.

Eriphyle Daughter of Talaus and Lysimache. When Polynices and the Seven Champions undertook the war against Thebes, she was appointed to arbitrate between her husband the seer Amphiaraus and her brother Adrastus, king of Athens. Adrastus, the leader of the expedition, wanted Amphiaraus to join it, but the latter knew through his powers of prophecy that it would fail, and that he himself, if he joined it, would perish. However, Polynices bribed Eriphyle to decide in favour of Adrastus by giving her the necklace of his ancestress Harmonia, Cadmus' wife. Amphiaraus had solemnly forbidden Eriphyle to accept any gifts from Polynices; and now, knowing that he was going to die, he made his children swear that they would avenge their father and go out themselves, in due course, to conquer Thebes.

Alcmaeon, son of Amphiaraus and Eriphyle, fulfilled both his father's commands. He led the Epigoni to the capture of Thebes, placing Thersander on the throne. Then, on his return from the expedition, he slew his mother Eriphyle. However, her avenging Furies drove Alcmaeon mad, and he could find no rest until he had settled in a country which had not seen the light of day at the time when his mother was slain. He finally came to such a land in alluvial deposit at the mouth of the River Achelous.

Eris A goddess, the daughter of Nyx ('night'). Her name means 'strife', and she is little more than a personification of discord. However, she appears in the myth of the marriage of Peleus and Thetis. She came to the ceremony uninvited, and flung a golden apple into the midst of the gathering, inscribed with the legend 'for the fairest'. At Zeus' suggestion the three goddesses who claimed the title, Hera, Athena and Aphrodite, referred the choice between them to Paris. Aphrodite, who had offered him as a bribe the most beautiful woman on earth, Helen, was selected; and from this came the origins of the Trojan War.

Homer describes the deeds of Eris on the battlefield in the train of Ares, declaring that she could not stop what she had once started and grew from a small size to a gigantic stature; she wanted to hear nothing but the groans of dying men.

Another goddess of the same name, or the same goddess under another aspect, represented the spirit of emulation. A later, moralising version of the myths relating to Heracles told how, early in his career – perhaps at the time of his slaying of the lion on Mount

Cithaeron – he met two beautiful women at a crossroads. One, Sloth, offered him a life of ease and luxury. But the other, whom he chose in preference to her, was Strife: what she offered him was a life of struggle and incessant toil, crowned with great glory.

Eros The god of love (*eros* in Greek means love of the sexual kind). The Romans called him Amor ('love') or Cupido ('desire'). There are several varying accounts of this divinity in Greek tradition. Hesiod says that Eros was born at the beginning of time out of Chaos (the Void), together with Tartarus and Gaia; and that he brought about the union of the original father and mother, Uranus ('sky') and Gaia ('earth'), and presided over the subsequent marriages of their offspring, the gods, and, eventually, of men. In this tradition Eros is little more than a personification of the generative power which infuses living creatures and causes their reproduction; he antedates Aphrodite, the goddess of love.

According to a different version, Eros was a much younger god, a son of Aphrodite and her lover Ares. In keeping with this view of his parentage, he is depicted in classical art and literature as a strong, handsome, athletic man. In the classical period he was often regarded as the protector of homosexual love between men and youths. His statue was placed in gymnasia, and he was taken by the Sacred Band at Thebes as their patron. As a god of fertility he was worshipped at Thespiae in Boeotia and at Parium in Mysia. The metics or resident aliens at Athens set up a statue with an altar on the Acropolis to Anteros, a form of Eros meaning 'love requited', in memory of two young men, Meles, an Athenian, and Timagoras, a metic. Timagoras loved Meles, who scorned his love and told him to leap from the Acropolis to prove it; when he did so, Meles was overcome by remorse and killed himself in the same way.

In Hellenistic times, as love became increasingly romanticised in art and literature, the alternative conception of Eros as a child or baby with wings and a quiverful of arrows gained ground; indeed the god was frequently made plural, as the Erotes (Latin: *Cupidines*), because the number of passions he represented seemed manifold. There arose the conceit that some of his arrows were tipped with gold to create passionate desire in his victims, and others with lead to turn people away from those who fell in love with them: thus Eros could both provoke love and frustrate it. This childlike Eros is familiar in the works of the Roman poets, and Virgil tells how Venus used him to make Dido fall in love with Aeneas. For the most famous of Cupid's myths, *see* PSYCHE.

Erysichthon Son of Triopas, king of Dotion in Thessaly, or of Myrmidon. Erysichthon (called Aethon, 'the blazing', by the historian Hellanicus) needed timber to build a banqueting-hall. An impious man, he cut down Demeter's sacred oak-grove where the nymphs were wont to dance. But as he laid his axe to the wood, blood flowed from the gash, and when a bystander objected, Erysichthon lopped off his head. The hamadryads (tree-spirits) of the grove called on Demeter, who came in the guise of her own priestess and begged him to spare the holy wood. However he only laughed at her. Whereupon the goddess, telling him to carry on with his plans, since he would find himself very much in need of a dining room, sent an Oread (mountain nymph) to Peina ('Hunger'), asking her to plague Erysichthon with a ravenous appetite; and Peina flew to his bedroom where he was asleep, and crept into his body. He woke up with a burning desire to eat, which could not be appeased. When he had consumed all his wealth in supplying himself with food, he had nothing left but his daughter Mestra, Poseidon's mistress. To procure further provisions, he sold the girl into slavery. She, however, asked Poseidon to rescue her, and he gave her the power to change into the shape of all manner of animals, so that she was able to find various kinds of food for her father. Even this gift, however, did not save Erysichthon for ever, and in the end he started to devour his own flesh and died.

Erythea *see* HESPERIDES.

Eryx Son of Aphrodite and Poseidon or Butes; king of part of north-western Sicily. On a mountain in that area he built the city of Eryx, founding a famous sanctuary for the worship of his mother. When one of Geryon's cattle wandered into his territory, Heracles came in search of it, and Eryx, as was his custom with newcomers, challenged him to a wrestling match; but Heracles killed him. Aeneas, the half-brother of Eryx, later visited the place, and honoured him as a hero or demi-god with sacrifices.

Etearchus *see* BATTUS I.

Eteocles *1*. An early king of Orchomenus in Boeotia, son of Andreus and Evippe or of the river-god Cephisus (a river in Boeotia).
2. Son of Oedipus, king of Thebes, and of his wife and mother Jocasta. When the incest they had committed became known to them, Jocasta hanged herself and Oedipus blinded himself with the pin of her brooch. Creon took over control of the state as regent. Eteocles and his brother Polynices twice insulted Oedipus, whom, according to one tradition, Creon had prevailed upon to stay in or near Thebes. The first insult is obscure and had to do with some of the silver vessels of Oedipus' father Laius, which the boys set before their blind father: this act for some reason offended Oedipus. The second insult is clearer. Even

after his fall, it was customary for the sons to bring the king the royal portion of meat, the shoulder; one day they tried to deceive him by giving him the haunch. Incensed by these wrongs, Oedipus solemnly cursed both his sons, praying that they might perish by one another's hands. Sophocles, however, recounts a different version, indicating that Creon, unwilling to let Thebes continue to be polluted by the presence of the incestuous king, sent Oedipus into exile immediately after his downfall, and that Oedipus cursed his sons for doing nothing to prevent his banishment.

When they were of age to rule, Eteocles and Polynices agreed to share the kingship between them, each ruling for an alternate year, while the other went abroad. According to Sophocles' *Oedipus at Colonus*, Polynices ruled first and banished Oedipus during his year of office. More often, however, it was Eteocles who was ascribed the first year's rule, either because he was the elder (though this is not the unanimous view), or as a result of the drawing of lots; and at the end of this time, supported by Creon, he was said to have refused to hand over the power to his brother. Meanwhile Polynices had gone to Argos, where he married Argia, King Adrastus' daughter, who bore him a son, Thersander. Eteocles had also married and begotten a son, Laodamas. According to the geographer Pausanias, the order of events was different. Polynices had left Thebes in order to avoid Oedipus' curse, and had settled in Argos, marrying Argia. When Eteocles came to the throne, he recalled Polynices; they quarrelled, and Polynices returned to Argos, intending to win the throne of Thebes by force.

When, for one reason or another, Eteocles had made it clear that he was not going to yield the throne to Polynices, Adrastus of Argos, Polynices' father-in-law, collected a large army together, including the Seven Champions who gave their name to Aeschylus' play *Seven Against Thebes*. Then, in spite of the warnings of the seer Amphiaraus that the expedition would fail disastrously, he besieged the city. First, however, Tydeus was sent to Thebes as an ambassador to demand the throne for Polynices; but his request was refused. According to one story, he now proceeded to participate in Theban athletic contests, with such success that Eteocles, in a fit of jealousy, had him waylaid on his way back: but Tydeus killed all his fifty assailants except one, Maeon.

The battle before Thebes was a disaster for Polynices' army. He himself attacked the gate which Eteocles was defending; the brothers met in single combat and fell at each other's hands, thus fulfilling Oedipus' curse. Creon was left as sole ruler of Thebes until such time as Eteocles' son should grow up. He ordered the Theban dead to be buried with honour, and Eteocles to be given a royal funeral. The enemy, however, and especially Polynices, were to be left lying outside the city to rot. According to Euripides' *Suppliant Women*, Theseus of Athens listened to an appeal by the mothers of the dead Seven Champions, and forced Creon to bury the Argives. There was also a tradition that Antigone, sister of Eteocles and Polynices, aided by Argia, dragged Polynices' dead body on to Eteocles' funeral pyre and gave him due burial in that way.

In addition to the versions of the story recounted by the three great Greek tragedians, the Roman poet Statius gave an account of it in his *Thebais*.

Eteoclus An Argive, the son of Iphis 2; one of the Seven Champions led by Polynices against Thebes. In spite of his royal birth, he was said to be a poor man, and respected for his honesty. He was killed in the battle by a Theban champion, Megareus, son of Creon, at the Neistan Gate.

Eubuleus ('of good counsel'). *1.* A euphemistic title of the god Hades, or another god of the Underworld.

2. Son of Dysaules, he is sometimes described as the brother of Triptolemus (who is sometimes, however, known as a son of Celeus). Eubuleus was a swineherd who, in one version of the story of Persephone's rape, told Demeter of her daughter's disappearance. When Hades' chariot returned to the Underworld carrying Persephone, his swine were swallowed up by the ground.

Euchenor Son of the seer Polyidus; he lived in Corinth and was very rich. He appears to have been under some obligation to join the expedition to fight the Trojan War; if he did not go, he would be liable to pay a heavy fine. His father predicted that his only alternatives were a swift death at Troy or a lingering death from disease at home. He chose the former: and Paris killed him with an arrow.

Eudora *see* HYADES.

Eudorus Son of Hermes and Polymele. When his mother married Echecles, his maternal grandfather Phylas brought him up. In the Trojan War he led one of the squadrons of Myrmidons under Achilles.

Eumaeus The faithful swineherd of Odysseus and of his father Laertes before him. He was a prince by birth, the son of Ormenus son of Ctesius, and his father was king of an island called Syrie. When a Phoenician ship had landed on this island, one of the sailors seduced a Phoenician slave-girl of Ctesius' household, and she escaped with them, bringing the child Eumaeus with her. The woman died at sea seven days later, and Eumaeus was sold to Laertes, king of Ithaca. Eumaeus served the royal household well, and during Odysseus' absence he tried to keep the pigs out of the hands of the greedy suitors. Odysseus, on his return, came first of all to Eumaeus' hut, disguised as an old beggar, and Eumaeus entertained him generously. It was in his hut that Odysseus revealed his identity to his own son Telemachus. Later in the great hall of Ithaca, the swineherd gave Odysseus help in defeating the suitors.

Eumelus *1.* King of Patrae in Achaea. Triptolemus taught him the cultivation of corn and became his close friend. His son Antheas was killed while trying to ride Triptolemus' chariot, which was drawn by winged serpents.
2. Son of Admetus and Alcestis, he became king of Pherae in Thessaly in succession to his father, and led a contingent to the Trojan War in eleven ships. He possessed superb mares, reared by Apollo for Admetus. With these he would have won the chariot race at Patroclus' funeral games, had not Athena intervened to help Diomedes, breaking the yoke of Eumelus' chariot. Eumelus married Iphthime, sister of Penelope.

Eumenides Literally 'the Kind Ones'; the title was usually applied as a euphemism to the Furies and in this respect was used by Aeschylus as the title of the third play in his trilogy the *Oresteia*. *See* FURIES.

Eumolpus ('sweet singer') *1.* Son of Poseidon and Chione *1* or *2*. His mother was ashamed to bear a bastard and flung her baby into the sea; but Poseidon caught him, and gave him to Benthesicyme, his daughter by Amphitrite, to rear. She was married to a king of the Ethiopians, who, when Eumolpus grew up, gave him one of his daughters in marriage; she bore him a son called Ismarus. But Eumolpus tried to rape his wife's sister and was banished together with his son. He fled to Thrace, where he was sheltered by Tegyrius, who gave

him his daughter in marriage. But Eumolpus plotted against his father-in-law and was banished once again, moving to Eleusis, where he made many friends. He was later asked back by Tegyrius who, being old and childless, made him his heir. When war broke out between Athens and Eleusis, Eumolpus came to the aid of the Eleusinians; but both he and his son were killed. Poseidon, in his anger, took vengeance on the Athenians by slaying their king Erechtheus.

Eumolpus is associated with the foundation of the Eleusinian Mysteries, in company with Celeus. He initiated Heracles into the Mysteries, after he had purified him for slaying the Centaurs. Eumolpus was the ancestor of the Eleusinian family of the Eumolpidae, and through his son Ceryx of the Ceryces family.
2. see TENES.

Euneus Son of Jason and Hypsipyle, queen of Lemnos. According to Euripides, he and his brother Thoas rescued their mother from captivity in Nemea; arriving by chance at the house, to which she admitted them, they recognised her and carried her off. Euneus supplied the Greek forces in the Trojan War with wine.

Eunomus Son of Architeles; he was the cup-bearer of Oeneus. After Heracles had married Oeneus' daughter Deianira, he accidentally killed Eunomus one evening, when the boy spilled wine over him; Heracles had merely meant to box his ears, but he underestimated his own strength, and the blow was so violent that it killed the youth. In consequence, Heracles went into exile.

Eupalamus ('handy', 'skilful') Son of Erechtheus and father of Daedalus.

Euphemus Son of Poseidon and Europe, whose father was Tityus. Euphemus, who lived on the Cape of Taenarum and was reputed for his swiftness, joined the Argonauts. When the *Argo* was returning home from the quest of the Golden Fleece, she was driven back from the Peloponnese to Libya, where she was deposited far inland by a great wave and stranded. The Argonauts carried their ship twelve days as far as Lake Tritonis, where they were at first unable to find an outlet to the sea. The god Triton then appeared to them in human form, pretending to be a local king, Eurypylus, son of Poseidon. He gave them directions, and presented them with a clod of earth, which Euphemus accepted. The clod represented sovereignty, and Euphemus had a dream in which it turned into a woman with whom he had sexual intercourse. He felt guilty after this act, according to his dream, but the woman comforted him by disclosing that she was Triton's daughter: if he gave her a home in the sea, Libya, her father's land, would nurse his children. When Euphemus awoke, Jason interpreted what he had dreamt, explaining that if the clod fell into the sea an island would grow from it, and there Euphemus' descendants would find a home. Moreover, from the island settlers would proceed to Libya and found a new colony there. Medea prophesied that if he let the clod fall into the sea at Taenarum, where there was an entrance to Hades' kingdom, the colony would be established in Libya in four generations; otherwise his posterity would have to wait much longer. Euphemus, however, dropped it into the sea some way north of Crete and the island of Calliste arose from it. Many generations later this island was settled by Euphemus' descendants, led by Theras, who renamed it Thera. These people had originally come from Lemnos (from which Euphemus' wife originated), but had been expelled from it by the Lydians. They had moved on to Sparta, and it was from there that they had made their way to Thera. Fi-

nally a descendant of these settlers, Battus, led a party of Therans to Libya, where after many tribulations he founded Cyrene.

Euphorbus Son of Panthous, a Dardanian. In the Trojan War, Euphorbus attacked Patroclus with his spear and hit him midway between the shoulder blades. Patroclus, by Apollo's agency, was stunned, but Euphorbus did not wait to fight him. When shortly afterwards Hector brought Patroclus down, Euphorbus wished to strip the corpse, but Menelaus spotted him. He warned Menelaus not to interfere and cast a spear at him, but in vain. Menelaus then pierced Euphorbus' throat with his spear and laid him low.

The Greek philosopher and mystic Pythagoras believed that he was a subsequent incarnation of Euphorbus, whose soul had transmigrated into his own body.

Euphrosyne *see* GRACES.

Eupithes An Ithacan nobleman whose life Odysseus saved when Eupithes, with the people of the Taphian Islands, had made a piratical raid on the Thesprotians. The Thesprotians wanted his head, but Odysseus protected him. His son Antinous showed ingratitude for this favour by his insolent behaviour, in Odysseus' absence, to his wife Penelope (of whom he was one of the principal suitors) and his son Telemachus. After Odysseus had killed Antinous and the other suitors, Eupithes led the people of Ithaca in a rebellion against him, but was killed by Laertes, Odysseus' aged father.

Europa Daughter of the Phoenician king Agenor and his wife Telephassa. Zeus saw the girl playing with her maidens by the sea, and fell in love with her. Taking the form of a handsome white bull, he wandered among the girls and lay down, allowing himself to be stroked (though some authorities held that the bull was not Zeus himself, but a bait he sent to lure the girl to him). Europa found him so gentle and sleek that she eventually climbed on his back, whereupon, rising up, he moved off into the sea and swam far out into the deep water. Eventually he and Europa disappeared from the view of Europa's companions, who never saw her again. She was carried to Crete, where the bull deposited her on the land and revealed itself as Zeus. He then made love to her either under a plane tree, which from that time onwards has been evergreen, or else in the Dictaean cave where he had been brought up. Europa bore Zeus three sons: Minos, Rhadamanthys, and Sarpedon. Zeus gave her three presents: an unerring spear, Laelaps the inexorable hound, and Talos, the bronze man who walked every day around Crete and drove off strangers. Asterius, king of Crete, eventually married Europa. She bore him a daughter, named Crete, and he adopted her sons as his own, making Minos his heir.

Europa's father Agenor was very anxious for the return of his daughter and sent his sons Cadmus, Phoenix, and Cilix to look for her, with instructions not to return without her. His wife went too; and he never saw any of them again.

Europa gave her name to the continent of Europe; the bull is commemorated in the stars as the constellation Taurus.

Europe Daughter of Tityus; mother of Euphemus.

Eurotas Son of Lelex; an early king of Laconia in the southern Peloponnese. His daughter Sparte gave her name to its chief city, founded by her husband Lacedaemon.

Eurus The south-east or, more loosely, east wind; like other winds, a son of Astraeus ('starry') and Eos ('dawn'). He was described as blustery and wet. The Romans also called him Volturnus.

Euryale *1. see* GORGONS.
2. Daughter of Minos; the mother, by Poseidon, of Orion.

Euryalus *1.* Son of Mecisteus, an Argive nobleman; an ally of the Epigoni. With Diomedes he became a guardian of Cyanippus, Adrastus' grandson and the heir to the throne of Argos. Euryalus accompanied Diomedes to Troy as one of the commanders of the Argive contingent. He was said to have sailed with the Argonauts (though elsewhere the same claim was made for his grandfather Talaus).
2. A Trojan companion of Aeneas. *See* GISUS.

Euryanassa ('ruling a broad land') Daughter of the River Pactolus.

Eurybates An Ithacan herald who came with Odysseus to the Trojan War. Agamemnon sent him with Talthybius to fetch Briseis from Achilles' tent. Later he took with him Agamemnon's offer of reconciliation and a large present, which Achilles refused.

Eurybia Daughter of Pontus and Gaia; she mated with Crius.

Euryclea Odysseus' old nurse, who recognised him on his return home from Troy. Odysseus had on his leg a great scar, made by a wild boar's tusk. This Euryclea recognised, as she bathed Odysseus' feet in Penelope's quarters; and in her excitement she dropped the basin. Penelope, however, did not detect the reason for her surprise, and Odysseus was able to hush Euryclea with a threat. Later, when he had slain the suitors, she was exultant and again had to be silenced. She then informed her master which of the serving women had betrayed him by consorting with the suitors, and they were put to death.

Eurydamas An Argonaut, a son of Irus.

Eurydice *1.* A Thracian Dryad (tree-nymph), loved by Orpheus. For her story, *see* ORPHEUS.
2. Mother of Danae; her husband was Acrisius and her father Lacedaemon, the king and founder of Sparta.
3. Wife of Creon, regent of Thebes. In Sophocles' tragedy the *Antigone*, Eurydice cursed her husband for the doom he had brought upon his whole family and then stabbed herself. All their children were dead, and the suicide of the youngest son Haemon over Antigone's corpse had been the final blow. The eldest, whose name was likewise Haemon, had been killed by the Sphinx, and the second, Menoeceus or Megareus, had immolated himself to save Thebes in the war against the Seven.
4. Daughter of Adrastus *2* and wife of Ilus, king of Troy.

Eurylochus Husband of Odysseus' sister. He was a nobleman from the island of Same (Cephallenia) and he accompanied Odysseus in the Trojan War and upon his return journey. It was he who led the first scouting party to Circe's palace; alone of his companions he refrained from entering the palace, and thus escaped drinking Circe's magic potion, which turned the rest of the men into swine. He brought back the news to Odysseus and could not be persuaded to return to the palace even after his leader with Hermes' help had tricked Circe into offering him unfeigned hospitality; but soon afterwards he overcame his fear. When Odysseus, later in his voyage, came to the island of the Sun-god Helios, Eurylochus persuaded his shipmates to kill the sacred cattle for food, although Tiresias had solemnly warned Odysseus against allowing this to be done. Only Odysseus himself had

no part in the sacrilege, since he was asleep. Zeus punished Eurylochus and the rest of the crew by wiping them out in a great storm, from which only Odysseus escaped.

Eurymachus Son of the Ithacan nobleman Polybus; a suitor of Odysseus' wife Penelope. He was the politest and least unacceptable of her suitors; and during the confrontation in the great hall of the palace he appealed to Odysseus. But Odysseus gave him no quarter and shot him with an arrow, second only after Antinous. His mistress was Melantho.

Eurymedon *see* GIANTS.

Eurynome *1.* Daughter of Oceanus and Tethys; she bore the Graces to Zeus. The epic poet Apollonius Rhodius cites an obscure tradition that before Cronos ruled Olympus, Eurynome and the Titan Ophion, her husband, had held sway there. She was depicted (especially in her temple at Phigalia in Arcadia) as a woman with the tail of a fish.
2. Daughter of Nisus, king of Megara; she married Glaucus, king of Ephyra (Corinth), and bore Bellerophon to the god Poseidon. Athena was said to have taught her great wisdom.

Euryphaessa *see* THEIA.

Eurypylus *1.* Son of Poseidon and king of part of Libya. When Triton aided the Argonauts at Lake Tritonis and gave Euphemus a clod of earth as a parting gift, he took Eurypylus' form.
2. A Mysian, son of Telephus, king of Pergamum, and of Astyoche, a daughter of Priam. His mother was most unwilling to allow him to depart to help the Trojans against the Greeks, until Priam bribed her with a golden vine. Euryplus then led a large force of Mysians to Troy. He slew Machaon the physician, Asclepius' son, and caused great havoc among the Greeks; indeed, he was pre-

vented from burning their ships only by
the arrival of Neoptolemus (son of Achilles, by this time dead), who killed him
with his sword.

3. Son of Evaemon from Ormenion in
Thessaly. A former suitor of Helen, he
led forty ships from Thessaly to the
Trojan War, and killed Axion, a son of
Priam, and Apisaon, son of Phausius,
but was hit in the leg by Paris with an
arrow. As he limped back to base, he
was met by Patroclus, who had been to
Nestor to get news of the fighting for
Achilles. Machaon being wounded,
there was no doctor available, and so
Eurypylus was tended by Patroclus.

He was one of the Greeks concealed
in the Wooden Horse. Then, when the
city was being sacked, he discovered a
chest, which had been left behind by
Aeneas or Cassandra because it would
be a curse to any Greek who took it.
Opening the chest, Eurypylus found in
it an ancient wooden image of Dionysus,
which had been carved by Hephaestus
and given to Dardanus by Zeus; it was
of such great sanctity that it drove
Eurypylus mad. The Delphic Oracle told
him that he would be cured only if he
took the image to a place where men
made an unfamiliar sacrifice. When he
reached Patrae, Eurypylus found the
people preparing to sacrifice a boy and
a girl to Artemis. Realising that this was
the sacrifice indicated by the oracle, he
showed the people the image of Dionysus; and it dawned on them that here
was the fulfilment of an oracle which
they, too, had received, bidding them
give up human sacrifice when a strange
king should come to them bringing a
strange god. Eurypylus was cured, and
the people of Patrae adopted the worship of Dionysus.

4. Son of Poseidon by Astypalaea; king of
the Meropes on the island of Cos. After
Heracles had sacked Troy and was on his
homeward voyage, Hera in her anger sent
against him a great storm which drove
him and his fleet on to the coast of Cos.

The Meropes thought that the Greeks
were pirates and tried to drive them off.
However Heracles captured their city by
night and killed Eurypylus, though he
was wounded in his turn by Chalcodon.

Eurysaces Son of Aias *1* and Tecmessa;
a king of Salamis.

Eurysthenes Son of Aristodemus and
the twin brother of Procles. The two
shared the rule of Sparta equally, thus
establishing the dual monarchy.

Eurystheus Son of Sthenelus and Nicippe or Menippe; king of the Argolid,
including Mycenae and Tiryns. He was
the bitterest enemy of Heracles, who
was enslaved to him while he performed
his Twelve Labours. For when Heracles,
Zeus' outstanding mortal son, was
about to be born to Alcmena, Hera,
jealous that she was to have no part in
the creation of the greatest of all heroes,
decided to deprive the child of his
human birthright, the rule of the Argolid. Zeus let fall the secret of Heracles'
impending birth by boasting to the gods
that 'that day a man would be born of
woman, of a race of Zeus' own blood,
who would rule those dwelling around
him'. However Sthenelus' wife Nicippe
(or Menippe) happened to be seven
months pregnant at the time, and as
Sthenelus was a descendant of Perseus,
his son would as truly fulfil the prophecy
as Heracles. Besides, after Amphitryon
had accidentally killed the previous king
of Mycenae, Sthenelus' brother Electryon, Sthenelus had seized its throne
for himself. So Hera, with the help of
Ilithyia, goddess of childbearing, accelerated the birth of Eurystheus and held
back Alcmena's delivery until the serving woman Galanthis tricked the goddess into abandoning her purpose: by
which time it was too late for Heracles
to fulfil Zeus' prophecy.

Thus Eurystheus became heir to the
Argolid, and when Heracles in a fit of

madness killed his wife Megara and their children, the Delphic Oracle ordered him to be enslaved to Eurystheus and perform ten (or twelve) Labours in that capacity. Jealous of Heracles' power and strength and of his right to the throne of the Argolid, Eurystheus imposed on him a series of tasks so formidable that no one but a true son and favourite of Zeus could have carried them out. Eurystheus, on the other hand, displayed cowardice: for example, when Heracles brought him the skin of the Nemean lion, he hid in a bronze storage-jar. Thereafter he refused to permit Heracles to enter his city (whether it was Tiryns or Mycenae is uncertain), and sent his uncle Copreus, a herald, to deliver messages to him. (In Euripides' play *The Children of Heracles*, he is depicted as cruel rather than cowardly.)

After Heracles' ascent to Olympus, Eurystheus continued to persecute him through his children. Ceyx, king of Trachis, declined to grant them his protection, since Eurystheus attacked him and ordered him to give them up; and so they fled to Attica. Here Demophon, son of Theseus, settled them at Marathon and fought a successful battle against Eurystheus. As the latter fled from Attica, Heracles' son Hyllus killed his persecutors at the Scironian Rocks on the Isthmus of Corinth. According to another version, Eurystheus was taken alive, but killed by order of Alcmena in spite of protests by the people of Athens. Since they had tried to spare him, Eurystheus promised the Athenians that his body would protect their land from invasion; and they buried him upon their frontiers.

Eurytion *1.* A Centaur who led the riot at the wedding of Pirithous and Hippodamia. He later attempted to rape Mnesimache, the daughter of King Dexamenus of Olenus, and was killed by Heracles, who was the king's guest. *See* CENTAURS.

2. The herdsman of the monster Geryon. *See* HERACLES.

3. Son of Actor and Demonassa, or of Actor's son Irus; king of Phthia. When Peleus took refuge there after murdering his brother Phocus, Actor purified him of the blood guilt and married him to his daughter Antigone, giving him a third of the kingdom. Eurytion sailed with Peleus on the *Argo*, and later accompanied him to the Calydonian boarhunt. But there Peleus, wildly casting his spear, accidentally killed Eurytion and did not dare return to Phthia. When Antigone heard the false report that Peleus was about to marry another woman, namely Sterope, the daughter of Acastus, she killed herself. After a year's exile Peleus returned to Phthia and, since Eurytion had not produced a son, took over his kingdom. *See* IRUS 2.

Eurytus *1.* King of Oechalia (of uncertain location; probably in Thessaly) and father of Iphitus. Eurytus held an archery competition, offering his daughter Iole to any man who could defeat himself and his son Iphitus. When Heracles won, Eurytus withheld the prize, as Heracles had already killed his children by Megara, and perhaps also Megara herself. Heracles left Oechalia in a fury, and at the same time a number of mares disappeared from Eurytus' stables. Later Eurytus was killed by Apollo for having dared to challenge him at archery. His son Iphitus (who, in Homer's account, was still alive at the time of Eurytus' death) went in search of the mares. According to this version, he had inherited his father's great bow, but gave this to Odysseus when he visited Sparta in the course of his search. Subsequently he went on to Tiryns and was entertained by Heracles, who killed him and kept the mares.

In another version of the story Eurytus was still alive at the time of the death of Iphitus, who had gone to Tiryns to ask Heracles to help him find the mares because, unlike his father, he believed in the hero's innocence of the theft. However Heracles killed Iphitus, either in anger at his presumption or in a fit of madness; and later he murdered Eurytus and abducted Iole – a deed which brought about his own death, since it prompted his wife Deianira to send him the tunic dipped in Nessus' blood, which burned him to death. Theseus gave Perigune, daughter of Sinis, to another of Eurytus' sons, Deioneus.

2. *see* GIANTS.

3. One of the Moliones.

Euterpe *see* MUSES.

Euthymus Son of the god of the River Ceacinus, in the toe of Italy. He was believed to have been a famous boxer, who enjoyed great success in the Olympic Games. Returning to Italy, he settled at the town of Temesa. There he discovered that the inhabitants were accustomed to sacrifice every year their most beautiful girl to the ghost of Odysseus' companion Polites, who had been stoned to death at this place for raping a Temesan maiden. They called his ghost 'the Hero'; and the Oracle of Delphi had warned them that this ceremony was necessary to appease its enmity. Euthymus, falling in love with the current victim, put on his armour and, when the ghost of Polites next manifested itself, attacked it, driving it down into the sea, from which it never reappeared. Then he made the girl designated as the victim his wife.

Evadne *1.* Daughter of Iphis and wife of Capaneus. After the siege of Thebes by the Seven, she flung herself on to her husband's funeral pyre and perished.

2. Daughter of Poseidon and the Laconian nymph Pitane. Her mother gave the child to Aepytus, son of Elatus, to look after. When she became pregnant, Aepytus consulted the Delphic Oracle and learnt that Apollo was responsible for his ward's condition. On returning from Delphi, however, Aepytus discovered that Evadne had already given birth to her child, which she had then concealed or abandoned. Apollo sent two serpents to care for the baby, which they fed with honey in a thicket among brambles and gilly-flowers. In due course Aepytus, under divine guidance, found the boy, whose name was Iamus (from *ia*, 'gilly-flowers'), and brought him up. Iamus inherited his father's gift of prophecy, and became the ancestor of a family of prophets, the Iamidae of Olympia. The story is told by Pindar.

Evander *1.* Originally a name of Pan or an Arcadian deity associated with him; he was especially honoured at Pallantion, a little town in Arcadia. According to one tradition, he was a son (like Pan) of Hermes (the Roman Mercury) and of Themis, a nymph of the River Ladon. In Italy he was sometimes identified with Faunus; in a more human form he was said to be a son of Echemus, king of Tegea.

In this humanised shape, he was introduced into the myth of Aeneas. According to the best known, Virgilian, version, he had emigrated from Arcadia sixty years before the fall of Troy, either under pressure from the Argives or because of an accidental homicide or a rebellion. His mother was believed to be Carmenta, a prophetic goddess like Themis. A connection between Aeneas and Evander was the Titan Atlas, the Arcadians' forebear, of whom Dardanus, ancestor of Aeneas, was a grandson. Faunus (an Italian equivalent of Pan, but a human king in this story) received Evander and his small company in Italy and offered him any of his land that he might desire. Evander, it was believed, chose the Palatine Hill, naming it Pallanteum after his home (Pallantion) in Arcadia; and thus he established a Greek settlement on the site of the future Rome. Already an old man when Aeneas came, he befriended the newcomer, and the two made common cause. Evander entertained Aeneas on the Palatine Hill and was his host at a festival commemorating a visit of Hercules to the place, when he had punished Cacus for stealing cattle and married one of Evander's daughters. Evander also had a son, Pallas, whom he entrusted to Aeneas as an ally at the head of a contingent of troops. But Pallas was killed by the enemy leader Turnus; and it was above all to avenge this deed that Aeneas, when he had Turnus at his mercy, refused to spare him.

2. Son of Sarpedon *1*; a king of Lycia.

Evenus *1.* Son of Ares by a mortal woman, Demonice. His daughter Marpessa was carried off by Idas, to whom Poseidon had given a chariot drawn by winged horses. Evenus pursued Idas until his own horses were worn out; then he killed them and drowned himself in the River Lycormas, which was thenceforth named after him. Idas carried his prize to Messenia, where Apollo in his turn tried to carry her off. But Zeus prevented him and gave her the choice between her two suitors. She selected Idas.

2. Son of Selepus; king of Lyrnessus near Troy. He was succeeded by his son Mynes, the husband of Briseis.

Evippe or **Euhippe** *see* PIERIDES

F

Fabula or **Faula** Acca Larentia, the wife of Faustulus – the shepherd who found Romulus and Remus in the she-wolf's lair and reared them – was, by virtue of her association with this animal, sometimes called *lupa*, which had a double meaning in Latin, since it signified both she-wolf and whore. Acca was therefore also called Faula, another name for whores, and this was sometimes altered to Fabula, literally 'legend' or 'story'.

A different tale also existed about Fabula. She was said to be a whore whom Hercules won at dice from the keeper of his temple when he visited the site of Rome in the time of Evander. Hercules played dice with the man for a free supper and a bedfellow, and won: whereupon the temple-keeper provided him with Fabula. She later married a certain Tarutius; but she had earned so much money from prostitution that she was able to leave a large estate to the Roman people.

Falernus *see* LIBER.

Fates (Greek: *Moirai*, Latin: *Parcae* or *Fata*) Usually conceived as three female deities who supervised fate rather than determined it. In the tale of Meleager's birth, however, the Fates seem to have a deciding role, and this myth suggests that their origin lay in the function of presiding over the birth of human beings and at that moment laying down what their lot in life was to be. For *Parcae* means 'those who bring forth the child' and *Moirai* the 'cutters-off' or 'allotters'. Seven days after Meleager was born, the Fates appeared to his mother and told her that he would die as soon as the brand burning in the fireplace was burnt out. She removed the brand, quenched it, and kept it until Meleager killed her brothers, whereupon she placed it on the fire again and Meleager died.

To Hesiod the Fates were three in number, the daughters of Nyx ('night'): Clotho ('the spinner'), Lachesis ('the drawing of lots') and Atropos ('inevitable'). He also called them the daughters of Zeus and Themis (whose name means 'order'). In this way he illustrated the ambiguity of their position: were they subject to Zeus or he to them? Could the gods alter the Fates' decrees? Many classical authors saw them as superior even to the gods, and indeed both Homer and Virgil describe how Zeus holds up an evenly balanced scale to discover what fate ordains, placing in it the respective lots of the heroes and seeing which way the balance will fall. In this way Zeus appears as an executor of destiny rather than its determining agent. Similarly Zeus knows that his son Sarpedon is fated to die at Patroclus' hands, and cannot, or will not, upset the decree of fate even to save one he loves so dearly. All he can do is to ensure that Sarpedon has a noble burial in his homeland of Lycia. And Aeschylus, in his play *Prometheus Bound*, likewise suggests that Zeus is subject to the decrees of fate.

In a later Greek tradition, the name Clotho with its reference to spinning gave rise to the picture of the Fates as three old women, spinning out men's destinies like thread: one drew them out, one measured them, and one cut them off.

In mythology the Fates played little part. They aided Zeus in his battles against the giants (in which they killed Agrius and Thoas with clubs) and against Typhon, whom they persuaded, when he was already under pressure from Zeus, to eat a diet of human food, assuring him, contrary to the truth, that it would strengthen him. Apollo, on the other hand, cheated the Fates on behalf of his friend Admetus by making them drunk, so that they allowed Admetus to live beyond his allotted span of time provided he could find a substitute to meet death in his place.

Faula see FABULA

Faunus An Italian god of the countryside, identified in due course with the Greek Pan. He possessed prophetic powers; the Romans believed that his voice issued from the Arsian forest on the night after a battle with the Etruscans, and pronounced that the Etruscans had lost one man more than the Romans. This caused the Romans to believe that they had won the battle, and they were consequently stimulated the next night into renewing the attack, whereupon they routed the enemy.

As a god, Faunus was considered to be the son of Picus and the grandson of Saturn. He was sometimes associated, even identified, with Evander, the Arcadian Greek who had settled on the site of Rome before Aeneas came. Pan was the god of Arcadia, and the name of Evander ('the good man') may have been believed to carry a similar significance to that of Faunus, since the latter was interpreted (with doubtful accuracy) as meaning 'favourable' or 'kind'. Faunus was also sometimes conceived of as a mortal: he was said to be a descendant of Mars who ruled over a kingdom on the Tiber and welcomed Evander the

Arcadian on his arrival in Italy, giving him land on the site of the future Rome. Faunus reputedly married a waternymph, Marica, and became the father of Latinus, king of the Latini at the time of the arrival of Aeneas, who eventually married his daughter Lavinia.

A myth related Faunus to the woodland god Picus and to Egeria, the waternymph loved by Numa Pompilius, the legendary second king of Rome. Egeria, who was very wise and imparted her wisdom to Numa, told him to leave wine at the spring where Faunus and Picus were accustomed to drink. By this means he caught them and obliged them to tell him how to summon the god Jupiter. When Jupiter appeared, Numa asked him how to avert the stroke of lightning, and induced him to list the ingredients of a sacrifice which would achieve this end: a head of garlic, human hair, a fish's life. These items represented Numa's clever alteration of Jupiter's intended demand for a human head and the sacrifice and life of a man.

Faunus was sometimes said to be the husband or father of the Bona Dea, who was also known as Fauna.

Faustulus The shepherd who found the babies Romulus and Remus in the she-wolf's lair after their abandonment by their great-uncle Amulius, king of Alba Longa. The name is a diminutive of the adjective *fautus*, 'lucky', 'propitious', perhaps a by-form or synonym (like 'Evander') of the name Faunus. He brought up the twins, suspecting their royal origin. He also preserved the cradle in which they had been cast on the Tiber by the royal servants; this helped their grandfather Numitor to recognise the pair.

Furies (Greek: *Erinyes*, Latin: *Furiae*) The Furies, female spirits of justice and vengeance, personify very ancient retributive ideas. They were usually said to have been born from the blood of

Uranus that fell upon Gaia, the Earth, when Cronos castrated him, i.e. they were chthonic (earth) deities. According to a variant account, they were born from Nyx (Night). Their number was usually left indeterminate, though Virgil, probably from an Alexandrian source, recognised three, Alecto, Megaera, and Tisiphone (respectively 'unceasing', 'grudging', and 'avenging murder'). In a wide sense, the Furies stood for the rightness of things within the established order. In the *Iliad*, for example, they silenced the horse Xanthus; and the philosopher Heraclitus declared that, if the Sun decided to change his course, they would prevent him from doing so. But for the most part they were understood as the persecutors of men and women who transgressed 'natural' laws, with special reference to those who broke kinship ties by committing parricide, killing a brother, or murdering a fellow-clansman. It was believed in early epochs that human beings might not have the possibility or even the right to punish such horrible crimes, and it was left to the dead man's Furies to pursue their perpetrator and exact retribution. The conception of Nemesis was similar, and indeed her function overlaps that of the Furies; she too ensured that vengeance was ultimately extracted.

In Aeschylus' *Eumenides*, the third play in the *Oresteia*, his trilogy on the death of Agamemnon and the vengeance of his children, the Furies haunted Orestes, who had murdered his mother Clytemnestra in revenge for her killing of his father Agamemnon. In this tragedy, which was said to have caused genuine terror to the audience at its first production, the Furies were the members of the chorus. From artistic representations it may be supposed that they appeared carrying whips and torches, and were perhaps wreathed with snakes. Only the deed which Orestes had committed interested the Furies, not its justice or any plea of mitigation. Even

Apollo was put about to combat their implacable vengeance, though he himself had sanctioned Orestes' murder of Clytemnestra, and had given him protection at Delphi, his most sacred shrine. The Furies however, it was said by Aeschylus, pursued him even there, and would not let him go, until persuaded by the gods to accept the verdict of the antique Athenian court of the Areopagus. There Athena, as patron of the city, intervened in order to equalise the votes, thus giving Orestes his acquittal, but only on condition of his fetching a sacred image of Artemis from the land of the Tauri; and the Furies, in the tamed form of the *Eumenides* ('kind-hearted') or *Semnai Theai* ('venerable goddesses'), were welcomed to Athens.

The Furies also haunted Alcmaeon, another slayer of his mother. Like Orestes, he had received Apollo's sanction for thus avenging his father, yet was pursued by the Furies across Greece until he found refuge in a new land which had not existed at the time of his mother's death – thus escaping the power of his pursuers.

The effect of the Furies upon their victim was madness; hence their Latin name (from *furor*). Whatever their Greek name *Erinyes* may have meant – for its derivation is uncertain – the Greeks hesitated to use the term openly, and it was to avert its evil omen that the Athenians preferred to employ the euphemisms mentioned above. In Arcadia there was a place containing two shrines of the Erinyes. At one of them, they were known as *Maniai* ('senders of madness'); this was the spot where, in black robes, they had first assailed Orestes. Nearby, according to the travel-writer Pausanias, was another shrine where they were associated with the Graces (*Charites*, 'spirits of forgiveness'); it was here that they had later blessed Orestes, in white robes, after his recovery. He offered a sin-offering to the Maniai and a thank-offering to the Charites.

The Furies were often thought of as having their natural abode in Tartarus, the Greek Hell, where, when not issuing forth on to the earth to punish living sinners, they applied everlasting torture to the eternally damned. This view of their dwelling-place harmonised with the stories of their birth from Earth or Night, but according to an alternative tradition they were actually believed to be sprung from Hades, god of Tartarus, and Persephone, in common with whom they had a dual nature, benign and malignant.

G

Gaia or Ge (Latin: *Terra* or *Tellus*)
The Earth. According to Hesiod's *Theogony*, this goddess was the first creature to be born from the primeval
Chaos, together with Tartarus (the Underworld), Nyx (Night), Erebus (Darkness), and Eros, the spirit of generative
love. Out of Gaia issued forth Uranus
(Sky), Pontus (Sea), and the Mountains.
Uranus then mated with his mother and
produced the Titans and Titanesses, including Cronos and Rhea, the parents
of Zeus, and his five siblings; and Oceanus and Tethys, deities of the great River
of Ocean coiling itself round the circle
of the lands. Uranus and Gaia also
brought forth the three original Cyclopes, Brontes, Steropes and Arges, and
the Hundred-Armed giants, Cottus, Briareos and Gyes. Meanwhile Nyx and
Erebus mated to give birth to Hemera
(Day) and Aether (the Upper Atmosphere).

Uranus hated the monstrous Cyclopes
and Hundred-Armed giants and refused
to let them see the light, pushing them
back down again into their mother's
womb so that Gaia's body was wracked
with pain. Infuriated with the tyranny
of her mate, she gave her son Cronos a
flint sickle and bade him castrate his
father when next he lay on her. This
Cronos did, flinging the severed genitals
far off into the sea. From the drops of
blood that fell upon the ground sprang
the Erinyes (Furies), the giants (distinct
from the Hundred-Armed giants: *see*
GIANTS), and the Meliae (Nymphs of
the ash trees). The member itself, however, floated upon the sea and came to
land at Paphos in Cyprus – or on the

island of Cythera near Laconia – where
the foam (*aphros*) that had gathered
about it was transformed into the goddess of love, Aphrodite.

But Cronos turned out to be as tyrannical to his family as his father Uranus
had been before him, casting his brothers the Cyclopes and Hundred-Armed
giants down into Tartarus and eating
his children by Rhea whenever she
brought them forth. This he did because
of a warning by Gaia and Uranus that
one of them would overthrow him. However Gaia helped Rhea to save the last
of her children, Zeus. For when Cronos
was about to swallow the child, she
offered him a great stone which he swallowed instead, and then she hid the baby
in a cave on Crete, where he grew up.

When Zeus came to maturity, he prepared to attack his father Cronos and
certain of the Titans who supported
him. Moreover Rhea, or Metis, gave
Cronos an emetic, causing him to spew
up his other children, the gods Poseidon
and Hades and the goddesses Demeter,
Hestia, and Hera. Zeus freed the captive
Cyclopes and Hundred-Armed giants
from Tartarus, arming them with thunderbolts, and the two parties engaged in
a great war lasting for ten years. When
Zeus had finally won, he imprisoned the
hostile Titans, including his father, in
the depths of Tartarus. But this offended
Gaia, who considered his imprisonment
of the Titans high-handed. Mating with
Tartarus, she brought forth the monster
Typhon as her champion, and she incited the giants (not the Hundred-
Armed), led by Eurymedon, Alcyoneus,
and Porphyrion, to rebel against Zeus:

the war was known as the Gigantomachy. She brought forth a plant whose juice would make the giants immortal and invincible in battle, but Zeus, causing darkness to reign everywhere, himself discovered the plant and removed it. Then, with much difficulty, aided by friendly gods and goddesses, he contrived to defeat his enemies, and locked them in the ground from which they had come.

However Gaia also performed a service for Zeus. For when he married his first wife Metis, she warned him that a son of the union would replace him as lord of the gods: whereupon he swallowed Metis and later brought forth Athena from his head. Gaia also attended the wedding of Zeus and Hera, giving Hera the golden apples which the Hesperides guarded.

She was closely associated with oracles and prophecy. It was she, according to tradition, who founded the oracular shrine of Delphi, originally devoted to her worship. She transferred it to Themis; but Themis surrendered her rights to the Titaness Phoebe, who in turn gave the oracle to Apollo. The earth-snake Python belonged to Gaia, and when Apollo killed it, he had to compensate for the murder by establishing the Pythian Games and by employing the Pythian priestess to oversee his oracle. Gaia supervised oaths, many of which were made in her name; she punished those who broke them and sent the Erinyes (Furies) to avenge her.

She mated with her son Pontus, and bore a number of marine deities, Nereus (father of the Nereids, including Thetis), Thaumas, Phorcys, Ceto, and Eurybia. She also brought forth many other children, several of them monsters: Echidna by a union with Tartarus, Erichthonius from the seed of Hephaestus, and (according to some accounts) Triptolemus from Oceanus. She created the scorpion which attacked the gigantic hunter Orion, when he threatened to destroy all the wild beasts of the earth, and stung him to death. Gaia possessed a widespread cult in Greece (although her husband Uranus had none).

Galanthis The slave girl of Alcmena who, when Ilithyia was endeavouring to prevent the birth of Heracles by sitting outside Alcmena's bedroom with legs and fingers crossed, deceived the goddess by a trick, thus allowing the child to be born. For, after seven days' waiting, she ran out of Alcmena's bedroom shouting 'Congratulate my mistress: she is safely delivered'. Thereupon the surprised Ilithyia, who had been sitting outside, rushed into the room, thus undoing the knotted pose she had assumed to block the delivery. Though she was no longer able to prevent the hero's birth, Ilithyia turned Galanthis into a weasel (*gale* in Greek).

Galatea Daughter of Nereus and Doris. Her name means 'milk-white'. She lived in the sea off Sicily, where the Cyclops Polyphemus pastured his flocks of sheep and goats. He became infatuated with her and pursued her. But Galatea, who preferred a young shepherd called Acis, a son of Pan and of the nymph Simaethis, spurned the overtures of Polyphemus, detesting his hideous appearance. Polyphemus was furiously jealous of Acis, but his grotesque serenades were merely mocked by the young pair. One day, catching them asleep together on a grassy bank, the Cyclops woke them and pursued Acis, picking up a huge boulder and crushing him beneath it. The broken-hearted Galatea caused a spring of water to issue from beneath the boulder, and made Acis into the god of the stream. In another version of the story there was no Acis, and Polyphemus, with his songs and piping, finally won the nymph's heart.

Ganymede Son of Tros, founder of

Troy, or of Laomedon, father of the Trojan king Priam. A youth of great beauty, he was abducted by the gods, according to Homer, to live among them as Zeus' cup-bearer. According to later authors, Zeus alone was the abductor of Ganymede, who was snatched up in a whirlwind or by one of Zeus' eagles, or by Zeus himself in the form of an eagle. Then Zeus sent Hermes to the boy's father, with news of the honour that had been done to his son; as a recompense, he offered the father a pair of immortal mares – from which the royal stud of Troy was descended – and a golden vine, the work of Hephaestus. Zeus became the lover of Ganymede and set him in the sky as the constellation of Aquarius, the water-carrier, with the eagle (Aquila) beside him.

Garamas see AMPHITHEMIS.

Gelonus see HERACLES (tenth Labour).

Geryon or **Geryones** or **Geryoneus** Son of Chrysaor and Callirrhoe the Oceanid. A three-headed, even three-bodied, monster, he lived on an island called Erythea ('the Red') far off to the West in the Ocean, beyond the Pillars of Heracles. His rich flocks of cattle were guarded by a herdsman called Eurytion and his two-headed dog Orthus ('straight') or Orthrus ('early'), offspring of the monsters Echidna and Typhon. Heracles' tenth Labour for Eurystheus was to steal Geryon's cattle and drive them to Mycenae. Heracles sailed out on the stream of Ocean in a golden cup which Oceanus or Helios, under the threat of his poisoned arrows, had bestowed upon him. Sailing to the West, he landed on Geryon's island and climbed a mountain there. Attacked by Orthus, he clubbed the dog to death and his master Eurytion as well. But as he was about to drive the cattle off, he was spied by Menoetes, Hades' herdsman, who told Geryon what had happened. Geryon pursued

Heracles as far as the river Anthemus, where the hero shot him dead.

Giants (Gigantes) Sometimes called *Gegeneis*, 'born from the Earth'.

The giants, who were mainly of human shape but had serpents' tails attached to their legs or feet, sprang from Gaia (Earth) where the blood from Uranus' genitals, severed by Cronos, touched the ground; together with them there also sprang up the Erinyes (Furies) and the Meliae (nymphs of the ash trees). (For the three distinct Hundred-Armed giants – likewise offspring of Uranus and Gaia – see the end of this entry.) When Zeus offended Gaia by imprisoning the Titans in Tartarus, she stirred up her sons, the giants, to make war upon the gods, a fight called the *Gigantomachia*. The attack was said to have taken place long after the offence which provoked it – the memory of Gaia being long and her patience infinite – but Zeus expected the onslaught. Since the giants were immune from death at the hands of the gods, he knew that the gods could not win without the aid of a mortal hero, and therefore prepared himself by giving a mortal woman a great and much-enduring hero, namely Heracles, as her son. Then Gaia brought forth a herb whose property was to render the giants both immortal and invincible at mortal hands. Zeus forbade the Sun (Helios), the Moon (Selene), and Dawn (Eos) to make their usual appearances until he had himself discovered the herb and removed it.

The battle took place at a spot known as Phlegra ('the Burning Lands') which was the abode of the giants; it was identified with Pallene (in Thrace) or with other volcanic regions. Led by Eurymedon, with Alcyoneus and Porphyrion as their most powerful champions, the giants advanced on the assembled gods throwing rocks and mountain-peaks and brandishing torches made of the entire trunks of oak trees. Attacking

Alcyoneus, Heracles shot him with a poisoned arrow, and, since the giant's immortality was only valid within his homeland of Pallene, dragged him off to die outside its bounds. Porphyrion tried to rape Hera, but Zeus hurled a thunderbolt at him, as at many of his comrades, and Heracles dispatched him with an arrow. Another giant, Ephialtes, was hit by arrows in each eye, from the bows of Apollo and Heracles. When his fellow-giant Enceladus fled from the field, the goddess Athena flung the island of Sicily on top of him and crushed him; he was not killed, but everlastingly imprisoned and his fiery breath still issued forth from Etna. Mimas suffered a similar fate; Hephaestus buried him under a mass of molten metal and he lies beneath the volcano of Vesuvius. Athena attacked the giant Pallas, whom she caught and flayed, covering her breastplate with his leathery skin. Poseidon buried Polybotes by throwing part of the island of Cos on top of him – it became a new island, Nisyrus. Hermes, wearing a cap of invisibility, overcame Hippolytus; Artemis shot Gration with her arrows; Dionysus struck down Eurytus with his staff (thyrsos); Hecate burned Clytius with her infernal torches; and the Fates killed Agrius and Thoas with bronze clubs. Each giant was finished off by Heracles with his arrows, for the poison of the Hydra, which tipped their heads, was lethal even to those vast bodies – and only a mortal man such as he was, could deliver them the death-blow.

According to other, less widespread, accounts of the Gigantomachy, the giants were defeated and put to flight by unfamiliar noises, the braying of asses ridden by Hephaestus and the Satyrs, or the strange sound of Triton's conch. Apollonius Rhodius tells how giants (Gegeneis) attacked the Argonauts in Mysia and were killed by Heracles' arrows.

The Hundred-Armed giants (Hekatoncheires, 'with a hundred arms and hands') Cottus, Briareos, and Gyes, the offspring of Gaia and Uranus, were three huge creatures possessing fifty heads and a hundred arms each. Their father pushed them back into the womb of their mother the Earth. For this act of cruelty Gaia in her pain persuaded Cronos to castrate his father and overthrow him. However, when Cronos became supreme, he too imprisoned the Hundred-Armed, locking them in Tartarus with their brothers the Cyclopes, because he was afraid of their power. Gaia was again angry and did all in her power to help Zeus overthrow Cronos and the Titans who supported him. But Zeus, to help him in the struggle, released the Cyclopes and the Hundred-Armed, to whom, since they were indispensable to his victory, he gave nectar and ambrosia, the food and drink of the immortals. At the end of the war, however, Zeus returned the Hundred-Armed to Tartarus, but this time as jailors, for they guarded the Titans imprisoned there. They remained Zeus' faithful allies and, when the other gods would have rebelled against Zeus, Thetis brought Briareos out of Tartarus to aid him.

Glauce 1. Otherwise known as Creusa, the daughter of King Creon of Corinth. When Jason married her, he repudiated his foreign wife Medea, who thereupon brought about the death of her rival by sending her a poisoned robe as a wedding gift. When Glauce put it on, she was burnt to death, and her father Creon as he embraced his dying daughter perished as well.
2. Daughter of King Cychreus of Salamis; the first wife of Telamon.

Glaucus ('grey') The name of several mythological characters. **1.** A sea-god, the son of Anthedon and Alcyone or Poseidon and Nais. The story of his origin, told by Ovid, is that he began as a fisherman living in the Boeotian city of Anthedon. One day he caught and landed some fish at a place where there grew a herb with the magic property of resuscitating fish and allowing them to return to the water. Glaucus ate some of this herb, which made him immortal but gave him the tail and fins of a fish. Oceanus and Tethys received him well and he was accepted among the deities of the sea, learning the art of prophecy at which they were skilled.

Glaucus fell in love with the Italian nymph Scylla, who rejected him. Thereupon he consulted the witch Circe, who herself became passionately fond of him. Since, however, he cared only for Scylla, Circe turned her into a monster from the waist down, with a row of dogs' heads round her loins. Scylla went to live in a submerged cave on the Straits of Messina from which she preyed on passing sailors.

Euripides in his play *Orestes* calls Glaucus a son of Nereus and says that he assisted Menelaus on his homeward journey with good advice. He also helped the Argonauts. It was believed that he was accustomed to come to the rescue of sailors in storms.

2. Son of Sisyphus and Merope; he inherited his father's kingdom of Ephyra (Corinth). Athena helped him to win Eurynome, daughter of Nisus of Megara. However Zeus hated Sisyphus, and decreed that his son should be 'father' to any man's son but his own. When, therefore, Bellerophon was born, Glaucus brought him up without knowing that his wife Eurynome had been seduced by Poseidon. Glaucus owned a team of mares, which he kept at Potniae in Boeotia, and made more high-spirited by depriving them of the company of males. When, however, he lost the chariot-race at Pelias' funeral games, his mares were so furious that they killed and ate him. His ghost haunted the stadium of the Isthmian Games near Corinth, where it continued for many generations to frighten horses.

3. Son of Minos. When, while still a small child, he was pursuing a mouse, he fell into a storage-jar of honey and was drowned. Polyidus the seer happened to be in Crete at the time, and fulfilled a strange condition described by the Curetes, for they had declared that whoever could find the most suitable comparison or simile for a prodigious calf in Minos' herds could both find Glaucus and restore him to life. Now a cow had calved in Crete and brought forth an offspring which changed colour, sometimes being white, sometimes red, at other times black. Polyidus proceeded to compare it to the fruit of the mulberry, which goes through these colours as it ripens. (Elsewhere, however, this prophecy was attributed to the Delphic Oracle, or the fruit described as that of the dog-rose.) Minos commanded Polyidus to find his son and bring him alive again. First of all, on the trapdoor leading to the storage room, the seer saw an owl (*glaux*) which was being plagued by bees; and from this he deduced the whereabouts of Glaucus' body. Next Minos shut him in a room with the corpse and commanded that he should be left alone. At first the seer had no idea what to do; but then a snake approached the body. Polyidus killed the snake, but to his surprise a second one appeared, carrying a herb with which it resuscitated the first. Polyidus applied the same herb to the body of Glaucus and he came to life again. (According to another version, Glaucus was revived by Asclepius.) Minos wished Polyidus to teach Glaucus the art of prophecy, and, in order to gain permission to leave Crete, the seer complied. He undid the gift, however, as he boarded the ship, for he made Glaucus spit into his mouth, whereupon the spitter totally forgot all he had learnt.

4. Son of Hippolochus, a Lycian, and, together with Sarpedon, the commander of the Lycian forces allied with Priam in the Trojan War. When he was face to

face with Diomedes, son of Tydeus, the two found that their families were linked by a bond of friendship, since Diomedes' grandfather Oeneus had entertained Bellerophon, the father of Hippolochus. They therefore gave up the mortal combat they were about to start, exchanged armour, and swore to avoid any future encounter in the war. Glaucus gave Diomedes golden armour in exchange for bronze, an act which Homer describes as foolish.

Glaucus was eventually killed by Aias, the son of Telamon, while they were fighting over Achilles' corpse. Apollo entrusted his body to the winds to carry back to his native Lycia, and set over his tomb a granite rock out of which ran a stream called Glaucus.

Gordius A Phrygian, the father of King Midas. As he was ploughing, an eagle perched on the yoke of his plough for a whole day. He went to Telmessus in Lycia, whose inhabitants had prophetic powers. There a girl, who was drawing water at a well, told him to offer sacrifice to Zeus. He married the girl, who bore him Midas (according to another version the child's mother was the goddess Cybele). When Midas grew up, the Phrygians were divided about who should be their ruler and they were told to expect a king to come to them riding on a waggon. Gordius, accompanied by his family, happened to approach by this means, and was made king; his waggon was dedicated to Zeus. Midas later became his successor. It was subsequently believed that whoever untied the knot on the waggon's yoke would rule all Asia. This feat was accomplished by Alexander the Great, who cut the rope.

Gorge Daughter of Oeneus; the wife of Andraemon, king of Calydon.

Gorgons Three female creatures of frightening aspect, daughters of Phorcys and Ceto, both denizens of the sea.

Their names were Stheno ('strength'), Euryale ('wide-leaping'), and Medusa ('ruler' or 'queen'). They lived in the far west by the shore of Ocean's stream. Their sisters were the Graiae and, according to some versions, Echidna. With the exception of Medusa, who was slain by Perseus, they were immortal. Poseidon was Medusa's lover, having taken her in a temple consecrated to Athena, and she was pregnant by him when Perseus killed her. Either the drops of her blood or her decapitated corpse gave birth to Chrysaor and Pegasus. (The mythologist Apollodorus adds a story that Asclepius got hold of Medusa's blood, which, being the god of healing, he used on his patients. One vein produced blood which had the power to revive dead bodies, but the blood coming from the other was lethal.)

Traditions vary about the appearance of the Gorgons. On the one hand they are sometimes described as beautiful, and it was said that Athena gave Perseus the power to kill Medusa (see Perseus) because she had boasted of excelling the goddess in beauty. Ancient art, on the other hand, depicts them with hideous round faces, serpentine hair, boar's tusks, terrible grins, snub noses, beards, lolling tongues, staring eyes, brazen hands, a striding gait, and sometimes the hindquarters of a mare. It was said that a glimpse of these creatures, or at any rate of Medusa, would turn a man to stone.

When Perseus had killed Medusa, he eventually gave her head to Athena, who set it in the centre of her breastplate (the aegis). However there was also a belief at Athens that the goddess buried the head under the city's market-place, and gave a lock of its hair to the city of Tegea to protect it in war. Medusa's ghost, like those of other mortals, went to Hades' kingdom, where it terrified the shades of the dead.

Gorgophone Daughter of Perseus and

Andromeda; wife of Perieres and later of Oebalus.

Graces (Greek: *Charites*, Latin: *Gratiae*) Minor goddesses who usually attended upon, or were associated with, Aphrodite. Their parentage was not agreed; Zeus and Eurynome, a daughter of Oceanus and Tethys, were most frequently given as their father and mother. Varying in number, though generally represented as three, they usually seemed little more than abstract personifications of beauty, gentleness, and friendship. They were favourite subjects in art, but played little part in myth. They were known by a variety of different names. Hesiod knew of a Grace called Aglaia ('the bright one'); she was sometimes said to be Hephaestus' wife, instead of Aphrodite. Homer, in the *Iliad*, calls her Charis. He also tells a story introducing a Grace named Pasithea. Hera, so that the gods could help the Greeks, wanted to lull Zeus to sleep, and to achieve this end she won the aid of Hypnos ('Sleep') by offering him Pasithea as his bride.

Graiae The three weird sisters of the Gorgons, daughters of Phorcys and Ceto. Their names were Enyo ('warlike', 'furious'), Pemphredo ('waspish'), and Deino ('dreadful'), though some writers omit the last and know only of two. Though Aeschylus (*Prometheus Bound*) said they looked like swans, their name *Graiae* means 'old women', for according to the usual tradition they were old hags from birth, grey-haired and wrinkled; they were also blind and toothless except for a single eye and a single tooth which they

shared between them. They lived in a cave in the side of Atlas' mountain. Like their sisters the Gorgons, they are known from the story of Perseus, who tricked them, by stealing their eye, into giving him information for his journey to the Gorgon's lair on the shore of Ocean.

Gration see GIANTS.

Grinnus see BATTUS *1*.

Gyes see GIANTS (Hundred-Armed).

Gyges This distant, mythical ancestor of the royal family of Lydia in Asia Minor was a simple shepherd in the service of the king of that time. Plato tells how, after an earthquake, he discovered a cleft in the ground, which he then entered. It led to a cavern containing a hollow bronze horse in which lay a corpse of more than human size. Gyges drew a ring from the finger of this corpse and returned above ground to his fellow herdsmen. As he sat among them, he discovered that by turning the bezel of the ring inwards, he could make himself invisible. He went to court where by using this power he seduced the queen and killed the king, while remaining invisible himself; and so he won the kingship. This Gyges was not the same as the famous King Gyges, a historical (though partly legendary) figure who reigned over Lydia from *c*. 685 to *c*. 657 BC, but his remote predecessor. The stories of the two men, however, as the account of Herodotus makes it clear have a number of elements in common.

H

Hades (*Haides*, in origin probably an epithet meaning 'the Unseen') The god of the dead and ruler of a subterranean kingdom, the 'Underworld', in which the shades of dead human beings, as well as certain mythological creatures such as the Titans, were thought to be confined. The name Hades rightfully refers to the god and not the place; its incorrect attribution to the latter arises from the elliptical Greek employment of the genitive case (*Haidou*) to mean 'house of Hades'. He was a son of Cronos and Rhea, and consequently brother of Zeus, Poseidon, Hera, Hestia, and Demeter, whose daughter was Persephone, his consort and Queen of the Dead. His name was considered unlucky and used as little as possible. He was often referred to by euphemistic titles such as *Plouton* (Pluto) 'the Rich', (translated into Latin as *Dis*, a shortening of *dives* 'rich'), a title recalling his nature as a chthonic (earth) deity. Like Persephone and Demeter, he was thought to make the crops grow and produce wealth. The Greeks also called him *Eubouleus* 'Good Counsellor', *Klymenos* 'Renowned', *Polydegmon* 'the Hospitable', *Pylartes* 'the Gate-fastener', and *Stygeros* 'Hateful'; and he was known as *Zeus Katachthonios*, 'Zeus of the Underworld', an appellation which shows his great power and absolute dominion over his realm. The Romans sometimes described him as *Orcus*, a name of uncertain origin.

Though the Greeks and Romans conceived Hades as a grim, cold deity, ruthlessly applying the rules of his kingdom to all without discrimination, they never thought of him as evil, Satanic, or unjust. His 'house' is therefore in no sense a hell, though it is a prison and Hades a jailor (he is often portrayed holding a key). The dead were regarded as mere shadows of their living selves, who lacked blood and consciousness, and dwelt in the Underworld without escape for ever, generally pursuing the activities of their former life in a wan, mechanical fashion. Their habitation (called the 'Plain of Asphodel') was dreary and offered no variety or social intercourse. On entering the Underworld escorted by Hermes, those shades who were able to pay the fare of a small coin (an *obolos*) were ferried across the River Styx by the ancient boatman Charon; the monstrous watchdog Cerberus prevented them from ever returning. When they reached the other shore they had to meet the infernal judges, Minos, Rhadamanthys and Aeacus. But little importance was generally attached to the result of their judgments – which seemed, for the most part, to be a mere empty continuation of their earthly functions – as the vast majority of the dead remained forever in the Plain of Asphodel. In one version a tiny band was admitted, owing to very special merits, to the 'Islands of the Blest' or *Elysium*. Yet even Achilles, according to Homer, was not chosen to receive this favour. For when Odysseus came to the Land of the Dead to consult the shade of Tiresias, he also encountered the shade of Achilles, although he declared that he would rather be a slave in the house of a landless man on earth than king among the dead. Even Heracles, who was received on Olympus as an immortal god, was also believed to be present in the Underworld in phantom form.

Besides being thought of as underground, the Land of the Dead was also associated with the West. When Odysseus sailed to Persephone's Grove, he came to a wild sunless coast at the edge of the world, where the River of Ocean flowed, and the infernal rivers debouched into its waters. When conceived of as being underground, Hades' kingdom was believed to have entrances in a cave on Cape Taenarum near Sparta, in the Alcyonian Lake at Lerna, and in Lake Avernus in Campania. At the bottom of the Underworld was Tartarus, a place of eternal blackness where the wicked were punished. But only a small number are mentioned as enduring its tortures. These include Tantalus, Sisyphus, Tityus, Ixion, the Danaids, and, in particular, the Titans who were guarded by the Hundred-Armed giants. Very few living mortals penetrated the Underworld and escaped: Heracles who fetched Cerberus, Orpheus for whom Persephone, by a unique act of mercy, released Eurydice, Odysseus who came to consult Tiresias, and Aeneas whom the Sibyl of Cumae guided, by way of Lake Avernus, in order that he might speak with the shade of his father Anchises. Theseus and Pirithous also came, in the hope of carrying off Persephone: Hades imprisoned them in chairs of forgetfulness which held them fast, but certain Athenian writers claimed that Theseus was later freed by Heracles.

Hades himself plays a part in very few myths. The account of his rape of Persephone is the only important story. He was, moreover, very little worshipped by the Greeks, who believed that his jurisdiction was confined to the dead and that he consequently possessed no interest in the living. For when the Universe had originally been shared out, he was considered to have been allotted the Underworld as his perpetual residence: Zeus received the sky, don the sea (the earth and Olym., were supposedly common ground). Hades, like Poseidon, had a connection with horses; when he seized Persephone his chariot was drawn by dark-blue steeds. He also owned flocks, which were pastured in the mythical western island of Erythea. His herdsman was Menoetes, who spied on Heracles when the hero was seizing Geryon's cattle.

Haemon *1.* The name of one or more sons of Creon of Thebes; *see* CREON *1.*
2. Son of Andraemon; the father of Oxylus.

Halirrhothius Son of Poseidon and a nymph, Euryte. Near the Acropolis in Athens he raped Alcippe, a daughter of Ares and Aglaurus, and for this Ares killed him. The god was arraigned by Poseidon at a court which met on the spot. This was the legendary origin of the court named the *Areopagus* ('Hill of Ares') which tried cases of homicide at Athens: it acquitted Ares of guilt. According to an alternative version of the story, Poseidon sent Halirrhothius to cut down Athena's sacred olive trees near the Acropolis, and the axe slipped and killed him.

Halitherses An Ithacan, son of Mastor, who favoured Odysseus and, being skilled in prophecy, predicted his return at a public meeting. After Odysseus had exterminated Penelope's suitors, Halitherses tried to prevent their kinsmen from attacking him.

Hamadryads *see* DRYADS.

Harmonia Wife of Cadmus of Thebes. She was commonly said to be a daughter of Ares and Aphrodite, but another tradition pronounced her to be the daughter of Zeus by Electra, daughter of Atlas. All the gods came to her marriage-feast. As wedding presents, Cadmus gave

Harmonia a fine wedding dress and a beautiful necklace made by Hephaestus, gifts which brought disaster on her descendants. *See also* CADMUS.

Harpalyce *1*. Daughter of Clymenus, king of Argos. She married Alastor, a son of Neleus, but while they were on their way home to Pylos, her father Clymenus pursued them and abducted Harpalyce, for whom he had conceived an incestuous passion. Harpalyce revenged herself on her father by killing her child by him (or her younger brother); she then cooked the corpse and served it to her father. When he discovered that he had eaten the child's flesh, he slew both his daughter and himself; or else his daughter, after praying to be removed from the sight of mankind, turned into an owl (according to one version of the story, this happened as she was fleeing from her father).

2. Daughter of Harpalycus ('ravening wolf'), a Thracian king. After the death of her mother, her father brought her up in the arts of war, and she fought alongside him. After his death she became a brigand. Sham fights were performed at her tomb.

Harpies (*harpyiai*, 'snatchers') Monstrous bird-like women, either three or four in number, who were held responsible for the disappearance of whatever could not be found. Hesiod gave Thaumas and the Oceanid Electra as their parents; they were thus sisters to the goddess Iris. As with the Gorgons, there were two traditions about them. In the earlier, Homeric version, they were like storm-winds, as their names Aello ('squall'), Okypete ('swift-flying'), Celaeno ('dark', like a storm-cloud), and Podarge ('swift-foot') indicate. Podarge mated with Zephyrus, the West Wind, and bore Achilles' horses Xanthus and Balius. They pounced on the daughters of Pandareos, whom Aphrodite and the other goddesses had reared after their parents' death, and, while Aphrodite was away talking to Zeus about their marriages, snatched them up and gave them to the Furies as their servants.

In art, however, the Harpies were represented as monstrous birds with women's faces like the Sirens (this caused them to be confused with ghosts or death-spirits, which were similarly represented), and it was as creatures such as these that they figured in their most famous myth, the plaguing of Phineus, a Thracian king who extended hospitality to the Argonauts during their voyage to Colchis. Flying into Phineus' dining-room, they seized his food and befouled his table with their droppings. He made a bargain with the Argonauts, agreeing to prophesy their future if they would rid him of this pest. In the usual version of the story, Calais and Zetes, the winged sons of Boreas, pursued the Harpies as far as the Strophades Islands in the Ionian Sea, where Iris appeared and told them to relinquish their pursuit, provided that the Harpies guaranteed to leave Phineus alone. In this version, they then went to live in a cave on Mount Dicte in Crete. According to another tradition, however, both pursuers and pursued failed ever to return, having died of starvation; and the river Harpys (Tigres) in the Peloponnese is said to have received its name because one of the Harpies, as they fled from Calais and Zetes, fell into its depths. Aeneas met the Harpy Celaeno at the Strophades, where she predicted that his Trojans would reach their new home only when hunger forced them to eat their tables. She and her companions raided the Trojans' meals, and since their feathers of steel were tougher than swords, it was impossible to drive them off.

Hebe ('youth', Latin: *Juventas*) Daughter of Zeus and Hera and sister of Ares, and a cup-bearer of the gods on Olympus. In the *Iliad*, after Ares had been wounded by Diomedes, she bathed his wounds. When Heracles met his end, burnt to death by the poisoned tunic that his wife Deianira had dipped in Nessus' blood, and the gods received him – purified of his earthly part – into their company on Olympus, they gave him Hebe as his new, celestial wife. For his sake she gave his nephew Iolaus his youth again so that he could go into battle against Eurystheus in defence of Heracles' children: and Iolaus was thus enabled to kill Eurystheus.

Hecabe (Latin: *Hecuba*) Daughter of Dymas, king of the Phrygians, or of Cisseus; her home was on the River Sangarius. According to Apollodorus, Priam, king of Troy, divorced his first wife Arisbe before making Hecabe his consort and chief wife. She bore him nineteen children. Her oldest son was Paris, whom she abandoned and exposed at birth because she had dreamed she bore a firebrand, an evil omen of destruction for Troy; but he was subsequently rescued (*see* PARUS). Among her other children were Hector, Helenus, Deiphobus, Troilus, Polites, Cassandra, Polyxena, and Creusa. In the *Iliad*, Hecabe remained in the background, appearing in order to lament her dead son Hector. Virgil makes Aeneas describe how, when Neoptolemus sacked Priam's palace, she prevented the old king from attacking him and sat at the altar as he and her son Polites were butchered. Hecabe was then given to Odysseus as a slave. Euripides in his play the *Hecuba* (*Hecabe*), tells of the discovery on the shore of the Thracian Chersonese of the body of her youngest son Polydorus, murdered by the Thracian king Polymestor, who had been meant to guard and rear him. In consequence, Hecabe persuaded Agamemnon to allow her to summon Polymestor to Troy, on the pretext that she would tell him where Troy's treasure was hidden. When he came, she killed his children and blinded him: whereupon he predicted that

Hecabe would be transformed into a bitch with fiery eyes. Hence the site of her tomb on the Chersonese was called *Cynos Sema*, 'the bitch's tombstone'. According to another tradition, she was stoned to death by Polymestor's Thracians, and as she died turned into a bitch; and in this form she was said to have haunted the Chersonese after her death. In his *Trojan Women (Troades)*, Euripides shows Hecabe accusing Helen before Menelaus so convincingly that he swears to kill her on his return to Sparta. She laments the murders of her daughter Polyxena, sacrificed to placate Achilles' ghost, and her grandson Astynax, whose funeral she supervises.

Hecale *see* THESEUS.

Hecate A chthonic (earth) goddess, unknown to Homer but important in Boeotia, the homeland of Hesiod. Her parentage is unclear. Hesiod named her as daughter of Coeus and Phoebe: a Titaness who kept her honours after the fall of the other Titans. But her father was also said to be Perses or Zeus himself; and her mother was usually identified as Leto's sister Asteria, though sometimes, also, she was called the daughter of Demeter or Pheraea. Her association with Demeter was enhanced by the belief that both goddesses looked after the fertility of the ground, Hecate being, perhaps, an importation from Caria in Asia Minor. Hesiod declared that Hecate (her name means 'she who has power far off') was honoured by Zeus more highly than any other divinity, and given power over land, sea, and sky. As an earth-goddess, however, Hecate became associated especially with the world of the dead (like Persephone, whose mother Demeter was sometimes believed to have been her mother also). She was a goddess of magic, and Medea invoked her aid to perform it both in Colchis and at Corinth. Crossroads were very important in magical rites, where they were often undertaken, and Hecate, although not identified with Artemis, was known as the Artemis of the cross-roads. She was portrayed with three faces, carrying torches and accompanied by baying hounds.

Hecaterus Father of five daughters from whom, according to Hesiod, the satyrs were descended.

Hecatoncheires *see* GIANTS (HUNDRED-ARMED).

Hector Son of the Trojan king Priam and of Hecabe. In the *Iliad*, when he prays for his infant son Astyanax, Hector seems to regard his son, through himself, as heir to the throne of Troy. But Paris must be regarded as older, in Homer's eyes, since at the time of Hector's death Helen declares it is nine-teen years since Paris had taken her to Troy: he must be regarded as about forty, whereas Hector is a younger man. He is, however, the Trojan war-leader – his name (a Greek word) means 'holder', 'resister' – and rebukes Paris for his dilatory behaviour, a rebuke which Paris accepts humbly. Before the war Hector had married Andromache, daughter of Eetion, king of Thebe in the Troad. In the *Iliad* she had already lost her father and brothers to Achilles' sword. According to Homer, Hector is open, frank, brave, cheerful in adversity, and tenderly compassionate: his parting from An-dromache and their child is one of the most touching scenes in the poem. Though he deplored Paris' seduction of another man's wife, even proposing to the Trojan Council that she should be returned to her husband, it was he who killed Protesilaus, the first Greek to step on Trojan soil, and thereafter he pros-ecuted the war with great vigour. By the time the events of the *Iliad* began, the Trojan army was penned inside the city walls; but the quarrel between Achilles and Agamemnon, causing the former to

withdraw from combat, provided several days' respite and gave Hector the opportunity to march out and attack the Greeks in the plain, eventually driv-ing them back into a stockade they had built round their beached ships. How-ever when Hector was on the point of setting the Greek ships on fire, Poseidon intervened and rallied the Greeks to stave off the crisis, and Patroclus entered the battle at the head of Achilles' Myrmi-dons, wearing Achilles' armour. This reinforcement gave the Greeks strength enough to throw the Trojans back.

But Apollo, who protected Hector, helped him to kill Patroclus and take the armour. The loss of his friend brought Achilles back into battle, to vent all his fury upon the slayer of Patroclus. Hector was warned by Polydamas to retreat before Achilles, yet refrained from making his withdrawal into the city. Next day, after the Trojans had been routed, Achilles with the help of Athena trapped Hector, and after a long chase round the city walls killed him. With his dying breath Hector prophesied the immi-nent death of his slayer. Stripping the corpse, Achilles fastened it to his chariot by thongs, and dragged it after him. Then he threw the body down by Patro-clus' bier, its face in the dust, and pulled it daily around Patroclus' tomb. He re-fused to give it back to Hector's family until his own mother Thetis had besought him to do so and Priam had come and begged for his dead son's return. Achilles then permitted Priam to ransom the corpse and convey it back to Troy, allow-ing an eleven-day truce for the funeral; meanwhile, Aphrodite had preserved the body by covering it with ambrosia. When Priam brought it home, Helen declared that Hector had been kinder than anyone else to her. The *Iliad* ends with his fu-neral. After the fall of Troy – which the Trojans knew that his death heralded – his son Astyanax was put to death, since the Greeks were afraid to let any of Hector's line live on to avenge him.

Hecuba *see* HECABE

Heleius Son of Perseus and Andromeda. Amphitryon made him ruler of the Taphian Islands.

Helen (*Helene, Helena*) Daughter of Zeus and Leda; the wife of Menelaus, king of Sparta, and subsequently of Paris, son of King Priam of Troy. Her name, which is not Greek, may originally have been that of a goddess; it is associated with birds and trees. Yet in the Homeric poems she is human, although she is ascribed a unique beauty and charm, regarded as the gift of Aphrodite, who clothes her with the power to attract whatever man she wishes.

Another account of Helen's birth makes her a daughter of Zeus and the goddess Nemesis (because she brought misfortune). Nemesis avoided Zeus' attentions and took the form of a goose, whereupon Zeus, in the form of a swan, seduced her. In a grove at Sparta she laid an egg, which shepherds found and took to Leda, King Tyndareos' wife. When Helen was hatched, Leda brought her up as her own. But the usual story is that it was with Leda herself that Zeus had intercourse, in the guise of a swan. Helen's brothers were Castor and Polydeuces, the Dioscuri, and her sister was Agamemnon's wife Clytemnestra. It was sometimes believed that, whereas Castor and Clytemnestra had Tyndareos as their father and were therefore mortal, Polydeuces and Helen were Zeus' children and immortal. Again, Leda is sometimes said to have laid two eggs, one containing the mortal and the other the immortal pair. In some stories Helen eventually died, but there was also a tradition, known to Homer, that Menelaus, when the hour of his death came, was admitted to Elysium simply because she was his wife.

At the age of twelve, Helen had been carried off by Theseus to be his bride. He locked her up at Aphidnae in Attica

under the care of his mother Aethra, while he aided his friend the Lapith Pirithous to take another daughter of Zeus for himself. Unfortunately for the two heroes, Pirithous chose Persephone, and when they went to the Underworld to fetch her, they were caught by Hades and shackled in chairs of forgetfulness. Meanwhile Helen was rescued by her brothers the Dioscuri and brought back to Sparta; and they carried off Aethra as well.

When the time came for Helen to be married, she was sought by all the eligible bachelors of Greece. They thronged Tyndareos' court, so that he was worried that those who were rejected would get out of hand and cause trouble. Odysseus, who was present as one of them, advised Tyndareos to make each of them swear to protect the life and rights of whichever succeeded in winning Helen as his bride. The suitors all agreed and duly swore the oath, standing on the remnants of a sacrificed horse to make their words more binding. Then Menelaus was chosen; presumably his riches commended him, and Helen's sister Clytemnestra was already married to his brother Agamemnon, king of Mycenae.

Helen bore Hermione to Menelaus; and either she or a slave girl was the mother of his son Nicostratus. (The poet Stesichorus also claimed that Helen bore Iphigenia and entrusted her to Clytemnestra to bring up, though Clytemnestra is more usually regarded as the girl's mother.) After a few years Paris, eldest son of Priam, king of Troy, visited Sparta. As a bribe for naming her the most beautiful goddess, Aphrodite had offered him the most beautiful woman in the world as his wife: when he saw Helen, he realised whom Aphrodite, had meant. Helen for her part succumbed to Aphrodite's powers and allowed Paris to convince her, so that when Menelaus was suddenly called away to Crete to arrange the funeral of his grandfather Catreus, they eloped together, taking with them rich presents for Paris from Menelaus' treasury. They reached Troy in three days of easy sailing – or else, according to different versions of the myth, were blown off course and went by way of Cyprus, Sidon, and even Egypt. When they arrived in Troy, the lovers were formally married in spite of the opposition of numerous Trojan leaders, including Hector, and lived together as man and wife until Paris was killed nineteen years later by an arrow from Philoctetes' bow. Then she married Paris' brother Deiphobus.

When Menelaus returned to Sparta and found her gone, he roused his brother Agamemnon and in addition all the leaders of Greece, who as Helen's ex-suitors had sworn to afford him their protection, to come and help him win his wife back. After a diplomatic intervention, headed by Menelaus and Odysseus, had failed to persuade the Trojans to return her, a great expedition was assembled, and sailed against Troy. Helen's own sympathies during the war and the siege were represented as ambiguous. At times, finding her position irksome, she reproached herself for her weakness and wickedness in staying with Paris; and when Odysseus came to Troy on a mission of espionage, she did not betray him even after he had killed a number of prominent Trojans – indeed, according to one account, she may even have helped him to steal the Palladium. Nevertheless, when the Greek leaders were hiding in ambush inside the Wooden Horse, she went to look at the horse with her husband Deiphobus, and deliberately tried to spring the trap by calling on each Greek leader, expertly mimicking his wife's voice. And yet she later helped Menelaus to kill Deiphobus. The relationship between Menelaus and Helen after the fall of Troy is described both in the *Odyssey* and in Euripides' *Trojan Women* (*Troades*). In the former, Menelaus, as he travels home to Sparta by way of

Egypt, spending seven years on the journey, becomes fully reconciled with Helen. But Euripides makes him very suspicious of Helen's true feelings, and when Hecabe has persuaded him that she has betrayed everybody and deserves only death, he promises to kill her on his return to Sparta.

Stesichorus, however, invented an entirely new story about Helen's adventures, and his new version was prompted by the following circumstances. It was said that, after writing a poem denouncing Helen's adultery, he had gone blind. Subsequently it so happened that a general from Croton in southern Italy, namely Leonymus, asked the Delphic Oracle how he might be cured of a wound. He had been told to go to an island, Leuce, in the Black Sea, where Aias (Ajax), the son of Oileus, would cure him. He duly went and came back with the story that the heroes of the Trojan War were still living there and that Helen, who was now married to Achilles, had told him that Stesichorus would regain his sight if he told the truth about her. And so the poet wrote a *Palinode* ('recantation'), in which he declared that Helen had never gone to Troy at all.

Euripides, in his romantic play *Helen*, developed the story. He declared that only a phantom Helen, made by Hera, was taken by Paris to Troy; for Zeus had ordered Hermes to conduct the real Helen to Egypt, where King Proteus then looked after her throughout the war years. Another version of the story was given by Herodotus, who reports that he had heard it in Egypt. Paris, according to this tradition, called at an Egyptian port on his way home with Helen, and his sailors told Proteus of her abduction. The king was indignant and detained Helen, sending Paris on his way. However when the Greeks besieged Troy, they would not believe that she was not there. It was only after sacking the city that Menelaus accepted the truth, and then he went off to Egypt to retrieve his wife. In Homer's story Menelaus and Helen were blown off course to Egypt on their way home together from Troy, because he had not sacrificed correctly to Zeus. While he was marooned on the isle of Pharos, Idothea, daughter of the sea-god Proteus, told him to catch her father asleep and hold him down, despite his transformations of shape, until he agreed to tell Menelaus how he could accomplish his return journey to Sparta. Menelaus acted accordingly, and Proteus instructed him to return to Egypt and perform the correct sacrifice.

On the day of their return to Greece, Orestes was being tried at Argos for the murder of Aegisthus and Clytemnestra. Euripides, in his *Orestes*, tells how Orestes' uncle Menelaus refused to defend him, whereupon Orestes and Pylades in desperation seized Helen and Hermione. But Helen, when they were on the point of killing her, vanished from sight and became a protector of sailors like Castor and Polydeuces, appearing in the form of St Elmo's fire.

But this is an unusual version of the story. She was generally said to have lived on long and happily at Sparta. Thus, when Telemachus came in search of news of his father Odysseus, she was there to entertain him. According to this tradition she outlived Menelaus, but after his death, his (or their) son Nicostratus drove her out to take refuge in Rhodes. There Polyxo, the widow of Tlepolemus, first received her with specious kindness, but then, in vengeance for the death of her husband in the Trojan War, commanded her women to dress up as Furies and hang Helen on a tree. So it was that Helen was worshipped in Rhodes as *Dendritis* ('of the tree').

Helenus Son of Priam and Hecabe; Cassandra's twin. As children, he and Cassandra were licked on their ears and

mouth by snakes while sleeping in the temple of Apollo at Thymbra, and as a result they learnt how to prophesy the future. Helenus was a good warrior as well as a prophet; and although he warned Paris of disaster if he persisted in making his voyage to Sparta, he himself fought bravely in the war. Towards the end of the siege, the Greeks captured him on Mount Ida by one of Odysseus' stratagems, whereupon Helenus told them how they could succeed in their enterprise. They must steal the Palladium, the image of Athena, from her Trojan temple, bring Pelops' bones to Troy, and persuade Achilles' son Neoptolemus and the marooned Philoctetes to take part in the fighting, the latter using Heracles' bow and poisoned arrows; and they must build the Wooden Horse. Philoctetes came; and it was he who shot and killed Paris. (According to a variant account, Helenus allowed the Greeks to capture him after Paris' death, because he was angry with the Trojans for giving Helen in marriage to Deiphobus rather than to himself.)

Helenus' prophecies came true and Troy fell. He attached himself to Neoptolemus, whom he warned not to sail home from Troy but to go overland, thus escaping the wrath of Athena and Poseidon. Neoptolemus gave him Hector's widow Andromache as his wife, and she bore him Cestrinus. Neoptolemus also allowed Helenus to build the city of Burthrotum in Epirus, and when Aeneas passed through that country on his way to Italy he found Helenus ruling a new 'Troy' there. The prophet gave Aeneas encouraging advice, but warned him his voyage would be long.

Heliades ('Children of the Sun') Helios, the Sun, had a number of children by different consorts. The Graces were sometimes described as his daughters by the nymph Aegle. By his wife Perseis or Perse, an Oceanid, his offspring were Aeetes, king of Colchis, Perses, king of the Tauri, Augeas, king of Elis, the witch Circe, and Pasiphae who married Minos. Neaera (or Clymene) bore him Phaethusa and Lampetia, who looked after his cattle on the Isle of Trinacria (often identified with Sicily). By Clymene his son was Phaethon, who perished driving his father's chariot, and by Rhode or Rhodos he begot seven sons who became the ancestors of the people of Rhodes. He told these seven that the first people to sacrifice to Athena would enjoy her presence for ever. The seven sacrificed to her at once, but had no fire. The Athenian Cecrops likewise performed a sacrifice; he was later than Helios' seven sons in doing so, but he used fire. In consequence both the Rhodians and the Athenians were believed to enjoy Athena's presence, and continued to sacrifice to her, the Rhodians still without fire. When Phaethon fell out of the sky after driving his father's chariot, his half-sisters buried him. Inconsolable, they sat for four months weeping for him by the River Eridanus, or Po, until the gods had pity on them and turned them into a row of poplars. Their tears were hardened by the sun into amber and dropped into the river.

Helicaon Son of Antenor. His wife Laodice fell in love with Acamas.

Helice Daughter of Selinus, king of Aegialus, and wife of Ion.

Helios The Sun, or rather its god, called *Sol* by the Romans. Hyperion ('going above') and Phoebus ('shining') were both once names or titles of his, but became dissociated from him. Hyperion was sometimes said to be Helios' father, and the name Phoebus was also applied to Apollo, who in later times was made into a sun-god and identified with Helios since the latter, like him, was equipped with arrows (the sun's rays).

As one who saw and heard everything, Helios was called upon to witness oaths; and Demeter consulted him to discover Persephone's whereabouts. But he was little worshipped and, apart from the story of Phaethon, occurs rarely in myth. In the story of Phaethon, Helios was described as a charioteer drawn by a team of four fiery steeds, traversing the sky by day from east to west, and heralded by Eos, the Dawn, who rode her carriage in front of his. According to later stories he returned to the east by night in a huge golden cup floating round by way of the Ocean, whose stream girdled the earth.

Helios had a large number of children by his wife, Perseis or Perse, and various mistresses (*see* HELIADES). He also seduced Leucothoe by appearing in the form of her mother Eurynome. Clytie, of whom he had formerly been the lover, in her jealousy told Leucothoe's father Orchamus, king of Persia, who consequently buried his daughter alive. Helios transformed Leucothoe into the frankincense tree. Clytie wasted away and became the heliotrope, whose head follows the sun's course across the sky.

The troubles of Helios in love were said to have been caused by Aphrodite, who was angry because Helios spied on her affair with Ares and told her husband Hephaestus. Helios once helped Heracles by lending him the golden bowl in which he sailed on the Ocean, so that the hero was able to reach Geryon's cattle on the isle of Erythea. But Heracles had threatened Helios on an earlier occasion, as he walked in the heat through the African desert, with an arrow from his bow.

When Zeus divided the lands among the various gods, Helios was away driving his chariot through the sky, and failed to receive a portion. Zeus compensated him by giving him the newly emergent isle of Rhodes, where he received special honours and three of his grandsons, Camirus, Lindus, and Ialysus, ruled, and gave their names to, the chief cities. The Colossus of Rhodes was a statue of Helios, crowned with a radiate crown, at the entrance of Rhodes harbour. Helios also disputed Corinth with Poseidon, and Briareos, appointed to arbitrate, awarded the citadel (Acrocorinth) to Helios. His son Aeetes ruled the place for a time.

Helle Daughter of Athamas and Nephele. When she and her brother Phrixus fled on the golden ram from Athamas and their stepmother Ino, Helle fell off its back into the sea, which was thenceforth called the Hellespont. *See* PHRIXUS.

Hellen The eldest son of Deucalion, the Greek Noah, and his wife Pyrrha. He gave his name to the Hellenes, whose name was originally restricted to a section of the Thessalians but was later applied to the Greeks as a whole. His wife, the nymph Orseis, was said to have given birth to the mythical forbears of the three great branches of the Greeks, Dorus the ancestor of the Dorians, Aeolus of the Aeolians, and Xuthus from whose sons the Ionians and Achaeans were descended.

Hemera ('day') Daughter of Erebus and Nyx. She came out of Tartarus (the darkest part of the Underworld), when her mother Nyx ('night') entered it, and *vice versa*. But at a very early date Helios (the Sun) and Eos (Dawn) came to personify these functions in place of Hermera.

Hemithea Daughter of Cycnus, king of Colonae, and sister of Tenes, who died defending her. *See* TENES.

Hephaestus (Latin: *Vulcanus* or *Mulciber*) Son of Hera, produced, according to Hesiod, without a mate. Other writers believed that Zeus was his father. He was the smith and metal-founder of the gods, and his worship was sometimes believed to have originated on the northern Aegean island of Lemnos, which contained a volcano on Mount Moschylus. He was also worshipped in Caria and Lycia in Asia Minor. His cult later spread to the volcanic regions of the west, Etna in Sicily, the Lipari Islands, and Campania in which Vesuvius is situated. He seems originally to have been a volcanic deity.

Hephaestus was twice flung out of Olympus. First of all, when he was born, Hera was offended by the sight of her ugly, deformed child (he was lame) and threw him out. The infant fell into the ocean, where Thetis and Eurynome the Oceanid found him and brought him up for nine years in their cave, unknown to the gods or Hera. It was here that he learnt his arts. He fashioned a golden throne for his mother and sent it to her; but he had concealed in it a trap whereby to gain his revenge, for when she sat on the throne she was imprisoned and none of the gods could help her. Hephaestus was invited to come to Olympus, where the other gods pleaded with him to release her. But he refused, until Dionysus, whom he trusted, made him drunk and wheedled the key to the device out of him. According to a variant story Hephaestus sent sandals to the gods, but those he sent to Hera were adamantine ones which caused her to fall flat on her face.

On Olympus he became a master craftsman, but was regarded as a figure of fun because of his limp, his sooty face, his bustling gait, and the dance that his errant wife Aphrodite led him. In particular, she committed adultery with Ares – bearing him a number of children – until Helios revealed to her husband what was going on. Hephaestus, in his fury, imprisoned the pair under a great net which descended upon them as they lay in bed. He had put it about that he was visiting his faithful people on the island of Lemnos. When he knew that the trap was sprung, Hephaestus called the whole company of Olympus to witness Aphrodite's shame. Only the male gods came, and they laughed greatly, though Hephaestus the cuckold proved as much of a joke as Ares. Finally Poseidon prevailed on him to accept a fine from Ares, going surety for its payment himself.

Hephaestus' second fall from Olympus showed he was reconciled to his mother Hera. She and Zeus were quarrelling over her vindictive persecution of Heracles, and Hephaestus spoke up for his mother so vehemently that Zeus took him by the leg and flung him down from heaven. He hurtled down all day and at nightfall landed half dead on Lemnos, where the Sintians tended him. That was why, according to this version, he became their protector, teaching them the arts of metalwork, at which they excelled all the Greeks.

Hephaestus was very useful to the Olympians. He built splendid halls and palaces and enabled the gods to live in great luxury. He even made armour for mortal men when a goddess could induce him to do so, for example Achilles' armour for Thetis, who had been Hephaestus' nurse, and Aeneas' armour for Aphrodite. He also created Pandora as a wife for Epimetheus so that Zeus might avenge himself on Prometheus for helping mankind. The site of Hephaestus' smithy was disputed. The Greeks generally thought he worked on Lemnos, where the Cyclopes acted as his workmates and were regarded – like the Cretan Dactyls, and the Telchines – as fire-gods. The Romans located Vulcan, whom they equated with him (and sometimes regarded as a personification of fire), under Mount Etna in Sicily. But he was also allotted a workshop on Olympus where, in the great battle of the gods and giants, he used molten iron to quell the giant Mimas. Hephaestus also forged the chain that bound Prometheus to the top of Mount Caucasus; and he made Zeus' thunderbolts and the arrows of Artemis and Apollo.

He was born from Hera before Athena sprang from Zeus – likewise without a mate, since she issued from his head: it was Hephaestus who had the task of splitting Zeus' cranium with an axe in order to release the goddess. He later fell in love with Athena, who repulsed him so violently that his seed fell on the ground, where it gave birth to Erichthonius. In the Trojan War, when Achilles was struggling with the River Scamander, Hephaestus dried the stream with blasts of flame and rescued the hero from drowning.

His children (mostly lame like himself) included the Argonaut Palaemon; Periphetes (also called Corynetes), a brigand of Epidaurus; and Ardalus, inventor of the flute. A large number of ancient rough-hewn images of the gods were believed to be his work.

Hera (Ionic Greek: *Here*, Latin: *Juno*) Wife of Zeus and queen of Heaven, she was Zeus' elder sister, the child of Cronos and Rhea. The name *Hera* may have meant 'the Lady', cf. *heros*, the masculine form, 'hero', 'warrior'. Her bird was the peacock, a symbol of ostentatious pride, and her province marriage and women's life.

Hera was swallowed at birth by her father, who suspected that his children would overthrow him. Only the sixth and youngest, Zeus, escaped this fate, through the cunning of Rhea and Gaia. When Zeus had established himself securely, he conducted love-affairs with a number of goddesses and nymphs, but decided that only Hera was great enough to be his consort. Even so, she was his inferior, working against him when necessary behind his back. Occasionally, in his anger, he punished her severely, and on one occasion, owing to her persecution of Heracles, he suspended her from a pinnacle of Olympus by the wrists, with her feet weighted by anvils.

There are several alternative versions
of the myths of Hera's birth and marriage. Some said that, after her birth
and her release from Cronos' stomach,
she was tended by Oceanus and Tethys,
while the gods fought the Titans. Others
said that she was brought up by Temenus in Arcadia, or by the Hours in
Euboea, or by the daughters of the River
Asterion in the Argolid. She was patroness of the city of Argos, after a dispute
with Poseidon: when the local river-
gods (Asterion, Inachus, and Cephisus)
awarded the rulership to Hera, Poseidon
dried their streams up and, in his spite,
flooded the whole surrounding country,
until Hera eventually persuaded him to
relent. One writer, Hyginus, even quotes
an account of her birth in which she
was not swallowed by Cronos but took
Rhea's place in rescuing her brother and
bringing him up out of sight of her
father. In one version of their marriage
story, Zeus found Hera wandering in
the woods near Argos, caused a rainstorm, and sheltered inside Hera's dress
in the guise of a cuckoo. When safely
hidden within her clothes, he resumed
his true form, embraced her, and promised on oath that he would make her his
wife. Alternatively, Zeus found Hera in
Euboea, ran away with her to Mount
Cithaeron, and took her in a cave. When
her nurse Macris came to find her, the
mountain warned her to go away, since
Zeus was in the cave lying with Leto.
Other seats of Hera's worship – Crete,
Samos, Euboea, and Naxos – made similar claims for themselves about the location of the divine wedding, and indeed
in many places throughout Greece the
institution of the Sacred Marriage,
whether performed by men and women
or represented by wooden images, was
observed in memory of their union.
Pomegranates and apples were sacred to
Hera: the former were given to brides
at Athens, where weddings traditionally
took place in Hera's month (*Gamelion*);
the golden apples of the Hesperides had

been presented to her by Gaia as a wedding gift.

At an early date Hera ceased to be
exclusively the patroness of women, and
played an important role in the myths
of wars and battles, being worshipped
by nobles and kings. In art she is portrayed as tall and stately, wearing a
diadem or wreath and carrying a sceptre. She bore Ares, Ilithyia, and Hebe to
Zeus, but produced Hephaestus without
his aid. When, however, Zeus acted likewise, giving birth to Athena out of his
head – with the help of Hephaestus' axe
– Hera in her jealousy, according to one
story, bore Typhon, to become Zeus'
most dangerous enemy (though this monster is usually called the child of Gaia).
Indeed, Hera was often moved by jealousy to take vengeance on Zeus' para-
mours and their children. The most
notorious targets of her vindictive persecution were Alcmena and her son
Heracles (although his name embodies
hers). She also persecuted Leto, who
was the mother of Apollo and Artemis,
Io, who was Hera's own priestess, and
Callisto and Semele.

Hera herself, as befitted the patroness
of monogamous marriage, was a model
of chastity. In the battle between the
gods and giants, Zeus, perhaps in order
to test her, filled the giant Porphyrion
with lust for her body. When, however,
Porphyrion attempted to rape her, Zeus
struck him down with a thunderbolt.
Ephialtes made a similar attempt, and
Artemis put him to death. When Ixion,
too, tried to make love to Hera thus
breaking the law of hospitality since he
was the guest of her husband on Olympus – Zeus formed a cloud into Hera's
shape, and Ixion lay with this. He was
subsequently punished with eternal torments in Tartarus.

Hera played an important part in
Homer's story of the Trojan War told
in the *Iliad*, though the Judgment of
Paris, in which she attempted to bribe
Paris with an offer of royal greatness,

receives only a brief allusion. It was because Paris failed to award her the prize for beauty that Hera persecuted Troy with such implacable fury. She was said by the poet Stesichorus to have saved Helen from dishonour by the substitution of a phantom which Paris took to Troy, while Hermes, in accordance with Hera's instructions, took the real Helen to Egypt. Hera often risked punishment by helping the Greeks against Zeus' orders, and on one occasion lured him to take her under a golden cloud while Poseidon spurred the Greeks on. In the *Aeneid* this enmity of Juno (Hera) extends to Aeneas too, until Jupiter prevails on her to allow a union between Trojans and Italians in a manner which will cause the Italians to play the dominant part. Jason, on the other hand, in his expedition to obtain the Golden Fleece, gained the support of Hera (who disguised herself as an old woman), but this was mainly to enable her to avenge herself on King Pelias of Iolcus, who had defiled her altar by the killing of Sidero, his stepmother. Subsequently Medea caused Pelias' daughters to cut him up and boil him in a cauldron.

A legend grew up at Plataea that on one occasion Hera left Zeus, on account of a supposed act of unfaithfulness on his part. According to this story Zeus, following the advice of the Plataean king Alalcomeneus or Cithaeron, made a wooden statue of a woman, which he caused to be drawn veiled on a cart. He made it known that this was his new bride, Cithaeron's daughter Plataea. When Hera heard of this she was so furious that she flew to the spot and overthrew the statue. But then she perceived the trick and was reconciled to her husband amid much laughter.

Hera and Zeus once had a great argument as to whether man or woman received more pleasure from sexual intercourse: each claimed that the other sex enjoyed it more. Since Tiresias had been both man and woman, they con-

sulted him. When he declared that a woman has nine times as much pleasure as a man, Hera struck him blind, whereupon Zeus gave him the gift of prophecy and long life. She also sent the Sphinx to ravage Thebes because Laius had not returned Chrysippus to his father Pelops, from whom he had kidnapped the youth.

Hera was worshipped by women all over the Greek world (though the function of presiding over childbirth passed to her daughter Illithyia over whom, however, Hera exercised great influence – the Romans, who called Ilithyia Lucina, later identified the two goddesses under the name Juno Lucina). At Stymphalus in Arcadia Hera was revered as Girl, Wife, and Widow – representing the whole female community. At Argos it was said that she recovered her virginity once a year by bathing in the spring of Canathus.

Heracles (Latin: *Hercules*) The most famous and popular of all the Greek heroes; the son of Zeus and Alcmena. His name, Heracles, literally 'Hera's glory', probably signified 'the glorious gift of Hera' and was related to his association with Argos, where Hera was worshipped. But the link seemed to be contradicted, in mythological terms, by that goddess's implacable persecution of Heracles because of her jealousy of Zeus' liaison with his mother. In rivalry with Argos, another city, Thebes, tried to take over the hero as its own at a very early date, and our only version of his birth locates it there. Our information about Heracles in the older Greek sources is scanty, and we have to make do with a couple of late, inferior authorities for our complete narrative, though there are plenty of incidental references elsewhere, in addition to Euripides' tragedy *Heracles* dealing with his madness. Nevertheless the character that emerges from the surviving traditions is clearly drawn. It is endowed with a superlative degree of valour, hardiness, endurance, good humour, pity for the weak, generosity, and adventurous spirit. His vices are equally conspicuous: violence of temper (especially against those he finds committing injustice), lust, gluttony.

For the story of Amphitryon's attempts to marry his mother Alcmena, *see* AMPHITRYON. For the conception and birth of Heracles at Thebes, *see* ALCMENA. Zeus had intended the throne of Argos, or at least Mycenae and Tiryns, as his birthright, but he had been swindled of this through the machinations of Hera. As a result, instead of turning into a great king, he became a slave to Eurystheus, a much worse man than himself. However Heracles, trained by a life of self-sacrifice, was destined in the end to rescue the very gods themselves, by defeating their enemies the giants.

He lost no time in showing himself a son of Zeus. Eight months after his birth, with his twin half-brother Iphicles, he was sleeping in the nursery in a shield for a cot. In the middle of the night Hera sent a pair of serpents to kill him. Iphicles saw them first and screamed, but Heracles seized one in either hand and throttled them. The parents rushed in, and Amphitryon realised at once which one was Zeus' child. According to a variant story, he himself had put the snakes in the cradle, in order to find out which child was which.

Many experts contributed to Heracles' education. Amphitryon showed him how to control horses and drive a chariot. Eurytus, king of Oechalia, made him proficient in archery. Autolycus gave him wrestling lessons, and Polydeuces instructed him in fencing. Linus, brother of the mistrel Orpheus, taught him how to play the lyre. Heracles was not a good pupil at this art, and Linus had cause to chastise the boy; whereupon Heracles, in a fury, picked up the instrument and brained Linus with it. In spite of his tender years, he was accused of murder, but argued the court into acquitting him, quoting a law of Rhadamanthys on the justification of self-defence.

After this Amphitryon sent Heracles off to herd his cattle on Mount Cithaeron near Thebes, and he quickly grew into a very strong, powerful man, though not tall (so Pindar; but later authorities added to his stature). His favourite weapon was the bow, but he was also a great wrestler and spearsman. At about the age of seventeen he fought and killed single-handed (though according to other traditions this was the deed of Amphitryon's father Alcaeus) a lion that had been mauling the flocks not only of Amphitryon but also of Thespius, king of neighbouring Thespiae. Before this exploit Thespius had entertained the young man in his house and allowed him to make love to his daughter – or, in a more extreme version of the tale, had detained him for fifty nights and sent into his bed a different one of his fifty daughters every night – or had even, according to Pausanias, sent them in all on one night, at a time when Heracles was so fuddled with wine that he thought he was having the same girl fifty times. Each of them in due course bore him a son.

On his way back to Thebes after slaying the lion of Cithaeron, Heracles fell in with the envoys of Erginus, king of the Minyans of Orchomenus. They were going to Thebes to collect an annual tribute the king had imposed owing to the death of his father Clymenus at Thebes. Erginus had defeated the Thebans, disarmed them, and ordered them to pay this tribute every year. Angered by his native city's humiliation, Heracles seized the envoys, lopped off their ears and noses (which he tied round their necks), and sent them back to their master. Then, armed by Athena, he routed Erginus in a mountain pass with the aid of the Thebans, who had armed themselves with weapons their ancestors had dedicated in the temples – although Creon, then king of Thebes, had previously offered to turn Heracles over to Erginus. Heracles then besieged Orchomenus, climbed its walls by night, and, unaided, burnt down Erginus' palace. He then imposed on Orchomenus twice the tribute that the Thebans had been obliged to pay.

In gratitude, Creon gave Heracles his daughter Megara in marriage. Megara bore Heracles three sons, Thersimachus, Creontidas, and Deicoon. Iphicles had already sired Iolaus, Heracles' future companion and squire, on Automedusa, Alcathous' daughter.

While Heracles was away in Argos, Creon died and the throne of Thebes was seized by Lycus, a Euboean usurper. Lycus, who was generally said to have murdered Creon, was afraid of the presence of the dead man's daughter and grandsons in the city, and was preparing to put them to death when Heracles unexpectedly returned and killed the usurper. In the rejoicing that followed, Hera suddenly struck Heracles with a fit of madness, in the course of which he took his bow and shot his three sons together with Megara, who tried to shield one of them with her body. He was about to kill Amphitryon too, when Athena struck him senseless with a rock. He was also said to have burned to death Iphicles' children, other than Iolaus (according to the version of the mythologist Apollodorus, however, Megara survived and married Iolaus).

Euripides, in his play *Heracles*, adopts a very different chronology for this story. There he makes Heracles perform his Twelve Labours for Eurystheus (see below) in the interval between leaving Thebes and coming back to find his family. After slaying Lycus, he was driven mad by Hera, killed his own wife and sons (thinking them to be Eurystheus and his family), and was taken to Athens by Theseus whom, in his last

Labour, he had rescued from the realm of Hades. This amended version, although it explains the lapse of time during which Creon died and Heracles' children grew to adolescence, removes the usually accepted reason for his having to serve Eurystheus, namely his blood-guilt for the murder of his wife and children.

In the more usual account of Heracles' life, it was as a result of his killing his family that he embarked on his Labours. Leaving Thebes, as was obligatory for a homicide, he took refuge with his old friend King Thespius of Thespiae, who purified him according to the established ritual. But Heracles, unable to find rest, went to consult the Delphic Oracle. There he was told to proceed to Tiryns, one of the cities of Eurystheus, and perform a number of tasks, in accordance with the king's demands. The number of the Labours is agreed to have been twelve, but most ancient authorities agree that, of these, two were rejected by Eurystheus for technical defects. It is, therefore, usually assumed that Heracles was originally ordered only to perform ten. (Alternatively Heracles had to spend twelve years in Eurystheus' service.) According to one source, it was only now that he received the name Heracles, being so addressed by the Pythian priestess, perhaps to placate Hera's wrath. Up till now he had been called simply Alcides, after Amphitryon's father Alcaeus. The priestess also promised him immortality if he succeeded in his Labours. But they constituted a dreadful imposition upon the proud hero, for Eurystheus was a weakling and must have seemed to Heracles the usurper of his rightful throne. Some said that it was after receiving this Delphic Oracle that Heracles flew into a frenzy and killed his family.

The order of Heracles' Labours appears to have been fixed by the scenes depicted on the metopes in Zeus' temple at Olympia (c. 460 BC), though Euripides changes the sequence considerably in his *Heracles*, and even introduces some different Labours at the expense of others. For example, he includes the killing of Cycnus, the clearing of pirates from the sea, and the supporting of the sky for Atlas (separate here from the apples of the Hesperides, see below No. XI). Even in the established 'canon', the eleventh and twelfth Labours (subsequently added because two were declared invalid) are often reversed. The order given in the following list was the most commonly accepted, since the Descent to Hades (XII) made an appropriate climax. The first six take place in the Peloponnese; the next two in remoter parts of the Greek world; and the remaining four in fabulous places, including the abode of the dead. Athena gave him unstinting help in these trials.

I The Nemean Lion. The first monster that Eurystheus told Heracles to overcome and deliver was the Nemean Lion, an invulnerable creature which had been suckled by Selene and was said to be sprung from Orthus and Echidna. Hera had sent it to Nemea in the Argolid in order to endanger Heracles. On arriving at Cleonae, he stayed in the hut of a labourer called Molorchus, who offered to sacrifice to him as a god. Refusing the honour, Heracles told him to wait a month, after which time he would either deserve sacrifice as a dead hero or would have killed the beast, in which case Molorchus could then sacrifice to Zeus the Saviour.

One evening Heracles came upon the lion on a hillside after it had eaten, and shot it from an ambush. However he quickly discovered its invulnerability, because his arrows, although gifts of Apollo, bounced off its hide. The lion charged, and Heracles held it off, fighting it with his bare hands and his olivewood club. He choked and battered it to death, breaking his club in the struggle, and skinned the corpse by using its own claws to cut the tough pelt. He cured the skin and always wore it thereafter. Zeus caused the lion to be placed in the stars as the constellation Leo. Molorchus was in the middle of his sacrifice to the hero when Heracles came back to Cleonae. On returning to Tiryns, he threw the skin down before Eurystheus, who was so terrified at its appearance that he jumped into a bronze storage-jar and hid himself. From that time onwards, he commanded Heracles to leave his trophies outside the city and to communicate with him indirectly, through the herald Copreus.

II The Hydra of Lerna. This monster, a water-serpent with a hound's body, was related to Heracles' first quarry, for it was once again the offspring of Echidna, with Typhon as its father. It lived at the spring of Amymone in the swamps of Lerna near Argos. It had a number of heads, estimated at various totals from five to a hundred; one was said by later mythologists to be immortal. Hera had apparently brought the Hydra up deliberately to imperil Heracles and had given it an ally, a giant crab, which served to create a diversion in the battle. When Heracles tried to kill the Hydra with his sword, he had to call in the help of his nephew Iolaus to cauterise the stumps of the monster's necks with a firebrand, because whenever one head was lopped off two more invariably grew up. Heracles smashed the crab with a blow of his foot, and Hera (who opposed him as vigorously as Athena helped him) promoted it to distinction as the constellation Cancer. After disposing of the mortal heads, he chopped off the immortal one and buried it under a rock by the road from Lerna to Elaeus. He then cut open the serpent's body and took its poison, which (to his own eventual undoing) he kept by him to poison his arrows. When he returned to Eurystheus, the king was said to have refused to count the exploit as a Labour, because Heracles had benefited from another's help.

III The Cerynitian Hind. It was not

agreed whether Heracles had to bring this beast back to Eurystheus alive or dead. Euripides claimed that it was a pest, which Heracles killed and dedicated to Artemis. Other sources said that he hunted it for a year and captured it alive. It had golden antlers and was sacred to Artemis, being one of four she had caught to draw her chariot. According to Pindar, the hind was a Pleiad, Taygete, whom the goddess had transformed into this shape to protect her from the attentions of Zeus. He says that Heracles went as far as the land of the Hyperboreans in its pursuit. According to others, it lived in the woods of Oenoe in the Argolid. Its connection with the Achaean town of Cerynia is obscure. Heracles tracked it down in Arcadia by the river Ladon, and caught it with a net as it slept. As he carried it away he met Apollo and Artemis, who reproached him and demanded the hind, but when Heracles laid the blame for its capture on Eurystheus, the goddess allowed him to take it to Tiryns and there to set it free unharmed. *See* TAYGETE.

IV The Erymanthian Boar. Heracles was next set the task of catching a huge boar that lived on Mount Erymanthus in Arcadia and plagued the land of Psophis. It was while Heracles was searching for this creature that the Centaur Pholus entertained him, with dire results for himself and his fellow Centaurs. The wild creatures were lured to Pholus' cave by the fumes of wine, to which they were unused, and after they had tasted the wine, they attacked Heracles in a drunken brawl. He was forced to defend himself with his poisoned arrows, and slew very many of his assailants. But one of the Centaurs who escaped from the massacre was Nessus who later brought about the hero's death. After this incident Heracles caught the boar by shouting outside its lair until it rushed out into a snowdrift. He then cast his net over it and carried it back to Eurystheus, who was said to have jumped into his bronze jar once again.

It was at this juncture that Heracles went off to join Jason's expedition to fetch the Golden Fleece from Colchis (*see* ARGONAUTS). He fits into that company rather badly, since he was by far the greatest of the heroes on board, and yet was represented as subordinate to Jason. Perhaps this is why he was imagined as leaving the expedition well before its arrival at Colchis; however it was also asserted that he was offered the leadership, but deferred to Jason's prior claim. There are several versions of the part he played in the saga. According to one account, he never even embarked, because the prophetic bowsprit, carved from Zeus' oak tree at Dodona, declared he would be too heavy for the ship. Apollonius Rhodius, the poet of the *Argonautica*, gives a version in which Heracles, accompanied by the youthful Hylas, son of King Theodamas of the Dryopes whom Heracles had killed in battle, sailed from Pagasae with Jason. After the Argonauts had dallied on Lemnos for a year with its husbandless women, he persuaded them to leave the island; and he killed the giants (*Gegeneis*) who plagued the Doliones of northern Mysia in Asia Minor. But when he broke his oar off the Bithynian coast, disaster ensued, for while he was cutting timber for a new oar, his squire Hylas, sent to fetch water, was stolen by the water-nymphs, who pulled him down into the spring. The Argonauts searched for a night, but on the advice of Calais and Zetes sailed off the next day, leaving Heracles behind. He eventually gave up the search, though only after compelling the local people to promise to continue looking for the boy every year thereafter. The Argonaut Polyphemus, who had heard Hylas' cries and told Heracles about them, was also left behind, and, after founding the city of Cius, saw to the maintenance of the search. Heracles later caught Calais and Zetes on the island of Tenos, where he slew them in revenge for their treachery.

V The Cleansing of Augeas' Stables.
Augeas was a son of Helios, the Sun-
god, and, like his father, possessed vast
herds of cattle, which he pastured in his
kingdom of Elis. Eurystheus ordered
Heracles to go to Augeas' stables, which
were so deep in dung that they had
become unusable, and to clean them out
in a single day. Although a bond slave
who was obliged to do what he was
told, Heracles attempted to bargain with
Augeas for the job, which he agreed to
complete in exchange for one tenth of
his cattle; Augeas' pledge was witnessed
by his son Phyleus. Heracles knocked
holes in the walls of the stables, and
diverted the waters of the river Alpheius
through them; then he returned the river
to its course before nightfall, blocking
up the holes again. The byres were then
fresh and pure, but Augeas refused to
honour his contract, claiming that Heracles was working under Eurystheus'
orders. Phyleus, angry at his father's
dishonesty, was sent into exile for speaking out. On his way back to Tiryns,
Heracles was entertained by Dexamenus, king of Olenus, and rescued his
daughter Mnesimache from the Centaur
Eurytion, who was forcing her into marriage, by putting her suitor to death. On
his return, Heracles found himself
doubly cheated, for because of his attempts to earn a reward, Eurystheus refused to count this task as one of the
Labours. Heracles later came back to
Elis and, after considerable difficulty,
conquered the country, killing Augeas
and replacing him with Phyleus.
VI The Stymphalian Birds. The last
Labour that Heracles performed in the
Peloponnese was the removal of these
birds – pests which infested the wooded
shores of Lake Stymphalus in Arcadia
and shot at people with their steel-tipped
feathers, besides ruining the crops with
their droppings. Heracles got rid of them
by means of a bronze rattle, manufac-
tured by Hephaestus and procured for
him by Athena. Scaring them off with

the rattle, he shot many of them with
his arrows as they flew up from their cov-
erts.
VII The Cretan Bull. Eurystheus now
sent Heracles further afield, and ordered
him to fetch the bull which Minos had
failed to sacrifice to Poseidon and had
become the object of Pasiphae's infatuation. Since the bull had caused him much
trouble and was dangerous, Minos did
not impede him. Heracles took it alive
to Tiryns, and then released it. It found
its way to Marathon, where it later
killed Minos' son Androgeos, king of
Paros, before falling victim to Theseus.
VIII The Mares of Diomedes. Heracles
was next ordered to Thrace, whence he
had to fetch the man-eating mares of
Diomedes, king of the Bistonians. It was
on his way through Thessaly that Heracles was entertained by Admetus, king
of Pherae, and rescued his wife Alcestis,
about to take the place of her husband
in the tomb, by wrestling with Thanatos
(Death) when he came to claim his
victim. Passing onwards to Thrace, Heracles took the mares and drove them
down to the sea to embark them. The
Bistones, roused by Diomedes who had
discovered his loss, then attacked him,
but Heracles routed them and captured
their king, feeding him to the mares,
which thenceforth became quite tame.
But in the meantime they had devoured
Heracles' young friend Abderus, whom
he had left in charge of them: Heracles
founded the city of Abdera in his
memory. After sailing the mares back to
Tiryns, Heracles released them. As they
wandered northwards, they were eaten
by wild animals on Mount Olympus.
(Some sources assert that it was at this
point that Heracles joined the Argonauts.)
IX The Amazon's Girdle. Since Admete,
his daughter, wanted a spectacular
present, Eurystheus now sent Heracles
to fetch the girdle or belt of Hippolyta,
queen of the Amazons, who lived near
the River Thermodon on the north coast

of Asia Minor. Heracles picked a body of companions, including Theseus and Telamon, and sailed off, calling at the island of Paros in the Cyclades on the way. When the Parians, whose king was Androgeos, a son of Minos of Crete, killed two of his men, Heracles besieged their town until they gave in, and took two of the king's sons, Alcaeus and Sthenelus, as hostages. In Mysia he helped King Lycus of the Mariandyni in a war against the Bebryces (Lycus founded Heraclea Pontica on the land won in this war) and thence sailed to the land of the Amazons. The girdle had been given to Hippolyta by her father Ares in token of her rule over the tribe; yet when Heracles asked for it, she offered it to him without demur. Hera was furious that he should have so easy a victory and, taking the form of an Amazon, she roused the others to attack Heracles, declaring that he was carrying their queen off; whereupon Heracles, under the impression that Hippolyta had broken faith, killed her, took the girdle from her body, and sailed away. Another version relates how Heracles captured Melanippe and Theseus seized Antiope, these being next in command under Hippolyta. Melanippe was returned to Hippolyta in exchange for the girdle and Theseus took Antiope home, because she was in love with him – for this reason she was said to have betrayed her people to the Greeks.

On his way home from the land of the Amazons Heracles agreed to help Laomedon, king of Troy, whose land was being ravaged by a sea-monster, sent by Poseidon in revenge for Laomedon's refusal to pay agreed wages for the building of Troy's city walls by Poseidon and Apollo. Laomedon was chaining up his daughter Hesione by the seashore to appease the beast, but Heracles came to her rescue, making a bargain that he would destroy the creature in return for the mares Laomedon had been given by Zeus. This he accomplished,

fighting from behind a wall that Athena built to protect him: though, in the end, he was swallowed by the beast, he succeeded in killing it from within. But Laomedon again went back on his word. Heracles swore to have revenge. (According to one account, this incident took place on Heracles' return from his voyage in the *Argo*.)

On his way back to Greece, Heracles landed at Aenus in Thrace, where he killed Sarpedon, brother of King Poltys, although the king had entertained him hospitably. He also captured the island of Thasos, turning it over to the Parians Alcaeus and Sthenelus. On his return to Tiryns, Eurystheus took the Amazon's girdle, and dedicated it in Hera's temple at Argos.

X The Cattle of Geryon. In performing the remaining Labours, Heracles had to travel to the ends of the earth and to the Underworld itself, a place described in the *Odyssey* as bordering the Western Ocean. On these journeys he also performed a number of incidental deeds (*parerga*) supplementary to his Labours. The cattle belonging to the three-headed ogre Geryon (perhaps originally another form of Hades) were pastured on the mythical island of Erythea ('Red Island') usually placed in the Western Ocean off Iberia (Spain): these Heracles had to steal and drive back to Argos.

Heracles began by going to Libya and marching westwards towards the Ocean. Irritated by the heat, he drew his bow on Helios. But instead of resenting this, Helios lent him the great golden bowl in which he returned each night to the east. In this bowl Heracles sailed the Ocean as far as Erythea, setting up the twin Pillars of Heracles as he passed the Straits of Gibraltar. After killing the guard-dog Orthus with his club, he slew the cowherd Eurytion in the same way, and drove the cattle into the gold bowl. Menoetes, who kept Hades' cattle in an adjoining pasture, informed Geryon of the robbery, and the ogre pursued Heracles; but was shot and killed by him on the River Anthemus. Then Heracles sailed on to Tartessus (an unidentifiable city in south-western Spain), where he returned the bowl to Helios and proceeded on foot, crossing Spain and southern France. Here a large force of Ligurians tried to seize the cattle and slay the hero, who ran out of arrows. But Zeus providentially dropped a shower of stones on the Ligurians, and Heracles also pelted them with stones. These, it was believed, are the boulders which still litter the countryside of Provence (where the Ligurians then lived).

Coming to a forest country north of the Black Sea, Heracles was robbed of his horses while he slept. When he looked for them, he came across a strange woman with a snake's tail, living in a cave. It was she who had seized the horses, but she refused to surrender them unless Heracles made love to her. She was the queen of that country, and he remained with her long enough for her to bear him three sons. They were called Scythes, Gelonus, and Agathyrsus, and gave their names to three mighty nations. Then, on handing over the horses, the snake-woman asked Heracles what should become of their sons. He left a bow with her, and told her to name the boy who could draw it as her successor. Scythes proved to possess this ability, and his descendants, the Scythians, became the strongest nation of southern Russia.

Heracles then drove the cattle southwards through Italy. Pausing at the site of Rome, he killed the monstrous Cacus, and was entertained by King Evander, and established his own cult at the *Ara Maxima* ('Greatest Altar'). Near the Campanian town of Baiae he built a huge causeway along the coast. When he reached Rhegium in southern Italy, a bull from the herd swam across to Sicily, and Heracles felt obliged to pursue it, leaving the rest of the herd under the protection of Hephaestus. When the bull

reached western Sicily, King Eryx placed it in his own herd and refused to give it up unless Heracles wrestled with him. Heracles beat him in three matches and killed him. As he drove the cattle across the Isthmus of Corinth, a giant, Alcyoneus, attacked him, flinging a stone so hard that it struck Heracles, bounced back, and killed the assailant.

However Heracles' troubles were not yet over, for as he drove the cattle on the last lap to Tiryns, Hera sent a gadfly which scattered them, and so he had the trouble of collecting them all over again. Eurystheus was most surprised to see Heracles, who had been away so long that he was given up for lost. The cattle were sacrificed to Hera.

XI The Golden Apples of the Hesperides. Heracles had now completed the statutory ten Labours imposed by the Delphic Oracle, but as Eurystheus had ruled two invalid, he had to perform two more. First (though the order of these two Labours, as was mentioned above, is sometimes reversed) he had to bring Eurystheus the Golden Apples of the Hesperides ('daughters of the evening'), sometimes said to be daughters of the Titan Atlas, who lived near their garden and supported the sky on his neck.

These apples, given by Gaia to Hera as a wedding present, were to be found in a garden at the edge of the earth where the Hesperides and the serpent Ladon (said to have a hundred heads) guarded them.

To begin with, Heracles had much difficulty in finding the garden. He first consulted the nymphs of the River Eridanus, who advised him to force the information out of Nereus, one of the sea-gods whose habit it was to change into fantastic shapes when efforts were made to catch him. Heracles found him, held him fast throughout all his transformations, and coaxed out of him the whereabouts of the garden in the distant West.

He met with a number of incidental adventures on the way. Killing the eagle that tormented the captive Prometheus, he freed the prisoner of his bonds; he slew Busiris, king of Egypt, who tried to sacrifice him to Zeus; in Libya he wrestled with the mighty Antaeus, Gaia's son, and killed him by holding him high off the ground; and he beat a son of Ares, Lycaon, who had challenged him to a fight. In Rhodes he stole a bullock, sacrificed it, and ate it, while its owner stood cursing him: and that, it was believed, was why for ever afterwards the Rhodians' sacrifices to Heracles were conducted to the accompaniment of curses.

There are two versions of Heracles' acquisition of the apples. The commoner story tells how, perhaps acting on a tip received from Prometheus, he persuaded the Titan Atlas to go for them while he himself, aided by Athena, held up the sky on the Titan's behalf. Atlas was glad of the rest and had no difficulty in getting the fruit from his daughters. On his return, however, he refused to receive the sky back, and decided to deliver the apples to Eurystheus himself. Heracles had to agree, but first asked Atlas to hold the burden for him while he padded his head. While Atlas complied, Heracles ducked out, picked up the apples, and made off with them to Greece.

In the version known to Euripides, Heracles himself killed Ladon and picked the fruit from the tree; being thirsty he made a spring gush forth by kicking the ground. (Later this water saved the Argonauts when they passed that way). There is also a tale that Emathion, a son of Eos and Tithonus, happened to be in the vicinity at the time of Heracles' attempt, and tried to prevent his theft of the apples, but was killed. Hera placed Ladon in the sky as the Constellation Draco. This version is consistent with the myth that Atlas had long before been turned into a great stony mountain, after Perseus had shown him the Gorgon's head. When Eurystheus received the apples, he at once gave them back to Heracles, since they were too holy for him to keep. Athena then took them and returned them to their garden.

XII The Descent to the Underworld for Cerberus. Heracles' last Labour (according to the usual reckoning) was the fetching of the infernal watch-dog Cerberus from the gate of Hades' House. In setting him this task, Eurystheus hoped to be rid of his enemy for ever. But instead Heracles defeated Hades in person, thus completing his claim to immortality. First he had to find his way to the Underworld: this he did by being initiated into the Eleusinian Mysteries by Eumolpus (for this purpose, as a foreigner, he had to be adopted by a citizen of Eleusis, Pylius) and purified of his killing of the Centaurs. He was now able to proceed to Hades' realm, fortified by the rites of Persephone. Some said that it was now that he rescued Alcestis from death. He went to Taenarum in the southern Peloponnese, where he was met and escorted down to the land of the dead by Hermes, the guide of the shades, and by Athena, his protectress. When they reached the Styx, its oarsman Charon was so frightened of Heracles that he speedily rowed him across (for which misdemeanour Hades later chained him up for a year). Heracles then had to fight Hades himself for admission, and wounded him in the gateway, so that Hades was obliged to depart to Olympus for Paeon's healing ointments, and agreed to Heracles' request for Cerberus – provided he was able to catch the beast without weapons. In the Underworld Heracles saw Theseus and Pirithous sitting in chairs of forgetfulness, where they had been imprisoned for trying to abduct Persephone. Hades agreed to the freeing of Theseus, since the latter had not sought to rape Persephone himself, but merely to help his friend; but Pirithous' doom remained sealed. Heracles also met the shades of the Gorgon Medusa and of Meleager. Hermes told him not to fear Medusa's shade, which could not harm him. The shade of Meleager told Heracles the story of his death, and when Heracles, moved by compassion, offered to marry his sister, he described Deianira's beauty to the hero. Heracles later fulfilled his promise. He also, it was said, freed Ascalaphus from the rock under which he had been pinned (for revealing that Persephone had eaten the pomegranate seeds), and killed one of Hades' cows to feed the shades. Persephone appealed to him to leave without doing any more damage, so he caught Cerberus, picked it up, and walked off, emerging from the Underworld to the upper world. On his way to Tiryns the terrible appearance of the hell-hound caused a number of fatalities: the plant aconite, a deadly poison, sprang up from its spittle, and Eurystheus was already in his bronze jar well before Cerberus' arrival. However Heracles took the monstrous dog straight back to Hades, as he had agreed to do.

Although his guarantee of immortality was now won, he still had to live out the rest of his life, and even to endure further spells of slavery before reaching his final haven. He began by divorcing Megara (if he had not killed her) and marrying her to his nephew Iolaus, on the grounds that he was himself now unworthy of her, since he had killed their children. He then took part in an archery contest organised by Eurytus, king of Oechalia, of which his daughter Iole was to be the prize. Heracles won, but in view of his unhappy matrimonial record Eurytus refused to honour the bargain, despite the pleas of his son Iphitus, who admired Heracles' valour. After the hero left in a rage, it was discovered that some mares, or cattle, had also disappeared (stolen, it turned out, by Autolycus), and Iphitus went after Heracles and asked him to

help search for them. Heracles took the boy to Tiryns, but then, perhaps resenting the implication of his request, hurled him down from his rooftop, or from the city wall.

Whether this murderous deed was self-inspired or the result of a madness inflicted by Hera, Heracles was visited with a serious bout of insanity. In his desire to be cured, he appealed to King Neleus of Pylos to purify him, but the king, a friend of Eurytus, refused. Heracles resorted to the Delphic Oracle, but the Pythian priestess, in abhorrence of his affliction, turned him away. Heracles then stole her tripod and threatened to destroy Delphi. Apollo came, and the two fought, until Zeus flung a thunderbolt to force his sons apart. Then at last the priestess gave Heracles the advice he needed. He was to accept another period of slavery, this time for three years. And he must pay his price to Eurytus as blood-money for the death of Iphitus – but Eurytus refused the fee.

Hermes took the hero and sold him to Queen Omphale of Lydia, the widow of Tmolus. In her service he performed many deeds, capturing the Cercopes of Ephesus and killing Syleus, a Lydian who forced travellers to work in his vineyard; Heracles struck him with his own hoe. He also defeated Omphale's enemies the Itoni and destroyed their city. Some authors claimed that Omphale made Heracles wear women's clothes and spin. Others asserted that she became his wife and bore Lamus to him. When he left her, his sanity came back to him.

Heracles now embarked on a programme of vengeance against the various people who had wronged him. He began with his enemies at Troy, raising an army and a fleet of eighteen galleys against them; Telamon of Salamis was his deputy. When he had beached his ships, Heracles left Oicles in charge of them, but the Trojans killed him and tried to burn the fleet. Heracles then besieged them in their city, and Telamon breached the wall. This success angered the jealous Heracles, who was appeased only when Telamon pretended to be building an altar for his worship. The hero killed Laomedon and all his sons except Podarces (whom Hesione ransomed with her veil) and Tithonus. Heracles took the mares which Laomedon owed him, and gave Hesione to Telamon, to whom she bore Teucer. He left Podarces in charge of Troy; he was now called Priam, and Greek etymologists wrongly believed that his name came from the verb *priamai* ('I buy'), on account of his being ransomed.

Heracles sailed away from Troy and was driven south to the island of Cos by a violent wind sent by Hera. This time Zeus punished her for her cruelty to his son by suspending her from Olympus by the wrists, her ankles being weighted by anvils. On Cos, the Greeks were attacked by the Meropes, whose king Eurypylus Heracles now killed. From this island Athena fetched Heracles to help the gods in their war with the giants at the Phlegraean fields. For Heracles was indispensable in the conflict because only a mortal man could deal the death-blow to their enemies. (See GIANTS.)

Next Heracles attacked Augeas, the king of Elis, who had refused to pay him the agreed fee for cleansing his stables of cow-dung (see Fifth Labour above). His first expedition failed, because Augeas was helped by the Moliones, Actor's sons, who were excellent generals. Being exiled by Eurystheus from the Argolid, Heracles moved to Pheneus in Arcadia and slew the Moliones from an ambush as they made their way as ambassadors to the Isthmian Games. It was at this point that he attacked Augeas again and slew him, placing his son Phyleus on his throne, and then, after sacrificing to his father Zeus at Olympia, reputedly founding the Olympic Games. Next he went on to Pylos, where he had an old score to settle with King Neleus, who had refused to purify him of the homicide of Iphitus. According to one account he had already killed Neleus and his sons at the time of Iphitus' death, and the madness which resulted in his servitude to Omphale ensued upon both these acts. At all events, of Neleus' sons only Nestor survived, because he was living away from Pylos at Gerenia.

Heracles then turned his attention to Sparta, where Hippocoon was king. This man had dispossessed his brother Tyndareos and had sided with Neleus against Heracles. Moreover, his sons had killed Heracles' cousin Oeonus for throwing a stone at a dog. So Heracles, enlisting the support of Cepheus, king of Tegea, attacked Sparta. In the battle his brother Iphicles, Cepheus, and most of Cepheus' sons were killed. However he slew his enemies and restored Tyndareos to the throne of Sparta. Cepheus' daughter Sterope defended Tegea from its enemies by holding up a lock of the Gorgon's hair which Athena had given to her father. Meanwhile Heracles had seduced Cepheus' sister Auge, who bore him Telephus.

Heracles then remembered his promise given to the ghost of Meleager to marry Deianira, and went to Calydon where Oeneus was king. He had to fight the river-god Achelous for Deianira, but won and broke the god's horn, and Deianira became his wife. Heracles helped the Calydonians to conquer the Thesprotians, and seduced King Phylas' daughter Astyoche, who bore him Tlepolemus. Either now or at a subsequent stage of their marriage, Deianira bore Heracles a son, Hyllus, and a daughter, Macaria. They had to leave Calydon because Heracles, in a fit of temper, struck down and killed the boy Eunomus, who, as he served at table, caused him annoyance by spilling wine on him. Though Oeneus forgave Heracles, he had to follow the custom applying to homicides and go into exile; and so, taking Deianira, he proceeded to Trachis. As they cross the River Evenus, the Centaur Nessus, carrying Deianira over the swollen river, tried to rape her and was shot by Heracles with one of his arrows steeped in the Hydra's venom. As Nessus died, he told Deianira to take his blood and use it as a charm if ever Heracles stopped loving her; and, unknown to her husband, she preserved it in a flask.

Arriving in Trachis, Heracles pursued a number of wars in aid of Ceyx, the country's king, defeating the Dryopes and the Lapiths and giving part of their territory to Aegimius, king of the Dorians. When Aegimius, in consequence, offered Heracles a home and land in his kingdom, he refused it for himself, but accepted it on behalf of his descendants, who in due course were believed to have allied themselves with the Dorian race.

Heracles then went into Thessaly, where at Itonus he was challenged to a duel by Cycnus, a son of Ares who was building his father a temple using his victims' skulls as bricks. He used to lie in wait for pilgrims on their way to Delphi, kill them, and take their offerings. When Ares intervened on his behalf, Heracles killed Cycnus and, with the help of Athena, fought against the god, whom he wounded. Zeus was said to have separated them by hurling a thunderbolt between them. According to one version, this incident took place in Macedonia, while Heracles was on his way to find the garden of the Hesperides.

The last war of Heracles' life was his expedition of vengeance against Eurytus who, after Heracles won his daughter Iole in an archery contest, had failed to hand the girl over. Heracles left Deianira in Trachis, and proceeded to Oechalia (which was probably in Thessaly, but perhaps in Euboea) with an army of allies. There followed a furious battle in which two of the sons of Ceyx were

killed; but Heracles was triumphant and slew Eurytus and all his sons. Iole tried to escape by leaping off the battlements, but her dress billowed out and broke her fall, so that her life was saved. Heracles took her as his concubine and sent her to Trachis with other prisoners. He also conveyed orders to Deianira to send him a clean tunic so that he might make a thank-offering to Zeus at Cape Cenaeum in Euboea. Lichas was sent to fetch the garment; but Deianira, afraid that Heracles cared more for Iole than for herself, dyed it in the blood of Nessus before handing it over. Lichas delivered the tunic and Heracles put it on.

After he had begun the sacrifice, the poisonous blood started to burn Heracles' flesh. In his agony he picked up Lichas and hurled him far out to sea. He tried to tear off the garment, but it pulled his skin away with it. He was taken by ship to Trachis, where Deianira, realising how Nessus had tricked her, hanged herself in grief. Heracles, too, understood what had happened, and remembered a prophecy that he would die not at the hands of the living but of one already dead. He sent an enquiry to Delphi, which thereupon told him to erect a pyre on Mount Oeta in Thessaly, climb upon it, and leave the rest to Zeus. Taking his son Hyllus, he obeyed the oracle. When Hyllus had built the pyre, however, and Heracles had mounted it, nobody could bring himself to apply a light until Poeas, a king of the Malians, who was passing with his sheep, was induced to do so by the offer of Heracles' bow and arrows, which were reputed to be unerring. As the flames burnt away the hero's mortal parts, there was seen a great flash of lightning, after which Heracles was found to have disappeared. It was believed that he ascended to Olympus, where he dwelt thereafter with the gods, reconciled to Hera and married to her daughter Hebe. Zeus made him into a constellation.

After his deification, Heracles occasionally appeared on earth to help his friends. He persuaded his new wife Hebe (whose name meant 'youth') to make Iolaus young again in order to defend Heracles' children in Attica against the attacks of the hero's old enemy Eurystheus, and he and Hebe accompanied Iolaus into battle in the guise of two stars which shone on Iolaus' chariot-yoke. Heracles later appeared to Philoctetes on Lemnos and commanded him to go to Troy and help the Greeks with the bow which Heracles had given his father Poeas; he also promised that Philoctetes' festering wound would be cured.

Heracles became a very popular god, and was identified throughout the Mediterranean with foreign gods who shared his characteristics; this caused his mythology to be inflated with a great number of additions. There is no extant epic poem about his deeds, but he is a prominent character in several plays, notably Sophocles' *Women of Trachis* and Euripides' *Alcestis* and *Heracles*.

His mythology developed vigorously in Rome and Etruria, partly under the influence of Phoenician traders, who brought to Italy their god Melqart, whom they identified with Heracles. Taking the attributes of Melqart, the Italian deity became a patron of merchants and bargains; the exclusion of women from his worship at his Great Altar (*Ara Maxima*) harmonises with this interpretation, since they would not have figured in the Phoenician cult. Among the Etruscans Heracles (known as Hercle) was a god of war, and also of both fresh and salt water; and in an attempt to link Etruria with Greece, the paternity of Tyrrhenus, eponym of the Etruscans, was attributed to him. In addition, perhaps because he had taken Cerberus from Hades, he was regarded as an important god of the Underworld. One Etruscan tradition claimed, for the sake of national pride, that it was not the Romans themselves but the god Hercle who had freed Rome from paying tribute to Etruria.

On his visit to the site of the future Rome this god, whom the Romans called Hercules, was believed to have overcome the monster Cacus, and subsequently to have married Evander's daughter Lavinia, who bore him two sons, Pallas (a name more often given to the son of Evander) and Latinus (usually the father of Lavinia). He taught Evander's Arcadian colonists the art of writing, it was said, and settled certain Greeks whom he had brought with him upon the Palatine Hill. While he was there, tradition recounted, he played dice with the custodian of a temple that had been dedicated to him. The custodian lost, and as a result had to furnish his master with a meal, a bed, and a woman: the woman he thereupon gave him was Fabula, a local prostitute. Another version of Cacus' story represents him as an Etruscan marauder who invaded Campania and was killed by Heracles, who defended the Greek settlers there.

Heracles the Dactyl see DACTYLS.

Hercules see HERACLES.

Hermaphroditus Son of Hermes and Aphrodite, brought up on Mount Ida in Phrygia. He was very handsome, and when, as a young man, he left home for Halicarnassus in Caria, the Naiad Salmacis fell passionately in love with him. He repulsed her, but when, later on, he inadvertently bathed in her spring, she embraced him and pulled him down into the pool, praying to the gods that she and he might for ever be united. Their bodies were joined into one, becoming a hermaphrodite, which has female breasts and proportions but male genitals. As a result of Hermaphroditus' prayers to his parents, the spring exercised a like effect on all men who bathed in it thereafter.

Hermes (Latin: *Mercurius*) Son of Zeus and of Atlas' daughter Maia. He was Zeus' messenger, the guide of shades to Hades' House, protector of travellers, bringer of luck, and patron deity of thieves and merchants. He was depicted in art as a young man wearing a wide-brimmed winged hat and winged sandals and carrying a herald's staff (*caduceus*) crowned with two snakes representing those which once attached themselves to the staff after Hermes had found them fighting and laid it between them. As a god of travellers, he was thought to have cleared the roads of stones. In memory of this, the herms, his monuments, were erected along roads and, because he was also a god of fertility, they were adorned with the phallus. The earliest herms were simply heaps of stones round a pillar. Later they often consisted of a head surmounting a square column adorned with a phallus, and herms of this more elaborate type were found in city streets, courtyards, and gymnasia. Hermes was popular among athletes, and the statues representing him as an athletic young man (*ephebos*) were commonly to be seen in ancient sportsgrounds.

His birthplace was Arcadia, where he was always popular. The story of his birth is told in the Homeric *Hymn to Hermes*. Zeus used to visit the nymph Maia, the daughter of Atlas and Pleione, in a cave on Mount Cyllene, while Hera was asleep. She eventually bore his son, Hermes. The child was born at dawn, but was highly precocious, for by noon he was big enough to walk out of the cave. On doing so, he found a tortoise, which he killed and turned into the first lyre ever made; he fitted it with a framework and seven strings, of sheepgut or gut from the cows he next proceeded to steal. For in the evening of the same day he went to Pieria in Macedonia and stole fifty cows from the herd of Apollo (who was away paying court to Hymenaeus, son of Magnes). He then dragged them backwards by their tails to Pylos in the Peleponnese, near the River Alpheius. On the way there, he tied brushwood to his feet to confuse his tracks. Then he sacrificed two of the cows to the twelve Olympian gods, but ate none of the meat himself. He burnt the hooves and heads to destroy evidence of his deed, and hid the animals, throwing his brushwood sandals into the river. He then returned to Maia's cave, where he crept innocently into his cradle.

Apollo soon came looking for his cattle (according to the Homeric *Hymn to Apollo*, Battus put him on the right track, and was later turned into a rock by Hermes for doing so) and was amazed to find Hermes lying there like a baby in his cot. The child denied all knowledge of the theft, even claiming not to know the meaning of the word 'cow'. Apollo searched the cave, and although he found nothing, summoned Hermes to Zeus' judgment seat. Here Hermes wove a cunning tale of his innocence, but while Apollo's back was turned filched his quiver and bow. Zeus saw through his lies and told him to return the cattle. But when Hermes had brought Apollo to the hiding-place, he took up the lyre and played with such mastery that Apollo was enchanted and desired to have the instrument for himself. Hermes therefore proposed a bargain, that Apollo, in exchange for the lyre, should consent to overlook the theft of the cows; and Apollo agreed. When Hermes handed back his bow and quiver, Apollo was greatly amused and became his firm friend, making him protector of herdsmen, granting him authority over divination by pebbles, and bestowing upon him his staff (Greek: *kerykeion*, Latin: *caduceus*) in recognition of his powers. Hermes was often portrayed in art carrying a ram on his shoulders, and he was known by the title *Nomios*, 'the pasturer'.

It was important, naturally, for Hermes to be reconciled with Hera, for she had an ugly reputation for her treatment of Zeus' children by others. And so, whether with her knowledge or without it, he dressed himself again in his swaddling-clothes – some say disguising himself as Hera's own son Ares – and sat on her lap, so that she suckled him. In this way she became his foster-mother, and had to treat him as her own child.

Hermes' exploits as messenger of Zeus and the gods are manifold. He saved Dionysus, when that god was a baby, from the wrath of Hera. Helping Zeus in his love-affair with Io, he had the task of securing her escape from the watchful Argus of the many eyes, whom he killed – the reason, it was believed, for his title *Argeiphontes*. When Ares was captured and imprisoned in a jar by the Aloadae, it was Hermes who rescued him. He also accompanied Zeus on his journeys across the earth, visiting Lycaon, and Philemon and Baucis. He arranged for the beauty contest between Hera, Athena, and Aphrodite, decided by the Judgment of Paris. He escorted Priam to the hut of Achilles to recover Hector's corpse. And he helped Odysseus to overcome the wiles of Circe and Calypso.

Hermes had a number of love-affairs. Among the goddesses his principal love was Aphrodite, who bore him Hermaphroditus and Priapus. At first she would have nothing to do with him. Zeus took pity on him, however, and sent his eagle to steal one of the goddess' golden sandals, as she bathed in the River Achelous. Hermes offered her the sandal back in return for her favours and she signified that she was willing.

He was the father of Pan by a nymph, or by a daughter of Dryops named Penelope. Another of his sons was Daphnis. He also fell in love with a number of mortal women, including Herse, a daughter of Cecrops. When her sister Aglaurus refused Hermes access to Herse's bedroom, the god turned Aglaurus to stone.

Herse bore him Cephalus. He also loved Apemosyne, who at first ran so fast that he could not catch her; but then he succeeded in trapping her by placing hides in her path, so that she slipped on them. When, however, her brother Althaemenes discovered she was pregnant, he kicked her to death.

Hermes performed his greatest service to Zeus after Typhon had cut out Zeus' sinews and hidden them in a cave in Cilicia, thus completely incapacitating him. Hermes took Aegipan to find the sinews and get them back from the serpent Delphyne, who was their guardian. Hermes was also associated with the Underworld, and escorted the shades of dead mortals down to the River Styx, where Charon ferried them across; in this capacity he was called *Psychopompos*, 'guide of souls'. He was sent by Zeus to negotiate with Hades for the return of Persephone, and helped Heracles on his quest for Cerberus. When Orpheus forfeited his right to bring Eurydice to the upper world, it was Hermes who conducted her back to Hades' House.

Herminius, Titus *see* HORATIUS COCLES.

Hermione Daughter of Menelaus and Helen. At the age of nine she was abandoned by her mother, when Helen went to Troy with Paris. According to Euripides, Orestes, after the murder of his mother Clytemnestra and her lover Aegisthus following the fall of Troy, seized his cousin Hermione as a hostage in order to force Menelaus to save him from the Argive people, who had condemned him to death. It was also sometimes said that Orestes and Hermione were already married before Menelaus' return from Troy, perhaps in a ceremony arranged by Tyndareos. A different tradition again recorded that Hermione was already betrothed to Orestes before the expedition to Troy, but that during the siege Menelaus changed his mind and promised her to Neoptolemus, Achilles' son, whom, after his return, she duly married. A little later, however, Neoptolemus went to Delphi to ask Apollo that he should receive recompense for the death of Achilles, and Orestes slew him there. According to another version Hermione, during her marriage to Neoptolemus, had tried to kill Andromache, her husband's Trojan concubine, whom she accused of making her barren by witchcraft. When Peleus, Neoptolemus' grandfather, put a stop to this attempt, Hermione fled to Orestes at Sparta, and Orestes subsequently killed Neoptolemus at Delphi. He then took Hermione and married her, and she bore him a son, Tisamenus.

Hero and **Leander** Hero was a priestess of Aphrodite at Sestos; Leander was a young man from Abydos, on the other side of the narrow Hellespont (Dardanelles). They met and fell in love, but Hero, because of her dedication to the goddess, was barred from marriage. To keep the affair secret, they arranged that he should swim across to her every night and back home every morning. To guide him, she put a light in the window of the tower where she lived. When winter came, her light blew out one night and he was drowned. Next morning she saw his body lying below her on the shore. In her grief she threw herself down from the tower and fell to her death. The story was told by the poet Musaeus.

Herse ('dew') Daughter of Cecrops and Aglaurus. Against Athena's command, she and her sister Aglaurus spied on the baby Erichthonius. Hermes fell in love with Herse and she bore him Cephalus.

Hersilia Romulus' wife, captured at the 'Rape of the Sabine women'.

Hesione Daughter of Laomedon, king of Troy. When Apollo and Poseidon

had agreed to build Laomedon the walls of Troy for a fee, he refused to pay them. In revenge Apollo sent a plague and Poseidon a sea-monster, to which an oracle declared that a maiden must be sacrificed. When the lot drawn for the victim had fallen on Hesione and she was already chained to a rock waiting to be devoured, Heracles offered to kill the monster for Laomedon, in return for two divine mares which his grandfather Tros had received from Zeus. Laomedon agreed; Heracles attacked the beast and, after a furious battle, killed it. But Laomedon once again refused to pay. In consequence, Heracles returned as soon as he could with an army, sacked Troy and captured Hesione, giving her as concubine to his ally Telamon, to whom she bore Teucer. Hesione was given the chance to choose one Trojan prisoner to be set free, and chose her brother Podarces, ransoming him with her veil as a token payment. He became King Priam, and subsequently asked for Hesione's return, which Telamon refused.

Hesperides Daughters of Atlas and Pleione, or Atlas and Hesperis, or Nyx (Night) and Erebus. These nymphs, four or seven in number, lived in a garden in the far West and, with the aid of a serpent, Ladon, guarded the golden fruit of an apple tree that grew there. The apples were a wedding gift which Hera received from Gaia. Their recreation was singing, and their names were Aegle, Erythea, Arethusa, Hestia, Hespera, Hesperusa, and Hespereia. When Heracles was ordered for his eleventh (or twelfth) Labour to deliver these apples to Eurystheus, he tricked Atlas, who stood holding the heavens on a nearby mountain, into obtaining them for him. After the theft, however, Athena took care to ensure their return to their garden from which they came.

Hesperus The evening star, originally a

son of Atlas, who was carried away by the wind from the summit of his father's mountain and transformed into the star.

Hestia Identified by the Romans with Vesta; the goddess of hearth and home. She was the eldest of the three daughters of Cronos and Rhea. Although she might have had Apollo or Poseidon as a husband, she refused marriage; and since she herself was a virgin, she insisted on that state in her priestesses, who at Rome were called the Vestal Virgins. She has no mythology.

Hilaira Daughter of Leucippus, betrothed to Lynceus and carried off by Castor.

Himerus A personification of sexual desire, sometimes said to be an attendant of Aphrodite.

Hippasus *1.* Son of Leucippe, one of the daughters of Minyas. When these women were driven mad because they refused to accept the worship of Dionysus, they drew lots to see which should offer sacrifice to the god. The lot fell on Leucippe, and her son Hippasus was torn to pieces.
2. Son of Ceyx, king of Trachis. He was killed fighting for Heracles against Eurytus.
3. Son of Admetus and Alcestis.

Hippe ('mare'). Daughter of the Centaur Chiron. She had conceived a child, Melanippe, by Aeolus, and was ashamed to tell her father of the child. Artemis was said to have taken pity on her and to have turned her, according to one account, into the constellation Equus, the horse (more usually identified with Pegasus).

Hippocoon A king of Sparta, the son of Oebalus and the Naiad Batia; he wrongfully drove his brother Tyndareos off the throne. Hippocoon offended Hera-

cles twice: first, because he refused to purify him of the murder of Iphitus, and secondly, because his sons killed Heracles' cousin Oeonus for throwing stones at their dog which had attacked him. In his campaigns of vengeance Heracles eventually killed Hippocoon and his twelve sons, and restored Tyndareos to the throne of Sparta.

Hippodamia *1. see* PIRITHOUS.
2. Daughter of Oenomaus, king of Pisa. After an oracle had warned him that her husband would cause his death, Oenomaus made it a condition of her marriage that her suitor should attempt to carry her off in a chariot. Oenomaus himself followed in full armour in his own chariot and attempted to spear the suitor along the road to the Isthmus of Corinth. After he had killed a dozen suitors in this way, Pelops came and bribed his charioteer Myrtilus to replace the linchpin of Oenomaus' chariot with a wax dummy, offering him a night in Hippodamia's bed and half the kingdom as bribes. When the chariot broke up, Oenomaus was killed, either in the crash or subsequently by Pelops, who then married Hippodamia. Later he murdered Myrtilus, who cursed him as he died.

Hippodamia bore Pelops several sons, including Atreus, Thyestes, and Pittheus. But she hated her husband's bastard son Chrysippus, whom Laius abducted. After the boy's restitution, Hippodamia persuaded her own sons to murder him; then, because Pelops heard of her complicity in the crime, she either hanged herself or fled to the city of Midea which Atreus and Thyestes were then ruling.

Hippolochus A Lycian; a son of Bellerophon and the father of Glaucus *4*.

Hippolyta or **Hippolyte** *1.* A queen of the Amazons, whose girdle or belt Heracles had to fetch as his ninth Labour. There were two versions of her story:

the first asserted that she was killed in the battle that took place over the girdle; according to the second, she lived on and led an attack on Athens to take vengeance for Theseus' abduction of Antiope. It was also sometimes said that after this attack failed, she was captured and married by Theseus and became the mother of Hippolytus (see next entry).

2. Daughter of Cretheus; the wife of Acastus.

Hippolytus *1.* Son of Theseus, king of Athens, and Hippolyta, queen of the Amazons, or her sister Antiope. After his mother had died, his father married Ariadne's sister Phaedra. According to one tradition Theseus, since he was heir to the aged Pittheus of Troezen, sent Hippolytus there to rule at the time of his remarriage. Theseus himself was later exiled from Athens and went to Troezen with Phaedra. There she fell in love with Hippolytus, who, as a follower of the virginal Artemis, would have nothing to do with her. In his *Hippolytus*, Euripides paints Phaedra as a modest woman who is driven by her intense passion to hang herself, leaving a letter for her husband incriminating Hippolytus. According to this play, moreover, the association of Hippolytus and Phaedra was rendered easier by Theseus' long absence in the Underworld. When he returned, he would not accept Hippolytus' protestations of innocence, and called on Poseidon – who was sometimes called his father, and had granted him three wishes – to rid him of his son. Hippolytus was therefore killed: when he was riding into exile along the shore at Troezen a monstrous bull rose out of the sea and frightened his chariot team, which threw him out and dragged him to his death. Theseus then discovered the truth from Artemis; and according to some versions the goddess could bring her devotee back from the dead, bribing Asclepius for this purpose. Hippolytus

refused to stay with his father and went instead, according to Italian stories, to Aricia in Latium, where he became king and instituted the cult of Diana (Artemis) at Lake Nemorensis (Nemi), assuming the name of a minor god, Virbius. At Troezen it was said that Hippolytus became the constellation of the Charioteer (Auriga); and girls, on their marriage, dedicated to him a lock of their hair.

2. *see* GIANTS

Hippomedon One of the Seven champions who attacked Thebes. His emblem was Typhon. He was killed by Hyperbius at the Oncaean Gate. His son Polydorus was one of the successors (Epigoni) who later avenged their fathers and sacked the city.

Hippomenes *see* ATALANTA.

Hippotas *see* AEOLUS *1.*

Hippotes *see* TEMENUS.

Hippothoon or **Hippothous** *see* ALOPE.

Horatii and **Curiatii** Two sets of triplets who were chosen to fight duels against one another in the legendary war between Rome and Alba Longa, at the time when Tullus Hostilius was believed to be king at Rome. As the two cities were afraid that a decisive battle would sap their resources beyond bearing, they agreed by an oath to settle their differences by means of a battle of champions between the two sets of brothers. Livy regards the Horatii as the Roman and the Curiatii as the Alban family, though he adds that it was disputed which was which. Clad in full armour, the triplets attacked each other with their swords. Before long the three Albans were all wounded, and two of the Romans were killed. The third, Publius Horatius (according to the version identifying the Horatii as the Romans), was still uninjured and fled. The Curiatii, though wounded, pursued, but at different speeds; so that Horatius was able to turn and kill them one by one. On his return to Rome, carrying the spoils of his three foes, he was met by his sister, who had been engaged to marry one of the Curiatii. On seeing the dead man's clothes, which she herself had woven, she burst into tears, whereupon her brother plunged his sword into her body with the cry, 'So perish all Roman women who mourn a foe!' Accused of treason for taking the law into his own hands, Publius Horatius was condemned to death. However he was so popular by now that – on appeal, it was believed, to the Assembly of the People – he was acquitted. His father purified him of blood-guilt by making him pass under a beam in token of submission to the law.

Horatius Cocles The legendary hero who defended the only bridge over the Tiber, when the new Roman Republic was threatened by the Etruscan Lars Porsenna, who wished to restore the exiled Tarquinius Superbus to the throne. He was held, according to some accounts, to be a descendant of Publius Horatius (*see* HORATII *above*).

The country people had taken refuge behind the city walls. The Janiculum, the hill which lay just over the Tiber and overlooked Rome, had been captured by the Etruscans, so that it was imperative to hew the bridge down. Horatius, who was leader of the party guarding the bridge, persuaded his fleeing comrades to stop and begin hacking the supports down. He himself, together with Spurius Lartius and Titus Herminius, stood at the other end of the bridge and kept the enemy at bay until the structure was about to fall. Then he compelled his companions to rush back to safety; and soon afterwards the bridge collapsed. As it crumbled, Horatius, with a prayer to the god of the

river, leapt fully armed into the Tiber and swam back to the river-bank through a hail of missiles. For this feat Horatius was said to have received the honour of a statue in the place of Assembly (Comitium) and a gift of as much land as he could drive a plough round in a day. The name 'Cocles' ('one-eyed') was apparently derived from a statue of a one-eyed personage (in fact, the god Vulcan) which, in historical times, stood at the head of the wooden bridge.

Horse, Wooden *see* EPEIUS; ODYSSEUS.

Hostilius *see* TULLUS.

Hours, the (Horae) Daughters of Zeus and Themis. The name means not 'hours of the day' but 'seasons of the year'. The number of Hours or Seasons varied from two to four, but generally there are three: Spring, Summer, and Winter. In Athens two or three were recognised, Thallo (Spring), Carpo (Harvest, Autumn, Fall), and sometimes Auxo ('Increase', i.e. Summer). In Hesiod they are given ethical names, Eunomia ('law and order'), Dike ('justice'), and Eirene ('peace'). They were wardens of the sky and when the gods went forth in their chariots, they rolled aside the clouds from the gate of Olympus.

Hundred-Armed (Hecatoncheires) *see* GIANTS.

Hyacinthus Son of Amyclas, king of Sparta, and Diomede, or of Pierus and the Muse Clio. He was a very handsome young man, and Thamyris (said to be the first homosexual) and later Apollo fell in love with him. He preferred the god. When the two of them engaged in a game of discus-throwing, Apollo accidentally hit Hyacinthus with his discus (some say that the west wind Zephyrus deflected it out of jealousy) and killed him. Unable to revive the youth, Apollo caused the blood from his wound to be transformed into the hyacinth flower (not ours, but a kind of iris), of which the petals were inscribed AI AI ('alas'!) in memory of his beloved. The god declared that a brave hero would one day be commemorated similarly – it was Aias (Ajax), the son of Telamon – and that Hyacinthus was to be venerated in Sparta.

Hyades ('Rainers') Five daughters of Oceanus and Tethys, or of Atlas and Pleione. As a reward for having nursed the god Dionysus as a baby on Mount Nysa, they were transformed into a cluster of stars. Another version of the story stated that they wept so much for the death of their brother Hyas (killed in Libya by a boar or a lion while out hunting) that they turned into stars.

Hyas see HYADES.

Hydra see HERACLES.

Hylas Son of Theodamas, king of the Dryopes, and the nymph Menodice. Heracles, after stealing one of Theodamas' oxen, fought him in a furious battle. Having killed the father, he carried off the son, a beautiful child, training him as his squire and becoming his lover. When Heracles accompanied the Argonauts, he broke his oar off the Bithynian coast and had to land to find a new one. Hylas, whom he sent to fetch water, was pulled down by the local water-nymphs into the pool and was never seen again. Heracles, wild with grief, was left behind in Mysia looking for the boy. Polyphemus the Lapith stayed behind, founded the city of Cius, and promised Heracles to continue the search for Hylas; though it proved unsuccessful.

Hyllus Heracles' son by Deianira. As Heracles lay dying on the pyre, he commanded Hyllus, when he should come

of age, to marry Iole, whom Heracles had won in an archery contest and fought for, when her father Eurytus would not give her up. It had been as a result of her jealousy of Iole that Deianira had brought about Heracles' death by sending him the tunic poisoned with Nessus' blood. Hyllus and Heracles' other children were protected by the hero's friend Ceyx, king of Trachis, until Eurystheus, Heracles' old enemy, decided to make war on them. Because of the weakness of Ceyx, the children of Heracles took shelter with Theseus, king of Athens (or his son Demophon). Eurystheus invaded Attica, but was killed either by Hyllus or by his cousin Iolaus, after Heracles' daughter Macaria had sacrificed herself in obedience to an oracle which declared that nothing but the immolation of a noble virgin could enable the Athenians to defeat Eurystheus. According to one account Eurystheus, when he had been taken prisoner, was killed on the orders of Heracles' mother Alcmena.

Hyllus married Iole, who bore him a son, Cleodaeus. Having misunderstood a Delphic oracle about his right to take his inheritance of the Argive kingdom, he invaded the Peloponnese. For Delphi had ordered him to wait for the 'third fruit': Hyllus supposed this to mean the third harvest, thus interpreting it to indicate that he could march after three years. But the oracle turned out to refer to the third generation, that is to say it imposed a delay of ninety years. In the war Hyllus was killed in single combat with Echemus of Tegea: it had been agreed that the duel would be regarded as decisive. It was not until Temenus, Hyllus' grandson, attacked the Peloponnese a hundred years later that the children of Heracles came into their own and the oracle was fulfilled.

Hymen or **Hymenaeus** A personification of marriage, the name being taken from the shout of the wedding guests *o*

hymen, hymenaie or *hymen hymenai' o.*
A myth was invented for him, according
to which he was a handsome Athenian
youth, too poor to marry the girl he
loved. But when pirates carried him off
in company with a band of rich Athenian girls, including his beloved, he succeeded in killing the brigands and restoring the girls to their families. He was
then accepted by the father of the
maiden he loved as a suitable son-in-
law. A son of Magnes, called Hymenaeus, was being courted by Apollo
when Hermes stole the god's cattle.

Hyperboreans A mythical nation living
far from Greece, to the north, east, or
north-west. The traditional interpretation of the name [*hyper borean,* 'beyond
the North Wind') sets them in the north;
but the name could also mean 'beyond
the mountains' and 'those who carry
(merchandise) across'. Apollo was said
to spend the winter months among
them, and his mother Leto was reputedly born in their land. Perseus visited
them in his search for the Gorgon, and
Heracles was said to have chased the
Cerynitian hind to their country. Pindar
saw them as a blessed people untouched
by human ailments, inhabiting a kind of
fairyland. It was said that two Hyperborean virgins, Opis and Arge (or Hypero-
che and Laodice), had come to Delos
with Leto, Apollo, and Artemis, and
had died on the island. Subsequently the
Hyperboreans, because the two maidens
never returned home, sent their offerings
to Delos through intermediaries, wrapping them in wheat-straw.

Hyperenor One of the 'Sown Men' of
Thebes, who sprang from the dragon's
teeth. *See* CADMUS.

Hyperion ('going over') A Titan. There
are two traditions about him. Hesiod
asserts that he was a son of Gaia (Earth)
and Uranus (Sky) and that he married
his sister Theia, who bore him Helios

(the Sun), Eos (Dawn), and Selene (the
Moon). More often Hyperion is simply
another name for the Sun-god Helios.

Hypermnestra or **Hypermestra** *1.*
Eldest daughter of Danaus, king of
Argos. When she and her sisters were
married to their fifty cousins, the sons
of Aegyptus, Hypermnestra was the only
one of the young women to disobey her
father's order that they should all slay
their bridegrooms. She helped Lynceus
to escape, and for this her father wished
to punish her. But he later became reconciled to her marriage, and her husband
Lynceus eventually avenged his murdered brothers on Danaus and his forty-
nine sisters-in-law. He took the throne
of Argos and was succeeded by Abas,
his son by Hypermnestra.
2. Daughter of Thestius; the wife of
Oicles and mother of Amphiaraus.

Hypnos (Latin: *Somnus*) Sleep, the
brother of Thanatos (Death), was a son
of Nyx (Night). His home was in a cave
on the island of Lemnos, or far off near
the land of the fabulous Cimmerians.
Here it was always dark and misty; the
waters of Lethe, the river of forgetfulness, flowed through the cavern, where
the god lay on a soft couch surrounded
by an infinite number of his sons, the
Dreams. Hera sent Iris to bid him send
one of them, Morpheus, to impersonate
Ceyx, after he had been drowned at sea,
to his wife Alcyone. Again, when Hera
wished to beguile Zeus during the
Trojan War, so that Poseidon might interfere on behalf of the Greeks after
Hector had driven them back to their
beached ships, she borrowed Aphrodite's girdle and went to the island of
Lemnos to see Hypnos, whom she tried
to persuade to lull Zeus to sleep. At first
he refused, recalling how, once before,
Hera had lulled Zeus to sleep in order
that she might attack Heracles, and
Hypnos had risked incurring severe punishment from which only Nyx had saved

him. However the offer of the Grace Pasithea as a wife persuaded Hypnos to comply with Hera's request. He flew to Mount Ida, where Zeus was sitting watching the battle, and perched on a pine tree in the form of a nightjar. Zeus made love to Hera, and Hypnos then lulled him to sleep. On another occasion the brothers Hypnos and Thanatos were sent by Apollo to carry his son Sarpedon's body home to Lycia.

Hypseus Son of the River Peneius and the Naiad Creusa; he was an early king of the Lapiths in Thessaly. He had three daughters, Cyrene, Themisto, and Astyagyia. Themisto married Athamas.

Hypsipyle A queen of Lemnos. When the other men in the island were all slain by the women, Hypsipyle saved her father Thoas, the king. She hid him in a chest, in which she then set him adrift; by this means he reached the island of Oenoe. When Jason and the Argonauts passed that way on their journey to Colchis, the Lemnian women, who by now felt the need of male company (and had lost the foul smell with which Aphrodite had cursed them), entertained the travellers for a year. Hypsipyle bore Jason two sons, Euneus and Thoas. After the Argonauts had left the island, the elder Thoas, Hypsipyle's father, returned and recovered his kingdom, and his daughter fled. She was captured by pirates, who sold her to king Lycurgus of Nemea. Another story is that the women of Lemnos learnt that Hypsipyle had rescued ·her father, and in anger at her treachery sold her into slavery. Lycurgus made her the nurse of his son Opheltes. But the Seven champions, on their way to attack Thebes, asked her for water. As she showed them the way to a spring, she put Opheltes on a parsley-bed; whereupon a snake came, bit the child, and coiled itself round his body. On their return, the Seven were horrified to learn from the seer Amphiaraus that this was an omen of their own doom. They killed the snake, buried the child under the name *Archemoros* ('beginning of doom'), and founded the Nemean Games in his honour. They also saved Hypsipyle from the wrath of Lycurgus. Euripides, in his play named after her, tells how, by a coincidence, her sons Euneus and Thoas came to Nemea, discovered their mother, whom they recognised with the aid of Amphiaraus, and carried her off to safety in Lemnos.

Hyrie see CYCNUS 4.

Hyrieus The founder and king of Hyria in Boeotia. He had no children; when he had entertained the gods Zeus, Poseidon, and Hermes, he asked them to give him an heir. They told him to fetch the hide of a bull and make water upon it. They then buried it. From the same place, nine months later, Orion grew up.

Hyrtacus King of Percote in the Troad. He married Merops' sister Arisbe, sometimes said to have been previously married to Priam of Troy, and they had at least two sons: Asius, who led the men of Arisbe to help the Trojans in the Trojan War, and Nisus, who accompanied Aeneas to Italy.

I

Ialmenus Son of Ares and Astyoche. *See* ASCALAPHUS *1*.

Ialysus Grandson of Helios. He gave his name to a Rhodian city.

Iambe A serving-woman in the house of Celeus of Eleusis. *See* DEMETER.

Iamus Son of Apollo and Evadne. He was born in the open country because Evadne, when she became pregnant, was terrified of her father's anger. She hid Iamus in a thicket, where a couple of serpents brought him honey. Evadne's father Aepytus, king of Phaesane, was told by the Delphic Oracle that the child was Apollo's, and would inherit his father's mastery of the prophetic art. He founded the clan of the Iamids, who were professional soothsayers.

Ianthe *see* IPHIS *3*.

Iapetus A Titan, son of Gaia and Uranus. Clymene, an Oceanid, bore him the Titans Prometheus, Epimetheus, Atlas, and Menoetius. In the war between gods and Titans, he was imprisoned by Zeus in Tartarus.

Iapyx An Illyrian, the son of Lycaon. He helped his brother Daunus to conquer southern Italy.

Iarbas A Numidian king. *See* DIDO.

Iasion or **Iasius** Son of Zeus, or Corythus, and of Atlas' daughter Electra. Homer seems to regard him as a mortal man, since the nymph Calypso, while complaining to Hermes of Zeus' order that she should let Odysseus sail home to his wife, compares her situation with that of another goddess, Demeter, who lay with Iasion in a thrice-ploughed fallow field. It was at the wedding of Cadmus and Harmonia that Demeter and Iasion were first believed to have met; and another version indicated that Harmonia was Iasion's sister. They produced a child, Plutus ('wealth'), but, according to Homer, Zeus, when he came to hear of the union, blasted Iasion with his thunderbolt and killed him. Ovid, however, asserts that Iasion lived on to a great age, and that Demeter deplored the greyness of his hair. His brother was Dardanus. A later writer, Hyginus, reported that Iasion and Demeter had a second son, Philomelus, who invented the waggon, for which reason he was turned into the constellation Bootes (*see* ICARIUS *2*, however). The historian Diodorus Siculus indicated that Iasion, after being instructed by Zeus in the Mysteries of Samothrace, married the goddess Cybele – who bore him Corybas – and was made immortal.

Iasus *1*. A king of Argos, the son of Triopas and brother of Agenor and Pelasgus, or else the son of Argus the all-seeing, and father of Io.
2. Son of Lycurgus; king of Arcadia. According to one version he was the father of Atalanta.

Icarius *1*. Son of Oebalus, king of Sparta, and of the Naiad Batia (though he was also said to be a son of Perieres and Gorgophone). He was involved in the expulsion of his half-brother Tyndareos from Sparta by his brother Hippocoon, though it is unclear whose part he took in the dispute. Tyndareos was later restored to the Spartan throne by Heracles; Icarius either joined him there or stayed in Acarnania, the country to which he had gone in exile. Icarius married a Naiad (water-nymph), Periboea, who bore him two daughters, Penelope and Iphthime, and five sons. When Odysseus had gained Penelope's hand in marriage, Icarius was reluctant to let her go. He tried to persuade Odysseus to live with him, and even followed the chariot in which the bridal pair were leaving, in order to persuade his daughter to return to him, but she veiled her head, thus indicating her refusal to leave her husband. Icarius erected a statue of Aidos ('modesty') on the spot.

2. An Attic farmer, the father of Erigone. They welcomed Dionysus to Attica. In exchange the god taught Icarius the arts of cultivating wine and maturing it in barrels, and presented him with several full wineskins to give pleasure to the country folk and spread the love of wine. But the first people to taste the vintage, simple peasants of the neighbourhood, got drunk and thought they had been poisoned. They clubbed Icarius to death and buried his corpse on Mount Hymettus. Erigone searched for her father, and when, with the help of the dog Maera, she had eventually found his grave, she hanged herself from a nearby tree. The dog, in its grief, jumped into a well.

According to some, the murderers took refuge on the island of Ceos, where a great drought soon ensued. The king, Aristaeus, consulted the Delphic Oracle, and was told to propitiate the shade of Icarius and sacrifice to Zeus, who sent the Etesian winds to relieve the sufferers.

At Athens Dionysus, angry at the treatment his servants had received, impelled the girls to go mad and, like Erigone, to hang themselves from trees. The Athenians discovered the cause of this affliction from Delphi and punished the murderers. They also instituted an annual ceremony held at the grape-harvest, the *Aiora*, at which girls swung themselves on swings suspended from trees. Dionysus also set Icarius, Erigone, and Maera among the stars as Bootes, Virgo, and the Dog-star (Canicula) respectively. (*See* IASION, however.)

Icarus *see* DAEDALUS

Icelus *see* DREAMS.

Idaea 1. Daughter of Dardanus, a king of Scythia. She married Phineus, king of Salmydessus, to whom she bore two sons, Thynius and Mariandynus. She was cruel to her stepsons, the children of Phineus' former wife Cleopatra, inducing him to blind them and cast them into prison. The Argonauts rescued the boys, and sent Idaea home to her father, who condemned her to death for her brutality.

2. A nymph of Mount Ida in the land of Troy. She bore a son, Teucer, to the river-god of the Scamander.

Idaeus King Priam's herald in the Trojan War.

Idas and **Lynceus** Sons of Aphareus, king of Messenia, and his wife Arene; though the father of Idas, the elder, was sometimes believed to be Poseidon. The two brothers were inseparable. Lynceus was gifted with such powerful vision that he could see clearly for great distances, and even through the ground. But Idas was not only the elder but the stronger of the two brothers. He was also notable for his insolence, a feature which eventually cost him his life. He married Marpessa, daughter of Evenus, whom Apollo also courted. In a chariot-race held by Evenus for the suitors of Marpessa, Idas, in a winged chariot lent him by Poseidon, proved the victor. Evenus, defeated in the race, pursued Idas as far as the River Lycormas, and then leapt into it; and thenceforward the river was named after him. Later Idas quarrelled with Apollo over Marpessa, and in his insolence came to blows with the god, who had carried her off and turned her into a kingfisher. Zeus parted the pair and asked the girl to choose; she chose Idas since, being mortal, he would grow old when she did.

Marpessa bore Idas a daughter, Cleopatra, who married Oeneus' son Meleager. In consequence, Idas and Lynceus took part in his boar-hunt at Calydon, being related by marriage to Oeneus who was king of the place. They also sailed with the Argonauts. Idas later invaded King Teuthras' kingdom of Teuthrania, but was driven out by Telephus, Heracles' son by Teuthras' wife Auge. Idas and Lynceus perished through a quarrel which Idas picked with the Dioscuri. For their deaths, *see* CASTOR and POLYDEUCES. After Idas had died, Marpessa killed herself, and since Aphareus now had no heir, he awarded the kingdom of Messenia to Nestor of Pylos (or his father Neleus).

Idmon ('knowing') Son of Apollo and Cyrene, but reputedly the son of a certain Abas. Idmon accompanied the Argonauts, even though, being a seer, he foresaw his own death while on the expedition. When the crew landed among the Mariandyni in Bithynia, he was killed by a wild boar. The Argonauts mourned him for three days. When Heraclea Pontica was founded, the Delphic Oracle told the settlers to build the city round a wild olive growing on his grave.

Idomeneus King of Crete and leader of the Cretan forces in the Trojan War. His father was Deucalion, son of Minos. His troops were said to have sailed to Troy in eighty ships – a very large contingent. Idomeneus, though he had been one of the suitors of Helen, was older than the other Greek leaders. During the war Poseidon, appearing to him disguised as Andraemon's son Thoas, tried to spur him to lead the Achaeans to fight harder against the Trojans who were threatening their beached ships. Meriones and he then took their stand on the left wing, where he killed several Trojans; but he was afraid of Aeneas, against whom he called for aid. Aiming his spear at him, Idomeneus killed Oenomaus instead.

Accompanied by his squire Meriones, he was one of those who lay in ambush in the Wooden Horse. According to one tradition he then sailed safely home and ruled Crete in peace. But another, contradictory story tells how, meeting with a great storm on his homeward voyage, he vowed to sacrifice to Poseidon the first living creature he met on landing in Crete. This turned out to be his own son, who was waiting to welcome him; but Idomeneus had to fulfil his vow. He was consequently banished from his kingdom, and settled, according to Virgil, on the south coast of Italy in the Sallentine Plain. According to a variant account a Cretan called Leucus seduced Meda, Idomeneus' wife, at the instigation of Nauplius. Leucus seized ten of the cities of Crete, killed Meda and her daughter, and drove Idomeneus away; and that was why he sailed to Italy. Idomeneus was also said to have brought upon the Cretans the reputation of being congenital liars, for this was the curse brought upon him by Medea when he awarded the prize for beauty to Thetis instead of to her.

Idothea or **Ido** Daughter of Proteus, the 'Old Man of the Sea'. When Menelaus was returning home from the Trojan War by way of Egypt, she advised him how to force her father to give him the advice he needed.

Idyia An Oceanid, the wife of Aeetes and mother of Medea.

Ilia *see* RHEA SILVIA

Ilione The eldest daughter of King Priam of Troy and Hecabe. She married Polymestor, king of Thrace, and brought up her youngest brother Polydorus, who was entrusted to her during the siege of Troy. According to one version, when Polymestor, for greed, or to gratify the Greeks, plotted to kill her brother, she saved his life by substituting her own son by Polymestor, Deipylus, whom his father then killed by mistake. Later she revealed the plot to Polydorus, who slew Polymestor with her help. When Aeneas passed through Thrace, Ilione presented him with her sceptre, which he later gave to Dido.

Ilithyia The goddess of childbirth. The name in Greek is *Eileithyia*, sometimes plural, *Eileithyiai*: Homer recognised a number of such goddesses. Hesiod called Ilithyia a daughter of Zeus and Hera. Her cult may have had a Cretan origin, for on a clay tablet from Cnossus she seems to be described, under the name of *Eleuthia*. Sometimes the *Eileithyiai* include Hera herself (as goddess of marriage) and Artemis (as the goddess of young creatures). Ilithyia was under the control of Hera, who on two occasions tried to prevent her rivals from giving birth by preventing her from offering her ministrations. Thus when Apollo and Artemis were due to be born, Hera tried to keep Ilithyia from their mother Leto, but the other goddesses lured her there by the bribe of an enormous gold necklace. Hera also prevented the birth of Heracles for a number of days, by making Ilithyia sit outside his mother Alcmena's room with her legs, arms, and fingers crossed. *See also* JUNO.

Ilus *1.* Whether an Ilus 'son of Dardanus' is to be distinguished from *2* is uncertain. If so, the 'tomb of Ilus' mentioned by Homer in the topography of the Trojan region would be his rather than his great-nephew's.

2. Son of Tros and Callirrhoe, a daughter of the River Scamander. He married Adrastus' daughter Eurydice, who bore him Laomedon and Themiste. Migrating from Dardania, of which his brother Assaracus became king, to Phrygia, he competed in games in which he won a prize of fifty men and fifty girls – and a dappled cow, which the local king gave him in obedience to an oracle. Ilus was commanded to found a city where the animal sat down. This it did upon a hill near Mount Ida, sacred to the goddess Ate (Infatuation). There, in consequence, he founded the city of Troy (Ilium). When Ilus asked for a sign, Zeus sent him the Palladium, a wooden image of Athena which dropped out of the sky in front of his tent. At this spot he founded a temple for Athena. It was believed that, as long as the Palladium was kept safe there, Troy could not fall. In the *Iliad*, Ilus' tomb is mentioned near a wild fig tree in the plain of Troy (*see 1*, however).

3. A king of Ephyra in Thesprotia, a son of Mermerus, and grandson of Medea. He refused to give Odysseus poison for his arrows.

Inachus The god of the River Inachus in the Argolid; a son of Oceanus and Tethys. When Poseidon and Hera were quarrelling about which of them should possess the land of Argos, he and his fellow-rivers Cephissus and Asterion settled the dispute by awarding it to Hera; whereupon Poseidon dried up the rivers and flooded the country – and thereafter they were dry, except after rain. Inachus was the mythical first king of Argos. He married his half-sister Melia (her mother's name was Argia), and their children included two sons, Phoroneus (to whom, in place of his father, the award of the land to Hera was sometimes attributed) and Aegialeus, and a daughter, Io. When Io was loved by Zeus, she was visited with dreams; and Inachus, in response to an oracle, sent her out of the country. After Zeus had subsequently abducted her, Inachus was said by some to have pursued him with curses, until the god sent the Fury Tisiphone to drive him mad. Inachus then flung himself into the River Haliacmon, which was thenceforth named after him. Ovid says that, when Io came to his stream in the form of a cow and wrote her name and story in the sand with her hoof, he recognised her. Argus drove her away, and Inachus hid himself in a cave at his source, weeping for his daughter and swelling his waters with his tears.

Ino Daughter of Cadmus and Harmonia; wife of Athamas, king of Orchomenus. She had two sons, Learchus and Melicertes. Her sister Semele, when she had borne the child Dionysus, perished in the fire which struck her as a result of seeing Zeus in all his glory. In spite of Ino's earlier disbelief in the child's divinity, Hermes persuaded her to nurse her little nephew and protect him from Hera's wrath. Ino dressed the child in girl's clothes and for a time the ruse succeeded; but then Hera discovered the truth, and drove Ino and Athamas mad. First Ino and her sisters Agave and Autonoe were stricken with a Bacchic frenzy (this was also regarded as a visitation from Dionysus for failing to recognise his godhead) in which they tore apart Agave's son Pentheus, king of Thebes, who was spying on them. Ino had earlier plotted to kill Phrixus and Helle, Athamas' children by his first wife the nymph Nephele, but their mother enabled them to fly away on the golden ram (see ATHAMAS). Finally, as Hera's supreme punishment upon Ino, she and Athamas killed the children she had borne him: he shot Learchus with arrows, and she either boiled Melicertes

in a cauldron, or rushed to the sea and jumped with him from the Molulian Rocks into the Saronic Gulf. Ino was then transformed into a sea-goddess, Leucothea ('White Goddess'), who with Melicertes − now renamed Palaemon − was believed to provide aid to sailors in distress.

A different version of Ino's story recounted that she ran away from Athamas' house before the death of her children, and stayed away so long that he remarried with Themisto who bore him two children. For this story, *see* THEMISTO. The Romans identified the goddess Leucothea with *Mater Matuta*, a goddess of growth, and Palaemon with *Portunus*. They had a story that Leucothea came to the goddess Carmenta, who gave her toasted cakes to eat in memory of the seed-corn Ino had parched in her plot to get rid of Phrixus.

Io Daughter of Inachus, the first king of Argos and a river-god, and of Melia; or of Iasus, son of Triopas. Though a virgin priestess of Hera, she earned Hera's hatred by attracting the attentions of Zeus. Io dreamed on a number of occasions that Zeus came and whispered to her in the night, begging her to come and lie with him in the meadows of Lerna. When Io told her father of these dreams, he consulted the oracles of Delphi and Dodona, and these, after a number of vague evasions, told him he must banish his daughter from his land for ever, or else his people would be wiped out by Zeus' thunderbolts. On being driven from the house of Inachus, Io was turned into a beautiful white heifer − either by Hera or by Zeus − and was continually stung by a gadfly, sent by Hera to stop the animal from settling anywhere long enough for Zeus to violate her virginity. Argus, a gigantic herdsman with a hundred unsleeping eyes − of which only two closed at any one time − was likewise set by Hera to watch over the cow, for the same purpose.

Zeus, however, continued to plot to have his will with Io. He began by sending Hermes to lure Argus away from the heifer, but he could not get past the all-seeing giant until he had first disguised himself as a herdsman and lulled Argus to close all his hundred eyes in sleep, telling him stories and playing lullabies on his pipes. As soon as all the eyes were shut, Hermes grabbed his sword and struck off the giant's head. But this did not prove of great assistance to Zeus, as the gadfly still kept Io on the move, and she was now constantly haunted by the ghost of Argus. She wandered over the earth, past Dodona where the prophetic oak greeted her as Zeus' future bride. And then she passed up the Adriatic Sea, part of which was thenceforth called Ionian in her memory, northwards to the place next to the Ocean, where Prometheus was bound to a rock. He gave her a prophecy of what was to come. She then travelled by way of Scythia, the Caucasus, the Black Sea coast, and the Bosporus ('cow-ford', named after her). From there she went east to the land of the Gorgons and the Graiae, coming eventually to Egypt where, in the city of Canopus, Zeus came to her, changed her back into a woman and, by touching her body with his hand, begot his son Epaphus ('he of the touch'). Epaphus ruled Egypt and Africa, and many dynasties, including the royal house of Argos, were descended from him.

This is Aeschylus' version of the myth, as told in his play *Prometheus Bound*. Ovid's story is different in a number of points. According to him Zeus saw Io walking near the river; he told her to meet him at noon in the woods, and spread a cloud over the place while he made love to her. Hera saw the cloud of darkness over Argos, and suspected what had happened, but Zeus turned Io into a heifer before the clouds dispersed. He pretended the animal was an ordinary heifer, but Hera

was not to be fooled. She asked to have it as a present, which Zeus could not reasonably refuse. Still suspicious, Hera set Argus to guard the heifer, which on arrival at the banks of the River Inachus wrote its story in the dust for Io's father to read. He realised what had become of his daughter and wept. Hermes then succeeded in deceiving Argus and slaying him, but Hera, after placing his eyes in her peacock's tail, sent a Fury in the form of a gadfly to drive Io all over the earth. Eventually she came to Egypt, where Zeus had mercy on her, and she begged Hera's forgiveness. Io was turned into a woman again, and was worshipped as the Egyptian goddess Isis. She bore Epaphus who was also worshipped as a god, identified as the bull-deity Apis.

Iobates *see* BELLEROPHON.

Iolaus Son of Iphicles and Automedusa, daughter of Alcathous; nephew and charioteer of Heracles. He attached himself to his uncle at the time of his Labours, and was particularly useful in the battle with the Hydra of Lerna; he also took part in the expeditions against Geryon and Laomedon, and in the hunting of the Calydonian boar. When Heracles renounced his marriage with Megara, whose sons he had killed in a fit of madness, he transferred her to Iolaus as his wife. After Heracles was dead, the aged Iolaus helped his children in Attica, when Eurystheus tried to kill them in a war. He prayed to Zeus, Heracles, and Hebe, Heracles' heavenly consort, and was restored to youth. This enabled him to lead his forces to victory, and to capture or kill Eurystheus with his own hands. Heracles and Hebe were said, in this battle, to have ridden in the form of stars on the pole of Iolaus' chariot.

According to a different tradition Iolaus was sent with Megara and a party of Heracles' fifty children by the daughter of King Thespius to colonise Sardinia. He was also said to have been buried at Thebes, where Pindar celebrated his memory in an ode.

Iole Daughter of Eurytus, king of Oechalia. In an archery contest Heracles won her as his prize; but her father would not give her up. She eventually married Heracles' son Hyllus. *See* HERACLES.

Ion Son of Xuthus or Apollo by Creusa, daughter of Erechtheus, king of Athens. There were two differing stories about his origin. According to one, Xuthus, the son of Hellen, a Thessalian, went to Athens, where he married Creusa, the youngest daughter of the reigning king, Erechtheus. He had two sons, Achaeus and Ion. Xuthus was eventually asked to select Erechtheus' heir from among the sons of the king and chose Cecrops, whereupon he was driven by the others from Athens. He took refuge in Achaea in the northern Peloponnese, then called Aegialus (the Coastland). When Xuthus died there, Achaeus returned to Thessaly and Ion tried to conquer Aegialus. But the king of that country, Selinus, offered Ion the hand of his daughter Helice, and made him his heir. When Selinus died, Ion renamed the inhabitants of Aegialus – hitherto known as Pelasgians – Ionians after himself, and on the Gulf of Corinth, at the mouth of the River Selinus, he founded the city of Helice, naming it after his daughter. Some time after these events, war broke out between Eleusis and Athens, and the Athenians invited Ion back to lead them in battle. The Athenians won, but Ion was killed and buried at Potami ('Rivers') in Attica. Later the Ionians were driven out of Aegialus by the descendants of Achaeus, and these were the circumstances, according to the myth, in which took place their historic migration by way of Attica to the central portion of the west coast of Asia Minor, which they named Ionia.

The second version of the story was told by Euripides in his play the *Ion*. He made Ion the son of Creusa and Apollo, who raped her when she was already Xuthus' wife. His mother exposed him in a cave under the Acropolis. Apollo then asked Hermes to take the infant boy to Delphi, where the Pythian priestess found him and dedicated him to the service of the god. Many years later Xuthus and Creusa, having no children, came to Delphi to ask what to do to remedy this situation. Xuthus was told by the oracle that the first man he met on leaving the temple would be his son. He met Ion: whereupon it was deduced that Ion must be an illegitimate child of Xuthus, and that Creusa would have to be told the news tactfully. Xuthus called him Ion because he met him 'on the way' (*ion* in Greek). Meanwhile an old slave and some women had filled Creusa's head with rumours, suggesting that Xuthus meant to replace the house of Erechtheus on the throne of Athens by a bastard of his own. Creusa therefore plotted to kill her husband's supposed bastard. Xuthus gave a feast in honour of Ion, and Creusa, after the libations had been poured, poisoned the young man's wine. But Apollo rescued his son. For after Ion heard a slave speak an ill-omened word, he ordered that the libations should be repeated; and when the wine from his own cup fell on the ground, one of Apollo's sacred doves drank it and died in agony. Thus it came to light that Creusa had tried to poison him. Ion was making ready to kill her when the Pythian priestess, horrified that the sacred precinct might be polluted by matricide, produced Ion's swaddling clothes and proved that he was Creusa's son. Ion was later believed to have become king of Athens and to have divided the people into the four Ionic tribes, Geleontes, Aegicoreis, Argadeis, and Hopletes, named after his own sons. Xuthus and Creusa had two sons, Dorus and Achaeus.

Iphianassa *1. see* IPHIGENIA.
2. see MELAMPUS.

Iphicles Son of Amphitryon and Alcmena, and the reputed twin brother of Heracles, whose father, however, was usually said to be Zeus. Amphitryon recognised that Iphicles was his own mortal son and not the child of Zeus from the terror the infant showed when Hera (or Amphitryon himself) sent two snakes into the nursery: whereas Heracles fought them and strangled them. Iphicles was the father 'of Iolaus, Heracles' charioteer, by Automedusa, daughter of Alcathous, king of Megara; there was a story that Heracles killed their other children together with his own by Megara in a fit of madness. He later married the younger daughter of Creon of Corinth and took part in the Calydonian boar-hunt. He helped Heracles in his wars against Augeas and Laomedon, and in the campaign against Hippocoon of Sparta he was killed. He was carried dying to Pheneus in Arcadia, where honours were later paid him at his tomb as a hero.

Iphiclus *1.* Son of Phylacus. *See* MELAMPUS.
2. Son of Thestius; perhaps killed by his nephew Meleager at the time of the Calydonian boar-hunt. Said also to have been an Argonaut.
3. Son of Cephalus and Clymene.

Iphigenia The eldest daughter of Agamemnon and Clytemnestra. She is usually identified with the Iphianassa mentioned by Homer. The Epic *Cypria*, however, differentiates between the two. (Stesichorus alleged that Iphigenia was in reality the child of Theseus and Helen, placed under the care of her aunt Clytemnestra as an infant.)

When Agamemnon, for the attack against Troy, had collected his army and fleet at Aulis in Boeotia, he was unable to set sail because of a contrary wind, which, as the prophet Calchas declared, had been sent by Artemis because Agamemnon had offended her or neglected a duty to her. The exact cause was variously described. Alternative versions indicated that Agamemnon had boasted of being a better huntsman than Artemis herself; that he had at an earlier time vowed to sacrifice to her the most beautiful thing born in the year of Iphigenia's birth, and since it was the child herself, he had broken his vow; or that Artemis was punishing him for a sin committed by his father Atreus, who had broken a vow to sacrifice the first lamb in his flock. Aeschylus, however, suggests that the reason for Artemis' hostility lay in an omen sent by Zeus to guarantee Agamemnon's future success at Troy, for two eagles, representing the Atridae, tore to pieces a pregnant hare in full view of the Greek army: whereupon Artemis, since she was protectress of all wild animals, became so angry at the suffering of the innocent creature that she prevented the sailing of the fleet. In any case, Artemis now demanded the life of Iphigenia. To obtain his daughter's presence – since she was at Mycenae – Agamemnon had to deceive his wife Clytemnestra, and so he sent a message that the girl was to be brought to him in order to be married to Achilles. When the sacrifice was over, Clytemnestra never forgave Agamemnon for the deed. (The *Iliad*, however, knows nothing of the sacrifice of Iphigenia, for there Agamemnon, long after his arrival at Troy, offers all three of his daughters in marriage to Achilles.)

There are two versions of what happened when Iphigenia was led to the altar. According to the tradition of Aeschylus (adopted by Lucretius), she was killed there by the priests in her father's presence. Euripides, however, following the *Cypria*, asserts that Artemis substituted a hind at the last moment, and carried the maiden off to the land of the Taurians in the Crimea to be her priestess at a temple where human sacrifice was performed. In this temple stood an ancient image of Artemis to which all strangers who came to the land were immolated; it was the duty of Iphigenia to prepare such victims for sacrifice.

Many years after these events Orestes, Iphigenia's brother, who had been driven mad by the Furies for avenging his father's murder on his mother Clytemnestra, was commanded by an oracle to fetch this statue of Artemis to Attica, in order to expiate his sin of matricide and thereby rid himself of his insanity. When he arrived in the land of the Taurians with his cousin Pylades, he was arrested by their king, Thoas, and duly delivered to Iphigenia for sacrifice to Artemis. After Iphigenia had heard that the pair were Greeks, and came from Argos, she offered to rescue one of them, if he would undertake to carry a letter to her brother Orestes; and this was how the brother and sister came to recognise each other. Plotting to get them both away, Iphigenia told Thoas of Orestes' matricide, which rendered him impure: all the sacrificial victims therefore, she declared, as well as the effigy of Artemis, and she herself as her priestess, must be washed in the sea, while the Taurians averted their eyes. The ruse was aided by Poseidon, and the three embarked on Orestes' ship with the statue. Athena appeared to Thoas to calm his anger and told him that Apollo and Artemis had decreed the removal of the image to Attica. It was set up in a temple in Attica – both Halae and Brauron claimed the distinction – where Iphigenia became the perpetual priestess of Artemis. Though human sacrifice to Artemis was discontinued (except, according to one tradition, among the Taurians), it was commemorated in historical times at Halae by a slight cut made in the throats of symbolic human 'victims' before the image. According to Hyginus, Iphigenia later met her sister Electra at Delphi.

Electra, believing that Iphigenia was a Taurian woman who had killed Orestes, tried to slay her, and was only prevented by the prompt arrival of Orestes himself.

Other stories of Iphigenia include the traditions that she died at Megara, where she had a shrine; that Artemis made her immortal; and that she was married to Achilles on Leuce (White Island) or in Elysium. In cult she seems to have been a virgin goddess akin to Artemis herself.

Iphimedia *see* ALOEUS.

Iphinoe *see* MELAMPUS.

Iphis *1.* A young Cypriot. *See* ANAXARETE.
2. Son of Alector and king of Argos. In order to compel Amphiaraus to take part in the war of the Seven against Thebes, he advised Polynices to bribe Amphiaraus' wife Eriphyle. His son Eteoclus and his son-in-law Capaneus were both killed in the expedition; and he bequeathed his kingdom to Capaneus' son Sthenelus.
3. Ovid tells the story of Iphis, the daughter of Ligdus of Cnossus in Crete and his wife Telethusa. Ligdus, who wished for a son, decreed that a daughter would have to be exposed. However the goddess Isis appeared to Telethusa in a dream, telling her to deceive her husband and bring up her daughter as a boy. When Iphis was thirteen, Ligdus betrothed her, in her male guise, to the beautiful Ianthe. The two fell in love; but Telethusa in her embarrassment postponed the ceremony as long as possible. However, Isis finally came to her aid and changed her daughter's sex, so that the young pair were able to marry.

Iphitus *1.* Son of Eurytus, king of Oechalia. When Heracles claimed Iole, whom he had won in an archery contest, and was accused of stealing some of

Eurytus' mares or cattle, Iphitus took Heracles' part against his father; but Heracles later killed Iphitus in a fit of madness. During his search for the animals, Iphitus had met Odysseus in Messenia, and as a result of their friendship gave him his father Eurytus' bow.

2. A king of Phocis who entertained Jason when he consulted the Delphic Oracle. Iphitus later joined the Argonauts. His sons Schedius and Epistrophus led the Phocians in the Trojan War.

3. An Elean whom Copreus killed.

4. A king of Elis who restored the Olympic Games after the Dorian invasion.

Iris A goddess, the daughter of the Titan Thaumas and the Oceanid Electra. Iris carried the messages of the gods. *Iris* means 'rainbow' in Greek, and the personification of this phenomenon was considered by the Greeks to connect sky and earth; hence her function as messenger. Callimachus portrays Iris as sleeping under Hera's throne, ever shod so as to be ready to carry her messages on the instant, but in Homer she usually runs errands for Zeus. Her husband was the west wind Zephyrus.

Irus *1.* A sturdy beggar in Odysseus' palace in Ithaca, whom the suitors favoured and Odysseus, himself disguised as a beggar, outfaced.

2. Son of Actor, king of Phthia, and father of the Argonauts Eurytion and Eurydamas. When Peleus offered him blood-money for the accidental killing of Eurytion, he would not accept it. Peleus then released the cattle he had intended to pay by way of fine, and a wolf which devoured them was turned into a rock, visible on the border of Phocis.

Isander Son of Bellerophon and Philonoe; killed in a campaign against the Solymi.

Ischepolis *see* ALCATHOUS.

Ischys *see* CORONIS.

Isis A great Egyptian goddess worshipped throughout the world of the later Greeks, and identified by them with Io.

Isemene Daughter of Oedipus and his mother Jocasta, and the sister of Antigone. As a character in tragedy she is a companion and foil for Antigone, helping her when the blind Oedipus was a fugitive in Attica and refusing aid when Antigone wished to bury their dead brother Polynices; though Ismene later volunteered to die with her.

Ismenius Thought at Thebes to be the father of Linus.

Itylos *see* AEDON.

Itymoneus An Elean whom Nestor killed in a cattle-raid.

Itys *see* TEREUS.

Iulus *see* ASCANIUS.

Ixion The first man to stain his hands with a kinsman's blood: the Greek Cain. He was a Thessalian king, the son of Antion, Phlegyas, or Peision. He ruled the Lapiths, and arranged a marriage with Dia, the daughter of Eioneus who may have been his kinsman. They had a son, Pirithous (though his father was sometimes believed to be Zeus). Ixion promised Eioneus a large bride-price, and invited his father-in-law to Larissa, the capital of Thessaly, to collect it. But by treacherously digging a pit filled with burning coals he trapped Eioneus, who duly fell into it and perished. Nobody would perform the rites of purification for such an unprecedented crime, until Zeus took pity on Ixion – perhaps because Zeus loved Ixion's wife Dia – and invited him to Olympus for the ceremony, giving him a place at the table of the gods. Thereupon Ixion tried to seduce Zeus' consort Hera. However Hera complained to Zeus, and he, to test Ixion, constructed a cloud which resembled her in every detail. With this cloud Ixion then committed adultery. Zeus caught him in the act, and condemned him to spend eternity in Tartarus, bound to a fiery, winged, four-spoked wheel which revolved everlastingly. The cloud, Nephele, brought forth a monstrous son, Centaurus, who mated with the wild mares of Mount Pelion in Magnesia and begot the race of Centaurs. Some said that the Centaurs themselves were Nephele's offspring; also that Ixion's wheel was covered with snakes rather than flames, and revolved in the sky rather than in Tartarus.

Iynx (Greek 'wryneck') A nymph, the daughter of Pan and Echo or Peitho. Iynx used magic to win the love of Zeus, either for herself or for Io. For this presumption Hera turned the girl into a wryneck, a dappled woodland bird tied by Greek witches to small wheels and used as a love charm, being revolved to the accompaniment of spells.

J

Janus (Latin: 'gate' or 'barbican') The Roman god of beginnings, doors, gates, and passageways; portrayed in art as having two faces (looking in opposite directions) or even four. He figured rarely in myth. Ovid tells a story of the nymph Carna, who beguiled her suitors by inducing them to go into a cave, with the promise that she would follow shortly after and let them make love to her: she then promptly ran away instead. But when she tried this trick upon Janus, he saw her departing with his second, backward-looking face; whereupon she granted him her favours, and he in return gave her the power to chase away nocturnal vampires – a power which she used to save their son Proca, later king of Alba Longa. When the girl Tarpeia allegedly betrayed the Roman Capitol to the Sabines, Janus stopped the enemy from entering by flooding the gateway with a hot sulphurous spring. He was also described as an early king of Latium, who welcomed Saturn (Cronos) when Zeus had expelled him from Crete. He was believed to have had a wife, Camise, and a son, Tiberinus, who was drowned in the River Tiber and so gave it its name.

Jason (Greek: *Iason* or *Ieson*) A Thessalian hero, the elder son of Aeolus' grandson Aeson, who should rightfully have been king of Iolcus in Magnesia, and of Alcimede or Polymede. When Aeson's father Cretheus died, Aeson's half-brother Pelias, son of Poseidon and Cretheus' wife Tyro, usurped the throne, allowing Aeson to live in Iolcus as a private citizen; or, in an alternative version, Pelias became regent for Jason after Aeson's death. In both versions Jason's mother, not trusting Pelias, employed the pretence of a funeral to send the boy secretly, either at birth or shortly after, to the cave of the Centaur Chiron to be reared by him. Chiron and his mother Philyra appear to have had other charges under their care as well, for in later years, when Jason set out on his expedition to fetch the Golden Fleece, old schoolfellows joined him in considerable numbers. Chiron gave Jason his name: it probably means 'healer', commemorating the skill in medicine which, among many other accomplishments, he taught the boy on Mount Pelion.

Meanwhile Pelias, who knew of Jason's existence, and had acquiesced, provided he stayed in humble circumstances in Magnesia, was warned by the Delphic Oracle to beware of a descendant of Aeolus who should come wearing only one sandal. For this reason he tried to extirpate the whole family, and Jason, who belonged to it, was in peril. However at the time of a great religious festival, when Pelias was about to sacrifice to his father Poseidon on the sea shore at Iolcus, Jason, now a grown man, determined to come to him and make known his claim to the throne. (There is another version that Pelias, knowing of his existence, invited him to attend.) On his way from Mount Pelion, Jason had to cross the River Anaurus, which was flooded at that season. As he prepared to wade through, an old woman begged him to carry her. Although he was eager to get on, he complied, but lost a sandal in the torrent. He went quickly on his way with no more thought for the old woman, and never knew that he had rendered a service to Hera, who hated Pelias for his neglect of her rites and from now onwards aided Jason until the day of Pelias' death. (Some said that Hera revealed herself to Jason and assured him of her assistance; others that it was a Magnesian custom to wear only one sandal, in order to make it easier to walk on mud.)

After being subjected to this test by Hera, Jason, wearing one sandal, came to the market-place at Iolcus in the midst of the festival, and asked to be shown to Pelias' house. Pelias' servants, however, who had long been expecting a man lacking a sandal, had already told him of the stranger's arrival; and the king hastened to the spot and asked Jason his name and business. Jason replied frankly, declaring that he was Aeson's son and heir, and had come to claim the throne. Pelias was thus placed in a dilemma. For, on the one hand, he knew he could not harm the young man in festival-time, or offend against the laws of hospitality; and besides, many of the people must have supported Aeson's son against the usurper. On the other hand, he was aware that Jason threatened his throne and his life, and must somehow be eliminated. This he planned to do by offering to name Jason as his successor subject to one condition: that he should fetch home the fleece of the golden ram which had magically carried Phrixus, son of Cretheus' brother Athamas, to Colchis. It was said that he asked Jason what, if an oracle should give warning that a man had come to kill him, he would do to that man. Jason replied that he would send the man to Aeetes' kingdom of Colchis in quest of the Golden Fleece; and that is what Pelias then ordered him to do. Alternatively, Pelias induced Jason to undertake the quest by pretending to be haunted by the ghost of Phrixus (killed by Aeetes),

which appeared to him in his dreams, ordering him to recover the fleece. In this version Jason was supported in his claim by Aeson's brothers Amythaon and Pheres and by their sons Melampus and Admetus. Jason demanded his father's throne, but offered to allow Pelias to keep his private wealth. Pelias therefore pretended that he was sending Jason to Colchis in the capacity of his own deputy and heir.

Having consulted the Delphic Oracle, Jason was joined by a band of the noblest heroes in Greece, including Heracles. A number of them were specialists at some skill, such as Argus the shipbuilder, Tiphys the pilot, Lynceus with his marvellous eyesight, Orpheus with the magical powers of his music, and Polydeuces the boxer. No two lists of members of this expedition agreed. For an account of its progress, see ARGONAUTS. On the journey Jason made love to Hypsipyle, queen of Lemnos, who bore him two sons, Euneus and Thoas. The witch Medea, Aeetes' daughter, gave him indispensable help in winning the fleece, and he brought her home with him from Colchis. He promised to marry her and consummated their union in the land of the Phaeacians, to which Aeetes' loyal fleet had pursued them. In consequence, Alcinous, the Phaeacian king, refused to give them up to the foe, and they eventually returned to Iolcus. During the voyage Jason was said to have displayed a smooth tongue and success with women, rather than courage or good judgment; indeed, Medea did most of his thinking for him. Hera, who was using Jason as an instrument for the punishment of Pelias, sought to achieve this purpose by enlisting the support of two fellow-goddesses: Athena, who gave him much help in his feats of valour, and Aphrodite, who overwhelmed Medea with love for him, so that she betrayed her father Aeetes and, in one version of the story, arranged the murder of her brother Apsyrtus.

On their return to Iolcus, the Argonauts found that Pelias, believing a rumour that the *Argo* had been wrecked, had done away with Aeson. Since Jason was sure that Pelias had no intention of handing over the throne to him, they deliberated what to do next. There are several versions of what ensued. Either the Argonauts gave Pelias the fleece and immediately sailed away to dedicate the *Argo* to Poseidon at the Isthmus of Corinth, or else they got rid of Pelias through Medea's magic (*see* MEDEA). At all events, Pelias' daughters cut their aging father up for the cauldron in the hope that Medea's magic could rejuvenate him, and on the failure of their scheme the Argonauts captured the city.

At this point Jason should have become king of Iolcus, but tradition is fairly consistent that he did not. Some said that he retired voluntarily to Corinth with Medea – who had a right to the kingship of that city since Aeetes had reigned there in the past – and handed Iolcus to Pelias' son Acastus. According to another story Jason was expelled by the Iolcans, who were disgusted at the savage murder of Pelias; and so, taking Medea with him, he sought and found sanctuary at the court of King Creon of Corinth. At this point Hera, her purpose achieved, deserted him.

Jason lived in Corinth with Medea for ten years, and they had sons, Thessalus, Alcimenes, and Tisander, or else Mermerus and Pheres, or else a son and daughter, Medeius and Eriopis. At the end of this time Jason was offered the hand of Creon's daughter Glauce, a marriage which could bring him great influence in the state. It meant, however, that he must disown Medea who, as a foreigner, had in Greek eyes no right to lawful marriage with a Greek (this version is incompatible with the story of Medea's right to the throne of Corinth). Jason therefore divorced Medea, and Creon banished her from Corinth. She,

overcome by anger and grief, resolved to punish her husband and wreck his new marriage. By an elaborate plot she killed Glauce and her own children, together with Creon, and then fled to Athens, some said on the chariot of Helios, drawn by winged serpents. (See the *Medea* of Euripides.) The deaths of the children, however, are sometimes attributed to the Corinthians, who, according to this story, killed them because of their apparent part in the plot. Jason now had no heir, unless, as one variant asserts, his son Thessalus escaped and later replaced Acastus as king of Iolcus.

One version of the myth indicated that Jason, too, died at Corinth, either at Medea's hands, or by suicide. But a much stronger tradition asserted that he lingered on for a while, a broken man dreaming of past glories, until one day, as he sat in the shade of his old ship at the Isthmus, part of the woodwork – perhaps the talking beam from Dodona which had served as the bowsprit – having rotted away, fell upon him and killed him.

The myth of Jason's life was told by Pindar, Euripides and Apollonius Rhodius.

Jocasta Daughter of Menoeceus and sister of Creon. Called by Homer Epicaste, she married first Laius, king of Thebes, and then their son Oedipus, after he had unwittingly murdered his father. She bore him two sons, Eteocles and Polynices, and two daughters, Antigone and Ismene. *See* OEDIPUS.

Julius *see* PROCULUS.

Juno A Roman goddess of women and marriage and the wife of Jupiter; identified from the earliest times with Hera. She was also associated with Ilithyia, the goddess of childbirth, whom the Romans called Juno Lucina. She had one Roman myth. Being angry because

Jupiter produced Minerva from his own head without the help of a mother, she was said to have complained to the goddess Flora. At the touch of a herb produced by Flora, Juno became pregnant and bore Mars (Ares), the god of War. In Greek myth Hera is also the mother of Ares, though Zeus is his father; on the other hand, Hera bears Hephaestus without male assistance. The Roman story may be no more than a legend invented to explain a feast of Juno, the Matronalia, on the first of March, the month dedicated to Mars. It is possible that the name Juno is cognate with *iuvenis*, 'young' in the sense of 'bride'; the Romans recognised an individual *iuno* as a spirit which protected a woman in the way the *genius* protected a man.

Juno was also associated with the moon, like Diana.

Jupiter or **Juppiter** The principal Roman god, originally a divinity of the sky. His name has the same origin as that of Zeus, with whom he was identified. *Ju-* is related to *Dyeu-*, 'sky', and -*piter* to *pater*, 'father'. Although his cult in Italy was widespread and vitally important to the national religion, he has few myths other than those borrowed from Zeus. He was thought to be responsible for weather of all kinds, especially lightning and rain. His special priest was the *Flamen dialis*, and his chief temple stood on the Capitoline Hill. It was dedicated supposedly to Jupiter Optimus Maximus ('Jupiter the Great and

Good') by Marcus Horatius at the beginning of the Republican period (*c.* 510 BC), though its origins probably went back to the earlier times of the Roman kingship.

Juturna An Italian water-nymph, the daughter of Daunus, king of Ardea in Latium, and hence sister of Turnus, whom she helped in battle against Aeneas. Jupiter had lustful designs on her and long pursued her; she hid from him by concealing herself beneath the waters of the River Tiber. Jupiter asked the nymphs to catch her for him, and all agreed except Lara, who was a chatterbox and even told Jupiter's wife Juno of the matter. But Jupiter had his way with Juturna, whom he recompensed for her lost virginity by making her a nymph and granting her power over springs and rivers. After successfully keeping her brother Turnus away from Aeneas, who she knew was ordained to kill him in single combat, Juturna, who had disguised herself as his charioteer Metiscus and had restored to him his lost sword made by Vulcan, was compelled by the warning of a Fury (sent by Jupiter) to give up the struggle to save her brother, and sank lamenting into her spring at Lanuvium. The spring was also identified with a pool or pond near the temple of Vesta on the Roman Forum, at which Castor and Polydeuces (the Dioscuri) were said to have watered their horses after the battle of Lake Regillus.

Juventas *see* HEBE.

K

Ker, Keres (Greek *ker*, plural *keres*, 'cutting off', 'destruction') Female spirits of death, resembling the Furies in appearance and function; they always brought destruction and woe in their train, and polluted those with whom they came in contact, causing blindness, old age, and death. In the *Iliad*, Ker was depicted dragging away wounded and dead alike to the gate of the Underworld. She had pointed claws, and wore on her shoulders a long cloak, red with the blood of corpses she had dragged off. Sometimes the word is used in the sense of 'fate', for Thetis offers her son Achilles the choice of two 'keres' – either to go home in obscurity or to stay at Troy and die in glory. Hesiod calls Ker a daughter of Nyx ('Night'), born without male participation together with her brothers Moros (Lot, Fate), Hypnos (Sleep), and Thanatos (Death), and a number of other personified abstractions.

Kore *see* PERSEPHONE.

L

Labdacus Son of Cadmus' son Polydorus and his wife Nycteis. When Labdacus was still an infant, he inherited the throne of Thebes from his father, and Nycteus, his maternal grandfather, ruled the city as his regent. On the death of Nycteus, his younger brother Lycus inherited the regency. Labdacus, when he became an adult, took over the royal authority, but fought an unsuccessful war against Pandion, king of Athens, and died shortly afterwards, leaving behind a son, Laius, only one year old; and so Lycus once more became regent.

Lacedaemon Son of Zeus and the Oread (mountain-nymph) Taygete; the mythical ancestor of the Lacedaemonians, who dwelt in Laconia. He married Sparte, the daughter of Eurotas, the Laconian king, and named his capital city after her. Their children were Amyclas and Eurydice, who married Acrisius. Amyclas inherited the throne, and founded the town of Amyclae near Sparta. His son was Hyacinthus.

Lachesis *see* FATES

Lacinius In one version of Heracles' theft of Geryon's cattle, he came to the south Italian town of Croton, where an aged hero (after whom the place was named) provided him with entertainment. Lacinius, a brigand of the district, made an attempt to steal the cattle, and in the fight that followed Heracles accidentally killed Croton.

Ladon *1*. A serpent with a hundred heads, the monstrous offspring of Typhon and Echidna. The beast was assigned the duty of defending the tree on which hung the golden apples of the Hesperides. Heracles was said, according to some accounts, to have killed it when he took the apples from the garden.
2. The god of the River Ladon in Arcadia; Daphne is sometimes called his daughter.

Laertes Father of Odysseus; the son either of Acrisius (Arceisius) and Chalcomedusa or of Cephalus and Procris. He married Anticlea, daughter of the famous thief Autolycus. Some authorities maintained that at the time of her marriage she was already pregnant with Odysseus by Sisyphus, but Homer knew nothing of this. When Odysseus grew up, Laertes yielded his royal authority to him, presumably because of his own old age. During Odysseus' absence in Troy and subsequent wanderings, Laertes was unable to defend Penelope and Telemachus from the suitors. Nevertheless on his son's return he came out of his miserable retirement and joined him in the final battle against the suitors' families, killing their leader Eupithes with the help of Athena. Later tradition made him a member of the Argonauts' expedition and the Calydonian boar-hunt.

Laestrygonians A race of man-eating giants who lived in a city called Telepylus founded by a certain Lamus, son of Poseidon. Their country was distinguished by the shortness of its night and the fine haven afforded by its harbour.

When Odysseus' fleet arrived there, the daughter of the Laestrygonian chieftain Antiphates led Odysseus' envoys to her father, who ate one of them. The party then retreated, pursued by the entire population, who sank the ships and speared the sailors as they floundered like fish, carrying them off to make their dinner. Only Odysseus' own ship escaped, since he had prudently moored his ship at the entrance to the harbour.

Laius Son of Labdacus and a king of Thebes. His father died when he was only a year old, leaving him in the care of a regent, Lycus, Laius' maternal great-uncle, who had already acted as regent in Labdacus' minority. But many years later, when Laius was a man, Amphion and Zethus usurped the throne of Thebes, and Laius was taken to the court of King Pelops at Pisa, where he was well looked after. When Amphion and Zethus died after a brief reign, Laius returned to Thebes to claim the throne, but as he did so he also carried off Pelops' young son Chrysippus, with whom, under the pretence of teaching him to drive a chariot, he had become infatuated. In consequence, as a result either of an imprecation uttered by Pelops or of the wrath of Hera, Laius fell under a curse. The fate of Chrysippus was variously stated – either he hanged himself for shame or he was recovered by Pelops and killed by his half-brothers Atreus and Thyestes at the instigation of their mother, Hippodamia, because they were jealous of him.

Laius, now established as king at Thebes, married Jocasta (or Epicaste), the daughter of Menoeceus. As they had no children he consulted the Delphic Oracle about a remedy, but instead received a blunt warning not to have a child, as his own son would kill him. He abstained for a time from his wife's bed, but eventually, when drunk, begot Oedipus. When the infant was born, he was exposed on a hillside, his feet being

pierced with a spike to hasten his death: but shepherds heard his screams and saved him. Years later, Laius was told of bad omens, which suggested that his predicted fate was about to befall him. Moreover (according to some) his kingdom was being plagued by the Sphinx which had been sent by Hera as a punishment for some sin. He set out for Delphi to consult the oracle, but when he came to a cross-roads near Mount Parnassus, his carriage met a young man on foot who refused to make way, A brawl ensued, in which Laius struck the youth with his staff or a goad; his adversary then slew him and all his servants except one, who escaped. Thus the prophecy was fulfilled, for his killer was Oedipus, who was on his way from Delphi into a self-imposed exile after hearing from the oracle that he was destined to kill his father and marry his mother. Laius was buried by Damasistratus, king of Plataea. However the tragedians Sophocles and Euripides place the arrival of the Sphinx in Thebes after the death of Laius, and explain his journey to Delphi by saying that he had reason to believe his son was alive and wished to consult the oracle on the matter.

Lamia Daughter of Belus and Libya. When Zeus fell in love with her, Hera caused her to devour her own children. She grew more and more savage until, completely wild, she retreated into a cave and lived by eating children whom she stole. In historic times, Greek mothers, when their children behaved badly, threatened them with this bogey-woman.

Lampus Son of Laomedon and one of King Priam's brothers. He lost a son, Dolops, in the Trojan War.

Lamus *1.* Son of Poseidon and the ancestor of the Laestrygonians.
2. Son of Heracles and Omphale.

Laocoon *1.* Son of Capys and brother of Anchises; a priest of Poseidon at

Troy. After he had warned the Trojans not to trust the Greeks' 'gift' of the famous Wooden Horse, and had cast his spear into its flank, he was killed, together with his two young sons, by two gigantic sea-serpents which swam over from the isle of Tenedos. (This scene is the subject of the 'Laocoon' marble group in the Vatican Museum.) Believing that Laocoon's death was a punishment inflicted by Poseidon or Athena upon him for doing violence to the horse, the bystanders dragged it from the plain, where they had found it, into the city. Their decision to do so was confirmed by the lying tale told by the Greek spy Sinon, who declared that the horse was an offering to Athena which would bring about the fall of Troy if the Trojans destroyed it, but would ensure the city's safety if brought inside the walls.

Two explanations were given for the violent death of Laocoon and his sons. One, favoured by Virgil, was that Athena wished to convince the Trojans of the truth of Sinon's story in order that they might be deceived by the horse and seal their own doom. However Hyginus gave a different reason, namely that Laocoon was a priest of Apollo and that his punishment had nothing to do with the war, but was visited upon Laocoon because he had married against the command of the god whom he served. In this version of the story the serpents, having killed Laocoon, hid in the temple of Apollo, whereas in the Virgilian account they made for Athena's temple, in which they hid behind the shield her statue carried.

2. Son or brother of Oeneus, king of Calydon. He accompanied the Argonauts, protecting his nephew or half-brother Meleager on the voyage.

Laodamas Son of Eteocles, king of Thebes. He was a small child when his father died in combat with his brother Polynices. Creon, Laodamas' great-

uncle, became regent or king of Thebes until the boy grew up. When the sons of the Seven, the Epigoni, attacked Thebes to restore Polynices' son to the throne, Laodamas took command and was defeated. He then led the remnant of his people to a new home in Illyria (or on Lake Copais).

Laodamia 1. Daughter of Acastus and Astydamia, and wife of Protesilaus, king of Phylace. who was the first Greek warrior to land on Trojan soil and was speedily killed by Hector, thus fulfilling an oracle and sacrificing himself for his comrades.

When Laodamia heard the news, she was inconsolable. Moved to pity by her prayers, the gods sent Hermes, who offered to restore her husband to her for three hours. At the end of this time Laodamia accompanied him back to the Underworld. A variant story asserted that Laodamia had a wooden statue made of her husband, which she used to embrace as she mourned for him. When a slave saw her doing this and reported to her father Acastus that she had a lover, he burned the statue, whereupon Laodamia flung herself into the same fire and perished in its flames.

2. Daughter of Bellerophon and mother of Sarpedon. Artemis slew her while she was still young.

Laodice The most beautiful of the many daughters of Priam and Hecabe. She was married to Antenor's son Helicaon. When the Greek Acamas, son of Theseus, was sent on a mission to Troy before the war broke out, in order to demand the return of the kidnapped Helen, Laodice fell in love with him and bore him a son, Munychus, of whom Aethra, Acamas' grandmother (now a slave of Helen), took charge. On the night when Troy was sacked, the ground opened and, in full view of many onlookers, Laodice was swallowed up in the chasm and never seen again.

Laomedon Son of Ilus 2, king of Troy, and Eurydice. His wife was Strymo, daughter of the River Scamander. His sons were Tithonus, Priam, Lampus, Clytius, and Hicetaon. When Laomedon succeeded him as king, the gods Apollo and Poseidon, who had rebelled against Zeus and were therefore obliged for a whole year to work in the service of a mortal man, came to him and offered to build a wall round Troy for a specified fee. It was alternatively said that the gods made this offer so as to test Laomedon, whose bad faith was already notorious. Either Poseidon built the walls and Apollo tended the king's herds on Mount Ida, or they both built the walls together. When Laomedon refused to pay, even threatening to shackle the two gods, cut off their ears, and sell them into slavery, Apollo sent a plague upon Troy, and Poseidon a gigantic sea-serpent which could be assuaged only by the offering of Laomedon's daughter Hesione. He was ordered to chain her to a rock. Laomedon duly chained his daughter up – according to one version a number of girls had already been offered to the monster in the same way. At this juncture, however, Heracles happened to arrive at Troy, and rescued Hesione, killing the serpent (see HERACLES). As a condition for providing his services, he had stipulated that he should be given the mares which Zeus had paid Laomedon in exchange for his cupbearer Ganymede, and according to some accounts he had demanded Hesione herself as well. Once again Laomedon went back on his bargain. Heracles did not return for many years, until he had finished his Labours. But then, as soon as he could, he sailed to Troy with an army in eighteen ships and, after an initial repulse, besieged the city. Telamon of Salamis breached the wall, and Heracles killed Laomedon. He was buried outside the Scaean Gate, and it was said that Troy's safety depended upon his tomb's integrity. Heracles

did not keep Hesione, but gave her to Telamon as a concubine; he killed all Laomedon's sons except Podarces – whom Hesione persuaded him to set free. The young man was renamed Priam and inherited the throne. Another son, Tithonus, also survived, because Eos had carried him off to be her husband. In the Trojan War the Greeks destroyed Laomedon's tomb.

Laothea A mistress of Priam of Troy and the mother of Lycaon.

Lapiths A Greek nation inhabiting the north of Thessaly; see AEGIMIUS, CAENEUS, CENTAURS, PIRITHOUS. They sent forty ships to the Trojan War under Polypoetes and Leonteus.

Lara A nymph, the daughter of the River Tiber, who refused to help Jupiter catch Juturna, with whom he was in love, warning her what was afoot and even informing Hera of the affair. Provoked by this interference, Jupiter pulled out her tongue and asked his son Mercury (Hermes) to take her to the Underworld, where she would have no alternative but to keep silent. It was said that Mercury, before completing his commission, fell in love with her and lay with her in a grove. She bore him the Lares, the household gods of the Romans.

Lars see PORSENNA.

Lartius, Spurius see HORATIUS COCLES.

Latinus According to Hesiod, the son of Odysseus and Circe; other Greeks made him a son of Heracles or Telemachus (Odysseus' son). Virgil, however, regarded the god Faunus and a local nymph, Marica as his parents. When Aeneas arrived in Italy, he found Latinus ruling at Laurentum in Latium. According to Virgil he was at this time an ineffective old man (though other

Roman writers believed him to be younger). His wife Amata wished to marry their only child Lavinia to Turnus, prince of the Rutulians of Ardea; and Latinus, in spite of his preference for Aeneas, and an oracle which had warned him to marry her to a foreign newcomer, was compelled to acquiesce in her proposal. At the end of the war, Amata having killed herself in the belief that Turnus was dead, Latinus gave Aeneas his daughter's hand. The city of Laurentum was refounded at a little distance away and named after the girl as Lavinium. According to Livy, on the other hand, Latinus, after pledging Aeneas Lavinia's hand, fought on his side against Turnus until he himself was killed, though Aeneas proved victorious. However it was also said that Latinus was not killed in the battle, but simply vanished and was received among the gods under the title of Jupiter Latiaris. Rome's homeland of Latium was held to have been named after this mythical king.

Latona see LETO.

Latreus A Centaur, slain by Caeneus in the battle against the Lapiths.

Lausus Son of Mezentius.

Lavinia see LATINUS, AENEAS.

Leander see HERO.

Learchus see INO, ATHAMAS.

Leda Daughter of Thestius, king of Aetolia, and wife of Tyndareos, king of Sparta. She was the mother of the Dioscuri Castor and Polydeuces, and of Helen (wife of Menelaus), Clytemnestra (wife of his brother Agamemnon), Timandra, Philonoe, and Phoebe. Nevertheless it was not agreed who the father of the Dioscuri was. Polydeuces was often said to be Helen's twin by Zeus,

and Castor their half-brother, begotten on the same night by Tyndareos, though he, too, was often said to be a son of Zeus (which is the meaning of the name Dioscuri). Helen's parentage was also disputed, for she was also said to be the child of Zeus – born from an egg, because the god had made love to her mother in the form of a swan. This story of Helen's birth from an egg was well known in antiquity (though Homer does not mention it) and was a favourite artistic subject. Helen was also sometimes said to have been hatched from an egg laid by the goddess Nemesis and to have been merely reared by Leda.

Lelex The name of an ancient king of either Sparta or Megara. He gave his name to the Lelegians.

Leonteus A Lapith leader in the Trojan War.

Leto (Latin: *Latona*) A Titaness, the daughter of Coeus and Phoebe. Before Zeus married Hera, he made love to Leto, and she bore him the two great archer-deities Apollo and his sister Artemis. If 'Leto', as is suggested, may be a corruption of the Lycian word *lada*, 'woman', this betrays the goddess' non-Greek origin. The story of her motherhood of Apollo and Artemis was as follows. When she was pregnant, Leto was constrained to journey through many lands, for none would offer her a place to rest. This was because the jealous Hera, knowing that Leto's children would be greater than any of her own, had forbidden every country to receive her. Moreover she had decreed that Leto's children might not be born in any place where the sun shone, and, when Leto approached Panopeus and Delphi, she found that the monstrous serpent Python had been sent by Hera to pursue her. It was also sometimes said that many places feared to admit the pregnant Titaness because they were afraid of her gigantic size, or of the terrible nature of the gods who were about to be born.

When Leto's time was come, Zeus ordered Boreas to carry her to Poseidon, who took her to Ortygia ('quail island', created when Leto's sister Asteria fell into the sea in the form of a quail while fleeing from Zeus in the form of an eagle) which, since it floated on the sea, was therefore no land at all; and he made a wave to curl over the island, so that it was hidden from the sun. There, clasping a palm tree, Leto brought forth her children. Some said, however, that Leto gave birth on the nearby island of Delos (which was also said to have been floating at one time and to have been originally called Ortygia), since the island was reassured by Leto's oath that her son would build his temple there. According to this version Leto leant her back against Mount Cynthus; and for this reason, Apollo and Artemis were known not only as *Delius* and *Delia*, but also as *Cynthius* and *Cynthia*. After the birth of the divine pair, Poseidon fastened Delos permanently down to the sea-bed by a pillar. According to an alternative version, however, the two children were born to Leto on different islands in succession, Artemis on Ortygia (that is to say, the island into which Asteria had fallen), and then Apollo on Delos. There all the goddesses except Hera and Ilithyia (the goddess of childbirth) attended the labouring Titaness for nine days, and finally they sent Iris to bribe Ilithyia to come and deliver the child Apollo without Hera's knowledge. It was believed that Leto took her babies to Lycia and wanted to wash them in the River Xanthus, but was prevented from doing so by some shepherds, whom wolves then drove away. Hence Leto called the country Lycia after the wolves (this story was based on a false etymology of Lycia from *lykos*, 'wolf') and turned the shepherds into frogs.

There was a close family loyalty be-tween Leto and her children. Apollo took vengeance on Python, the dragon which had persecuted his mother when she was pregnant. He also killed Tityus, a Euboean giant who tried to rape Leto, and saw to it that his shade was eternally tortured in Tartarus. Moreover Apollo and Artemis slew Niobe and most of her children, because she had rashly vaunted her superiority as a mother over Leto.

Leucippe One of the daughters of Minyas. When they had neglected the rites of Dionysus, and had consequently been driven mad, her son Hippasus was torn to pieces. Leucippe and her sisters were then turned into bats.

Leucippus *1.* Son of Perieres and Gorgo-phone, and joint king of Messenia with his brother Aphareus. His daughters were Arsinoe, Phoebe, and Hilaira.
2. Son of Oenomaus of Pisa. *See* DAPHNE.

Leucothea *see* INO.

Leucothoe *see* HELIOS.

Leucus *see* IDOMENEUS.

Liber An Italian god of the countryside, usually worshipped in conjunction with Ceres and Libera. In due course the three were identified with Dionysus (Bacchus), Demeter, and Persephone. In one story told about Liber, his identification with Dionysus is clear. While he was passing through Campania in southern Italy, he was entertained at the table of a poor peasant, Falernus, on Mount Massicus. The fare was rustic and there was no wine. Liber filled the cups with red wine, over which Falernus fell asleep: when he awoke, the mountain was covered with grapevines. Such was the mythical origin of the Falernian wine which the Romans so greatly prized.

Libera *see* LIBER.

Libitina A Roman goddess associated with death.

Libya Daughter of Epaphus and Memphis. To Poseidon she bore Belus and Agenor, who were twins, and Lelex. Libya, a Greek name applied to large areas of Africa, was called after her.

Lichas Heracles' herald, whom he sent to fetch a clean tunic from Deianira when he wished to sacrifice at Cape Cenaeum in Euboea. Deianira gave Lichas the tunic dipped in the fatal blood of Nessus and Lichas conveyed it to Heracles. When the poison ate into him, Heracles flung Lichas out to sea, where he was transformed into a rock.

Licymnius Son of Electryon, king of Argos, and of a slavewoman, Midea. The boy was brought up by Amphitryon and Alcmena and was a friend and supporter of Heracles. He married Amphitryon's daughter Perimede, who bore him three sons, Oeonus, Argeius, and Melas. Oeonus was stoned to death by his cousins, the sons of Hippocoon, at Sparta; Heracles avenged him. Argeius and Melas were killed fighting for Heracles in Oechalia. Licymnius in his old age, after fighting for the children of Heracles in Argos, was accidentally killed by one of them, Tlepolemus, who was sent into exile as a consequence.

Lindus Grandson of Helios. He gave his name to a Rhodian city.

Linus A musician of whom several incompatible stories are told, perhaps indicating the diverse origins of the myths invented to interpret the harvest song *ailinon* (usually considered to be a lament for the death of the year and perhaps derived from the Phoenician *ai lanu*, 'alas for us!') as *ai* Linon, 'alas for Linos'. An Argive story asserts that Linus was the son of Psamathe, a princess of Argos and the daughter of King Crotopus. The child's father was Apollo. When he was born his mother abandoned him, and he was eaten by Crotopus' dogs. (In another version he was rescued and brought up by shepherds.) Then Apollo brought a plague upon Argos, until Crotopus discovered its cause and propitiated the god by instituting this dirge, to be sung annually in memory of the child. Some said that Crotopus killed Psamathe because she told him of the birth giving of her son. It was also recounted that the plague sent by Apollo wiped out all the children in Argos.

In central Greece there was a story that Linus was a son of Amphimarus and the Muse Urania, and was killed by Apollo for claiming to sing as skilfully as the god: whereupon the Linus song was sung by the people in mourning for his death. He was also said to have been a son of Apollo or of Oeagrus and a Muse. It was believed that he discovered the rules of harmony, brought the Phoenician alphabet to Greece, and tried to teach Heracles to play the lyre. Some claimed that, when he tried to chastise Heracles, the young hero killed him by striking him with the lyre. At Thebes he was held to have been a son of Ismenius, and to have taught Thamyris and Orpheus how to play music.

Liriope ('Lily-voice') A nymph; the mother of Narcissus by the River Cephissus.

Lityerses *see* DAPHNIS.

Lotis *see* DRIOPE; PRIAPUS.

Lotus Eaters Odysseus landed in the mythical country of these people after rounding Cape Malea on his way home from Troy. Some of his sailors tasted the lotus plant, and as a result forgot everything and only wanted to stay there for ever, eating the fruit in blissful oblivion. They had to be dragged back to the ships by force.

Lua *see* SATURN.

Lucina The Roman goddess of child-birth, identified with Ilithyia.

Lucretia Wife of the Roman leader Lucius Tarquinius Collatinus. When the Roman forces were besieging Ardea, he and his fellow-commanders discussed the merits of their respective wives; and Collatinus suggested they should ride to Rome and discover, in proof of their claims, what their womenfolk were actually engaged in doing. Lucretia was the only wife to live up to her husband's claims for her: she was sitting quietly weaving at home, whereas the other wives were using their husbands' absence as an excuse for carousing. One of the men who rode to Rome, Setus Tarquinius, the son of the Roman king Tarquinius Superbus, was so greatly aroused by Lucretia's beauty and virtue that a few days later he returned secretly to Collatia, where she gave him honourable entertainment. During the night he burst into her bedroom and raped her at the point of a dagger. She then wrote summoning her father and husband, who came with Valerius Poplicola and Lucius Brutus. She made them promise to avenge her honour, and then stabbed herself to death. According to Roman legend it was as a result of this event that the Roman nobles rose against their king and founded the Republic, of which, according to one tradition, Collatinus and Brutus were the first consuls.

Lucumo *see* TARQUINIUS PRISCUS.

Luna *see* SELENE.

Luperca, Valerias Sister of the early, and perhaps mythical, Roman consul Valerius Poplicola or Publicola. At an advanced age, she was said by a historian of the Valerian family to have instigated the wife and mother of Coriolanus

to intercede with him when he was threatening Rome with extinction.

Lycaon *1.* Son of Pelasgus and Meliboea; an early king of Arcadia. He had fifty sons by a number of wives; and he had daughters of whom one was Callisto. There were two traditions about his character: some said he was the virtuous father of vicious sons, others that he was as bad as they were. Whichever may have been the case, Lycaon was punished for the wickedness of his court when Zeus and Hermes toured Arcadia. To test Zeus, Lycaon was said to have served him human flesh, the flesh of a Molossian slave. Zeus blasted all Lycaon's sons except one, Nyctimus, with a thunderbolt, transformed the king himself into a wolf (**lykos** in Greek), and then, after saving Philemon and Baucis, caused the great flood. According to another version Zeus turned Lycaon into a wolf for having sacrificed a child at the altar of Lycaean Zeus, which Lycaon had founded. From that time onwards, every time sacrifice was made at the altar of Lycaean Zeus in Arcadia, a man was turned into a wolf; if, however, after eight years the wolf had not eaten human flesh, it reverted to human form. (This is a version of the werewolf tradition.) *See also* CALLISTO. *2.* Son of King Priam and Laothea. While cutting fig-wood to make chariot rails he was captured by Achilles, who sold him as a slave in Lemnos; but a friend of Lycaon's, Eetion, bought him back. Lycaon managed to return to Troy but twelve days later Achilles caught him again, unarmed, and this time, in spite of his entreaties for safety and offers of ransom, put him to death. *3.* An Illyrian king, the father of Daunus and Peucetius. *4.* Son of Ares. He challenged Heracles to a fight and was killed. *5.* A king of Zeleia in Lycia. *See* PANDARUS.

Lycomedes A king of Scyros. Theseus,

after he had been banished from Athens, went in exile to his court, since he had estates on the island. Lycomedes received him courteously, but secretly feared that Theseus might supplant him as king, and pushed him over a cliff to his death. Some said he did this to please Menestheus, who had usurped Theseus' throne at Athens. It was to Lycomedes that Thetis brought her young son Achilles, in fear that he would be summoned to the Trojan War and be killed; she urged him to dress the boy in girl's clothes and hide him from the Greek captains. After the ruse had been detected and Achilles had left for Troy, Lycomedes' daughter Deidamia bore the departed hero a son, Neoptolemus.

Lycurgus 1. Son of Dryas and king of the Edonians in Thrace. When the youthful Dionysus came with his nurses seeking refuge, Lycurgus repelled him, driving off the god and his followers with an ox-goad and accusing him of encouraging immoral behaviour. Thereupon Dionysus leapt into the sea, where Thetis welcomed him and the Nereids gave him shelter. Lycurgus also imprisoned Dionysus' nurses, or his train of Maenads, and was consequently punished. According to Homer Zeus blinded him and brought him to a speedy end. According to other traditions he went mad; the imprisoned women were miraculously released; and Dionysus returned and made Lycurgus drunk on wine, so that he failed to recognise his own mother and tried to rape her. When he realised who she was, he went into the country and started slashing the vines with an axe. While doing so he killed his own son Dryas, thinking his legs were vinestems. As a result of his crimes Thrace was visited with famine, and an oracle predicted that there would be no relief until Lycurgus was put to death. He was therefore bound and led to Mount Pangaeus, where wild horses devoured him. In other versions of this myth Lycur-

gus killed himself; or he killed his wife and son, and Dionysus then caused his death by delivering him to the panthers of Mount Rhodope.

2. A king of Nemea. *See* HYPSIPYLE

3. A king of Arcadia; the son of Aleus. When his brothers Cepheus and Amphidamas sailed away in the *Argo*, Lycurgus remained in Arcadia and ruled on behalf of their father. Lycurgus killed King Areithous in a narrow pass where his great iron mace could not save him. He later gave Areithous' armour to his squire Ereuthalion. As Lycurgus' son Ancaeus had been killed by the Calydonian boar, he was succeeded by his nephew Echemus, the son of Cepheus. Lycurgus is also sometimes said to be the father of Iasus, father of Atalanta.

Lycus 1. A king, or regent, of Thebes; the son of Chthonius, one of the 'Sown Men'. Lycus and his brother Nycteus were brought up in Euboea; but because of their murder of Phlegyas, king of Orchomenus in Boeotia, they were exiled to the Boeotian town of Hyria. They subsequently moved to Thebes, where they were made citizens by King Pentheus. According to another version they originated not from Thebes but from Hyria or Euboea and were sons of the god Poseidon by the Pleiad Celaeno.

At Thebes they quickly rose to high favour. Nycteus' daughter Nycteis married King Polydorus, the son of Cadmus, and when the king died, Nycteus became regent for the dead man's son Labdacus. Nycteus' daughter Antiope was seduced by Zeus and, in fear of her father's anger, fled to Sicyon, where Nycteus then proceeded in pursuit of her. He was killed trying to recover her, or else, in shame at her dishonour, committed suicide; before dying he made Lycus promise to punish Epopeus, the king of Sicyon, who had given her shelter. Lycus, who inherited the regency of Thebes from his brother, marched to Sicyon, where he overthrew Epopeus and seized Antiope, dragging her back to Thebes. On the way, upon Mount Cithaeron, she gave birth to Zeus' sons, the twins Amphion and Zethus. Lycus forced her to abandon her babies in a cave on the mountain, where shepherds found them and brought them up. Lycus put Antiope in the charge of his wife Dirce, who treated her like a slave and kept her in a dungeon.

When Labdacus came of age, the rulership was ceded him by Lycus, but he had only reigned a year or two when he was killed in a war with Pandion of Athens. Lycus once more became regent, this time for Labdacus' son Laius, and it was said that he planned to make himself king in Laius' place. Many years later, when Antiope's sons Amphion and Zethus, now fully grown, came to Thebes, they put Lycus to death (though according to another version Hermes saved him). Their mother Antiope having escaped from Dirce, they had inflicted on Dirce the same punishment that she intended for Antiope (tying her to a bull which gored her to death), and now they made themselves masters of Thebes. Lycus and Dirce had a son, Lycus 2.

2. Son of above and Dirce. After his father's death, he escaped to Euboea. Some time after the defeat of the Seven, but before the attack on the city by their sons the Epigoni, he seized power in Thebes, killing the aged Creon, who was regent for Laodamas, the son of Eteocles. Heracles, who had married Megara, Creon's daughter, was absent from Thebes at the time of the usurpation. But when he returned, he found that Lycus was on the point of killing Megara and his children (as well as Amphitryon, Heracles' stepfather), since he believed Heracles to be dead and was afraid of his family's influence at Thebes. According to Euripides' *Heracles*, this event took place during the twelfth of Heracles' Labours, when he was visiting the Underworld in quest of Cerberus. The commoner version of the story, however, places these events before the Labours, and makes the command of Delphi to perform them the result thereof. Heracles in his anger killed Lycus, restored Laodamas to the throne, and rescued his wife and children from the executioner. But then, in a fit of madness, he killed his children and perhaps Megara too, believing them to be Eurystheus' children.

3. A king of the Mariandyni in Bithynia. He or his father Dascylus entertained the Argonauts when they passed by his kingdom on their way to Colchis. He sent his son Dascylus with them as far as Thermodon, to ensure a friendly reception. Heracles, engaged upon his quest for the Amazon's belt, also stayed with him, and gave him useful help against the barbarous Bebryces, who had attacked his country.

4. Son of Pandion, king of Athens. After Pandion's death his three sons at first divided the kingdom between them, but subsequently Aegeus drove the other two out. Lycus went to Messenia, where he enhanced the worship of Demeter and Persephone in their sacred grove at Andania. He also developed prophetic powers. According to Herodotus, Lycus took refuge in the southern part of Asia Minor, giving to the country whose people had previously been known as Termilae, the name of Lycia after him. He was also said to have settled there in the company of the Cretan exile Sarpedon. The Athenian clan of the Lycomedae, who were priests of Demeter and Persephone, claimed him as their ancestor.

Lynceus *1*. The only one of Aegyptus' sons to be spared by his bride on his wedding-night. He became king of Argos and was succeeded by his son Abas. *See* HYPERMNESTRA.

2. see IDAS.

Lyncus A king of Scythia who, according to Ovid, tried to kill Triptolemus in order to claim for himself the credit for the gift of corn to mankind. Demeter punished him by turning him into a lynx.

Lysimache Wife of Talaus, king of Argos; her father was Abas, son of Melampus.

Lysippe *see* MELAMPUS.

M

Macar or **Macareus** ('blessed') *1*. Son of Aeolus. He committed incest with his sister Canace and, when his sister was killed by their father, put himself to death.

2. A seaman of Odysseus who settled near Caeta. According to Ovid he recognised his lost comrade Achaemenides in the Trojan fleet of Aeneas, to whom he recounted the story of Odysseus' voyage from Troy.

Macaria A virgin daughter of Heracles and Deianira who sacrificed herself to win victory for Iolaus and the children of Heracles in Attica, when Eurystheus invaded the country to take vengeance upon them for his humiliation at their father's hands.

Machaon ('warrior') Son of Asclepius by Epione. He and his brother Podalirius ruled Tricca, Ithome, and Oechalia in Thessaly, and inherited their father's talent for healing. Machaon married Anticlea, and she bore him three sons, who likewise practised medicine: Nicomachus, Gorgasus, and Alexanor. Either because they had been among Helen's suitors, or as a result of their reputation in medicine, Machaon and Podalirius were asked to join the expedition to Troy, to which they led a contingent of thirty ships from their Thessalian kingdom. In the war, they served as physicians to the Greek army. Machaon healed Menelaus, but was himself wounded by Paris and tended by Nestor; he was subsequently killed by Eurypylus or Penthesilea. Nestor took his bones back to Greece and buried

them at Gerenia, where a shrine with healing powers was established.

Macris Daughter of Aristaeus; she nursed the infant Dionysus in Euboea. When Hera, jealous of this son of Zeus by another woman, drove her from her home, she took refuge in a cave on the island of Drepane or Scheria, which was subsequently (or even at that time) inhabited by the Phaeacians. Here, for her sake, Demeter taught the people how to sow corn.

Maenads ('frenzied women') Women who followed Dionysus and, in a state of ecstatic frenzy, celebrated his rites with song, dance, and music in the mountains, dressed in the skins of fawns or panthers, carrying the thyrsus (a staff crowned with a pine-cone), and wreathed with ivy, oak-leaves, or fir. They also carried torches, snakes, and bunches of grapes. Reckless of normal conventions, they were inspired with great physical strength, which enabled them to tear wild beasts to pieces and devour them. Asian Maenads accompanied Dionysus on his triumphal progress from Lydia to Greece, where they were joined by Greek women, much to the disgust of their husbands, who often tried to interfere. As a result of his prying upon the Maenads, Pentheus of Thebes was killed. They were also called Thyiades ('inspired') and Bacchae or Bacchants ('women of Bacchus').

Maeon Son of Haemon. Eteocles sent him with fifty Thebans to ambush Tydeus, who killed them all except

Maeon, whom he spared because of an omen.

Magnes Son of Zeus and Thyia; he gave his name to Magnesia in Thessaly.

Maia *1*. The eldest of the Pleiades, daughters of Atlas and Pleione, and the mother of Hermes. She lived in a cave on Mount Cyllene in Arcadia. Zeus loved her and visited her late at night, when his wife Hera was asleep. She bore him Hermes who grew up so rapidly that he stole Apollo's cattle on the very first day of his life. Maia seems to have been immune from the jealousy usually displayed by Hera; indeed, she shielded from her the less fortunate Callisto, or rather the baby she bore to Zeus, Arcas, whom Hermes gave to his mother to rear (*Maia* means 'mother' or 'nurse').
2. An obscure Italian spring goddess after whom the month of May was called.

Manes A Roman name for the spirits of the dead in the Underworld, usually called *di manes*. In later times the term Manes was used in a topographical sense for 'Underworld', and was also employed sometimes to refer to its gods, Hades (Pluto) and Persephone (Proserpina). The Romans believed that the Manes of their ancestors (*di parentes*) emerged from their tombs for a few days every February (*parentalia*, 'all souls' day', *feralia*, 'day of offerings') when they had to be propitiated with offerings.

Manlius Marcus Manlius Capitolinus, a Roman of consular rank – perhaps mythical – was believed to have been in charge of the garrison which held out in the Capitol after the rest of Rome had been captured by the Gauls in 387 BC (as a matter of historical fact, the Capitol probably fell when the rest of the city was taken). When Camillus sent a

messenger to consult the garrison, a Gaul saw him climb up the cliff and enter the citadel, and a night attack was made by the same route. However the sacred geese, which were kept in the temple of Juno Moneta, cackled and awoke Manlius and his party, who repulsed the Gauls. Next day the Romans flung the captain of the watch, who had been on duty but had failed to hear the attackers, over the cliff and rewarded Manlius who became known as Capitolinus for his exploit.

Manto Daughter of the Theban prophet Tiresias, herself gifted with prophetic (mantic) skill. When the Epigoni, sons of the Seven against Thebes, captured that city, they dedicated Manto to Apollo at Delphi as the finest prize, together with a number of other Thebans. While at Delphi, Manto bore to Alcmaeon (leader of the Epigoni) two children, Amphilochus and Tisiphone, both of whom were reared at Corinth by King Creon. Manto eventually led the other Theban prisoners from Delphi to Asia Minor, where they had been directed by the oracle to found a colony. Manto herself was said to have founded Apollo's oracle at Clarus near Colophon, where she also married the Cretan Rhacius. They had a son, the famous seer Mopsus *2*.

Marathon Son of Epopeus, king of Sicyon. He founded the town of Marathon in Attica to escape from his father's bad government. When Epopeus died, Marathon took his kingdom and divided it between his sons Sicyon and Corinthus, after whom the cities of Asopia and Ephyra were renamed.

Marcius, Ancus Ancus Marcius, who may or may not be wholly mythical, was believed to have been the fourth king of Rome. It was said that he was the son of King Numa Pompilius' daughter. Tradition recounted that Ancus Marcius, unlike his predecessor Tullus Hostilius, was a peaceful ruler. He was believed to have built the first (wooden) bridge over the Tiber, and to have colonised the port of Ostia. He enlarged the city boundaries. His descendants, the Marcii, were in historical times an extremely important family, but were of plebeian origin, a fact which may have encouraged them to invent their royal forbear or exaggerate his importance.

Marica An Italian water-nymph. She was the mother of Latinus by Faunus.

Maron Son of Euanthes and priest of Apollo at Ismarus in Thrace. He was the only inhabitant of Ismarus whom Odysseus, in his attack on the Cicones, spared. In return Maron gave him the strong wine with which he later befuddled the Cyclops Polyphemus.

Marpessa *see* IDAS.

Mars The Roman god of war, identified with Ares; though originally he had been a god of more general characteristics or specifically of agriculture. His name, of unknown meaning, had earlier taken the form *Mavors*, in some dialects *Mamers* (Etruscan: *Maris*). His function appears to have developed as the Romans themselves evolved from an agricultural to a warlike nation. He had a highly developed cult at Rome, being considered, next to Jupiter, the greatest patron of the State; he was particularly revered by the army, in relation to which he had the title *Gradivus*. He gave his name to the month of March (*Martius mensis*), on certain days of which the priesthood of the Salii danced a war-dance and sang ritual songs. It was appropriate to his agricultural function that his major festivals were held in spring and early summer. There was also an ancient song sung by the Arval Brethren (an old priestly college of twelve) at the Ambarvalia, during May,

in which he was asked to protect the people and the fields. In the earliest times he was identified with the pastoral god Silvanus. The Romans believed that the goddess Juno bore Mars after she had been impregnated by a flower; whereas the Greeks attributed the paternity of Ares to Zeus. Mars was married to a minor goddess called Nerio (a word meaning 'strength'). In the religion of the Roman State his worship was of paramount importance, since it was believed that his fatherhood of Romulus by Rhea Silvia, a Vestal Virgin, founded the Roman race. He had come to Rhea Silvia, it was said, while she was asleep, and she bore him twin sons, Romulus and Remus. Their great-uncle Amulius tried to drown the babies in the Tiber, but they had been saved by a she-wolf; and when he grew up Romulus founded the city of Rome.

The wolf and the woodpecker, which had likewise helped to save the infants, were sacred to Mars; Picus, the woodpecker, was an ancient Roman god who served as his companion.

Equally independent of the Greek myths associated with Ares were two other stories told of Mars. One referred to the sacred shield (ancile), which fell from the sky in the time of King Numa Pompilius. As the fate of Rome was thought to depend on the safe keeping of this shield, Numa had eleven more made in its likeness and hung the twelve in the temple of Mars, so that no one who wanted to steal the original would know which it was. The priestly order known as the Salii were appointed to guard it and its replicas. In the other story, Mars fell in love with Minerva and asked the aged goddess Anna Perenna to act as go-between. Eventually Anna told Mars that Minerva would marry him. He then went to take his bride, but on raising the veil of the goddess who had been presented him discovered that she was not Minerva but the old Anna Perenna herself. The other gods enjoyed the joke.

Mars gave his name to the Campus Martius, a field where the Roman males practised warlike skills. In the time of Augustus he was given the title *Ultor*, 'Avenger', in memory of the emperor's part in the victory over Julius Caesar's assassins. Soldiers sacrificed to Mars before and after battle, in association with the goddess Bellona, who was variously described as his wife, sister, or daughter.

Marsyas A Phrygian satyr. Athena made a double flute to imitate the lamentations of the Gorgons for their sister Medusa. Since, however, the playing of the instrument distorted her face, she threw it away with a curse. Thereupon Marsyas found the flute and, undeterred by the beating Athena gave him, played it, becoming so proficient that he challenged Apollo to a contest. Its rule was that the winner should use the loser in any way he wished; and the judges were to be the Muses. Both competitors performed equally well, until Apollo challenged Marsyas to play his instrument upside down – a thing possible on the lyre but not the flute. Consequently Marsyas lost and Apollo flayed him alive, hanging him on a pine; and his blood, or the tears of his friends the nymphs and satyrs, formed the River Marsyas. The flute, which Apollo flung into the River Maeander, was found at Sicyon, and dedicated to Apollo by Sacadas, a shepherd or musician.

In Roman times, the name of Marsyas, somewhat unexpectedly, stood for the freedom of Roman citizen communities (*coloniae* and *municipia*) and for the jurisdiction that guaranteed it.

Mastarna An Etruscan hero, possibly, though not certainly, historical; identified by the Emperor Claudius with the sixth king of Rome, Servius Tullius. Mastarna's exploits played a great part in the legends of Etruria. It was believed that he belonged to the Etruscan town

of Vulci, but that he was driven from Etruria with Caeles and Aulus Vibenna, in whose company he then occupied the Caelian Hill at Rome. According to an Etruscan tradition, preserved on paintings from Vulci, Mastarna rescued Caeles Vibenna from 'Tarquinius the Roman' (one of the kings of that name of Rome?), who was killed. It is possible that he himself, if he was a historical figure, likewise became king of Rome, though in that case he was not one of the traditional seven.

Mastusius When Demophon, king of Elaeus in the Thracian Chersonese, in order to avert a plague of which an oracle had warned him, instituted the annual sacrifice of a virgin of noble birth, he used to draw lots for the victim, without including his own daughter. Mastusius protested against the king's practice, and as a result of this his own daughter was immediately sacrificed. Then, pretending to accept this decision calmly, he invited Demophon and his daughters to a sacrifice, knowing that the king would arrive late. By the time he came his daughters had all been killed, and he was offered a cup of their blood mixed with wine, which he unwittingly drank. Then Demophon threw Mastusius into the harbour, together with the bowl, which became the constellation of Crater ('the mixing-bowl').

Mecisteus An Argive warrior (a son of Talaus) whom Apollodorus names as one of the Seven against Thebes. Although he was said to have been killed attacking the Proetid Gate, which was held by Melanippus, an incompatible tradition stated that he subsequently competed in the funeral games held for Oedipus at Thebes, and won many prizes.

Medea Daughter of Aeetes, king of Colchis (son of Helios, the Sun-god), and the Oceanid Idyia, whose name, like

Medea's, means 'cunning', 'knowing'. From her earliest days, Medea, taking after her aunt Circe, was a skilful witch and devotee of Hecate. When Jason came to Colchis with the Argonauts in his quest for the Golden Fleece, Hera, who wished to punish Pelias, king of Iolcus, caused Aphrodite to make Medea fall violently in love with Jason, who was both handsome and persuasive. Aphrodite sent Eros to shoot her with an arrow, and appeared to her in the form of Circe in order to persuade her to overcome her scruples. As a result Jason, when presented by Aeetes with seemingly impossible tasks as a condition for winning the Golden Fleece, asked Medea to help him, and she, in return for a promise of marriage, complied (according to Ovid) because she knew her father meant to destroy the Argonauts and had no intention of surrendering the fleece. She performed elaborate rituals to propitiate Hecate, gave Jason a magic ointment making him impervious to the onslaught of the fire-breathing bulls, told him how to defeat the soldiers who would spring from the dragon's teeth, and killed or drugged for him the serpent which guarded the Golden Fleece in a sacred grove. Then, realising that Aeetes meant to kill the Argonauts in the night, Medea went to them secretly and urged them to flee at once. As they went to the ship, she took Jason to the grove, and he stole the fleece.

There are two versions of Medea's treatment of her brother Apsyrtus. According to one story he was a small boy whom she took with her as a hostage and cut to pieces as her father's pursuing fleet approached, leaving the fragments in prominent places so that Aeetes was forced to delay his flight in order to pick them up. Alternatively, he was a grown man, and himself led the pursuit of her across the Black Sea and up the Danube. Then, on an island in the Adriatic, she tricked him into an interview with Jason, who treacherously murdered

him. Circe later purified the pair of their guilt, but on hearing the details of their crime afflicted them with a curse. In the mythical land of the Phaeacians, Medea finally escaped her father's pursuit by consummating her marriage with Jason in a cave and thus inducing the Phaeacian king Alcinous to guarantee her safety. Towards the end of the journey Medea helped Jason by killing Talos, the bronze man of Crete, who protected the island for Minos by running round it thrice a day and preventing intruders from landing; he would burn his victims to death or sink their ships with stones. Medea removed the nail – lodged in his heel – which stopped up his great vein, and he bled to death.

When the Argonauts reached Iolcus, Medea was said to have rejuvenated Jason's father Aeson. She did this by magical means, using a charm by which she filled Aeson's viens with a brew she had boiled in a pot from herbs, or alternatively, actually boiling him in the pot. She offered to do the same for Pelias, Jason's uncle who had usurped Aeson's throne, and then induced his daughters to cut him up for the pot, having first offered them a demonstration with a ram: in this way the girls were tricked into murdering their father, and the Argonauts were able to take Iolcus.

As a result of this crime, Jason and Medea – now deserted by Hera – left Iolcus for Corinth, where (according to one version) Medea had a right to the throne, since her father had been king there years before. They had a number of children; but then Jason, to ingratiate himself with the Corinthian king Creon, proposed to divorce Medea and, for the sake of their children's future, to marry again, taking the king's daughter Glauce as his wife. Medea had her revenge, burning Glauce alive with a poisoned wedding-dress, which she sent by the hands of her children. They too met their deaths, either murdered by herself or killed by the Corinthians for helping their mother in her plot. Creon, the king, was also slain by the wedding-dress as he tried to help Glauce. The name and number of Medea's children vary in different versions of the story: some of these identified two sons, Mermerus and Pheres, others three, Thessalus, Alcimenes, and Tisander, of whom Thessalus, it was said, was not killed.

Medea escaped from Corinth in the magic chariot of her grandfather the Sun, drawn by winged serpents. She went to Athens, where the king, Aegeus, owed her an obligation, having vowed to protect her, if the need should arise, in return for a guarantee that the king, who believed he was childless (though in fact he had begotten Theseus) would have children. Medea now married him and bore him a son, Medus. When, a few years later, Theseus came to Athens to claim his inheritance, Aegeus did not understand who he was, but Medea knew and poisoned Aegeus' mind against him, persuading him to pit the boy against the dangerous bull of Minos which was infesting Marathon. When Theseus succeeded in this task, Medea tried to kill him by offering him a cup of poison, but Aegeus now recognised the tokens Aethra had given him and dashed the cup out of his hand. Medea fled or was exiled, and returned to Colchis with her son Medus. She sent her son ahead of her. At Colchis Perses, who had killed his brother Aeetes and seized the throne, now imprisoned the boy, believing that a descendant of Aeetes was destined to kill him, and suspecting Medus of being such, in spite of his claim to be a Corinthian, Hippotes, the son of Creon. The Colchian crops failed as a result of his deed. Medea now arrived, disguised as a priestess of Artemis, and offered to end the drought if Perses would allow her to perform a rite in which the boy would be killed. It was even sometimes said that before she saw him Medea actually believed Medus' claim to be a son of Creon, and wished to get rid of him, since she had caused so much harm to his family. She planned an elaborate ritual, in the midst of which she discovered that the young man was in fact her own son Medus. She then gave him a sword, and he turned and stabbed Perses, thus avenging his grandfather Aeetes. Other accounts made Medea herself kill the king. Medus, who took the throne, conquered the land of the Medes (Media) and named it after himself. Of Medea's end nothing was said.

Medon ('ruler') *1.* Son of Codrus and last king of Athens.
2. Son of Oileus, king of Locris, and Rhene. Being exiled for homicide, he went to Phylace and fought in the Trojan War. He took command of the force from Methone when Philoctetes was marooned on Lemnos, but was later killed in battle by Aeneas.
3. An Ithacan herald, loyal to Odysseus in his absence.

Medus *see* MEDEA.

Medusa *see* GORGONS; PERSEUS.

Megaera *see* FURIES.

Megapenthes *1.* Son of Proetus. He handed over the throne of Tiryns, which he had inherited from Proetus, to Perseus in exchange for the throne of Argos. According to one story he later killed Perseus in revenge for the death of Proetus, who had been turned to stone by the head of the Gorgon.
2. A bastard son of Menelaus by a slave-woman. Menelaus loved the boy dearly and gave him a daughter of Alector as his bride. After Menelaus' death he drove Helen from Sparta, but failed to take the throne, which was given to Orestes.

Megara Daughter of Creon of Thebes.

She was married to Heracles and bore him two or three children, whom Heracles slew in a fit of madness. Some accounts asserted that he killed Megara at the same time, others that he married her to Iolaus because of his own unworthiness of her.

Megareus *1.* A king of Onchestus who helped Nisus in his wars with Minos of Crete. He was either killed in battle at Megara, or else survived Nisus and married his daughter Iphinoe, succeeding him as king of Megara, to which he gave his own name. His sons having died, he made Alcathous, who killed the Cithaeronian lion, his heir.
2. Son of Creon at Thebes. He defended the Neistan gate at Thebes against Eteocles in the attack of the Seven. According to Sophocles he was killed leaping from the walls of the city in a self-immolation demanded by Ares; but Euripides attributed this act to another of Creon's sons, Menoeceus.

Meges Son of Phyleus, king of Dulichium (later named Leucas). He was among Helen's suitors and led forty ships to the Trojan War, but was shipwrecked off Euboea on his way home.

Melampus ('black foot') A great seer, who founded an important family of prophets. Melampus was the son of the Thessalians Amythaon and Idomene, who migrated to Messenia: he and his brother Bias were brought up in Pylos. When Melampus accompanied King Polyphantes into the country, a serpent bit one of the king's slaves, and the king killed it. Melampus, however, found the nest containing its young in an oak-tree. He piously cremated the parent's body and reared the young snakes, who repaid him by licking his ears when he was asleep, so that, when he awoke, he found that he could understand the speech of animals and birds. Melampus also had relations with Apollo, whom

he met beside the River Alpheius, and with Dionysus, whose cult he helped to propagate. As a result he became an expert prophet.

When his brother Bias fell in love with Pero, the beautiful daughter of Neleus, king of Pylos, Neleus refused his consent to the match unless Bias could produce as bride-price the cattle of Phylacus, king of Phylace in Thessaly. According to Homer Neleus had already announced that this bride-price must be paid by any suitor for Pero. Melampus was so fond of Bias that he undertook to drive off the cattle, which were guarded by a wild, unsleeping hound; but he was caught in the act and imprisoned for a year. According to one tradition Phylacus had already agreed to give the cattle to anyone who would endure a year's imprisonment. Homer also suggests, in an alternative version of the tale, that Neleus seized Melampus' goods and forced him to flee the country, and that it was he, not Bias, who loved Pero.

At the end of a year Melampus one day heard certain woodworms in the roof of his cell say that they would finish devouring the main beam that night. Melampus persuaded his jailer to move him to another cell, and the roof duly collapsed. Phylacus was so impressed by his prophetic powers that he consulted him about the impotence of his son Iphiclus (or Iphiclus consulted him about himself). Melampus offered to solve the problem in return for the cattle. When this was agreed, he sacrificed two bulls and invited the birds to the feast. The last bird to arrive was an old vulture who remembered that Phylacus had frightened his son when he was small: he had been gelding rams and had approached the boy with the bloody knife in his hand. The boy screamed, and Phylacus, going to comfort him, buried the knife-blade in a sacred oak, where he had forgotten it. The knife was now found deep in the tree's bark, and on Melampus' directions Iphiclus took a potion of wine containing the knife's rust for ten days in succession. Iphiclus was thus cured and begot two sons, Podarces and Protesilaus.

Melampus now drove the cattle back to Pylos, where he demanded the hand of Pero for Bias. He was also said to have avenged himself on Neleus (according to the version indicating that Neleus had confiscated his property).

Among Melampus' other deeds was the healing of Proetus' daughters from the madness from which they suffered. Homer tells how the seer went to live in Argos, Proetus' kingdom, and offered to cure the girls in return for a third of the kingdom; but Proetus refused. Their madness may have been due to their rejection of the rites of Dionysus. In any case, it now spread to the other women of the country, who roamed the mountains, imagining themselves to be cattle, and killed their own children. Proetus now accepted Melampus' offer, but the seer raised his price, demanding another third of the kingdom for his brother Bias. Proetus agreed to this too, and the brothers drove the frenzied women into Arcadia or Sicyon, and purified them at a temple of Artemis there. In the chase one of the girls, Iphinoe, had died, but Bias (whose wife Pero had also perished) and Melampus married the other two, Iphianassa and Lysippe respectively. Melampus had three sons, Abas, Mantius, and Antiphates (the grandfather of Amphiaraus). According to Pindar, Melampus gave up his prophetic career on becoming king of Argos. Bias and Pero had a son, Talaus; his second wife, Iphianassa, bore him Anaxibia, who married Pelias, king of Iolcus.

Melanippe ('black mare') Daughter of Aeolus and Hippe; she bore two sons to Poseidon, Aeolus, and Boeotus. In consequence, her father blinded her and abandoned the babies, who were suckled by a cow and reared by shepherds. They gave the infants to Theano, who was childless and was about to be banished for this reason by her husband Metapontus, king of Icaria. Theano then bore two sons of her own. When the four boys grew up, Metapontus preferred the elder pair, and Theano urged her own sons to kill them, explaining that their supposed brothers were foundlings; but a battle ensued in which Poseidon brought about the deaths of Theano's sons. Thereupon she killed herself, and the sons of Melanippe returned to the shepherds who had preserved them in their infancy. Poseidon revealed himself to the youths, ordering that they should rescue their mother, whom her father Aeolus had imprisoned. They killed Aeolus, Poseidon restored Melanippe's eyes, and Metapontus married her, adopting the 'sons' whom he had always preferred to his own children by Theano.

Melanippus ('black horse') *1. see* COMA-ETHO.

2. A Theban nobleman. He was a son of Astacus, and fought against the Seven, killing Mecisteus and Tydeus. But Tydeus also gave him his death-blow in the same battle, and afterwards ate his brains, as he himself lay dying.

3. Son of Theseus and Perigune, daughter of the outlaw Sinis. Melanippus was a noted runner and won a race at the Nemean Games held by the Epigoni. He had a son called Ioxus, whose descendants refrained from burning asparagus. *See* SINIS.

Melanthius or **Melantheus** ('the black') A goatherd in the service of Odysseus at Ithaca, who betrayed his master's interests and served the suitors of Penelope. When Odysseus returned in the disguise of a beggar, Melanthius and his sister Melantho were insolent to him; but Melanthius suffered a painful death at the hands of Eumaeus and Philoetius. His father was Odysseus' faithful servant, Dolius.

Melantho A servant in Odysseus' house, who became the mistress of one of the suitors, Eurymachus. *See* MELAN-THIUS.

Melanthus A descendant of Neleus, king of Pylos. He brought a host of Messenians, whom the Dorians had driven from their homes, to Attica. There he supplanted the descendants of Theseus on the throne and became king himself. His son and heir was Codrus.

Melas *1.* Son of Portheus, king of Calydon. Melas' eight sons were killed by his nephew Tydeus, who had to leave Calydon in consequence.
2. see PHRIXUS.

Meleager A prince of Calydon, the son of Oeneus and Althaea, or of Ares and Althaea. He was said to have taken part in the expedition of the *Argo*, on which his uncle or half-brother Laocoon looked after him. He returned, having according to one version killed Aeetes, and married Cleopatra, daughter of Idas. A little later, Artemis sent a great wild boar to ravage the land of Calydon, because Oeneus had failed to sacrifice to her. Meleager invited all the heroes of Greece to come to hunt the boar – compelling them to remain with him in the hunt because they had accepted his hospitality – and Oeneus collected many helpers offering the boar's skin to whoever should kill it. After nine days' feasting the hunt began. The Arcadian Ancaeus and a number of others were killed by the beast. Then Atalanta, the virgin huntress, drew first blood with an arrow, and Amphiaraus scored a hit also. But it was Meleager who killed the boar and won the right to the spoils.

A quarrel subsequently broke out in which Meleager killed one or more of his uncles, Althaea's brothers; and the neighbouring Curetes attacked Calydon. In sources other than Homer the explanation given is that Meleager had awarded the prize to Atalanta (rejected by many of the heroes as a member of the hunting-party, owing to her sex), because he was in love with her and because she had drawn first blood. Althaea's brothers Toxeus and Plexippus then tried to take the prize from Atalanta, and it was in consequence of this that Meleager killed one or both of them. His mother cursed him for this deed, praying that he might fall in battle, and in the subsequent war with the Curetes Meleager in consequence stayed at home and lay in bed. As a result of his defection the Curetes were winning the war, besieging and burning Calydon itself, until finally Cleopatra by a desperate plea persuaded Meleager to relent. He saved Calydon in the nick of time, but won no reward, since he had changed his mind too late.

Meleager died, Homer implies, before the Trojan War, perhaps in this very battle. The story of his death as given by other writers – Aeschylus, Bacchylides, and Ovid – asserts that, when Meleager was born, the Fates had visited Althaea's bedroom: two of them predicted courage and glory for the baby, but the third declared that Meleager would die as soon as a certain brand, which was seen burning at that moment in the hearth, had been consumed. Althaea had then seized the brand and stored it away, quenching the fire. But now, when she heard of the death of her brothers at Meleager's hands, she immediately thought of the brand once again. Taking it from its hiding-place she threw it in the fire, thus bringing about her son's immediate death. His sisters, who mourned him at his funeral, were turned into guinea-hens (*meleagroi*). Althaea was said to have repented and hanged herself.

Meles *see* EROS.

Melia Daughter of Oceanus and Argia. She married Inachus.

Meliae The nymphs of ash-trees, born from the drops of blood which fell when Zeus castrated his father Cronos.

Melicertes *see* INO.

Melpomene *see* MUSES.

Memnon Son of Eos and Tithonus. His brother was Emathion. Their skin was black, supposedly because of their mother, the dawn-goddess, since in childhood they, like her, were constantly in company with the sun (Helios), whose chariot they accompanied every day across the sky. Memnon and his brother thus went to the hottest parts of the world, where in due course Memnon became king of Ethiopia, and Emathion king of Egypt. After a campaign in Persia, where he captured Susa, Memnon in the tenth year of the Trojan War came to Troy with a force of Ethiopians to help his uncle Priam. Wearing armour made for him by Hephaestus, he killed Achilles' friend Antilochus, son of Nestor, and many others. Finally Achilles attacked him and they fought with one another, while their two mothers, both goddesses, pleaded with Zeus for their lives. However Memnon fell; and Eos asked Zeus to show him some special honour. Some versions declared that Zeus made him immortal; others that the god caused the smoke from Memnon's pyre to turn into birds, which, dividing into two groups, circled the flames and killed each other, falling into the fire as offerings to the hero's ghost. Then, every year thereafter, fresh flocks of these birds, called Memnonidae, came to his tomb and performed the same death-ritual, falling dead upon the mound.

Memphis Daughter of the god of the River Nile. She married Epaphus.

Menelaus The younger son of Atreus, king of Mycenae, and of Aerope (or,

according to a less familiar version, of Atreus' son Pleisthenes). He and his brother Agamemnon spent their youth at Sicyon and in Aetolia, while Atreus' brother Thyestes was in control of Mycenae. When they were old enough to rule, Tyndareos of Sparta helped them to expel Thyestes. Agamemnon married Tyndareos' daughter Clytemnestra and, using his influence with his father-in-law, urged the cause of Menelaus as a suitable match for Clytemnestra's half-sister Helen, who was a daughter of Zeus. The other suitors of Helen had been numerous and quarrelsome, but agreed to Odysseus' proposal that they should swear an oath to protect whichever of them Helen eventually chose as her husband. She chose Menelaus, and they had a daughter, Hermione. Menelaus also had two bastard sons, Megapenthes by a slave-woman and Nicostratus by a nymph. In his old age Tyndareos made Menelaus his heir to the throne of Sparta, and abdicated in his favour.

Ten years later Paris, son of King Priam of Troy, came to Sparta, where Menelaus lavishly entertained him. In spite of a warning oracle, which he had not understood, Menelaus left Paris alone with his wife while he went to supervise the funeral of his grandfather Catreus in Crete. Thereupon Paris eloped with Helen, taking many rich treasures as well. On his return, Menelaus went to Troy with Odysseus to demand that Helen should be given back, but they were rejected and insulted. Then Menelaus' brother Agamemnon, now king of Mycenae, collected a huge army from the whole of Greece, reminding Helen's former suitors of their oaths to protect her husband, and claiming that the honour of the Greeks had been affronted.

In the war, which lasted ten years in all, Menelaus was ascribed a secondary role to Agamemnon and the other outstanding heroes. He was a brave fighter, but not particularly skilful. In the tenth year of the war he fought an arranged duel with Paris in order to settle the issue for good, and would have killed his enemy had not Aphrodite, who supported Paris, rescued him and whisked him off to Helen's bedroom. Later, after Paris' death, the Trojans gave Helen to his brother Deiphobus, in whose house, on the night of the fall of Troy, Menelaus found her. He had meant to kill her on the spot, but her beauty and Aphrodite's power deterred him. He promised the captive Trojan women that he would kill her when he got her back to Greece, but long before that he had forgotten his anger.

Menelaus and Helen had a difficult return voyage to Greece, because he had omitted to appease the gods of defeated Troy. He lost all but five of his fifty ships, and Apollo shot his helmsman; the remainder were driven to many countries, and finally to Egypt. Here, by capturing Proteus, the prophetic Old Man of the Sea, on the island of Pharos, Menelaus was able to discover what he must do in order to return home safely. He then made the sacrifices demanded and quickly sailed back to Greece with a favourable wind, bringing with him much wealth that he had acquired on his travels. On his way back to Sparta, he came to Mycenae at the time of the funeral of Aegisthus and Clytemnestra, whom her son Orestes had slain in revenge for his father Agamemnon. Orestes, who was in danger of being condemned to death for the murder, appealed to Menelaus for help. When Menelaus refused, Orestes and his sister Electra seized Helen and Hermione; they tried to kill the former, but she was rescued by Aphrodite. Menelaus then persuaded the people to commute the sentence to a year's exile.

Telemachus, on his voyage to find his father Odysseus, arrived at Sparta after Menelaus and Helen were peacefully installed there once again. Menelaus gave his news of Odysseus, which he had received from Proteus. As Proteus had also foretold, Menelaus, when he died, became immortal and went to the Elysian Fields in company with Helen. Orestes took the kingdom of Sparta at his death. For alternative versions of the myth, *see* HELEN.

Menestheus Son of Peteos and great-grandson of Erechtheus. When Theseus, king of Athens, was imprisoned by Hades in the Underworld, Menelaus usurped his throne. He persuaded the people to accept his rule since Theseus had stolen Helen from Tyndareos, and her brothers the Dioscuri (Castor and Polydeuces) had invaded Attica to recover her from her abductor; indeed, one tradition has it that they were invited to intervene by Menestheus, and then placed him on the throne.

When Theseus returned up to the earth after being released by Heracles, Menestheus expelled him from Attica and induced King Lycomedes of Scyros to kill him. Theseus' sons took refuge in Euboea. Menestheus was one of the suitors of Helen, and led fifty ships from Athens to the Trojan War, in which, according to one version, he died. The usual story, however, is that he survived the war, but that since Demophon, Theseus' son, returned from it to Athens as king, Menestheus had to content himself with the isle of Melos, whose king, Polyanax, had died without issue.

Menippe *see* CORONIDES

Menodice A nymph who bore Hylas to Theodamas, king of the Dryopes.

Menoeceus *1.* A descendant of the 'Sown Men' at Thebes, and the father of Creon and Jocasta. Some sources also make him the father of Hippomene (mother of Amphitryon and Anaxo).
2. Grandson of the above, the son of Creon and Eurydice. According to Euripi-

des, Menoeceus sacrificed himself to save the city during the siege by throwing himself off the city walls into the dragon's lair to appease the wrath of Ares for the slaying of this beast by Cadmus, since the serpent had been a son of the god. This act he undertook at the time of the attack of the Seven, because Tiresias had prophesied that Thebes could be saved only by the self-sacrifice of a virgin male descended from the 'Sown Men'. Creon did his best to prevent the sacrifice, but Menoeceus insisted on immolating himself, because he was the only man in Thebes suitable for the deed. (Sophocles, however, attributes it to Megareus, another son of Creon.)

Menoetes The heardsman of Hades' cattle. *See* HERACLES (tenth Labour).

Menoetius *1.* A Titan, the son of Iapetus and Clymene.
2. Father of Patroclus. He was a son of Actor and Aegina, and sailed in the *Argo*. His wife was Acastus' daughter Sthenele. When Patroclus during his boyhood killed a comrade in an argument over a game of dice, his parents fled with him to Phthia, where Peleus, another Argonaut, sheltered them. There Patroclus got to know Achilles, to whom he became devoted.

Mentes A Taphian chieftain, the son of Anchialus: Odysseus knew him well. Athena took his form to persuade Odysseus' son Telemachus to leave Ithaca in search of him.

Mentor An old Ithacan of noble family whom Odysseus appointed to bring up Telemachus and take charge of his household in his absence. He was a constant companion and support to Telemachus. Athena, on occasion, impersonated him.

Mercury (Latin: *Mercurius*) A Roman god, presiding over trade (Latin: *merx*, trade). *See* HERMES.

Meriones A Cretan, son of King Idomeneus' brother Molus; the king's squire and second in command. On the night of the spying raid on the Trojan camp, he gave Odysseus a helmet, which Odysseus' grandfather had stolen from Amyntor. Meriones helped Menelaus to rescue Patroclus' corpse from the battlefield, and won the prize for archery in Patroclus' funeral games.

Mermerus *see* JASON; MEDEA.

Merope *1.* One of the Pleiads.
2. Daughter of Oenopion. *See* ORION.
3. Wife of Polybus, king of Corinth, and foster-mother of Oedipus.
4. Daughter of Cypselus and the wife of Cresphontes, king of Messenia.
5. Wife of Sisyphus.
6. Daughter of Pandareos.

Merops *1.* A king of Egypt who married the nymph Clymene.
2. A seer of Percote near Troy. His sister Arisbe married Hyrtacus, king of Percote. The sons of Merops, Adrastus and Amphius, went to the Trojan War with troops from Apaesus – in spite of their father's pleas, for he knew by his prophetic art that they would be killed – and Diomedes slew them.

Mestor Son of Perseus and Andromeda. His daughter Hippothoe married Pterelaus.

Mestra Daughter of Erysichthon, who was cursed by Demeter with an insatiable appetite but purchased food by continually selling Mestra into slavery. As she had the power to change her shape – given by Poseidon in exchange for her favours – she constantly escaped and could be sold again. Ovid asserts that she married Autolycus, the thief.

Metabus A King of the Volscians. *See* CAMILLA.

Metanira Wife of Celeus, king of Eleusis in Attica. When Demeter was searching for Persephone, she came to Eleusis in the guise of an old woman, and sat down on a rock to rest. Celeus' daughter asked her in for a drink and a rest, and Metanira gave her the post of nurse to her baby son Demophon. Offered wine, Demeter preferred a cup of *kykeon*, which was barley meal and pennyroyal mixed with water. She tried to make Demophon immortal by placing him in the fire at night and anointing him with ambrosia, but Metanira, catching her in the act, screamed with terror, so that Demeter threw the baby on the ground. She then resumed her divine appearance and rebuked Metanira. *See* DEMETER.

Metapontus *see* MELANIPPE.

Metioche *see* CORONIDES.

Metion When Xuthus chose Cecrops as Erechtheus' successor on the Athenian throne, it was said that Metion and Pandorus, the younger sons of Erechtheus, drove him into exile. Metion's sons subsequently rebelled against Pandion, Cecrops' son, but in their turn they were driven out by Pandion's sons.

Metis ('thought', 'counsel') Daughter of Oceanus and Tethys; Zeus' first consort. Zeus persuaded Metis to give his father Cronos the emetic which caused him to regurgitate Zeus' brothers and sisters. Although at first she had changed her shape to avoid his bed, Metis in due course became Zeus' first wife. But Gaia prophesied to him that if Metis bore a daughter, she would be his equal in wisdom, and that she would then bear a son who would be mightier than Zeus and would overthrow him. In consequence he tricked Metis and swallowed her while she was pregnant, subsequently bringing forth her baby, full

grown, from his own head: Athena. Moreover he gained Metis' powers of wisdom, which were now within him and helped to prevent him from being overthrown.

Metope A river-nymph, the daughter of the River Ladon; she married the River Asopus.

Mettius Fufetius *see* TULLUS HOSTILIUS.

Mezentius An Etruscan king from Caere, who joined Turnus' forces in opposing Aeneas. According to Virgil, he was a ruthless, godless brute whom the people of Caere had expelled for his tyrannical behaviour. Aeneas killed him, after first killing his son Lausus. Cato the elder asserted that Mezentius had imposed a tribute of wine upon all the Latins, and that both Turnus and Aeneas were killed in the war, but Mezentius survived: Aeneas' son Ascanius eventually defeated him, after which Mezentius became an ally of the Trojans and Latins.

Midas Son of Gordius, and of Cybele or a prophetess of Telmessus. Midas was said to have inherited the throne of Phrygia from his father. Several myths were told of him. In one, old Silenus, who acted as Dionysus' tutor, was captured drunk by the country folk of Lydia and brought, chained with flowers, before King Midas, who, recognising Dionysus' companion, treated him kindly and entertained him lavishly for ten days and nights. Then Midas took Silenus back to Lydia and restored him to the god. Dionysus in his joy at the return of Silenus offered Midas whatever he wished; the king chose that all he touched might be turned to gold. Midas was at first delighted with the results, but his joy turned to horror when he realised that his food and drink were also being transformed. He finally prayed to lose his gift, and was told by the god to wash in the River Pactolus, the sands of which were thenceforth filled with gold dust.

A variant of this tale asserts that when Midas realised that Silenus used to come secretly at night to drink at the fountain in his garden he pumped wine into the water, so that Silenus became drunk. Midas captured him, curious to learn his wisdom, which was then imparted to him.

Another story concerned a music contest between Apollo and Pan (or, according to another tradition, Marsyas). When Tmolus, acting as judge, awarded the prize to Apollo, Midas expressed his disagreement. Apollo thereupon gave him an ass's ears for his folly. Although Midas succeeded in hiding his humiliation from everybody else by wearing a Phrygian cap, he had to show his ears to his barber. This man, although ordered to keep the secret on pain of death, felt unable to keep quiet about it, so he dug a pit in the ground, whispered the news into its depths, and filled the pit in. Unfortunately for Midas, the ground put forth reeds which, when rustled by the breeze, whispered the truth to the whole world: 'King Midas has ass's ears!'

Midea A Phygian slave-woman; the mother of Licymnius by Electryon.

Milanion or **Meilanion** see ATALANTA

Miletus Son of Apollo by one of his mistresses – usually said to be Acacallis. He was loved by the three sons of Zeus and Europa, Sarpedon, Minos, and Rhadamanthys, but Miletus preferred Sarpedon, and Minos drove the pair of lovers from Crete. They separated on their journey, Sarpedon going to Lycia and Miletus to the town of Anactoria in Caria, which he conquered and renamed Miletus. He had two children by the nymph Cyanea, a son Caunus and a daughter Byblis.

Mimas see GIANTS.

Minerva An Italian goddess of household arts, possibly of Etruscan origin. She was early identified with Athena, and Roma was depicted in her guise.

Minos Son of Zeus and Europa. He became king of Crete after a dispute with his brothers Rhadamanthys and Sarpedon, who left the country and went elsewhere, Sarpedon to Lycia and Rhadamanthys to Boeotia. (According to one story the three had quarrelled over the handsome Miletus, whom each of them loved.) The three brothers had been adopted by Asterius, the former king, to whom Zeus had married Europa after he had made love to her. The quarrel for the succession was settled when Minos prayed to Poseidon for a worthy sacrificial victim, and the god sent him a magnificent bull from the sea. Minos' claim to the throne was vindicated, but the bull was so handsome that Minos neglected to sacrifice it. Indeed, his wife Pasiphae, the daughter of Helios, fell in love with the animal, and the exiled Athenian craftsman Daedalus built a hollow image of a cow in which she hid; whereupon the bull mounted her. Some said that this was the vengeance of Poseidon for Minos' failure to sacrifice the animal, others that Aphrodite caused Pasiphae to conceive her unnatural passion because of Helios' treacherous spying on herself and Ares. Pasiphae had many children by Minos: Catreus, Deucalion, Glaucus, Androgeos, Acacallis, Ariadne, Phaedra, and Xenodice. Now, however, she bore a monster, the bull's son, which had the body of a man and a bull's head. It was called *Minotauros*, 'the bull of Minos'. Minos then commissioned Daedalus, who was living at his court, to build an underground maze at Cnossus: the Labyrinth, in which the Minotaur was shut away.

Minos made himself ruler of the seas and subjugated much of Greece. He was said to have been on intimate terms with his father Zeus, who received him every nine years on Mount Ida and gave him laws to impose on Crete (the pre-Hellenic civilisation of the island is known as Minoan after this mythical figure). He was believed to have made war on Megara and Athens, defeating them both. His victory over King Nisus of Megara was due to the treachery of his enemy's daughter, who fell in love with him and cut off her father's talismanic hair. In spite of the girl's deed, Minos repudiated her and drowned her. Athens had offended Minos because his son Androgeos had died there – either through the treachery of the Athenian King Aegeus or because he was gored to death by the bull of Marathon. Minos could not take the city, but as a result of his prayers it was infested by so grave a pestilence that Aegeus had to agree to offer up an annual or nine-yearly tribute of seven boys and seven girls which must be sent to Crete to be fed to the Minotaur. Only by paying this tribute, the Delphic Oracle declared, would the city be released from the plague.

Because of Minos' love affairs, Pasiphae, who as a daughter of Helios had family connections with witches such as Circe and Medea, plied him with drugs, so that he would infect any woman he made love to with a virulent poison. Minos is said to have been cured by Procris, whom he rewarded with a magic hound and an unerring spear.

When eventually Theseus came to Crete as a member of one of the groups of victims, he killed the Minotaur and carried off Minos' daughter Ariadne, who had helped him. Daedalus was also implicated in his deed, for it was he who had made the clue of thread which showed Theseus his way back out of the Labyrinth; so Minos imprisoned him in

it, together with his son Icarus. Daedalus eventually escaped and, after making wings of wax and feathers, flew away, though Icarus fell to his death.

Minos pursued Daedalus to the west, but had great difficulty in finding him. The king presented the rulers he suspected of harbouring the refugee with a spiral shell, demanding that a thread should be passed through it. When Cocalus of Camicus in Sicily returned the shell duly threaded, Minos knew that Daedalus was hiding there – for no one else could have achieved this – and demanded his surrender. Cocalus pretended to comply, but meanwhile offered Minos a bath. Through pipes which he had installed, Daedalus scalded Minos to death with boiling water, and so was rid of his foe. Succeeded in Crete by his son Deucalion, Minos himself became a judge in the realm of Hades, together with his brother Rhadamanthys. This privilege was given him because he had received laws from Zeus.

Minotaur A monster with a bull's head and a man's body, the son of Pasiphae and a bull. The word means 'Minos' bull'. *See* MINOS; PASIPHAE; THESEUS.

Minthe or **Menthe** A Naiad (water-nymph) who became the mistress of the god Hades. Persephone heard of their association and trampled Menthe underfoot, whereupon she turned into the aromatic plant mint (this is the meaning of her name), of which the scent is sweeter the more it is trampled.

Minyas The mythical founder of Orchomenus in Boeotia; he gave his name to the Boeotian or Thessalian clan of Minyans, to whom the Argonauts were said to belong. He was said to have been a rich man, and to have built a treasury. He had three daughters, Alcithoe, Leucippe, and Arsippe, who refused to participate in the rites of Dionysus. On the god's feast-day, however, as they wiled away the time telling each other stories, all of a sudden the looms at which they were working sprouted grape-vines and their threads tendrils. The room was filled with smoke and the glow of fire, and the house with the sound of unseen revellers, so that the girls fled in terror to remote corners where they turned into bats. According to some accounts Diony-sus himself appeared and drove them mad, so that they killed Leucippe's son Hippasus as a sacrifice and then joined in the revels. The Maenads, in horror at the girls' murderous deed, put them to death. Another daughter, Clymene, married Cephalus after the death of Procris.

Misenus According to Virgil, Cape Misenum in the Bay of Naples was named after the Trojan Misenus, formerly one of Hector's men and later Aeneas' trum-peter. He had aroused the jealousy of the sea-god Triton, and, when the Trojans landed near Cumae, he was dragged into the waves and drowned. Aeneas buried him on the cape which bears his name.

Misme *see* DEMETER.

Mnemosyne A Titaness; the mother, by Zeus, of the Muses.

Mnesimache *see* DEXAMENUS.

Moreae *see* FATES.

Moliones or **Molionidae** The two sons of Actor and his wife Molione or, accord-ing to Homer, of Poseidon and Molione. Their names were Eurytus and Cteatus, and according to certain accounts, they were Siamese twins. Renowned for their great strength and valour, they took part in a siege of Pylos and in the Calydonian boar-hunt. Their greatest achievement was the war they fought on behalf of their uncle King Augeas of Elis against Heracles, who wished to punish Augeas for refusing to pay him a promised debt.

They beat off Heracles' army, killing his brother Iphicles and Dameon, son of Phlius. Heracles, supposedly ill at the time, had to withdraw. He later killed the Moliones treacherously by ambush-ing them as they were making their way to the Isthmian games, thus violating a sacred trust since at such times peace was declared to prevail.

Molorchus *see* HERACLES (first Labour).

Molossus Son of Neoptolemus and Andromache. He gave his name to the Molossians of Epirus.

Momus Son of Nyx (Night); he personi-fied the spirit of grumbling. In certain stories he turns up as a constant critic of the gods' dispensations: for instance, he blamed Zeus for placing the bull's horns on its head and not on its shoul-ders, where the animal is strongest.

Moon *see* SELENE.

Mopsus *1.* A Thessalian seer, the son of Ampycus (or Ampyx) or of Apollo, and of Chloris. He took part in a number of heroic enterprises: the battle between the Centaurs and Lapiths, the Calydo-nian boar-hunt, and the voyage of the *Argo*, where he gave Jason advice based on the flights of birds. On the Argo-nauts' return journey he was killed in Libya, when he trod on a snake.
2. Son of the Cretan Rhacius and of Tiresias' daughter Manto. After the fall of Thebes to the Epigoni, Manto and her followers, who had been dedicated as spoils at Delphi, went to Asia Minor, where they founded the oracle of Clarus near Colophon. There Manto married Rhacius, who had already settled in the region. When their son Mopsus grew up, he took charge of the oracle and defeated the neighbouring Carians. After the Trojan War the Greek prophet Cal-chas came to Clarus with Amphilochus,

Manto's son by Alcmaeon, and a famous contest took place between the two diviners (see CALCHAS). Mopsus and his half-brother Amphilochus then proceeded to found the dream oracle of Mallus in Cilicia, but when Amphilochus went away to Epirus, where he founded the city of Amphilochian Argos, Mopsus refused to readmit him, and the two killed each other in a duel.

Moros A personification of Fate, and a son of Nyx.

Morpheus Son of Hypnos (Sleep); a dream-god who made human shapes appear to dreamers. The name is derived from *morphe* ('form') and therefore means 'transformer'.

Mucius see SCAEVOLA.

Mulius Son-in-law of Augeas, king of Elis. Nestor killed him.

Munychus The bastard son of Acamas and Laodice. He was cared for by Aethra.

Musaeus A vague mythical character, said to have been the son or teacher of Orpheus. He was also believed to have had a connection with the Mysteries of Eleusis and to have issued oracles.

Muses Daughters of Zeus and the Titaness Mnemosyne (whose name means 'memory'). They were the goddesses of the fine arts, music, and literature, and in later times of a wider range of intellectual pursuits, such as history, philosophy, and astronomy. The importance of the Muses arises from their popularity with poets, who attributed to them their inspiration and liked to invoke their aid. Their name (akin to the Latin *mens* and English *mind*) denotes 'memory' or 'a reminder', since in the earliest times poets, having no books to read from, relied on their memories.

The Muses, who were generally depicted as winged, had their principal abodes on mountains, particularly Helicon (near Ascra) in Boeotia and Pieria near Mount Olympus. They were originally considered to be three in number, Melete ('Practice'), Mneme ('Memory') and Aoede ('Song'). Pausanias says that the Aloadae first settled them on Helicon. At Delphi they were named after the three strings of the early lyre, Bottom, Middle, and Top (*Nete, Mese, Hypate*). Hesiod, however, had ascribed them the traditional number of nine and had allotted each of them a name, though their functions were not differentiated until very much later, and even then without complete agreement. They were usually identified as follows: Calliope, 'fair voice' (epic poetry), Clio 'renown' (history), Euterpe 'gladness' (flute-playing), Terpsichore 'joy in the dance' (lyric poetry or dance), Erato 'lovely' (lyric poetry or songs), Melpomene 'singing' (tragedy), Thalia 'abundance, good cheer' (comedy), Polymnia 'many songs' (mime), and Urania 'heavenly' (astronomy). The Muses were associated with Apollo who, as god of music and prophecy, was their leader. It was believed that they danced with him and other deities, the Graces and the Hours, at festivals of the gods on Olympus. They also attended the weddings of Cadmus and Harmonia, and of Peleus and Thetis.

The Muses figured in few myths. When the Thracian bard Thamyris boasted of being their superior, the Muses met him at Dorium in Messenia, where they blinded him and deprived him of his memory. To others, such as Demodocus, they gave the art of minstrelsy in compensation for blindness. The Pierides, the nine daughters of Pierus, a Macedonian, and of his wife Evippe, challenged the Muses (who were likewise known as Pierides on occasion) to a contest and lost, the judges being a panel of nymphs. As a result of their presumption the Pierides were turned into jackdaws. For a similar boast by the Sirens, the Muses plucked their feathers. Clio bore Hyacinthus to Pierus, and Calliope bore Orpheus and Linus to Apollo (or else Linus was the son of Urania and Amphimarus). King Rhesus' mother was a Muse; and the Corybantes were said to be the children of Thalia. The Romans identified the Muses with certain obscure Italian water-goddesses, the Camenae.

Mutto A king of Tyre. *See* DIDO.

Mygdalion Son of Cinyras, king of Cyprus.

Mygdon A king of the Phrygians. King Priam of Troy was his ally in a war which he and Otreus fought against the Amazons on the River Sangarius. During the sack of Troy, his son Coroebus was killed making a hopeless counter-attack.

Myrrha, **Smyrna** or **Zmyrna** *see* CINYRAS.

Myrtilus The charioteer of King Oenomaus of Pisa. Pelops bribed him in order to win the hand of Hippodamia. Myrtilus was a son of Hermes and a daughter of Aeolus, Cleobule, or of Hermes and a Danaid, Phaethusa. For the myth, *see* PELOPS. The constellation of Auriga was sometimes identified with Myrtilus, placed in the sky by Hermes.

N

Naiads *see* NYMPHS.

Nais *see* DAPHNIS.

Nana *see* ATTIS.

Narcissus Son of the River Cephissus in Boeotia and the nymph Liriope. When he was a baby, his mother asked the seer Tiresias if her son would live a long life. Tiresias answered 'He will, if he never knows himself': an enigmatic response that nobody understood at the time. As a youth Narcissus was so beautiful that many lovers, both men and women, courted him, but he repulsed them all. Then the nymph Echo fell in love with him; but she, whose constant chatter had warned Zeus of Hera's approach as he made love to other nymphs, had incurred the punishment of the goddess, who had taken away from her the power of speech, with the sole exception that she could repeat the last syllable of any word she heard. Narcissus ignored her, and she wasted away to a mere voice. The youth, however, was eventually requited for his cruelty. A lover rejected by him prayed to Nemesis, who condemned Narcissus to the contemplation of his own beauty reflected in a pool on Mount Helicon. The more he looked, the deeper he fell in love with himself. This futile passion held him in its grip, as he lay day after day beside the pool, until he wasted away and died. The gods turned him into the narcissus flower. *See* AMEINIAS.

Nauplius ('seafarer') *1*. Son of Poseidon and Amymone; an early navigator who founded the port of Nauplia near Argos. He invited Egyptian sailors, who came to Argos with his father-in-law Danaus, to settle in his city.

2. His descendant and often confused with him in ancient sources; the son of Clytoneus. He was an Argonaut, and later, as king of Nauplia, became an active slave-trader. When Aleus' daughter Auge was pregnant by Heracles, he entrusted her to Nauplius, with instructions to drown her or sell her. She was sold to King Teuthras. Catreus, the son of Minos, gave Nauplius his daughters Aerope and Clymene, since an oracle had predicted that one of his children would cause his death. Nauplius sold Aerope to Atreus and married Clymene himself. She bore him three sons, Palamedes, Oeax, and Nausimedon. Palamedes was subsequently stoned to death by the Greeks at Troy – the victim of Odysseus' vindictiveness – and Nauplius sailed there to demand satisfaction for his son. When the Greeks refused to help him, Nauplius made a tour of the captains' homes, urging their wives to cuckold them. Moreover, when the Greek fleet was sailing home, he lit false beacons on Cape Caphereus, and by this means, when a storm arose, lured many to their deaths on the rocks. As a result of this act, he had to flee his kingdom and was said to have taken refuge in Chalcidice. According to one account he died, as he had caused others to die, as a result of being deceived by a false beacon.

Nausimedon *see* NAUPLIUS 2.

Nausicaa The young daughter of Alcinous, king of the Phaeacians, who gave Odysseus clothes and advice when he was washed up on the shore; he found her playing ball with her maids. Alcinous would have given her to him in marriage, but Odysseus declined because he was eager to return to his wife Penelope.

Neaera *1.* A nymph; a consort of Helios.

2. Daughter of Perseus, wife of Aleus, and mother of Auge and Cepheus.

Neis *see* AEDON.

Neleus Son of Poseidon by Tyro. He and his twin brother Pelias were abandoned by their mother when it was decided that she was to marry her uncle Cretheus, or because of the cruelty of her father Salmoneus and stepmother Sidero. However the boys were discovered and brought up by some horse breeders. Pelias eventually killed Sidero but, after quarrelling with Neleus, expelled him from Iolcus. Neleus took refuge with his cousin Aphareus, king of Messenia, who gave him a strip of coastal land, provided he could win it for himself. He conquered Pylos and drove out its founder of the same name.

Neleus married Chloris, the only daughter of Niobe to survive the arrows of Artemis. Neleus and Chloris had twelve sons and a daughter, Pero, whom Bias married. Heracles quarrelled with Neleus because the latter refused to purify him of the homicide of Iphitus, being a friend of Eurytus, the murdered man's father. In his campaign of revenge, Heracles came to Pylos and sacked it, killing Neleus and all his family save Nestor, who was absent at Gerenia in Laconia and subsequently came back to become king of Pylos. Homer, however, tells another story, implying that Neleus survived Heracles' attack and subsequently fought the

people of Elis, winning extensive spoils from them. The Corinthians maintained that he died in Corinth during the reign of its king Sisyphus, and was buried in a secret grave on the Isthmus.

Nemesis A goddess, the daughter of Nyx (Night). She came to personify the power of retribution for evil deeds, and was also thought of as the punisher of heartless lovers. When Zeus fell in love with Nemesis and pursued her, she sought to escape by assuming the forms of a variety of animals and even fish. Finally she became a goose and he a swan, whereupon, according to one story, he made love to her, and she laid the egg which became Helen. In one version of Nemesis' tale, Aphrodite caused her downfall by assuming the form of an eagle and pretending to pursue the Zeus-swan; the latter took refuge in Nemesis' lap and, when she fell asleep, had intercourse with her so that she laid the egg. There was a tradition that the constellations of the Swan and the Eagle were formed to commemorate this exploit of Zeus. Whatever the manner of her impregnation, Nemesis' egg was taken by a shepherd who found it (or by Hermes) to Leda, wife of Tyndareos, who reared Helen when she was hatched. (It was also said, however, that Leda, not Nemesis, had laid the egg.)

Neoptolemus Also called **Pyrrhus**. Son of Achilles by Deidamia. When Thetis, seeking to conceal her son from notice so that he might not have to fight at Troy, entrusted him to Lycomedes, king of Scyros, the young Achilles, who was dressed in girl's clothes and kept in the women's quarters, made the king's daughter Deidamia pregnant. The child subsequently born to her was called Pyrrhus ('red-haired'), either because he had red hair or because the disguised Achilles had been known at Lycomedes' court as Pyrrha. Deidamia brought the boy up until he reached adult years. Achilles now being dead, the Greek leaders before Troy discovered from the captured prophet Helenus that the city could fall only if certain conditions were fulfilled; and these necessitated the presence in the army of both Pyrrhus and Philoctetes. Odysseus and Phoenix went to fetch Pyrrhus from Scyros, Phoenix giving him the name Neoptolemus ('young warrior') because of his youth. Odysseus presented him with the armour of Achilles which, in spite of the objections of Aias the son of Telamon, he had been awarded as a prize.

The youth won speedy renown by killing many Trojans, including Eurypylus, son of Telephus. But it was a difficult task to persuade Philoctetes, suffering from his wound on the island of Lemnos, to co-operate with the Greeks. According to Sophocles, Odysseus sought to trick the unwilling Philoctetes by a plot involving the young Neoptolemus, whom he had taken to Lemnos with him; but Neoptolemus was too honest to comply. Heracles' sudden appearance, however, saved the day, and Philoctetes agreed to accompany them to Troy.

Neoptolemus was one of those concealed in the Trojan Horse. During the sack of Troy he ruthlessly slaughtered Priam at the altar of Zeus; and later he immolated Priam's daughter Polyxena at the tomb of his father Achilles, since Achilles' ghost had demanded her as his prize. Neoptolemus' own prizes were Andromache, Hector's widow, and Helenus, her brother. He returned safely to Greece. His route was disputed. Some writers said he sailed to Phthia where Achilles' father Peleus reigned (though according to another account Peleus had been driven out by the sons of Acastus, and was now reinstated by his grandson Neoptolemus). At all events he avoided the storm that Athena sent to wreck the other Greek ships, because Thetis made him wait a few days before sailing. Some sources maintained, however, that Thetis made him go home by land and avoid the sea, because she knew that Apollo was angry with him for his defilement of Zeus' altar in the palace courtyard with Priam's blood. There was also a tradition that because of Apollo's anger Neoptolemus never reached home, but instead went to Epirus, whether overland or driven across the sea by a storm. There he created a kingdom for himself, establishing his capital at Ephyra; and he allowed Helenus to found the town of Buthrotum.

One tradition maintained that when Neoptolemus was asked to arbitrate between Odysseus and the relatives of Penelope's murdered suitors, he tricked Odysseus out of the island of Cephallenia. He was also believed, at some stage, to have claimed the hand of Menelaus' daughter Hermione, who had been promised to Orestes as well. When Neoptolemus fetched her, he left Andromache in the hands of Helenus.

The manner of Neoptolemus' death was much disputed. Some said that he was killed by Orestes, others by the people of Delphi after he had defiled their sanctuary, or else at Hermione's instigation even though he was innocent of any such defilement. The story relating to his fatal quarrel with Orestes was on the following lines. Hermione, according to this version, had not only been promised to her cousin Orestes, but had actually married him during the course of the Trojan War. Menelaus her father, however, sought to win the favour of Neoptolemus, without whose aid Troy could not be taken, by proposing that he should marry Hermione. After the war, when Orestes, as a result of slaying his mother, had gone mad, Neoptolemus went to Sparta in order to claim his bride, and Hermione was duly taken from Orestes to become his wife.

Neoptolemus then went to Delphi: his motive was variously recorded. Either he sought to buy Apollo's pardon for the slaughter of Priam and the sacrilege it involved, or he wanted to enquire why Hermione bore him no children, or he desired to punish Apollo for slaying Achilles by destroying his temple. According to one version, Orestes took advantage of Neoptolemus' absence at Delphi to rescue Hermione; then, going there himself, he plotted with some Delphians and killed Neoptolemus himself (or persuaded the Delphians to do so) in the same way as Neoptolemus had killed Priam, at the altar of a god (hence the Greek saying 'Neoptolemus' punishment' for an act of poetic justice). Hermione was also sometimes said to have urged Orestes to kill him, since she hated and feared him because of his harsh treatment of Andromache. There was also a story that Neoptolemus pillaged and burnt Apollo's temple and was killed for this outrage by the priest of Apollo, or the people of Delphi.

Andromache had borne Neoptolemus three sons, Molossus, Pielus, and Pergamus; and after their father's death Helenus married Andromache and became their guardian. Helenus also obtained part of Neoptolemus' kingdom. However Molossus remained and ruled a kingdom of his own, calling its people Molossians. Neoptolemus' other two sons emigrated. He himself was buried in Delphi (though some said his ashes were scattered in Ambracia). The Delphians despised the grave until his ghost helped to save them from an attack by the Gauls, after which they gave it the honours due to a dead hero.

Nephele see ATHAMAS.

Neptune see POSEIDON.

Nereids Nymphs of the sea; the fifty daughters of Nereus and his wife Doris. Among them were Thetis, a goddess whom both Zeus and Poseidon wanted at one time to marry; Amphitrite, the wife of Poseidon; Psamathe; and Galatea.

Nereus A marine deity, older than Poseidon himself. His parents were Pontus (the Sea) and Gaia (the Earth). Like other sea-gods, he had both the power of prophecy and the ability to change his shape. He used the second art to avoid revealing the first. Heracles forced Nereus to tell him the way to the Garden of the Hesperides. Proteus, another Old Man of the Sea, was sometimes confused with him.

Nerio see MARS.

Nessus The Centaur who brought about Heracles' death long after his own. For when Nessus carried Deianira across the swollen River Evenus, he tried to rape her on the way; and Heracles shot him with a poisoned arrow. As he expired, Nessus, with specious repentance, told Deianira to smear Heracles' tunic with his blood: this powerful charm, he assured her, would win back Heracles' love if ever it waned. Years later, when Heracles captured Iole in Oechalia, Deianira thought he preferred his captive to herself, and sent him a tunic smeared with Nessus' blood: the Hydra's poison which it contained caused Heracles to die in agony, and Nessus had his revenge.

Nestor The only son of King Nereus to survive Heracles' attack on Pylos was Nestor, who was away in Gerenia, a coastal town of Laconia. He therefore became heir to the throne of Pylos. In the time of Neleus there was said to have been a good deal of cattle-raiding between Elis and Pylos, and Nestor, in his reminiscences in the Iliad, describes his exploits in those battles. In a raid into Elis he killed Itymoneus and stole his herds, including fifty head of cattle and a hundred and fifty horses. This raid was a reprisal against Augeas, king of Elis, for stealing a chariot-team sent to take part in the Olympic Games. Neleus tried to prevent Nestor from taking part in the raid by hiding his horses; but the young man fought on foot and outshone the charioteers, killing Augeas' son-in-law Mulius and many others. He then routed the people of Elis and captured fifty chariots. He was skilful in many kinds of sport, and won numerous prizes at the funeral games of Amarynceus. Another of his exploits was to slay an Arcadian champion, Ereuthalion, in single combat on the River Celadon. He took part in the Calydonian boar-hunt but had to take refuge in a tree.

We know of him mainly from the *Iliad*, where he is a highly respected elder statesman, much older than the other chiefs: he is always heard patiently, although given to long, rambling tales about the distant past, and offering advice which is often superfluous or ineffective. He took ninety ships from Pylos to the Trojan War, accompanied by his sons Antilochus and Thrasymedes. It was he who suggested the spying raid on Hector's camp, in which Dolon was killed. However his scheme to persuade Achilles, by diplomatic means, to rejoin his allies failed. After Achilles had been killed and the Greeks heard the strange dirge of Thetis and the Nereids mourning for their dead, it was Nestor who restrained them from a stampede, by explaining what the noise was. When Memnon attacked the Greek army, Nestor was almost killed, owing his preservation to his son Antilochus who gave his life for him. At the time of the departure of the Greeks after their capture of Troy, Nestor was deeply suspicious of the leaders' conduct of affairs and sailed off on his own, narrowly missing the great storm with which Athena wrecked so many of the others. Thus he returned home safely to Pylos where his aged wife Anaxibia (or Eurydice) was still alive. Ten years later, when Telemachus came seeking news of his father, Nestor received him and advised him to consult Menelaus.

We know nothing of the old man's death. He had seven sons – one of whom, Pisistratus, accompanied Telemachus to Sparta – and two daughters.

Nicostratus A son of Menelaus. He drove Helen from Sparta after his father's death.

Nike The goddess of victory, of which she is a personification. She was said to be a daughter of the Titan Pallas and of Styx, but in the battle between the gods and Titans she deserted her father's side. She escorted Heracles to Olympus. She was portrayed with wings, holding a crown of victory above the heads of conquerors.

Niobe *1.* Daughter of the Lydian king Tantalus and of Dione; she married Amphion of Thebes, bearing him six sons and six daughters (or seven of each, according to variant sources). On the feast day of Leto at Thebes, Niobe expressed scorn of the goddess, whose two offspring, Apollo and Artemis, she compared unfavourably with her own dozen. Leto was affronted by the insult to herself and her children, and called on them to avenge it. Apollo and Artemis therefore assailed Niobe's children with arrows, killing them all; they were buried by the gods at Thebes. (According to another version, two were spared: her daughter Chloris, because she prayed for mercy, and her son Amyclas.) Niobe was overwhelmed with grief and bitterly regretted her affront to Leto, but it was too late. She survived long enough to eat a meal; then the gods, in pity, turned her into a block of marble which spouted streams of water like tears. This block stood on Mount Sipylus in Lydia.

2. The first woman, a daughter of Phoroneus, who, according to Argive traditions, was the first man. She was Zeus' first human mistress, and bore him

Argus, king of Phoronea, after whom the city was re-named Argos.

Nisus *1.* A king of the city later known as Megara; the son of Pandion, king of Athens, who, on being driven out of his kingdom, took the throne of Megara. Nisus and his brothers Pallas and Lycus helped their half-brother Aegeus to recover the throne of Athens. Nisus had a crop of red hair, or else a single red hair, on which his life depended. When Minos attacked the family of Pandion in Athens and Megara because of the death of his son Androgeos, Nisus was betrayed by his daughter Scylla: after either falling in love with Minos, or accepting a bribe from him, she cut her father's hair while he slept and thus killed him. She expected gratitude from Minos, but instead, in his horror at her deed, he drowned her (or else she drowned herself). Nisus was turned into an osprey and Scylla into a sea-bird. In addition to her, Nisus had two other daughters, Euronyme, the mother of Bellerophon, and Iphinoe, whose husband Megareus succeeded Nisus and gave his name to Megara. The port of Nisaea was named after Nisus.

2. Son of Hyrtacus and a companion of Aeneas on his voyage to Italy. He and Euryalus, whom he loved, tried to break through Turnus' lines when Aeneas was away from camp. They got out by night and killed several of their Italian enemies, but at daybreak, after losing his way, Euryalus was captured. Nisus tried to free his friend but saw him perish before his eyes, and was then killed in his turn.

Notus The South Wind; usually said to be a brother of Boreas and Zephyrus. Though generally personified as gentle and warm, he brought storms in autumn, and was feared as a destroyer of crops.

Numa Pompilius The mythical second king of Rome, invited to succeed Romulus; according to tradition he reigned from 715 to 673 BC. He was said to be of Sabine origin, and it was for his piety that the Romans asked him to rule them. They attributed to him the foundation and formulation of most of their religious rituals, including the worship of Janus; he was believed to have established the college of Vestal Virgins. It was thought that his mistress, the water-goddess Egeria, who lived in a grove near the Capena gate, gave Numa much instruction in religious and legal matters. When his wife Tatia died, Numa married the nymph. Numa was contrasted in the Roman mind with Romulus, for he was as peaceful as his predecessor had been warlike. Later writers sometimes said that Numa learnt his wisdom from the Greek philosopher Pythagoras (who, in fact, for all his legendary aspects, was an historical figure, and lived long after Numa's traditional epoch). This may be explained by the strength of Pythagorean mysticism in Southern Italy.

During Numa's reign the *ancile*, a sacred shield in the figure of eight, was dropped from heaven by Jupiter as a talisman of Rome's safety. Numa had eleven similar shields made, and placed them in his royal palace, the Regia, instructing his priests (the Salii) to guard them. He was also credited with having called Jupiter down from heaven by using the magic revealed to him by Faunus and Picus, two rural gods he trapped by mixing wine with their water. Having secured Jupiter's presence, he was able to trick the god into foregoing human sacrifice (*see* FAUNUS).

Numitor Son of Proca; a king of Alba Longa in Latium, and the father of Rhea Silvia. His throne was usurped by his brother Amulius. Rhea's sons Romulus and Remus, after discovering their real origin, restored Numitor to his throne.

Nycteis Daughter of Nycteus and wife of Polydorus, king of Thebes.

Nycteus A king of Thebes. The eldest son of Chthonius, one of the 'Sown Men', and brother of Lycus. Nycteus and Lycus were brought up in Euboea. (According to one account, they were not Thebans at all but Euboeans, sons of Poseidon by Celaeno. They were later made citizens of Thebes by Pentheus.) Subsequently exiled for killing Phlegyas, king of Orchomenus in Boeotia, they moved to Hyria. Nycteus' daughter Nycteis married Cadmus' son Polydorus – who was the third king of Thebes – and bore him Labdacus. When Polydorus died, Nycteus was appointed regent and guardian of his infant grandson.

Nycteus, however, had another daughter, Antiope, whom Zeus had courted in the form of a satyr. When she realised she was pregnant, the girl fled to Sicyon in fear of her father. Nycteus died in his grief at her departure, or, according to another version, killed himself for shame at her dishonour, or else was killed fighting a war with King Epopeus of Sicyon, Antiope's protector and subsequent husband, against whom Lycus eventually took vengeance.

Nyctimene Daughter of Epopeus, king of Lesbos. Raped by her father, she went to the woods and hid herself away. But Athena saw her and turned her into the 'night-bird', i.e. the owl, to save her shame; her name comes from *nyx*, meaning 'night'.

Nyctimus Son of Lycaon, king of Arcadia. He was the only one of Lycaon's sons to survive Zeus' thunder-bolts.

Nymphs (Greek *nymphe*, 'young woman', 'bride') Female spirits of divine or semi-divine origin – often daughters of Zeus – whom the Greeks believed to reside in particular natural phenomena;

it is possible that they were originally localised nature-goddesses. They were considered to be immortal, or at any rate very long-lived (but *see* HAMADRYADS below). They possessed an amorous disposition, and were credited with many love-affairs with gods and men, resulting in the births of numerous children. The ancients imagined the nymphs as youthful and beautiful women, often to be found in the company of gods (especially Pan, Hermes, Apollo, Dionysus, and Artemis), and in association with satyrs and Sileni. Generally speaking, they are incidental rather than central to the myths. They resemble the fairies of later folklore, and, like them, could be cruel as well as kind (e.g. *see* DAPHNIS).

The Greeks did not systematise their belief in these creatures, though certain broad classes were recognised. There were *Dryads*, tree-nymphs; *Hamadryads*, whom some believed to inhabit individual trees and to die with them; *Meliae*, the nymphs of ash trees, who were said to be sprung from the drops of blood which fell from the castrated genitals of Uranus; *Oreads*, or mountain-nymphs; *Naiads*, water-nymphs; *Nereids*, sea-nymphs (daughters of Nereus, an Old Man of the Sea); *Oceanids* (daughters of Oceanus and Tethys); and others named after geographical features such as sand, meadows, springs, and streams, sometimes with particular locations: for example, the *Acheloids*, who were nymphs of the River Achelous.

Nyx (Greek 'night') The goddess of night. She was considered to be among the first deities ever to exist, having originated from primeval Chaos at the same time as Erebus, Gaia, Tartarus, and Eros. From Nyx were born some of the most powerful and portentous of the personified forces: Thanatos (death), Hypnos (sleep), Moros (fate), Ker (doom), Oneiroi (dreams), Momus, Nemesis (retribution), Oizys (pain), Eris (strife), Geras (old age), the Three Fates, and many others. These she brought forth without male cooperation; to her brother Erebus she bore Hemera (day) and Aether (the air). When Zeus was about to eject Hypnos from Olympus, Nyx protected her son and even the king of the gods had to yield.

O

Oceanids Sea-nymphs; the three thousand daughters of Oceanus and Tethys, sisters of the river-gods. They were believed to look after the waters covering the earth – and even under it, for Styx was one of their number. Another of them, Doris, married Nereus, an Old Man of the Sea, and bore the Nereids. Her sister Amphitrite (alternatively described as a Nereid herself) was particularly eminent among them, for she married Poseidon. Metis achieved a similar eminence by becoming Zeus' first wife and conceiving his daughter Athena. Clymene formed an alliance with Helios, the Sun-god, and bore him Phaethon. Her sister Perseis presented the same deity with Aeetes, Circe, and Pasiphae. Calypso, who ruled the island of Ogygia, fell in love with her visitor Odysseus; but he finally left her. Together with Apollo, the Oceanids had the duty of bringing young men to their prime.

Oceanus A Titan, the son of Gaia and Uranus – though Homer calls him the parent of all the gods. He ruled the Ocean, the wide mythical stream which was believed to wind its way in a circle round the edge of the earth. Oceanus and his consort (and sister) Tethys did not join their fellow Titans in their war with Zeus, and so were left peacefully in control of their wide realm. They brought forth all the gods and nymphs of the rivers, lakes, and seas, including the three thousand Oceanids. During the great war between Zeus and the Titans, Rhea brought her daughter Hera to Oceanus and his wife Tethys for protection. However Oceanus quarrelled with

Tethys, and Hera sought to reconcile them. Oceanus obtained from his son-in-law Helios his golden cup or bowl, in order to lend it to Heracles, so that he could sail on it upon the Ocean stream to fetch Geryon's cattle.

Ocrisia or **Ocresia** Mother of the sixth legendary king of Rome, Servius Tullius. She was believed to be a slave-woman who had been taken at the fall of the town of Corniculum. The story which grew around the origin of the king elevated his mother to royal birth. But the identity of his father was surrounded by a mystery suggesting divine origin. It was said that Ocrisia saw a phallus rise out of the hearth, and reported the phenomenon to her master King Tarquinius Priscus of Rome. After consulting his wife Tanaquil, the king made Ocrisia stand before the fire dressed in a bridal gown. She was mysteriously impregnated, and subsequently gave birth to Servius Tullius.

Odysseus King of Ithaca. One of the leading personages in the *Iliad* and the central figure of the *Odyssey*.

Odysseus was held to be the only son of Laertes and Anticlea. However his paternity was sometimes questioned, for it was also said that Anticlea, at the time of her marriage, was already pregnant by Sisyphus – and that this paternity explained Odysseus' cunning, since Sisyphus could outwit even Autolycus, Anticlea's father, who was a famous thief and trickster. Autolycus happened to visit Ithaca a day or two after Odysseus' birth. Euryclea, the baby's nurse, placed him in Autolycus' lap, and suggested that he might think of a name for his grandson since nobody else could. He suggested 'Odysseus', meaning 'victim of enmity', because he himself, throughout his life, had collected such a host of enemies, or, alternatively, because he himself hated so many men (Greek *odyssesthai* 'to hate', 'to be angry'). Autolycus also offered Odysseus a rich endowment when he should be able to come and claim it at his home on Mount Parnassus. When the time to do so arrived, and Odysseus was out hunting with his uncles, he received a long scar on his thigh from a boar's tusk. Later Odysseus was sent to Messenia to recover some sheep that had been stolen from Ithaca in a raid. There he met Iphitus, son of Eurytus, who was looking for the mares that had disappeared at the time of Heracles' departure from Oechalia. The two became friends and exchanged gifts. Iphitus gave Odysseus the great bow that had won Eurytus his fame – the weapon with which Odysseus subsequently tested the strength of Penelope's suitors. This bow Odysseus never used in war, though he obtained poison to dip his arrows in; for although Ilus, Medea's grandson, refused to provide him with the necessary poison, Anchialus, a prince of the Taphians, gave him all he wanted.

When the time came for Odysseus to find a wife, his eye lit on Penelope, daughter of Icarius, the king of Sparta. In winning his bride, Odysseus first showed the cunning for which he was to become proverbial. He joined the crowd of suitors wooing Helen, the beautiful daughter of the king's brother Tyndareos (who had also been king himself), but knowing he was far too poor for his courtship to succeed, he brought her no gifts. Instead, he offered Tyndareos a sound piece of advice. The suitors were at daggers drawn with one another, and it appeared that if Tyndareos chose one of them, the rest would run riot. Odys-

seus therefore suggested that they should all swear an oath to protect the suitor whom Tyndareos chose for Helen whoever he might be against any harm that might come from the marriage. This meant that when Tyndareos came to choose Menelaus, everyone had to accept him: and later, after Paris had abducted Helen, they found themselves obliged to fight the Trojan War to help him retrieve her. Meanwhile, as a reward for his advice, Tyndareos spoke to Icarius, and Odysseus was awarded Penelope – though Icarius was loth to let her go. (According to one version of the story he instituted a foot-race to decide who should become his daughter's husband, and Odysseus won it.) As the bridal pair were leaving Laconia, Icarius pursued them, caught up with them, and begged Penelope to return to him, suggesting that Odysseus too should come and live with him in Sparta. But he refused and, growing angry, ordered Penelope to make her choice; whereupon she silently covered her head with her veil, thus signifying her obedience to her husband. Icarius later founded a shrine on the spot and dedicated it to *Aidos* (modesty). Penelope bore Odysseus only one child, Telemachus, who grew up in his father's absence.

In due course Laertes abdicated his throne in favour of his clever son Odysseus. Now king of Ithaca, he became the favourite of Athena, who admired both his cunning and his piety. When Paris took Helen from Sparta and refused to return her to Menelaus, and Agamemnon, on his brother's behalf, wanted to remind Helen's former suitors – including many of the princes of Greece – of their promise to protect the rights of the husband and the honour of Greece, Menelaus and Nauplius' wily son Palamedes were sent around the rulers of the different states, to remind them of their duty. Among the places they visited was Ithaca. But when they arrived there,

Odysseus feigned madness; pretending that he proposed to sow the sands with salt, he yoked a horse and an ox together and started to plough. Palamedes called his bluff by placing the baby Telemachus on the sand in front of the plough, whereupon Odysseus proved his sanity by pulling up sharp. After this Odysseus had to go to Troy; but he bore Palamedes an undying grudge.

Because of his cunning (even though it had failed him this time), Agamemnon sent Odysseus with Nestor to persuade Achilles to join the army; and it was through a ruse of the Ithacans that Achilles was discovered hidden in the women's quarters of Lycomedes' palace. Odysseus, whose kingdom included the islands of Cephallenia and Zacynthus as well as mainland territories, brought twelve shiploads of men to fight the Trojans. When the fleet was becalmed at Aulis, Odysseus tricked Clytemnestra into sending her daughter Iphigenia by pretending that she was to marry Achilles; whereas, in fact (according to the principal version of the story), she was sacrificed to Artemis, in order to avert the goddess's anger. It was on Odysseus' suggestion that the Greeks marooned Philoctetes on the island of Lemnos, and he saw the meaning of the oracle telling Achilles how to cure Telephus' wound.

When the Greeks finally reached Troy, Odysseus beached his ships in the middle of the fleet, and it was from his prow that the heralds spoke to the army. At the outset he was sent with Menelaus on a deputation to demand Helen's return. However the two of them would have been killed by the Trojans had not Antenor protected them. Odysseus' best friend in the army was Diomedes, and they performed many valiant deeds together. One infamous action, however, was the slaying of Palamedes, whom the army stoned as a result of a treacherous plot by Odysseus (with or without the connivance of Diomedes; or else, according to an alternative story, Odysseus

and Diomedes drowned him as he was fishing.

In the *Iliad* Odysseus is prominent not so much as a fighter but as a speaker and schemer. In debate his contribution is presented as outstanding. Though he was small and broad of stature, and seemed stiff and lifeless as he made ready to speak, once he began the whole assembly hung on his every word. Chosen to accompany Aias (the son of Telamon) and Phoenix in their attempt to persuade Achilles to resume his participation in the war, he spoke most eloquently; but, for once even his great resourcefulness failed to achieve its purpose. He took part in at least two spying expeditions. On the first occasion, when Hector was gaining the upper hand and had established a Trojan camp on the plain, it was Odysseus who went by night with Diomedes to examine their dispositions. They encountered the Trojan spy Dolon, whom they questioned and killed; then they stealthily slaughtered the newly-arrived Thracian chieftain Rhesus and many of his noblest followers. On a later occasion Odysseus (whether or not accompanied by Diomedes) entered Troy clad in beggar's rags. While he was within the city, Helen recognised him but decided not to betray his identity. She bathed his body, gave him clothes, and swore not to give him away; in return he told her the Greeks' plans, and she was glad to know that she would soon be rescued. During his visit he killed a number of Trojans and learnt of the enemy's plans, which he was later able to report to his compatriots. Some said that he also stole Athena's image, the Palladium; and that the wife of the Trojan king Priam himself, Hecabe, recognised who he was, but, like Helen, failed to denounce him.

When Achilles was shot dead by Paris, Aias the son of Telamon saved his body and brought it off the field while Odysseus protected his rear. Then there arose a dispute between the two warriors as to which of them should be awarded

Achilles' immortal armour. Since Odysseus was much the better speaker of the two, he easily persuaded the army that he had served the Greek cause better than his opponent, and won the vote. Aias, considering his honour lost, succumbed to a bout of madness in which he tried to kill the Greek leaders, and then committed suicide.

When Paris was finally slain, Helenus, the Trojan seer, left Troy because he felt slighted, since Helen's new husband was to be Deiphobus rather than himself. When, therefore, Odysseus captured Helenus on Mount Ida, his prisoner was glad to inform him, out of his prophetic powers, of the conditions the Greeks must fulfil in order to capture Troy. In the fulfilment of these conditions Odysseus was much concerned. He persuaded Achilles' son Neoptolemus to join the army, giving him his father's armour; and he led an expedition to Lemnos, where, with the help of Neoptolemus, he tried to trick Philoctetes, owner of Heracles' great bow, into coming to Troy. Fortunately the deified Heracles appeared and, despite Philoctetes' hatred of Odysseus, who had marooned him on the island, commanded him to comply.

When these events had duly taken place, Odysseus had the idea of deceiving the Trojans by the introduction into Troy, in the guise of a religious offering, of a wooden horse, filled with Greek warriors who, under the command of Odysseus, would subsequently emerge from its interior by night and seize the city. After Epeius had constructed the horse, it was duly abandoned on the plain outside Troy, and the Greek fleet ostensibly sailed away. Thereupon the Trojans dragged the horse into their city through a breach in the walls, or through a gate which they enlarged. Helen and Deiphobus came to see it, and Helen spoke to the men inside, perfectly imitating the voices of their wives, in order to try to spring the trap, if

there was one. Odysseus needed all his resourcefulness to prevent his companions from answering. Subsequently, when the Greeks burst out from the horse, Odysseus did not forget his debt to Antenor, on whose door, in consequence, he hung a panther-skin as a sign to spare him when the other Trojans were slaughtered.

On the other hand, Odysseus was instrumental in the killing of the little Astyanax, Hector's son; for he declared that none who could claim the throne of Troy and take vengeance on the Greeks must be left alive. He also tried to avert from the Greeks the wrath of Athena, after Aias, the son of Oileus, had raped Cassandra in front of the goddess's image – to which she had been clinging for sanctuary – for Odysseus urged that Aias should be stoned to death. When Athena subsequently sent a storm to avenge herself on the Greeks' ships, Odysseus was not among those killed. Nevertheless he incurred the enmity of the gods, especially (as will be seen) Poseidon, and was the last Greek to reach home alive, after ten years of wandering.

His adventures during this period, and those that befell him after he had reached home, form the subject of Homer's *Odyssey*. From Troy he sailed to the Thracian Chersonese, where Hecabe – now, after the death of her husband Priam, Odysseus' slave – discovered that her son Polydorus had been murdered by King Polymestor of the Bistones. She took vengeance on the Thracian monarch by contriving a plot in which she and her attendants stabbed his two sons and blinded him with their pins. Hecabe then turned into a bitch and ran in a frenzy into the sea.

Odysseus sailed on to another part of Thrace, where he sacked the city of the Cicones but lost many men in a subsequent battle. Maron, the priest of Apollo, whom alone he spared, gave him a rich gift including the wine with which he later befuddled the Cyclops Polyphemus. Then, while attempting to return to his home in Ithaca, Odysseus was blown off course by a storm off Cape Malea, and came to the land of the Lotus eaters. He next landed on the island of the gigantic Cyclopes (which was later identified with Sicily). There, with twelve of his men, he sought the hospitality of Polyphemus, telling him his name was *Outis* ('Nobody'); but the giant shut them in his cave, barricading its entrance with a great rock, and ate six of his companions. Unable to get out, because he could not move the rock, Odysseus resorted to the strategem of blinding Polyphemus with a red-hot stake, after he had made him drunk with Maron's wine so that he fell asleep. None of the other Cyclopes came to help Polyphemus, because he cried out that 'Nobody' was killing him. When day broke, Polyphemus opened his cave to let his flocks out, and Odysseus and his surviving six men escaped clinging to the undersides of the sheep. After he had regained his ship, Odysseus could not help shouting his real name to Polyphemus, at which the monster hurled a great rock which all but sank the vessel. It was for his blinding of Polyphemus that Odysseus incurred the anger of Poseidon, who was the giant's father; and he would never have reached Ithaca again but for the aid of Athena. As it was, he came home only after many years – and alone, in a ship that was not his own.

After escaping from Polyphemus, he had first reached Aeolia, the island of Aeolus, Lord of the Winds, who gave him a bag containing all the winds except the West; this he allowed to blow so that it could waft Odysseus home. His sailors, however, believing the bag to contain gold, opened it on the voyage while their chief slept, and the storm which ensued blew them all the way back to Aeolia. But this time Aeolus, in fear that Odysseus was cursed by the gods, drove them away.

Their next landfall was among the Laestrygonians, savage man-eating giants. The captains of Odysseus' fleet, in excessive confidence, anchored in the harbour, where the Laestrygonians crushed their ships with great rocks and devoured their crews. The only ship which escaped was that of Odysseus himself.

In this he sailed on and next reached Circe's island of Aeaea. A powerful enchantress, Circe, bewitched the party sent to explore the island, turning them into swine, with the single exception of Eurylochus, who was too suspicious to enter and returned to the ship. Odysseus got the better of Circe with the help of Hermes, who then gave him a herb which rendered him immune to spells. He overpowered Circe and made her turn his men back to their human form. She also swore an oath to do him no harm nor to emasculate him in her bed; and so he spent a whole year in her company.

His men finally persuaded him to continue his voyage, and with Circe's advice and information he made the terrible journey to the edge of the Ocean, where the shades of the dead would come to meet him, and the ghost of the prophet Tiresias would instruct him how he might return home. On the shore Odysseus dug a trench and offered libations; then he killed a ram and a black ewe, offering them to Hades and Persephone. The blood flowed into the trench and the shades flocked to drink it, but he held them at bay with his sword until Tiresias had drunk and spoken. Elpenor, a comrade who had been killed accidentally on Aeaea and left there unburied, made an appearance, and so did Odysseus' mother Anticlea, who had died in sorrow for his long absence and supposed death; but he resolutely kept them off. Then Tiresias came, and after drinking the blood gave Odysseus the advice he needed. His was the only shade in the Underworld which still retained its mental powers unimpaired; and he gave Odysseus a special warning. This was that the cattle of Helios in the isle of Thrinacia must not be touched; if they were, Odysseus' return would be almost impossible, and all his men would be killed. Tiresias also gave him other predictions about his future, and told him that his home was occupied by a band of suitors for the hand of Penelope. Then the shade of Odysseus' mother Anticlea gave him further information about how things stood at home. After that Odysseus conversed with the shades of many of the heroes who had been his comrades at Troy, and he spoke also with the shades of many beautiful women. Agamemnon, in view of his own terrible death, counselled him to be very cautious when he at last returned home. Then, finally, he met the shade of Heracles.

On leaving the abode of the dead, Odysseus returned to Aeaea, where he buried Elpenor and received further advice from Circe; then he sailed in the direction of his home. When the Sirens' island was near, he filled his men's ears with wax to prevent their being ensnared by their singing. He himself listened to it, but first he had himself bound to the mast; following his previous instructions, the crew tied him yet tighter, when, fascinated by the singing, he ordered them to release him. He then passed between Scylla and Charybdis (subsequently located in the Straits of Messina), and chose to go closer to Scylla – which seized six men from the ship. On the island of Thrinacia (later identified with Sicily), on which his men compelled him to land, he was delayed for a month by an adverse wind. Ravenous with hunger his men, against all his pleadings, ventured to kill some of Helios' cattle, while Odysseus was asleep. After six days of feasting on the meat, they set sail on a favourable wind, but as soon as they lost sight of land, they were wrecked by a terrible storm,

sent by Zeus at Helios' request. Only Odysseus survived. He lashed together the mast and keel and drifted as far as Charybdis, where his craft was swallowed up. He clung to an overhanging tree until the remains of his vessel surfaced again. He then rowed off with his hands, drifting astride a spar for nine days until he was washed up on Ogygia, the island of the beautiful Oceanid Calypso, who wished to marry him and make him immortal. He spent seven years living with Calypso, but after that time his tears of longing for his home and wife moved the gods, who sent Hermes to bid Calypso show him how to build a raft so that he could get away. She found Odysseus sitting on the shore, looking forlornly out to sea, as he constantly did. He did not believe her news at first, and made her swear she was not trying to hurt him.

While Poseidon, still his implacable enemy, was absent among the Ethiopians, Athena ensured that Odysseus sailed away. When, however, the god returned after seventeen days, he sent a mighty tempest which wrecked Odysseus' raft. Then Leucothea, a sea-goddess, came to him in the guise of a seagull and advised him to swim for his life. She also gave him a veil which he could wrap about him to prevent himself from drowning. He swam in huge waves for two days, and finally, when Athena made them still, he was washed up on the coast of Scheria, the land of the Phaeacians, where (as previously ordered by Leucothea) he threw the veil back into the water with averted face, and lay down to rest in some bushes.

Next morning he was discovered there by Nausicaa, daughter of Alcinous, king of the Phaeacians. She had come to the river with the maids to wash the royal linen; and as the girls played ball, Odysseus crept out, hiding his nakedness with a branch, and begged the princess, with words of flattery, to help him. She lent him clothes and told him the way to her father's palace. Following her instructions, Odysseus entered the palace unobserved and knelt down in supplication before Queen Arete. Alcinous and his court accepted Odysseus' pleas, and made him an honoured guest. They also agreed to give him transport back to Ithaca.

On the day that followed there were games, and at the evening feast Odysseus revealed his identity and told his story. Nausicaa looked upon him with admiration, but he would not consider being parted from Penelope any longer. Finally a Phaeacian ship took him home to Ithaca by night, the crew setting him on the sand in his sleep, together with a rich treasure that Alcinous had given him. On its return journey to Scheria, owing to the wrath of Poseidon, the ship was turned to stone. Alcinous then remembered a prophecy that Poseidon would one day punish the Phaeacians for their hospitality to shipwrecked sailors.

When he awoke, Odysseus found himself wrapped in thick mist, and suspected that he had been tricked. But Athena, who had created the mist for his protection, appeared and revealed herself to him. She disguised him as an old beggar and told him first to consult Eumaeus, his swineherd. Meanwhile she herself escorted Odysseus' son Telemachus back from Sparta, to which he had gone in search of news of his father. Eumaeus had remained loyal to Odysseus, and, true to his master's example, entertained the 'beggar' hospitably, giving him a full account of the situation that prevailed at Ithaca. More than a hundred suitors for Penelope's hand were passing their time idly in Odysseus' palace, eating up his substance and insulting his wife and son. Many of the servants pandered to their wants and favoured their excesses. Odysseus' father Laertes had left the court, partly in disgust, but mainly in grief at losing Odysseus and his wife Anticlea; the old man

was living a humble life in a rough hut in the country. Odysseus did not reveal himself to Eumaeus, but pretended to be a Cretan who had fought at Troy and knew something of the Ithacan king.

Telemachus then returned, guided by Athena, and came to Eumaeus' hut. He gave the supposed beggar a kindly welcome, but could not invite him to his father's palace because he was afraid of the reception the suitors would give him. Eumaeus left to report Telemachus' arrival to Penelope, and it was now that Odysseus revealed himself to his son, and they made a plan of campaign against the suitors.

Next morning Odysseus and Eumaeus set out for the palace, having a brush with the disloyal goatherd Melanthius on the way. At the palace the hound Argus recognised his master; he was too weak to rise from the dunghill where he lay, but he wagged his tail and then died. After entering the great hall in his beggar's disguise, Odysseus went around begging from the suitors, who gave him food, all but Antinous who struck him with a stool. Irus, a sturdy young beggar, tried to cow him with threats, but Odysseus felled him with a single blow. Penelope then announced to the suitors that she would soon be making her choice of a second husband, since after twenty years Odysseus could no longer be expected to return. She reproached them, however, for their greed and insolence, so that Odysseus was struck with admiration for his wife. Melantho, Melanthius' sister, insulted Odysseus, and there would have been a fight had not one of the suitors, Amphinomus, persuaded the others to go home.

This was the signal for Odysseus' preparations to begin, and he and his son stripped the hall of all the weapons that were there, laying them up in the storeroom. Penelope then told the 'beggar' how she had kept the suitors at bay for more than three years by pretending to weave a shroud for Laertes and secretly unpicking it every night. She had heard that the 'beggar' had news of her husband, and Odysseus, still claiming to be a Cretan, predicted his own imminent return. Euryclea, his old nurse, washed his feet and recognised him by the scar on his thigh. But he obliged her to swear not to give his secret away, even to Penelope. Odysseus then heard Penelope's decision to hold a competition among the suitors, who would be invited to string her husband's bow and shoot an arrow through the holes in twelve axe-heads in line, as he himself had often done: and the man who succeeded would gain her hand in marriage. Odysseus urged her to hasten the contest, assuring her that her husband would return before anyone else succeeded in the task she had set.

Next morning preparations were made for a great banquet in the hall, and numerous animals were brought in to be slaughtered for the feast. Telemachus placed Odysseus in a strategic position by the door; when the suitors noted the young man's new-found authority, there was an ugly scene; and the seer Theoclymenus predicted imminent doom for those present. After the meal Penelope fetched the bow Odysseus had received from Eurytus and announced the contest. All, led by Telemachus, then tried to string the great bow, and failed. Meanwhile Odysseus revealed himself to Eumaeus and to Philoetius the cowherd; Euryclea and Philoetius barred the doors, and he and Eumaeus went in. After much discussion Telemachus insisted that Odysseus should be allowed to take part, and ordered Penelope to her room. Then, to the astonishment of the suitors, the 'beggar' strung the bow and, from a seated position, shot an arrow through the axe-heads.

Next, in company with Telemachus and Eumaeus, Odysseus began to butcher the suitors with his arrows, sparing only Phemius the bard and Medon

the herald. Athena joined Odysseus in the guise of Mentor, Telemachus' tutor. In the fighting Melanthius brought armour to the suitors, as Telemachus had left the storeroom unlocked. But Eumaeus and Philoetius caught Melanthius in the storeroom and hanged him there. And soon all the suitors, too, were dead, piled high throughout the building.

When Euryclea saw them, she wanted to exult, but Odysseus forbade it. He told her to collect the treacherous women-servants, whom he then compelled to carry the corpses out into the yard and cleanse the hall. After that Telemachus hanged them. Euryclea woke Penelope from her sleep to tell her the good news of Odysseus' return, but she would not believe it. It took a long time to persuade her – and only the revelation of a secret they both shared was able to convince her. This was the information that the foot of their bed, which Odysseus had himself made, was carved from a tree-trunk that was still rooted in the ground, so that the bed could not be moved.

Next day Odysseus revealed himself to his father Laertes, going up to the orchard farm where the old man passed his weary days. Other faithful servants met him there, and plans were laid to meet the expected counter-attack from the suitors' families. Laertes dressed in a fitting robe, and Athena made him taller and stronger. Then the whole party, including the servants, armed themselves, and were ready for the suitors' kinsmen as they approached. Their leader Eupithes, father of the arrogant Antinous, was killed with Athena's help by Laertes with his spear. A battle was about to break out when the goddess, in the form of Mentor, appeared and separated the two parties. She gave a great cry, which sent the Ithacans flying; Odysseus would have pursued them, but Zeus flung a thunderbolt to warn him to refrain. Peace followed – and this is where the *Odyssey* ends.

Odysseus' subsequent adventures were indicated by prophecies described in that work. He did what Tiresias had told him to do in order to ensure for himself a peaceful old age. That is to say, he crossed to the mainland and walked inland, carrying on his shoulders an oar, until he met a traveller who asked him why he carried a winnowing fan. There, far from the sea, he fixed the oar in the ground, and sacrificed a ram, a bull, and a breeding boar to Poseidon. Thus reconciled with the god, he returned to Ithaca and lived with Penelope to a great age; and then a gentle death came to him out of the sea.

But a number of quite different and contradictory tales were also told of Odysseus' closing years. He went, it was said, to Thesprotia and married its queen, Callidice, while Penelope was still alive. There, leading the Thesprotians against the Brygi – for whom Ares was fighting – he lost a battle, and was succeeded as king of Thesprotia by Polypoetes, his son by Callidice. He was also believed to have been killed by Telegonus, his son by Circe, who had been sent by his mother to find him and, in a raid on Ithaca, unwittingly killed him, striking him with a spear tipped with a sting-ray, and thus bringing him a death out of the sea – though not a gentle one. When Penelope learnt who Telegonus was – according to this version – she went with him to Aeaea and buried Odysseus there. There were even stories that Penelope then married Telegonus, and Circe married Telemachus.

Another tradition asserts that the suitors' kinsmen were able to bring Odysseus to justice and that Neoptolemus, who acted as arbiter, found in their favour and condemned Odysseus to exile, in the hope of being able to annex from him the island of Cephallenia. Odysseus was stated to have gone to Aetolia and joined Thoas its king, marrying his daughter – who bore him a son, Leontophonus – and subsequently spending the rest of his life in Aetolia.

Oeagrus A Thracian king, sometimes said to be the father of Orpheus and Linus.

Oeax ('rudder') Son of Nauplius 2. In his bitterness over the death of his brother Palamedes at Troy, Oeax went to Clytemnestra at Mycenae and told her that Agamemnon was returning home with a Trojan concubine whom he preferred to her. Clytemnestra therefore took Aegisthus as her lover, and they plotted to kill Agamemnon on his return (when he brought with him the captive Trojan princess Cassandra). Oeax was also hostile to Agamemnon's son Orestes, whom he urged the people of Argos to banish for killing his mother Clytemnestra.

Oebalus A king of Sparta; the father of Tyndareos, Hippocoon, and Icarius, by Gorgophone or the nymph Batia.

Oedipus ('swollen foot') A king of Thebes; the son of Laius and his wife Jocasta (Epicaste in Homer). The Homeric version of his story differs from the later tradition used by Sophocles in his three Theban plays, *Oedipus the King, Oedipus at Colonus*, and *Antigone*, by Aeschylus in *Seven against Thebes*, and by Euripides in his *Phoenician Women* and other plays that are now lost.

King Laius, while a refugee at the court of Pelops at Pisa, abducted his host's son Chrysippus; from this deed many believed the curse of the house of Laius to have sprung. On his return to Thebes, Laius married Jocasta, the daughter of Menoeceus, one of the 'Sown Men'. But shortly afterwards an oracle warned him that any son Jocasta bore him would kill him. When, therefore, his wife bore him a son, he took the infant, pierced his feet with a spike (perhaps to hasten his death, or after his death to prevent his ghost from walking), and abandoned him on Mount Cithaeron. However the Theban shepherd charged with this task disobeyed his orders, and instead handed the baby to a Corinthian shepherd, who took him to his king, Polybus; and he, a childless man, decided to adopt the child, calling him Oedipus.

When Oedipus had grown up, he was taunted one day at a banquet with being not Polybus' own son, but a bastard. He therefore went to Delphi to enquire the truth and was there informed that he was destined to kill his father and marry his mother; and the horrified priests drove him away from Delphi. Still believing that King Polybus and Queen Merope were his parents, he resolved never to return to Corinth, and made his way back to Boeotia. At a crossroads he met a stranger – King Laius, though he did not know it – riding in a carriage; and its driver ordered Oedipus to make way in the narrow road. Oedipus refused and the driver pressed forward, running a wheel over Oedipus' foot. Furthermore the rider in the carriage, in passing, struck him a blow with his staff; and Oedipus, enraged, killed the rider and all the rest of the party, except one servant who ran away.

Continuing his journey, Oedipus came to Thebes, where he found the people in great distress. King Laius, it appeared, had recently been killed on the way to Delphi, to which he had been going to consult the oracle about the Sphinx, a dangerous monster that was plaguing Thebes. For she had been eating its citizens whenever they could not answer its riddle: 'What creature walks on four legs in the morning, on two at noon, and on three at evening, and is weakest when it walks on most?' She had already devoured many people, including, it was said, Haemon, son of the regent Creon (though in other versions of the story he was younger, and survived to be betrothed to Antigone; or it could be supposed that Creon had two sons of the same name). Now that

Laius was dead, Creon offered the throne, together with the hand of his sister, Laius' widow Jocasta, to any man who would rid Thebes of the pest. This Oedipus did, by replying correctly that the answer to the riddle was Man, who walks on all fours as a baby and leans on a stick in old age. In this way he brought the oracle to completion for, having already unintentionally killed his father Laius, he now married his mother Jocasta.

In Homer's version of the story, Jocasta, who had married her son in ignorance, was quickly made aware of her sin and hanged herself, whereas Oedipus himself, in spite of his grief at his two unwitting crimes, continued to rule Thebes for many years. The geographical writer Pausanias concludes from this that another woman, whom he calls Eurygania daughter of Hyperphas, bore him his sons; of his daughters Homer knows nothing. He also knows nothing of his exile and says that he died in battle.

The version adopted by Sophocles is quite different. Oedipus and Jocasta, aided by Jocasta's brother Creon, ruled over Thebes happily for several years, having two sons, Polynices and Eteocles, and two daughters, Antigone and Ismene. Then Thebes was struck by plague once again, and the whole country became barren, so that all births ceased. Creon went to Delphi to enquire what should be done, and brought back the command to drive out the murderers of Laius. The prophet Tiresias backed up the oracle and angered Oedipus by declaring that he was the guilty man. At that same time King Polybus of Corinth died, and the Corinthians, believing Oedipus to be his heir, sent him a message asking him to become their king. He told the messenger that he could not, as he was afraid to go near his mother Merope, Polybus' wife. The messenger – the Corinthian shepherd who had long ago handed over the infant

Oedipus to Polybus – denied that Oedipus was Merope's son. Oedipus, following up information received from him, arranged that the Theban shepherd, who had received him from Laius, should be found and, in spite of the man's warnings, elicited from him the dreadful truth about himself. Jocasta hanged herself, and Oedipus blinded himself with her brooch. Creon took over the regency, and banished Oedipus as the Delphic Oracle had commanded.

How long a time elapsed before he went into exile was variously reported. One tradition maintained that Oedipus spent many years in Thebes while his children grew to manhood and Jocasta's brother Creon acted as regent. During this period it was said he quarrelled violently with Eteocles and Polynices, solemnly cursing them because they served him a meal on Laius' royal plate which he considered cursed; and on another occasion, when they gave him the second-best portion of meat, he regarded it as unfit for a king, and prayed that they might kill each other. Finally Creon was believed to have cast him out – perhaps at the time when Eteocles became king of Thebes – and Oedipus wandered away from the city, accompanied by his elder daughter Antigone, who was betrothed to Creon's son Haemon. In *Oedipus at Colonus*, however, Sophocles makes Oedipus accuse Polynices of having driven him out of Thebes.

The curses Oedipus had pronounced against his sons took effect shortly afterwards, for both of them claimed the throne at Thebes, and an agreement to take turns year by year collapsed when Eteocles, after his year of office, refused to surrender the throne. In consequence King Adrastus of Argos, who was the father of Polynices' wife, brought an army to Thebes to restore his son-in-law and attacked the city at all its seven gates. Before this attack, however, Polynices went to Colonus, near Athens, where Oedipus had found a refuge, and begged for his blessing – since an oracle had forecast success to the side Oedipus supported: but received a curse instead. Because of the same oracle Creon, who supported Eteocles, tried to kidnap Oedipus from Colonus, desiring to bury his body at Thebes; for this, it was prophesied, would save the city. But he was driven off by Theseus' Athenian troops. In his gratitude, Oedipus assured Theseus that the presence of his body would guarantee Athens' safety against any future attack from Thebes. Then he died at Colonus, leaving his blessing upon Attica, the land that had given him his last refuge. Only Theseus knew the site of his tomb. Another tradition, consistent with the Homeric story of Oedipus, states that the Thebans, after celebrating magnificent funeral games for their king, buried him outside their city at Ceus, but a plague afflicted the place, whereupon his bones were secretly moved by night to Eteonus. The Eteonians, unhappy about the matter, consulted the Delphic Oracle; but it bade them leave the tomb alone, for Oedipus was now a guest of Demeter, in whose grove he lay.

Oeneus A king of Calydon, the son of Portheus and Euryte. His wife Althaea, daughter of Thestius, bore him a number of children, including Meleager. When Dionysus came to Calydon, Oeneus hospitably allowed him to sleep with Althaea, and the result of their union was Deianira, who married Heracles. Dionysus repaid Oeneus with the gift of viticulture and, according to some accounts, named wine (Greek *oinos*) after him. It was also said that Ares was the father of Meleager. Oeneus entertained Bellerophon and Alcmaeon and may have given a refuge to Agamemnon and Menelaus during their exile. Oeneus was pious as well as hospitable. Nevertheless one year he failed to include Artemis in his harvest sacrifices; and in consequence the goddess sent a monstrous boar to ravage Calydon – the beast which Meleager, in company with a noble band of warriors, eventually killed. After the hunt, there broke out a fierce quarrel as a result of which his mother Althaea, in her anger over his part in the slaying of her brothers Toxeus and Plexippus, caused his death. Then, in her grief, she killed herself.

Oeneus won himself a new wife, Periboea, daughter of Hipponous, either by an attack on her father's kingdom of Olenus, or by seducing her. It was also suggested that Hipponous, when she became pregnant by another man, sent her to Oeneus with the request that he should dispose of her. She bore him two sons, Tydeus and Olenias. Tydeus, because of his prowess as a warrior, proved a great support to Oeneus, until he was exiled for homicide. Then Oeneus' brother Agrius, or his sons, seized Calydon, driving the old king out. Tydeus was killed in the siege of Thebes, but after the Trojan War his son Diomedes succeeded in expelling Agrius' sons and recovering the Calydonian throne. Oeneus was by this time too old to rule, so Andraemon, husband of his daughter Gorge, became king, and Oeneus accompanied Diomedes to Argos, where he died at a great age. Some said, however, that he was killed in an ambush in Arcadia by Agrius' sons, who were anxious to avenge their expulsion from Calydon.

Oeno see ANIUS.

Oenomaus 1. A king of Pisa. See HIPPODAMIA; PELOPS.
2. A Trojan, slain by Idomeneus.

Oenone A nymph of Mount Ida near Troy, and a daughter of the River Cebren. She married Paris before he knew he was a Trojan prince. Later, influenced by the prophetic gift she had received from Rhea, she tried to dissuade him from going to find Helen in Sparta. In spite of his refusal to listen, Oenone told Paris to come to her if he were ever wounded, for she had great skill as a healer. Years later, when Paris was wounded by Philoctetes, he was taken to Oenone, but now, on account of his desertion of her, she refused to help him. Paris was carried back to Troy. Then, repenting, she rushed after him, only to find him dead on her arrival. In her grief she hanged herself.

Oenopion ('wine-drinker') A son of Dionysus and Ariadne. In Crete he learnt the cultivation of the vine. Later he received the island of Chios from Rhadamanthys. He married a nymph, Helice, and promised their daughter Merope in marriage to Orion if the giant would clear Chios of wild beasts. However he retracted his pledge; whereupon Orion got drunk and raped Merope. As the giant lay there in a drunken stupor, Oenopion put out his eyes, and then he drove him out of Chios. Subsequently Orion, his sight restored, came to Chios to seek vengeance, but could not find Oenopion, who was hiding in an underground house built for him by Hephaestus. Orion departed and Oenopion reigned in Chios for the rest of his life.

Oeonus A friend and cousin of Heracles, killed at Sparta by the sons of Hippocoon. Heracles later avenged his death.

Ogygus A very early king of Boeotia, or Lycia, or Thebes in Egypt. He was said to have survived a flood, like Deucalion. He was also believed to have fathered a number of offspring after whom Attic and Boeotian towns took their names.

Oicles An Arcadian seer, the father of Amphiaraus. He helped Heracles on his expedition against Troy.

Oileus Son of Hodoedocus. His mother Agrianome was a daughter of Poseidon.

He was a king of Locris and an Argonaut. He had two sons: one was Aias, and the other Medon, a bastard by Rhene.

Olus *see* VIBENNA.

Omphale A daughter of Iardanus and queen of Lydia; for she married Tmolus, an early king of the country. After her husband's death, she ruled in her own right, and when Heracles was sold into slavery she bought him, making him wear women's clothes. On her behalf he performed many deeds, killing the outlaw Syleus, destroying a monstrous serpent that was plaguing the country, and sacking the city of the hostile Itoni. She bore him a son, Lamus.

Oncius An Arcadian king. *See* DESPOINA.

Opheltes *see* HYPSIPYLE.

Ophion *see* EURYNOME *1*.

Opis or **Upis** One of two Hyperborean maidens (the other was Arge) who accompanied Leto and her children Apollo and Artemis to Delos. After being held in great honour there, the two eventually died and were buried in Artemis' sacred precinct. Because of their failure to return home, the Hyperboreans ceased to send envoys to Delos. According to one story Artemis killed the giant Orion for raping Opis.

Ops The Roman goddess of abundance, identified with Rhea, the wife of Cronos, and therefore sometimes paired with Saturn, but more usually with Consus.

Oracle, Delphic *see* APOLLO; PYTHON; GAIA.

Orchomenus The eponyms of the two Greek cities of this name. *1*. In Boeotia; the son of Zeus and the father of Minyas (alternatively he was described as Minyas' son).

2. In Arcadia; one of the sons of King Lycaon whom Zeus destroyed in the flood.

Orcus *see* HADES.

Oreads *see* NYMPHS.

Orestes Son of Agamemnon and Clytemnestra, and king of Mycenae, Argos, and Sparta. Orestes was still a boy at the time of his father's murder by his mother and Aegisthus. To save his life he was taken by his sister Electra or his nurse to Phocis, where King Strophius, an old friend and brother-in-law of Agamemnon, brought him up with his own son Pylades. The two boys became inseparable friends and accompanied each other in the terrible events that were to follow. According to Clytemnestra in Aeschylus' *Agamemnon*, Strophius sent for Orestes well before Agamemnon's murder in case he should be injured in a popular revolt. Nine years later Orestes, now fully grown, asked the Delphic Oracle what he should do about his father's murder. The oracle ordered him to kill both Clytemnestra and her lover. Proceeding secretly with Pylades to Mycenae, he made himself known to Electra (whom, according to Euripides, Aegisthus had married to a peasant in order to degrade her). Thereupon Electra supported Orestes and even helped him to kill their parents, and the deed was done. There are several versions of these stories, which form the background to three Attic tragedies: Aeschylus' *Choephori* (Libation Bearers), Sophocles' *Electra*, and Euripides' *Electra*.

What happened next was variously recounted. Homer, who knew of the events so far described, lauded Orestes' deed and, followed by Sophocles, indicated no evil consequences. But Greek tradition also knew of the Erinyes or Furies, primeval Earth-spirits whose function was to punish those guilty of great sins, especially parricide; and the lyric poet Stesichorus, who in his *Oresteia* set the scene in Sparta, asserted that Apollo had given Orestes a bow, because he had to drive the Furies away.

The version followed by Aeschylus and Euripides makes the Furies assail Orestes with madness immediately after his mother's death and hound him all over Greece and beyond. But first, according to some accounts, he was put on trial at Mycenae by Clytemnestra's father Tyndareos. Oeax, who hated Agamemnon for letting his brother Palamedes be stoned, urged the banishment of Orestes. Euripides, in his play *Orestes*, said that Orestes and Electra were actually condemned to death, and only saved because Menelaus, who had originally refused to help them, was ordered by Apollo to tell the Mycenaeans to be content with one year's banishment. Orestes was believed to have tried to coerce Menelaus by seizing Helen and their daughter Hermione (who was betrothed to him). Helen was saved by Zeus, who took her up into the sky, but Hermione was held hostage for a while.

Aeschylus' version of the story was that Orestes went to Delphi for help, since Apollo had ordered the death of his mother. There the oracle sent him in Hermes' care to Athens so that he might offer himself for trial by the Areopagus, a court of elders founded by the gods when Ares was tried for the manslaughter of Halirrhothius. There both Athena and Apollo, as well as the Furies, took part in the trial. Apollo acted as Orestes' advocate, the Furies as prosecutors. When the votes of the Athenian jury turned out to be equal, the goddess as president gave her casting vote in favour of Orestes, on the grounds that a father took precedence over a mother.

Even then, according to one tradition, the Furies did not leave Orestes alone, though Aeschylus implies that they did. Apollo told Orestes that in order to secure his final release he must travel to

the land of the Tauri in the Cimmerian Chersonese (Crimea), and bring back a most holy image of Artemis. These adventures are the subject of Euripides' *Iphigenia in Tauris*. When Orestes and Pylades reached the country, they were captured as sacrificial victims for Artemis, the fate of all strangers who came to the country. At the last moment, however, they learnt that the priestess who was preparing them was the long-lost sister of Orestes, Iphigenia – she had offered to spare one of them when she learnt they came from Argos, if he would promise to take a letter to Orestes. Iphigenia now tricked the Taurians into turning their backs while she pretended to wash her victims in the sea, on the grounds that their pollution by matricide had to be cleansed; then they hastened on board Orestes' ship with the sacred image. On their way back to Greece, Orestes and Iphigenia were said to have found yet another member of the family on the isle of Zminthe, for Chryseis had borne Agamemnon a son, Chryses. Thoas, king of the Taurians, chased Orestes this far, but now was turned back and perhaps killed by Orestes and the young Chryses.

On returning to Greece, Pylades married Electra, and Iphigenia became priestess of Artemis once more. Orestes took the throne of Mycenae and Argos – according to some killing a Mycenaean usurper, his half-brother Aletes, the son of Aegisthus and Clytemnestra – and, when Tyndareos died, he became king of Sparta too; he also conquered a large part of Arcadia. He made Hermione his wife, for she had been betrothed to him during the Trojan War and taken from him in his madness by Neoptolemus, to whom Menelaus had married her on his return from Troy. Orestes was sometimes said to have brought about Neoptolemus' death as he tried to regain his wife, for when Neoptolemus was at Delphi Orestes himself killed him at

Apollo's altar or persuaded the Delphians to do so on the grounds that Neoptolemus intended to pillage the temple. Hermione seems to have preferred Orestes, and bore him a son, Tisamenus, who became his heir.

Several places recorded shrines commemorating Orestes' cure from madness. The most spectacular, at Megalopolis, was said to be at a place where Orestes, attacked by the Furies, bit off one of his own fingers. The Furies then became benign, and he was sane again.

Orestes died of a snake-bite in old age, and was buried at Tegea in Arcadia. Centuries later, according to one tradition, a Spartan was guided by a Delphic oracle to locate Orestes' bones beneath a blacksmith's forge in Tegea. The Spartans removed these remains to their own city, and thereafter, in their wars with Tegea, they were always victorious.

Orestheus A king of Aetolia. He was a son of Deucalion and grandfather of Oeneus. A bitch he owned was pregnant and brought forth a piece of wood. Orestheus buried this and a vine sprang up. The Ozolian Locrians were said to be named after its branches (*ozoi*).

Orion A giant hunter, after whom, as early as Homer, a constellation was named. One story about his birth went as follows. Hyrieus, the founder of Hyria in Boeotia, lacked children, and after hospitably entertaining Zeus, Hermes and Poseidon he asked them to remedy this deficiency. They told him to fetch the hide of the bull he had sacrificed to them; then, after he had made water upon the hide, they buried it. Nine months later, at that place, there grew a boy whom Hyrieus named Orion (from *ouria* 'urine'); he turned into a giant. A variant tradition, however, makes Poseidon and Euryale, daughter of Minos, his parents. He was so tall that he could walk on the seabed and still keep his head and shoulders well above water. He had a number of mistresses. His wife Side ('pomegranate') bore him the Coronides, Menippe and Metrioche. Side, however, was arrogant and compared her beauty to Hera's, so she was sent down to the house of Hades. Orion then went to Chios, where king Oenopion promised him his daughter Merope if he would rid the island of wild beasts; but later the king went back on the deal. Then Orion got drunk and raped Merope, and Oenopion blinded him, throwing him down on the shore. Orion rose and waded over to Lemnos, where at Hephaestus' forge he picked up the boy Celadion and put him on his shoulders, and then, with him as his guide, re-entered the sea and waded eastwards into the sun's rays, which restored his eyesight. He then returned to Chios and tried to kill Oenopion, but the king, with the help of Hephaestus, had hidden himself in an underground chamber.

Orion next went to Crete, where he hunted in Artemis' company, but Eos, goddess of the dawn, fell in love with him and carried him off. The gods, and particularly Artemis, were jealous that a goddess should take a mortal lover, and on the island of Delos, where she herself had been born, Artemis killed Orion with her arrows. She is likewise associated with other variant accounts of Orion's death. According to one of them he died because he rashly challenged the goddess at discus-throwing; and another story recounted that she shot him for trying to rape Opis. Again he was said, while clearing Chios of wild animals, to have tried to rape Artemis herself, but she brought from the ground an enormous scorpion which stung him to death. Or else she did this because she was afraid that he would kill all the animals on earth; or, alternatively, she actually contemplated marriage with Orion, whereupon her brother Apollo tricked her into killing him by pointing to an object far out to sea and betting that she could not hit it. She tried and succeeded, but the target she had hit turned out to be Orion's head, for he was swimming or wading far from the shore. In her grief at the accident she placed her beloved in the sky as a constellation. Another explanation of Orion's constellation, however, was that the giant saw Atlas' daughters the Pleiades in Boeotia and chased them in amorous pursuit. They and their mother Pleione fled, and all were turned into stars; and that is why Orion seems to be hunting the Pleiades in the sky.

Orithyia An Attic princess, the daughter of King Erechtheus of Athens and Queen Praxithea. As she danced by the River Ilissus in Attica, she was snatched up by Boreas, the North Wind, and carried to Thrace, where he forced her to become his wife. She bore him the winged pair Calais and Zetes, who joined the Argonauts, and two daughters, Cleopatra and Chione.

Ormenus The name of several mythical personages, the chief of whom gave his name to the city of Ormenium in Thessalian Magnesia. There were also two Trojan warriors of the same name, and a king of Syrie, the father of Eumaeus.

Orneus Son of Erechtheus. His son Peteos was the ancestor of Athenian kings.

Ornytion Son of Sisyphus; the father of Phocus 2.

Orpheus The supreme minstrel of Greek mythology: his loss of his wife Eurydice forms the most famous of romantic myths. He was the son, or pupil, of Apollo (or of Oeagrus, king of Thrace), his mother being the Muse Calliope. He was also a devotee of Dionysus, a god whose worship is likewise closely connected with Thrace. The mystic religious cult of Orphism was named after Orpheus, and perhaps founded by him if, as is possible, he was (divested of his myths) a historical character.

According to the traditional stories Orpheus was so marvellous a musician that when he sang and played the lyre the whole of nature would listen entranced, and all creatures would follow him. Even trees and stones were believed to come and hear his music. He joined the Argonauts on their voyage to Colchis, lulling the waves in their path and calming the unruly spirits of the crew. He took them to Samothrace, where he initiated them into the mysteries of the Cabiri; and when they arrived in Colchis, some said that he lulled to sleep the serpent that guarded the tree in Ares' grove from which Jason took the Golden Fleece. He also drowned the Sirens' songs with his lyre, making them unable to seduce the Argonauts from their purpose.

On his return to Thrace, Orpheus married a Naiad or Dryad, Eurydice, whom he loved passionately. Soon after, Aristaeus was pursuing her amorously through the meadows, when in her haste to escape him she trod on a snake, which bit her leg so badly that she died. Overwhelmed with inconsolable grief, Orpheus ceased to sing and play, but moped in silence. Finally he wandered to Taenarum in Laconia, where he made his way into the passage leading to the Underworld. When he came to the Styx and the gate kept by the watchdog Cerberus, he once again played his lyre so beautifully that even Charon and Cerberus were moved to let him pass. The shades were entranced by his music, and even Hades and Persephone were softened. They granted him a favour, allowing him to recover Eurydice on one condition: he must lead the way and not look back at her until they reached the upper air again. According to the oldest version of the story Orpheus succeeded in his task and thus bore witness to the power of his lord Dionysus even over death. But in the story as told by Virgil and Ovid, just as he had the end of the passage in sight and the light was visible ahead, he could not refrain from turning and gazing at his wife's face: and through this excess of love he lost her, for she turned into a wraith of mist and vanished back to the house of Hades. He tried to follow again, but this time the way was barred and all his music could not prevail.

And now Orpheus was like a lost soul, living the life of a recluse and avoiding above all the company of women. However the Thracian Maenads, among whom he had often celebrated Dionysus' orgies, soon bore him a grudge for his neglect of their company; and one day they found him, and tore him to pieces, as Zagreus had been torn to pieces by the Titans. According to some accounts they all lusted after him, and it was while quarrelling over him that they tore him apart. Only his head was saved. It fell into the River Hebrus, and was washed down to the sea, rolling this way and that and constantly crying 'Eurydice!' Eventually it came ashore on Lesbos, where the people buried it, founding a shrine and an oracle and winning for themselves the gift of poetic skill. The Muses gathered the fragments of Orpheus' body and buried them in Pieria. His lyre was placed in heaven as a constellation.

Orpheus was said to have taught other Greek bards: Musaeus, Eumolpus, and Linus.

Orseis A nymph; the wife of Hellen and mother of Dorus, Aeolus, and Xuthus.

Orislochus *see* CRETHEUS.

Orthrus or **Orthus** *see* HERACLES (tenth Labour); GERYON

Othryoneus *see* CASSANDRA.

Otreus A Phrygian king, whom Priam in his youth helped in fighting against the Amazons in a battle on the River Sangarius.

Otus and **Ephialtes** These two giants, the Aloadae or 'sons of Aloeus', were the children of Poseidon and of Iphimedia, Triops' daughter. Their mother, after her marriage to Aloeus, fell in love with the god and sat by the seashore, longing for him and allowing the waves to wash over her lap, until she conceived the twin giants. They grew so quickly that at the age of nine they were eighteen yards (sixteen metres) high. Their first exploit, while they were still in their childhood, was to capture the god Ares and imprison him in a great bronze jar. He stayed there for thirteen months until the giants' stepmother Eriboea revealed his whereabouts to Hermes, who rescued him when he was on the point of death. It was said, however, that Aphrodite had given Adonis into the protection of Otus and Ephialtes, and that they imprisoned Ares for killing him.

The pair then fell in love with two goddesses, Artemis and Hera, and planned how to capture them. Though not yet fully grown, they determined to assault heaven by piling up mountains, Ossa upon Olympus and then Pelion on Ossa, until they could scale the sky itself. But Apollo and Artemis brought about their destruction, either by shooting them down with arrows, or by letting a deer (which according to some accounts was Artemis herself) run between them: each of the twins aimed his spear at it, but instead hit his brother. This was said to have occurred in Naxos, but tradition maintained that the bodies were conveyed to Anthedon in Boeotia and buried there. Although Otus and Ephialtes are sometimes said to have introduced the cult of the Muses and founded the city of Ascra, where they received worship, they were punished in Tartarus for their insolent behaviour, being bound with writhing serpents back to back against a column.

Oxylus Son of Andraemon or his son Haemon; king of Elis. When Oxylus had been banished from his native Aetolia to Elis on account of his accidental killing of his brother Thermius, he met on his homeward journey the Heraclids (descendants of Heracles) who, in obedience to the Delphic Oracle's command to wait for three generations, were preparing to invade the Peloponnese. Oxylus was driving a one-eyed mule at the time, and the Heraclids, who had received an oracle bidding them make the 'three-eyed one' their leader, asked him to guide them. He took them south-wards through Arcadia rather than through fertile Elis, which he wished to save for himself. The Heraclids under Temenus defeated Orestes' son Tisamenus; Oxylus returned to Aetolia and led an army of his compatriots to invade Elis. The king, Dius, resisted, and the matter was settled by a single combat between two champions, an Elean archer, Degmenus, and an Aetolian slinger, Pyraechmes. The Aetolian won, and Oxylus ruled Elis in peace. He shared his rule with Agorius, because Pelops, an early king of Elis, was Agorius' ancestor.

P

Paeon *1.* Homer knew of a god of healing of this name, who cured Hades when, defending the gate of the Underworld, he was wounded by one of Heracles' arrows. Hades came to Olympus to be cured in Zeus' palace, where Paeon spread ointments on his wound; he performed the same service for Ares too, after Diomedes had wounded him in battle. Later the name Paeon became simply an epithet of other gods associated with medicine, Apollo and Asclepius.
2. Son of Endymion, king of Elis, and Calyce.

Palaemon *1. see* INO
2. Son of Hephaestus; an Argonaut.

Palamedes Son of Nauplius *2* by Clymene, daughter of Catreus. His name means 'handy' or 'clever'. He was believed to be the inventor of draughts (checkers) and dice games, as well as of several letters of the Greek alphabet. He was a useful servant to Agamemnon, and was sent with Menelaus to round up the former suitors of Helen for service in the Trojan War, since they had taken an oath to come to the aid of her husband, whoever he might prove to be. Odysseus, though it was he who had proposed the oath, tried to avoid service by a trick, but Palamedes saw through his deception and forced him to come. For this reason Odysseus bore him implacable hatred, and duly took vengeance on him when they reached Troy. First he carefully hid a quantity of gold beneath Palamedes' tent (or told Agamemnon of a dream which made it neces-

sary to move the camp for a day, and hid the gold where Palamedes' tent had been). Then he forged a letter from Priam to Palamedes, promising him the same amount of gold if he would betray the Greek camp. The letter was intercepted in the hands of a Phrygian slave and read by Agamemnon, who ordered a search. When the gold was found, Agamemnon handed Palamedes to the army to be stoned to death. Another tale was that Odysseus and Diomedes told Palamedes there was gold in a well and, when he climbed in to look, flung stones down on top of him. A third version asserted that they drowned him while he was fishing at sea. Achilles and Aias gave him an honourable burial. Palamedes' father Nauplius came to Troy to demand satisfaction for the death of his son, but was sent away empty-handed. He gained his revenge, however, by turning the Greek leaders' wives against them and by wrecking many ships when the fleet sailed home.

Palici Twin gods of Sicily. The nymph Thalia was pursued by Zeus but feared Hera; so she implored her lover to let her be swallowed up by the ground. Some time later her twin sons sprang up from the spot and were called Palici ('coming again'). According to an alternative story they were the sons of Hephaestus and the nymph Etna. The place where they were thought to have emerged contained pools giving off natural gas. At this spot a place of sanctuary for suspected criminals was founded. Anyone who swore his innocence there was believed, for if he lied, it was said that the Palici would immediately punish him.

Palinurus Aeneas' helmsman on the voyage from Troy to Italy. After leaving Carthage, the Trojans put in at Elyma in Sicily because of a storm, and waited until it abated. As Juno had sent the storm to wreck them, she was angry that they had escaped and demanded the life of at least one Trojan. She therefore sent Somnus (Hypnos, 'sleep') who lulled Palinurus to sleep at his helm so that he fell overboard. He was washed ashore and killed by the Lucanians. Aeneas met his ghost in the Underworld and promised him burial; he later carried out his promise by burying him at Cape Palinurus, which still bears his name.

Pallas (stem *Pallad-*) A title of Athena, of which the original meaning was lost. Stories were invented to explain it. According to one of them Pallas was a small girl, Athena's ward, the daughter of Triton. One day she and her guardian quarrelled, and Pallas struck at the goddess with her spear, a blow which Zeus warded off with his magic breastplate or aegis. Athena struck back and killed Pallas; but afterwards she regretted her deed, and herself assumed the girl's name, making an image of her clad in the aegis. This was the Palladium, which fell from heaven into Troy during the reign of Ilus. It was said that Zeus threw the image out of Olympus, because the Pleiad Electra, when Zeus was pursuing her, clung to it for safety; and when Ilus prayed for a sign from Zeus, it fell in his camp. The Palladium brought luck to Troy, and that was why Odysseus stole it in the Trojan War.

Another story is that Athena took the name of Pallas from a giant of that name whom she slew. *See* PALLAS 2.

Pallas (stem *Pallant-*) *1.* A Titan, the son of Crius and Eurybia. By Styx he

was father of Cratos, Bia, Zelus, and Nike; and perhaps also of Selene the Moon.

2. A giant killed by Athena in the war with the gods. She then flayed him and used his skin to make armour for herself. Some said that she took the name Pallas for this reason.

3. Son of Pandion *2*, king of Athens. He at first helped his elder half-brother Aegeus to take the throne, but later quarrelled with him. His fifty sons, the Pallantids, were eventually killed by Theseus.

4. See EVANDER.

Pamphylus Son of Aegimius, king of Doris.

Pan The god of the pastures, especially of sheep and goats. Like his father Hermes, Pan possessed close links with Arcadia. His name is associated with his pastoral function, since it means 'shepherd' or literally 'feeder' (early Greek *Paon*). A wide diversity of parents were attributed to him in antiquity. His father was variously identified as Hermes, Zeus, Apollo, Cronos, and others; and his mother as Callisto, Penelope (probably the name of a daughter of Dryops), Hybris, and a she-goat. At all events, when his mother first saw what she had produced, she leapt up and left him; the nymphs, therefore, reared him instead. For he had the legs of a goat and little horns on his head. (The medieval image of the devil was derived from this picture of Pan.) But in spite of his odd appearance, Hermes was very proud to introduce him to the gods on Olympus. Being a rustic god, Pan was lustful and constantly chased the nymphs. He was also held to be responsible for the fertility of the flocks and herds. When they did not reproduce, his statue was flogged with squills.

Like Apollo, he was a musician, though not such a good one. In Lydia they once had a contest, which Tmolus judged, giving Apollo the prize; for his stupid comments, Midas received ass's ears. Pan's instrument was the *syrinx*, or Pan-pipes, to which the nymphs and satyrs used to dance. He obtained his pipes on one of his amorous adventures, when he was chasing the nymph Syrinx or Nonacris. She reached the River Ladon, and finding, in despair, that she was unable to cross it, asked the nymphs to make her into a reed-bed. They complied with her request. Pan cut the reeds and set pieces of different lengths together to make his pipes. Pan also loved Selene, the Moon-goddess. luring her into the woods by the offer of a beautiful white fleece of wool.

Pan was sometimes a frightening god, as the derivation of the word *panic* from his name suggests; and above all he was angry if his sleep was disturbed, both at night and at noontide. He was a favourite of the pastoral poets, thus resembling his half-brother Daphnis, whom he greatly loved and mourned after he was dead. Pan also showed favour to the Athenians, for when Pheidippides ran from Athens to Sparta to ask for help at the time of the battle of Marathon (490 BC), it was said that, as he crossed Mount Parthenium in Arcadia, the god called him by name and asked him why the Athenians did not worship him, since he had so often come to their assistance. After the victory at Marathon, therefore, at which the Persians had fled 'in panic', Athens instituted a shrine and sacrifices and processions in his honour. Pan had also, it was believed, instilled panic into the giants when they fought against the gods, by means of a great shout which struck terror into their hearts. The Romans identified him with their woodland god Silvanus.

Panacea ('cure-all') Daughter of Asclepius.

Pandareos A king of the city of Miletus. He stole a golden dog from a shrine of Zeus in the island of Crete and lent it to Tantalus, king of Lydia, who refused to return it, denying that it was in his possession. Since, however, the dog had guarded Zeus' temple as it had earlier guarded Amalthea at the time of his birth, he punished both Pandareos and his wife Hermothoe by putting them to death. Aphrodite and the other goddesses rescued his two younger daughters, Cleothera and Merope, and brought them up: Athena taught them domestic crafts, Artemis made them taller, Hera gave them beauty and understanding, and finally Aphrodite arranged their marriages. But while she was on Olympus consulting Zeus about this matter, the girls were carried off by storm-winds to be slaves to the Furies. Their eldest sister Aedon, who had married Zethus, also came to an unhappy end, for she accidentally killed her own son Itylus. Because of her grief, she turned by Zeus into a nightingale, constantly singing her son's name.

Pandarus Son of King Lycaon of Zeleia in Lycia, and an ally of the Trojans. He went to war as an archer, having learnt that skill from Apollo himself. In obedience to orders from Athena, he disguised himself as Laodocus, son of Antenor, and shot an arrow at Menelaus, thus breaking the truce whereby Menelaus and Paris were to settle the issue by single combat. He was subsequently killed by Diomedes.

Pandion *1.* Son of Erichthonius and the Naiad Praxithea, the sixth of the mythical kings of Athens. He married his aunt, Praxithea's sister Zeuxippe. His sons were Erechtheus and Butes, his daughters Procne and Philomela. During his reign a war was believed to have been fought against Thebes under King Labdacus, and Pandion allied himself with the Thracian king Tereus, to whom he gave Procne in marriage. During Pandion's reign both Dionysus and Demeter visited Attica and their worship was instituted.

He was succeeded by Erechtheus, named as his son in later myths but described in the earlier stories as brought forth from the earth.

2. Son of Cecrops and Metiadusa; a great-grandson of the above. After succeeding his father as king of Athens, he was ousted by the sons of his uncle Metion. Taking refuge in Megara, he married King Pylas' daughter Pylia. When Pylas slew his uncle Bias, he was exiled from Megara, and Pandion became king. His son Aegeus eventually drove the sons of Metion out of Athens with the help of his brothers Pallas and Lycus. Another son, Nisus, inherited the throne of Megara.

3. Son of Phineus and Cleopatra.

Pandora The first woman, created by Zeus as a pest for mankind, in order to discredit Prometheus, who had acted as man's friend, so that Zeus could gain the vengeance he desired. Her name means 'all gifts'; she was fashioned by Hephaestus out of clay, given life and clothes by Athena, granted beauty by Aphrodite so that men would love this new plague, and taught guile and treachery by Hermes: he gave her to Epimetheus, Prometheus' foolish brother, who accepted her as his bride. The gods had given into her hands a sealed jar or casket containing all the evils that were ever to plague mankind; the only good it contained was Hope, right at the bottom. Epimetheus had been warned by Prometheus never to accept a gift from Zeus, and Pandora now brought about the ruin of mankind. With her natural feminine curiosity she opened the casket, and out of it flew all the sorrows, diseases, quarrels, and woes that have ever since afflicted human beings. She hastily snapped the lid back on but it was too late to prevent the plague of evils escaping into the world. The spirit Hope, which was trapped inside, cried to be let out in order to alleviate the ills which were now re-

leased to plague mortal men. Thus the males who had hitherto exclusively comprised the human race and had lived an existence free from care and toil were now obliged to labour and suffer in order to make their living.

In another version of the story the casket belonged to Prometheus and contained all the good gifts which he had won for mankind and was keeping in store for them. Pandora found it in the house and in her curiosity opened the lid, releasing the benefits which flew away never to be recaptured, and keeping only Hope, which was slower than the rest and was trapped inside.

Pandora bore Epimetheus a daughter, Pyrrha, who married Deucalion and, with him, survived the Great Flood.

Pandorus Son of Erechtheus and Praxithea. He helped his brother Metion to expel Xuthus from Athens.

Pandrosus ('dewy') For obeying Athena's command not to look at the baby Erichthonius, Pandrosus received honours on the Acropolis and Athena's olive was planted in her precinct. *See* AGLAURUS 2.

Panthous Son of Othrys; he was a Trojan elder and a priest of Apollo. His sons, all Trojan warriors, were Polydamas, Euphorbus, and Hyperenor.

Paphos Daughter of Pygmalion and mother, or wife, of Cinyras.

Paraebius A poor man of Thynia in Thrace, who, in spite of all his hard work, grew ever poorer. The seer Phineus, king of Salmydessus, told him that he had unwittingly killed a Hamadryad (tree-nymph) by chopping down her tree, and was consequently under a curse. After sacrificing to appease the nymph's ghost, his luck turned. When Phineus was pestered by the Harpies, Paraebius in gratitude helped him.

Parcae *see* FATES.

Paris Son of Priam, king of Troy, and of his wife Hecabe. Homer prefers to call him Alexander (Alexandros).

There was confusion over Paris' place in the order of Priam's sons. Homer depicts him as second to Hector, but according to the *Iliad* Paris had been sent to Sparta as an envoy nineteen years before the death of Hector, and Hector appears considerably younger. It was also the privilege of primogeniture that allowed Paris to keep Helen against such powerful opposition. The contrary suggestion that he was one of the younger sons was presumably intended to support the impression of his outstanding good looks.

The stories of Paris' birth and upbringing are not mentioned by Homer, and may be of later invention. A little before his birth his mother dreamed that she brought forth a firebrand by which the whole city was set on fire and destroyed, or a hundred-armed monster which tore the place apart. A seer (Aesacus, son of Priam by the nymph Alexirrhoe) or a Sibyl warned Priam that the dream foretold disaster, and that the child must die: he therefore entrusted Paris, at birth, to a shepherd, Agelaus, who abandoned him on Mount Ida, but five days later discovered him still alive, since a she-bear had suckled him. Agelaus then took pity on the baby and reared him as his own child.

He grew into a strikingly handsome man, and in due course was reconciled with his family. Priam sent men to the mountain to fetch a bull to be the prize in funeral games he was holding. The bull chosen was Paris' favourite, and he followed the men to Troy, determined to compete in the games and win the animal back. In this he was indeed so successful that he aroused the jealousy of Priam's other sons; and when Deiphobus drew a sword on him, Paris took refuge in the courtyard at Zeus' altar.

Cassandra, who saw him there, recognised him as Priam's lost son and he was received back, Hecabe's vision forgotten. He had already married a nymph, Oenone, daughter of the River Cebren, and continued to pass his time with her on Mount Ida, pasturing his father's sheep amongst his boyhood friends.

It was here that Hermes, on Zeus' command, led Hera, Athena, and Aphrodite, who contested the golden apple thrown down by Eris (Strife) at the wedding of Peleus and Thetis and inscribed 'for the fairest'. Each of the three goddesses tried to bribe the handsome judge, offering him respectively dominion over the earth, victory in battle, and the most beautiful woman in the world. The last of these bribes appealed to Paris the most, and he awarded the prize to Aphrodite, who thereafter protected him and arranged his marriage with Helen. Then Priam, no doubt under Aphrodite's influence, sent Paris on a deputation to King Menelaus of Sparta. Paris may have put it about that he intended to bring Helen back with him, for her beauty had a wide reputation, owing to her courtship by all the eligible princes of Greece. It was said that Helenus and Cassandra predicted doom for Troy if he went; and Oenone, foreseeing he would desert her, told him that he must come to her on Mount Ida if ever he should be wounded, and she would use her healing skill to cure him.

When Paris reached Sparta, Menelaus entertained him hospitably while Helen his wife, on an impulse sent by Aphrodite, fell deeply in love with the visitor. After nine days, however, Menelaus was forced to sail to Crete in order to bury his grandfather Catreus, and Paris eloped with Helen, taking with him a magnificent treasure from Menelaus' coffers. The time they took to reach Troy was disputed. Some said they were blown to Sidon in Phoenicia by a storm sent by Hera and that, while they were

there, Paris captured the city. Another
version of the tale asserted that he
reached Troy in three days. But it was
also declared, by those concerned to
whitewash Helen, that Hera substituted
a cloud-image of her for the real woman,
and that this was what Paris loved and
took to Troy, while Helen herself was
spirited away by Hermes to Egypt.

After a number of years, since it had
proved impossible to recover Helen by
diplomacy, a huge force, drawn from
many kingdoms and principalities of
Greece, attacked Troy under the supreme command of Menelaus' brother,
Agememnon. Homer's *Iliad* recounts
mythical events of the tenth year of the
siege. In this account Paris, in spite of
his distinguished appearance, played a
somewhat inglorious part. Homer's
name for him, Alexander (Alexandros),
means 'defender of men' and implies
great valour. But it is as if, by choosing
the prize that Aphrodite had offered
him, he had lost after his Judgment all
the manliness with which Hera and
Athena might have endowed him.
During the battle against the Trojans,
the one duel he fought face to face was
a single combat with Menelaus, which
was supposed to decide the fortunes of
the whole war. In this Paris appeared as
a coward because, as Menelaus was haul-
ing him off, defeated, by his helmet,
Aphrodite caused the chin-strap to break
and whisked him away to Helen's bedroom, wrapped in a thick mist. Few
respected him, and Hector was very sar-
castic about his unmanly ways. Yet it
was Paris who finally killed Achilles,
though the arrow with which he did so
was guided by Apollo. Thereafter Paris
himself very soon met his end, again
through an arrow-shot, dispatched from
the bow of Heracles which was now in
Philoctetes' hands. As he lay wounded,
he bade his attendants carry him to
Mount Ida, where Oenone had promised
to cure him. But now, after a desertion
of nineteen years, she had changed her

mind, and he was taken back to Troy.
Shortly afterwards Oenone repented,
but it was too late and Paris was dead:
so she hanged herself for grief.

Parthenopaeus Son of Atalanta; his
father was Milanion or Meleager, or the
god Ares, or Talaus. His name was explained by Atalanta's long virginity
(Greek *parthenos*, 'virgin'); or because
she abandoned and exposed him, as an
infant, on Mount Parthenium; or because she did so to hide the loss of her
virginity. He was a close friend of Heracles' son Telephus, whom he accompanied to Teuthrania. In the assault on
Thebes by the Seven Champions, of
whom he was one (flaunting a sphinx
on his shield), he was killed at the
Borrhaean gate by Periclymenus, who
crushed the life out of him by throwing
a rock. His son Promachus, fighting
among the Epigoni, avenged his death.

Parthenope *1*. Daughter of Stymphalus.
She gave Heracles a son, Everes.
2. A Siren; she gave her name to the city
of Naples in Campania (formerly called
Parthenope).

Pasiphae Daughter of Helios the Sun-
god and the Oceanid Perseis. She became
the wife of Minos, king of Crete, and
bore him many children, but succumbed
at last to a violent passion for a bull – a
punishment inflicted by Poseidon upon
her husband for failing to sacrifice the
animal to him. Daedalus made a wooden
cow, into which Pasiphae inserted herself
in order to have sexual relations with
the bull. Having satisfied her passion,
she bore the Minotaur. Then Pasiphae,
enraged by Minos' constant amours, bewitched him so that he gave a painful
disease to the women to whom he made
love. He was cured of it by Procris.

Pasithea *see* GRACES.

Patroclus Son of Menoetius of Opus.

As a youth, in a quarrel over a game of dice, Patroclus was guilty of the accidental homicide of Clitonymus, son of Amphidamas. He had to go into exile, and his father took him to Phthia, where King Peleus purified him. There Patroclus formed a firm friendship with Achilles, who was still a boy at the time but later accepted him as his devoted companion. After Peleus decided to send Achilles to fight at Troy, Menoetius dispatched his son with special instructions to keep an eye on the impetuous prince. When Achilles, in the last year of the war, withdrew from battle as a protest against his treatment by Agamemnon, Patroclus, as second-in-command of the Myrmidon contingent, also retired. But when he saw the Greeks being worsted, he felt pity for them. In consequence, following a suggestion made by Nestor, he borrowed Achilles' armour, led the Myrmidons into battle, and drove the Trojans from the ships; but then, when Achilles ordered him to return to camp, he disobeyed, killing Sarpedon the Lycian and advancing to the walls of Troy. Then Euphorbus inflicted a wound upon him, and Hector, with a spear-thrust, put him to death. Over his body a long struggle took place in which Hector succeeded in seizing the armour of Achilles, but the body was rescued by Menelaus and Aias the son of Telamon. Achilles, when he heard the news of Patroclus' death, vowed that he would not bury his friend until he had taken vengeance on the Trojans: and so it was the death of Patroclus that brought Achilles back into the fight and led to his killing of Hector. Later, at Patroclus' funeral, at which the body (which Thetis had preserved with ambrosia) was cremated, Achilles killed twelve Trojan captives. After Achilles too had been slain, the two were buried in the same tomb, their ashes mixed together.

Patron see SMICRUS.

Pedias see CRANAUS.

Pegasus see BELLEROPHON.

Pelagon A king of Phocis. See CADMUS.

Pelasgus A king of Argos. See DANAUS.

Peleus Son of Aeacus, king of Aegina, and Endeis. When he and his brother Telamon killed their half-brother Phocus with a discus – either because they were jealous of him, or to please their mother – Aeacus banished them from Aegina. Peleus went to Phthia, where the king, Actor, after purifying him, presented him with a share of his kingdom and gave him the hand of his daughter Antigone, who bore him Polydora.

Peleus then took part in the expedition of the Argonauts and went to Calydon to help Meleager kill the great boar. Unfortunately he killed Eurytion, Actor's son, and was again banished, this time from Phthia. He went to Iolcus where Acastus, a fellow Argonaut, was king and took part in the funeral games for Acastus' father Pelias, in which he wrestled with Atalanta. But then another misfortune overtook Peleus: Acastus' wife Astydamia fell in love with him. Peleus had no wish to cuckold his host, and repulsed her pleas. In her spite, therefore, she pretended that Peleus was about to marry her daughter Sterope, and sent Antigone this message. Antigone, in her distress, hanged herself. Still not content, Astydamia now told Acastus that Peleus had made advances to her. Acastus, who had purified Peleus of the homicide of Eurytion, was unwilling to kill his guest and resolved to get rid of him by guile.

He therefore took Peleus hunting on Mount Pelion, challenging him to trap more game than he himself could in the day: for he hoped, by these means, to tire Peleus out. Peleus, however, in order to prove his victory, cut out the tongues of his catch and displayed them when Acastus accused him of having caught nothing. During the night Acastus hid Peleus' sword, a weapon made by Hephaestus, beneath a heap of cow dung, and abandoned him asleep on the mountain, hoping that the wild Centaurs would kill him. Chiron, however, prevented such an outcome and returned his sword to Peleus. Then Peleus, realising the truth of the matter, gathered some of his old comrades from the *Argo* and attacked Acastus, killing Astydamia and marching his army between the severed halves of her corpse; some said that he killed Acastus as well. He then gave Iolcus to the Thessalians, and himself returned to Phthia, where he possessed a kingdom. For the virtue he had shown in repulsing the advances of Acastus' wife, Zeus rewarded him with an extraordinary privilege, marriage to the goddess Thetis. This reward, however, was not without an ulterior motive, for Zeus, having himself wished to form a liaison with Thetis, had learnt to his horror from Prometheus that her son was fated to be greater than his father. He therefore made haste to marry her to a mortal. To win his bride, Peleus had to capture her in a sea-cave in Magnesia and wrestle with her, or hold her while she changed herself into a variety of shapes. The wedding feast was magnificent, and all the gods except Eris (Strife) were invited. Each brought a gift, among them the immortal horses Xanthus and Balius and a suit of armour made by Hephaestus. Eris came uninvited and cast down as her gift the famous golden apple that Paris later awarded to Aphrodite.

Thetis bore a son, Achilles, and was most anxious to ensure his immortality. She did this by placing him in the fire at night and by anointing him with ambrosia. Peleus, however, seeing his son in the fire, cried out. For this interference Thetis left him and returned to the sea. Some said she also dipped her baby in the River Styx to make him proof against all wounds but failed to wet the

heel by which she held him, so that this became vulnerable – the traditional Achilles' heel. Peleus, left to rear the child, entrusted him to his old friend Chiron, who kept a school in the mountains where he had brought up Jason. Thetis, however, still loved her son dearly and often visited and consoled him. But according to some accounts Chiron was already dead by this time, for Homer attributed Achilles' education to Phoenix, a refugee from the court of his father Amyntor of Ormenium; Peleus made him king of the Dolopes. Other refugees came to Peleus' court, including Epeigeus of Budeum and Patroclus with his father Menoetius.

After Achilles' death in the Trojan War, the elderly Peleus was driven out of Pththia by the sons of Acastus, and took refuge in the island of Cos. After the war his grandson Neoptolemus reconquered Pthia and ruled it for a time. While Neoptolemus was absent in Epirus, Peleus defended the Trojan princess Andromache, his concubine, from Hermione and Menelaus, who wished her ill. Finally Thetis fetched Peleus to join her in the sea and enjoy immortality with her there.

Pelias Pelias and Neleus were twin sons of Poseidon and Tyro, daughter of Salmoneus. Being afraid of her step-mother Sidero's anger, Tyro abandoned and exposed her infant sons. They were found and reared by a horse-breeder, and Pelias was named after a livid mark (*pelios*) that a mare had made when it kicked him. On attaining manhood, the two discovered who their mother was. Tyro recognised them from the basket in which she had abandoned them. Owing to her ill-treatment of her stepdaughter Tyro, Pelias seized Sidero – although she had fled to Hera's altar for refuge – and put her to death. Hera never forgave Pelias this insult to her honour, especially as he refused to sacrifice to her ever again.

After her association with Poseidon, Tyro had married Cretheus, the king of Iolcus, and borne him three sons, Aeson, Pheres, and Amythaon. But Pelias usurped the throne of Iolcus from his half-brother Aeson, who, as Cretheus' son, had a right to the kingship, whereas Pelias had none. Pelias married Anaxibia, the daughter of Bias, who bore him Acastus and a number of daughters, including Alcestis. Meanwhile Aeson lived quietly in Iolcus, and when his wife bore him a son, Jason, he pretended it was dead; the boy was entrusted to the Centaur Chiron.

Years later, Pelias was warned by an oracle he received from Delphi to beware of a stranger of the house of Aeolus, a man wearing one sandal, who would cause his death. Subsequently Jason arrived back at Iolcus wearing a single sandal, for he had lost the other while carrying Hera disguised as an old woman across the swollen River Anaurus; and so he was destined by the goddess to serve as the instrument of Pelias' destruction. Jason now demanded the throne of Iolcus that was rightfully his father's. With specious kindness Pelias asked Jason how, if he knew of a man who intended to kill him, he would advise him to get rid of him; and Jason replied that he would send such a man to fetch home the Golden Fleece from the kingdom of Aeetes in Colchis. And so Pelias told Jason, if he wanted to be king of Iolcus, to do just that: if he could bring home the fleece, he would be Pelias' heir. While Jason was absent on the seemingly impossible task, Pelias killed his father Aeson and his brother Promachus; and his mother committed suicide. After several years, however, Jason unexpectedly returned, bringing with him a wife, the witch Medea, and it was she who accomplished Hera's purpose. For she tricked Pelias' daughters into cutting up their father and putting him into a stew-pot, in the hope that by so doing they would achieve his

magical rejuvenation. Jason now held Iolcus in his power, but because of the murder of Pelias, he and his wife left the city, and Acastus, Pelias' son, succeeded to the throne. At the funeral games he held for his father, one of the events was Peleus' wrestling match with Atalanta.

Pelops Son of the Lydian king Tantalus either by the goddess Dione or by a Pleiad.

A story concerning his childhood asserted that Tantalus was honoured by a visit from the Olympian gods, whom he entertained to dinner. He decided to test his guests' omniscience by cutting up his son Pelops, stewing his body, and serving it at table. His divine guests recognised their fare, all except Demeter, who ate a portion of the shoulder. The gods brought the child back to life, and Demeter gave him an ivory shoulder; thenceforward the shoulders of his descendants continued to display a white birthmark. The poet Pindar however, rejects this story, declaring that the gods had no desire to dine with Tantalus and did not do so, but that Poseidon fell in love with Pelops and carried him to Olympus. When Tantalus' reign came to its wicked end, the gods returned Pelops to Lydia, giving him a team of fabulous winged horses and teaching him how to handle them. However he was driven out of his kingdom by Ilus, king of Troy, and went with his followers to Greece.

There he took part in the competition for the hand of Hippodamia, princess of Pisa. Her father Oenomaus insisted that the man who would marry her must first bear her off in a chariot. However he himself was accustomed to give chase to her suitors and then spear them between the shoulder-blades. Either he himself was in love with Hippodamia or, according to an alternative version, he had been warned that he would die at the hands of her husband. Wearing a suit of armour given to him by Ares, he fixed the racecourse as the whole distance between Pisa and Corinth, some ninety miles. Moreover his horses were immortal, being a gift from Ares.

Pelops won Hippodamia by deceitfully bribing Oenomaus' charioteer Myrtilus, whom he offered a night in Hippodamia's bed and a half of the kingdom if he would replace the lynchpins of his master's chariot with new ones made of wax. (According to one tradition Hippodamia, being in love with Pelops, made the arrangement with Myrtilus on his behalf.) Pelops had a good start, while the father of his prospective bride was sacrificing to his patron Ares. Then, as soon as Oenomaus mounted his car, the wheels came off and he crashed to the ground. Pelops, who had expected this, was hanging behind, and now returned and plunged his spear into Oenomaus' back. The dying man understood that Myrtilus had caused his fall and cursed him, forecasting that he too would be killed by Pelops. And that is just what happened, for Pelops, who was now king of Pisa and may have been jealous of Myrtilus, invited him for a ride in his magic chariot; then, as they passed over the sea, he pushed him into the water. As he drowned, Myrtilus cursed Pelops as he himself had been cursed, and in his curse he included Pelops' descendants as well.

Pelops felt remorse because of his treacherous murder of Myrtilus. In the stadium at Olympia he set up, in honour of his victim, a monument which was called Taraxippos ('horse-scare') because it was believed to be haunted by Myrtilus' ghost, which caused horses to bolt at the sight of it. He also tried to propitiate Myrtilus' father Hermes by instituting the god's worship throughout his territories.

Pelops became a very powerful king, adding the whole of Elis, Arcadia, and other lands to his kingdom, so that the whole of southern Greece was called Pelops' Island, the Peloponnese. Arcadia he won by deceit, for after pretending to befriend its king, Stymphalus, he murdered him and thus caused his kingdom to be plunged into a famine which was alleviated only by Aeacus' prayers.

Pelops was believed to have possessed a large family, including the sons after whom Epidaurus, Sicyon, and the Troezen were subsequently named. Better known are Pittheus, Alcathous (king of Megara), Letreus, and Sciron (alternatively regarded as the offspring of Poseidon). Pelops' most famous sons, however, were Atreus and Thyestes, on whom Myrtilus' curse had the greatest effect. He also had a bastard son, Chrysippus, by a nymph. This child, who was particularly handsome, was Pelops' favourite, so that Hippodamia and her sons became jealous. Moreover Laius of Thebes, a refugee at Pelops' court, abducted the lad for a while. But Chrysippus was killed in an ambush laid by Atreus and Thyestes at the instigation of their mother. When Pelops discovered what had happened, Hippodamia fled to Midea in the Argolid, where her sons were now rulers. His daughters, Astydamia, Nicippe, and Lysidice, he gave in marriage to Perseus' sons, who ruled Argos: they married Alcaeus, Sthenelus, and Mestor respectively.

Of Pelops' death we know nothing. He was honoured at a precinct at Olympia, founded, according to one tradition, by his descendant Heracles. In spite of his murder of Myrtilus, Pelops left a reputation for hospitality and piety, and sacrifices were performed for him in his precinct. Some of the Greeks believed that he founded the Olympic Games, though Heracles was also credited with that honour.

Pelorus One of the 'Sown Men' of Thebes. *See* CADMUS.

Pemphredo *see* GRAIAE.

Penates The *Di Penates* were the Roman gods of the store-cupboard (*penus*), and were the objects of family worship from a very early date. Later the Penates of the Roman state were elevated to special importance. These national Penates were kept in the temple of Vesta in the Forum, and were considered to be protectors of the whole nation. They were connected, in mythology, with the supposed Trojan origin of Rome, and were believed to be the household gods of Aeneas – or else the gods from the citadel of Ilium – which he had carried in his arms out of the burning city of Troy, brought in his ships to Italy, and established in a temple at the city he founded at Lavinium in Latium. Subsequently, when Rome itself was founded, it was believed that they were brought there by Aeneas' descendants. The national Penates were in the form of two seated warriors holding spears, originally contained in earthenware jars which still remained at Lavinium. They were sometimes identified with other pairs of gods, the Dioscuri and the Cabiri.

Peneius The god of the river which flowed through the vale of Tempe in northern Thessaly. He was a son of Oceanus and Tethys; a nymph called Creusa bore him a son, Hypseus, and three daughters, Cyrene, Daphne, and Stilbe.

Peneleos A Theban leader during the Trojan War. He acted as regent for Tisamenus, king of Thebes, after his father, Polynices' son Thersander, had been killed during the Trojan War in an attack on the Mysians. He himself was killed in battle by Eurypylus.

Penelope *1.* Daughter of a Spartan king, Icarius, and his wife, the nymph Periboea. Her father was unwilling to lose her, and when Tyndareos persuaded him to marry the girl to Odysseus, he did his best to persuade the young man to stay and live in Sparta. When this proved unsuccessful and the young couple departed, he nevertheless rode after them, and Odysseus challenged Penelope to choose between himself and her father. Silently veiling her head, she chose her husband. For the myths associated with her married life, see ODYSSEUS.

Penelope's name is a byword for marital fidelity and patience. She waited more than twenty years for Odysseus' return, keeping her suitors at bay for three years by pretending to weave a shroud for her father-in-law Laertes, and unravelling it secretly every night. When she was at the end of her tether, her husband returned and killed her suitors. He did not reveal himself to her until he felt that it was safe to do so; and even then she accepted him only when he described the special construction of their marriage-bed. They had a son, Telemachus, who was about twenty when Odysseus returned, and now she bore him a second son, Ptoliporthes ('sacker of cities'). After Odysseus' death (according to late writers) Penelope married Telegonus, a son of Odysseus by Circe, and bore him a son, Italus, from whom Italy took its name. Circe made Penelope and Telemachus, whom she herself had married, immortal.

The name Penelope (Greek: 'duck') was sometimes explained by a story that Nauplius, in his anger at the death of his son Palamedes, whom Odysseus had treacherously slain, spread a false report of Odysseus' death: whereupon Penelope tried to drown herself in the sea, but was saved by the ducks.
2. Daughter of Dryops; she was the mother, by Hermes, of Pan.

Penthesilea Queen of the Amazons; a daughter of Ares and the Amazonian Queen Otrere. Having accidentally killed an ally – or her sister Hippolyta – she was purified of the homicide by King Priam of Troy. In consequence, she came to his aid in the Trojan War. The Amazons killed many Greeks in battle, but in the end she herself was killed by Achilles. After he had stripped her of her armour, he gazed on her corpse and fell in love with it. Thersites, however, jeered at Achilles for his sentimentality, whereupon the hero laid him out with a single blow. In later myth a son, Caistus, was attributed to Achilles and Penthesilea.

Pentheus The second (or, according to Pausanias, third) king of Thebes. Pentheus was the son of Cadmus' daughter Agave and of Echion, one of the 'Sown Men'. His reign was short, for he soon fell foul of Dionysus, whose divinity he refused to recognise. In his play the *Bacchants* (Bacchae), Euripides shows how the young Pentheus arrogantly flung Dionysus into jail but was then inveigled by him into wanting to go up Mt. Cithaeron and spy on the Maenads, whom he suspected of sexual licence. While the women of his family, under the influence of Bacchic frenzy, roamed the mountain with the Maenads, Pentheus, disguised as a woman, climbed a tree to watch their revels. His mother and aunts saw him there and, thinking in their madness that he was a lion, tore him to pieces which they scattered far and wide. In this way Dionysus was revenged on Pentheus for his unbelief and on his mother and aunts because they had scorned their sister Semele, who was Dionysus' mother. The women were exiled from Thebes.

Penthilus Son of Orestes and Erigone 2.

Perdix see DAEDALUS.

Pergamus The youngest son of Neoptolemus and Andromache; the conqueror of Teuthrania in Mysia and founder of the city of Pergamum.

Periboea or **Eriboea** 1. Daughter of Al-

cathous; the mother, by Telamon, of Aias 1.
2. see ICARIUS 1.
3. Daughter of Hipponous. She was Oeneus' second wife and the mother of Tydeus and Olenias.

Periclymenus 1. Son of Poseidon who helped in the defence of Thebes against the Seven. He killed one of them, Parthenopaeus, by hurling a rock on him, and tried to kill Amphiaraus, who was, however, swallowed up by the earth.
2. Son of Neleus; an Argonaut. His grandfather Poseidon gave him the power to change his shape. When Heracles attacked Pylos, Periclymenus used this gift, assuming the shape of an eagle and tearing at the hero's face. But Heracles shot him with a poisoned arrow.

Perieres 1. Son of Aeolus and Enarete. After the death of Polycaon he became king of Messenia. He married Perseus' daughter Gorgophone and had two sons, Aphareus and Leucippus.
2. The charioteer of Menoeceus. See CLYMENUS 2.

Perigune When Theseus killed Perigune's father Sinis, she became his mistress and bore him Melanippus.

Perimede Daughter of Amphitryon and wife of Licymnius.

Periphetes Son of Hephaestus or of Poseidon. He was lame and became an outlaw, terrorising travellers in the region of Epidaurus with his bronze club, so that he came to be called Corynetes, 'bludgeoner'. Theseus killed him and thereafter carried Periphetes' club himself.

Pero see MELAMPUS.

Perseis or **Perse** see HELIOS.

Persephone or **Persephassa** (Latin: *Pros-*

erpina) The daughter of Zeus and Demeter; later known simply as Kore ('Virgin'). As the wife of Zeus' brother Hades, she became queen of the Underworld, but she was originally a goddess of grain, like her mother. To the Greeks the fertility of the ground was closely associated with death, and the seed-corn was buried in the dark during the summer months before the autumnal sowing. This return of life after burial is symbolised in the myth of Persephone's abduction and return, and gave rise to the ritual of the Eleusinian Mysteries, in which the worshippers believed that the restoration of the goddess to the upper world promised the faithful their own resurrection from death.

Persephone was exceptionally beautiful, and her mother Demeter shut her away in her favourite island of Sicily to keep her safe. There, in the woods near Henna, Persephone used to pass her time with the Oceanids. But one day, when they were picking flowers together, Persephone wandered apart from the rest and saw a large dark-blue narcissus, placed there by Zeus, who had accepted his brother Hades' request to marry the girl and, in the face of Demeter's known objections, hoped to trick her into accepting an accomplished fact. Now that Persephone was safely alone, Hades rose in his chariot from the earth, seized her despite her screams and carried her off. The nymph Cyane, who witnessed the abduction, protested in vain, and in her grief melted into water. When Demeter eventually discovered Persephone's whereabouts, she could only contrive to win her back on the condition that while in her wooer's house she had eaten nothing. Ascalaphus, however, was able to tell Hades that the girl had eaten a few pomegranate seeds, so Hades claimed his rights as husband. A compromise was arranged, however, and Hermes brought Persephone and Demeter before the throne of Zeus, who decreed that Persephone must pass four (or, some

said, six) months a year with Hades as queen of the Underworld, and the rest of the time on earth.

Persephone seems to have accepted her role as queen of the dead, for in the myths she always acts in concert with her husband. Indeed, according to certain sources, she was not Demeter's daughter at all, but the child of Styx, and had always been queen of the dead. She plays little part in other myths (but see ADONIS; PIRITHOUS; ZAGREUS), but fulfilled an important role in religious ritual in many places, especially at Eleusis, Thebes, and Megara, and in Sicily and Arcadia.

Perses *1.* A Titan of outstanding wisdom, son of Crius and Eurybia. He married Asteria, who bore him the goddess Hecate.

2. Son of Helios. After the theft of the Golden Fleece from Colchis, he usurped Aeetes' throne. However he was subsequently killed by his niece Medea or by her son Medus.

3. The eldest son of Perseus and Andromeda, whom they left in the care of Cepheus and Cassiopea. When he grew up he won himself a great empire, and the Persian nation was named after him.

Perseus Son of Zeus and Danae. Perseus was born in a bronze tower, or a tower fitted with doors of bronze, in which his grandfather Acrisius, king of Argos, had imprisoned his mother, terrified by an oracle which declared that her son would cause his death. Zeus saw Danae, and desired her. In order to take possession of her body, he turned into a shower of golden rain, which fell into her lap and made her pregnant. When the baby Perseus was born, the horrified Acrisius planned to end the lives of his daughter and her dangerous child, and launched them on the sea in a chest. But Zeus protected them and they came safely ashore on the island of Seriphos.

There they were found by a kind

fisherman, Dictys ('net'), who happened to be the brother of the local king Polydectes. Perseus grew up in the fisherman's house, but when he was a young man, Polydectes fell in love with his mother Danae and persecuted her with demands of marriage. Perseus, however, proved a formidable defender of his mother, and Polydectes sought an opportunity to get him out of the way. His plan was to raise a tax of horses from the islanders (according to alternative versions this was intended for a bridegift he meant to offer for the hand of Hippodameia of Pisa). Now Perseus had no horses, but offered to procure him anything else he could; this suited Polydectes' scheme for ridding himself of the impediment to his marriage, and so he told Perseus to fetch the head of the Gorgon Medusa – a seemingly impossible task.

Athena, however, who hated Medusa for making love to Poseidon in a temple dedicated to herself, appeared to Perseus and, presenting him with a bronze shield, told him how to proceed. He first had to go to the cave of the Graiae, three old hags living in the mountains of Africa who shared but a single eye and a single tooth, both of which they passed between them from hand to hand. Since they were the Gorgons' sisters, it was necessary for Perseus to persuade them to help him, and this he did by a trick: putting out his hand for the eye as it passed around, he seized it, and then demanded to know the way to the Gorgons and to certain nymphs, from whom Athena had told him to seek help for his exploit. When the Graiae had reluctantly divulged their information, Perseus flung their eye into Lake Tritonis, to prevent them from warning their sisters of his approach. The nymphs, who lived nearby, gave Perseus three important aids for his task: a cap of invisibility, a pair of winged shoes, and a wallet into which he was to put Medusa's head. As he left the nymphs, he was met by

Hermes who, admiring his handsome looks, presented him with an extra gift, a curved sword made of 'adamant' (a hard metal, such as iron); and, according to some accounts it was he, not the nymphs, who gave him the winged shoes.

Using these shoes and the cap of invisibility, Perseus flew over the stream of Ocean to its shore where the Gorgons lived. He found them asleep, and, keeping clear of Stheno and Euryale who were immortal, advanced towards Medusa, watching her reflection in his bronze shield: for if he had looked directly at the face of the Gorgon he would have been turned instantly to stone. Then he struck off her head with Hermes' sword and hid it in his wallet. Medusa's sisters, who awoke and flew at him, were foiled in their pursuit when he made himself invisible, and so he escaped.

In Ovid's version Perseus, after being buffeted by storm-winds, returned to Greece by way of the territory of Atlas, who, hearing that his father was Zeus, tried to turn him away by force, since Themis had warned him that a son of Zeus would one day steal the apples of the Hesperides. Ovid adds that Perseus, in his anger, petrified Atlas with a view of Medusa's head, turning him into a vast mountain on which the sky rests (a story in conflict with the usual version of Heracles' quest for the golden apples, in which Atlas was still alive – several generations later).

Perseus passed over Egypt, where he saw his ancestors' home at Chemmis. Then, as he flew along the coast of Phoenicia, he glanced down and beheld Andromeda, chained to a rock to be devoured by a sea-monster, for the oracle of Ammon had commanded that she should undergo this fate as a penalty for the boastfulness of her mother Cassiopea.

Her father Cepheus, king of Joppa, declared that he would offer her in marriage to Perseus with his kingdom as dowry, if only he would get rid of the monster. And so, as it swam up to eat Andromeda, Perseus attacked the beast and slew it with Hermes' sword, and plans for their wedding proceeded. Phineus, the king's brother and Andromeda's former betrothed, tried to disrupt the wedding feast, and Perseus was forced to turn him and his host of followers into stone by means of Medusa's head. Andromeda bore him a son, Perses, whom Perseus left behind with Cepheus, designating him heir to the throne of Joppa, when, a year later, he took Andromeda back to Seriphos.

There he found that Danae and Dictys had been forced by Polydectes' persecution to take sanctuary in a temple. He confronted Polydectes, who poured scorn on his claim to have brought back Medusa's head : whereupon Perseus displayed it to him, and he was turned to stone. Now that Perseus' task was accomplished, Athena left him, with instructions that he should give the weapons back to Hermes, to be returned by him to their various owners. Perseus left Dictys as king of Seriphos and, with Andromeda, went to Argos, the kingdom of his grandfather Acrisius. But Acrisius, hearing of his approach, fled to Larissa in Thessaly to avoid the fulfilment of the oracle that a son of his daughter would kill him. Perseus followed him – with no evil intensions – and arrived in time to take part in funeral games which the Thessalian king Teutamides was holding for his father. When, however, Perseus threw a discus, he accidentally hit his grandfather, thus fulfilling the prophecy.

On returning to Argos, Perseus found that Proetus (the twin brother of Acrisius and according to one tradition Perseus' real father) had usurped his brother's throne; Perseus killed him by turning him into stone, and became king of Argos himself. But because he had killed its former monarch, he preferred

not to rule the kingdom, exchanging it for Tiryns, the realm of Megapenthes.

Hyginus, however, gave a different version of all these mythical events, according to which Polydectes was a kindly man who married Danae and brought Perseus up in the service of Athena, and Acrisius was accidentally killed by Perseus on Seriphos at Polydectes' funeral games. Hyginus also indicated, here in agreement with Ovid, that Perseus was killed by Megapenthes, in vengeance for the death of his father Proetus. The usual story, however, was that Perseus and Andromeda ruled Tiryns for many years, and founded new cities in neighbouring regions of the Argolid, at Mycenae and Midea. Andromeda produced five more sons, Alcaeus, Sthenelus, Heleius, Mestor, and Electryon, and a daughter, Gorgophone ('slaying of the Gorgon').

Although myths about Perseus were very well known and formed the subject of a number of lost plays, surviving traditions about his end are sparse. It was said that Perseus quarrelled with the followers of Dionysus, whose worship was thought to have reached the Argolid at this time. He was also reported to have thrown an image of Dionysus into the lake at Lerna and to have fought a battle with certain 'women from the sea'. Athena placed Perseus and Andromeda, and the sea-monster, and Cepheus and Cassiopea in the sky as constellations.

Peteos Son of Orneus. *See* MENESTHEUS.

Peucetius An Illyrian, the son of Lycaon. He conquered southern Italy.

Phaea *see* THESEUS.

Phaedra Daughter of Minos and Pasiphae. Although Theseus had abandoned or lost Minos' elder daughter Ariadne, once Minos was dead her brother

Deucalion made an alliance with the Athenian king and gave him another of his sisters, Phaedra, as his wife. Some time thereafter Phaedra fell violently in love with Hippolytus, who was Theseus' son by an earlier marriage with an Amazon queen and had become the ruler of Troezen, the kingdom inherited by Theseus from his grandfather Pittheus. When Phaedra saw that Hippolytus was horrified by her declaration of love, she denounced him to his father, alleging that he had tried to seduce her. She then hanged herself; and Hippolytus, cursed by Theseus, was soon dead as well. Phaedra bore Theseus two sons, Demophon and Acamas.

Phaenon A beautiful boy whom Prometheus made. Zeus placed him in the sky as a planet (Jupiter).

Phaestus A Cretan, the son of the bronze man Talos. He gave his name to a city in Crete.

Phaethon *1*. Son of Helios, the Sun-god, and of the Oceanid Clymene. As a youth, he was taunted by his friend Epaphus, who declared that Helios was not his father at all. Clymene, by this time married to Merops, king of Egypt, sent him to Helios' palace in the East, at the rising of the sun. After a long journey he arrived, and Helios, in order to show his fatherly affection, offered to grant him any wish he might choose to express. Phaethon demanded to drive the sun-chariot across the sky for a day. Helios was horrified by the rash request, but had to comply.

The four horses were yoked to the gleaming chariot, and Phaethon took the reins. His father had given him anxious instructions, but, once in the sky, the boy lost his head, and the horses ran away with him. They first blazed a great gash across the heavens, which became the Milky Way. Then, as Phaethon became more and more dizzy, they plunged downwards and scorched the earth, causing a drought and turning the skins of the equatorial peoples black. Alarmed to behold the destruction that Phaethon was causing, Zeus flung a thunderbolt which hurled the boy out of the chariot. His blazing corpse fell into the River Eridanus. There his sisters, the nymphs, who had seen his fall, stood on the banks of the river and wept for him. They were turned to poplars, which are still common along the shores of that river (now the Po). Cycnus, king of the Ligurians, who was a kinsman of his, also came to mourn and was turned into a swan (which is the meaning of his name): and the 'swan song' is derived from his dirge. Some said that Zeus sent the flood to cool the earth after this disaster, and it was believed that the constellation of Auriga, the charioteer, commemorated Phaethon.

2. Son of Eos (Dawn). Aphrodite carried him off and made him her priest at a Syrian temple. Adonis was one of his descendants.

Phaethusa *1*. Daughter of Helios.
2. Daughter of Danaus, and the mother, by Hermes, of Myrtilus.

Phegeus *1*. A king of Psophis in Arcadia (his city was known earlier as Erymanthus). He had two sons, Temenus and Axion, and a daughter, Arsinoe or Alphesiboea. When Alcmaeon, after killing his mother Eriphyle, came to him to seek refuge, Phegeus purified him and married him to Arsinoe, to whom Alcmaeon gave Harmonia's wedding gifts as a present. Later Alcmaeon had to leave Psophis and Arsinoe owing to the anger of the Furies; when he tried to trick Phegeus into giving him Harmonia's wedding gifts, Phegeus' sons ambushed Alcmaeon and killed him. Arsinoe, who had still loved him, cursed her father for the act, and Alcmaeon's sons by his last wife, Callirrhoe, avenged him by killing Phegeus and his wife and sons.

2. A Trojan, the son of Dares. Diomedes killed him.

Phemius The bard of Odysseus' household in Ithaca.

Pheres *1.* Son of Cretheus, king of Iolcus, and Tyro. When Pelias usurped the throne of Iolcus, Pheres and his brother Amythaon fled, and he founded a new city near Iolcus which he named Pherae. He had two sons by Minyas' daughter Periclymene, Admetus and Lycurgus. He supported Jason against Pelias, and sent Admetus in the *Argo*. After the *Argo's* return, he abdicated in Admetus' favour, but, when it was time for Admetus to die, he refused to volunteer as a substitute for him. His son Lycurgus became king of Nemea.
2. Son of Jason and Medea.

Philammon A famous minstrel, son of Apollo and Chione, Daedalion's daughter; he was thus the half-brother of Autolycus. Philammon served at his father's shrine at Delphi, and won many musical contests there. He loved a nymph from Parnassus named Argiope, but when she was pregnant by him he refused to receive her in his house. When, therefore, their son Thamyris was born, she took him far away and brought him up in Thrace. When the forces of Phlegyas, king of Orchomenus, attacked Delphi, Philammon led a force of Argives in its defence, and was killed in the battle.

Philemon *see* BAUCIS.

Philoctetes Son of Poeas (*poia, poa* 'grass'), a shepherd or king of Malis, and of Demonassa. Either Poeas or Philoctetes was passing by on Mount Oeta, looking for his sheep, when the dying Heracles lay in agony upon the pyre he had built there. As none of his followers would light their master's pyre while he was alive, Heracles offered the passer-

by his bow and poisoned arrows in exchange for this service. Poeas may have served with Heracles as an Argonaut.

Philoctetes, who had been one of Helen's suitors, took seven shiploads of archers from Malis to the Trojan War. When the fleet reached Tenedos, it was decided that sacrifice must be offered to Apollo on the island of Chryse, and Philoctetes guided the commanders of the expedition to the place. While they were sacrificing there, however, a water-snake bit Philoctetes' foot, and the wound festered and would not heal. Some authorities recorded that the snake was the guardian of the shrine, or that it had been sent by Hera because of the help Philoctetes had given to Heracles; others that it was not a snake which fell on to his foot, but one of the arrows poisoned with the Hydra's blood. So great was Philoctetes' pain that he would constantly cry out, uttering curses and oaths which terrified the army; moreover the stench of the festering wound was unendurable. At Odysseus' suggestion, therefore, Philoctetes was marooned on the island of Lemnos, while the fleet continued to Troy, including his contingent which passed under the command of Medon, a bastard son of Oileus. During his lonely stay on Lemnos, Philoctetes kept himself alive only thanks to his bow and arrows, which never missed their target. He lived on the birds and wild animals he shot; and his wound grew no better.

Ten years later Odysseus captured the Trojan prophet Helenus, who among other things told him that Troy could never fall to the Greeks unless Philoctetes could be persuaded to come and fight with Heracles' bow. Knowing how greatly Philoctetes must hate him for having proposed his abandonment, Odysseus resorted to a stratagem. Taking with him to Lemnos Achilles' son Neoptolemus, who had not been with the Greek army at the outset, he arranged that the youth should offer Philoctetes safe passage home to Greece. Philoctetes responded by entrusting his bow to Neoptolemus, who then revealed to him the plot to take him to Troy. According to Sophocles' play *Philoctetes*, Neoptolemus began to feel ashamed of his part in the trick and proposed to keep his word to the wounded man and send him back to Greece after all, but Heracles, now a god, appeared and ordered Philoctetes to go and fight at Troy, where he would be cured. Other versions of the story named Diomedes as Odysseus' companion and made no reference to Heracles' intervention.

At Troy the physician Machaon, or Podalirius, or both of them, cured the wound of Philoctetes, and he killed Paris with one of the poisoned arrows. According to the *Odyssey* Philoctetes returned home safely, but other sources asserted that he was driven by storms to southern Italy where he founded the city of Crimissa near Croton; and there, at a shrine he himself built, he dedicated his weapons to Apollo as protector of travellers.

Philoetius Odysseus' faithful cowherd in Ithaca, who helped Eumaeus in the defeat of the suitors.

Philomela Daughter of Pandion, king of Athens. *See* TEREUS.

Philomelus *see* IASION; DEMETER.

Philonoe Wife of Bellerophon.

Philonome *see* CYCNUS 2; TENES.

Philyra Daughter of Oceanus and Tethys, whom the god Cronos found in Thessaly as he looked for the infant Zeus whom his wife Rhea had concealed. Cronos took on the appearance of a horse, either to escape Rhea's notice or because Philyra, in order to avoid him, had assumed the form of a mare. When her baby was born, Philyra was so shocked to see a creature in the form of a

Centaur that she prayed the gods to change her shape: Zeus then turned her into a lime tree – which is what her name means. Her son was Chiron, the first and best of the Centaurs. In another version of the myth Philyra did not become a tree but eventually took up her dwelling in Chiron's cave on Mount Pelion and helped him to educate the Greek heroes.

Phineus *1.* Brother of Cepheus; Andromeda's uncle. *See* PERSEUS.
2. A king of Salmydessus in Thrace and a soothsayer. He is variously described as a son of Poseidon, or of Agenor, king of Tyre, or of the latter's son Phoenix. When the Argonauts came to his home on their way to Colchis, they found him a pathetic figure, not only blind, but half-starved because the pestilential Harpies snatched up his food and fouled his table. He was rescued from this predicament by Calais and Zetes (the Boreades), who chased off the Harpies; and in return he told the Argonauts how their enterprise was destined to turn out.

How Phineus came to be afflicted in this way is not clear. According to one well-known version he was related to Calais and Zetes, having married as his first wife their sister Cleopatra. When she died, he married a Scythian woman, Idaea, daughter of King Dardanus, who ill-treated Cleopatra's sons Pandion and Plexippus, accusing them falsely of trying to seduce her. As a result either Phineus or Idaea blinded and imprisoned the boys; according to the former version, Zeus, to punish him for his unjust deed, offered Phineus the choice of death or blindness, and he chose blindness. Helios who, as god of the sun, resented Phineus' preference for long life over the power of sight, then assailed Phineus further by plaguing him with the Harpies. (There were also traditions that it was Helios rather then Zeus who blinded him – or that the Argonauts were responsible.) Some said that the Argonauts rescued the sons of Cleopatra, but did not themselves punish Idaea, preferring to send her back to her native Scythia, where her father, hearing of her treacherous behaviour, killed her. A further version of Phineus' story asserts that he was punished by Poseidon for telling Phrixus the way to Colchis. It was also asserted that Phineus himself, rather than his food, was carried off by the Harpies, who deposited him in Scythia. Yet another account maintained that his first wife Cleopatra did not die before he remarried, but was then imprisoned together with her sons. Calais and Zetes freed them all and killed Phineus who tried to resist. Whereupon Cleopatra, now queen of Salmydessus, returned Idaea to her father.

Yet another version of Phineus' story made him a servant of Apollo and a prophet (blindness and prophetic skill often went together) who offended Zeus by revealing to men more than was good for them, and was for this reason plagued by the Harpies.

Phlegyans A warlike nation living in Boeotia; see PHLEGYAS.

Phlegyas Son of Ares. Upon the death of Eteocles who was childless, he became king of Orchomenus in Boeotia and gave his name to a warlike tribe in that region. He himself had two children, Ixion and a daughter Coronis, who was the mother of Asclepius by Apollo. As the renown of Asclepius as a healer spread, his grandfather Phlegyas began to persecute him, spying upon his birthplace at Epidaurus and attacking Delphi, whose oracle supported Asclepius' claim to divine parenthood. There Phlegyas killed Philammon, but was subsequently killed by Nycteus and Lycus who were either Thebans or Hyrians. According to an alternative version, Apollo himself shot him as he attacked his temple at Delphi. In Virgil's account, Aeneas saw Phlegyas undergoing torture in Tartarus and crying a warning to all mankind:

'Be warned, learn righteousness, and despise none of the gods!'

Phlogius see AUTOLYCUS 2.

Phobos see DEIMOS.

Phocus 1. The bastard son of Aeacus, king of Aegina, and the Nereid (seanymph) Psamanthe, who appeared to Aeacus in the form of a seal (*phoke*) from which her son derived his name. Since Phocus was a handsome youth of outstanding athletic ability, Endeis, Aeacus' wife, persuaded her own sons Telamon and Peleus to kill him. The two drew lots and Telamon slew him on the sports-field; Aeacus then banished them both. This Phocus is often confused in ancient sources with the second.
2. Son of Ornytion (who was the son of Sisyphus), or of Poseidon. He emigrated from Corinth, and founded and named the kingdom of Phocis near Mount Parnassus. When Antiope, whom Dionysus had driven mad, wandered into his kingdom, Phocus cured her of her frenzy and married her. It was they who were probably the parents of Panopeus, Crisus, and Naubolus, though their parentage is also attributed to the other Phocus. He and Antiope were buried together at Tithorea, where the people believed that they could ensure a good harvest by sprinkling the grave with soil from the graves of Amphion and Zethus.

Phoebe ('bright') 1. A Titaness, daughter of Uranus and Gaia. By Coeus she was the mother of Leto and Asteria. According to Aeschylus, she was the third protectress of the Delphic Oracle, after Gaia and Themis.
2. Daughter of Leucippus. See CASTOR and POLYDEUCES.
3. Daughter of Tyndareos and Leda.
4. A late name for Artemis.

Phoebus ('bright one') A late name for Apollo.

Phoenix *1*. The eponym of Phoenicia; a son of Agenor and Telephassa. He was sometimes said to be the father of Phineus, Europa, and Adonis.

2. Son of Amyntor, king of Ormenium. His mother Cleobule persuaded Phoenix to seduce Amyntor's mistress and thus turn her affection away from Amyntor. When, however, Phoenix spent a night with the girl, Amyntor found out and placed him under a curse, asking the Furies to deny him children, a prayer which was fulfilled. Phoenix wished to kill his father, but did not do so, and instead, escaping from his room where his kinsmen were guarding him, fled the country. (In a lost play Euripides asserted that Phoenix, though innocent of seducing Amyntor's mistress, was blinded by him and later cured by Chiron at Peleus' request.) He went to the court of Peleus in Phthia, where he was well received and made king of the Dolopians. After taking part in the Calydonian boar-hunt, he was charged by Peleus with the training of the young Achilles in the use of arms. Later he accompanied Odysseus to Scyros to persuade the youth to go to Troy, and then he himself, despite his age, took part in the expedition as Achilles' lieutenant. During Achilles' absence from battle owing to his feud with Agamemnon, Phoenix remained in action and was a member of the deputation which offered Achilles full compensation and an apology from Agamemnon. Achilles' refusal to accept this offer deeply grieved him, as he had always regarded him as a son. After the fruitless deputation he remained with Achilles, and when the war was over returned home with Achilles' son Neoptolemus, but died on the journey.

Pholus *see* CENTAURS.

Phorbas *1*. A Lapith, the son of Lapithes, or of his son Triopas, or of another. His home was variously ascribed to northern Thessaly or Elis. He took part in the battle with the Centaurs that broke out at Pirithous' wedding. He was also said to have migrated to Rhodes, where he rid the island of snakes. His attribution to Elis permitted the belief that he was the father of Augeas.

2. A Phlegyan of Panopeus in Boeotia, who terrorised travellers to Delphi by challenging them to box with him and then killing them. However Apollo came in the guise of a wayfarer and put him to death.

Phorcys One of the 'Old Men of the Sea'. His parentage was attributed to Pontus (Sea) or Nereus, and Gaia (Earth). His monstrous sister Ceto bore him a strange progeny: the Gorgons, the Graiae, Echidna, Ladon, and perhaps the Sirens, Tritons, and Hesperides. He was also said to be the father of Scylla (by Cratis) and of Thoosa.

Phoroneus Son of the River Inachus and the Oceanid Melia. Phoroneus was claimed as the mythical founder of Argos, which he called Phoronea. A nymph, Teledice, who was loved by Zeus, bore him Apis and Niobe (according to another tradition Niobe was the wife, not the daughter, of Phoroneus), and his wife Cerdo presented him with a son, Car, who became king of Megara. The Argives credited Phoroneus with the discovery of fire, and kept an eternal flame burning in his memory. He was also believed to have inaugurated Hera's great sanctuary the Heraeum near the city.

Phosphorus ('light-bringer') The morning star personified; the son of Eos (Dawn) and Astraeus or Cephalus.

Phrasius A Cypriot seer. *See* BUSIRIS.

Phrixus Phrixus and Helle were the children of Athamas, king of Orchomenus,

and the cloud-nymph Nephele. After
Nephele left him, Athamas married Ino,
who bade her husband obey an oracle
which she pretended came from Delphi,
ordering that Phrixus should be sacrificed to Zeus. Athamas was unwilling
to kill his son. According to one version,
however, Phrixus volunteered to die. As
the king was preparing to cut Phrixus'
throat, there appeared a fabulous ram,
which Nephele had sent to rescue her
child. The ram had a fleece of spun gold
and could talk. It told Phrixus to mount
its back, and Helle, whom Ino likewise
wished ill, joined him. It then rose in
the air and flew away.

As the ram flew over the sea dividing
Europe from Asia, Helle fell off into the
straits, which were thereafter called the
Hellespont. The ram carried Phrixus on
to the East, coming finally to land at
Aea, the capital of Aeetes' kingdom of
Colchis, which lay at the eastern end of
the Black Sea. Aeetes welcomed Phrixus,
marrying him to his daughter Chalciope; and Phrixus, acting either on the
ram's own instructions or his mother's,
sacrificed the animal to Zeus. He placed
the fleece in Ares' grove, where a fire-
breathing serpent protected it. When,
however, Aeetes was warned by an
oracle that a Greek stranger would cause
his death, he put Phrixus to death (according to another account, however,
he died of old age). His four sons by
Chalciope, Argus, Phrontis, Melas, and
Cytissorus, escaped from Aea on a raft,
and after its wreck drifted on a beam to
the mythical island of Ares, or Dia,
where the Argonauts shortly afterwards
found them and took them back to Colchis as guides and helpers. When Jason
fled with the fleece, they escaped a
second time.

Phronime see BATTUS _1_.

Phrontis see PHRIXUS.

Phylacus King of Phylace in southern
Thessaly. His parents were Deion of
Phocis and Diomede; he married
Clymene who bore him Iphiclus and
Alcimede, mother of Jason. See MELAM-
PUS.

Phylas _1_. A king of the Thesprotians.
When Heracles was staying in Calydon
with his father-in-law King Oeneus, he
made war on Phylas to help Oeneus,
and captured the city of Ephyra. There
Heracles seduced Phylas' daughter Astyoche or Astydamia, who bore him Tlepolemus, a Rhodian king.
_2_. A king of the Dryopes of Mount
Parnassus who, because of his attacks
on the Delphic Oracle, was assailed and
defeated by Heracles. Heracles then enslaved the Dryopes to Apollo, but many
of them found their way to Asine in the
eastern Peloponnese. Phylas' daughter
bore Heracles a son, Antiochus.
_3_. Father of Polymele; whether the same
as either of the above is uncertain.

Phyleus Son of Augeas; he quarrelled
with his father at the time of Heracles'
cleansing of the stables, and had to flee
from Elis. He went to the island of
Dulichium (now Leucas) where he
founded a kingdom. Years later Heracles
returned to Elis, deposed the aged Augeas,
and placed Phyleus on his father's throne;
but Phyleus did not stay long, preferring
to return to Dulichium. He married a
daughter of Tyndareos, Timandra, who,
having deserted Echemus in his favour,
bore him a son, Meges.

Phyllis Daughter of King Phylleus of
Thrace; she is connected in myths with
both of Theseus' sons, see ACAMAS; DE-
MOPHON.

Phyllius see CYCNUS _4_.

Phytalus An Athenian who welcomed
Demeter into his home on her wanderings, and was consequently rewarded by
her with the gift of the fig tree.

Picus There were two distinct traditions about Picus. The first treated him as an ancient Italian king and the founder of Laurentum. He was considered to be the son of Saturn (or Stercutus), the husband of the nymph Canens, and the father of Faunus. There was a story that Picus was changed into a woodpecker (which is the meaning of his name) through the jealousy of the witch Circe ('hawk'), who was angered by his refusal to respond to her advances. According to the other tradition Picus was a country god who, possessing the power to change his shape, preferred the form of Mars' sacred bird, the woodpecker. He had prophetic powers, and used them to give oracles at one of Mars' shrines, sitting on a wooden column. Picus and Faunus were once lured into a trap by King Numa Pompilius, who introduced wine into their drinking water. They became very drunk and were easily captured; they changed their shape to foil him, but at last agreed to tell him how to bring Jupiter down from heaven (see FAUNUS). Picus was also said to have guided the Piceni, an eastern Italian people, to new homes – this was regarded as an explanation of their name; and there was a tradition that he helped the she-wolf to feed Romulus and Remus.

Pielus Son of Neoptolemus and Andromache.

Pierides *1. see* MUSES.
2. see PIERUS.

Pierus A Macedonian king who gave his name to Mount Pierus, lying to the north of Olympus. He was king of Pella and his father was the Thessalian Magnes. He learnt about the Muses from an oracle in Thrace and introduced their cult into the region. His wife Evippe had nine daughters (the Pierides); these girls practised the arts, at which they became so proficient that

they challenged the Muses to a contest. The Muses turned them into jackdaws for their presumption. However the Muse Clio bore Pierus a son, Hyacinthus; and his son Oeagrus married another Muse, Calliope, who bore him, according to one tradition, Orpheus and Linus, though their parentage was variously ascribed.

Pilumnus *see* DAUNUS *1*.

Pimplea *see* DAPHNIS.

Pinacus *see* POLYDORUS.

Pirithous A king of the Lapiths of Thessaly and a close friend of Theseus. He was Zeus' son by Ixion's wife Dia. He succeeded Ixion on the throne of Thessaly, but was soon involved in a war with the Centaurs who, as Ixion's sons, claimed a share of his kingdom. After a fierce struggle the dispute was settled amicably, the Centaurs being given Mount Pelion as their land.

Pirithous had heard much of the fame of Theseus, king of Athens; and he therefore tested the hero by making a cattle raid upon Marathon. Theseus pursued him and caught up with him, and a battle was about to take place when the pair suddenly embraced each other and swore a pact of lifelong friendship. They served together in the Calydonian boar-hunt and, according to some accounts, in the expedition of the Argonauts. They also conducted a joint expedition against the Amazons, in which Theseus carried off an Amazon queen as his prize.

Pirithous now proposed to marry Hippodamia (or Deidamia), daughter of Butes. He invited to his wedding a great array of guests including Theseus and Nestor of Pylos. He also invited the Centaurs of Pelion, whom he now believed to be his friends. They, however, being unused to wine, got violently drunk and attempted to carry off the bride and her Thessalian bridesmaids. A fierce battle ensued in which many were killed on either side, but the Lapiths finally proved the victors. The Centaurs were then driven out of Thessaly and took refuge in the Peloponnese, with the single exception of Chiron, who had taken no part in the fight and stayed on Mount Pelion until his death.

Hippodamia bore Pirithous a son, Polypoetes, who led a contingent of forty ships to Troy. When she and Theseus' wife Phaedra died, the two widowers resolved to wed daughters of Zeus. Theseus chose Helen, and Pirithous helped him to kidnap her from Sparta. Since, however, she was still too young to marry, they shut her up in the stronghold of Aphidnae in Attica, under the care of Aethra. Then they went in quest of a bride for Pirithous. He, however, in defiance of the gods, chose Persephone, wife of Hades. Pirithous and Theseus descended to the Underworld through the passageway at Taenarum in Laconia. They succeeded in forcing Charon to ferry them over the Styx, and somehow passed the guardian hound Cerberus. Then they openly demanded Persephone from her husband. Hades gave them chairs to sit in, but once they were seated the pair stuck fast and moved no more, for they were chairs of forgetfulness. Heracles, it was said, subsequently released Theseus and brought him back to the upper world, but when he grasped Pirithous, the ground shook and he had to give up.

Pitane A Spartan nymph whom Poseidon raped. She bore Evadne 2.

Pittheus Son of Pelops and Hippodamia of Elis. He and his brother Troezen settled in the Argolid where Aetius, a grandson of Poseidon, was the ruler. When Aetius was dead, Pittheus and Troezen held joint rule for a time until Troezen too died and Pittheus, left as sole king, founded a city which he named after his brother. Pittheus was a shrewd and learned man, and when Aegeus, king of Athens, came to him with an oracle he could not interpret, he understood it to foretell that Aegeus' son would be a great hero. He therefore made Aegeus drunk and put him to bed with his daughter Aethra. In due course Aethra bore Theseus (though it was also commonly said that Poseidon was Theseus' real father). Theseus grew up at Pittheus' court and was named heir to his throne. When, in later years, he became king of Athens instead, he sent his son Hippolytus to live with Pittheus at Troezen and succeed to the throne of that city.

Pityreus A king of Epidaurus. See DEIPHONTES.

Pleiades The seven daughters of the Titan Atlas and the Oceanid Pleione. Their names were Maia (mother of Hermes by Zeus), Electra (mother of Dardanus and Iasion by Zeus), Taygete (mother of Lacedaemon by Zeus), Celaeno (mother of Lycus by Poseidon), Alcyone (mother of Hyrieus, Hyperenor, and Aethusa by Poseidon), Sterope (mother of Oenomaus by Ares), and Merope (who bore Glaucus to a mortal, Sisyphus). Some sources asserted that Electra married a mortal, Corythus, who may have been the father of her sons. According to another story, Artemis turned Taygete into a hind in order to help her to avoid Zeus' attentions, and this was the Cerynitian hind which Heracles hunted for a year and then brought back to Eurystheus.

The Pleiades were so distressed at the death of their sisters the Hyades that they all killed themselves, and Zeus placed them in the sky as a cluster of seven stars. It was also said, however, that Zeus turned them into stars to save them and their mother Pleione from Orion, who had chased them for seven years. He too became a constellation which appears to be ever pursuing the

Pleiades. One of the seven stars shines fainter than the rest; it was believed to be either Merope, ashamed of her passion for a mere mortal, or Electra, grieving for the fate of her son's city of Troy. The name Pleiades is derived from a Greek word meaning 'to sail', because the seven stars are visible during the summer months, comprising the season which the ancients reserved for navigation.

Pleisthenes He was either a son of Pelops or a son of Pelops' son Atreus (in which case he, rather than Atreus, was thought of as the father of Agamemnon and Menelaus); and his wife was either Aerope or Cleolla, daughter of Dias.

Pleisthenes was also sometimes said to be a bastard son of Thyestes and Aerope and the brother of Tantalus. Another Pleisthenes, a son of Atreus, was believed to have been killed by Thyestes.

Plexippus *1*. Son of Thestius, slain by his nephew Meleager.

2. Son of Phineus, king of Salmydessus.

Pluto *1*. A name of Hades (literally 'rich one').

2. A Titaness, the mother of Tantalus.

Plutus Son of Demeter and Iasion. After the wedding of Cadmus and Harmonia, Iasion made love to the goddess in a field in Crete. Plutus' name means 'wealth' and he protected the abundance given by fertile fields. He was worshipped with his mother at Eleusis. There was a tradition that Plutus was blinded by Zeus to make him impartial in his distribution of riches and to prevent him from making the rich even richer. In Aristophanes' play named after him Plutus' sight is restored, so that he may be able to distinguish honest men from the dishonest.

Podalirius ('lily-foot') Son of Asclepius

and Epione; the brother of Machaon. Podalirius and Machaon accompanied the Greek army to Troy, where they acted as surgeons. They also led an army from their kingdom in Thessaly. Podalirius was sometimes believed to be the more competent of the two and to have learnt his art from Machaon, who was older. He was also said to have specialised in medicine, whereas Machaon was more of a surgeon. When Eurypylus, son of Evaemon, was wounded in the fighting at the Greek ships Podalirius was unable to help as he was himself heavily engaged. Podalirius or Machaon cured Philoctetes of the wound in his leg, and enabled him to shoot Paris; then he became a member of the party concealed in the Wooden Horse. He survived the Trojan War. In the company of the prophet Calchas, he travelled to Clarus near Colophon, and later went to Delphi to consult the Pythian Oracle, which bade him live in a place where he would not be injured if the sky fell. He chose the peninsula of the Carian Chersonese in southern Asia Minor – where he had been shipwrecked – since it was surrounded by high mountains. He was rescued from the wreck by a goatherd named Bybassus, after whom he called the city he founded there. He married a king's daughter, Syrna, who had fallen from a roof and been cured by him of her injuries. He also founded a city named Syrnos after her.

Podarces *1*. The younger son of Iphiclus. When his brother Protesilaus was killed at the beginning of the war, Podarces took command of the force from Phylace.

2. The original name of Priam.

Poeas *see* PHILOCTETES.

Polites *1*. Son of Priam and Hecabe. He took part in the Trojan War as a warrior and scout. He was killed by Neoptolemus at the altar of Zeus in Priam's courtyard before the eyes of his parents; Virgil describes his death.

2. A comrade of Odysseus. *See* EUTHY-MUS.

Pollux *see* CASTOR and POLYDEUCES.

Poltys A king of Aenus in Thrace. He entertained Heracles, who then killed his brother Sarpedon.

Polyanax *see* MENESTHEUS.

Polyboea An alternative name for Merope, the wife of king Polybus of Corinth.

Polybotes *see* GIANTS.

Polybus *1.* A king of Corinth, who, since he was childless, adopted Oedipus when he was brought to Corinth as a foundling by a shepherd. His wife's name was Merope.
2. A king of Sicyon the son of Hermes and Chthonophyle, daughter of the eponym of Sicyon. He inherited the throne of Sicyon from his grandfather; he had a daughter, Lysianassa, whom he married to Talaus of Argos. After a long reign he was succeeded by Talaus' son Adrastus, who had taken refuge at his court.

Polycaste Daughter of Nestor; she bathed Telemachus on his visit to Pylos and later married him.

Polydamas Son of the Trojan priest Panthous, he was an able debater and fighter in the Trojan army, and several times gave Hector good advice. When Achilles returned to the battle, he advised Hector to retire into the city. Hector ignored his counsel and was killed.

Polydamna An Egyptian woman, wife of Thon, the governor of the Nile Delta; she was said to have taught Helen the art of medicine.

Polydectes The king of Seriphos who sent Perseus to fetch the Gorgon's head. His parents were Magnes, son of Aeolus, and a Naiad; his brother was Danae's protector Dictys. *See* PERSEUS.

Polydeuces *see* CASTOR.

Polydora Daughter of Peleus and Antigone, daughter of Eurytion. She bore Menestheus to the River Spercheius; and then married Borus, son of Perieres.

Polydorus *1.* A king of Thebes, said to be the only son of Cadmus and Harmonia. According to Apollodorus he succeeded his nephew Pentheus and, after a brief reign, left his throne to his baby son Laius by his wife Nycteis, daughter of Nycteus. Pausanias, on the other hand, names him as Cadmus' direct heir.
2. One of the Epigoni; the son of Hippomedon.
3. Priam's youngest son. According to the *Iliad*, his mother was Laothoe, daughter of king Altes of the Leleges. He was an excellent runner, but Priam, because he loved him best, forbade him to fight in the Trojan War. Achilles, however, slew him, rousing Hector's furious anger. A different tradition, followed by Euripides in his *Hecabe*, makes Polydorus a son of Hecabe. Since his parents wished at least one Trojan prince to survive the war, they sent him to Polymestor, king of the Thracian Bistones, asking him to take charge of the boy, and giving him a quantity of gold as Polydorus' inheritance. However, when Troy fell, Polymestor murdered the boy and took the treasure. But his deed was discovered by Hecabe, who had been brought to his kingdom by Odysseus on his way home. In Euripides' play Polydorus' ghost appeared and told of his murder; then Hecabe found his body on the shore. To avenge her son's death, she lured Polymestor into her tent with the offer of a further sum,

killed his children, and put out his eyes. When Aeneas visited the peninsula of the Thracian Chersonese, intending to found his city there, the tomb of Polydorus was revealed to him because some branches his men picked there bled, and his voice warned them of the inhospitality of the place. So the Trojans, after sacrificing to him, departed.

In yet another version Polydorus was brought up by his sister Ilione – who was Polymestor's wife – together with her own son Deipylus. Then after the war the Greeks bribed Polymestor to kill Polydorus, offering him a great treasure and the hand of Agamemnon's daughter Electra. But when the two children were babies Ilione had exchanged them, keeping the knowledge of their two identities to herself: so Polymestor killed his own son instead. At a later date Polydorus, who believed himself to be Deipylus, went to the Delphic Oracle, which told him that his city had been burnt, his father killed, and his mother enslaved. Finding all well at home, he taxed his mother with the oracle, and was told his true identity; whereupon together they killed Polymestor.

Polyidus An Argive prophet descended from Melampus. He aided Bellerophon to tame Pegasus, and miraculously cured Minos' son Glaucus (see GLAUCUS). From Crete Polyidus went to Megara, where he purified Alcathous of the homicide of his son Callipolis. In one version Minos attacked Megara for harbouring Polyidus, against whom he bore a grudge for not allowing Glaucus to become a seer. Polyidus had a son, Euchenor.

Polymele A mistress of the god Hermes, to whom she bore Eudorus. She married Echecles.

Polymestor King of the Bistones. See POLYDORUS 3.

Polymnia or **Polyhymnia** see MUSES.

Polynices or **Polyneices** ('much strife') The elder son of Oedipus and Jocasta. For the myths associated with his life, see ETEOCLES. In Sophocles' play *Oedipus at Colonus*, Polynices tried to win his blind and banished father's support for his attack on Thebes, claiming that Eteocles had unfairly won the Thebans over to his cause. Oedipus, however, cursed him, arguing that it was Polynices who, as the first of the brothers to rule Thebes, had been responsible for his own expulsion, and praying that, in the forthcoming attack of Polynices' Argive supporters, Thebes might be spared but his two sons might die at each other's hands. Polynices and Argia had a son, Thersander, and perhaps two others, Adrastus and Timeas.

Polyphantes A king of Messenia. See MELAMPUS.

Polyphemus *1.* A Cyclops, the son of Poseidon by the sea-nymph Thoosa. When Odysseus came to his island, identified in later literature with Sicily, and asked Polyphemus for hospitality, telling him that his name was *Outis*, 'Nobody', the monster only laughed at him and then shut him up with his companions inside the cave where he lived and stabled his flocks of sheep and goats. Then, at intervals, he began to devour his Greek prisoners. Odysseus dared not kill him, because the Greeks were quite unable to move the stone blocking the entrance. But he hit on the stratagem of blinding him instead, after first making him drunk with a very potent wine. When Polyphemus appealed to them for help, crying that 'Nobody' was injuring him, the other Cyclopes only laughed. After the blind giant had opened the entrance next morning, the Greeks made their escape strapped to the underside of his sheep. Back on his ship, Odysseus taunted Polyphemus as he sailed away, and was nearly shipwrecked by a massive rock the giant hurled in his direction.

Polyphemus, before his blinding, had a tragi-comic love affair with the nymph Galatea. During this time he was warned by a seer, Telemus, that he would lose his sight to a man called Odysseus. He heedlessly declared that he had already lost his heart to another.

2. An Argonaut from Thessaly. He remained with Heracles when the latter lost Hylas, and founded the city of Cius in Bithynia. He was later killed fighting the Chalybes, a nation of eastern Asia Minor.

Polyphontes A descendant of Heracles who usurped the throne of Messenia. See AEPYTUS *1*.

Polypoetes *1*. The eldest son of Pirithous and Hippodamia; he and Leonteus, grandson of Caeneus, led a Thessalian contingent of forty ships to the Trojan War.

2. A king of Thesprotia; the son of Odysseus and Callidice.

Polyxena Daughter of King Priam of Troy and Hecabe. When the Trojan women were captured after the fall of Troy and distributed to the Greek captains, the ghost of Achilles rose from the tomb and demanded that, as his share of the spoils, Polyxena should be slain on his tomb, so that her shade would be the companion of his own in the Underworld. In consequence Neoptolemus, Achilles' son, duly put her to death. In later times there arose a romantic tale that Achilles had been in love with her during his life, having seen her sacrificing at the temple of Apollo at Thymbra; Hector had prevented their marriage, but after Achilles had killed him, Polyxena went to the temple by arrangement to meet Achilles. There Paris, from a concealed position behind a statue, treacherously shot him, thus gaining revenge for Hector. Euripides alludes to the myth in his *Trojan Women*.

Polyxenus Son of Agasthenes *1*; leader of the Eleans in the Trojan War.

Polyxo *1*. The old nurse of Queen Hypsipyle of Lemnos, skilled in prophecy, who persuaded the other women of the island to kill their husbands; for they had abandoned their wives on account of a stench with which Aphrodite had cursed them for neglecting her rites. When, however, the Argonauts came to Lemnos, Polyxo realised that the Lemnian women could not forever manage the island without male offspring, and at her suggestion the Argonauts were welcomed and remained for a year, providing the women with plenty of children.

2. The widow of Heracles' son Tlepolemus, king of Rhodes, who was killed by Sarpedon in the Trojan War. When Menelaus and Helen landed in Rhodes on their return voyage from Egypt, Polyxo, who blamed her husband's death on Helen since it was she who had caused the Trojan War, told the Rhodian women to burn the ship. Menelaus disguised a slave-girl as Helen and stood her on the deck; the Rhodian women killed her and gave up their attack. In another version of the story Helen took refuge in Rhodes after the death of Menelaus and was hanged on a tree by the Rhodian women, who had disguised themselves, on Polyxo's instructions, as avenging Furies.

Pomona A Roman goddess of fruit and its cultivation (*pomum* 'apple', 'fruit'). The god Vertumnus fell in love with her, but she rejected him. He, since he had the power to change his shape (his name comes from *vertere* 'turn'), transformed himself into an old crone, and spoke on his own behalf so eloquently that, when he reassumed his true form, Pomona gave herself to him after all.

Pompilius *see* NUMA.

Porphyrion *see* GIANTS.

Porsenna, Lars An Etruscan prince, generally said to have been the ruler of Clusium (now Chiusi). He is likely to be mythical rather than historical, since his name is a compilation of two aristocratic titles, *larth* ('a champion') and *purthna* ('leading citizen'). In the legends of the early Roman Republic, he is the principal ally of Tarquinius Superbus, himself an Etruscan, who, after being expelled from the Roman kingship, asked his countrymen to lend him military support to restore him to the throne. According to these stories Porsenna, at the head of a massive confederation, besieged Rome, taking the Janiculum Hill which overlooks the city on the right bank of the Tiber. He was only prevented from capturing Rome by the heroism of Horatius Cocles, who defended the bridge over the Tiber. Subsequently, during a protracted siege, Mucius Scaevola made an attempt on Porsenna's life but killed the wrong man instead, because he was ignorant of the king's appearance. Porsenna, however, was so impressed by Scaevola's courage and determination that he made a treaty with the Romans, agreeing to lift the siege and abandon the cause of Tarquinius Superbus in exchange for a party of Roman hostages, the children of the most eminent citizens. A Roman girl called Cloelia finally achieved Porsenna's total reconciliation to the Romans by another act of signal courage, and he withdrew with his army to Clusium.

Portheus or **Porthaon** A king of Calydon, the son of Agenor and Epicaste. His wife Euryte bore: him Oeneus, Alcathous, Melas and Agrius. Laocoon was said to be his bastard son.

Portunus *see* INO.

Poseidon The principal Greek god of seas and waters, whom the Romans identified with an old Italian water-deity Neptunus (Neptune), investing him with Poseidon's mythology. The name Poseidon (Doric *Poteidan*) seems to mean 'lord (or husband) of Earth', an origin consistent with his common epithet *gaieochos* 'earth-holding'. He is also linked with earthquakes, whence his titles *enosichthon, enosigaios* 'shaker of earth'. The animals chiefly associated with him are horses and bulls.

Poseidon was one of the greatest gods in both cult and myth, and became a frequent artistic subject, being represented as a tall, bearded figure holding a trident (a three-pronged tunny fisherman's spear made by the Cyclopes or the Telchines), and sometimes a fish. He seems to have supplanted a series of older, more peaceful sea-gods, Nereus, Phorcys, and Proteus, the 'Old Men of the Sea', and to have assumed many of their attributes. Poseidon, however, adds a note of violence absent from their myths, since he is often represented as bad-tempered, vindictive, and dangerous. That is to say, he represents the might of the sea-storm, and his activity displays its destructive power.

He was a son of Cronos and Rhea and, according to Hesiod, Zeus' elder brother. Like all his brothers and sisters except Zeus, Poseidon was swallowed at birth by his father, who feared his children's future rivalry (though the Arcadians claimed that Rhea substituted a foal for Poseidon; and there was also a story that Rhea took him to Rhodes, where the Oceanid Capheira, aided by the Telchines, brought him up). When Metis had given Cronos the emetic which released his children, Poseidon helped Zeus to overthrow the Titans and bind them in Tartarus. Then the three sons of Cronos divided the universe between them, leaving earth and Olympus as common ground: to Poseidon's lot fell the sea, into which (in a variant of his usual birth-story) Cronos had flung him as soon as he emerged from Rhea's womb. Zeus was given the supreme rank – Homer calls him the eldest brother – but Poseidon frequently rebelled, acknowledging himself beaten only in extremity. Once he even made a plot with Hera and Athena to overthrow Zeus, and they bound him up; but Thetis saved Zeus by fetching Briareos from Tartarus to release him.

Most of Poseidon's children, both human and divine, inherited his violence. His wife was said to be Amphitrite, a daughter of Nereus or Oceanus. When Poseidon courted her, she took fright and fled to Atlas. Delphin, a dolphin-like sea creature, found her and persuaded her to marry Poseidon, in reward for which he was placed in heaven as a constellation. Amphitrite gave her husband three children, Triton, Rhode, and Benthesicyme. But he had a great many other children by goddesses, nymphs, and mortal women. He also took Demeter in the form of a horse, since she, to avoid him, had become a mare (perhaps she was his original consort as the relationship between their names suggests), and she bore him the divine horse Arion and a daughter Despoina. Poseidon also loved the Gorgon Medusa, while she was still a beautiful woman; he made love to her in a temple of Athena, in consequence of which the virgin goddess turned her into a repulsive monster and helped Perseus to kill her. From the severed head of Medusa, who had been pregnant by Poseidon, sprang Chrysaor and the winged horse Pegasus. Poseidon also begot the giant Antaeus on his grandmother Gaia; other giants whom he fathered included Otus and Ephialtes, who tried to storm Olympus, and Polyphemus the Cyclops, whose blinding by Odysseus caused Poseidon to pursue the perpetrator of the deed with implacable hatred. Further children of Poseidon were of normal size, but ferocious nature: Cercyon and Sciron, evil-doers killed by another of his sons, Theseus; Amycus, put to death by Zeus' son Polydeuces; and Busiris, slain by Heracles.

More ordinary mortals claiming Poseidon as their father included his sons by Epaphus' daughter Libya, namely Belus, Agenor, and Lelex; Theseus, the most famous of all, whose mother was Aethra and reputed father Aegeus; the great seafarer Nauplius, son of Amymone; Pelias and Neleus, son of Tyro; Cycnus, son of Calyce, king of Colonae; and many others.

Poseidon was very important to Homer. This was largely because of his hostility to the Trojans, which impelled him to intervene on behalf of the Greeks even against the express command of Zeus. This hatred sprang from the earlier servitude of Poseidon and Apollo to King Laomedon, Priam's father. They had agreed with him to build the walls of his city of Troy for a certain sum, but in the end he had refused to pay the fee. Apollo seems to have felt that the plague he sent was sufficient punishment, for he supported the Trojans in the subsequent war. But Poseidon was relentless. Not content with having dispatched a sea-monster which almost devoured Laomedon's daughter Hesione, he continued to persecute the Trojans throughout the fighting. However his anger did not spare the Greeks either, for he helped his niece Athena to punish them for the sacrilege Aias the son of Oileus had committed by his rape of Cassandra in Athena's temple. Indeed, Poseidon killed the offender himself by destroying the rock to which he clung as he defied the gods and boasted of having saved himself after being shipwrecked on his return journey; and the other Greek captains were storm-tossed for refusing to punish him for what he had done. Odysseus, who had proposed stoning Aias for his crime, escaped this persecution, but received the brunt of Poseidon's anger later when he blinded the god's son Polyphemus. After that, his return home was greatly delayed, and achieved only after the loss of all his companions; and meanwhile Poseidon punished the sea-faring Phaeacians for the aid they gave Odysseus and other travellers by blocking their harbour with a mighty mountain range and by turning into a rock the ship in which they conveyed Odysseus. However Poseidon, in quieter mood, liked to visit his faithful Ethiopians, who gave him rich sacrifices, and it was this accident that allowed Odysseus to escape his notice more than once.

Poseidon lived in a submarine palace near Aegae (there were two places of this name, in Achaea and in Euboea). He travelled over the sea in his chariot at incredible speeds, passing from Samothrace to Aegae in four strides – and when he took part in a battle, Hades was afraid that the ground would collapse under the earthquakes he created, and the roof of the Underworld cave in. Poseidon claimed a number of lands as specifically his own, and quarrelled with other gods over them, often getting the worst of the disputes. Thus he came into conflict with Athena over Athens and Troezen. In the former case, a contest was held: Athena created an olive tree, but all Poseidon could manage to produce was a spring of brackish water where he struck the rock of the Acropolis with his trident. The local people judged Athena's gift the more useful of the two: and to punish them for their choice, Poseidon flooded the surrounding plain of Attica. Zeus later reconciled him with the Athenians, and thereafter they honoured him greatly. At Troezen Zeus gave equal honour to his brother Poseidon and his daughter Athena. Even there, however, Poseidon flooded the country, until the Troezenians honoured him with the title *Phytalmios*, 'the raiser of plants'. It was near Troezen that he sent the sea-bull which killed Theseus' son Hippolytus. At Argos Poseidon had a furious struggle with Hera, but Hera was rated more highly by the local river-gods, because she had been the original patroness of the city. In his anger Poseidon dried up all the rivers and flooded the land with sea-water. (Nevertheless it was at Argos that he later met one of Danaus' daughters, Amymone, who delighted him so much that he showed her the way to certain springs and made love to her; and she bore him Nauplius *1*.) One city, however, Poseidon did gain as his own. He quarrelled with Helios over the ownership of Corinth, and the dispute was referred to Briareos, whose impartial decision was to give the lofty hill overlooking the city (the Acrocorinth) to the Sun-god, and the whole of the Isthmus, flanked as it was by water on both sides, to Poseidon.

Poseidon had a violent quarrel with Minos, king of Crete. When the king asked Poseidon to send him a bull to sacrifice, he complied and sent a magnificent specimen out of the sea, so fine indeed that Minos preferred to keep it rather than sacrifice it. Poseidon, in his anger at this, caused Minos' wife Pasiphae to conceive a bestial passion for the bull. Then, when Theseus came to Crete to kill their monstrous progeny the Minotaur, Minos threw his ring into the sea and ordered Theseus to retrieve it – thus challenging him to prove that Poseidon was really his father. When Theseus dived in, the Nereids (sea-nymphs) immediately returned the ring to him, and Amphitrite added a gold crown, which Theseus kept for himself.

Poseidon valued honours rendered to him inland, as well as beside the sea. This was shown by the instruction by Tiresias' shade that Odysseus should propitiate the god by sacrificing to him so far away from the sea that people did not even recognise an oar he carried on his shoulder. Poseidon was worshipped inland, both in Boeotia and at Delphi – where he was even said to have shared the Delphic Oracle with Gaia before Apollo took it over. (At Delphi the people of the island of Corcyra were accustomed to offer a bronze bull to the god, in memory of a bull which had stood on their sea-shore and shown the fishermen the position of shoals of tunny fish – but only after receiving instructions from Delphi to give the god a tithe of their catch, if the Corcyreans were able to net the fish.)

In addition to his destructive acts, Poseidon performed certain deeds of mercy. Thus he turned Thessaly, which had been an enormous lake, into dry land. This he did by a huge earthquake which hollowed out the Vale of Tempe, through which the River Peneius flowed. He also saved Ino and her son Melicertes when they flung themselves into the sea, changing them into the sea-gods Leucothea and Palaemon. He appointed Castor and Polydeuces, the Dioscuri, as protectors of sailors, giving them the power to lull storms. His aid was also invoked against earthquakes, and for this purpose the Greeks appealed to him as *Asphalios* 'preventer of slips'.

In his capacity as a god of horses, Poseidon was known as *Hippios* ('Lord of horses'); at Athens Athena was associated with him under the title *Hippia*. He presented horses to a number of his favourites. Thus to Pelops, whom he loved, he gave the horses with which he won Hippodamia; to Idas those with which he carried off Evenus' daughter Marpessa; to the Thracian Rhesus those that Odysseus and Diomedes stole; to Peleus at his wedding with Thetis the immortal steeds Xanthus and Balius that Achilles inherited. He was also associated with rams, for when he abducted Theophane, he assumed the shape of this animal and turned her into a sheep to avoid her suitors, who were in pursuit of them. Then Theophane was said to have borne the ram with the fleece of gold that Nephele gave her son Phrixus to save him from sacrifice at the hands of Athamas. All sea-gods had the power to alter their shape, but Poseidon also transformed many human beings. After raping Caenis, he turned her at her own

request into a man, and he metamorphosed Alope into a spring of water. He gave his son Periclymenus the power to change his form at will; and to Mestra, whom he had seduced, he gave the same gift. He made his son Cycnus invulnerable.

Praxithea Wife of Erechtheus, king of Athens. *See also* DEMETER.

Prayers (*Litai*) Prayers were occasionally personified as daughters of Zeus who carried the petitions of mortal men to their father. *See* ATE.

Priam The king of Troy at the time of the Trojan War. Originally called Podarces, he was a son of Laomedon of Troy and (among other accounts) of Strymo, a daughter of the River Scamander. When Heracles destroyed Troy because of Laomedon's refusal to pay him for saving Hesione, he spared Podarces at her request. She ransomed him with her veil, as a result of which the ransomed man was said to have been given the new name of Priam, from the Greek verb *priamai* 'I buy' (this, however, is not the true origin of the name, which is non-Greek). As the only surviving son of Laomedon, Priam inherited the kingdom and ruled it for many years, building it into a very prosperous place with dominion over a wide area. At the time of the fall of his city to the Greeks he was a very old man. His principal wife was Hecabe, daughter of Dymas, king of the Phrygians (or of Cisseas), and he possessed a large number of concubines as well. He had fifty sons, the eldest of whom was Paris or Hector (the others included Deiphobus, Helenus, Troilus, Polites, and Polydorus), and fifty daughters, including Cassandra, Creusa, Laodice, and Polyxena. The nymph Alexirrhoe, daughter of the River Granicus, bore him the prophet Aesacus.

The chief myths regarding Priam's life related to a battle against the Amazons at the River Sangarius; the abandonment and exposure of the infant Paris – regarding whom Hecabe had dreamed that she gave birth to a firebrand – and his rediscovery by Cassandra; Paris' abduction of Helen from Menelaus and Priam's subsequent ratification of the marriage of the pair; the refusal of his sons and counsellors to return Helen to Menelaus, and the war and siege of Troy which then followed; the death of his favourite son Hector and his redemption of Hector's body from Achilles; and finally, when Troy fell, his own death beside Zeus' altar in the courtyard of his palace. He had lost most of his sons in the war, and in his last moments he witnessed the death of another, Polites; after a feeble attempt to arm himself and fight, he was butchered by Neoptolemus without pity.

Priam, according to the *Iliad*, was a gentle, amiable old man, who showed kindness to Helen. The only Trojan the Greeks trusted, it was he who was summoned to the oath-taking before the duel between Menelaus and Paris. When he came to Achilles for Hector's body, though nervous in the presence of his supreme enemy, he retained his dignity and self-respect. It was because of his great piety that the gods kept him safe on this mission, though he was doomed before long to perish with Troy itself.

Priapus A god of gardens, of late arrival in the Greek world, coming probably from Phrygia. He was borne, it was said, by Aphrodite to Dionysus or Hermes, but disowned by his mother because of his ugliness, for he possessed a grotesque little gnarled body, to which a massive phallus was attached. After an upbringing by shepherds, he joined the retinue of Dionysus. He loved the nymph Lotis, and crept up on her as she slept, but, just as he lay at her side, an ass brayed and woke her; and when she saw what Priapus was trying to do, she was horrified and ran away. He followed in hot pursuit, until the gods at length took pity on her and changed her into a tree, the lotus. Ever after, Priapus hated asses, and was content that they should be killed in his honour. A different explanation of his hatred of asses attributed it to an argument he had with an ass to which Dionysus, in return for a favour, had given the power of speech. The argument was about the respective size of their genitals; Priapus lost and beat the animal to death.

Proca A king of Alba Longa, the father of Numitor and Amulius.

Proclea Wife of Cycnus 2 and mother of Tenes.

Procles A Spartan king, the son of Aristodemus and twin brother of Eurysthenes. The twins were protected by Theras in adolescence, and when they came of age divided the kingship equally between them, establishing the dual monarchy.

Procne *see* TEREUS.

Procris Daughter of Erechtheus, king of Athens. *See* CEPHALUS.

Procrustes (Greek *prokroustes* 'stretcher'). Said to be a son of Poseidon. A notorious scoundrel whose real name was Polypemon; he had another nickname, *Damastes* 'the tamer'. He lived by the side of the road between Eleusis and Athens, and was accustomed to offer hospitality to wayfarers, whom he then seized, fastened to a bed (a long one for short people and a short one for the tall) and lopped or racked to fit it. Theseus gave Procrustes the treatment he had given to others, adjusting him to the size of the bed by cutting off his head.

Proculus, Julius A mythical settler at Rome, from Alba Longa, at the time of its foundation by Romulus; he claimed on oath to have seen the deified Romulus after the latter's death. Romulus, he declared, had looked taller and fairer than in life, and had worn shining armour. He had ordered Proculus to report to the Romans that he was now a god, whom they should henceforth honour under the name Quirinus, and that Rome would be the most glorious and powerful city in the world. In historical times the Julian family claimed him as an ancestor, but Cicero declared that he was a man of peasant origins (not a patrician as was believed) and that he told his story in response to a bribe from the senators, who had put Romulus to death.

Proetus A king of Tiryns; the son of Abas, king of Argos, and of Aglaia, and the twin brother of Acrisius. Even in their mother's womb the twins quarrelled, and thereafter they never ceased. When Abas left them his kingdom jointly, they fought each other for its possession. Acrisius eventually drove Proetus out, alleging that he had seduced his daughter Danae, though Danae herself declared that her lover had been Zeus. Proetus took refuge in Lycia, where King Iobates welcomed him and presented him with his daughter Stheneboea (or Antia) as his wife. He also gave him an army, which attacked Acrisius at Epidaurus. Since a single combat between the twins proved indecisive, they decided to divide the kingdom: Acrisius took the south, keeping Argos as his capital; Proetus built a new city further north, calling it Tiryns. Tradition maintains that the Cyclopes built its city-walls.

Proetus lost his wife Stheneboea, who hanged herself for love of Bellerophon. She had borne Proetus three daughters, Iphinoe, Lysippe, and Iphianassa, and a son, Megapenthes, who inherited the kingdom. The daughters were driven into a frenzy by Dionysus or Hera for despising the worship of one god or the other; they roamed the countryside committing all kinds of unseemly acts. Eventually Proetus tried to strike a bargain with Melampus to cure them – but the seer's price, a third of the kingdom, proved too high. The situation then worsened, for many other Argive women were driven mad as well. Proetus then agreed to pay Melampus an even higher price, two-thirds of the kingdom, if he would cure the women. This he did successfully, except that Iphinoe was accidentally killed. It was said that Proetus eventually drove Acrisius from the throne of Argos and took it for himself, for which reason Acrisius' grandson Perseus turned Proetus into stone with the aid of the Gorgon's head. Megapenthes was believed to have avenged his father by killing Perseus.

Promachus _1._ The younger son of Aeson. _2._ One of the Epigoni; the son of Parthenopaeus.

Prometheus A Titan, the son of Iapetus and of Themis (or Clymene, daughter of Oceanus). He was the mythical archrebel and champion of mankind against the hostility of the gods; his name, meaning 'forethought', illustrates his character. In the earliest form of the story he was probably nothing more than a clever trickster who outwitted Zeus. But Greek writers, especially Hesiod in his _Theogony_ and Aeschylus in _Prometheus Bound_, developed him into man's creator and saviour, whereas Zeus (subject to the further developments in the rest of Aeschylus' Promethean trilogy) appeared as a cruel tyrant.

In the battle between the gods and Titans, resulting in Zeus' imprisonment of his foes in Tartarus, Prometheus, who, as his name indicates, had knowledge of what was to come, advised the Titans to use cunning; when they ignored his advice, he joined Zeus' side. After the battle, however, Prometheus found himself at loggerheads with Zeus over mankind. According to Hesiod's story, Prometheus himself had created the human race, out of clay he found at Panopea in Boeotia; as a mastercraftsman, he was able to mould the figures, and Athena helped by breathing life into them. (According to some accounts he showed the individual models to Zeus for approval, but omitted to do so in the case of one particularly beautiful boy, called Phaenon ('shining bright'). When Zeus discovered the omission he carried the boy to heaven and turned him into the planet now known as Jupiter.) However because of the faults of mortal men, Zeus determined to destroy them, or so Prometheus thought, and make a new and better creature instead. At all events Zeus started by depriving them of fire. He also tried to starve them by demanding offerings of the best of man's food; but Prometheus defeated his attempt by the following trick. At Mecone (afterwards Sicyon) a meeting was arranged between gods and men to determine which part of the victuals should be set aside for the gods. Prometheus, as arbiter, produced an ox and carved it up, dividing the meat into two bundles. One, consisting of the entrails, he wrapped in fat; but it was the other, contained in the stomach, which was the choicer of the two. He then told Zeus to choose a bundle. Zeus, thinking he had seen through the deception, fell into the trap, for he chose the fatty bundle; and for this reason, from then onwards the sacrifices offered by mankind always consisted of the fat and entrails.

It was now that Zeus, in his anger, decided to deprive men of fire. Prometheus rebelled against this decree by secretly taking fire in the stalk of a fennel plant from Olympus, or from Hephaestus' forge, and bringing it to mankind (he also taught them many other arts, such as metalwork) and at the same time deprived them of knowledge of the future, which they had previously pos-

sessed, lest it should break their hearts. By night Zeus, seeing the earth covered with a myriad of glowing lights, fell into a great rage, and summoned his servants Cratos and Bia, together with Hephaestus, to arrest Prometheus and chain him to a mountain peak (perhaps the Caucasus) at the edge of the stream of Ocean, far from mankind. There he sent his eagle every day to gnaw at the prisoner's liver, which grew whole again every night; for Prometheus, being a Titan, was immortal (or, according to one tradition, Chiron, when he died, had transferred his own immortality to him). Then, according to Aeschylus, when Zeus first heard Prometheus taunting him and refusing to disclose the secret of his safety, he flung a thunderbolt at the rock where his captive lay bound, so that he was driven to Tartarus, rock and all.

Finally, after long ages, Zeus allowed Prometheus to be freed in exchange for a vital piece of information – that it was fated that the son of Thetis (whom both Zeus and Poseidon had long been pursuing) should be greater than his father. Then Heracles, son of Zeus, came and shot the eagle, and freed the captive from his bonds. In exchange for this favour, it was asserted that Prometheus advised Heracles how best to obtain the apples of the Hesperides, which he was then seeking: he should send Atlas to fetch them and offer to carry the sky for him in his absence. Had he not received Prometheus' information, Zeus would have wedded Thetis and been overthrown by a more powerful son, just as he had overthrown Cronos.

There was also another story of the gods' cruelty to men, according to which they created the first woman, Pandora (until then only men had existed, made from clay by Prometheus), giving her all kinds of evil traits, but making her seductive and beautiful. They presented her to Prometheus' gullible brother Epimetheus, who, in spite of Prometheus' frequent warnings, accepted her. Her daughter Pyrrha married Deucalion, the only man who survived the flood, in which Zeus wiped out all the rest of Prometheus' creations. Some said that it was Prometheus who told Deucalion and Pyrrha to throw their mother's bones over their shoulders so as to remake the human race; though others attributed the advice to his mother Themis. She was also believed to have been Prometheus' original teacher of wisdom.

Prometheus was worshipped in Attica as a god of craftsmen. His wife was very variously named.

Protesilaus A king of Phylace in Thessaly; the son of Iphiclus. A little after his marriage to Laodamia, daughter of Acastus, before his new house was even complete, he was summoned to join the Greek expedition to Troy, to which he contributed a force of forty ships. It was learnt from an oracle that the first Greek to tread on Trojan soil would also be the first to die; and in consequence the rest of the army hesitated to disembark. But Protesilaus leapt ashore and killed a number of the enemy before Hector cut him down. (Catullus attributed his death to his failure to offer due sacrifice to the gods before building his house.) For the fate of his grief-striken wife, *see* LAODA-MIA.

Proteus An ancient sea-god, one of the 'Old Men of the Sea'; he is occasionally described as a son of Poseidon, but was probably a more ancient deity. He herded the flocks of seals and sea-creatures for Poseidon, and possessed the gift of prophecy, but was unwilling to disclose what he knew and tried to escape questioners by assuming a variety of shapes, including fire and water and the forms of wild beasts. He was said to live in a number of different places, including the islands of Carpathos and Pharos. Menelaus, on his return journey from Troy, took the advice of Proteus' daughter Idothea and disguised himself as a seal. As a result, he was able to catch her father and bind him as he slept, and thus prevailed on him to reveal the right way to get back home. Similarly Aristaeus, who had offended Orpheus and the nymphs, so that his bees were mysteriously dying, caught Proteus as he basked among his seals at noontide and made him tell what offence he had committed to cause the blight. Proteus instructed Aristaeus how to appease the nymphs and keep his bees alive.

In Euripides' *Helen* Proteus was said to be a king of Egypt, Pharos' son, to whom, in consideration of his justice and honesty, Hermes brought Helen for safe keeping while what Paris took to Troy was merely her phantom. After a time, according to this story, Proteus died, and his son by the Nereid Psamathe, Theoclymenus, tried to make Helen agree to marry him. Helen was only saved by her own wits and the timely arrival of Menelaus. Herodotus claims that it was Paris himself who had brought Helen to Egypt: Proteus then drove him off, and later returned Helen to her husband.

Psamathe A Nereid. *See* AEACUS; LINUS; PROTEUS.

Psyche The tale of Cupid (Eros, Amor) and Psyche, known to us from a story told in Apuleius' *Metamorphoses*, is a romantic myth containing many familiar elements of folk-tale and fairy-story.

A certain king had three daughters. The youngest, Psyche, was so beautiful that the people ceased to worship Venus (Aphrodite) and turned their adoration to the girl, who would, however, rather have received offers of marriage than divine honours. Venus herself, enraged by the princess's usurpation of her rites, however involuntary, resolved to punish her. She ordered her son Cupid to make

Psyche fall in love with the ugliest creature he could find. When he saw her, however, he fell in love with her himself, and he could not obey his mother's command. He asked Apollo to give Psyche's father an oracle that she must get ready for marriage and stand, decked in her wedding gown, upon a lonely mountain peak, where an evil spirit would take her for his wife. In great sorrow the king obeyed. Psyche, however, was wafted on the gentle breeze of Zephyrus down from the mountain to a hidden valley, in which she saw a fairy palace with jewelled gates and golden floors. She entered and was waited upon by unseen hands. A friendly voice guided her round and advised her that she need fear nothing. When night came she went to bed, where she was joined by Cupid in human form. He told her that he was her husband, and that she would enjoy the happiest of lives if only she would refrain from seeking to find out who he was or trying to see him: if she did not obey, her baby would be denied the immortality it would otherwise inherit.

She began to love him deeply. Nevertheless after a few days she felt lonely – since she saw no one – and asked her unseen husband if she might be visited by her sisters. With great reluctance he agreed to fetch them; but at the same time he warned her not to listen to any questionings from them about his identity. The west wind Zephyrus wafted them, as he had wafted Psyche, to the palace and, as soon as they saw it, they were madly jealous. On a second visit her sisters discovered that Psyche had never seen her husband, and terrified her into believing he would turn into a serpent which might creep into her womb and devour her and her baby. Torn at first between the warnings of her husband and the importunity of her sisters, she finally gave in to her curiosity and fear, and when she next went to bed for the night took a lantern and a dagger with her. After Cupid had fallen

asleep, she lit the lamp and held it to his face, raising the dagger to slay him. But when she saw the beautiful features of the god of love she was so startled that she let a drop of hot oil from the lamp fall down on his shoulder, and he awoke. Realising that Psyche now knew who he was and that his secret would be out, Cupid rose and flew away.

Psyche, in despair, searched everywhere for him, but in vain. When her sisters learnt of her husband's identity, they too wanted to marry him, but when, seeking to imitate her, they leapt off the mountain in wedding gowns, they fell to their death on the rocks below. Meanwhile Psyche wandered about in search of Cupid, and, after receiving no help from Juno (Hera) or Ceres (Demeter), who could not assist an enemy of their fellow-goddess Venus, she came to the palace where Venus herself was living. The goddess let her in but made her a slave and set her impossible tasks to perform. First she had to sort out a roomful of assorted grains before nightfall; a colony of ants came to her assistance by dividing the grains into piles. Next Venus told Psyche to bring a hank of wool from a flock of man-eating sheep; this time a reed told her how to obtain the wool, when the sheep were asleep in the afternoon. Then Psyche had to fill a jug with the water of the River Styx in a mountainous part of Arcadia; an eagle which owed Cupid a favour turned up in time and fetched the water. Lastly she had to obtain a jar containing beauty from Proserpina (Persephone). Psyche saw that this order meant that she must perish, for Proserpina was queen of the Underworld; so she climbed a high tower, resolving to leap to her death. The tower, however, addressed her and gave her careful instructions how to achieve her task. She entered the house of Hades by way of Taenarum in the Peloponnese, carrying two obols and two cakes. With these she twice placated Charon and

Cerberus, at the same time escaping a number of traps that Venus had set for her. Proserpina offered her a chair and a meal, but she wisely sat on the ground and ate only bread. The goddess also gave her a jar in response to Venus' request, carefully sealed. And now Cupid, who desperately missed his lost wife, approached Jupiter's throne and made a clean breast of his disobedience, pleading that Psyche had been punished enough and begging that he might be allowed to make her his lawful wife. Jupiter consented. Meanwhile, however, Psyche, as she approached the passage leading back to the upper world, felt herself overcome by curiosity and so greatly desired to win back Cupid's love that she was unable to resist opening the jar she had been given, ignoring the advice of the tower that she should do no such thing; whereupon she was overpowered by the deathly sleep which was what the jar really contained. It was in this condition that Cupid now found her, but he brought her back to life and carried her up to Olympus. The marriage of Cupid and Psyche was celebrated by the gods. Venus forgot her anger, and Jupiter himself handed her a drink of nectar which made her immortal. She bore Cupid a daughter, Voluptas (Pleasure).

Apuleius, in his story, hints at an allegory of the soul (*psyche*) in pursuit of divine love (*eros, amor*).

Pterelaus A king of the Taphian islands near the mouth of the Gulf of Corinth. Pterelaus was a son of Poseidon, who had placed a single gold hair on his head, ensuring that he could not die, or else that his city could not be taken, unless the hair were removed. Pterelaus claimed the land of Tiryns through his mother (Hippothoe, daughter of Mestor and grand-daughter of Perseus), and sent his six sons there to raid the cattle of Electryon, king of Mycenae. In the raid all but one of Pterelaus'

sons were killed, and every one of the sons of Electryon. When Electryon's son-in-law Amphitryon came to take vengeance for the raid, Pterelaus' daughter Comaetho fell in love with him and pulled out her father's gold hair, so that he died and the city was taken. But Amphitryon killed Comaetho for her treachery.

Publicola or **Poplicola** *see* VALERIUS.

Pygmalion *1. see* DIDO.
2. A king of Cyprus who, according to Ovid, had a lifelike ivory statue of his ideal woman made for him, since no real woman came up to his standards. He fell in love with the statue, and Aphrodite, taking pity on him, brought it to life (the name given to it, Galatea, has no ancient authority). Pygmalion married her and she bore him a daughter, Paphos, who was either the mother or the wife of Cinyras. According to others, their daughter was not Paphos but Metharme, who became Cinyras' bride.

Pylades Son of Strophius *1*, king of Phocis, and his wife Anaxibia, Agamemnon's sister. His cousin Orestes, in order to be safe from the usurper Aegisthus, was brought to Strophius' court by Electra, and Pylades grew up as his companion. Pylades helped Orestes in the killing of Clytemnestra, and Strophius banished him from Phocis for his part in her death. According to one account Pylades fetched Iphigenia (who, in this version, had not been sacrificed at Aulis) home from the Tauric Chersonese. He also killed Neoptolemus at Delphi, and married Electra, who bore him two sons, Medon and Strophius *2*.

Pylas or **Pylos** A Lelegian, said to have been exiled from his kingdom of Megara for killing his uncle Bias. Pandion, his son-in-law, took over Megara, while Pylas went to the Peloponnese and founded

Pylos, from which, however, Neleus expelled him. The Lelegians were the earliest indigenous inhabitants of Greece.

Pylia Daughter of Pylas and wife of Pandion 2.

Pyraechmes *see* OXYLUS.

Pyramus and **Thisbe** According to a myth told by Ovid in the *Metamorphoses*, Pyramus and Thisbe lived next door to each other in Babylon, and became friends and then sweethearts, but their parents would not hear of their marriage, and they had to keep their passion secret. In the wall between their houses there was a small chink which only the lovers knew: through this they whispered and exchanged sighs and kisses. Then they decided to meet each other one night at Ninus' tomb outside the city. Thisbe, her face veiled, arrived first. When, however, a lioness, its jaws bloody from a fresh kill, came to drink at an adjoining spring, the girl ran into a cave nearby for shelter. As she ran, she dropped her veil, which the lioness mauled and stained with blood.

When Pyramus arrived, he saw the blood-soaked veil and the animal's footprints. Falsely concluding that his beloved was dead, he stabbed himself with his sword beneath a mulberry tree. The blood streamed from his side and tinged the fruit dark red, a colour mulberries, previously white, have retained for ever afterwards. Shortly afterwards, Thisbe

found his lifeless body and joined him in death, stabbing herself with his sword. Their parents buried their ashes in a single urn. Two rivers in Cilicia (south-eastern Asia Minor) took their names from Pyramus and Thisbe.

Pyrrha Daughter of Epimetheus and Pandora. *See* DEUCALION.

Pyrrhus *see* NEOPTOLEMUS.

Pythia *see* APOLLO.

Python A monstrous serpent which inhabited Delphi before the coming of Apollo and gave the place its first name, Pytho. It was said to have been female and to have protected the original oracle, which was in the hands first of Gaia (Earth), then of Themis and Phoebe. Python was sometimes identified as the serpent which Hera set in pursuit of the goddess Leto when she was pregnant with Apollo and Artemis: for this reason Apollo, when still newly born, hunted it to Delphi and slew it there, subsequently propitiating Gaia by its burial and by the establishment of the Pythian Games in its honour. In memory of the original ownership of the oracle, Apollo's prophet at Delphi always continued to be a woman and was always called Pythia. Others said that Apollo killed Python because it was the guardian of the chasm at Delphi which he wanted to enter in order to establish his oracle.

Q

Quirinus An early Italian high god or war-god, somewhat analogous to Mars. He gave his name to the Quirinal Hill, one of the Seven Hills of Rome, because of his temple there. Quirinus was perhaps a Sabine god by origin, the Quirinal having, according to a persistent tradition, been first settled by Sabines. His name may be derived from the Sabine town of Cures, and according to some interpretations the Latin word Quirites, 'citizens', went back to the same origin. For his identification with the deified Romulus, *see* PROCULUS; ROMULUS.

R

Racilia Wife of Cincinnatus.

Rea *see* RHEA SILVIA.

Remus Son of Mars and Rhea Silvia. For the myths of his birth and early life, *see* ROMULUS, his twin brother. It was because of Remus' arrest by his great-uncle Amulius, king of Alba Longa, that the twins were discovered by their grandfather Numitor, to whom Remus had been handed over by Numitor's brother Amulius, on the grounds that he had raided Numitor's flocks. When Romulus and Remus subsequently decided to found a city of their own, they could not agree which of the two should lead the undertaking, and so left the issue to an omen to be provided by birds in the sky. Remus, from his vantage point on the Aventine Hill, saw only six vultures, whereas Romulus, from the Palatine Hill, saw twelve, and was awarded the right to rule. While the walls of Rome were being built on the Palatine, Remus, in a fit of jealousy, jumped over the foundations with a contemptuous taunt, whereupon Romulus or one of his followers, Celer, felled him with a spade. Remus died from the blow and Romulus, although he had condemned Remus' insult, finally broke down and wept at his brother's funeral. Another version of Remus' death, however, asserted that he was killed in a brawl fought between the followers of the twins, since each side claimed that the omen provided by the birds had supported their own cause.

Rhadamanthys A judge of the dead. Rh-adamanthys was either a son of Zeus and Europa and a brother of Minos and Sarpedon or else a son of Phaestus, son of Talos (the bronze man of Crete). According to one account Rhadamanthys ruled Crete before Minos, and gave the island an excellent code of laws, which the Spartans were subsequently believed to have copied. However, when the three brothers quarrelled over a handsome youth, Miletus, Minos drove out Rhadamanthys and Sarpedon; and Rhadamanthys now went to rule the southern Aegean Islands, of which the inhabitants had already made him their king out of respect for his laws.

After his death he was believed to have been made a judge or ruler of the Underworld. Alternatively, he was described as the king of Elysium, that part of the Underworld where the most blessed shades passed their time in bliss. According to Homer, Rhadamanthys acted not as a judge of the deeds men had performed during their lives, but as an arbiter in the quarrels between the shades. Virgil, however, presents him as punisher of the wicked in Tartarus.

After the death of her husband Amphitryon, Rhadamanthys was said to have married Alcmena – either in Boeotia, while they still lived on earth, or in Elysium. The sons of Rhadamanthys, Gortys and Erythrus, had Cretan towns named after them.

Rhea A Titaness, the daughter of Uranus and Gaia, and consort of Cronos. She bore Cronos six divine children, Hestia, Demeter, Hera, Hades, Poseidon, and Zeus; but her husband, having learnt from Gaia that one of his children would overthrow him and rule in his stead, attempted to swallow them as they were born. He succeeded with all save Zeus, for whom Rhea substituted a large stone wrapped up to look like a baby. According to some accounts, Poseidon too was saved, his substitute being a foal. When Zeus had rescued his brothers and sisters by persuading Metis to give Cronos an emetic, Rhea sent her daughter Hera to the home of Oceanus and Tethys so that in the war between the gods and the Titans she might be safe.

Rhea was an important goddess in Crete, where the birth of Zeus was believed to have taken place, and in Arcadia, which told the myth of Poseidon's rescue. In Phrygia she was often identified with Cybele. Like Gaia herself, she seems to have been a mother-deity. The Romans identified her with Ops, an ancient Italian goddess of plenty.

Rhea (or **Rea**) **Silvia** Rhea Silvia, or Ilia, was the mother of the twins Romulus and Remus. Her father, of whom she was the only child, was Numitor, a king of Alba Longa deposed by his brother Amulius. To ensure his own safety, Amulius imposed perpetual virginity upon her by forcing her to become a Vestal Virgin. The god Mars, however, came to her while she drew water at a spring in his sacred grove, and made her the mother of his twin sons, one of whom, Romulus, was destined to found Rome. When she had given birth to her children, Amulius exposed them and imprisoned Rhea; she was subsequently released many years later by her sons. According to a different version, however, she was drowned or beheaded. The name Ilia is derived from an early variant of the story, in which she is a daughter of Aeneas, and was consequently named after his homeland of Ilium (Troy).

Rhesus A Thracian king and ally of

Priam of Troy. Homer calls him a son of Eioneus, but in the play *Rhesus*, which may be by Euripides, his father was the god of the River Strymon and his mother the Muse Euterpe. In a late version of his myth (not mentioned by Homer), it was prophesied that if Rhesus' magnificent horses (the gift of Poseidon) should taste the Trojan pastures or drink from the River Scamander Troy could never fall to the Greeks.

Rhesus did not arrive at Troy until the tenth year of the war, the day before Hector's great assault on the Greek ships; his lateness, according to one tale, was caused by a force of Scythians which had invaded Thrace. On his way to Troy Rhesus had visited Cius, where he married Arganthoe who, like himself, enjoyed hunting. On landing near Troy, he bivouacked on the plain outside the city at the extremity of the Trojan camp. That night Odysseus and Diomedes made a spying raid on the Trojans and, helped by Athena and by the captured Trojan spy Dolon, took Rhesus' contingent by surprise, killing Rhesus and twelve of his men in their sleep, and driving off his team of horses. After his death his body was carried off by his mother the Muse and taken to Thrace, where his spirit inhabited a cave on Mount Rhodope and issued prophecies. It was also said that Arganthoe, on hearing of his death, came to Troy and died of grief over his body.

Rhexenor Eldest son of Nausithous, king of the Phaeacians; he died shortly after his marriage. His daughter Arete married his younger brother Alcinous.

Rhode or **Rhodos** ('rose') Daughter of Poseidon and Amphritrite or Aphrodite; the nymph after whom the island of Rhodes was said to have been named. She bore to Helios, the patron god of the island, seven sons, one of whom, Cercaphus, became the father of the men after whom the island's chief cities were named Ialysus, Cameirus, and Lindus.

Rhoetus A Centaur, killed at Pirithous' wedding feast.

Rhome ('strength', 'might'). The eponym of Rome, according to an early Greek tradition. She was said by a Greek author to be the sister of Latinus, king of Laurentum. According to the Greek historian Hellanicus, Rhome was a Greek slave-woman who was brought to Latium by Aeneas and burnt his ships, so that it was impossible for him to sail away again. Alternatively, she was described as a Trojan captive of Greek settlers.

Rhomus A Greek name for the founder of Rome, said to be a son of Aeneas; he was sometimes identified with Romulus.

Romulus The mythical founder of Rome in the year 753 BC. The name simply means 'Roman'. The various forms assumed by his story have roots in Greek mythology.

Romulus and Remus were the twin sons of Rhea Silvia, daughter and only child of Numitor (a descendant of Aeneas), who was deposed from the kingship of Alba Longa by his younger brother Amulius. In order to prevent Numitor from having a grandson and heir, Amulius forced Rhea Silvia to become a perpetually celibate Vestal Virgin, but the god Mars raped her in his sacred grove. When Amulius discovered her pregnancy, he imprisoned (or drowned) her and told his servants to kill her twin sons by immersing them in the Tiber. However the servants, more kind-hearted than their master, instead placed the cradle on a plank, which they then proceeded to launch on the floods created by the swollen river. As the waters receded, the plank settled on the mud near a fig tree (its name, Ruminal, was believed to be derived from *ruma* 'breast'). Here Mars' sacred animals, a she-wolf and a woodpecker, came and

tended the twin children; and after a short time they were found by one of the king's shepherds, Faustulus, who took them home, saying nothing to his royal master. His wife Acca (or Acca Larentia) brought the boys up. They grew into sturdy and intelligent young men, who led the sons of the shepherds in raids on the local brigands – or even on Numitor's herds. But one day, on the occasion of Pan's festival of the Lupercalia, their party fell into an ambush and Remus was captured. He was led before King Amulius, who, hearing that the youth was accused of stealing Numitor's cattle, turned him over to his brother for punishment. Numitor questioned Remus and drew from his answers the conclusion, already reached by Faustulus, that the twins were his lost grandsons; and his supposition was confirmed when he inspected the twins' cradle. Soon afterwards Numitor was restored to his throne by a rebellion organised by the two youths, who attacked Amulius' palace and killed their great uncle.

Romulus and Remus, however, were not content to live in Alba Longa under their grandfather, and, although only eighteen years old, resolved to found a city of their own. They chose a site not far away, just by the Tiber where they had been exposed. But then they quarrelled about which of them should take charge of the building operations – and become the official founder of the city. So they decided to settle the issue by means of augury, or divination by birds. Romulus, standing on the Palatine Hill, saw twelve vultures – twice as many as Remus saw on the Aventine. Now, however, the dispute broke out afresh, since Remus' followers declared that he had received his sign first. Romulus went ahead, marked out the walls of his city upon the Palatine Hill with a ploughed furrow, and began the work of building on the Parilia, Pales' feast on 21 April. But Remus was angry, and insulted his brother by leaping over the incomplete city wall, contemptuously asking how such a feeble barrier would ever keep the city safe. Thereupon Romulus or, according to an alternative account, his foreman Celer ('swift'), picked up a spade and killed Remus with a blow (in one version Faustulus, as he tried to separate his foster-children, was also killed). Romulus then declared 'so die any foe who crosses my walls!' However at Remus' funeral on the Aventine Hill, so it was said, Romulus dropped his austere pose and wept sincerely for his brother.

He peopled his new city by making it an asylum for fugitives and runaway offenders. It soon had a large surplus of males. But unfortunately for the new settlers, they were viewed so unfavourably by their neighbours that they were quite unable to find brides from the country round about. Romulus hit on an ingenious solution to this problem: he invited people from the Sabine and other townships around to visit his new city and attend a great festival, the Consualia, at which there would be games and theatrical performances. Then, when the visitors least expected it, the Romans seized their wives and daughters ('the Rape of the Sabine Women'), driving the menfolk away. The girls were at first terrified of their captors, but Romulus, with smooth words, was soon able to talk them into accepting their new situation. Shortly afterwards their neighbours returned to Rome to fight for the restoration of their women. At first they all came in small, disorganised raiding parties. In defeating Acron, king of the men of Caenina, Romulus was believed to have been the first Roman to dedicate the *spolia opima* (spoils won by a king from any enemy king killed in single combat). The men of Crustumerium and Antemnae were easily vanquished, and Hersilia, Romulus' wife, persuaded him to let the people

of these Latin towns migrate to Rome, if they wished. Finally the Sabines of Cures, under their king Titus Tatius, arrived and blockaded the city, eventually taking the Capitoline outpost through the treachery of Tarpeia, and then attacking the Romans on the flat ground (later the Roman Forum) beneath the Capitoline and Palatine Hills. Just as the Sabines were compelling the Romans to fall back in retreat, Romulus appealed to Jupiter to stop the rout and restore the situation, vowing him a temple as *Stator* ('the Stayer') on the spot. His appeal was heard. Then, as the battle was still being hotly fought, the women themselves ran between the two armies, protesting that they could not idly stand by and see their husbands and fathers killing each other. And so a treaty was arranged: the Romans and the Sabines agreed to merge in a single federation, making Rome their capital and Romulus and Titus Tatius their joint rulers.

Forty years later, after a peaceful and prosperous reign, Romulus disappeared from the earth. While he was reviewing his army on the Campus Martius (Field of Mars) near the marsh of Capra ('she-goat') there was a violent thunderstorm, in which he was enveloped in a cloud and vanished from human sight. His divinity was at once acclaimed by those who had witnessed the miracle. Shortly afterwards Romulus appeared in a more than human form to a certain Julius Proculus, and assured him that all would be well with the city. He bade the Romans to practise arms, and to worship him in future as the god Quirinus.

Such is one of the canonical Roman versions of the end of his life. But there were also many variants and rationalisations, both of these and of many other features of his career; they were often inspired by political and family interests of later, historical times.

S

Sabine Women *see* ROMULUS.

Sacadas *see* MARSYAS.

Sagaritis *see* ATTIS.

Salmacis A Naiad. *See* HERMAPHRODITUS.

Salmoneus Son of Aeolus and Enarete; Salmoneus was driven out of Thessaly by his brother Sisyphus and migrated to Elis, where he founded a city and named it Salmone after himself. His first wife was Alcidice, daughter of Aleus, who bore him Tyro. After Alcidice's death he married Sidero, who, after Tyro claimed to be pregnant by Poseidon, treated her cruelly. Salmoneus after his death is placed by Virgil in the lowest depths of Tartarus on account of his impious arrogance: for it was said that he pretended to be the equal or even the superior of Zeus, and that in order to prove his claim he flung torches to resemble thunderbolts and drove his chariot furiously, dragging along pans and dried hides in order to imitate thunder. He even took Zeus' share of sacrifices. Finally, therefore, Zeus struck him and his city with a thunderbolt, and blotted king and people from the face of the earth.

Sandoces A Syrian, descended from Tithonus. *See* CINYRAS.

Sarpedon *1.* Son of Zeus and Europa and brother of Minos and Rhadamanthys. When the three brothers all fell in love with the same young man, Miletus,

and Sarpedon won his favours, Minos drove both his brothers out of Crete and ruled the island alone. Sarpedon and Miletus went to southern Asia Minor, but separated after a time. Then Miletus moved to the western coast, where he founded the city named after him; whereas Sarpedon, with a band of Cretan followers, stayed in the south of the peninsula, meeting there his uncle, Europa's brother Cilix, who had founded a kingdom in Cilicia. The two made war on the Solymi, whom they defeated, and Sarpedon and his Cretans (called Termilae) moved into their land. Sarpedon was then joined by Lycus (who had been exiled from Athens by his brother Aegeus), and shared his kingship with him: Lycus gave his name to the people he ruled, who were then known as Lycians. Sarpedon's son Evander married Bellerophon's daughter Deidamia, and succeeded to the Lycian throne.

2. A king of Lycia and the greatest warrior among Troy's allies in the Trojan War. Early writers identify him with the above, explaining the chronological discrepancy by the assertion that Zeus allowed him to live for three generations of men (though, according to the usual mythical genealogies, the difference is nearer six). Others preferred to make him the son of Evander and Deidamia, and hence the grandson of *1.* To Homer, however, he is the son of Zeus and Laodamia (probably to be identified with Deidamia), a daughter of Bellerophon. According to this reckoning his predecessor as king of Lycia would have been Iobates or one of his sons. His cousin Glaucus, who accompanied him to Troy as second-in-command of the Lycian forces, was the son of Hippolochus, Laodamia's only surviving brother. Sarpedon killed Heracles' son Tlepolemus, and led the assault on the wall the Greeks built round their ships. But when his turn came to die – struck by a spear cast by Patroclus – his father Zeus wanted to postpone the death of his beloved son. At this, Hera rebuked her husband, and Zeus had to obey the law of fate. However he ordered Apollo to carry Sarpedon's body off the battlefield and entrust it to Sleep and Death to bear to Lycia, where it was given honourable burial.

3. Brother of Poltys, king of Aenus in Thrace. See HERACLES (ninth Labour).

Saturn An ancient Italian rustic god, usually equated with the Greek Cronos. He differs from Cronos, however, in that he was regarded as an early king of Latium, whose reign was a Golden Age when life was easy and happy. He taught men how to till the fields and enjoy the gifts of civilisation. He was believed by the Romans not to be native to Italy but a foreigner who, after fleeing from Jupiter (Zeus), had taken refuge in Latium. His festival, the Saturnalia, which took place in late December, was the merriest of the year. The Romans identified his wife as Lua, though in later times he was associated with Ops, who was equated with the Greek Rhea.

Satyrs Woodland creatures who accompanied the Maenads in Dionysus' revels. According to Hesiod they were descended from the five daughters of a certain Hecaterus, who married an Argive princess, the daughter of King Phoroneus; their sisters were the Oreads. They were renowned for their lascivious appetites and mischievous behaviour. In later times they were endowed with certain animal features, such as pointed ears, horses' legs, hooves, and small horns on their heads.

They seemed to personify the unrestrained fertility of Nature in the wild; and what they particularly enjoyed was pursuing the nymphs, on whom they hoped to gratify their lust.

In literature the satyrs, like the Sileni, were debased and comic figures, for it was the custom of the tragic poets, after presenting a trilogy of plays recounting one of the serious mythological dramas, to terminate their contributions to the festival of Dionysus with the performance of a light comedy based on the activities of these un-tragic folk. *See also* SILENUS.

Scaevola, Gaius Mucius A legendary Roman hero who, during a siege of Rome by the Etruscans, resolved to kill their king Lars Porsenna of Clusium. Mucius dressed himself as an Etruscan and infiltrated the enemy camp, but when he found himself standing in the crowd of soldiers, the army's pay was being distributed and a secretary was sitting at a desk with the appearance of authority. Mistaking this man for the king, Mucius stabbed him to death. Placed under arrest and disarmed, he was taken to Lars Porsenna for interrogation. Thereupon, in indignation at his failure, he plunged his right hand in the fire of a nearby altar, looking steadfastly at the king as he underwent the ordeal. Moved by his courage, Porsenna returned Mucius his sword. He received it with his left hand – for which reason he was henceforth known as Scaevola, from *scaeva*, 'left hand'. In response, Mucius undertook to disclose what no punishment could have extorted. Three hundred Romans, he declared, all as determined as he, were hiding in the camp waiting to assassinate Porsenna: he had drawn the lot to be first, and was glad that he had failed, because Porsenna deserved to be Rome's friend rather than her foe. A truce was then made between Rome and the Etruscans, and the siege was raised.

Scamander The river-god of the stream which flowed near Troy; the gods called it Xanthus ('yellow'). He supported the Trojans in the war, and when Achilles filled his waters with Trojan corpses after the death of Patroclus, he was angry. A battle took place between him and Achilles, and Achilles would have been drowned had not Hera sent her son Hephaestus, god of fire, to scorch the river and dry it up with a flame. *See* TEUCER I.

Scamandrius *see* ASTYANAX.

Schedius Son of Iphitus, and a leader of the Phocians in the Trojan War.

Schoeneus A king of Orchomenus in Boeotia. He was the son of Athamas and Themisto. He was said to be the father of Atalanta in the Boeotian version of her story. His wife was Clymene.

Sciron Son of Poseidon or of Pelops. He infested the Scironian Way, the road between Megara and Eleusis. At a point where there were precipitous rocks overlooking the sea, he would stop travellers and make them wash his feet. As they stooped to do so, it was his custom to kick them over the edge of the cliffs; at the bottom, a giant turtle ate their remains. Theseus, however, requited him with his own medicine. According to a divergent Megarian account, Sciron was a son of Pylas, king of Megara, and disputed the succession with Nisus, son of Pandion. Aeacus, king of Aegina, arbitrated in the dispute, and made Nisus the king of Megara and Sciron the commander of its army. Endeis, Sciron's daughter, married Aeacus.

Scylla ('whelp') *1.* Daughter of Nisus, king of Megara. *See* NISUS I.
2. A sea-monster which infested the Straits of Messina. Originally Scylla was a beautiful nymph, said to be the daughter of Phorcys and Cratais (though her parentage was much disputed). She spent her days in the sea, playing with the sea-nymphs, and rejected all lovers. When the sea-god Glaucus fell in love with Scylla, he went to the witch Circe for a love-potion, but Circe forthwith fell in love with him herself. When he repulsed her, in her jealousy she turned her rival Scylla into the monstrous form she thereafter displayed, with six heads, each with a mouth containing triple rows of teeth, and twelve feet; according to one account her waist was surrounded by a ring of dogs' heads, which bayed and ravened for prey. Scylla was immortal; and the only defence against her was to invoke the aid of her mother, the sea-nymph Cratais. She made her lair in a cave opposite the whirlpool of Charybdis, and when sailors (including Odysseus) ventured through the straits, she used her multiplicity of mouths to seize as many men as possible from the decks of the ship. She was finally turned into a rock, and that was how Aeneas found her when he passed that way.

Scyrius A king of the island of Scyros; according to one tradition he was the father of Aegeus, king of Athens.

Scythes The mythical ancestor of the Scythians. *See* HERACLES (tenth Labour).

Seasons *see* HOURS.

Selene ('moon'). The goddess of the moon, known to the Romans as Luna. Her parents were said by Hesiod to be Hyperion and Theia; otherwise they were given as Pallas or Helios and Euryphaessa. To Zeus she bore two daughters, Herse ('dew') and Pandia; and Pan seduced her with the gift of a beautiful white fleece. Her best known myth connects her with Endymion, whom she put to sleep for ever. When, in later times, Artemis came to be connected with the moon, Selene receded from the attention of mythological writers.

Selinus King of Aegialus (Achaea); he married his daughter Helice to Ion.

Semele or **Thyone** Daughter of Cadmus and Harmonia and mother of the god Dionysus. 'Semele' is not of Greek origin, and seems to be a corruption of a word used by the Thracians, Zemelo ('earth'), which was perhaps their name for the mother of Diounsis (Dionysus).

In the Greek tradition Zeus appeared to Semele in Thebes in order to become her lover in the form of a mortal man, and she conceived a child. Then Hera, who knew and was jealous, disguised herself as Semele's old nursemaid Beroe, and put it into Semele's mind that her lover's claim to be Zeus might be false: to prove his identity, she must persuade him to appear in his true nature. Semele, therefore, induced her lover to grant her a boon, and then made her demand, which was that he should appear before her in his full splendour. He did his best to dissuade her but had to carry out his promise, and the flashes of his lightning burnt her up. But the child in her womb was immortalised, for, after Hermes had rescued him, Zeus had him sown into a gash cut within his own thigh. Three months later Dionysus was born. Semele's tomb at Thebes continued to smoulder for years. But her sisters, Agave, Ino, and Autonoe, refused to believe this account of what had happened or to accept Dionysus' divinity, and were subsequently punished for their scepticism. When Dionysus came to manhood, he fetched Semele from the Underworld and took her to Mount Olympus to receive immortality from Zeus.

For the Orphic version of the myth, *see* ZAGREUS. *See also* DIONYSUS.

Semnai Theai ('venerable goddesses').

Usually identified with the Furies (who were also known as Eumenides, or 'kindly ones'). They were two or three in number, and were worshipped in a cave on the Areopagus at Athens.

Servius Tullius The sixth in the traditional list of Rome's legendary kings, ascribed to the sixth century BC. He may have been a historical figure, and even, as the most familiar version recorded, a Latin intruder between the Etruscan monarchs (the Tarquins) who terminated Rome's king-list. But his story is almost pure myth. There are two traditions about him. An Etruscan tale, reported by the Emperor Claudius, equates him with Mastarna. The Roman myth, known from Livy and other writers, is as follows. In the court of King Tarquinius Priscus there was a slave-woman, Ocrisia, who gave birth to a son. There were variant accounts of his paternity. The first maintained that his father was called Servius Tullius, prince of Corniculum, a recently conquered town, and that his mother, though now a slave, had formerly been the prince's wife. The other explanation asserted that Ocrisia was impregnated by the god Vulcan in the shape of a phallus which rose out of the hearth. The child's destiny was brought to the attention of the court by a flame of innocuous fire which played round his head as he lay in his cradle. Tarquinius' queen Tanaquil declared that he must not be disturbed; and when he awoke, the flame departed. Then the royal pair, impressed by the omen, decided to bring up the baby as their own son, and when he was fully grown, they married him to their own daughter. Tanaquil, although she had sons of her own, continued to support him; and when Tarquinius Priscus was assassinated by the sons of his predecessor Ancus Marcius, she concealed her husband's death and claimed that he was merely wounded, until such time as Servius was able to establish himself in power. Then, when the truth came out, he was able to occupy the throne without difficulty, and his rivals had to flee the country.

According to the Roman tradition Servius' reign was highly successful. He defeated Veii, it was said, and divided the citizen body into classes and 'centuries', based on property; he increased the size of the city, building the famous 'Servian Wall' around its new circumference (though the surviving portions of the wall described by that name belong only to the fourth century BC); he introduced the worship of the Latin goddess Diana; and he confirmed his rule by an overwhelming popular vote. The patricians, however, were believed to have always resented his rule. But it was the grandsons (or, according to Livy, the sons) of his predecessor Tarquinius Priscus, married by Servius to his daughters, who eventually brought about his downfall and death. First, Livy asserts, one of these girls, the younger Tullia, who was particularly ambitious, had contrived the murders of her sister and of Tarquinius' more passive grandson Arruns; then she married her brother-in-law Lucius Tarquinius, later called Superbus. Next these two assassinated Servius after a reign of forty-four years. Tarquinius refused the body the rite of burial, and Tullia rode her carriage over her father's body as it lay bleeding in the street.

Seven against Thebes The Argive champions who besieged Thebes on behalf of Polynices. When Eteocles, son of Oedipus, refused to hand over the throne of Thebes to his brother Polynices after his year of office, as had been agreed between the two of them, Polynices took refuge in Argos, where Adrastus was king. There he and Tydeus, who had also taken refuge there after being banished from Calydon for homicide, quarrelled over a couch in the palace porch. Adrastus separated them; and, noting that Polynices and Tydeus wore a lion-

skin and a boarskin respectively, or else had a lion and a boar emblazoned on their shields, he remembered an oracle commanding him to marry his daughters to 'a lion and a boar'. He further promised to re-establish the two young princes in the states that had exiled them. It was decided to restore Polynices first, and Adrastus gathered a huge army to help him. The seven leaders of the principal contingents were Adrastus, Polynices, Tydeus, Parthenopaeus (an Arcadian), Capaneus and Hippomedon (both Argives), and a further most unwilling Argive, Amphiaraus. Two alternative names were often included: Eteoclus, son of Ophis, instead of Adrastus; and Mecisteus, Adrastus' brother, instead of Polynices.

The army proceeded to Thebes in an over-confident mood, paying heed neither to Amphiaraus' predictions of doom, nor to Oedipus' curses directed against his sons; for he had prayed that they might kill one another. Tydeus carried out an unsuccessful mission to Thebes, to try and negotiate a settlement. On his way back he encountered fifty Thebans in an ambush and wiped out forty-nine of them. The Thebans, however, had grounds for confidence, since Tiresias had promised them victory if an unmarried male descended directly from the 'Sown Men' immolated himself for the city: and this self-sacrifice one of Creon's sons, Menoeceus (or Megareus), took upon himself.

After founding the Nemean Games in honour of Opheltes (see HYPSIPYLE), the army besieged Thebes, one champion attacking each of the seven gates. According to Aeschylus, in his play *Seven Against Thebes*, Tydeus attacked the Proetid Gate, defended by Melanippus; Capaneus the Electrian Gate, defended by Polyphontes; Eteoclus the Neistan Gate, defended by Creon's son Megareus; Hippomedon the Oncaean Gate, defended by Hyperbius; Parthenopaeus the Borrhaean Gate, defended by

Actor; Amphiaraus the Homoloid Gate, defended by Lasthenes, and Polynices the Hypsistian Gate, defended by Eteocles. Capaneus mounted the wall, crying that not even Zeus could prevent him from entering the city, for which boast the god slew him with a thunderbolt. Parthenopaeus was struck on the head and killed by a stone dropped by Periclymenus from the walls. Mecisteus and Eteoclus were slain in single combat. When Tydeus, himself severely wounded and dying, had killed his foe Melanippus, Athena, his protectress, begged Zeus to allow her to make him immortal. But Amphiaraus, who bore a grudge against all his allies, cut off Melanippus' head and tossed it to Tydeus – who began to devour the brains, thus alienating Athena's sympathy, so that he was not preserved from death. Amphiaraus was chased by Periclymenus and fled in his chariot, only to be swallowed up by the earth, which Zeus opened with a thunderbolt. Since it was known that whichever side Oedipus backed would win, Polynices had tried to win his support, and on Eteocles' behalf too Creon had tried to secure Oedipus' return to Thebes. But he withheld assistance from either side and maintained his curse, which was fulfilled when his two sons slew each other in single combat. Adrastus was the only one of the Seven to escape, thanks to his swift horse Arion, the foal of Poseidon and Demeter.

Creon now became king or regent of Thebes, and refused burial to the invaders who had perished, including Polynices. According to one account Argia his wife, in association with Antigone, dragged Polynices' body on to Eteocles' pyre. Sophocles, in his play *Antigone*, tells how his sister Antigone performed Polynices' burial rites unaided, by sprinkling a few handfuls of dust on the rotting corpse. Another version, recounted by Euripides in his *Suppliant Women*, asserted that Theseus, king of Athens, invaded Thebes and compelled Creon to bury the enemy dead in response to the supplications of Adrastus and the women of Argos at the altar of Demeter at Eleusis, where they were joined by Theseus' mother Aethra.

Ten years later the sons of the Seven, the Epigoni, avenged their fathers' deaths.

Sibylla or **Sibyl** The name of a mythical female who lived at Marpessus near Troy; she devoted herself to the service of Apollo, who gave her the gift of prophecy. She was believed to have expressed her oracles in riddles, and to have written them down on leaves. On account of the renown she gained, her name came to be used as a generic appellation, and many places claimed the presence of a Sibyl. Most famous were those of Erythrae, Libya, and Cumae.

The Sibyl of Cumae, Deiphobe, was once offered anything she liked by Apollo, if she would take him as her lover. She accepted his gift, asking for as many years as a pile of sweepings contained grains of dust; and the grains numbered a thousand. Unfortunately she had not asked for perpetual youth, and, as she changed her mind about becoming the god's mistress, she continued to age. She was finally so old that she hung from the ceiling of her cave in a bottle, all shrivelled up, and when children asked her what she wanted, she simply said, 'I want to die.'

Virgil describes Aeneas' descent into the Underworld accompanied by the Sibyl of Cumae, who showed him how to pluck the talismanic Golden Bough, as a passport to the realm of Hades, in the woods beside Lake Avernus. She also came to Tarquinius Superbus, the last king of Rome, with nine books of riddling prophecies, and demanded a huge price for them. He mocked her, however, and sent her away: and then she burnt three, and offered him six for the same sum. When he still refused to pay, she burnt three more and came once again to offer him the last three, still at the original price. This time Tarquinius consulted a board of priests, the augurs, who deplored the loss of the six books and advised him to buy those that remained. The books which he then acquired were traditionally identified with collections of oracles which still existed in historical times, having been preserved for many years in the temple of Capitoline Jupiter, so that they could be consulted in national emergencies. They were burnt in a fire which destroyed the temple in 83 BC.

Sicelus see SICULUS.

Sicinus Son of Thoas, king of Lemnos, and of Oenoe.

Siculus The eponym of the Sicilian race; also stated, according to one account, to have founded a city at Rome before the coming of Aeneas.

Side ('pomegranate') The first wife of the giant Orion; because she rivalled Hera in beauty, Zeus cast her into the Underworld.

Sidero ('woman of iron') Wife of Salmoneus and hard-hearted stepmother of Tyro, whose sons, Pelias and Neleus, after being abandoned and brought up by horse-dealers, later discovered who their mother was, and how cruelly Sidero had treated her. They avenged her by pursuing Sidero to a temple of Hera, where Pelias stabbed her to death.

Silenus, Sileni Silenus, an elderly companion of the Maenads in the revels of Dionysus, was a son of Pan or Hermes and of a nymph. He had a snub nose and the tail and ears of a horse; he was bald and pot-bellied, and often rode on a donkey. By origin a water-spirit, he had a reputation for practical wisdom, and the power of prophecy. In this character he was believed to have been the

young Dionysus' tutor, and was said to be the king of Nysa, the mythical land in which the god was brought up by the nymphs. Virgil tells how two shepherds once caught Silenus, and how he sang them legendary stories. He was also captured by King Midas of Phrygia, who wanted to share his wisdom. The king mixed wine with the waters of a forest spring, and when Silenus drank it, he fell asleep and was seized by the king's servants. They brought him before their master, to whom he imparted the secret of human life: that the best thing for man is not to be born at all, and the next best thing is to die as early as possible.

Silenus had a number of sons by the nymphs. In the satyr-plays (see SATYRS) written by the tragedians, these creatures, the Sileni, who took after their father in appearance, bore little resemblance to the wise old prophet described above. For they, as well as their father, became drunken, cowardly fellows, always wanting to be on the winning side; and they resembled the satyrs in their inability to keep their hands off the nymphs.

Socrates was compared with Silenus, on account of his physical appearance and method of argument.

Silvanus ('of the forest') An Italian woodland god, sometimes identified by Classical Latin writers with Pan and the satyrs, or with Mars in his capacity as a rural divinity.

Simaethis A nymph; the mother of Acis.

Sinis Surnamed *Pityokamptes*, 'pine-bender', because of an evil habit he possessed. For he was a brigand who infested the Corinthian Isthmus, stopping travellers and fastening their arms and legs to a couple of pine trees he had bent down together: then, having tied them in this way, he would release the trees, tearing his victims asunder. (According to another version he made his victim help him bend a pine to the ground and then suddenly released it so that the other was flung into the air.) Theseus, however, killed him by the same method that he had been accustomed to employ against others. He then discovered Sinis' beautiful daughter Perigune, who had been hiding from him in a dense clump of wild asparagus, vowing never to root them up or burn them if they would only protect her. It was not long, however, before she was in love with Theseus, and became his mistress, presenting him with a son, Melanippus. But eventually Theseus married her to Deioneus, son of Eurytus.

Sinon When the Greeks left the Trojan Horse standing in the plain outside Troy, one of their number, Sinon, stayed behind and deliberately allowed himself to be captured by the Trojans. Though a kinsman of Odysseus (Autolycus was grandfather of both), he pretended to the Trojans that he had been a follower of Palamedes, treacherously killed by Odysseus. He threw himself on the Trojans' mercy, telling them that Odysseus hated him and declaring that the Greeks, in response to an oracle from Apollo, had chosen him as a human sacrifice in order to win a favourable return journey. He also explained the pretended purpose of the Wooden Horse, assuring the Trojans that it was an offering to propitiate Athena for her loss of the Palladium, the image which Odysseus and Diomedes had stolen from the citadel of Troy. The prophet Calchas had declared, Sinon asserted, that if the Trojans burnt the horse, they would be ruined, but if they took it into their city, they would be safe from any further siege, for Troy would then become impregnable. As a result of these lies the Trojans breached the wall or enlarged the gateway and dragged the Horse into the city, at the same time giving Sinon

sanctuary. Later that night he sent a fire signal to the Greeks on the isle of Tenedos, and then opened the Horse, so that the warriors hidden inside it emerged, and Troy was taken by the Greeks.

Sirens Bird-like women not unlike the Harpies in form and effect. The number varies in different accounts. Where there were three, their names were Leucosia ('white'), Ligeia ('shrill'), and Parthenope ('maiden-voice'); where two, Himeropa ('gentle-voice') and Thelxiepeia ('enchanting speech'); where there were four, Thelxiepeia, Aglaopheme ('lovely speech'), Peisinoe ('persuasive'), and Molpe ('song'). Their parentage was much disputed: they were said to be the daughters of a Muse and of Phorcys or a river-god, the Achelous. They lived on an island, Anthemoessa ('flowery'), near the straits where Scylla and Charybdis lurked, and sang so sweetly that any sailor who heard them was compelled to stay and listen for ever: the ground around them was white with the bleached bones of sailors. According to one account their victims were shipwrecked on the rocks.

It was prophesied that when any ship should sail past their island without succumbing, the Sirens would leap into the sea and drown. Strangely, this condition was fulfilled on two occasions. In the first place Orpheus, when he sailed past in the *Argo*, was able to drown their singing with his music so that only one man, Butes, heard them and leapt overboard. Aphrodite, who loved him, saved Butes' life. Secondly Odysseus escaped, for, on the advice of Circe, he blocked his men's ears with beeswax, and made them tie him to the foot of the mast so that he could not be drawn away by the Sirens' song. When he begged to be released, the crew had orders to tighten his bonds.

The Sirens were said to sing prophecies and songs relating to the kingdom of Hades. They were connected with Persephone, for according to one version they had been the goddess's companions who allowed Hades to carry her off; they were changed into their grotesque shape as a punishment for this crime. They were once induced to compete in singing against the Muses (their parents, according to one account): they lost, and the Muses plucked their feathers to make themselves crowns. One of the Sirens, Parthenope, was believed to have reached the site of Naples, which originally bore her name.

Sisyphus Son of Aeolus and Enarete. He founded the city of Corinth, though to begin with he named it Ephyra. He was proverbial for his cunning and craft: for this reason he was sometimes associated (with scant regard for mythical chronology) with Autolycus the master thief. It was said by late authors that Autolycus stole his cattle, but that he recovered them. Having made notches beforehand in their hooves, he was able to prove Autolycus' denials of the theft to be false; and then he got his own back on the thief by seducing his daughter Anticlea – so that he, rather than her husband Laertes, was sometimes rumoured to be the father of Odysseus, whom she subsequently bore.

When Sisyphus founded Ephyra, he established the Isthmian Games there in honour of Melicertes, whose body he had found and buried there; and he fortified the neighbouring high hill of the Acrocorinth as a citadel and watchtower. One day he caught sight of Zeus as he was carrying off the river-nymph Aegina, daughter of the river-god Asopus and of Metope; Zeus took her to the isle of Oenone, where he ravished her. Asopus gave chase, and asked for information from Sisyphus, who promised to tell what he knew, in return for a spring of fresh water on the Acrocorinth, which Asopus immediately produced (the spring of Pirene). Zeus was

furious at Sisyphus' disclosure, and punished him by sending Thanatos (Death) to take him off to the house of Hades. Sisyphus, a master of cunning, somehow tricked Thanatos, bound him, and threw him into a dungeon, with the result that mortals ceased to die. Then the gods, disturbed by this abnormal phenomenon, sent Ares to release Thanatos, who came looking for Sisyphus once again. However Sisyphus had given his wife, the Pleiad Merope, careful instructions what to do in such an eventuality: she left his body unburied and made none of the customary offerings to the dead. Thus Sisyphus tricked Hades, for that god was so angry at Merope's neglectfulness that he, or his wife Persephone, allowed Sisyphus to return to the upper world to punish Merope and make her bury his body. On returning to Corinth, however, Sisyphus did no such thing, but resumed his life and lived on to a great age in defiance of the gods of the Underworld. It was felt to be because of this impiety, quite as much as for his tale-telling about Zeus, that his shade was punished in Tartarus after his death. For he was forced to roll a great stone eternally up a hill: when he had nearly pushed it to the top, it always rolled down again to the bottom.

After a long reign Sisyphus was buried on the Isthmus. He left four sons: Glaucus (father of Bellerophon), Ornytion (father of Phocus 2), Thersander, and Almus.

Sleep see HYPNOS.

Smicrus (Greek *smikros* 'small'). A lost child, descended from Apollo, whom the wealthy Patron took as a servant into his household. When Smicrus and Patron's other servants caught a swan, they wrapped it up in a cloth and presented it to their master. On unwrapping it, he discovered that it had turned into a woman. She instructed Patron to take special care of Smicrus, who would bring him luck, and, in consequence, Patron married him to his daughter. Their son was Branchus, founder of the oracle of Branchidae.

Smintheus see APOLLO.

Smyrna see MYRRHA.

Somnus see HYPNOS.

Sosipolis A divine child, brought by an unknown woman to Olympia and given by her to the people of Elis, who were under attack from the Arcadians. She declared that a dream had warned her to hand her baby over to the Eleans as their ally. When, therefore, the battle-line was drawn up, the Elean general placed the naked child in front of his army: and, as their Arcadian enemies approached, it turned into a serpent, at which they fled in terror. The serpent then vanished into the ground. The Eleans dedicated a temple to the child under the name Sosipolis, 'safety of the state'.

Sown Men or **Spartoi** The five warriors who sprang from the dragon's teeth that Cadmus sowed at Thebes, and survived the ensuing battle. Their names were Echion ('serpent') the father of Pentheus, Udaeus ('of the ground'). Chthonius ('of the earth'), Hyperenor ('superman'), and Pelorus ('giant'). They made peace with Cadmus and accepted his rule as king of Thebes; and they became the ancestors of the Theban nobility.

Sparte Wife of Lacedaemon and eponym of Sparta.

Spartoi see SOWN MEN

Spermo see ANIUS.

Sphaerus ('sphere', 'wheel') The chariot-eer of Pelops, who was buried on an island near Troezen, which was called Sphaeria after him. Aethra conceived Theseus upon the island, which she re-named Hiera ('sacred').

Sphinx or **Phix** ('the throttler') A winged monster with a woman's head and a lion's body. The daughter of Echidna and Typhon (or the hound Or-thrus), she was dispatched by Hera to plague Thebes in revenge for Laius' ab-duction of Chrysippus, an offence against the goddess of marriage. Accord-ing to another account, Apollo or Diony-sus sent her – the latter in order to punish the Thebans for neglecting his rites. For she would ambush young The-bans in a lonely place outside the city, or else would fly to the citadel and trap her victims there. Then, sitting on a wall or a rock, she challenged them to answer her famous riddle. It was this: 'There is on earth a two-footed, four-footed, and three-footed thing under one and the same name – the only creature to change its nature of all that go on land, through air, or in the sea; but the speed of its limbs is weakest when it walks on most feet.' When the men she challenged failed to answer, as was in-variably the case, the Sphinx jumped on them, carried them off, and devoured them. One of Creon's sons (sometimes identified as Haemon) was killed like this. It was ordained that if ever any of her victims gave the right answer, the Sphinx would dash herself to death on the rocks, or at any rate leave Thebes for ever. In despair after the death of King Laius of Thebes, Creon, as regent, offered the kingdom to anybody who would rid Thebes of the Sphinx. This was achieved by Oedipus, who was accosted by the beast while on his way to the city. His reply to the riddle was: 'You mean man who, when he walks the earth, is at first a baby on all fours; and, when he gets old, bent down and scarcely able to raise his head, leans on a stick as his third foot.' On receiving this correct answer the Sphinx hurled herself to her death.

Staphylus ('bunch of grapes') *1*. Son of Dionysus and Ariadne, who, together with his brother Phanus, accompanied the Argonauts. His daughter Rhoeo bore Anius to Apollo.

2. A goatherd in the service of Oeneus of Calydon. He discovered the grape, when one of his goats was found eating the fruit of a wild vine. He gave a bunch to his master, who squeezed the juice out of the grapes, and drank it. Then Dionysus showed Oeneus how to ferment the juice into wine.

Stentor A proverbial herald who, according to Homer, had a voice equal to the voices of fifty men. He invented the trumpet, but, after failing to beat Hermes in a shouting contest, died.

Stercutus The Roman god of dunglaying. *See* PICUS.

Sterope *1* see PLEIADES.
2. see CEPHEUS *2*.
3. see ACASTUS; ANTIGONE *2*.

Steropes *see* CYCLOPES

Stheneboea *see* BELLEROPHON.

Sthenelus *1*. Son of Perseus and Andromeda. He was king of Mycenae, and married Pelops' daughter Amphibia or Nicippe, who bore him Eurystheus, Alcyone, and Medusa. When Amphitryon accidentally killed the former king of Mycenae Electryon, Sthenelus, who was the brother of the dead ruler, seized the throne, and Tiryns too. He also gave the town of Midea to his brothers-in-law Atreus and Thyestes.

2. The companion of Heracles on his campaign against the Amazons. Apollonius Rhodius made him a son of Actor, and asserted that he was killed in the campaign and that his ghost was later seen by the Argonauts. The mythographer Apollodorus represented him as a son of Androgeos and brother of Al-

caeus *2*, and stated that he lived on the island of Paros which Androgeos ruled as king. The two brothers were given as hostages to Heracles after he had besieged the town. He took them on his quest for the Amazon's belt, and after his return presented them with the island of Thasos, which he conquered for them.

3. Son of Capaneus and Evadne. He was a close friend of Diomedes, whom he accompanied in the attack of the Epigoni on Thebes. Then, as one of the suitors of Helen (who were under an oath to protect whoever became her husband), he was obliged to take part in the Trojan War. Though he himself was king of a third of the Argolid (having a better claim to the throne than Diomedes himself), he was unable to fight on foot because of an injury received in falling from a wall during the siege of Thebes. In consequence, he went into battle driving Diomedes' chariot. He did, however, take part in the ambush of the Wooden Horse, and returned to Argos with Diomedes. There it proved that his son Cometes had seduced Diomedes' wife Aegialia. Another son, Cylarabes, became king of the whole of the Argolid.

Stheno or **Sthenno** *see* GORGONS.

Stilbe A nymph, the daughter of the River Penieus and the Naiad Creusa. In one version she was mother of the Centaurs and Lapiths by Apollo.

Strophius *see* PYLADES.

Strymo Daughter of the River Scamander; the wife of Laomedon.

Stymphalian Birds *see* HERACLES (sixth Labour).

Stymphalus Son of Elatus, son of Arcas; king of Arcadia. He founded the city of Stymphalus in north-eastern Arcadia.

When Pelops, king of Elis, tried to conquer Arcadia, he feigned friendship with Stymphalus and then treacherously murdered him, scattering his bones far and wide. This impiety brought a drought on the whole of Greece; and it was only alleviated by the prayers of Aeacus. His daughter Parthenope bore Heracles a son, Everes.

Styx ('abomination') The eldest daughter of Oceanus and Tethys. She ruled the river which, branching off from the Ocean, ran from Mount Chelmus in Arcadia through a wild gorge down into the Underworld. There it divided into several branches, including Cocytus ('wailing'), and wound nine times around Hades' kingdom of the dead.

In the Underworld Styx lived in a palace which was splendid with silver pillars. She married the Titan Pallas, and bore Cratos (Might), Bia (Force), Zelus (Zeal), and Nike (Victory). When Zeus fought Cronos and the Titans, she was the first to come to Zeus' aid, and her children were of great value in his victorious campaign. Zeus made them his closest attendants and decreed that an oath sworn by the waters of Styx should never be broken even by the gods: whenever a god swore an oath, Iris fetched a jar of this water and poured a libation of it as the oath was pronounced. The breaker of such an oath went into a deathlike stupor for a Great Year (usually said to be nine ordinary years), after which he was exiled from Olympus for nine more Great Years.

Sun see HELIOS.

Sychaeus see DIDO.

Syleus An outlaw in Lydia who forced passers-by to till his vineyard. Heracles, when in Omphale's service, killed him with his own hoe.

Syrinx (also called Nonacris) An Arcadian nymph who passed her time hunting in the company of Artemis. One day Pan amorously pursued her. In order to preserve her virginity, she begged the nymphs of the River Ladon, which she could not cross, to help her: and they turned her into a bed of reeds. When Pan reached the river, he made his pipes from the same reeds, and called them *syrinx* after his love.

Syrna see PODALIRIUS.

T

Tages A divine child of Etruscan mythology. One day an Etruscan ploughman was tilling a field in the neighbourhood of Tarquinii, when a head stuck out of the furrow; he uncovered the body, and found a small child, Tages, with the grey hair of an old man. Tages addressed the ploughman, who summoned his neighbours. The child was then taken to the twelve princes of the twelve Etruscan cities, who received him with great honour and listened to his teaching. His words were written down in the Books of Tages (*libri Tagetici*), from which the Etruscan soothsayers derived their knowledge. The chief of the twelve princes was Tarchon, who, according to some accounts, was the ploughman who unearthed Tages. The child, his mission accomplished, returned to the soil. *See* TARCHIES.

Talaus The eldest son of Bias and Pero; he inherited Bias' kingdom in the Argolid, and was an Argonaut. His wife was Lysimache, and several of his sons joined the expedition of the Seven against Thebes. Eriphyle, his daughter, supported them against the wishes of her husband Amphiaraus. The sons of Talaus were Adrastus, Mecisteus, Pronax, Aristomachus, and perhaps Hippomedon and Parthenopaeus.

Talos The bronze man of Crete. He was a giant and the last survivor of the men of bronze. He had a single vein running from his head to his ankles, containing ichor – the blood of the gods – and sealed at the bottom by a bronze nail or a membrane of skin. Some said that Zeus gave him to Europa to guard her island, others that Hephaestus made him for Minos. His business was to run around the coast of Crete three times every day, and repel any invaders who appeared. In order to do this, he pelted their ships with rocks, or burnt them by making himself red hot and clasping them in his arms. He finally succumbed to Medea, who, when the Argonauts wished to land, sang spells which put the giant to sleep; she then pulled out the nail in his foot – or cut the membrane – and he died. There are also other accounts of how Medea killed him. For example, it was asserted that she gave him a drug; or she gained his confidence by promising to make him immortal; or she simply talked him into injuring his own foot, so that the ichor ran out. Alternatively, the Argonaut Poeas was said to have pierced his membrane with an arrow.

Talthybius A Spartan; the herald of Agamemnon in the Trojan War. He was the colleague of Eurybates, but authors later than Homer made Talthybius the more important of the two. He performed a number of unpleasant duties for his master: the removal of Briseis from Achilles' tent, the capture of Astyanax from Andromache so that he could be put to death, and the announcement to Hecabe that Polyxena had to be slain in order to appease Achilles' ghost. He also helped Odysseus fetch Iphigenia to Aulis to be sacrificed there. Subsequently, he returned to his native Sparta to die.

Talus *see* PERDIX.

Tanaquil An Etruscan noblewoman of Roman mythology; though, denuded of her myths, she could also be a historical figure. She was said to have married Tarquinius Priscus – the son of a Greek who had settled in Etruria – and to have persuaded him to move from Tarquinii in that country to Rome, where he gained possession of the throne. She was instrumental in promoting the interests of Servius Tullius, and when Tarquinius Priscus was killed by the sons of his predecessor Ancus Marcius, Tanaquil ensured Servius' succession. Some sources, however, gave Gaia Caecilia as the name of Tarquinius' wife; whether she was thought of as the same person as Tanaquil is uncertain.

Tantalus *1.* Son of Zeus and the Titaness Pluto ('wealth'). He was a Lydian, and ruled the region of Mount Sipylus in that country. As his mother's name, and the Greek saying 'the talents of Tantalus' (*Tantalou talanta*) suggest ('talen', a large measure of gold), he had a great reputation for riches. He married Dione, a daughter of Atlas, or Euryanassa, a daughter of the River Pactolus. Their children were Pelops, who migrated to Elis in Greece, Niobe, who married Amphion, and the sculptor Broteas, who carved the first image of Rhea or Cybele.

Tantalus offended the gods, and was punished for eternity in Tartarus. By eating at the gods' table and listening to their conversation, he had become immortal. But how he earned the dire fate which then descended upon him was variously recounted. For one thing, he invited the gods to dine with him, and when they came he presumptuously tested their omniscience by killing his son Pelops, cooking his flesh, and serving it up to them in a stew. All the gods realised the gruesome character of the dish except Demeter, who, in her grief for her lost Persephone, absent-mindedly gnawed Pelops' shoulder. Then Hermes fetched Pelops from the Underworld and the gods restored him to life, replacing his damaged shoulder with ivory; but thenceforth Tantalus was hateful to them. He was also said to have stolen nectar and ambrosia from the gods' table to give to his friends, and to have told mortals the secrets he had heard there. Yet another story of his wickedness tells how Pandareos stole from a shrine of Zeus a wonderful golden guard-dog, which he gave to Tantalus to look after. Hermes was sent by Zeus to claim the dog, and Pandareos later asked for it back, but on both occasions Tantalus swore an oath that he knew nothing of the dog and had never seen it.

For some or all of these various offences Tantalus was punished in Tartarus. For he was kept perpetually famished and parched, standing chin-deep in water and with laden boughs of fruit trees just above his head; he could not reach the water to drink it, and whenever he tried to take the fruit, it receded from him. (The English verb 'tantalise' is derived from his name, because of this punishment.) Alternatively (or additionally) a great stone hung over his head, suspended by a thread, so that he lived in everlasting terror.

2. Son of Thyestes; he was Clytemnestra's first husband, but Agamemnon killed him and his child and married the widow.

Tarchetius In an Etruscan version of the myth of Romulus' and Remus' birth – differing from the Roman tradition – Plutarch tells how Tarchetius, a wicked Etruscan king of Alba Longa, saw a male organ rise from the hearth in his palace and stay there for many days. An oracle pronounced by Tethys told him that, if a virgin had intercourse with this phallus, her son would be of great importance. Tarchetius told his daughter that this was what she must do, but she was ashamed and made her slave-girl take her place. When Tarchetius learnt the truth, he imprisoned both women – he was prevented from killing them by a dream in which Vesta, goddess of the hearth, appeared to him – and made them weave a tapestry by day, which he subsequently caused to be unpicked every night. The slave-girl eventually bore twin sons, whom Tarchetius gave to a servant, Teratius, to expose. He placed them beside the river, where a wolf suckled them and birds brought them titbits. Finally a cowherd spied them and saved them. He brought them up, and when they were men, they killed Tarchetius. Similar stories were told of the birth of Servius Tullius.

Tarchies An Etruscan seer (perhaps to be identified with Tages) who taught Tarchon the art of divination from animals' entrails.

Tarchon Son of Tyrrhenus, mythical leader of the migration of the Lydians, the future Etruscans, to central Italy. Tarchon (his name is of the same origin as Tarquinius and Tarpeia) was said to have founded the city of Tarquinii and to have encouraged his followers to found the other eleven cites of Etruria. When Cacus, represented by some accounts as a fellow-Lydian who had joined the emigration to Etruria, tried to usurp Tarchon's authority, Tarchon imprisoned him, but he escaped and caused disturbances in Campania, where Hercules killed him in defence of the Greeks. Tarchon also had trouble with his vassal Mezentius, who tyrannised Caere and was exiled; when Mezentius opposed Aeneas' settlement on the Tiber, Tarchon took this as a sign that he himself must join Aeneas' allies, since only under foreign leadership could Mezentius effectively be crushed. Tarchon learnt the art of the *haruspices*, Etruscan soothsayers, from Tages and Tarchies.

Tarpeia Daughter of Spurius Tarpeius,

commander of the Capitoline fortress when, at the beginning of Romulus' reign, it was attacked by the Sabines under their king Titus Tatius. There were many variants of her myth, and many different motives were assigned to her. She was said to have sought an interview with Tatius and to have proposed to him that she obtain the keys and surrender him the fortress, for which service (or, according to another tradition, in return for his love) what his soldiers wore on their left arms must be given up to her. The usual story was that she wanted their gold bracelets and rings; another version maintained that she really wished to deprive them of their shields, which were actually what they wore upon their left arms. She let the Sabines in by the gate at night, crying to the Roman defenders that they must flee. When the Sabines had the hill in their control, according to the best-known tradition they gave up their shields to her, throwing them at her so that she was overwhelmed by them and died, but in the alternative version it was she who insisted on having their shields. Her intention, according to this view, was to obtain the enemy's shields and, when she had gained them and held the Sabines in her power, she sent Romulus a message to send a force: the messenger, however, deserted to the enemy, and the Sabines, learning of her plot, put her to death. It was therefore disputed by Roman mythologists whether she was a heroine or a traitress. The early name of the Capitol was the Tarpeian Hill, and traitors were cast over the Tarpeian Rock at its edge; this was said to be in recollection of the arch-traitress Tarpeia. *See* TARCHON.

Tarquinius, Arruns *1.* Son or grandson of King Tarquinius Priscus of Rome. He was murdered by his brother Lucius Tarquinius Superbus at the instigation of his wife Tullia, in a political intrigue to overthrow Tullia's father, King Servius

Tullius, and win the throne back for the Tarquin family.

2. Son of Tarquinius Superbus. In the war waged with the aid of Veii to re-establish the expelled house of the Tarquins on the throne of Rome, he fought in single combat against Lucius Junius Brutus, and both combatants were killed.

Tarquinius Collatinus, Lucius A great-nephew of Tarquinius Priscus, who appointed him as governor of the little Alban town of Collatia. After the Roman leaders, while conducting the siege of Ardea, had argued about the virtues of their wives, they proceeded to pay them a surprise visit to see which was behaving best – a contest which Collatinus' wife Lucretia won. She was then brutally raped by Sextus Tarquinius. Collatinus joined the movement to avenge Lucretia and to set up a republic, under the leadership (according to one tradition) of Lucius Junius Brutus. Appointed as one of the consuls of the first year, Collatinus had to resign his post because of popular resentment against his name, which was associated with the royal family. He resigned on the suggestion of Brutus and went into exile at Lanuvium.

Tarquinius Priscus, Lucius The fifth king of Rome who reigned, according to tradition, from 616 to 579 BC; whether he is a mythical or (at least to some extent) a historical figure is uncertain. According to Livy he was the son of a Greek immigrant to Tarquinii named Demaratus, a Corinthian from whom he inherited great wealth; his mother was an Etruscan, and he was originally called Lucumo (an Etruscan word meaning 'prince'). Although the Etruscans scorned him as a foreigner, he married an ambitious Etruscan woman named Tanaquil (or a woman called Gaia Caecilia, perhaps to be identified with Tanaquil), who persuaded him to move to

Rome. When they reached the Janiculum Hill, Lucumo received an omen of his future power from an eagle, which removed the cap on his head and then replaced it again; Tanaquil interpreted this as a sign of his future kingship. After his arrival in Rome, he took the Roman name Lucius Tarquinius Priscus (Priscus means 'the original', 'the first'). He made himself indispensable to King Ancus Marcius by his services, and when Ancus died he was elected king, even though Ancus had left two sons of his own. He then strengthened his position, it was said, by enrolling a hundred of his supporters into the Senate.

Priscus was believed to have reigned for thirty-eight years, during which time, it was believed, he had founded the Circus Maximus, started to wall the city with stone, annexed a number of Latin towns (called the 'Ancient Latins'), and defeated the Sabines. He was also credited with the draining of the marshy land between the Palatine and Capitoline Hills – which thus became the Roman Forum – and with initiating the construction of the temple of Capitoline Jupiter. Two shepherds in the pay of the sons of Ancus Marcius murdered him by cleaving his head open with an axe. He was succeeded, however, by his son-in-law Servius Tullius, whom Queen Tanaquil had promoted to high position. At first she kept the news of Priscus' death a secret, pretending he was merely wounded. It was only when Servius was well established, after the murderers had been dealt with and Ancus' sons had gone into exile, that she allowed the truth to come out.

Tarquinius Superbus, Lucius 'the Proud' The seventh and last legendary king of Rome: perhaps recalling a historical figure (for there must have been a last king of Rome) but embodying many myths. He was believed to be a son or grandson of Tarquinius Priscus. He achieved power through the ambition of Tullia (daughter of King Servius

Tullius, successor of Priscus), who incited him to kill his previous wife and Arruns Tarquinius (his brother and her first husband) so that he and Tullia could marry: for Tullia despised her father's humble origins, and saw in Tarquinius Superbus a man of the right mettle to rule Rome as a despot. When they had duly become man and wife, she pressed him to eliminate her father and seize the throne. Taking a clique of his young followers, Tarquinius Superbus occupied the Senate House and sat on the king's throne. Servius Tullius appeared and ordered him out: whereupon Tarquinius attacked the old man bodily, casting him out of the building, and had him stabbed by his followers in the street. Then, as Tullia rode triumphantly through Rome, her carriage ran over her father's corpse. Tarquinius refused the dead king burial and killed his supporters. Named Superbus, 'arrogant', he embarked on a rule of terror, and trumped up charges against the senators, in order to get his hands on their wealth and estates. He was cunning as well as cruel, as his conquest of the town of Gabii without a struggle serves to illustrate. He sent his son Sextus Tarquinius to the town in the guise of a fugitive and a suppliant. Sextus pretended he had been persecuted by his father, and rapidly gained the trust of the leading citizens of Gabii. He urged them to make war on Rome, and was soon made commander-in-chief. Then Sextus sent his father a secret messenger, to enquire what to do next. Tarquinius merely took the messenger in the garden and knocked off the poppyheads with his stick. Sextus took the hint, assassinated the chief men of Gabii, and had no difficulty in presenting his father with a conquered town.

Tarquinius Superbus was an excellent commander, and brought under the rule of Rome such Latin states as had remained outside its sphere. He was thought to have completed the temple of Capitoline Jupiter and, according to one tradition, to have laid the Cloaca Maxima ('great sewer') through the Forum. Subsequently, while he was besieging the Rutulian town of Ardea, his son Sextus raped Lucretia, the wife of his cousin Lucius Tarquinius Collatinus, at Collatia: an action which was believed to have precipitated the fall of the Roman monarchy, followed by the inauguration of the Republic. Led (as one version had it) by Lucius Junius Brutus, the leading citizens, in their disgust and anger at Sextus' deed and at the cruelty of his father, closed the gates of Rome in the face of the royal family, while it was attempting to return to the city from Ardea. Tarquinius Superbus fled to Caere and persuaded the Etruscans of Veii and Tarquinii to attack Rome on his behalf. Meanwhile at Rome the Senate, after debating what to do with the property of his family, refused either to restore it or confiscate it; instead they turned the people loose to pillage from it whatever they wanted. The Field of Mars (Campus Martius) was created out of royal lands. A plot to restore Tarquinius, which involved certain young patricians including Brutus' sons, was uncovered by a slave.

The war with Veii and Tarquinii was won with difficulty by Rome. Tarquinius then took refuge with the king of a further Etruscan city, Lars Porsenna of Clusium, who also failed to restore him, whereupon he retired to Tusculum. But the Romans, it was believed, continued to be afraid he might appear; and he fought them at the battle of Lake Regillus, where he was wounded. He was said to have died a few years later at Cumae in Campania.

Tarquinius, Sextus The youngest of the three sons of Tarquinius Superbus. He won control of the city of Gabii for his father, but provoked the overthrow of the monarchy by his rape of Lucretia. After the expulsion of the Tarquins from

Rome, he took refuge in Gabii, where he was assassinated. *See* TARQUINIUS SUPERBUS, LUCIUS.

Tatia The first wife of Numa Pompilius.

Tatius, Titus *see* ROMULUS.

Taygete A Pleiad (a daughter of Atlas), Taygete was the nymph of the Taygetus range of mountains west of Sparta. She served Artemis and hunted with her; but Zeus made love to her, and fathered upon her Lacedaemon, ancestor of the Spartans. Artemis was said to have vainly turned Taygete into a doe, to enable her to escape the attentions of Zeus. The poet Pindar suggested that this doe, or another which Taygete offered to Artemis in thanks for her efforts, was the Cerynitian Hind that Heracles pursued as his third Labour.

Tecmessa Daughter of a Phrygian king, Teleutas. She was the mistress of Aias (son of Telamon), to whom she bore Eurysaces.

Tegyrius A Thracian king who gave shelter to Eumolpus.

Telamon ('shield-strap') Son of Aeacus, king of Aegina, and of Endeis. He and his brother Peleus, at the instigation of their mother, and perhaps also from motives of personal jealousy, killed their bastard half-brother, the athlete Phocus. Although they hid the body, Aeacus discovered the crime and exiled both his sons. Telamon made his new home in Salamis, an island off the coast of Attica. The pair later claimed that the homicide was accidental; or Telamon declared that he, for his part, had taken no part in the actual murder. He sent Aeacus a herald, asking to be allowed to return. Aeacus permitted him to approach the shore in a ship and plead his case from its deck, but rejected the plea and re-fused to allow him to land. Telamon married Glauce, daughter of King Cychreus of Salamis, and, when the king died, leaving no son, inherited the throne. Glauce appears to have died soon afterwards, for it was by his second wife, Eriboea or Periboea, daughter of Alcathous, that Telamon became father of Aias (Ajax) *1*.

Telamon sailed with the Argonauts and joined the Calydonian boar-hunt. He also aided Heracles in the sack of Troy, when the hero punished Laomedon for his dishonesty. Telamon was instrumental in breaching the city wall and entered the city first – a feat which Heracles would have bitterly resented, had not Telamon at once built an altar and declared that he was dedicating it to Heracles the Victor. For the part he had played in the victory, Heracles gave him Laomedon's daughter Hesione as his slave. The hero also asked his father Zeus to send Telamon a brave son; in response to his prayer, an eagle appeared, providing a good omen. The child was called Aias after the eagle (aietos). When Heracles visited Salamis, he wrapped the boy in his Nemean lion-skin, thus rendering him invulnerable. Hesione also bore Telamon a son, Teucer, who accompanied Aias to the Trojan War. Telamon may have given Heracles further support by joining him in his war against the Amazons. His death was variously described, for the people of Elis claimed to have killed him when he was helping Heracles to fight them, whereas the usual tradition is that he died in Salamis much later on, after banishing Teucer for failing to save Aias from death at Troy.

Telchines Magicians who lived at Ialysus, in the island of Rhodes. The historian Diodorus makes them the children of Thalassa (the sea) and says they were Rhodes' original inhabitants. They helped Capheira to nurse Poseidon in his childhood, perhaps when Cronos wished to devour him. They were able to alter the weather, cure diseases, and make wonderful objects out of metal. For example, they were believed to have made Poseidon's trident (more usually, however, attributed to the Cyclopes, with whom they were sometimes confused) and Cronos' sickle, and the first images of the gods. Their ability as smiths is attested by the names of three of them, Chryson ('gold-worker'), Argyron ('silver-worker'), and Chalcon ('bronze-worker'). But at the same time they were considered to be malevolent. For they were adept at putting the evil eye on the works of men: for example, they destroyed crops by mixing sulphur with the waters of the Styx and sprinkling the poisonous mixture on the island. Zeus therefore grew to hate them, and drowned them in a great flood – even though they had foreseen it, and had fled to Asia Minor to escape the engulfing waters. According to a variant account, however, they were driven from Rhodes by the sons of Helios, the god of the island.

Teledice see PHORONEUS.

Telegonus see ODYSSEUS.

Telemachus Son of Odysseus and Penelope. Homer's *Odyssey* shows us his development from a timid youth to a self-confident and resourceful man. When his father was summoned to go off to the Trojan War, he was still a baby. Odysseus had tried to avoid enrolment by pretending to be mad and sowing salt on the sea-shore he had ploughed. Palamedes, however, detected his ruse by placing Telemachus on the ground in front of the plough, whereupon Odysseus, after displaying his sanity by failing to run him over, abandoned his pretence.

During the nineteen years of his father's absence, Telemachus saw his mother besieged by a flock of suitors,

against whom he had not the strength to prevail. But Athena, appearing first in the form of a Taphian, Mentes, and later as Mentor, the Ithacan who was charged with his education, inspired him with boldness and persuaded him to sail off to seek news of his father. He went to Nestor in Pylos and Menelaus at Sparta – the latter providing him with grounds for hope. Meanwhile the suitors, irked by his criticisms, had conspired to lay an ambush for him on his return voyage, but Athena directed him back to Ithaca by a different route. When he reached home, Odysseus was already on the island. Telemachus henceforth showed courage and resource. He first went for news to the swineherd Eumaeus, in whose hut he met his father. After a moving reunion, father and son plotted the downfall of the suitors. Telemachus cleared the palace hall of the weapons hanging on the walls, so that, after the contest with the bow, the suitors were powerless to oppose Odysseus in the massacre that he inaugurated. In that battle Telemachus fought energetically beside his father. After the defeat of the suitors, however, traditions about him diverge. According to one account he married Nestor's daughter Polycaste, who had bathed him at Pylos – or Nausicaa, whom Odysseus had met in Scheria. A later tradition recounts how Telemachus was banished by Odysseus because of an oracle which foretold that his son would kill him. After Odysseus' death at the hands of Circe's son Telegonus, he returned home and then went with Penelope to Aeaea, where he buried Odysseus and married Circe. The witch made him immortal, and gave him a son, Latinus.

Telemus A Cyclopian prophet, the son of Eurymus. He foretold Polyphemus' blinding at the hands of Odysseus.

Telephassa Wife of the Phoenician King Agenor; she bore Cadmus and Europa and a number of other children. When her husband sent his sons out in quest of Europa, whom Zeus had seduced, she left him, and accompanied Cadmus to Thebes.

Telephus Son of Heracles and Auge, the daughter of King Aleus of Tegea. Aleus, because he knew of an oracle predicting that any son of Auge would cause the death of one of his sons, installed her as priestess in Athena's temple, a post requiring perpetual virginity. However when Heracles came to Tegea he seduced her. On discovering that she was pregnant, Aleus was furious and sent his daughter to the sea to be drowned; on the way there, she bore a son, Telephus. When they reached Nauplia, King Nauplius placed both mother and son in a chest, and set it adrift; they eventually landed in Mysia, where Auge brought Telephus up. Another version of the story asserts that she bore the child in Athena's temple and hid it there, as a result of which the goddess in her anger caused the land to be barren. Her father enquired the reason for this pestilence, and discovered his daughter's offence. He therefore abandoned and exposed the child on Mount Parthenium, and sent Auge to Nauplius for sale as a slave overseas. She was sold to Teuthras, king of Teuthrania on the River Caicus in Mysia. Telephus was discovered by some shepherds in the care of a doe (*elaphos*) which was suckling him (*thele*, 'a teat'), and in consequence the shepherds named him *Telephus*. They brought him up in the company of Parthenopaeus, who had been abandoned nearby. The two were great friends. Some said, however, that Auge herself abandoned Telephus on Mount Parthenium to hide her shame, or that she bore him there on the way to Nauplia.

When Telephus grew up, he was anxious to know the identity of his parents – according to one story, because he had been taunted at Aleus' court with being a nobody. On receiving this affront, he killed the person who mocked him and the dead man turned out to be one of Aleus' sons. In any case, it is agreed that Telephus consulted the Delphic Oracle, which sent him to Mysia to find out about his origins. Accompanied by Parthenopaeus, he sailed to Teuthrania, where, at the head of an army of Greek invaders, he helped to drive out Idas. Teuthras, who had no son, made him his heir. In one version Teuthras had married Auge. In another, however, he had adopted her as his daughter, and now insisted on marrying her to Telephus as part of his reward. Auge, though unaware she was his mother, was opposed to the match, according to some accounts because she wished to remain faithful to Heracles' memory. So she took a sword to bed with her, intending to stab the young man. But suddenly an enormous snake appeared in the bed between them, and now Auge, in her terror, confessed her intention. Telephus, understandably outraged, prepared to kill her; whereupon she called on Heracles for his help, and Telephus asked why she had appealed to the hero. Then she told him the story of her seduction, and the two thus came to recognise each other. In this version of the story (told by Hyginus), Telephus then married Argiope, Teuthras' daughter. His wife was alternatively given as Astyoche (or Laodice), a daughter of Priam.

While Telephus was on the throne of Teuthrania, the Trojan War broke out; as Priam's son-in-law, he supported the Trojan side. The Greeks mistakenly landed in Mysia, believing it to be Trojan territory. Telephus fought against them, killing Polynices' son Thersander, but was himself wounded by Achilles when his foot caught in a grapevine. After the Greeks returned home, Telephus' wound had still not healed up. He consulted an oracle and was told, 'he that wounded shall also heal'. Then, dressed in beggar's rags, he went to Mycenae, where the Greek captains were preparing another expedition against Troy. He confided his plight to Clytemnestra, who advised him that the only way to gain his point with the kings was to seize the child Orestes and supplicate Agamemnon. He did so, urging that Achilles should cure him. The Greek leaders, who had received an oracle that they could reach Troy only if Telephus guided them there, supported his plea. Achilles declared that he had no experience as a doctor; but Odysseus saw a deeper meaning in the oracle, and suggested that it referred to Achilles' spear rather than to Achilles himself. So a little rust from the spear was applied daily to the wound, and in a few days it had healed. Telephus guided the Greek fleet to Troy, but refused to join them. After his death, his son Eurypylus, in the tenth year of the war, led Mysian reinforcements to aid Priam. The myth of Telephus was in later times fostered by the Attalid kings of Pergamum in Mysia.

Telethusa *see* IPHIS *3*.

Tellus or **Terra** Mother Earth; *see* GAIA.

Telphusa The nymph of an oracular spring at Haliartus in Boeotia. On his way from Delos to found his own oracle, Apollo stopped at Haliartus and asked the nymph's advice. When she heard his plan, Telphusa got rid of him as quickly as possible by sending him on to Delphi, into the lair of the Python which lurked there. When Apollo discovered her trick, he returned to Haliartus and covered Telphusa's spring with rocks. Tiresias died after drinking its water.

Temenus *1.* Son of Pelasgus and king of Stymphalus in Arcadia. He founded three temples to Hera at that city, as Girl, Wife, and Widow. A local tradition declared that he himself brought the god-

dess up at Stymphalus, and that later, after a tiff with Zeus, she returned there for a time.
2. Son of Phegeus, king of Psophis.
3. A descendant of Heracles; the son of Aristomachus and elder brother of Cresphontes and Aristodemus. When the Delphic Oracle predicted that the children of Heracles (the Heraclidae) would conquer the Peloponnese in the 'third crop', Temenus reproved the oracle for an apparent inaccuracy. The Pythian priestess, however, replied that the mistake had been theirs, as 'crop' meant not 'year', but 'generation'. In consequence Temenus, three generations after the original attack on the Peloponnese under Hyllus, renewed the attempt with a large band of Heracles' descendants. After a false start, in which Temenus' father Aristomachus – in obedience to an earlier oracle given to Hyllus, telling him to travel by 'the narrows' – was killed trying to cross the Isthmus of Corinth, they tried again, going this time over the 'narrow seas', the Gulf of Corinth between Naupactus and Rhium. For failing to consult the Delphic Oracle at the outset of the expedition, Aristodemus was killed by lightning or by Apollo's arrows. (His twin sons Procles and Eurysthenes took his place and later founded the dual kingship at Sparta.) Then, because a member of the army, Hippotes, had killed a soothsayer mistaken for a spy or hostile magician, the fleet was shipwrecked. In their last attempt, however, they safely crossed the Corinthian Gulf to Rhium. The leaders also followed Delphi's advice in engaging a 'three-eyed one' as their leader. This was the exiled Aetolian Oxylus whom they met as he drove a one-eyed donkey; he guided the Heraclid army to Argos, where Temenus crushingly defeated Tisamenus, the son of Orestes. In the distribution of territory that followed, Argos fell to Temenus. He married his daughter Hyrnetho to another Heraclid, Deiphontes: but, because of

his favour towards this son-in-law, his own sons overthrew him and murdered him. One of them, Creisus, tried to make himself king and sent his brothers to Epidaurus to persuade Hyrnetho to leave her husband. When she refused, they tried to kidnap her and she died in the struggle. The Argive people elected Deiphontes as their king and drove out the sons of Temenus, one of whom was then said to have founded the Macedonian royal family.

Tenes Son of Cycnus, king of Colonae near Troy, and of Proclea. Subsequently he claimed Apollo as his father. When his mother died, Tenes had to endure a wicked stepmother, Philonome, who first tried to seduce him, and then, after he had repulsed her, complained to his father that he had tried to rape her (the story of Phaedra and Hippolytus is similar). When a flute-player named Eumolpus supported her story with false witness, Cycnus set Tenes and his sister Hemithea adrift in a chest, in which, with the help of Poseidon, they floated to the isle of Leucophrys. There the inhabitants made Tenes their king, and he renamed the island Tenedos. Cycnus later discovered the truth about his son and wished to be reconciled to him. He punished Philonome by burying her alive and Eumolpus by stoning him to death. Then he sailed to Tenedos, where he had learnt that his son was now king. When, however, he tried to land, Tenes cut his ship's hawser with an axe, casting his father adrift as his father had done to him. (That is the derivation of the Greek proverb 'axe of Tenes', for a rash deed.)

Achilles was warned by Thetis that he must not injure Tenes, or Apollo would avenge his son. Nevertheless he landed on Tenedos, and when Tenes tried to defend Hemithea from Achilles' lust (or was stoning Achilles' ship as it landed), put him to death. Henceforward the dead man was worshipped on

Tenedos as a hero; at his shrine fluteplayers were not admitted, nor might Achilles' name be mentioned. Later on, when Paris shot Achilles with his bow, Apollo guided his hand.

Teratius *see* TARCHETIUS.

Tereus A Thracian (or perhaps Daulian) king, son of Ares. He brought help to the Athenian king Pandion in his war against Labdacus, king of Thebes. In his gratitude, Pandion gave Tereus his daughter Procne as bride. The wedding ceremony was ill-omened; but in due course Procne gave birth to a son, whom she called Itys. After five years Procne asked her husband to allow her to return to Athens to see her sister Philomela, or else to fetch Philomela to stay with them. Tereus preferred the latter course, and went in person to ask Pandion's permission for Philomela's visit. Philomela was very beautiful, and on seeing her Tereus was infatuated, but for the time being gave no hint of his feelings. Philomela, anxious to see Procne, persuaded her father to let her go to Thrace.

When they reached his kingdom, Tereus took Philomela to a stronghold in the middle of a forest and refused to let her go. There he raped her and, in order to stop her cries and prevent her revealing what he had done, he cut out her tongue. Thereafter she remained his prisoner for a whole year, while Tereus assured Procne that her sister was dead. But Philomela hit on the idea of representing a picture of her sufferings on a tapestry, which she wove and sent by a servant to Procne at her palace. Procne examined the tapestry and understood everything. Then, since a festival of Dionysus was at hand, she went, in the guise of a Bacchant, to the stronghold where her sister was held, and dressed Philomela likewise so that she could be smuggled back to the palace. Her heart full of anger, Procne sought means of revenge. She dragged her son Itys, who closely resembled Tereus, to a remote room, where she stabbed him to death, thus depriving Tereus of his heir. Philomela helped Procne to cut up the child's body, and they cooked his flesh and served it to Tereus at a meal. When the king realised what he had eaten – for Philomela had come in after the meal and thrust the boy's gory head at her ravisher – he attempted to kill both her and her sister. But as he chased them, they turned into birds, Procne into a nightingale and Philomela, since she had no tongue, into a swallow – which merely chatters. (Latin authors reversed the position, making Philomela the nightingale, perhaps because they preferred the sound of her name.) The tale explains why the nightingale sings the plaintive song *ityn, ityn* for her dead son. Tereus too was transformed into a bird, in his case a hoopoe. This version of the story is told by Ovid in the *Metamorphoses*.

Terpsichore *see* MUSES.

Terra Mother Earth; *see* GAIA.

Tethys A Titaness, the wife of Oceanus, with whom she dwelt in the farthest reaches of the earth. She gave her mighty husband innumerable sons, the river-gods, and three thousand daughters, the Oceanids – nymphs who under Apollo's supervision had charge of young men, whom they protected until they were fully grown. When Zeus fought the Titans, Oceanus and Tethys supported him against their own kind, and took care of Hera for him while the war lasted. Later, when Tethys quarrelled with her husband, her foster-child Hera tried to reconcile the pair. Tethys was fond of Hera and, to gratify her, excluded Callisto's constellation, the Great Bear, from the stream of Ocean, so that she eternally revolved round the Pole Star. This was to punish her for presum-

ing to make love to Zeus. *See also* AESACUS.

Teucer (Greek: *Teukros*) *1*. The first mythical king of the land of Troy, whose people were sometimes known as Teucrians; he was the son of the local river-god Scamander and the nymph Idaea. He gave his daughter Batia to the immigrant leader Dardanus, who inherited the kingdom in due course. A different tradition about Teucer's origins, however, was known to Virgil. In the *Aeneid* he was a native of Crete, who, during a famine in the island, migrated with his father and a third of the Cretan people to Troy. He discovered his new home through a prophecy of Sminthian Apollo, which had instructed him to settle in a place where the inhabitants attacked him by night. Such an attack took place on the River Xanthus, which Teucer renamed Scamander after his father, a Cretan of that name.

2. The bastard son of Telamon and Hesione, Laomedon's daughter. He was an active fighter in the Trojan War, employing the bow and the spear with expert skill. He generally stood next to his half-brother Aias *1*, using his shield for shelter. He killed a large number of Trojans and, if Hector had not hit him first with a rock, might well have proved a match for him. He later gave Sarpedon a grievous wound. In Patroclus' funeral games, Teucer came second to Meriones in the archery contest. When Aias killed himself over the arms of Achilles, Teucer was away on an expedition in Mysia. On his return he disputed Agamemnon's decision not to bury his half-brother's body. Odysseus saved an ugly situation by inducing Agamemnon and Menelaus to relent. Teucer was in the Trojan Horse, and returned to Salamis safely. But when he arrived, his father would not let him land, because he had not prevented his brother's suicide. Teucer pleaded his case from his ship, but Telamon was adamant. On the instructions of an oracle Teucer sailed on to Cyprus, where he founded a new Salamis and married a daughter of King Cinyras. According to a variant story Belus, king of Syria, conquered Cyprus and gave it to Teucer.

Teuthras The founder of the kingdom of Teuthrania on the River Caicus in Mysia. He bought Auge as a slave and either made her his wife or adopted her. He made Telephus (her son by Heracles) his heir.

Thalia *see* MUSES.

Thamyris or **Thamyras** A Thracian minstrel, the son of Philammon and the nymph Argiope. His mother, when pregnant, was repudiated by Philammon; and so she went far away to Thrace to be delivered of her son. Thamyris was the first man to fall in love with a boy, conceiving a passion for Hyacinthus. Having won singing competitions at Delphi, he ventured to challenge the Muses at song, but in the contest, which took place at Dorium in Messenia, he was the loser. The Muses paid him back for his impudence by blinding him and removing his gift of minstrelsy; and after his death he was punished among the presumptuous in Tartarus.

Thanatos The personification of Death. He was a son of Nyx (Night) and the brother of Hypnos (Sleep). In mythology he possessed the function of an angel of death, coming to mortals when their allotted timespan had run out, cutting off a lock of their hair to dedicate them to Hades and then carrying them away. With the help of Hypnos he removed Sarpedon's body from the battlefield at Troy, and fetched Alcestis from Pherae, when she had taken her husband's place on the bier. In the latter story, as Euripides tells it, Thanatos advanced on the doomed woman clad in a black robe and bearing a sword. But Heracles wrestled with him, and forced him to give

Alcestis up. Another mortal who had dealings with Thanatos was Sisyphus, who tricked him once but suffered everlasting torments as a punishment.

Thaumas An ancient sea-god (his name means 'wonder'), son of Pontus (Sea) and Gaia (Earth); he married the Oceanid Electra, who bore him Iris and the Harpies.

Theano *1. see* MELANIPPE.
2. see ANTENOR.

Thebe A Boeotian nymph who was married to Zethus and gave her name to the city of Thebes, previously Cadmeia.

Theia ('divine') A Titaness, daughter of Uranus and Gaia. To Hyperion she was said to have borne Helios (sometimes identified with Hyperion), Eros, and Selene. She was the mother of the Cercopes by Oceanus. She was also called Euryphaessa.

Theias *see* ADONIS.

Thelxiepeia One of the Sirens.

Themis ('justice', 'order') A Titaness, daughter of Uranus and Gaia (Earth). To Zeus, of whom she was the second consort after Metis, she presented the Hours and the Fates as offspring. Her original husband, however, was the Titan Iapetus, by whom she bore Prometheus. To her son she imparted much of her wisdom, for she knew the future, including secrets of which even Zeus himself was ignorant, such as that Thetis' son was fated to be greater than his father. It was through this knowledge that Prometheus eventually gained release from Zeus' punishment. Succeeding Gaia as possessor of the Oracle of Delphi, Themis gave Deucalion and Pyrrha the secret knowledge enabling them to re-people the earth after the flood. She also warned Atlas that a son of Zeus would one day come and steal the golden apples of the Hesperides – and it was for this reason that Atlas refused to respond to Perseus' plea for help. She eventually ceded the Delphic Oracle to her sister Phoebe (or, alternatively, to Apollo himself after his return from Tempe, where he had been purified for the slaying of Python).

Themison *see* BATTUS *1*.

Themiste Daughter of Ilus *2*, king of Troy. The mother, by Capys, of Anchises, the father of Aeneas.

Themisto Daughter of Hypseus, king of the Lapiths. After his wife Ino, who was mad, had been away so long that he believed her to be dead, Athamas, king of Orchomenus, married Themisto. She bore him a number of children (her sons were identified as Leucon, Erythrius, Schoeneus and Ptous; but the names Presbon, Sphincius, and Orchomenus were also given). But in due course Ino returned, cured of her insanity. Thereupon Themisto became ferociously jealous of Ino's children, Learchus and Melicertes, and plotted to murder them. She told their nurse to dress her own children in white and Ino's in black, so that when during the night she entered their bedroom they all shared, she would have no difficulty in telling them apart. But Ino reversed the colours, and Themisto killed two of her own sons. Then, in horror at her mistake, she committed suicide. This version of the story (which echoes the relationship between Ino and Nephele, Athamas' first wife) was given in Euripides' lost play *Ino*. *See* ATHAMAS.

Theoclymenus *1*. An Argive prophet descended from Melampus. When Theoclymenus was fleeing from his kinsmen, one of whom he had killed, Odysseus' son Telemachus gave him passage from Pylos to Ithaca. After arriving in Ithaca

Theoclymenus warned Penelope's suitors of their impending deaths, but they only reviled him.

2. A king of Egypt, the son of Proteus. According to Euripides' *Helen*, he buried his father near the gate of his palace, so as to behold the tomb whenever he passed. He tried to compel Helen, to whom his father had given refuge, to marry him; Menelaus arrived just in time to save her.

Theodamas King of the Dryopes and father of Hylas. Heracles picked a quarrel with him, demanding a fine ox he was using to plough a field. When Theodamas refused, Heracles killed him and carried off Hylas.

Theophane The beautiful daughter of Bisaltes, who gave his name to a Thracian tribe living on the River Strymon. Poseidon fell in love with her and, since she had many suitors, carried her off to an island. The suitors, however, instituted a search for her and discovered her whereabouts. To foil their plans, therefore, Poseidon turned her and the islanders into sheep, and when the suitors began to eat the sheep, he transformed the eaters into wolves. He himself became a ram, mating with Theophane and fathering a lamb which turned out to have a fleece of gold. This lamb grew into the talking, flying ram which Nephele sent to save Phrixus and Helle from Ino's wiles; its fleece was later sought and won by Jason and the Argonauts in Colchis.

Theras Son of King Autesion of Thebes. When his brother-in-law Aristodemus died in the Dorian invasion of the Peloponnese, Theras had become guardian of his nephews Procles and Eurysthenes, whose mother was his sister Argia. Aristodemus had possessed the right to a third share of the conquests of the invading force, and Theras made sure that the twins were not deprived of their inheritance. When lots were drawn, Messenia was the most sought-after territory, and Cresphontes won it by a trick. Procles and Eurysthenes drew Sparta, and Theras ruled it on their behalf for many years.

When the twins grew up, Theras decided to emigrate and found a colony on Calliste ('most beautiful'), a treeless volcanic island to the north of Crete, occupied at that time by descendants of the Phoenicians. He was joined in his colony by some inhabitants of Mount Taygetus, called Minyans because they were descended from the children of the Argonauts and the women of Lemnos; they had been expelled from Lemnos by their neighbours there. These people had barely escaped death at the hands of the Spartans, who resented their arrogance; they were saved only by the forethought of their Spartan wives, who sent them out of Sparta to the mountains dressed as women.

Theras took three ship-loads of Spartans and Minyans to Calliste. The inhabitants of the island accepted his kingship and welcomed the settlers, and the island was henceforth known as Thera. According to a story inconsistent with the above, the island had grown from a clod of earth which had been given to the Argonaut Euphemus by the god of Lake Tritonis, and had been dropped by him into the sea on his homeward voyage. In this version there were people descended from Euphemus in the Minyan party that accompanied Theras, and one of their descendants, Battus, founded a colony in Libya at Cyrene.

Theras' grandchildren later died because the avenging Furies of Laius and Oedipus (who had already compelled Theras' father Autesion to give up the throne of Thebes) continued to persecute the descendants of Polynices whom Oedipus had cursed. Therefore sacrifices were made and temples built, as the oracles directed, and the curse was then lifted.

Thermius Son of Andraemon; his brother Oxylus accidentally killed him and was consequently exiled from Aetolia.

Thersander *1*. Son of Polynices and Argia; king of Thebes. In order to bribe Eriphyle to persuade her son Alcmaeon to lead a second expedition against Thebes – the expedition of the Epigoni ('Successors' to the Seven who had failed ten years earlier) – Thersander used the divine wedding-dress of his ancestress Harmonia. Although the Epigoni won, they destroyed much of the city, and, when Thersander became its king, it was a weakened kingdom that he inherited. He invited the Thebans who had fled to return home, and rebuilt the lower part of the city. His wife was a daughter of Amphiaraus and Eriphyle, Demonassa, who bore him Tisamenus, his successor. Later Thersander went to the Trojan War and led the mistaken landing in Mysia (when the Greeks had lost their way), but Telephus struck him down with a spear and he was killed. He was buried at Elaea.
2. Son of Sisyphus. His sons, Coronus and Haliartus, were adopted by their uncle Athamas, and gave their names to two Boeotian towns, Coronea and Haliartus.

Thersites In the *Iliad*, Thersites is the only low-born character among the Greeks who are portrayed; though he was subsequently given a noble pedigree and identified as the son of Oeneus' brother Agrius. Homer describes him as physically repulsive: lame, bandy-legged, round-shouldered, and almost bald, with an egg-shaped head. He had an unbridled tongue and loved to mock the leaders. When he upbraided Agamemnon for stealing Briseis from Achilles, and suggested that the army should return home to Greece, Odysseus beat him over the back with his staff for his impudence. In later Greek literature it was said that, when he mocked Achilles for falling in love with the dead body of the Amazon queen Penthesilea, he was struck dead by the hero. Achilles therefore had to go to Lesbos to be purified of the murder. There he sacrificed to Leto and her children Apollo and Artemis, and Odysseus performed the required ritual.

Theseus The greatest Athenian hero. He was the son of either Aegeus or the god Poseidon, and of Pittheus' daughter Aethra. When Aegeus consulted the Delphic Oracle and asked how to remedy his childlessness, the oracle bade him not to loosen the spout of his wine-flask before he returned to Athens. Not understanding the message, Aegeus went to Troezen and told his friend Pittheus, king of Troezen, of the oracular words; whereupon Pittheus, interpreting them as prophesying that Aegeus was going to beget a son on his return home, induced Aegeus to accompany him to a small island, Sphaeria, where he made him drunk with wine and put him to bed with Aethra. Aegeus soon realised what had taken place, and also learnt, before leaving Troezen for Athens, that Aethra was with child. He then took her to a place where there was a great boulder, which he raised, placing beneath it his sword and sandals and setting the rock down over them again. He told Aethra that should her child be a son, she must wait until he was strong enough to raise the boulder and then send him to Athens: if the youth lifted the rock and brought him the sword and sandals, he would acknowledge him as his son and make him heir to the Athenian throne – though Aegeus' tenure of the throne was in any case precarious, as his half-brother Pallas and his fifty sons declared him to be merely an adopted child of Pandion, and claimed the sovereignty for themselves. Meanwhile at Troezen, Pittheus put out the story that his daughter's lover was

Poseidon, and that it was therefore the god's son whom she was due to bear. In later days the belief that Theseus was the son of Poseidon became widespread at Athens; and he was said to have claimed such parentage himself.

When Theseus came to manhood, Aethra showed him the boulder and told him the secret of his royal birth. He lifted the stone with ease, retrieved the sword and sandals, and set out to walk to Athens, preferring the circuitous land journey round the Saronic Gulf to the quick and easy passage by ship. For the young man had heard of the numerous brigands that beset the land route and, in passionate admiration for his kinsman Heracles, wished to prove himself.

Near Epidaurus Theseus came face to face with Periphetes, a son of Hephaestus, who was called *Corynetes*, 'clubbearer', because he used to bludgeon wayfarers to death with his enormous club. Theseus, who was a skilful wrestler, managed to wrest the club from him, and dealt with him as Periphetes had treated so many others. Theseus kept the club, and it became his emblem as the lionskin was the emblem of Heracles. At the Isthmus of Corinth he was accosted by Sinis, an outlaw who made his victims help him bend a tree down (whence he was nicknamed *Pityokamptes*, 'pine-bender'), after which he released it suddenly, hurling them into the air; or else he fastened them to two pines he had himself bent down to the ground and then, releasing the trees, tore them in two. Theseus killed Sinis with his own pine trees. He then discovered his beautiful daughter Perigune hiding in a bed of wild asparagus and became her lover. She bore him Melanippus and later married Deioneus, son of Eurytus of Oechalia.

At Crommyon Theseus rid the people of a notorious pest in the form of a grey sow named Phaea ('grey'), a beast sprung from monstrous parents, Echidna and Typhon, which was ravaging the countryside. According to other versions, however, this menace was a brigand, or a depraved woman who was nicknamed the Sow.

As Theseus entered the territory of Megara, he came to a place where the road ran between a mountain and high cliffs called the Scironian Rocks, which overlooked a bay. Here lurked Sciron, a ruffian who robbed wayfarers and then compelled them to wash his feet: next, as they knelt before him, he would kick them over the cliffs to feed a great turtle that lived on the shore of the bay. Theseus pretended to comply, but as he bent down he seized Sciron's legs and hurled him over the rocks to feed the turtle himself. (At Megara, however, Sciron was said not to be a robber but a great soldier.)

The next contest that Theseus had to face was at Eleusis, in those days a city independent of Athens. Its king, an Arcadian called Cercyon, forced strangers to wrestle with him, on the understanding that the loser was put to death. However Cercyon met his match in Theseus, who by killing him won the throne of Eleusis. He later added it to the Athenian kingdom, making Hippothoon, Cercyon's grandson, its governor.

At Erineus near Mount Aegaleos Theseus was stopped by Procrustes ('the Stretcher'), who was accustomed to receive travellers at his inn. Once they were safely inside he made them lie on a long bed if they were short, and on a short bed if they were tall; fastening them down, he would then rack them or cut them to size until they fitted the bed exactly. Theseus killed him by the same method, cutting his head off since Procrustes was very tall. Procrustes was also known as *Damastes* ('the Tamer') and *Polypemon* ('the Baneful'). When he subsequently reached the River Cephissus, Theseus was accorded the first friendly welcome he had received throughout his entire journey, for the descendants of Phytalus, whom Demeter

had given the fig tree, purified him of the murders he had committed and offered him lavish hospitality. Theseus subsequently made them priests.

Coming to Athens, he found everything in turmoil, as Aegeus had no lawful son and Pallas' fifty sons were plotting to seize the throne. Aegeus was living with Medea, who hoped that her own son Medus would inherit the throne of Athens, in spite of his mother's foreign origin. Theseus, though he received a warm welcome on account of his exploits on the road, did not give his identity away. Medea, however, recognised him and persuaded Aegeus, for the sake of her own son, to allow her to poison him at a banquet, telling the old man that her proposed victim was in league with the sons of Pallas. Just in time, however, Aegeus realised his son's true identity, for Theseus prepared to carve the meat with his father's sword that he had brought from Troezen, displaying the weapon in a manner that could not fail to inspire Aegeus' recognition. Thereupon the old man dashed Theseus' cup to the ground and Theseus perceived the danger in which he had stood. Medea fled from Athens, where she was never seen again. Aegeus embraced his son and named him as his successor.

Next Theseus had to deal with the threat which the fifty sons of Pallas presented to his father's power and his own right to the throne; for now that Theseus was proclaimed heir, they rebelled openly. Half of them marched against Athens, and half lay in ambush for Theseus' supporters. However a herald, Leos, reported this plan to Theseus, who caught the ambush party by surprise; and the other force, on hearing this news, took to flight.

Then Theseus went to Marathon, in the east of Attica, to kill the wild bull which was ravaging the countryside. Whether he performed this exploit before Medea tried to poison him and was sent on the dangerous adventure by his father at her request, or else left after her departure, is disputed in our sources. The bull was the one which had been given to Minos of Crete by Poseidon and had been loved by Minos' wife Pasiphae. Heracles had brought it to Greece as his seventh Labour, and it had wandered into Attica. Minos' son Androgeos had already been sent against the brute by Aegeus, and had died in trying to kill it. Now Theseus set out, and on his way was entertained hospitably by a little old woman named Hecale. She vowed to make a thank-offering to Zeus if the young man returned safely, but while Theseus was still away she died. On his return after capturing the bull he instituted a local ceremony in honour of her memory. Then he drove the bull to Athens and sacrificed it to Apollo.

As a result of this adventure Theseus learnt the story of Androgeos' death and of the tribute that his father Minos had imposed on Athens as a punishment for it. As a result of a successful war against that city, in which the Athenians were laid low by a plague, Minos had obliged them to send seven adolescent boys and girls every year (or, according to Plutarch, every nine years) to be offered up to the Minotaur (the progency of Pasiphae and the bull, which possessed the body of a man and the head and horns of a bull) in the Labyrinth which Daedalus, an Athenian exile, had built on Minos' instructions to house it. At this juncture, the tribute was once again due; and according to one tradition, Minos specifically demanded the inclusion of Theseus among the party. Most writers, however, including Plutarch, assert that the common people of Athens were displaying anger that the king's son alone should be exempt from inclusion among the victims – who were normally drawn by lot – whereupon Theseus deliberately insisted that he himself should be one of the victims. (Another version asserts that Theseus

merely insisted on being among those whose names were included in the lot – and that it was his name which emerged.) Distressed at his son's imminent departure, Aegeus told him that if, by any chance, he should ever manage to return alive, he was to change the colour of his sail on the homeward voyage from black to white (or scarlet).

According to some, the Minotaur ate the victims offered up to it in the Labyrinth. Other sources maintained that they simply wandered about until they starved to death. They had to go to Crete unarmed; but it was also decreed that if one of them should succeed in killing the monster and find his way out, the tribute would be cancelled in future.

It was disputed whether the Minotaur's victims were taken to Crete in an Athenian or a Cretan ship. The former version accords with the story that Theseus, if he returned, would have his own vessel to return in and could thus change the sails to warn his father of his safe return; the latter with a tradition that Minos on the outward voyage tried to interfere with one of the girls, a daughter of Alcathous, king of Megara, whereupon Theseus indignantly defended the girl from molestation and Minos grew angry. At that juncture, the two men declared one another to be bastards; but each proved his paternity, Minos by praying his father Zeus to send a thunderbolt from the blue sky, Theseus by diving into the sea and miraculously recovering the gold ring that Minos had contemptuously flung into Poseidon's domain. Not only did Poseidon hand the ring over to Theseus, but Amphitrite, Poseidon's consort, presented him with a gold crown which he wore as he triumphantly emerged from the sea. Theseus then returned the ring to the astonished Minos.

Theseus was a pious youth, and before sailing to Crete he had propitiated Apollo, to whom he was particularly attached, and had asked Aphrodite for her especial favour. When he reached Crete, this forethought stood him in good stead, for it was by the love of Minos' daughter Ariadne that he was enabled to perform his task. In the passion the mere sight of him inspired in her, she consulted Daedalus, and extracted from him the information that the only way to escape from the complex maze of the Labyrinth would be to follow back a thread fastened to the entrance. Ariadne then introduced herself to Theseus and, after he had promised to marry her, secretly gave him a clue of thread and, according to some authorities, a sword. Leaving his companions near the entrance, Theseus advanced to the centre of the Labyrinth, playing out his thread. When he came upon the Minotaur he killed it, using the sword or, according to another version, his fists. He then returned to the entrance, where Ariadne released the party from the Labyrinth and they made their way back to the Athenian ship in the harbour. There, under cover of night, Theseus and his companions bored holes in the bottoms of Minos' ships, so that they could not set out in pursuit, and so the Athenians set sail for home. Another account had it that Theseus and his friends were compelled to fight their way back to their ship, and killed Minos' son Asterius in the battle.

However there was also quite a different rendering of the events which were said to have happened in Crete. According to Philochorus, an Attic historian of the fourth century BC, Theseus took part in the games which were held on his arrival on the island, and in the wrestling match beat the unpopular local champion Taurus ('bull'), who was also Pasiphae's lover. In this version Minos released Theseus and his companions because he admired his prowess and he was glad to see Taurus humiliated.

Theseus and his men now sailed safely away, taking Ariadne with them. The first land they touched was the island of Dia (later known as Naxos), where they went ashore; and when they sailed on, Ariadne was left behind. The earliest version suggests that Theseus was somehow bewitched and forgot her. Later writers, however, attributed the desertion to deliberate treachery on the part of Theseus, who was in love with Aegle, daughter of Panopeus. Homer, who is not explicit on the point, says that Dionysus brought about Ariadne's death by asking Artemis to shoot her. Perhaps this is an earlier rendering of the most famous of these stories, which recounted that, after Theseus' departure, the god himself came to Dia and whisked Ariadne away on his magic chariot to become his heavenly queen. The story was rationalised by a version explaining that it was not Dionysus himself but his priest on the island, one Oenarus, who took her as his wife, after Theseus had deserted her for another woman. Dionysus was also sometimes said to have fought Theseus for her hand. (A Cypriot author, Paeon, claimed that Theseus' ship was blown off course to Cyprus and that Ariadne, now pregnant and seasick, was set on shore; but the ship was immediately driven out to sea again by the violent waves, and Theseus could not come back to her. When he eventually managed to return to Cyprus, he found that she had died in labour before she could bring forth their child.)

After Dia, Theseus' next landing was at Delos, where the Athenian party introduced the serpentine Crane Dance in memory of their experiences in the twisting passages of the Labyrinth. From there they sailed for Athens, but Theseus was so pleased to be returning that he totally forgot to change his sail: his father saw the expected homeward-bound ship, concluded him to be dead, and flung himself from the cliffs (or from the Acropolis) to his death. Meanwhile Theseus landed at the Athenian port, Phalerum, and completed his thank-offerings to the gods before he heard the news of Aegeus' death.

Theseus was now king of Attica. After conducting Aegeus' funeral, he was believed to have instituted a reform to subordinate the communities of Attica to Athens herself, and it was said to have been as a result of this that Athens, now the political centre of the country, grew into a large town. It was also he who reputedly gave the city its name; and in honour of its namesake Athena he was credited with the institution of the great Panathenaic festival, to take place every four years, as a ceremony to be observed by the whole of Attica. He brought Megara, formerly the territory of his uncle Nisus, into his kingdom, and founded or re-founded the Isthmian games at Corinth in honour of Poseidon. At some point he also inherited the kingdom of Troezen from his maternal grandfather Pittheus.

Some time after this, Theseus embarked on an expedition against the Amazons of Themiscyra on the Black Sea. There he captured one of the Amazon leaders, Antiope, the sister of their queen Hippolyta – or, according to variant accounts, it was Hippolyta herself whom he captured. Either she had fallen in love with him or else (in another version) when the Amazons sent him gifts of friendship, he invited their bearer to come aboard his ship and simply sailed off with her. Resenting her loss, the Amazons pursued Theseus back to Attica. Invading his kingdom and attacking Athens itself, they occupied the hill of the Pnyx and besieged the Acropolis, and on the ground between the two hills there was fought a great battle, which Theseus won. His adversary (usually said to be Hippolyta, or Antiope in an alternative tradition – if his prisoner was not she) withdrew to Megara, where she died. Later his wife – for he had married his captive – bore him a son, Hippolytus, and died soon after.

Another version of the story asserts that Theseus captured his Amazon wife in the battle on the Pnyx. Yet another account places the birth of Hippolytus before the Amazon assault on Athens, and indicates that his Amazonian mother was killed by a javelin in the battle, while she was fighting at Theseus' side. According to some versions of this episode, Theseus' attack on the Amazons was a joint venture with Heracles, who had been commanded by his master Eurystheus to fetch the belt of the Amazon queen (Heracles' ninth Labour).

Theseus is sometimes added to the lists both of the Argonauts and of the hunters of the Calydonian boar. He intervened at Thebes after the failure of the attack by the Seven, and forced Creon to allow the Argive dead to have honourable burial. He also gave Oedipus and his daughter Antigone sanctuary at Athens, and when Creon's men sought to compel Oedipus to leave Attica and return to Thebes (to lend his support to Eteocles in his war against the Seven), he prevented it.

Theseus' greatest friend was Pirithous, king of the Thessalian nation of Lapiths. Hearing of Theseus' heroic qualities, Pirithous had determined to meet him. He had therefore raided Theseus' herds of cattle at Marathon and had driven them off, and when he heard that Theseus was in pursuit, he turned to face him. But the two did not fight: Pirithous extended his hand to the Athenian king, who took it and, instead of punishing Pirithous for his marauding, swore eternal friendship with him. Thereafter the two performed many exploits together (including, perhaps, the expedition to the land of the Amazons and the successful battle of the Pnyx). When Pirithous married Hippodamia, Theseus attended the wedding and helped his friend in the ensuing battle with the drunken Centaurs, who tried to carry off the bride and the Lapith women who were present.

In spite of his abandonment of Minos' daughter Ariadne, Theseus was said to have become the husband of another of his daughters, namely Phaedra. Minos himself was dead, and the marriage sealed the friendship of Theseus with Deucalion, who had inherited his throne. Phaedra bore Theseus two sons, Acamas and Demophon. Some time after this marriage Pallas, with his sons, made his last attempt to drive Theseus from his throne, but Theseus killed him and wiped out his entire family. Because of this homicide of his kinsmen, he was sentenced to a year's exile from Athens. He therefore took his wife and family to his other kingdom of Troezen, where his son Hippolytus, now a man, was ruling as viceroy (or was being brought up by his grandfather Pittheus).

Hippolytus was a shy, retiring young man devoted to hunting and consequently the favourite of Artemis; he was averse to the idea of marriage and scorned to worship Aphrodite. However his stepmother Phaedra had fallen in love with him the first time she saw him, when he had been initiated into the Mysteries of Eleusis. Now that she was living in close proximity to him at Troezen, her passion flared up. Theseus left Troezen for a time, in order to consult the Delphic Oracle, and while he was away matters came to a head. Phaedra's old nurse, pitying her mistress's emotional plight, revealed her passion to Hippolytus, who was shocked and revolted but swore to keep the matter secret. However Phaedra, on learning of Hippolytus' scorn, hanged herself and left Theseus a lying letter in which she accused his son of seducing her. When Theseus returned, he believed the letter and pronounced a curse upon Hippolytus, asking Poseidon, who had once granted him three wishes, to bring about his son's death. Then Theseus sent Hippolytus into exile: but as the youth rode in his chariot along the sea-shore near Troezen, a monstrous bull emerged from

the sea and startled his horses, so that he was flung out and killed. Then Theseus learnt the truth of the matter from Artemis. (Some sources assert it was now that Phaedra committed suicide, having openly accused Hippolytus of the alleged seduction on Theseus' return from Delphi.) Theseus and Pirithous, who were now both widowers, made an agreement to help each other to win wives they considered worthy of their rank, and both chose daughters of Zeus. First they went to Sparta to obtain Helen, daughter of Leda, to be Theseus' bride. (According to Plutarch the two kings drew lots to see which of them should marry her.) Although only twelve years of age, she was already renowned for her beauty. They found her dancing in the temple of Artemis and carried her off to Aphidnae in Attica, where Theseus placed her in the care of his mother Aethra until she should be old enough to wed him. It was now Pirithous' turn to secure a bride for himself, and he chose Hades' wife Persephone. He and Theseus made their way down to the Underworld, where Hades pretended to receive them respectfully. When he invited them to sit down, however, the two newcomers found themselves locked into their seats; and they lost all memory of who they were, for they were sitting in the Chairs of Forgetfulness. There Pirithous remained for ever, and so, according to a tradition preserved by Virgil, did Theseus; but in the better-known version he was released after a while by Heracles, who had come to fetch Cerberus. According to some sources it was Theseus who, after Heracles had killed his children by Megara in a fit of madness, gave him a home.

When Theseus returned to Athens he found the city in turmoil and himself the object of great unpopularity. For the Spartans, led by Helen's brothers the Dioscuri, had invaded Attica to rescue Helen, sacking Aphidnae and carrying Aethra off with them. Athens had fallen under the sway of Menestheus, a descendant of King Erechtheus, and Theseus' sons Acamas and Demophon had taken refuge on the island of Euboea. Forced to flee from Athens, Theseus decided to go to the isle of Scyros, where he had inherited estates from his grandfather Scyrius (this corresponded with a tradition that Theseus' father Aegeus was the son of Scyrius and not of Pandion). The Scyrian King Lycomedes apparently gave him a kind welcome, but secretly feared the presence of so powerful and dangerous a man in his kingdom. So he took Theseus to the top of a cliff, ostensibly to show him his estates on the island, and then treacherously pushed him off the edge. So died the greatest hero of Athens and its reputed founder.

It was believed that Menestheus continued to rule Attica until the Trojan War, in which he was killed. Then Theseus' son Demophon, who had rescued Aethra in the sack of Troy, returned to Athens and inherited his father's kingdom. In about 475 BC the Athenian general Cimon, as a popular gesture, fetched Theseus' supposed bones back from Scyros and reinterred them in a temple dedicated to the hero, whom the Athenians believed to have helped them at the battle of Marathon (490 BC).

Thespius The eponym of Thespiae in Boeotia. *See* HERACLES.

Thesprotus The eponym of the land of Thesprotia in Epirus. He provided shelter to Pelopia, daughter of Thyestes, and gave her in marriage to her uncle Atreus.

Thessalus Son of Jason and Medea. The sole survivor of Medea's murder of her children at Corinth. He succeeded Acastus on the throne of Iolcus, and gave his name to the land of Thessaly, in which Iolcus lies.

Thestius A king of Pleuron in Aetolia;

the son either of Ares and Demonice or of Agenor and Epicaste (in which case Demonice was his sister). He had a number of children: Althaea the wife of Oeneus, Hypermnestra the wife of Oicles, Leda the wife of Tyndareos (who, exiled from Sparta, had taken refuge with Thestius), and two sons, Toxeus and Plexippus, whom Althaea's son Meleager subsequently slew.

Thestor *see* CALCHAS.

Thetis A Nereid (sea-nymph). Though a sea-goddess, Thetis was brought up on Mount Olympus by Hera, whom she loved dearly. However after her return to the depths of the sea, when Hera flung her son Hephaestus out of Olympus because she was ashamed of his lameness, Thetis and her sister Eurynome rescued him. Hephaestus stayed with the two Nereids for nine years in their watery home. But Thetis parted company with Hera when the latter, aided by Poseidon and Athena, plotted to revolt against Zeus and tie him up. Thetis got wind of the conspiracy and went to Tartarus; from there she brought the Hundred-Armed giant Briareos who, ever loyal to Zeus, rescued him from his assailants. When the youthful Dionysus was attacked by Lycurgus on Mount Nysa, he leapt into the sea, and Thetis received him and sheltered him for a while; in return for this favour he gave her a golden bowl or vase. Thetis was distinguished by her outstanding beauty, for which both Zeus and Poseidon wished to marry her. However fate had decreed that Thetis' son must be greater than his father. Prometheus knew this destined outcome, having learnt it from his mother, the Titaness Themis, but he refused to reveal the secret to Zeus until the god ordered his release from his place of torture where he was fastened to a rock at the edge of the world or in Tartarus. Finally Zeus consented to Prometheus' liberation, and learnt how near he had been to disaster, for, according to one version of the oracle, the son Thetis would have borne him was destined to overthrow him as he himself had overthrown his father Cronos.

Zeus accordingly decided that Thetis must at all costs be married off to some-one relatively insignificant, and the choice fell on the mortal Peleus, king of Phthia, for although not a great man he was highly honoured by the gods. First, however, this bridegroom had to catch her, for Thetis had no intention of com-plying with Zeus' plan. Peleus was warned by Chiron that, since she was a sea-goddess, she had the power to change her shape and would do all she could to escape him. He found her rest-ing in a cave on the coast of Magnesia, and pounced upon her there. In spite of the many forms she assumed – appear-ing as water, fire, wild animals, and frightening marine creatures – he held on, until she finally agreed to be his wife. The gods were all invited to the wedding, and out of respect for Thetis all attended, bringing handsome gifts. The one exception was Eris (Strife), whom it was thought better to exclude: but she forced her way in and threw down the golden apple of contention, over which Hera, Athena, and Aphro-dite proceeded to quarrel since it was intended as a prize for the most beautiful goddess.

For a time Thetis lived with Peleus as a dutiful wife and, according to one version of the myth, bore him seven sons. Six of them she tested with fire or boiling water to discover whether they had inherited her own immortality. None of the six stood the test; and finally Peleus prevailed on her to spare the seventh boy, Achilles, who was brought up as a mortal. Other authori-ties know nothing of Achilles' brothers, but assert that, after his birth, Thetis used to place him in the fire by night to burn away his mortality, anointing him

with ambrosia by day to render him immortal. When Peleus found his son lying in the fire he was so angry or distressed that Thetis left him and re-turned to the sea. In another story about Achilles' infancy it was said that Thetis dipped him in the River Styx to make him invulnerable, but failed to ensure that his heel, by which she held him, was wet.

When the ship *Argo*, which Peleus and his fellow-Argonauts were aboard, was faced with disaster at the Wander-ing Rocks, Thetis and her sister Nereids pushed the vessel past these dangerous obstacles. She was a constant support to Achilles during his short life, and was saddened by the knowledge of his im-pending doom. She did all she could to keep him out of the Trojan War, conceal-ing him on the isle of Scyros among King Lycomedes' daughters. When Achil-les was angry with Agamemnon for seizing his concubine Briseis, Thetis im-plored Zeus, on her son's behalf, to turn the tide of war in the Trojans' favour so that Achilles would have to be begged to return to battle. She offered him com-fort on the loss of Patroclus, and under-took to obtain new armour for him from the forge of Hephaestus, to replace the armour which he had lent Patroclus and which had been taken for his corpse. When Achilles was slain, Thetis and the Nereids lamented over his body with such a terrible wailing that the Greek army fled in terror. After his fu-neral she placed his bones in the golden vase that Dionysus had given her, and buried the vase in the tomb. According to one account she then made Achilles immortal and took him to live on the island of Leuce in the Black Sea, where he later married Helen, while Thetis herself lived there with Peleus, on whom she likewise conferred immortality.

Thisbe *see* PYRAMUS

Thoas *1.* Son of Dionysus and Ariadne;

king of the island of Lemnos. His wife was Myrina. The women of Lemnos neglected the rites of Aphrodite, so that the goddess caused them all to stink, and their husbands took Thracian mistresses. The Lemnian women then killed their husbands in revenge, but Thoas' daughter Hypsipyle saved him and smuggled him off the island, setting him adrift in a chest. Dionysus helped him to float to the isle of Oenoe. There he married the nymph after whom the island was named, and she bore him a son, Sicinus. Another version, however, maintained that the Lemnian women found and killed Thoas before he left the island.

2. Grandson of the above; son of Jason and Hypsipyle. He and his brother Euneus rescued their mother from slavery at the court of Lycurgus, king of Nemea, and took her home to Lemnos. Thoas inherited the throne from his grandfather.

3. Son of Andraemon and Gorge. His father had gained control of the kingdom of Aetolia, originally ruled by Gorge's father Oeneus, since all the sons of Oeneus had died. This kingdom Thoas inherited, and led a contingent of Aetolians in forty ships to the Trojan War. His son was Haemon; Haemon's son was Oxylus.

According to one tradition (in conflict with the *Odyssey*) Odysseus, on his return to Ithaca, discovered that Penelope had been unfaithful during his absence; and he sent her back to her father Icarius. Then he, in his turn, was driven out of Ithaca because Neoptolemus, called on to arbitrate between the massacred suitors' families and Odysseus, gave his verdict against Odysseus so that he himself might take possession of Cephallenia. Odysseus was then said to have fled to Aetolia and married one of Thoas' daughters, who bore him a son, Leontophonus.

4. The king of the Tauri, a barbarous nation inhabiting the Crimea. Artemis made Iphigenia her priestess at her temple in Thoas' kingdom. Orestes and Pylades eventually rescued Iphigenia and carried her off by sea, together with a statue of Artemis from her temple. Thoas' fleet pursued Orestes' ship as far as the island of Zminthe, where Chryses, the son of Agamemnon and Chryseis, rescued the Greeks and helped Orestes, his half-brother, to kill Thoas.

5. A giant; together with his brother Agrius he was killed by the Fates. He was also called Thoon.

Thoon *see* THOAS 5.

Thoosa A sea-nymph, the mother of the Cyclops Polyphemus by Poseidon.

Thrasymedes Son of Nestor. He and his brother Antilochus accompanied their aged father to the Trojan War. Thrasymedes returned home and was at Pylos when Telemachus came there in search of Odysseus.

Thyestes Son of Pelops and Hippodamia. For the story of his share in the death of his half-brother Chrysippus, his long feud with his brother Atreus, and his incest with his daughter Pelopia who bore him Aegisthus, *see* ATREUS. After the death of Atreus, Thyestes took his kingdom of Mycenae, where he had already reigned for a brief period previously. When Atreus' sons Agamemnon and Menelaus, who had fled from Mycenae to Sicyon at the time of their father's death, were old enough and strong enough, they returned with an army – aided by their father-in-law Tyndareos, king of Sparta – and drove Thyestes from the Mycenaean throne: he took refuge on the island of Cythera, where he died. His expulsion was subsequently avenged by his son Aegisthus, who killed Agamemnon and ruled in his stead, taking Clytemnestra, who had helped him to carry out the murder, as his queen.

Thymoetes A Trojan elder and counsel-

lor of Priam. According to a variant of
the myth of Paris' birth, Thymoetes'
wife bore Priam a bastard son on the
same day as Paris was born. Priam abandoned and exposed this child instead of
Paris, in response to Hecabe's dream
which foretold that her son would cause
Troy's downfall. According to Virgil,
Thymoetes was the first to propose that
the Wooden Horse should be moved
inside the walls of Troy.

Thyone *see* SEMELE.

Tiberinus Son of Janus and Camise, or
else a descendant of Aeneas and king of
Alba Longa (his father being in this
case, King Capetus); he was drowned in
the River Albula or was killed on its
banks. As a result of his death there the
river was renamed Tiber.

Tilphusa *see* TELPHUSA.

Timagoras *see* EROS.

Timandra Daughter of Tyndareos; she
married Echemus, but left him for Phyleus.

Tiphys The original helmsman of the
Argo. He was the son of Hagnias or
Phorbas, and a Boeotian. When the ship
came to the land of the Mariandyni in
Bithynia, Tiphys died of an illness, and
his place was taken by Ancaeus or Erginus.

Tiresias The great blind Theban seer, a
son of Everes – a Theban nobleman
descended from Udaeus, one of the
'Sown Men' – and of Chariclo, a nymph.
There were two alternative myths to
explain Tiresias' blindness. According
to one of them his mother was the
favourite of Athena and bathed with her
at a spring. One day the youthful Tiresias was hunting nearby when he caught
sight of Athena naked. The goddess at
once covered his eyes with her hands

and blinded him. Then, to comfort
Chariclo in her distress at her son's punishment, Athena purged his ears so that
he could understand the speech of birds.
She also gave him a cornel-wood staff
able to guide him as well as if he could
see, and endowed him with a life seven
generations long, as well as granting
him the gift of prophecy.

The other explanation was that Tiresias saw two snakes copulating on
Mount Cithaeron, or on Mount Cyllene
in Arcadia. He seized his stick and
lashed out at them, killing the female.
At once he was transformed into a
woman, and remained so until seven
years later, when he chanced to see a
pair of snakes coupling once again. This
time he struck the male, and became a
man again. (According to another version of the myth, he had not killed the
first snake, and it was the same pair
that he saw once more on the second
occasion.) When Zeus and Hera were
arguing one day whether a man or a
woman derives the greater pleasure from
sexual intercourse, it was Tiresias whom
they consulted as the only creature able
to answer from his own experience.
Hera had stated that a man enjoys it
much more than a woman: so when
Tiresias declared that a woman's pleasure was nine times greater than a man's,
she struck him blind in her rage. Zeus
could not undo his wife's act, but compensated the blinded man by giving him
the gift of unerring prophecy, based on
his understanding of the speech of birds.
Tiresias had a special dwelling-place
near Thebes where he practised divination, in the company of a boy who
assisted him in his sacrifices.

Tiresias played a part in many myths.
When Dionysus first came to Thebes
and was rejected by the impious Pentheus, Tiresias and Cadmus joined his
revels. Pentheus would not listen to Tiresias' warning to respect the god, and as
a result of his disbelief was torn to
pieces by a band of Maenads which

included his own mother. It was Tiresias, too, who revealed to Oedipus that he had killed his father Laius and married his mother Jocasta. When the Seven attacked Thebes, Tiresias warned Creon that the only thing that could save the city from conquest would be the self-sacrifice of an unmarried Theban nobleman to Ares: whereupon Creon's son Menoeceus leapt from the city walls into the lair of Ares' dragon that Cadmus had slain. After the failure of the attack, Tiresias solemnly warned Creon to bury Polynices' body: and because Creon was too late in obeying, he lost his son Haemon, his daughter-in-law Antigone, and his wife Eurydice.

In the subsequent successful attack on Thebes by the sons of the Seven, the Epigoni, Tiresias predicted the fall of the city and advised the king, Eteocles' son Laodamas, to arrange a withdrawal of the people from the city by night. According to one variant of the myth, Tiresias died on this journey after drinking water from the spring of Telphusa at Haliartus. In an alternative version he died there after being captured by the Epigoni, while they were taking him and his daughter Manto to Delphi to be offered to Apollo as prizes of war. Tiresias was buried by the spring of Telphusa. Yet another story asserts that when Manto migrated to Colophon in Asia Minor, he accompanied her and died there, being buried by Calchas and other seers who gathered to do him honour.

Odysseus was sent to the edge of the earth by Circe to consult Tiresias' shade. His was the only shade to keep its intelligence after death, a privilege which was given him by Athena or Zeus or Persephone. He was still able to utter prophecy, and, after drinking the blood of the black ewe which Odysseus slew, told him, with many warnings, all that would befall him, first on his homeward voyage, and then in his house which was occupied by Penelope's suitors, and

subsequently after his victory over the intruders for the rest of his life.

Tisamenus *1.* Son of Thersander and of Amphiaraus' daughter Demonassa. When his father was killed in the Trojan War, Tisamenus inherited the throne of Thebes. His son Autesion succeeded him.
2. Son of Orestes and Hermione. After his father's death, he ruled his kingdom of Sparta and Argos until the descendants of Heracles (the Heraclids) invaded the Peloponnese and drove him off his throne. After taking refuge in Achaea in the northern Peloponnese, Tisamenus was either killed fighting the Heraclids, or else died in a subsequent battle between his followers and the Ionians, when the latter tried to eject him from Achaea. His men beat the Ionians and settled there, burying Tisamenus at Helice.

Tisiphone *1. see* FURIES.
2. see ALCMAEON.

Titans and **Titanesses** The race of gods begotten by the union of Uranus (Sky) and Gaia (Earth). The Greeks thought of them as gigantic beings who had ruled the world in a primitive age. The principal Titans were Cronos, Rhea, Oceanus, Tethys, Iapetus, Hyperion, Coeus, Crius, Phoebe, Themis, Mnemosyne, and Theia. Some of their children were also regarded as Titans: Helios (the Sun; often simply called 'The Titan'), Prometheus, Epimetheus, and Atlas. The children of Cronos and Rhea, however, were not Titans but members of the divine race of the gods which eventually supplanted them. Just as Cronos overthrew his father Uranus for his high-handed behaviour, so Zeus deposed Cronos from the rule of the universe in a mighty battle, in which the gods and Titans were pitted against one another. Prometheus and some of Gaia's other children, the Hundred-Armed giants

(Hecatoncheires) and Cyclopes, helped the gods; and a large number of Titans, including Oceanus and Helios, as well as all the Titanesses, took no part in the fight. The Titans took Mount Othrys as their stronghold, and the gods Olympus. After a conflict lasting ten years Zeus won by bringing the Hundred-Armed giants from Tartarus as his allies. He then threw his Titan enemies down into Tartarus, in the nethermost depths of the Underworld, as far beneath Hades as the sky was above the earth. In this place of eternal gloom the Titans were everlastingly imprisoned behind bronze doors, with the three Hundred-Armed giants as their jailers. Atlas was punished by being forced to support the corner of the sky on his shoulders.

Whether the reign of the Titans was barbarous or, on the contrary, a golden age of great ease and prosperity, was disputed by the Greeks. There was also an alternative myth about Cronos' fate, which asserted that after his fall from power he became king of the Isles of the Blessed in the Western Sea.

The origin of the word Titan is unknown. The names of the Titans and Titanesses are very varied in origin: some are non-Greek, others personifications of abstract ideas, such as Mnemosyne 'memory', Phoebe 'bright', Theia 'divine', and Themis 'order'.

Tithonus Son of Laomedon, king of Troy, and (according to some accounts) of the nymph Strymo. When Eos, the goddess of the dawn, set eyes on the handsome youth, she fell in love with him and carried him off to be her husband and lived in her palace in the farthest East, by the stream of Ocean in Ethiopia. Eos bore Tithonus two sons, Memnon and Emathion. The latter, a king of Arabia, tried to prevent Heracles from taking the golden apples of the Hesperides, and was killed by him. Memnon brought a force of Ethiopians to Troy, and died there fighting the Greeks.

Eos begged Zeus to grant Tithonus immortality, and Zeus consented to her request. Some time afterwards, however, she noticed that her husband was visibly ageing: he went grey and then white, and his skin sagged and became wrinkled. Eos realised that she had failed to ask Zeus to supplement his gift of immortality by eternal youth; and now it was too late. As Tithonus gradually withered into a desiccated shell, Eos locked him in one of her palace rooms, which was barred with bronze doors. According to a variant of the myth Eos turned him into a cicada, so that he might please her with his constant chirruping and put off his aged skin once a year.

Titus Tatius see ROMULUS.

Tityus A giant, said to be the son of Gaia (Earth) or of Elare, daughter of Orchomenus (according to the latter interpretation his father was said to be Zeus). Tityus lived on the island of Euboea, and Phoenician sailors took Rhadamanthys to see him there. Hera beguiled him into making an attempt to rape Leto, mother of Apollo and Artemis, as she was crossing the fields of Panopeus on her way to Delphi. Thereupon Artemis (or Apollo) shot Tityus, and Zeus flung a thunderbolt at him; he was then bound to the ground in Tartarus, where he covered a couple of acres. A pair of vultures eternally pecked his liver (according to the ancients, the seat of sexual desire), and his hands were unable to drive them off.

Tlepolemus Son of Heracles and Astyoche, daughter of Phylas; king of Ephyra in Thesprotia. When Tlepolemus grew up, he took refuge at the court of King Ceyx of Trachis, together with Heracles' other sons; and later he went to Athens. Tlepolemus and Licymnius, half-brother of Heracles' mother Alcmena, settled at Argos, and it was there that Tlepolemus killed Licymnius, either in a quarrel, or by accident when Licymnius tried to stop him from beating a slave. For this murder Tlepolemus was exiled from Argos and took his wife Polyxo and a large company of followers to found a kingdom on the island of Rhodes. There his people settled in three districts, Lindus, Ialysus, and Cameirus. He had been one of Helen's suitors and took nine shiploads of Rhodians to the Trojan War. There, however, he was killed by Sarpedon of Lycia. His son by Polyxo was Deipylus.

Tmolus The god of Mount Tmolus in Lydia, or a king in the same region, who adjudicated the musical competition between Pan and Apollo.

Toxeus *1.* Son of Thestius and brother of Althaea. Meleager killed him in a quarrel over the Calydonian boar.
2. Nephew of above, a son of Oeneus and Althaea; he was killed by his father for jumping over the ditch dug to fortify the city.

Triopas *1.* Son of Phorbas and king of Argos. His children included Agenor, Iasus, and Pelasgus.
2. Son of Poseidon and Canace, daughter of Aeolus *2.* Triopas' children were Phorbas, Iphimedia, and Erysichthon. He was king of Dotion in Thessaly.
3. A Rhodian, the son of Helios and Rhode.

Triptolemus A young man of Attic extraction whom Demeter chose as the transmitter of her gift of grain and agriculture to the nations of the world. He was variously stated to be a son of Celeus and Metanira of Eleusis (identified, in some accounts, with the child whom Demeter tried to render immortal); or of the hero named Eleusis (after whom that town was named); or of Oceanus and Gaia (Earth). Triptolemus was depicted in Greek art as carrying a wheatsheaf and sitting in the magic

chariot given him by Demeter, which was drawn by a pair of winged serpents. In this vehicle he flew the length and breadth of the earth, scattering seeds of grain and teaching the inhabitants of each place how to cultivate crops, and giving them laws and justice. In Scythia, however, the king of the country, named Lyncus, was consumed with jealousy of Triptolemus' powers, and resented his role as benefactor of mankind. Lyncus tried to murder Triptolemus in his bed, but Demeter saved her favourite by restraining Lyncus, as he was about to drive his dagger home, and turning him into a lynx. Antheas, son of King Eumelus of Achaea, tried to drive Triptolemus' magic chariot, but fell out and killed himself. In Thrace King Carnabon slew one of the winged serpents and imprisoned Triptolemus in a dungeon. But Demeter again rescued him and gave him another serpent; and to remind mortals of Carnabon's sin, she placed him in the sky as the constellation Ophiuchus, the serpent-holder. Some ancient authorities claimed that Triptolemus invented the wheel. The Athenians moreover believed that after his death he became one of the judges of the dead, along with Minos and Rhadamanthys.

Triton A minor sea-god cast in the shape of a merman; the son of Poseidon and Amphitrite. He was a popular subject of ancient art, but his depiction was varied, and it was even uncertain whether he was one or many. His commonest representation was as a creature with a human head and torso, but with the tail of a fish. When a huge tidal wave had taken the Argonauts far inland in Libya, and they had carried their ship to Lake Tritonis (in what is now southern Tunisia), Triton appeared in the form of a handsome young man called Eurypylus, and showed them which direction to take in order to find the sea again. As a parting gift, he gave Euphemus a clod of earth, after himself receiving as a present from the Greeks a golden tripod which the Argonauts had brought from Delphi; and this clod, when Euphemus dropped it from the ship north of Crete, became the island of Calliste (Thera).

The men of Tanagra in Boeotia regarded Triton, or one of the beings described by this name, as a menace, since when their women were bathing in the sea before sacrificing to Dionysus, he used to attack them; and so a fight took place between the two gods, which Triton lost. On another occasion a Triton was caught at Tanagra and beheaded. It was said that he had preyed upon the cattle of the locality, but had subsequently been lured into a trap when intoxicated by a gift of wine.

Triton was associated with spiral conch-shells, since he used one of them as a trumpet in order to calm the stormy seas. In the battle between the gods and giants, he employed a shell in this way in order to terrify some of the giants. He also carried a trident, like his father Poseidon. Whether he was identified with the sea-monster called Triton whom Heracles overcame at wrestling is unclear. In a myth about the childhood of Athena, Triton was said to have had a daughter, Pallas, with whom the goddess played and, in a fit of anger, killed. *See* ATHENA.

Trivia (Latin 'of the crossroads') An epithet of Hecate or Diana (Artemis).

Troezen Son of Pelops and Hippodamia. With his brother Pittheus he ruled the towns of the eastern Argolid which, after his death, Pittheus combined into a single city and called Troezen after him.

Troilus Son of either Priam or Apollo; his mother was Hecabe. He was still a young man when, as he either drove his chariot or accompanied Polyxena at nightfall to draw water at a well, he was ambushed by Achilles near the temple of Apollo at Thymbra. In the first version of the myth, the one known to Virgil, Troilus' horses bolted when Achilles attacked him; the youth was dragged along behind the chariot. In the second version Achilles slaughtered him upon the altar of the temple. There was also a tale that Achilles killed him because he knew Troy would never be taken if Troilus was allowed to reach his twentieth year.

Trophonius and **Agamedes** Sons of Erginus, king of Orchomenus in Boeotia; Trophonius, however, was also called a son of Apollo. These two were fine architects and builders: they built Alcmena's bridal chamber at Thebes, a temple of Poseidon in Arcadia between Tegea and Mantinea, and the shrine of Apollo at Delphi. When they constructed a treasure-house, either for the Boeotian king Hyrieus or for Augeas, king of Elis, they cheated their employer by placing a loose stone slab in the wall of the building, which they alone knew how to remove. They then began a series of thefts which the king could not understand, since the treasure-house was supposed to be proof against thieves. He set a trap to catch the robber, and Agamedes, who on that occasion had been the first of the pair to enter the building, found himself caught and unable to escape. When Trophonius came in, he realised at once that his brother could not possibly be rescued: and so he cut off his head, thus at the same time saving Agamedes from dreadful tortures and himself from any danger of identification, since only a headless body remained. So Trophonius escaped detection. Nevertheless he soon lost his life; for when he was at Lebadea in Boeotia, he was swallowed up in a hole in the earth. In later times the oracle of Apollo at Delphi ordered the Boeotians, when they were troubled by a drought, to consult Trophonius' oracle. They did not know how to find it, but one of their envoys, called Saon, followed a swarm of bees into a cave, where Trophonius appeared and disclosed to the visitor that he was now the god of an oracle at that spot. For those who wished to consult it, an elaborate ritual was ordained, including a ceremony of purification and various sacrifices; then the enquirer went down into the cave and put his questions, ostensibly to Trophonius in person.

A different version of the myth declares that Trophonius and Agamedes, after building Apollo's temple at Delphi, asked the god for a reward. They were told that they should enjoy themselves for six days and that their reward would arrive on the seventh. After six days' happiness they died in their sleep.

Tros A king of Troy; the son of Erichthonius and Astyoche, daughter of the River Simois. His wife was also a river-nymph, Callirrhoe, daughter of the Scamander. Their children were Ilus, founder of the city of Troy (Ilium), Assaracus, who ruled the kingdom of Dardania, and Ganymede, the handsome boy whom Zeus carried off to be his cup-bearer. To recompense Tros for the loss of his son (which had caused him great distress), Zeus gave him a team of immortal horses, which Heracles afterwards coveted. The land of Troy was named after Tros.

Tullia see TARQUINIUS SUPERBUS.

Tullius see SERVIUS TULLIUS.

Tullus Hostilius The third king of Rome – whether mythical, or a historical personage round whom myths accumulated, is not certain. His grandfather, Hostus Hostilius, was believed to have won a battle against the Sabines. Tullus was elected king after the death of Numa Pompilius, and proved a contrast to his predecessor, being active and belligerent as opposed to Numa's peace

and piety. After a battle of champions fought between the Horatii and Curiatii, he conquered Alba Longa. When the Alban king Mettius ·Fufetius, now his tributary, deserted his side during a battle against the cities of Veii and Fidenae, Tullus had him bound to two chariots facing in opposite directions; and he was torn apart by the horses. He then forced the people of Alba to come and live in Rome, and razed their former city to the ground. The population of Rome was thus doubled, and Tullus felt himself strong enough to declare war on the Sabines, over whom he won a notable victory. A shower of stones then fell on the Alban Mount, and a festival was inaugurated to expiate the abandonment of Alba's shrines.

At the end of his life, after a reign of thirty-two years, Tullus fell ill and turned to superstition. This change of heart brought about his death, for, while trying to propitiate Jupiter Elicius with a formula taken from the books of King Numa, he was struck by lightning and killed.

Turnus *1.* Son of Daunus and Venilia. Turnus was a prince of the Rutulians, an Italian nation centred upon Ardea. He was betrothed to Lavinia, the daughter of Latinus, who was the king of his Latin neighbours, but the engagement was disrupted by the arrival of the Trojan Aeneas. Amata, Latinus' queen, continued to support Turnus' ambition to win Lavinia's hand, and Turnus broke a treaty between the Trojans and Italians according to which the issue was to be decided in single combat between himself and Aeneas: his sister Juturna, a water-nymph, helped him escape from the Trojans. Finally Venus put a stop to Turnus' attempts at flight, and Aeneas succeeded in killing his rival. Virgil, although favourable to Aeneas, presents the character and death of Turnus with pathos and a measure of sympathy.

2. A man of Aricia who spoke against Tarquinius Superbus at an assembly of the Latins: Tarquinius, under the pretext that he intended rebellion, had him drowned.

Tyche The goddess of Fortune; a daughter of Oceanus (or Zeus) and of Tethys.

Tydeus Son of Oeneus, king of Calydon, by his second wife Periboea or his daughter Gorge. His uncle Agrius, who had usurped Oeneus' throne, exiled him from Calydon for homicide. Whom he had killed, however, was variously stated – it was either his brother Olenias, or his uncle Alcathous, Oeneus' brother, or else the eight sons of Melas, another of his uncles. After his murderous deed, Tydeus took refuge at the court of King Adrastus of Argos. There he had a quarrel with another refugee, Polynices of Thebes. Adrastus stopped the fight, and married his daughters Deipyle and Argia to the pair in response to an oracle which had bidden him give them in marriage to a lion and a boar – for Tydeus was clothed in the hide of a boar draped over his shoulders, and Polynices wore a lionskin, or else the two bore these beasts as emblems on their shields.

Adrastus undertook to restore the two princes to the thrones of their respective cities. He gave Polynices his first attention, and Tydeus accompanied the army that went to Thebes. When the army reached the River Asopus, Tydeus was sent to negotiate with the Thebans, but failed to achieve a settlement. He did, however, beat the Thebans at a number of athletic contests, which so greatly aroused their jealousy that, while he was on his way back to the Asopus, fifty of them attacked him from an ambush. He fought single-handed against this troop and slew all but one, Maeon, whom he sent back to Thebes with the tale. In the siege of Thebes, Tydeus, whose emblem was Night, at-tacked the Proetid gate and fought a duel with Melanippus. Each dealt the other a mortal blow. The goddess Athena, who loved Tydeus dearly, approached him as he lay in his death-throes, intending to endow him with immortality; but Amphiaraus, who knew her purpose and hated Tydeus for having persuaded Adrastus to undertake the ill-starred expedition, severed Melanippus' neck and tossed the head to Tydeus, who seized it and devoured the brains. Athena was disgusted and turned away, and so Tydeus was allowed to die the death of a mortal. Deipyle gave Tydeus a son, Diomedes.

Tyndareos A king of Sparta. His father was either Oebalus or Perieres; his mother Batia or Gorgophone. On the death of Oebalus the previous king, Hippocoon, a brother or half-brother of Tyndareos, expelled him from Sparta. Tyndareos took refuge in Messenia or Aetolia, and later married Leda, daughter of King Thestius of Pleuron in Aetolia. After Heracles had killed Hippocoon and his twelve sons, he placed Tyndareos on the Spartan throne. Leda had a number of children, some of whom claimed Zeus, rather than Tyndareos, as their father. Helen was a daughter of Zeus, who was usually also said to be the father of the Dioscuri, Castor and Polydeuces. Leda's other daughters, Clytemnestra, Timandra, Philonoe, and Phoebe, were usually assigned to the paternity of Tyndareos.

After Thyestes had killed their father Atreus, Agamemnon and Menelaus took refuge in Sparta. Tyndareos married them to his daughters, Clytemnestra and Helen respectively, and helped them win back the kingdom of Mycenae for Agamemnon, the elder. Clytemnestra was, in fact, already married to Thyestes' son Tantalus, but Agamemnon killed this man and his infant son and married the widow. Helen was sought after by all the eligible princes of Greece because of her beauty. Indeed, Theseus of Athens had already stolen her from Sparta with the intention of marrying her; but before he could do so her brothers the Dioscuri had come to her rescue. Now her suitors gathered at Sparta, and Tyndareos was at a loss how to appease them all. Finally at Odysseus' suggestion he sacrificed a horse and made all the suitors stand on the hide and swear to support the chosen bridegroom, whoever he turned out to be, and protect his marriage-rights. This oath was what led the Greek princes to go to Troy to win Helen back from Paris. Tyndareos married Helen to Agamemnon's brother Menelaus, whose presents were the richest, and rewarded Odysseus by gaining him the hand of his niece, Icarius' daughter Penelope.

Tyndareos quarrelled with Aphrodite and laid a chain around her statue in her temple at Sparta. He also omitted to offer sacrifice to her. As a result she punished him by making not only his wife but also his daughters unfaithful: Clytemnestra with Aegisthus, Helen with Paris and Deiphobus, and Timandra (who had married Echemus, king of Arcadia) with Augeas' son Phyleus.

Tyndareos, having lost his sons in their battle with Idas and Lynceus, nominated Menelaus as his heir. According to Euripides he lived long enough to arraign Orestes, the son and slayer of Clytemnestra, on a charge of matricide before the Areopagus at Athens.

Typhon or **Typhoeus** After Zeus had defeated the Titans and locked them in Tartarus, or after the Olympian gods had conquered the army of the giants, Gaia (Earth) mated once more, this time with Tartarus, and in the Corycian Cave in Cilicia (in south-eastern Asia Minor) brought forth the terrible monster Typhon. He had a hundred serpentine heads, each flickering its dark tongue, and flashing fiery eyes. Moreover in every head he had a frightening voice, and these voices spoke the speech of the gods, or bellowed like a bull, or whis-

tled, or barked like a dog. As soon as he was fully grown, Typhon made war on Zeus; and Zeus, well aware of the threat he posed to his sovereignty, determined upon his suppression. When Typhon emerged into the daylight, Zeus assailed him with a hail of thunderbolts and drove him back to Mount Casius in Syria. There Typhon made a stand, and a fierce battle took place. He grasped hold of Zeus, took away his *harpe* or sickle, and with it removed the sinews of the god's limbs, leaving him lying helpless on the ground. Then Typhon seized Zeus' thunderbolts and gave his sinews to another monster, Delphyne, part woman and part serpent, to guard under a bearskin in the Corycian Cave; and he deposited the helpless Zeus there as well. Some time later Hermes and Aegipan came to the cave, beguiled Delphyne into allowing her attention to wander, and stole the sinews, which they fitted once more into Zeus' limbs. Zeus then escaped and flew back in a winged chariot to Olympus, where he acquired a new supply of thunderbolts. With these he renewed the attack on Typhon, driving him to the mythical Mount Nysa. There Typhon had a meeting with the Fates, and when they suggested that he should eat the food of mortal men to give him strength he trusted and believed them: though after doing so he was, in fact, gravely weakened. He then faced Zeus again on Mount Haemus in Thrace: the ancients believed that the blood (Greek *haima*) he shed there gave its name to the mountain range. Zeus now had the upper hand, and chased Typhon southwards to the sea off Italy, picking up an island from the sea and flinging it on top of him. The island in this new position was later known as Sicily, and Typhon's fiery breath became Mount Etna, for he was immortal and could not die.

In Hesiod's version of their battle Zeus simply set Typhon on fire with his shower of thunderbolts: the whole world shook in the fray, and Tartarus itself trembled. Then Zeus seized him and flung him down into the depths of Tartarus, where he joined the imprisoned Titans. There the captive became the father of all the winds that cause men harm, and that is why the word typhoon is derived from his name. It was also said that during their great struggle the other gods fled in terror to Egypt, where, to disguise themselves from Typhon, they assumed the shapes of animals: this was told in explanation of the animal forms with which the Egyptians invested many of their gods. The Greeks identified Typhon with Set, the monster which pursued Osiris. It was even supposed that Zeus accompanied this flight and disguised himself as a ram: this accounted for the cult of Zeus Ammon (Amun) in the shape of that animal.

The ancients also believed that before his defeat Typhon mated with Echidna, and brought forth the Chimaera, Orthus, Ladon, the Sphinx, the Sow of Crommyon, the Nemean Lion, and the eagle that tortured Prometheus.

Typhon was occasionally differentiated from Typhoeus and said to be the latter's offspring; it was sometimes said to be the son rather than the father who mated with Echidna.

Tyro Daughter of Salmoneus, a king of Elis, and his first wife Alcidice. After Tyro's mother died, her stepmother Sidero treated her with great cruelty. When Poseidon saw Tyro, he fell in love with her and took advantage of the girl's infatuation for the River Enipeus by disguising himself as the river-god and then ravishing her, making a wave of the river curl over their bodies as they lay together. Tyro gave birth to twins, Pelias and Neleus, who were abandoned and exposed by her and brought up by a horse-trainer. The reason for Sidero's cruelty was sometimes believed to have been her discovery of Tyro's pregnancy and her refusal to believe the story of Poseidon's visit. However Tyro was married to her father's brother Cretheus, king of Iolcus in Thessaly, and bore him three sons, Aeson, Pheres, and Amythaon. But her son by Poseidon, Pelias, eventually supplanted Aeson as heir to the kingdom of Iolcus, and killed Sidero for her cruelty to his mother.

Tyrrhenus A native of Maeonia in Lydia, and the son of the Lydian king Atys. According to tradition, he led the migration of Lydians to Italy, after a great famine had made Lydia itself uninhabitable. The Etruscans were named after him, and some of the ancient writers, notably Herodotus, held that they were the descendants of these migrants from Lydia. Tyrrhenus also gave his name to the Tyrrhenian Sea west of Italy.

U

Ucalegon (Greek *ouk alegon* 'not caring') A counsellor of Priam, king of Troy.

Udaeus One of the five 'Sown Men' (*Spartoi*), who were sprung from the dragon's teeth that Cadmus sowed, and were the ancestors of the Theban nobility. Tiresias was his grandson.

Ulixes The Latin name of Odysseus.

Ulysses see ODYSSEUS.

Underworld see HADES.

Upis see OPIS.

Urania see MUSES.

Uranus (Greek *ouranos* 'sky'). After Earth (Gaia) was born out of Chaos, she produced Uranus without the aid of a male. She then mated with her son, and their offspring was the race of Titans and Titanesses, the gigantic immortals who preceded the race of gods. One of these Titans, Cronos, helped Gaia to take vengeance on Uranus, for Uranus was jealous of his children and, when the time came for them to be born, tried to push them back into the body of Gaia. She gave her son a flint sickle (*harpe*), and the next time Uranus came to lie upon Gaia, Cronos castrated him with the sickle. The drops of blood gave birth to the Furies, the Giants, and the nymphs of ash trees; the genitals themselves fell into the sea and floated on the foam to the island of Cyprus or, according to an alternative version, Cythera, where they were transformed into the goddess of love, Aphrodite. Uranus had not further role in mythology, and the Greeks never accorded him worship.

V

Valeria *see* LUPERCA.

Valerius Publicola or **Poplicola, Publius** The colleague – whether mythical or historical is not certain – of Lucius Junius Brutus as first consul of the Roman Republic, after the expulsion of the last king, Tarquinius Superbus. Son of a certain Volesus and brother of another legendary figure, Valeria Luperca, he was one of the leaders brought to Lucretia by her father at her urgent summons, after she had been raped by the king's son, Sextus Tarquinius. In the first battle between Roman forces and the Etruscan allies of Tarquinius Superbus, Valerius led the infantry, defeating the men of Veii but finding the soldiers from Tarquinii stiff opponents. The Romans were finally recognised to have the victory when the voice of the god Silvanus that night proclaimed that the Etruscans had lost one man more than the Romans. Valerius celebrated a triumph, but soon found himself unpopular, as the people suspected him of fostering royal ambitions. Thereupon, according to one tradition, he called a meeting of the commons at which he had the *fasces* (bundles of rods symbolising the consul's authority) lowered, acknowledging the people's sovereign power. He then agreed to move the house he had started to build from the top of the Velian slope – where it would have enjoyed a commanding position over Rome – to the foot of that hill. He also reputedly instituted the right of appeal to the people against the decisions of state officials, a very popular move, for which he was said to have been accorded the surname *Poplicola*, from *populum colere*, 'to favour the common people'. He then held elections to appoint his colleague in the consulship, since Brutus had been killed in single combat with Tarquinius Superbus' second son, Arruns. Valerius was believed to have served a second term as consul in the following year, during which he continued to lead the Roman forces against Tarquinius Superbus whose principal Etruscan ally was now Lars Porsenna of Clusium. At a later stage he interceded with Porsenna to protect certain hostages whom Cloelia had rescued from the Etruscans who held them, and eventually persuaded him to make friends with Rome. Two further consulships were ascribed to him, and he was believed to have died a poor man, receiving a state funeral at public expense. The women of Rome mourned him for a year.

Vegoia An Etruscan nymph with prophetic powers who gave oracles to Arruns Veltumnus, a prince or priest of Clusium.

Venilia *see* CANENS.

Venus An Italian goddess who presided over ploughland and gardens, making them trim and neat. She was identified from very early times with the Greek Aphrodite, and endowed with her mythology. The story of her son Aeneas' wanderings and final settlement in Italy was particularly important to the Romans, for it was claimed that the Julian House, to which Augustus and his successors belonged by adoption, were descended from Aeneas' son Iulus, and thus from Venus herself. It was Venus who helped Aeneas to escape from the burning city of Troy and protected him from the enmity of Juno. She made Dido, queen of Carthage, fall in love with him and grant him refuge at a time of great stress. She also helped him in his final battle with Turnus, placing his spear, which was lodged in a tree stump, back in his hands.

Vergilia *see* CORIOLANUS.

Verginia During the period of aristocratic government at Rome under the decemvirate or Board of Ten (451–450 BC), it was traditionally held, in circles hostile to the Claudian family, that the decemvir Appius Claudius conceived the desire to debauch Verginia, the beautiful daughter of a centurion, Verginius, who was away with the army at Mount Algidus. In order to get her into his own hands Appius instructed one of his dependents, Marcus Claudius by name, to assert that Verginia was in reality his own slave, the daughter of a woman who had previously belonged to his household. Then Appius, in the absence of Verginia's father, immediately handed her over into Marcus Claudius' custody. But Icilius, to whom she had been promised in marriage, and her uncle Numitorius appeared, and she was placed in their control pending the arrival of her father. Though Appius sent messages to the army commanders to detain Verginius, he came with all speed to the hearing of the case. He led his daughter into the Forum, dressed in mourning. Appius then gave judgment – that Verginia was a slave and must be surrendered to her owner. When Marcus Claudius tried to take her, Verginius resisted, but a force of armed men appeared. With a show of subjection, Verginius obtained a few minutes' respite, in which he took his daughter to a butcher's shop nearby and stabbed her in the heart, cursing Appius

and declaring that her death was better than her dishonour. Verginius got away from Rome to the army, which he roused with the tale of Appius' outrageous conduct. The common people and the ordinary soldiers then seized the Aventine Hill, and later seceded to the Sacred Mount, as they were also said to have done fifty years previously (though the historicity of both events is dubious). These events, it was believed, led to the suppression of the decemvirate and the restoration of the tribunes, the traditional protectors of the common people against aristocratic oppression.

Vertumnus *see* POMONA.

Vesta The Roman goddess of the hearth, identified with the Greek Hestia. At Rome she was considered to be protectress of the nation, and the Vestal Virgins were appointed to superintend her worship.

Veturia *see* CORIOLANUS.

Vibenna The surname of two Etruscan brothers, Aulus (Olus) and Caeles Vibenna, great heroes in the mythology of Etruria, and allies of Mastarna. Their legend was obscure even in Roman times; it was believed however, that they captured Cacus (described in an Etruscan story as a great seer, and inspired by Apollo) in a sacred wood where they forced him to reveal his secrets. The brothers were driven out of Etruria and exiled. According to the historian Tacitus, Caeles was granted one of the hills of Rome by Tarquinius Priscus or another Roman king, and it was subsequently named the Caelian Hill after him.

Virbius A minor Italian god associated with the worship of Diana; he had a cult at the town of Aricia in Latium. It was said that Hippolytus, the son of Theseus, after Asclepius had raised him from the dead, was brought to Italy by Artemis, and settled there under the name of Virbius (*vir bis* 'a man for a second time').

Volumnia *see* CORIOLANUS.

Volupta ('Pleasure') Daughter of Cupid and Psyche.

Vulcan (Latin: *Vulcanus*) An ancient Italian god of fire, occasionally called Mulciber, worshipped at Rome, and identified with the Greek god of metal-work and craftsmanship Hephaestus. He has no mythology apart from what he acquired from his Greek counter-part.

X

Xanthus *1.* Xanthus and Balius were Achilles' immortal horses, born on the banks of Ocean where their mother grazed in the form of a filly, and given by the gods to his father Peleus as a wedding present. Their names meant 'Bay' and 'Piebald' respectively, and they were the sons of the West Wind Zephyrus and the Harpy Podarge ('fleet-foot'). Achilles took them to Troy and lent them to Patroclus when the latter led the Myrmidons into battle. After Patroclus had fallen, the two horses wept bitterly for his death, and Zeus took pity on them and regretted having given them to a mortal man so as to become involved in the sufferings of those miserable creatures. Zeus gave them strength to escape Hector, and they dashed back to the Greek lines.

When Achilles himself returned to battle, he reproached the pair of horses for having failed to bring Patroclus back safe from battle. Xanthus then reminded Achilles that Patroclus had died not through any fault of theirs, but because Apollo had decreed it in order to give glory to Hector, and he added that Achilles' death too was now close at hand. At that point the Furies struck Xanthus dumb, and he never spoke again. Achilles, however, declared that the prophecy of his death was nothing new, since he had heard it before.

2. A river of Troy, usually called Scamander, and its god.

3. A river of Cilicia, and its god.

Xenia *see* DAPHNIS.

Xuthus Son of Hellen and the nymph Orseis, or of Aeolus and Enarete. According to the former (and more commonly accepted) version of his parentage he was the brother of Dorus and Aeolus: they were believed to have been the ancestors of the Doric and Aeolic branches of the Greek race, and he was ancestor of the Ionians and Achaeans. After ruling the Thessalian town of Iolcus for a time, Xuthus was driven out by his two brothers, on the grounds that he had stolen their patrimony. He then went to Athens, where he gave the king Erechtheus valuable help in a war against Chalcodon in Euboea, and received his daughter Creusa as his wife. When Erechtheus died, his sons asked Xuthus to choose one of them as the new king. He chose the eldest, Cecrops, whereupon the other drove Xuthus out of Athens. He took his wife and sons, Achaeus and Ion, to the northern Peloponnese, and died in the land of Aegialus there: it was later renamed Achaea, after his son Achaeus.

According to the *Ion* of Euripides, however, Xuthus was a son of Aeolus, and succeeded Erechtheus on the throne of Athens. In this account Ion was a child of Apollo and Creusa, and Dorus and Achaeus were Xuthus' own sons. The play tells how the existence of Ion, who had been brought up at Delphi in the service of Apollo, was miraculously revealed to Xuthus and Creusa, and how Xuthus accepted him as his own and Creusa's son.

Z

Zagreus A Cretan god who was usually identified with Dionysus and played an important part in the beliefs of the sect practising the Mysteries of Orpheus.

According to their account, after Demeter bore Persephone as his daughter, Zeus then fathered Zagreus on Persephone, intending him to be his heir. But the Titans, who were opposed to Zeus' power, lured the child from his parents by offering him toys, and then tore him to pieces and devoured him, all but the heart, which Athena rescued and gave to Zeus. From the heart Zeus remade his son in the body of Semele, and punished the Titans for their crime by blasting them to ashes. Out of the soot so formed was created mankind. When Semele's child, made from the heart of Zagreus, was born, Zeus called him Dionysus. Then the Orphic story substantially followed the usual version of Dionysus' myth.

Zelus ('emulation'). A companion of Zeus, together with his brothers Bia and Cratos and his sister Nike. He was a son of the Titan Pallas and of Styx.

Zemelo see SEMELE.

Zephyrus The god of the West Wind; one of the sons of Astraeus and Eos. He fell in love with the beautiful Hyacinthus, a young man of Amyclae near Sparta. When Apollo also courted Hyacinthus and gained his favour, Zephyrus took revenge by causing a discus, which Apollo had flung, to swerve and hit the youth on the head, so that he died. Zephyrus was the father of Apollo's im-

mortal horses Xanthus and Balius, having made their mother, a Harpy, pregnant when she was grazing in the form of a filly in meadows beside the Ocean. In general the West Wind was considered the gentlest and most welcome of winds, and was frequently compared to his advantage with the harsh North Wind, Boreas. It was Zephyrus who wafted Psyche to the castle of Cupid (Eros). His wife was sometimes said to be Iris, the goddess of the rainbow.

Zetes see CALAIS.

Zethus see AMPHION.

Zeus The supreme ruler of the Greek gods. The etymology of his name – he is one of the few major Greek gods whose name is Indo-European – associates him with the heavens: it is cognate with Sanscrit *dyaus div-* ('sky'), Latin *dies* ('day'), and the first syllable of *Jupiter* ('Father Sky'), with whom later the Romans identified him. Though Zeus' name may originally have designated the daytime brightness of the sky, he appears always to have been a weather-god, particularly responsible for rain, hail, snow, and thunder. Thunderbolts were his constant and infallible weapons; and one of his commonest Homeric epithets was 'Gatherer of Clouds'. Consequently the Greeks came to believe that he lived on a mountain, namely Olympus (by origin a non-Greek word). However it is clear – for example, from the myth of Otus and Ephialtes who piled other mountains on top of

Olympus to reach the gods in heaven – that the Greeks must have very early abandoned their literal belief that Zeus lived on the summit of the mountain. In the *Iliad* he sometimes sits on the peak of Mount Ida to observe the fighting at Troy.

Zeus' functions were generalised at a very early time, and every aspect of the affairs of the Universe was considered to be under his jurisdiction. He was commonly, and especially by Homer, called 'father of gods and men'. In the strict sense he was not their father: several gods were his brothers, sisters, or distant relations; and he did not create or beget mankind, who were formed by Prometheus out of clay, and received the breath of life from Athena. His 'fatherhood' must therefore be interpreted in the sense of the master of a household; Zeus was a king, and human kings were under his special protection. Thus in the *Iliad* Agamemnon is described as having a sceptre which Hephaestus had made for Zeus, and Zeus had given to Pelops.

Zeus was therefore the protector of the city's integrity: *Zeus Polieus* ('god of the state') corresponds with his female counterpart, dating from pre-Greek times, Athena Polias. Zeus was also the interpreter of destiny: he held up a pair of scales, in which he tested the fates of men, ensuring that when a man was doomed to die, not even the intervention of a powerful god, or even his own affection for a dear son such as the Lycian hero Sarpedon, could prevail upon him to annul this fated doom. In this respect Zeus was also a giver of portents: his sacred oak tree at Dodona in Epirus told mortals of the future, and thunder and lightning too were regarded as omens. Zeus protected strangers and travellers and severely punished those who broke the laws of hospitality. He was therefore called *Zeus Xenios*, 'protector of strangers'. When Paris, as a guest of Menelaus, stole his wife Helen,

Zeus was determined that he should not escape scot-free, even though he had acted on the instigation of a powerful goddess, Aphrodite.

Hades was sometimes called *Zeus Katachthonios*, 'Zeus of the Underworld', a title implying that the Greeks saw the name Zeus as signifying 'ruler' and 'king'. In fact, the Underworld was the one realm where Olympian Zeus was believed to have interfered very little, though he did adjudicate between Hades and Demeter over the rape of Persephone. In the visual arts he was portrayed with a beard, and his most famous statue of all, carved by Phidias and installed in the temple of Zeus at Olympia, showed him seated upon his throne. Sometimes he appeared helmeted, and generally he carried one of his thunderbolts, in the form of a winged spear; frequently, too, he wore the aegis, a tasselled breastplate or apron of goatskin. He was accompanied by his attendant bird, the eagle. Other characteristics of Zeus are indicated by his titles *Meilichios* 'the Mild', *Ktesios* 'protector of property', *Herkeios* 'of the courtyard', i.e., the protector of the household, and *Hikesios* 'protector of suppliants'; for any violation of the immunity of any man who asked for the protection of the gods, or any infringement of the right of sanctuary at their altars, was punished by the wrath of Zeus. In this respect he was also called *Soter* 'protector, saviour'.

According to Homer Zeus was the eldest, according to Hesiod and other ancient authorities the youngest, of six children of Cronos and Rhea. Hesiod's account, given in the *Theogony*, tells how Cronos, in jealousy and fear of a rival, swallowed all his offspring until the exasperated Rhea, helped by her mother Gaia (Earth) who had herself suffered similar injury from her husband Uranus, dressed a great stone in swaddling clothes for Cronos to swallow, and smuggled Zeus, her last baby, to Crete, where the nymphs took charge of him, hiding him in a cave at Lyctus (Lyttus). There he was fed on the milk of the goat Amalthea, and the Curetes danced wild dances outside the cave, clashing their weapons together to hide the baby's cries from his suspicious father. According to the Arcadian version, Zeus was born on Mount Lycaeus in Arcadia and from there taken to Lyctus, but the Cretans asserted that he was born in a cave on Mount Ida or Mount Dicte.

When Zeus reached manhood, he determined to overthrow his tyrannical father, and courted the wise Titaness Metis, whom he persuaded to put an emetic in Cronos' drink. Cronos accordingly brought up the five children he had swallowed, as well as the great stone which had been the substitute for Zeus; it was placed at Delphi at the centre of the earth, and became known as the earth's navel. With the help of his brothers Poseidon and Hades, and of Gaia's sons the Cyclopes who forged Zeus' thunderbolts, and the three Hundred-Armed giants Cottus, Briareos, and Gyes, Zeus overthrew Cronos and those of his brother Titans who supported him, in a conflict lasting ten years, and confined them in the depths of Tartarus, where the Hundred-Armed giants guarded them ever after.

The three divine brothers Zeus, Poseidon, and Hades now decided to divide the Universe between them, drawing lots for three different realms. Zeus became lord of the sky, Poseidon of the sea, and Hades of the Underworld. Mount Olympus and the earth were regarded as common territory, though Hades very seldom visited them. Zeus' paramountcy was also recognised, as he had led the revolt against Cronos and the Titans and had rescued his brothers from their father's belly. Some versions said that it was in gratitude for this that the other gods elected him to be their ruler.

As the Greeks did not at any stage practise polygamy they rejected the notion of a polygamous Zeus. Nevertheless they possessed widespread traditions according to which Zeus begot a large number of children on various goddesses, nymphs, and women. Many of the goddesses he took as partners were originally earth divinities, for the marriage of the sky-god with the earth-goddess appears to have been a basic image of Greek religion, linking (according to one plausible theory) the male-oriented society of the Indo-European immigrants with their new homes on the Mediterranean where a mother-goddess had previously been the chief deity. The solution finally adopted by the Greeks regarding Zeus' numerous mistresses was to suppose that he first married a number of goddesses, one after the other, before eventually settling down to a permanent marriage with Hera; and that subsequently he had many extra-marital relationships both with goddesses and with mortal women.

His first wife was the Oceanid Metis, whose name means 'thought'. When she was pregnant for the first time, Zeus learnt from Gaia that if she conceived again the infant would turn out to be a god superior to Zeus himself, who would replace him as ruler of the Universe. For this reason – and because he wished to acquire his wife's wisdom – Zeus swallowed her, together with the baby in her womb. The embryo grew inside Zeus and eventually emerged from his head (after Hephaestus had cloven it open with an axe) as the fully grown, fully armed warrior-maiden Athena. His next wife was the oracular Titaness Themis, an earth-goddess, whose children by him were the Hours and the Fates. Subsequently he left Themis for Eurynome, another Oceanid, who bore the Graces and other daughters; after which his sister Demeter, goddess of the earth and its fruits, bore him Persephone. Next he took the Titaness Mnemosyne ('memory'), who gave birth to the nine Muses. Then, according to some, he made love to Leto, who bore him Apollo and Artemis. Hera, another of his sisters, whom Tethys had taken into her care during the war with the Titans, now became his last and permanent wife, and presented him with three children, Ares, Hebe, and Ilithyia. Zeus had another consort, Dione, whom Homer calls the mother of Aphrodite: she may have been little more than a local form of Hera, for her name is a byform of Zeus' own and simply means 'Zeus' wife'.

Zeus also had one other divine mistress, Maia, the Pleiad, who bore him Hermes. Of her Hera showed no jealousy; generally speaking, however, she pursued all his mistresses, whether nymphs or mortals, with unremitting fury, whenever she was able to identify them. (When she herself produced Hephaestus without male cooperation, she did this, according to some accounts, out of spite because of Zeus' unaided creation of Athena.) As for the beautiful Nereid Thetis, both Zeus and Poseidon noticed her charms and vied to seduce her. Just in time, however, Zeus learnt from the Titan Prometheus that the son of Thetis was destined to be greater than his father, and in consequence he hastily married her to a mortal, Peleus, lest he be supplanted by a more powerful son. Years before, Zeus had punished Prometheus by fastening him to a high rock by the edge of the Ocean and causing an eagle to devour his liver each day. This torture was the price of Prometheus' championship of mankind, against Zeus' hostility. For after the creation of human beings at Prometheus' hands Zeus had wished to destroy them and had ordained that their life should be uncomfortable and short. To console his creatures, Prometheus stole fire from the gods and gave it to men. He also tricked Zeus into choosing the inferior share of the meat when there were sacrifices, and, when Zeus intended to de-

stroy the whole race by a flood, warned his son Deucalion to build a ship. For this opposition to his plans, Zeus had ordered that Prometheus should be confined and tortured, until, ages later, Heracles freed him, and it was now that Zeus learnt from Prometheus the dangers of a union with Thetis.

Zeus had determined to destroy the human race in the flood because of the impiety of the Arcadian king Lycaon, who tried to serve human flesh to the gods. He later consigned Tantalus to Tartarus for the same sin, and for revealing the gods' secrets to men. Ixion suffered likewise for betraying Zeus' hospitality and for trying to seduce Hera. Zeus also slew Asclepius, for breaking his universal law by the raising of the dead: in response, Apollo tried to avenge his son by killing the Cyclopes who made Zeus' thunderbolts. Zeus nearly destroyed Apollo on the spot, but at Leto's entreaty relented and simply made Apollo serve a mortal man, Admetus, for a year.

Zeus had occasional difficulties with the gods, and punished them firmly when they transgressed. When Hera, Poseidon, and Athena rebelled and tried to throw him into chains, he was rescued by Thetis, who fetched Briareos from Tartarus to save him. When Hera once went too far in her persecution of Heracles, he suspended her from heaven, her feet weighted down by an anvil. He also flung Hephaestus out of Olympus for trying to help his mother in her predicament. He made both Apollo and Poseidon act as slaves to Laomedon for some rebellious act. He was also relentless in his punishment of human wrong-doers, particularly those who arrogated his majesty to themselves, such as Salmoneus or Ceyx.

The first mortal woman whom Zeus seduced was Niobe, daughter of Phoroneus, king of Argos. He also had designs on another Argive woman, Io, whom Hera for a long time persecuted; Io finally bore him Epaphus, ancestor of the kings of Egypt. He took Europa, a Palestinian princess, in the form of a bull, and carried her off on his back to Crete. Zeus generally appeared to mortal women in the form either of an animal or of an ordinary man. However after his seduction of Semele, mother of Dionysus, Hera tricked the girl into asking him to prove his identity by appearing to her in true form, and she was shrivelled to a cinder at the sight; Zeus then had to carry the embryo of Dionysus in his own thigh until it was ready for birth. He visited Danae, the mother of Perseus, and made love to her in the form of a shower of gold, since her father Acrisius had locked her up in a tower. He seduced Leda, mother of Helen and the Dioscuri, in the form of a swan: Helen was therefore born in an egg. By Antiope Zeus was the father of Amphion and Zethus, kings of Thebes. His last mortal mistress, to whom he came in the form of her own husband Amphitryon, was Alcmena, mother of Heracles – the hero destined to save the gods in their decisive war with the giants.

For Gaia, the Earth, was by now as weary of Zeus' high-handed ways as she had been of those of Uranus and Cronos. She therefore brought forth the race of giants, who attacked Olympus. She also produced a herb which, if the giants had eaten it, would have rendered them immortal and invincible; but Zeus prevented the sun, moon, and stars from shining so that they could not find the plant, and he himself found it instead in the darkness. Nevertheless it was only with the help of a mortal hero that the gods could vanquish these

giants; and Zeus' mortal son Heracles stood by and finished each of them off with a poisoned arrow, since none of the gods had the power to put them to death.

After the failure of this attempt to overthrow Zeus, Gaia again conceived, and now produced the most dangerous of all the gods' adversaries, the immortal monster Typhon. Zeus was nearly defeated by this creature, but finally buried him beneath the island of Sicily. The last external threat to Zeus' authority was the assault mounted by Otus and Ephialtes, who piled up the mountains Ossa, Pelion, and Olympus to reach the gods in heaven. They were defeated by Apollo, and Artemis and Zeus consigned them to the depths of Tartarus.

It is impossible to include here all the myths in which Zeus played an active role, or to enumerate the many amours attributed to him in various myths. In the *Iliad* and *Odyssey* he is portrayed as a majestic and impartial overseer of life, both human and divine. The fact that he does not, as far as we know, appear as a character in any Greek tragedy indicates the special awe in which he was regarded by both playwrights and audiences; yet many are the odes in which these playwrights and other poets honoured his exalted grandeur. Like Xenophanes before him, Socrates, according to Plato, roundly condemned the myths that described Zeus and the gods as immoralists and philanderers.

Zeuxippe A Naiad (water-nymph). She married her nephew Pandion, king of Athens, and bore him twin sons, Erechtheus and Butes, and two daughters, Procne and Philomela.

Genealogical Trees

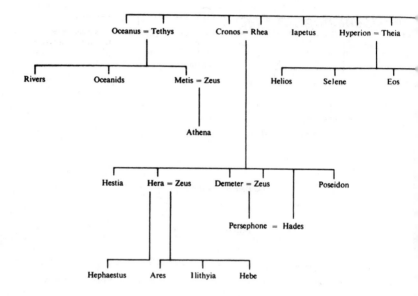

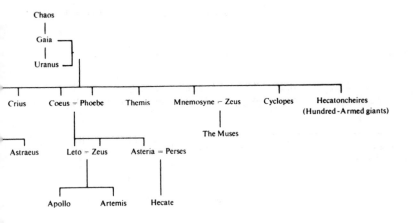

The Descendants of Perseus

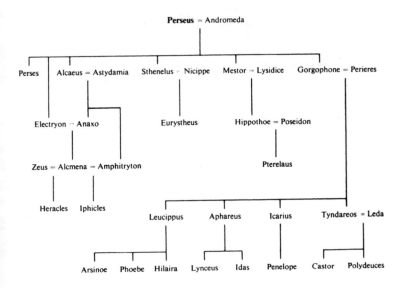

The Descendants of Proetus

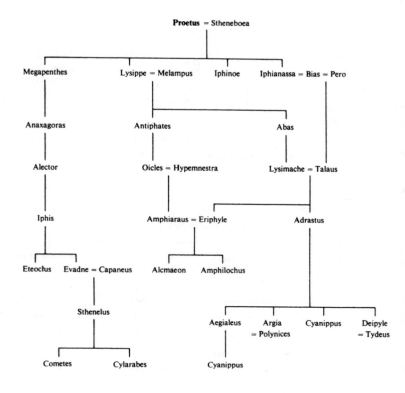

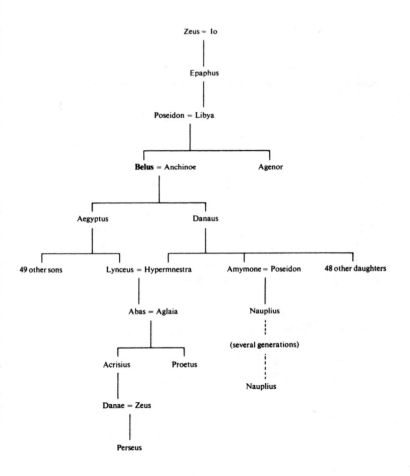

The Descendants of Belus

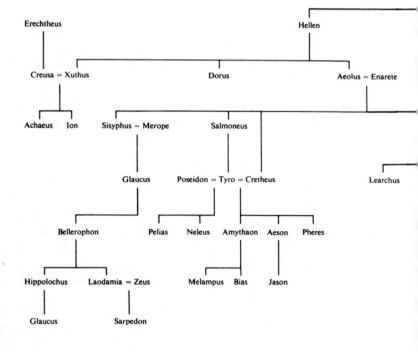

Erechtheus

Hellen

Creusa = Xuthus   Dorus   Aeolus = Enarete

Achaeus   Ion   Sisyphus = Merope   Salmoneus

Learchus

Glaucus   Poseidon = Tyro = Cretheus

Bellerophon   Pelias   Neleus   Amythaon   Aeson   Pheres

Hippolochus   Laodamia = Zeus   Melampus   Bias   Jason

Glaucus   Sarpedon

The Descendants of Prometheus

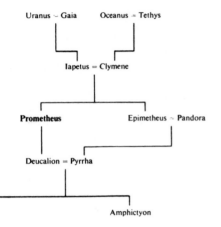

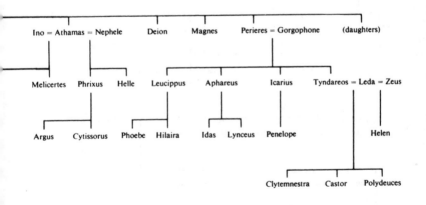

The House of Leda

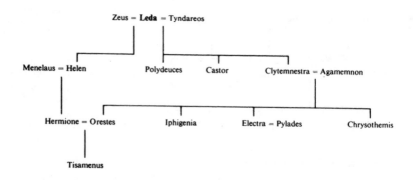

The House of Minos

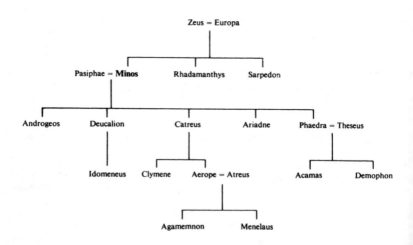

The Royal House of Thebes

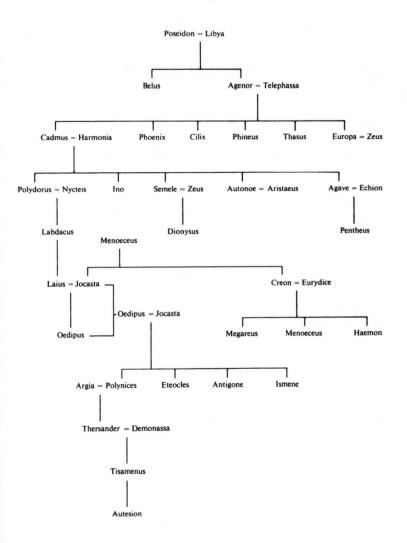

The Royal House of Athens

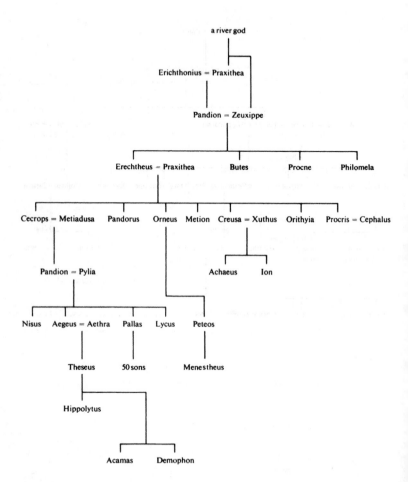

The Descendants of Tantalus

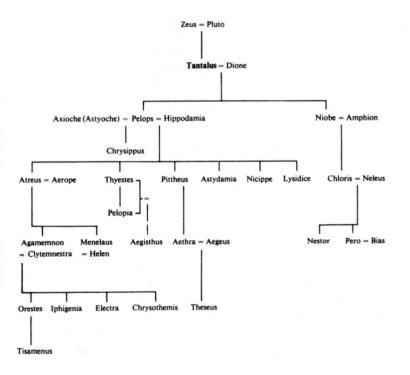

The Royal House of Troy

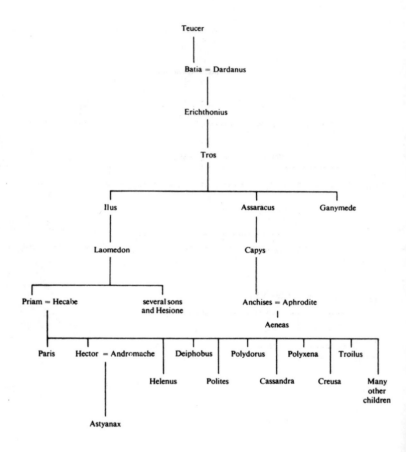

The Descendants of Aeneas

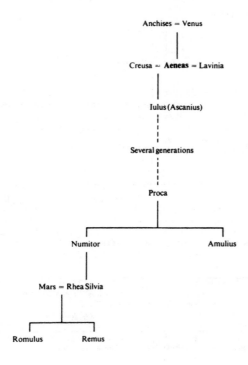

List of Greek and Latin writers referred to in the dictionary

Aeschylus Greek tragic playwright, 525 to 456 BC; Athenian. Extant works: seven poetic dramas:- *Persians, Seven against Thebes, Agamemnon, Libation-Bearers* (*Choephori*) and *Kindly Ones* (*Eumenides*) (these three forming a trilogy, *The Oresteia*), *Suppliant Women,* and *Prometheus.* Many of his plays are lost.

Apollodorus Greek mythographer, born *c.* 180 BC, lived at Athens, Alexandria and Perganum. His *Library* (*Bibliotheca*) exists in a condensed form, abridged from his original work in the first century AD. He also wrote on other subjects: history, religion, geography and etymology.

Apollonius Rhodius Greek epic poet born *c.* 295 BC; lived in Alexandria, retired to Rhodes for a time in early life, whence his surname Rhodius 'the Rhodian'. Extant work: *Argonautica*, an epic telling the story of Jason's quest for the Golden Fleece.

Apuleius Latin prose author, born *c.* AD 123 at Madaurus in Africa; educated in Carthage, Athens and Rome. Lived mostly in Africa. His principal surviving work is the romance, *Metamorphoses*, now generally known as *The Golden Ass.* A few speeches and translations from the Greek also survive.

Aristophanes Greek comic playright, *c.* 457 to *c.* 385 BC; Athenian. Extant works: eleven poetic comedies, of which the majority had a satirical purpose: *Acharnians, Knights, Clouds,* *Wasps, Peace, Birds, Lysistrata, Thesmophoriazusae, Frogs, Women in Parliament* (*Ecclesiazusae*), *Plutus.* Many of his plays are lost.

Aristotle Greek philosopher, scientist and political theorist, 384 to 322 BC. Born at Stagirus in Chalcidice; lived in Athens, Lesbos, and Macedonia. Founded a college (the Lyceum), and initiated a school of philosophy (the Peripatetics). A wide variety of extant works on philosophy (including the *Nicomachean Ethics*), politics, and science (especially biology).

Athenaeus Greek prose writer, *c.* AD 200; born at Naucratis in Egypt. *Sophists at Dinner or Connoisseurs in Dining* (*Deipnosophistai*). Fifteen 'books' of table talk about many subjects relating to ancient Greece (more than twelve books survive).

Bacchylides Greek lyric poet, *c.* 505 to *c.* 450 BC; born on the island of Ceos. Choral poems of various kinds.

Cato the Elder Latin historian, orator and agriculturalist, 234–149 BC; from Tusculum; held many offices of the Roman state. His works (including the *Origines* which tell the legends of early Rome) are lost, with the exception of the greater part of his treatise *On Agriculture* (*De Agri Cultura,* or *De Re Rustica*).

Catullus Latin lyric poet, *c.* 84 to 54 BC; born at Verona; lived in Rome. Short lyrics on love and other themes, and longer poems on a variety of subjects.

Cicero Latin orator; composer of ethical, rhetorical, religious and political treatises; poet; and letter-writer, 106–43 BC. He was born at Arpinum, and held the consulship at Rome in 63. His surviving works include 58 speeches, 18 treatises, and more than 900 letters.

Cypria *see* EPIC CYCLE.

Diodorus Siculus Greek (Sicilian) historian, wrote *c.* 60–30 BC; born at Agyrium in Sicily. His *Library of History* (*Bibliotheke Historike*) was a history of the Mediterranean world from its beginnings. Fifteen of its forty 'books' survive.

Ennius Roman epic, tragic and comic poet, 239 to 169 BC; born at Rudiae in Calabria (S.E. Italy), and served under Roman commanders and governors. 550 lines of the eighteen books of his epic chronicle of Rome, *The Annals*, survive.

Epic Cycle (Cyclic Poems). The name given by Proclus, writer of a handbook of Greek Literature in about the fifth century AD, to groups of epic poems (now almost entirely lost) attributed to poets other than Homer and Hesiod. These included sequences on the mythical stories of Oedipus (*Oedipodeia*), Thebes (*Thebaid* and *Epigoni*) and Troy (including the *Cypria, Aethiopis, Little Iliad, Sack of Troy (Iliu persis), Homecomings,* and *Telegonia*). In the tradition of Hesiod's *Theogony* were the *Gigantomachy* and *Titanomachy*. *See also* HOMER and HESIOD.

Euripides Greek tragic playwright, *c.* 480 to *c.* 406 BC; Athenian, he died at the court of Macedonia. Extant works: eighteen poetic dramas:- *Alcestis, Medea, Hippolytus, Trojan Women (Troades), Helen, Orestes, Iphigenia at Aulis, The Bacchants (Bacchae), An-*dromache, Children of Heracles (Heraclidae), Hecuba (Hekabe), Suppliant Women (Supplices), Electra, Heracles (Hercules Furens), Iphigenia in Tauris; Ion, Phoenician Women (Phoenissae); and perhaps the *Rhesus* is by him. Also one 'satyr-play', the *Cyclops*.

Herodotus Greek historian, *c.* 480 to *c.* 425 BC; born at Halicarnassus in Caria (S.W. Asia Minor), lived at Athens and travelled widely. His *History*, subsequently divided into nine books, narrated the Persian Wars, with a vast introduction and digressions.

Hesiod Greek epic and didactic poet, probably of the eighth century BC; born at Ascra in Boeotia, son of an immigrant from Cyme in Aeolis (W. Asia Minor). Long poems: *Works and Days* and the *Theogony*. He, or more probably writers of his school, also wrote the *Shield of Heracles* (480 lines) and the *Catalogue of Women* (*Eoeae*) (fragments survive). *See also* EPIC CYCLE.

Homer Greek epic poet, probably of the eighth century BC; born in Ionia (W. Asia Minor), where many cities, including Smyrna and Chios, claimed his birth-place. Long poems traditionally attributed to him (though they may be by different authors): the *Iliad* and the *Odyssey*. Other 'Homeric' poems sometimes ascribed to him in antiquity are more likely to be by members of his school: e.g. *Thebaid* and *Margites* (both lost), and *Battle of Frogs and Mice* (*Batrachomyomachia*) (parody). *See also* EPIC CYCLE *and* HOMERIC HYMNS.

Homeric Hymns A collection of thirty-three Greek poems in epic metre, addressed to deities; often attributed to Homer in ancient times but composed at various epochs, mainly between the eighth and sixth centuries BC.

Horace Latin lyric, philosophical and

satirical poet, 65 to 8 BC; born at Venusia in Apulia (S. Italy), lived at Rome and then in the Sabine hills (central Italy). Poems: four books of *Odes; Secular Hymn; Epodes*; two books of verse *Epistles* (including the *Art of Poetry [Ars Poetica]*); *Sermones* (Satires).

Hyginus Spanish freedman (ex-slave) of Augustus and librarian of the Palatine library at Rome, *c.* 64 BC to AD 17. His name is attached to a Latin collection of mythological material, the *Genealogies* or *Fables*, which appears, however, to belong to the second century AD. It is translated from a lost Greek original. A work on astronomy (*De Astronomia*) was likewise wrongly ascribed to Hyginus.

Iliad *see* HOMER.

Ilias Parva (Little Iliad) *see* EPIC CYCLE.

Iliu Persis (Sack of Troy) *see* EPIC CYCLE.

Livy Latin historian, 64 (or 59) BC to AD 12 (or 17); born at Patavium (Padua), lived at Rome. Thirty-five of the 142 'books' of his *History of Rome* survive, and two sets of abridgements (Epitomes).

Lucretius Latin philosophical (Epicurean) poet, probably born in the 90s and died in the 50s BC; little or nothing is known about his origin and life. Didactic poem: *On the Nature of the Universe* (*De Rerum Natura*), in six books.

Musaeus Greek poet of the fourth or fifth century AD; author of an extant poem on the myth of Hero and Leander.

Naevius Roman poet of the third century BC. He served in the First Punic War and was an actor. Only fragments

of his works survive. He wrote comedies, tragedies, and an epic poem entitled the *Punic War*.

Odyssey *see* HOMER.

Ovid Latin quasi-epic, elegiac and tragic poet, 43 BC to *c.* AD 17; born at Sulmo (central Italy), lived at Rome, died in exile at Tomis (now Constanta in Romania). Hexameter poem, on mythological subjects: *Changes of Shape* (*Metamorphoses*), in fifteen books. Elegiac poems: the *Loves* (*Amores*), *Heroines* (*Heroides*), *Cosmetics* (*Medicamina Faciei*), *Art of Love* (*Ars Amatoria*), *Cures for Love* (*Remedia Amoris*), *Calendar* (*Fasti*), *Poems of Sadness* (*Tristia*), *Letters from the Black Sea* (*Epistulae ex Ponto*). Of doubtful ascription are the following: in hexameters, *Halieutica* (mainly lost), on marine creatures of the Black Sea; in elegiacs, *Ibis* (a curse) and the *Nut-Tree* (*Nux*). He also wrote a lost tragedy, *Medea*.

Pausanias Greek travel-writer of the second century AD. He travelled widely, but his descriptions of topography, with much historical and religious detail, are concerned with Greece. His work, which still survives, bears the title *Description of Greece* (*Periegesis tes Hellados*): its ten books cover the ten sections of mainland Greece.

Pherecydes Greek chronicler, probably of mid-fifth century BC; born on the island of Leros, lived at Athens. Mythological and genealogical *History*, in ten 'books' (lost).

Philochorus An Athenian writer on religion, myth and antiquities. He lived *c.* 340 to *c.* 260 BC. His surviving work consists of fragments of a large historical chronicle, the *Atthis*.

Pindar Greek lyric poet, *c.* 518 to 438 BC; born at Cynoscephalae in Boeotia, and lived at Athens; visited Sicily etc., and died at Argos. Collections of lyric odes (*Epinicia*, celebrating victories in the Games): *Olympian*, *Pythian*, *Nemean* and *Isthmian*. Poems of other types survive mainly in fragments.

Plato Greek philosophical writer, *c.* 429 to 347 BC; Athenian; founder of the Academy. His surviving twenty-six prose works ('dialogues' except for the *Apology*; there are also a number of doubtful authenticity) purporting to describe the philosophical beliefs of Socrates (died 399 BC), include narrations of myths, notably in the *Phaedo*, *Symposium*, *Phaedrus*, *Republic*, *Critias* and *Timaeus*. Thirteen prose epistles (some spurious) and a number of poems (preserved in the Greek Anthology) are also attributed to him.

Plautus Latin comic dramatist, *c.* 254 to *c.* 184 BC. Born at Sarsina (Umbria); lived at Rome. Complete extant works: twenty poetic comedies, of which the best known are the *Amphitruo*, *Pot of Gold (Aulularia)*, *The Two Bacchises (Bacchides) The Prisoners of War (Captivi)*, *The Two Menaechmuses (Menaechmi)*, *The Ghost (Mostellaria)*, *The Braggart Soldier (Miles Gloriosus)*, *The Trickster (Pseudolus)*, *The Rope (Rudens)*, *Trinummus*.

Plutarch Greek essayist and biographer, *c.* AD 46 to *c.* 127; born at Chaeronea in Boeotia. Extant works: numerous treatises and dialogues on philosophical, religious, scientific and literary subjects (the *Moralia*); and twenty-three pairs of *Parallel Lives*, biographies of Greeks and Romans (both mythical and historical).

Proclus *see* EPIC CYCLE.

Propertius Latin elegiac poet, *c.* 50 to *c.* 16 BC; born at Asisium (Assisi) in Umbria, lived at Rome. Four books of elegies, including much antiquarian and mythological material.

Pythagoras Semi-legendary Greek philosopher, sixth century BC; born at Samos, lived at Croton in south Italy. Although 'Pythagorean' doctrines, theories and institutions were quoted, it is uncertain whether he left any writings.

Sophocles Greek tragic playwright, *c.* 496 to 406 BC; Athenian. Extant works: seven poetic dramas:- *Ajax (Aias)*, *Antigone*, *Oedipus the King (Oedipus Rex* or *Tyrannus)*, *Women of Trachis (Trachiniae)*, *Electra*, *Philoctetes*, *Oedipus at Colonus (Oedipus Coloneus)*.

Statius Latin epic poet, AD *c.* 40 to *c.* 96; born at Neapolis (Naples), lived at Rome. Extant works: the *Thebaid*, *Achilleid* (unfinished) and *Silvae* (miscellaneous pieces).

Stesichorus A Greek lyric poet, who lived between *c.* 632 and *c.* 553 BC. He lived mainly at Himera in Sicily. His poems were frequently on mythological subjects, including Heracles' quest for the cattle of Geryon and the Calydonian boar-hunt, but only scanty fragments survive.

Theocritus Greek pastoral poet, *c.* 310 to *c.* 250 BC; born at Syracuse, lived at Cos and Alexandria. Extant works: nearly thirty 'Idylls' on pastoral (bucolic) and other themes. Some of the poems in the Theocritean corpus are not by him.

Theogony *see* HESIOD.

Virgil (Vergil) Roman poet, 70 to 19 BC; born near Mantua (N. Italy), lived at Rome and Neapolis (Naples). Extant works: the *Eclogues* (ten pastoral poems), *Georgics* (four longer poems glorifying agriculture and Italy), and *Aeneid* (in twelve 'books'). A number of minor poems (in the *Appendix Vergiliana*) were regarded as his juvenile works, but most of them are not his.

Works and Days *see* HESIOD.

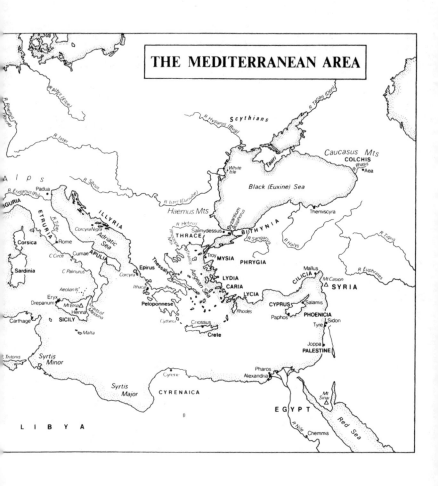

THE MEDITERRANEAN AREA

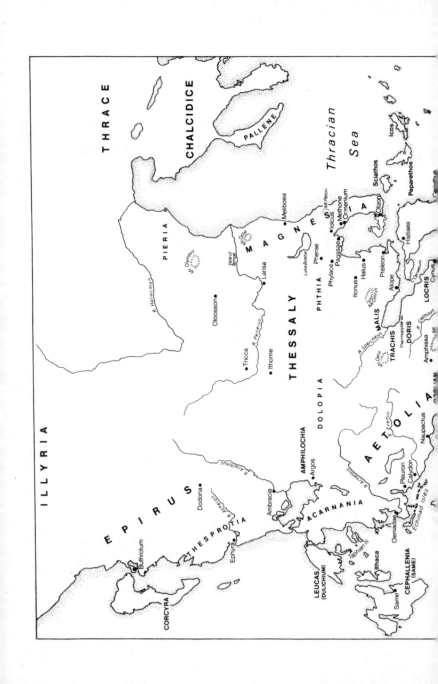

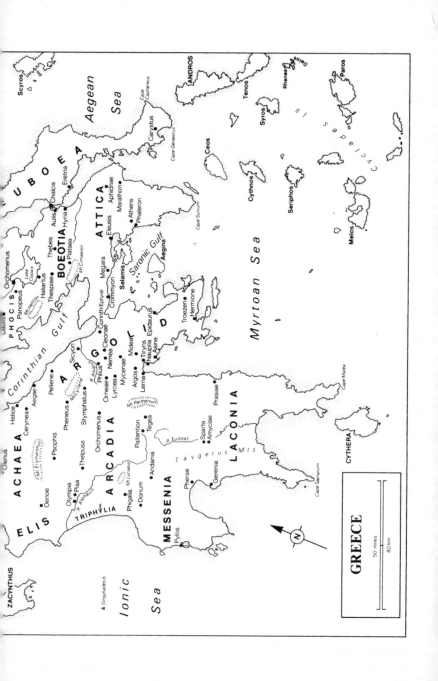

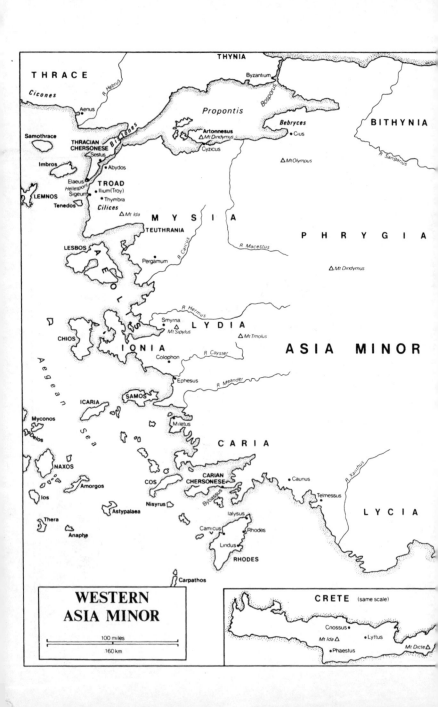

THRACE

Cicones

R. Hebrus

Aenus

THYNIA

Byzantium

Propontis

Artonnesus

△ _Mt Dindymus_

Cyzicus

Bosporus

Bebryces

• Cius

BITHYNIA

R. Sangarius

Samothrace

THRACIAN CHERSONESE

Sestus

Imbros

Elaeus

Hellespont

Sigeum

Abydos

TROAD

• Ilium (Troy)

• Thymbra

Cilices

LEMNOS

Tenedos

△ _Mt Ida_

M Y S I A

△ _Mt Olympus_

TEUTHRANIA

LESBOS

Pergamum

R. Caicus

R. Macestus

P H R Y G I A

△ _Mt Dindymus_

A E O L I S

R. Hermus

Smyrna

△ _Mt Sipylus_

L Y D I A

△ _Mt Tmolus_

CHIOS

I O N I A

Colophon

R. Cayster

Ephesus

R. Meander

A S I A   M I N O R

_A e g e a n   S e a_

ICARIA

SAMOS

Myconos

Delos

Miletus

C A R I A

NAXOS

Amorgos

Ios

COS

CARIAN CHERSONESE

Bybassus

• Caunus

R. Xanthus

Thera

Anaphe

Astypalaea

Nisyrus

Ialysus

Telmessus

Camicus

• Rhodes

L Y C I A

Lindus

RHODES

Carpathos

C R E T E   (same scale)

Cnossus •

Mt Ida △

• Lyttus

• Phaestus

Mt Dicte △